ONE AFTER ANOTHER

ONE AFTER ANOTHER

Rectification & Prediction
using Planetary Sequence

Kennet Gillman

First published online October 2009.

Second web edition placed online December 2009.

Initial print edition, May 2010.

Considerations Inc.
3 Lake Street, Goldens Bridge, New York 10526

ISBN: 978-0-557-43517-3

Contents

Acknowledgements

I am beholden to Alexander Ruperti for his unselfish encouragement during the early years of my research, and for his permission to freely use and adapt his explanation of the seven-way development of a cycle.

I remain forever deeply grateful for the support and intellectual stimuli provided by my long-time friend and ally Prier Wintle, who left this world just as my book neared its completion.

I am most thankful to Anne Whitaker and the late Elaine Krengel for taking the time to read some of the early chapters and for providing astute and extremely helpful criticism. The corrections suggested by Noah Mullette-Gillman and Axel Harvey have been very much appreciated.

My thanks to Rob Hand for allowing me to quote on page 59 from his stimulating 2005 York lecture.

I am indebted to Joan Schleicher of the Anodos Foundation for allowing me to reproduce Ellen Auerbach's photo of Arthur M. Young on page 227. This comes from Arthur's astrological autobiography *Nested Time*.

The many drawings in this book are the work of two hands. The irreplaceable Hal Barnell crafted most of them. A few others, those notable for their lack of any artistic sense, were drawn by the author.

The cover photos, both front and rear, are by Michael Gillman

For my children, the fruit of a fifth house planet in its own sign:

Gabi, Noah, O'Dhaniel and Michael.

Introduction

The list of words in David Copperfield *is almost the same as the list of words in* The Catcher in the Rye. *Both draw upon the vocabulary of an educated native speaker of English. What is completely different about the two books is the order in which the words are strung together. Similarly, when a person is made, or when a mouse is made, both embryologies draw upon the same dictionary of genes: the normal vocabulary of mammal embryologies. The difference between a person and a mouse comes out of the different orders in which the genes, drawn from the same mammalian vocabulary, are deployed, the different places in the body where this happens, and its timing.*

Matt Ridley
Nature via Nature

I was born in a country in which the moment of a child's birth is rarely recorded; birth certificates state the day but not the time, exceptions being royal and multiple births. To understand and to predict my future and that of others, many of whom, like me, knew only their day of birth, I have experimented with several ideas over the past forty-plus years to quickly identify whether the birth occurred during the daytime or at night, and which was the first planet to rise to the eastern horizon in the hours following birth. These methods are based on the sequence in which the planets follow each other across the sky. This book is about two of them, which I have named the Decan and the Septenary. In combination they provide a swift and effective rectification of the approximate birth time and also make available a considerable amount of information concerning the different phases through which an individual lives his or her life, which enables the astrologer to understand and to predict just how a life will flow over time. Those planets that become emphasized at particular times in an individual's life, due to their initial place in the planetary sequence at the birth, strongly color and dominate the meaning of any transits, returns, progressions or directions that occur during these same periods. An understanding of the sequence of the planets at birth is essential for the astrologer to interpret the succession and nature of events in an individual's life. Growth and dissolution patterns can be clearly observed.

Many births occur with each of the planets in the same signs and with identical aspects, it is the order in which they come into the life that matters.

In addition to their value in prediction and rectification, these methods are excellent tools for understanding how the different components within the horoscope operate in relation to each other. Virtually no computation is necessary once the natal chart has been erected; there is no need to refer to an ephemeris for transits, no necessity to compute progressions or directions; a detailed understanding of the complete life is easily achieved from a rapid visual examination of the chart that contains the planetary positions at birth.

The natal horoscope is a snap shot, the birth moment one of pause. It is the primal blink of an eye that stills the continuous movement of the Earth; the revolving planets and the expanding universe are halted, for just the briefest of fleeting seconds. The relationship

1

between the planets and a single location on the Earth is evoked at this moment of a new birth. At this unique time the newly born is exposed to an indelible impression of the nature and relative positions of the planets. Immediately thereafter movement continues, the universe expands still further, providing room for its latest inhabitant, the Earth continues her diurnal rotation, and each of the planetary bodies in turn comes to rise in the eastern sky. As each body crosses the horizon it will take over the direction and pattern of growth of the person.

Various systems to allocate periods of life to different planets have been used by astrologers in the past. This book also relates periods in an individual's life to a sequence of governing planets but it differs from those others in that while most of them utilize a constant sequence of ruling planets the approach explained here uses the sequence that is actually present in an individual's horoscope.

The most widely used of these other systems divides the life into nine 'dasas' involving the seven classical planets and the two nodes of the Moon. These nine dasas or parts are in a specific sequence that is unchanging. It is the same for everyone. The exact part of a dasa that commences the sequence for a particular individual is determined by the degree of the Moon at the time of birth. If, for example, the Moon is found to indicate that the starting dasa is the one ruled by Venus, then the following dasa will always be that ruled by the Sun, and the one after that the dasa governed by the Moon, and so on in an unvarying sequence of the planets. There is no reference to the actual sequence of the planets in the individual's horoscope. The dasa system has countless adherents in India and the Far East but tends to be ignored in the West.

Another system, the Firdaria or Alfridary, which apparently comes from ancient Persia and has received some attention in recent years, also uses a constant sequence that varies only by whether an individual was born during the night or in the daytime.

Western astrology responded to the Indian dasa system with Profections, a system that appears to have been popular up to the 18th century. The method is described by William Lilly in his *Christian Astrology*: "Profections and Progressions are all one, and are no more than a regular or orderly change of the Significators according to the succession of Signs." According to Lilly, profections commence either with the rising sign, the sign on the midheaven, or the signs occupied at birth by the Sun, Moon, Fortuna, Saturn, Jupiter or Mars. They then proceed in an anti-clockwise direction through the signs, allocating them one by one to succeeding years. Profections were originally described by the 2nd century astrologer Vettius Valens, and tend to be ignored nowadays. By following the sequence of signs, profections will take into account the sequence of planets but only strictly so when there is just one planet in each sign. When there is more than one planet in a sign the multiple bodies are combined as if they were a single entity.

The alternative sequencing of governing planets described here provides a system for finding the time of day when people with unrecorded birth times were born, something the other systems have problems doing. As rectification is really prediction in a backwards direction, using an individualized sequence of time rulers also provides methods for effectively predicting a person's future.

In the past, doubtless like many others, I have found someone's expressive oratory, talented writing or reputation has too easily persuaded me to believe that a particular approach to astrology was meaningful. Too often I spent many days and hours investigating such persuasive ideas only to eventually discover the research had been fruitless, the highly touted concepts failed to produce the results their advocates had promised. To minimize the likelihood that readers will be thwarted in this way, all that is stated herein has been extensively tested on over nine thousand years of happenings in people's lives and the detailed results of this research, with statistical significance tests, are provided. To ensure readers are not put off by the presence of these probability tables, they are accompanied by details of events in the lives of various well-known individuals who experienced the appropriate direction in their lives.

The first edition of *One After Another* was completed on 30th August 2009. It was first viewed on the web on 26th October 2009. The second web edition appeared a month later. It added chapter numbers, completely revised Appendix A, and corrected some spelling errors. Other than the format changes necessary in going from the web to the printed page, this first print edition does not differ from the second web edition.

You are welcome to enter into my world. I ask only that, besides wiping your feet on the doormat, you put to one side those comforting beliefs and prejudices you habitually carry around with you; they'll still be there for you to pick up should you wish to do so when you leave. Enjoy your visit!

22nd February 2010
Goldens Bridge, New York

Chapter 2

Night or Day ?

There is a priceless but little known tool that is invaluable for an astrologer who has the task of rectifying an individual's time of birth. It is a feature of what was known in earlier times as the decennial, but which I prefer to call the 129-year cycle.

When asked to interpret an individual's horoscope, the first question the astrologer should need to answer is whether the birth occurred in the daytime or at night. Is the Sun located above or below the horizon in the birth chart? Each of the planets has different strengths and weaknesses that are interpreted very differently according to whether the birth chart is diurnal or nocturnal. In a diurnal chart the Sun, for example, tends to act as the benefic that Western astrology teaches; but when it is below the horizon, in a nocturnal chart, the Sun frequently acts very much as Hindu astrology says, as a malefic.

The astrologer faced with an unknown time of birth can, by a quick review of the ages when major life-changing events occurred in the native's life, together with their nature, immediately identify whether the Sun was above or below the horizon.

If a person was born during the daytime, when the Sun was above the horizon, then early in that person's nineteenth year, usually around the age of 18¼, a major event will occur that will change the direction of the person's life. The timing of this life-altering event may not occur precisely at the age of 18¼ years, but it will certainly occur close to that age.

If the person was born during the night, with the Sun below the horizon, such a life-direction changing event will occur early in the twenty-fifth year, usually close to the age of 24¼.

The nature of these life changing events will be symbolized by the planet that at the moment of birth is next ahead in the zodiac from the appropriate light, ahead of the Sun for a diurnal birth, ahead of the Moon for a nocturnal one.

Why these two ages? Why 18¼ and 24¼?

As life begins at the moment of conception, a person we would nowadays say is 18¼ years old has in fact experienced nineteen years of life up until that time—nine months within the womb and 18¼ years outside of it. What is so important about nineteen years? The period of 19 years belongs to the Sun and it relates to the Metonic cycle. The Greek astronomer Meton is said to have inaugurated this cycle in Athens on June 27, 432 BC, at what was then the beginning of the summer solstice. Every nineteen years an eclipse returns to the same degree of the zodiac. 235 lunations occur in these nineteen years. This same 19-year cycle was earlier well-known in Babylon where it was the basis for the cyclic calendar and was used to identify the annual dates of the solstice, equinox and the rising of Sirius. To the present day the Christian ecclesiastical calendar in its Easter dating continues to maintain the basic principle of this 19-year solar cycle. The first nineteen years of life of anyone born during daylight hours will be ruled by that person's Sun.

Similarly, for a nocturnal birth it is the Moon that rules the early life and the appropriate event that will radically redirect the individual's life will occur in the nine months immediately prior to the 25th birthday, usually close to age 24¼. The age of 24¼ years identified for this life-altering event is due to the 25-year lunar period commencing, like that of the 19-year period of the Sun, at the time of conception. The length of the Moon's period relates to the phases of the Moon occurring on the same days of the year every 25 years. A year here is an Egyptian year of 365 days: twelve months, each of thirty days, with five additional days at the end. In these 25 Egyptian years there are exactly 309 lunation cycles. The Moon rules the first twenty-five years of anyone born at night.

Some daytime births:

Barack Obama was several months shy of his nineteenth birthday when he moved from Hawaii to Los Angeles.

George Washington was similarly some months short of his nineteenth birthday when he made his only trip outside of continental North America, to Barbados, where he stayed for two months and caught small pox.

Alexander Hamilton, the first Treasury Secretary of the United States, was also a daytime birth. He was born January 11, 1755 on the island of Nevis in the West Indies, and was eighteen years and five months old when he came to New York to attend college. He never returned to the West Indies. By contrast, at age 24¼ he was in his third year as George Washington's ADC, hoping to be given a diplomatic assignment to France, which Congress denied him.

John Lennon was a few months past his eighteenth birthday when he and Paul McCartney formed their song-writing team. The key event at 24¼ was passing his driving test.

Adolf Hitler's mother died in the early morning hours of December 21, 1907, when he was eighteen years and eight months old. Four months earlier he had received his patrimony and gone to sit the examinations of the Academy of Fine Arts in Vienna, which he failed. With Adolf gone, his mother, who had undergone an operation in January 1907 to remove a cancerous breast, is said to have "let herself go and became an old woman." No life-changing event occurred in Hitler's 25th year to suggest he was born at night.

The philosopher Bertrand Russell was born on May 18, 1872. On June 24, 1890 he first attended Cambridge University. Within two months, at which time he would have been 18¼ years old, influenced by the writings of John Stuart Mill, he had declared himself an atheist.

King Juan Carlos of Spain was born on January 5, 1938 with the Sun high above the horizon. In March 1956, aged eighteen years two months, he accidently shot and killed his brother.

Some night births:

Abraham Lincoln was born at night. He was 24¼ when his village store failed and his partner died. He was left badly in debt. He survived by getting appointed as the town's postmaster. Shortly thereafter he began to study law.

Richard Nixon, born January 9, 1913, graduated from Duke University Law School on June 7, 1937, at age 24 years 5 months.

Jacqueline Bouvier, born July 18, 1929, was a month short of becoming 24¼ years old on September 12, 1953 when she married John Fitzgerald Kennedy.

Charlie Chaplin, born April 16, 1889, was 24 ¼ in July 1913 when the Keystone Film Company first offered him a contract to become "a moving picture actor…"

The Noble Prize-winning novelist Doris Lessing was another night birth. She married Gottfried Lessing, an enemy alien and communist, when she was in her twenty-fifth year. At age 18¼ she had been working in a telephone exchange, filling her spare hours with drinking, dancing and flirting.

Josef Stalin was aged twenty-four years and eight months on July 7, 1903 when Tsar Nicholas II signed the order for him to be exiled to Siberia. Four months earlier Stalin had instigated a riot at Batumi Prison, where he had been imprisoned since April 1902.

When Peter the Great of Russia set off on his Great Embassy to the West he was 24 years 10 months old. This is seven months after the suggested age of 24¼. However, several months earlier he had sent fifty Russians to Western Europe to study seamanship, navigation and shipbuilding, so it appears that this revolutionary concept that radically altered his life direction took some time in becoming actualized.

Jack Nicholls D.Sc. and Ross Harvey, in *Considerations* VII:4 stated that they had used this diurnal-nocturnal discrimination procedure *"many times without a failure."*

Chapter 3

Which Planet Will Rise First ?

The Decan

Once the astrologer has decided whether the birth occurred in the daytime or at night, the next step is to find which planet will first come to the ascendant following the moment of birth.

Planetary sequence was first introduced in the journal *Considerations* in 1983 in a two-part article that described the application of the septenary in the life of the Mahatma Gandhi. Since that time I have learnt much more. Although I discovered the septenary in the early seventies, several years before I stumbled on the decan, I will describe the decan first as it is more effective than the septenary for rectification.

Every horoscope contains ten planets, the seven known in classical times and the three discovered in recent centuries, together with the four angles, and these are identified as being located among the twelve signs of the zodiac. Many hundreds of newborn babies are born on the same day with similar aspects or planets in the same house or sign. One way in which these individuals can differ is in the order in which the planets come to affect the life.

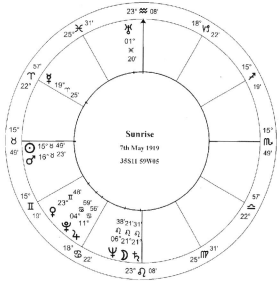

A word of caution here: it is the order of the planets at the moment of the birth that is used; the birth sequence is fixed; any alteration in it, such as the Moon passing another body, that occurs at any time after the moment of birth should be ignored.

If the time of birth is unknown, use the method described in the previous chapter to decide if the birth occurred in the day or at night, and then separate the diurnal bodies from the others. The simplest way to do this is to erect a chart for sunrise at the birth location; one of the planets below the horizon at sunrise will usually be the first to rise if this is a diurnal birth, while the Sun or one of the planets above the horizon at sunrise will usually be the first to rise if it is a nocturnal birth.

Note the use of the word 'usually' in the preceding paragraph. There can be instances in which a planet designated by the above rule as a nocturnal- or diurnal-riser—Uranus in the chart illustrated here is a perfect example—could be the first to rise were the birth either diurnal or nocturnal. As several hours of daylight still remain after the planets in Leo have risen above the ascendant, Uranus could then become the first planet to rise in a diurnal chart. Following sunset Uranus would continue to be the first to rise but the chart would now be a nocturnal one.

The planets are the Sun and Moon (termed planets here), Mercury, Venus, Mars, Jupiter, Saturn, Uranus, Neptune and Pluto. No other bodies are involved. Chiron, the Nodes, any asteroid or other body hypothesized by different authors or schools are not used.

Celestial longitude is usually sufficient to determine the sequence of the planets. However, which planet in a close conjunction is ahead of the other is best determined by the methods of primary direction, see Appendix A. A planet in the first house with a positive altitude cannot be the first to rise; one in the twelfth with a negative altitude can.

The horoscope of Eva Peron will be used as an example. The chart for sunrise on her birthday at her birth location is on the previous page. Uranus and Mercury were above the horizon when the Sun came to the ascendant. They will have risen over the ascendant some time during the night. Between the rising of Mercury and the moment of sunrise the Sun will have also been the first body next to rise.

Just three bodies, Mercury, Uranus and the Sun, could have been the first body to rise if this is a night birth. Each of the remaining seven planets (plus Uranus) can be the first to rise over the ascendant into a daytime sky once the Sun has risen. The Moon crossed Saturn shortly after sunrise, some time between the rising of Mars and the later rising of Venus, while the Sun did not pass over Mars until the next day.

The first planet to rise after birth will rule the first ten years of life. The second planet to rise will rule the second ten years, and so on. Each planet as it comes in sequence to the ascendant will take over control of the life for a period of ten years.

Applying the day-night method described in the previous chapter to discriminate between day and night, there can be no doubt but that Eva Peron was born during the night—her life radically changed in her 25th year when she met her future husband, Juan Peron. Their romance and marriage was like a fairy tale or the climax of a movie, quite against all rational expectations. Nothing at all comparable occurred in her 19th year that would argue for a daytime birth.

We are left with three planets that could be the first that rose after her birth: Uranus, Mercury or the Sun. To decide which of these is appropriate; let's consider what occurred to Eva in each of the decades in which she lived.

Eva Peron died when she was 33 years old, only the following sequences of decan rulers are therefore possible:

Age	Night birth			Day birth							
0 - 9	♅	☿	☉	♂	♀	♇	♃	♆	♄	☽	♅
10 -19	☿	☉	♂	♀	♇	♃	♆	♄	☽	♅	☿
20 - 29	☉	♂	♀	♇	♃	♆	♄	☽	♅	☿	☉
30 - death	♂	♀	♇	♃	♆	♄	☽	♅	☿	☉	♂

As a child she was Eva Maria Ibarguren. She experienced humiliation and poverty from the year she was born. Her father abandoned the family, forcing them to move into a rural slum. To keep the family from starving, her mother was forced to sew clothes for the villagers. The Sun could rule this decade. It is afflicted by its conjunction with Mars, which is more than usually malefic in Taurus, the sign of its detriment, and it is also squared by the very difficult Moon-Saturn conjunction. Uranus, with its well-known effect of disrupting home life could also rule these same ten years. Mercury seems the least likely.

Eva had ambitions to become an actress and at age fifteen she used her good looks and willingness to provide sexual favors to get taken to Buenos Aires, where she changed her name to Maria Evita Duarte. In Argentina's capital city she had a series of affairs but only managed to get bit parts in the theater. All three rising planets could rule this second decade. Either the Sun or Mars would signify Eve's attempt to improve her life by doing whatever was necessary, while Mercury in Aries cannot be completely ruled out.

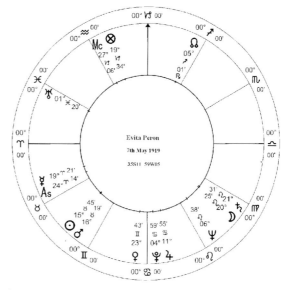

Everything changed once Eva became twenty years old. This was the start of a miraculous decade. She quickly obtained a part in a new radio soap opera and was such an instant success that she was soon able to form her own radio company and rapidly became one of the best-paid radio actresses of the time. Then came "my marvelous day" when she met Juan Peron, a prominent army officer with a ministerial position in the army-ruled government. The pair fell immediately in love and together began to live on an exhilarating switchback that swung rapidly from the depths of despair to the peaks of success. It culminated in Eva moving into the Unzue Palace as the wife of the newly elected president. Only Venus of the three planets that could rule Eva's twenties is appropriate for these events.

At the start of the following decade, Eva was found to have cancer but was not told. She suffered great pain without knowing its cause, and was deceived by her doctors, seemingly on the orders of her husband. She died in Buenos Aires at 8:25 PM local time on 26th July 1952, at age 33. Congress had given her the title "Spiritual Leader of the Nation", a title without precedent. There was national mourning. To the people she had become Santa Evita. Her body was embalmed and three exact copies of it were made. All found their way to Europe. Her true body was buried under an assumed name in Italy. Only Pluto of the three possible bodies can have ruled this final decade.

With Venus ruling Eva's third decan and Pluto her final one, we can now say with confidence that the Sun was the first body to rise, and that her ascendant is therefore somewhere between 20° Aries and 15° Taurus. This agrees with various sources, all of which place the birth close to 5 AM local time, at which time Mercury is already above the ascendant and the Sun is the first body to next arrive at the eastern horizon, followed in turn by Mars, Venus and Pluto.

Fraser and Navarro write "At some time after five o'clock on 7th May 1919, an Indian woman went on foot to a house west of the village to deliver a child." The former mayor and publisher of the local paper, as cited by astrologer Marion March, and Paul Montgomery in *Eva Evita* agree on the same time. On a June 1979 Thames TV program *Queen of Hearts* it was stated that she was born "early in the morning".

AstroDataBank gives 5:14 AM LMT from Marc Penfield, but he has her born in 1908, eleven years earlier than the other sources. To complicate matters there are three birth dates given in the official records: 21st November 1917 in the ledger at the Comedia Theatre in Buenos Aires for Evita Duarte; 7th May 1919 in the Los Toldos church register for Eva Maria Ibarguren; and 7th May 1922 on her marriage certificate as Maria Eva Duarte.

We'll come back to Eva Peron later. For now let's consider another example.

Adolf Hitler

Adolf Hitler was born on 20ᵗʰ April 1889 in Branau, Austria. The recorded time was 6:30 p.m., which places Uranus just above the eastern horizon, with the Moon first the rise after the birth. However, events in the six decans of Hitler's life lead me to suggest that Uranus had not yet risen over the ascendant when he was born. In brief these events were as follows:

Ages	Events	Sequence	
		A	B
0 - 9	Father retires from the Austrian custom service and becomes a bee farmer	☽	♅
10 - 19	Younger brother dies. Elder brother runs away from home. Father dies. Mother dies. He is ambitious to become an artist.	♃	☽
20 - 29	Period of poverty. Joins the German army. First World War. Twice awarded the Iron Cross for bravery. Miraculously escapes death.	☿	♃
30 – 39	Attends lectures at university. Much public speaking. Political organizing. Imprisoned. Writes *Mein Kampf*.	☉	☿
40 - 49	Election success. Becomes Chancellor of Germany. Fame.	♂	☉
50 - death	Starts the Second World War. Successful invasions. Has great power. Exterminating the Jews. Poor health. Defeat. Suicide.	♀	♂

There is no doubt that Hitler was born in the daytime. His mother died in the early morning hours of December 21, 1907, when he was 18 years and 8 months old. The event coinciding with 18¼ years was Hitler receiving his patrimony and leaving Linz to go to Vienna to sit the examinations of the Academy of Fine Arts. With Adolf gone, his mother, who had undergone an operation in January 1907 to remove a cancerous breast, is said to have "let herself go and became an old, sick woman." No life-changing event occurred in Hitler's 25ᵗʰ year to suggest a nocturnal birth.

Sequence B, with Uranus below the horizon and the first planet that will rise into the eastern sky after birth, is clearly the more appropriate sequence. Each of the planets in Sequence B better symbolizes events in Hitler's life in each ten-year period than do the alternative planets in Sequence A.

Hitler's twenties were difficult. To better understand the rulership of Jupiter, the Greater Benefic, during these years, we see that it is located in Capricorn, the sign of its Fall; and closely conjunct a debilitated Moon. While the Moon conjunct Jupiter can be wonderfully positive it will not be so at all when it occurs in Capricorn the sign in which both bodies are weakened. Also Jupiter, a naturally diurnal planet, is inappropriately located be-low the horizon in this daytime chart. Despite these difficulties, Jupiter acted in a protective manner and brought Hitler safely out of the deadly trenches of the First World

War. A biased observer may have wished that Jupiter had also received several square aspects to have severely weakened its protective mode and allowed the world to avoid the many horrors Hitler subsequently brought about.

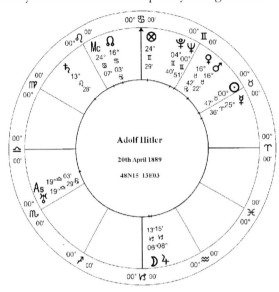

Attending lectures at university, the public speaking, the political organizing, and writing his best-selling book can all be associated with Mercury ruling Hitler's thirties. This again points to B being the correct sequence.

Becoming the ruler of Germany when the Sun ruled the decan is obviously right, as are the events of the Second World War, which coincided with Mars ruling his decan after 1939. Both of these rulerships are listed in Sequence B, and confirm that it was Uranus and not the Moon that would be the planet first to rise to Hitler's ascendant following his birth. The illustrated chart has Uranus arbitrarily placed just a few arc-minutes from the ascendant, but the ascendant could in theory be several degrees earlier in Libra. Greater accuracy is not necessary in order to apply the decan as a prediction tool

John Lennon

John Lennon's birth time has long been a subject of controversy. The times, each seemingly given with great authority, alternate between seven in the morning and six-thirty in the evening. Sunrise at Liverpool on his birthday was at 7:33 a.m., and the sunset was at 6:24 p.m. Was Lennon born during the day or night?

In early 1959, when Lennon was 18¼ years old, the turning point appropriate for a daytime birth, he and Paul McCarthy formed their song-writing team. Mercury is sextile Venus and squares both the Moon and Pluto, forming a T-cross with these two bodies.

By contrast, 1965, which would have been a year of change had he been born after sunset, was a year of drugs and constant touring. There were however happenings in his life that could be associated with Saturn taking over rulership of his life: that year John received his MBE (Member of the Order of the British Empire), a reward for work well done; there was a frenetic tour of the United States during which he upset that country's religionists, a saturnine establishment; and the Beatles made their final live performance.

However, I believe the 1959 formation of the Lennon-McCarthy song-writing duo points to Mercury taking over the rulership from the Sun. This seems to be confirmed by the Moon-Pluto opposition with which Mercury is connected, the three-body combination symbolizing the worldwide popularity of the Beatles, their music and their songs. That argues for John Lennon being born during daylight hours. It doesn't say however whether he was born shortly after sunrise or just before sunset, either of which would fit with the two different suggested times.

Decade	Diurnal			Nocturnal							
0 - 9	☿	☽	♄	☉	♂	♆	♀	♇	♅	♃	♄
10 - 19	☽	♄	♃	☿	☉	♂	♆	♀	♇	♅	♃
20 - 29	♄	♃	♅	☽	☿	☉	♂	♆	♀	♇	♅
30 - 39	♃	♅	♇	♄	☽	☿	☉	♂	♆	♀	♇
40 - death	♅	♇	♆	♃	♄	☽	☿	☉	♂	♆	♆
	A	**B**	**C**								

During Lennon's first ten years of life his parents separated and he lived mostly with his uncle. In Lennon's second decan both his uncle and his mother died.

The twenties were the years of the Beatles' phenomenal success: their initial record came out when John was 20 years old. The partnership ended ten years later. I associate this with Jupiter or Uranus ruling the decan, which rules out Saturn.

Lennon's thirties began with him quitting Britain and moving permanently to the United States. There was a period of public feuding with the other members of the Beatles; he then became involved in politics and sued the US government; and he and his new wife Yoko separated and led an on-again off-again marriage, always in the public eye. This sounds very much like Uranus.

He was assassinated at the start of his forties when Pluto took over rulership in Column B.

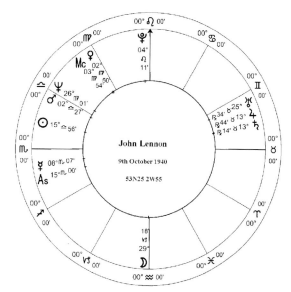

John Lennon
9th October 1940
53N25 2W55

Given the nature of the events that occurred in each of these decans and the associated planetary rulers, there can be little doubt that the Moon was the astrological body that first rose to the eastern horizon following his birth (sequence B). This means that Lennon's was a diurnal birth and that his natal ascendant is in Scorpio, Sagittarius or Capricorn. In the illustrated chart I have arbitrarily placed the ascendant at 15° Scorpio.

The prediction of future happenings in the life and their general nature does not require the ascendant to be specifically determined with any greater accuracy than this. Knowing which planet will be the first to rise to the eastern horizon after birth is enough to allow the general happenings within a life to be forecast. However, knowing the sign and degree of the ascendant and the sign and degree culminating, the location of the ascendant ruler, the house positions of the different planets, etc., namely the standard features within the natal horoscope, will add colorful detail to any forecast of general happenings within the life.

Winston Churchill

The usually accepted chart for Britain's wartime prime minister has the last degree of Virgo on the ascendant with Mars in Libra the first planet to rise after birth. However, based on the sequence of rising planets in the Decan, I don't believe this is correct.

All of the available evidence points to the birth having occurred at Blenheim, England in the early hours of November 30th 1874, sometime between midnight and sunrise, which tells us that only one of four planets, Mars, Jupiter, Mercury or the Sun, could have been the first to rise after birth.

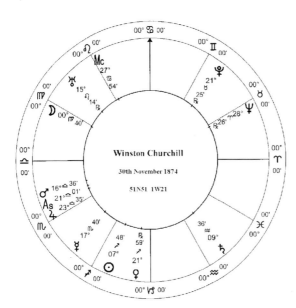

The table opposite lists the four alternative sequences of planets that could govern each of the different ten-year periods in Churchill's long life, together with major events occurring in each of these periods, depending on which of the four planets first arrived at the ascendant after his early-morning birth.

Churchill was born at night. He was aged 24¼ when he resigned from the army. By contrast, at age 18¼ he was studying to take his entrance exams to go into the army.

There is a distinct difference between the nature of events in Churchill's life

14

when he was in his thirties as opposed to those that occurred when he was in his forties. He was thirty-one years old when he was given a post in the government. Two years later he was promoted into the Cabinet, subsequently becoming Home Secretary and then the First Lord of the Admiralty. This was a phenomenally fast rise to power for anyone at such an early age. In the same period he married and his wife gave birth first to a daughter and then a son. The nature of these events would appear to rule out the two sequences of events labeled as C and D, which would have Saturn or Neptune ruling the period.

Rising planets				Age	Events
♂	♃	☿	☉	0-9	Father quarrels with Prince of Wales. In Ireland. Unhappy when away at school.
♃	☿	☉	♀	10 - 19	Father self-destructs his political career. Injuries. In trouble with authorities. To Harrow school. Studying to go into the army.
☿	☉	♀	♄	20 - 29	Father dies. Goes into army. To India. Resigns from the army. War correspondent. To South Africa. Captured by Boers but escapes. Famous. Elected MP.
☉	♀	♄	♆	30 - 39	Marries. Becomes Home Secretary, then 1st Lord of the Admiralty. Children born.
♀	♄	♆	♇	40 - 49	First World War. Resigns. In trenches. Depression. Back in the Cabinet as Colonial Secretary. Buys & repairs Chartwell Manor. Mother dies. Inheritance.
♄	♆	♇	♅	50 - 59	Chancellor of Exchequer. Out of office. Loss of money in market crash. Much writing.
♆	♇	♅	☽	60 - 69	Warns against Hitler. Abdication crisis. Attacks weakness of Britain's air defenses. Daughter elopes. Writing. Second World War. Back in Cabinet. Becomes Prime Minister. Battle for Britain's survival. He & Stalin split up Eastern Europe.
♇	♅	☽	♂	70 - 79	Victory. Loses election. Large financial gains. Painting. Again Prime Minister. Feeble concentration. Noble Prize.
♅	☽	♂	♃	80 - 89	Sadly resigns his office. Strokes. Painting. Physical pain & discomfort. Daughter commits suicide.
☽	♂	♃	☿	90	Death.
A	B	C	D		

By contrast Churchill's forties were extremely difficult. The First World War was happening, and the combination of naval setbacks and failure in the Dardanelles, for both of which he was largely responsible, forced him to resign his office and to go to France as a soldier and experience life in the trenches under fire. He then helped the White Russians, who were badly defeated by the Bolsheviks. Later in this same period two daughters were born, his mother died, he received an inheritance and purchased the derelict Chartwell Manor, which he then repaired and moved into. As events during this ten-year period appear much more likely to be ruled by Saturn than by Venus, the sequence of planetary rulers in column B of the preceding table has my vote, which means that the first planet to rise after Churchill's birth was Jupiter.

Examination of each of the other ten-year periods and associating them with the time ruler listed in column B confirms that this sequence is more appropriate than the sequence listed in column A, the one associated with the time of birth usually accepted, or with those in the other two candidate sequences, C and D. Accordingly, I submit that Winston Churchill's ascendant was after 16½° of Libra and earlier than 23½° of the same sign. The ascendant of the accompanying chart has arbitrarily been given the 20th degree of Libra. The clairvoyant Charubel associated this degree with *The sun shining brightly*, and wrote that it *"denotes a great man; a public character; one who will be noted in his day and whose presence among mankind will be considered essential. The world will ever appreciate the presence of such a one."* Those present in London during the blitz of the Second World War will appreciate just how appropriate Charubel's words are for Churchill.

Individual Decan Years

Now let's return to Eva Peron and use the decan to go deeper into her short life.

Eva Peron's chart is a difficult one. Each of the two Lights is closely conjunct an afflicted malefic. The Sun is with Mars in Taurus, the sign of its detriment; and the Moon is with Saturn in Leo, where Saturn is in its detriment. And these two extremely difficult pairings square each other.

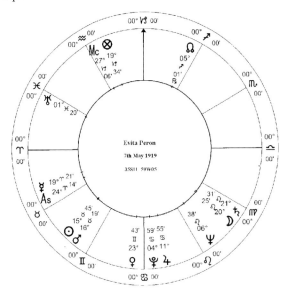

The chart has overall a bowl shape; the two tight conjunctions square each other, both contain a light and a malefic; there is a trine between the Moon and Mercury; Venus is sextile to Saturn; and there is a wide Jupiter-Pluto conjunction.

The ascending degree is a clear line of demarcation. A body with a positive altitude has already risen; it cannot be the first body in the sequence.

The woman known as Eva Peron was born roughly 1¾ hours before sunrise. The first planet to rise, the Sun, represents her future; it symbolizes the central theme around which her life will be involved. The body that rose last before the birth, Mercury for Evita, may tell us something about her immediate past, possibly it informs us of abilities that are innate within her, talent she was born with and which, given the right circumstances, will assist her in this life. Eva Peron was first a successful radio actress. Later her speeches to Argentina's masses brought her their adulation.

The initial year of each decan is entirely of the nature, defined in terms of its Zodiac position, house placement and aspects, of the planetary ruler of the decan. This year, the first of ten is invariably one of new beginnings, stimulated by and of the nature of this ruling planet. It is a year of potentials.

The second year within each set of ten is described in terms of the planet ruling the decan coming, by direction, to the natal position of the first body it meets after rising above the horizon, going in a clockwise direction around the natal chart. In the previous year the decan ruler was brought from below the Earth to the eastern horizon. Now it is lifted up further to the position of the planet that rose immediately before it did.

Eva Peron's first year of life is characterized by the Sun rising in the east. Her second year is then described by the Sun being directed higher in the sky and coming to the position of her natal Mercury, the planet that rose immediately before the Sun. The new situation that manifested itself the previous year, associated with the rising of Evita's Sun, is now becoming a more complete part of her life.

Her third year has the Sun coming to Uranus, the next planet it meets as the ruler continues to move around the horoscope in a clockwise direction. The following year the Sun will come to Saturn, and this circling of the chart will continue as the decan ruler is directed to each of the planets in turn, spending a year with each of them. It will eventually arrive at Mars, the final one of the ten, which occurs on the ninth birthday. The following year, at age ten, Mars will become the new decan ruler and its place will become the new ascendant. At age eleven Mars, the ruler of this second decan, will rise up to conjunct the Sun, and the year after that it will come to Mercury and so on, in its turn circling the chart and being directed to each of the planets until it gets to Venus, the next ruler.

This process continues throughout an individual's life. Each planet in sequence will rule a ten-year decan, and it will move around the wheel coming to each of the other planets in turn. The table on the next page shows the ages when each of the conjunctions will occur. Rising sequence simply means the order in which a planet will rise above the ascendant following the birth. For Eva Peron the sequence is: first the Sun followed in turn by Mars, Venus, Pluto, Jupiter, Neptune, the Moon, Saturn, Uranus, with Mercury as the last of the ten.

The first planet to rise in Eva Peron's birth chart is the Sun. It is a nocturnal Sun and as such not placed where it is strongest, in the sky above. Where the Sun is located in the horoscope indicates where the individual can shine. When found below the Earth at birth, as it is here and as it usually will be when it is the first to rise after birth, the shining, the attention the individual receives, the compliments, honors and so forth, will be deeply desired but they are not going to be automatically available, not his or hers simply by right. Any demands for attention may receive no immediate response; they may be ignored and in that case can become internalized. This in turn can strengthen the need for attention and reinforce the individual's ambition.

With the Sun as the first body to rise after birth, circumstances often occur during the initial ten years of life that will force the child to become independent and stand on his or her own feet years before he or she is mature enough to cope with the experience. The child is forced to stand up for himself against others at an early age, often at too early an age, long before it possesses the physical or mental strength to do so. A child born with the Sun first to rise after birth tends to be an only child, or be without playmates of its own age; he or she may be born to elderly parents, into a broken marriage, or with one, perhaps both, absentee parents. Sometime during the decan the child may be sent away from the parental home to live with relatives or boarded at a distant school. These children are frequently left too soon to their own devices, forced to become independent and self-reliant too early in their lives. Yet the desire for affection is rarely absent, it doesn't go entirely away. It can grow into a craving for adulation, a need to be placed on a pedestal.

Ages when each decan ruler is directed to each receiving planet

Rising sequence of decan ruler	*Rising sequence of Receiving Planet*									
	1	**10**	**9**	**8**	**7**	**6**	**5**	**4**	**3**	**2**
1	**0**	1	2	3	4	5	6	7	8	9
2	11	12	13	14	15	16	17	18	19	**10**
3	22	23	24	25	26	27	28	29	**20**	21
4	33	34	35	36	37	38	39	**30**	31	32
5	44	45	46	47	48	49	**40**	41	42	43
6	55	56	57	58	59	**50**	51	52	53	54
7	66	67	68	69	**60**	61	62	63	64	65
8	77	78	79	**70**	71	72	73	74	75	76
9	88	89	**80**	81	82	83	84	85	86	87
10	99	**90**	91	92	93	94	95	96	97	98

In the above table the ages (0, 10, 20, 30, etc) when a decan ruler rises to the ascendant are highlighted, the row and column having the same rising sequence value. For example, age 30, when the fourth ruler comes to the ascendant, is shown at the junction of row 4 and column 4.

Evita's Sun is in Taurus closely conjunct Mars. The natural malignancy of Mars is heightened in Taurus, the sign of its detriment, and further added to by being combust a Sun that is below the horizon in this nocturnal chart.

Both Eva and Juan Peron were born with the Sun conjunct Mars. Eva's was in Taurus, Juan's in Libra. Thus both conjunctions occurred in signs difficult for Mars, and in the case of Juan difficult also for the Sun. For both there was an energetic quest for fame, power, and the dominion of and building up of an empire. Sex was subordinate in their lives to ambition. Both were ruthless taskmasters, working themselves and others to the point of sheer exhaustion and able to get more accomplished than most other people. Eva put everything she had into whatever she was doing at any particular moment. This conjunction attracts attacks from others.

Eva's father abandoned the family the year she was born.

After coming to the ascendant the decan ruler proceeds in a clockwise direction to conjunct each of the other planets one after the other. The Sun arrives at her Mercury when Eva is one, at her Uranus when she is two, and at her Saturn when she is three, and so on. In each

Age	Decan Ruler's direction
0	☉ ♂ As
4	☉ ♂ ☽
6	☉ ♂ ♃

of these years events of the nature of the two bodies involved in the directed conjunction can be expected to occur. For young children such events are often happenings that occur directly to other members of their family, but which alter the world in which the child is living.

When Eva is four, at which time the rising Sun moving in a clockwise direction has come to her Moon, she is badly burnt by boiling frying oil that falls on her, the oil covering "her entire body". She is extremely lucky. There are no scars but she is left with a parchment skin, quite transparent, for which she is later famed. Not only is her Sun conjunct a debilitated Mars, and her Moon conjunct a debilitated Saturn, but there is also a square aspect between these two difficult conjunctions. One positive feature of what at first sight appears to be an impossible situation is that the Sun and Moon are in a mixed Mutual Reception—the Sun is in Taurus the Moon's sign of exaltation, while the Moon is in Leo the sign the Sun rules.

She is six when the Sun comes to Jupiter. That year her absentee father dies in a car accident. Jupiter often indicates the father, or someone with authority over the native. Jupiter's wide conjunction with Pluto may explain his abandonment of the family—Pluto tends to bring about separations.

It is not hard to understand that Eva's next decan, ruled by the afflicted Mars, would be difficult. She will find herself in a hostile world, one in which she must battle in order to survive and pursue her objectives.

I know nothing of events in Eva's life for the first five years of her second decan.

At age fifteen, when the decan ruler Mars has moved around to her natal Moon, she decides to become an actress. Despite having a boyfriend, a soldier in the local garrison—with Mars ruling her decan Eva will have instinctively been drawn to military people—she leaves her home and heads for Buenos Aires, going as the mistress of Augustin Magaldi, a tango singer. Once in the capitol city she obtains a part in a radio program, finds an apartment for herself, and abandons Magaldi.

At sixteen, Eva's Mars comes to her Neptune. Mars directed to Neptune often indicates a year in which the individual will encounter unreality. It can be a time when a person's efforts all end in failure. The radio program ends and she begins seeking work in theaters. She is short of money and food. For a short run she has a role as a maid, then two other parts before becoming unemployed again. She is described as having become so skinny it was pitiful. At the end of the year she obtains a job in a touring company.

Age	Decan Ruler's direction
15	♂ ☌ ☽
16	♂ ☌ ♆
17	♂ ☌ ♃
18	♂ ☌ ♇
19	♂ ☌ ♀

Mars comes to Jupiter when she is seventeen. Although Jupiter is strong in Cancer, the sign is an unfriendly place for Mars. The malignant Mars has Eva encounter several people represented by the exalted Jupiter. She acts in a touring company, playing a nurse who is ministering to a man dying from syphilis in "The Fatal Kiss." While on the road she is forced to sleep with the company manager. After she leaves the touring company and is back in Buenos Aires, she gets other parts by sleeping with a theater producer so grossly fat that he is nicknamed "the Toad".

At eighteen, with Mars still in Cancer but now on her Pluto, she experiences great difficulties but survives by acting bit parts.

The bit parts continued into the start of the next year, the final one of the ten, as Mars comes to her Venus in Gemini. Venus is most benefic when she rises after the Sun in a nocturnal chart, as it does here. We would therefore expect an improvement in her situation, some relief from the difficulties she has been experiencing. For six months she lives with an actor who says he wants to marry her, but then deserts her. She starts frequenting the offices of a movie magazine, trying to get herself mentioned in its gossip columns. There are several affairs with men who she believes could help advance her acting career. She is learning how things work, and intuitively preparing to take full advantage of the coming decan, when Venus will take over as her ruler.

Eva is twenty when her Venus-ruled decan begins. Her circumstances immediately change when she obtains a part in a new radio soap opera, aimed at stay-at-home housewives in the afternoons. She does well and is very successful in several other radio soaps. Feature stories about her begin to appear in the magazines, including a cover photo by a well-known fashion photographer.

The next year, with Venus coming to Mars, her success in radio continues. Mars is unable to work his malignant tricks; he can only be subservient to Venus, who rules Taurus, the sign it occupies.

At age twenty-two Venus comes to the Sun in Taurus. With the aid of her brother, who has become an executive for a cosmetic and soap company (products we associate with Venus and the signs she rules), Eva is able to get a sponsor to back her radio programs. She also gathers together a group of radio actors, and forms her own company.

At twenty-three Venus arrives at Mercury in Aries, a sign in which Venus is always uncomfortable. Her radio company is becoming a success but does so without her; Eva disappears from all of her usual haunts for the first six months of 1943. What happened? She has become pregnant and has a back-street abortion in which the bottom of her uterus is perforated. She nearly dies from the resulting peritonitis.

Age	Decan Ruler's direction
20	♀ ☌ Aₛ
21	♀ ☌ ♂
22	♀ ☌ ☉
23	♀ ☌ ☿
24	♀ ☌ ♅
25	♀ ☌ ♄
26	♀ ☌ ☽
27	♀ ☌ ♆
28	♀ ☌ ♃
29	♀ ☌ ♀

Venus comes to Uranus the following year. Venus is exalted in Pisces the sign Uranus occupies. Events proceed appropriately. This year, at age twenty-four, she is hired at Radio Belgrano and becomes one of the best-paid radio actresses of the time. She moves into an apartment in the city's best residential district. While fund-raising for the victims of an earthquake (because of their unpredictable disruption to normal life, earthquakes are symbolized by Uranus) she first meets Juan Peron, a prominent army officer with a ministerial position in the army-ruled government. For the rest of her short life Eva will refer to the date of their meeting as "my marvelous day". They immediately begin an affair. She personally dismisses Peron's former mistress and moves in with him. The same year she has her first starring film role, and then negotiates the largest contract ever in radio. This is also the year in which she first bleaches her hair.

At age twenty-five Venus comes to Saturn. Saturn is uncomfortable in Leo but Venus is not. Even so the influence of Saturn in the sign of its detriment clearly makes itself felt during the year. Eva is elected president of the newly formed broadcasting performers union. She begins making nightly radio broadcasts pushing for Peron to become President. She attends meetings of Peron's closest supporters, something that was shocking in those days in Argentina, quite unheard of, a thing incomprehensible to his supporters. She is acting in three radio programs daily and becomes ill. Her doctor orders her to rest and to take things easier. By exchanging celluloid, which in very short supply, Peron arranges for Eva to be given the starring role in the film *The Prodigal*. This is the last film that she will ever make. Before it can be premiered her acting career (twenty plays, five movies, more than twenty-six radio soaps over ten years) has been swallowed up in her life with Peron.

A comment on Eva's Moon conjunct Saturn: anyone born with this conjunction tends to suffer from a chronic physical disability. They will know hardship and frustration, even failure and poverty. They will fear insecurity and may feel resentment. They may be kindhearted, but usually they have few close friends. In Eva's case the negativity invariably associated with the Moon conjunct Saturn occurred in early life but it is somewhat counteracted by the square from the Sun-Mars conjunction, the Sun-Moon mutual reception, and the strong Jupiter located between the two conjunctions. However, the negativity manifested itself again at the end of her short life.

The following year, with Eva now twenty-six years old, the decan ruler Venus comes to the Moon. Any Moon-influenced year can be expected to involve many ups and downs in the life, changes of both place and fortune. This is no exception. The Moon is located in Leo, conjunct Saturn and in a mutual reception with the Sun in Taurus. Under pressure from the Army, Peron resigns as War Minister and from the army. There are many threats against his life. Eva and Peron leave Argentina to go to Paraguay. Hunted by the army and the police, they hide on a small island but are quickly discovered. Peron is arrested and imprisoned. After her initial shock, Eva begins to organize his release. She is told that in prison Peron has become sick with pleurisy. The unions march in from the suburbs and take control of Buenos Aires. They call for Peron's release. The army capitulates; Peron is released and takes control of the country. Amid scenes of triumph seemingly taken directly out of one of her films, Eva and Peron are married. Elections are called. Eva stands beside her husband during the election campaign, something no candidate's wife has ever done before in Argentina. With her help, Peron is elected President of Argentina.

Eva is twenty-seven years old when her husband is inaugurated president. Venus has now come to her Neptune and this is truly a Neptunian year, one in which she is living a life that in her early years could only be considered so much fantasy. The couple moves into the Unzue Palace. Eva begins visiting factories and working in the newly created Ministry of Labor. She attends many meetings with the unions. As first lady she enjoys receiving many presents, especially jewels. She is learning how to act and to dress for her new position. She purchases a newspaper using borrowed money. It will become a propaganda organ she will use to ensure full details of Peron's programs are communicated to the masses. While she is greatly criticized by the upper classes and by the political opposition, there is vast identification with her, due to affection or empathy, by Argentine housewives. She is invited to visit Spain and Italy.

She arrived in Buenos Aires without a penny to her name. She acted in hopeless theatres where her pay was a cup of coffee with milk. She was nothing or less than nothing then: a sparrow at an outdoor laundry sink, so skinny it was pitiful... [then] she began to make herself look pretty with a passion. She wove a chrysalis of beauty, little by little hatching a queen... She rose like a meteor from the anonymity of minor roles to a throne on which no woman had sat: that of Benefactress of the Humble and Spiritual Head of the Nation. She managed to do so in less than four years. In September 1943 (aged 24) she was hired at

Radio Belgrano. In July 1947 [aged 28] she was on the cover of Time *magazine. She had just returned from a tour of Europe that was baptized as "going over the rainbow."[1]*

At age twenty-eight Venus has arrived at her exalted Jupiter in Cancer, and, despite her fear of flying, Eva flies off to Europe. Her fame has preceded her. She is on the cover of *Time* magazine. She receives a great welcome by Franco in Spain, enjoys successful visits to Paris and Lisbon, and has an audience with the Pope in Rome. However, her vanity is wounded when she is told the British royal family will be away from Buckingham Palace when she is due to visit London—she cancels that visit. On her way home, she stops off to visit Brazil. Her tour is generally successful but it exhausts her physically. This is the year in which Argentinean women first get the vote.

In the final year of this third ten years of life, Venus comes to Pluto. By antiscion, there is a close conjunction between Venus and Pluto. Eva is speaking more and more in public. She speaks fluently, dramatically, with passion: always emotionally—appropriately for Venus directed to Pluto, these are public confessions of her love for Peron. The Maria Eva Duarte de Perón Foundation is created (it is later renamed the Eva Perón Foundation). Its aim is to help the poor. She runs it, working long hours to distribute her love. Eva uses the Foundation to create the Children's Football Championship; to sponsor universal pension schemes (only later will the state take these over); to build nursing homes; and to remove inequality from health care.

Age	Decan Ruler's direction
30	♀ ♂ As
31	♀ ♂ ♀
32	♀ ♂ ♂
33	♀ ♂ ☉

At thirty a new decan begins, one ruled by Pluto in Cancer. By equal sign, Pluto is in the fourth house. It indicates a need to transform past traditions, to leave the past behind through a series of upheavals that can occur in the home, in property or real estate. Just as Pluto is the outsider planet so when emphasized in life, which it is when it becomes ruler of a decan, it indicates just how an individual will separate himself from society's existing mores and customs and want to change them. The stronger Pluto is at birth—here it can be considered angular and conjunct the two naturally benefic planets, Venus by antiscion and the exalted Jupiter by wide conjunction—the more it can compel an individual to work to shatter society's *status quo*. It can become an obsession. Pluto, of course, and especially when located in the fourth house, is also associated with the end of things, with death.

Eva begins the year by founding the Peronist Women's Party, which she dominates. It is an outstanding success. She is incessantly in the public eye. She works fervently for the Foundation—"my vocation"—distributing money and help to others. She uses the Foundation to improve public medical care and to build a Children's City. She will not stop working. Eventually this catches up with her and she faints. She is rushed to hospital for an emergency appendectomy. Tests taken at the time show that she had cancer of the

---

[1] Tomas Eloy Martinez, *Santa Evita.*

uterus, but she is told she has anemia not cancer. A hysterectomy is recommended, which she refuses.

At thirty-one Pluto comes to her Venus, ruler of her previous decan. She continues her Foundation work: providing bargain burials, operating food and liquor stores. She is again working excessively, through the night, sleeping only two hours nightly. She eats little. The business of giving people things fills her life. With a ghostwriter she works on her autobiography. She mediates in a nation-wide railway strike. People begin saying she should become Vice President.

She was the emissary of happiness, the gateway to miracles… She gathered up the troubles that were lying around loose and made a bonfire of them that could be seen from afar. She did the job too well. The fire was so thoroughly going it also burned her.[2]

The following year Eva is thirty-two years old. Pluto comes to her Mars in Taurus. If we give Pluto co-rulership of Scorpio with Mars, then Taurus the opposing sign will be a sign in which Pluto is uncomfortable, in its detriment. This is not a good year for Argentina's first lady. She has lost weight, is thin and much paler than before; her face is drawn, her legs permanently swollen, and she suffers from intense abdominal pains. There is immense support from the masses for her to become Vice President. She is now at the zenith of her political career. 22nd August 1951 becomes known as *Evita's Day of Renunciation*, the day she publicly rejects the people's plea that she become Vice President. She is exhausted and in constant pain. Some days she is unable to get out of bed at all. Advanced cancer of the uterus is confirmed but the doctors continue to lie to Eva. They never tell her the true nature of her illness. On the day of an attempted coup against Peron that is foiled by the unions, she has to have blood transfusions before having strength enough to record a radio message, thanking the workers for rescuing Peron. Her autobiography is published and is an instant best seller. The poor and the workers begin praying publicly for her. When she has a hysterectomy operation, a crowd of twenty thousand waits in the street outside the hospital. Peron is reelected. Eva is convalescing. The cancer is spreading. Her rare public speeches become more and more violent—they are her cries of pain and impotence.

At age thirty-three Pluto arrives at Eva's Sun in Taurus. In June Peron is again inaugurated as president. Eva attends the ceremonies. She is dosed with painkillers and held up in the open car by wires. She is losing weight every day. Radiotherapy treatment has little effect. It badly burns her and she suffers greatly from it. Congress gives her the title of *Spiritual Leader of the Nation*, one without precedent. She is only intermittently lucid. She starts to write a second book, *My Message*, which is never published. She writes her will, giving all of her possessions to the people. She dies at 8:25 pm local time on 26th July 1952. There is national mourning and a genuine sense of intense loss.

---

[2] *Santa Evita.*

Eva's story does not however end with her death. Her body is embalmed, a process that takes a year. Then, after a military junta overthrows Peron, her body disappears (the year Pluto comes to Saturn). The new leaders fear the cult of her memory and hide her body until 2nd September 1971 (Neptune, ruler of Eva's sixth decan, is now on Pluto), when it is dug up in a monastery burial ground in Milan, Italy, where it has for years been buried under a false name. Three years later (Neptune at Eva's Sun) her body is returned to Buenos Aires, but it is not handed over to her family until 22nd October 1976 (Neptune has come to her elevated Uranus), when finally it is laid to rest in her family's mausoleum.

Generalized Meanings of Each of the Years within a Decan

These generalized meanings combine personal observation with ancient Pythagorean doctrine, which in turn appears to have been derived from Sumerian teachings.

Ages that end in 0: The initial year of each decan, the Monad, is entirely of the nature, defined in terms of its Zodiac position, house placement and aspects, of the planetary ruler of the decan. This year, the first of ten is invariably one of new beginnings, stimulated by and of the nature of this ruling planet. It is a year of potentials, which because it gives rise to everything else can be chaotic. Situations will occur, usually out of the individual's control, which can alter the whole direction the person's life has been taking up until this time. The change of direction is unlikely to be something the native can do very much about. He can either adapt and happily go in the direction circumstances are taking him, or he can resist and be led complaining down the same road. Events or situations over which the individual has no real control—whether he believes he does or not—will manifest and he will either ride along with them, sitting up front in the belief that he controls his life, or be dragged along behind, a victim of fate. There is really no choice. The astrologer will be greatly aided in his interpretation of the effects of this year, and of the meaning of the whole decan, by erecting a chart with the ruling body at the ascendant.

Ages that end in a 1: The second year of the ten, the Dyad, can be difficult. The native is changing. Situations alter; people come and go; interests are redirected. How things were over the previous decan is not the same. There may be conflict between how life was in the previous ten years and the direction in which the current decan ruler wants it to go: the future battling to overturn the grasp of the conservative past and separating from what has been. Life does not stand still; it is only motionless in the grave, where it is absent. The planet the ruler meets this year will give shape to the ruler's raw potential that was awakened in the previous twelve months. To others the individual may appear more opinionated now than in earlier times, more impulsive, more reckless. He is instinctively becoming aware of a new direction his life can take, a fresh opportunity that is being offered, and is eager to shed the restraints of the past and move on. This is a coming-to-be year.

Ages that end in a 2: The third year of the decan, the Triad, is often the first in which the potential of the decan ruler starts to become actualized. The individual has learned from the conflict of the previous year and gained experience from what has happened in the past. He should know now how to act correctly, with moderation, prudently avoiding what is excessive or defective. As a result he can look ahead to the future with cautious confidence.

Ages that end in a 3: Events during the fourth year, the Tetrad, usually solidify the direction of the decan. There will be growth, the individual's world gradually expanding to encompass this decan's intent. The planet the ruler meets now will define what is possible in these ten years. As such all that follows in the remaining years of the decan will most probably be produced from how this pair of bodies combine and manifest this year. It represents a second start to the decan.

Ages that end in a 4: In the fifth year, the Pentad, the individual may go off in an entirely new direction and encounter new experiences indicated by the planet to which the decan ruler has come. He is responding to an impulse that seeks for what is missing from his life, despite being unbalanced this will energize the decan.

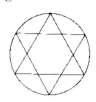

Ages that end in a 5: The sixth year, the Hexad, is frequently one of balance and the setting of limits, of settling down again after the distractions and excitement of the previous year. What may have been contrary and at variance should now be brought together. Where at all possible, these conflicts will be reconciled.

Ages that end in a 6: The seventh year, the Heptad, is often the most critical time of the decan. In some manner the individual will be tested. A crisis is likely to occur. Many things will be brought to completion and unstable situations will result. Either a new force upsets the harmony and balance that were achieved in the previous year or an entirely new impulse appears. Many different outcomes are possible: health or sickness, generation or destruction. If the critical moment is seized, the result could be rebirth into a new transformative process. If the opportunity is missed, expect the life to follow more of the same.

Ages that end in a 7: The eighth year, the Octad or Ogdoad, should rebalance the instability of the previous one and set the stage for further development. If last year's critical challenge was faced positively, this year could contain another beginning, perhaps the first step on the path toward some form of spiritual transformation.

Ages that end in an 8: The ninth year, the Ennead, contains all that has been accomplished in the decan. It is a time either of completion and attainment or of failure and shortcoming. This is the Finishing Post. Either the opportunities provided by the decan ruler have been accepted and made use of, in which case progress is likely to continue, or they were ignored and there was really no progress at all.

Ages that end in a 9: The final year of the ten, the Decad, is one that realizes what has been accomplished over the whole decan. It reintegrates the sequence of planetary influences the ruling planet has experienced into a new and more refined whole. The planet the ruler meets now will rule the upcoming decan. It will be the prime mover of the next ten years of the life, the body that will organize all of the changes the individual will experience in the immediate future. There should be indications this year, especially in the final four months, of the direction in which the next decan will head.

The above descriptions of what may be expected in each of the ten years of any decan are of course generic. They will be greatly modified by the natal strength of the decan ruler and its relationship to the planet and sign it comes to in each of these years. The planets in the septenary, the ruler and the body and sign to which that ruler is directed, will also greatly modify happenings in any specific year.

Each of the different decans can also be related to the above-generalized meanings. Thus, for example, an individual's sixties, his seventh decan, can be described in very much the same way as is the seventh year within a decan. It will be a critical period in which the individual either responds to the new impulse and eagerly looks forward to the opportunities retirement from the workplace will present or, not knowing what to do with himself, he simply allows himself to lose interest in life. Details of how to divide individual decan years into finer parts are given in Appendix B.

Chapter 4

The Septenary

We've seen how the decan, the sequence in which the ten planets come in turn to the ascendant, can be of great use in finding the first planet to rise after birth. That is one way of using the sequence of planets. We will consider now another approach that uses only

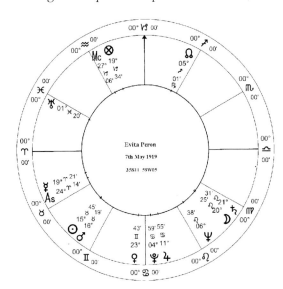

Evita Peron
7th May 1919
35S11 59W05

the seven bodies that have been known since classical times, the septenary. To show the added dimension the septenary brings to that of the decan, I'll again use the chart of Eva Peron. Using a chart that was also used for the decan will help to demonstrate how each of these two methods can provide differing views of the same events in a person's life. The different planetary symbolism of the septenary compliments that of the decan.

The process is exactly the same as has just been described for the decan except that Uranus, Neptune and Pluto are now ignored. Thus, for Eva Peron, the first body to rise to the ascendant is again the Sun, as it was in her decan, and the Sun will rule her first seven years—just seven years now as we are only making use of the seven classical bodies. Mars is still the second body to come to the ascendant and Venus the third.

The fourth planet to rise in the decan was Pluto, but this is now ignored. Instead, in the septenary the fourth ruler is Jupiter, and this planet will rule the fourth set of seven years in Eva Peron's life. After Jupiter we skip over Neptune and come to the Moon. As Eva Peron died at age 33, her death occurred during the rulership of this fifth septenary ruler. The different rulers and the years they ruled in her life are listed in the accompanying table:

Age	Eva's Septenary Ruler
0 - 6	☉
7 - 13	♂
14 - 20	♀
21 - 27	♃
28 - death	☽

What we know about the first years of Eva's life involves her father. He abandoned the family the year Eva was born and he died when she was six years old. The Sun is a symbol of the father. These two major events cover the range, 0 to 6, when the afflicted Sun was ruling Eva's septenary.

Little is known of events during the next Septenary, ruled by Mars. Her grandmother died, she started school, and the family moved twenty miles to another town.

When her Venus-ruled septenary began she had a boyfriend but soon abandoned him to go to Buenos Aires as the mistress of Agustin Magaldi, a tango singer. She wanted to become an actress. Once in the capital city, she left Magaldi and for the remaining years of the septenary pursued her dream of becoming a famous actress but without any great success. Venus is associated with the glamour of the theater and with love affairs, of which Eva reportedly had several during these seven years.

This all changed with the advent of Eva's Jupiter-ruled septenary. Jupiter is in Cancer at her birth, the sign in which it is exalted. She got a part in a new radio soap opera and was an immediate success. So much so that within just a few years she had become one of the best-paid actresses on radio. Then, when she was 24, she met Juan Peron. The two fell immediately in love. Two years later, with Eva's help, Peron was elected Argentina's president. Eva and Juan were married and moved into the presidential palace. She quickly became idolized by her country's masses, the women fantasizing themselves into her position. It was truly seven years ruled by an exalted Jupiter, a Cinderella-like rags-to-riches fairy tale.

Her badly afflicted Moon rules Eva's final septenary. It is conjunct the debilitated Saturn in Leo and squares the difficult Sun-Mars conjunction in Taurus. The year-week started with Eva traveling on a good will tour to Europe, but she quickly began to suffer increasing pain and died from a cancer in her uterus.

The planets ruling each of the seven-year periods, like those ruling each of the ten-year periods of the Decan, describe the general direction of Eva's life during the times they had rulership. We'll confirm this with another example, again using someone we have already discussed.

Adolf Hitler

In the decan of Adolf Hitler Uranus ruled the initial ten years of life. In the septenary the first classical planet to arrive at the ascendant following the birth is the Moon. It is an afflicted Moon, in its detriment in Capricorn. The Moon's close conjunction with Jupiter in the sign of its fall increases this affliction. When the Moon is the first body to reach the ascendant following the birth there are often indications of an erratic personality, of the individual in later life being subject to sharp mood changes. This appears to be so whether the Moon is the first in the septenary or in the decan. These indications are more certain to manifest in later life when the Moon is afflicted.

Hitler's first septenary ends when he is six years old. This is when his father retires from his job as an Austrian customs official and set himself up as a beekeeper. His irritable and

Age	Septenary Ruler
0 - 6	☽
7 – 13	♃
14 - 20	☿
21 – 27	☉
28 - 34	♂
35 - 41	♀
42 - 48	♄
49 - 55	☽
56 - Death	♃

violent father, unused to being at home, disrupts what had until then been fairly contented years that young Adolf had spent in the company of his mother and brothers.

His elder brother runs away from home when Adolph is seven, at the start of the Jupiter-ruled septenary. The next year Adolph is briefly intoxicated by religion and wants to become a priest. The following year his younger brother dies. A year later Adolph tries to run away from home to escape his bullying father. Adolph is thirteen when his father dies. At the time he is ambitious to become a great actor. Jupiter in Capricorn can be associated with each of these happenings.

Mercury, opposed by Uranus and badly afflicted by being combust the Sun, rules Hitler's third septenary. It is a very bad period. Despite failing several subjects at school he is allowed to graduate. He applies to attend the Art Academy in Vienna but is rejected. His mother dies. He fails in an attempt to write plays. There is little money and he soon becomes a tramp, begging on the street, humiliated and apathetic.

The Taurean Sun rules the next septenary. Hitler's interest in politics begins at the start of these seven years, when he is twenty-one. He is painting now, and beginning to sell his paintings. His finances improve. He moves from Vienna to Munich, and enlists in the German army when war begins. He is in several fierce battles, his bravery being rewarded with an Iron Cross. He writes much poetry during these years. The painting and the poetry of the period can be related to the Sun's natal placement in Taurus, a sign ruled by Venus. Hitler's active role in the German army, a sharp contrast to the general failure and apathy of his previous septenary, is explained by the Sun's rulership of these years.

The war is still going on when Hitler's next septenary begins. He is twenty-eight. Mars rules the septenary. It is in Taurus, the sign of its detriment, and conjunct Hitler's ascendant ruler, Venus. This is a difficult combination but by itself it is not the worst that can happen. The awful signature that cosmic forces burned into Hitler's soul, which conspired to make him the monster he became, is the connection this conjunction of Mars and Venus has with the elevated Saturn. Saturn is in Leo, the sign of its debility, and it is squared by the Mars-Venus conjunction. Again, this forms a difficult combination but it is not the worst. What makes the combination lethal is that the antiscion of Saturn falls at 16° 34' Taurus, where it is between Mars, at 16°22', and Venus, at 16°42'—just 2' from their exact midpoint. The triple conjunction of Mars and Saturn with the ascendant ruler is deadly. More so because it is located in the 8th house, and in a chart that also has a close conjunction of the Moon and Jupiter in Capricorn, and Uranus very close to the ascendant.

It is with the advent of his Mars Septenary, when Hitler becomes twenty-eight years old, that his true self first really begins to appear.

He wins a second Iron Cross but loses his dog and his paintings. He is starving, barely escapes a choking death from poison gas, and is blind for several weeks. Wounded and demoralized by Germany's defeat he is in black despair, ashamed by the ignominy. He has a vision, the memory of which will stay with him until his death. He leaves the army, learns oratory, and joins the German Workers Party, which he quickly reorganizes. He is speaking frequently in public, living in a revolutionary atmosphere. He adopts the swastika as the party's symbol, gains control of the party, has it buy a newspaper and he becomes recognized as a political force in Bavaria. Party membership increases. He realizes he must use force to increase the power of the party. Communists defeat his party in a street battle and he is wounded. The putsch fails and he ends the septenary in prison.

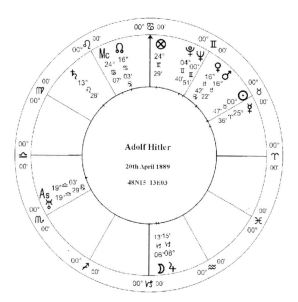

The Venus septenary starts when he is thirty-five years old. He is in prison writing *Mein Kampf*. The book quickly becomes a best seller. On his release from prison he buys a house and a new car. He is known publicly as *Der Fuhrer*. He has a 16-year-old girl as his lover. She attempts suicide. He changes her for a different girl friend; this one is again nineteen years younger than he is (Hitler's attraction to much younger women is indicated by Mercury close to his descendant). He decides that *Lebensraum* and the Jewish danger are intertwined, and plans to destroy the Jews. Germany's economic depression and high unemployment provide him with the political weapons he needs. The Party is successful in elections and he becomes famous internationally.

When Hitler is forty-two the third planetary member of his deadly trio, the 10th house Saturn, takes over rulership of the septenary. He becomes a German citizen and stops eating meat. His girl friend commits suicide. The economic depression in Germany has worsened. The Reichstag fire triggers a general election and Hitler becomes Chancellor. He has achieved power. At his direction Germany quits the League of Nations and trebles the size of its army. Jewish-owned businesses are boycotted, and concentration camps opened. Hitler's Nazis becomes the only permitted party in Germany. He has his rivals murdered and becomes the Fuehrer. He moves from the lawful and legal to the illegal and unlawful, and fears he has throat cancer. The Olympic Games are held in Berlin. His armies occupy the Rhineland and then Austria.

When Hitler is forty-nine the Capricornian Moon again becomes the ruler of his septenary. He has health concerns but invades Czechoslovakia and declares war on the Jews. Eva Braun moves in with him. He starts the Second World War by invading Poland, and then quickly defeats France. He believes he is "more godlike than human," the first of a new race of supermen, the first and only mortal to have emerged into a 'superhuman state'— hence not bound by any human morality or convention, and 'above the law'. He invades Russia, declares war on the USA, and starts the mass extermination of the Jews. He has more *de facto* power than anyone in history. He is paranoid, swinging between extreme optimism and extreme rages, refusing to listen to anyone's advice. His health is failing, and he is defeated at Stalingrad and in North Africa. There are assassination attempts. He falls into a deep depression; he is losing allies and the war. The septenary ends as he faces total defeat. This is a Moon that is completely out of control as indicated by its location in Capricorn and its close conjunction with Jupiter. Both the Moon and Jupiter are in a sign in which they are totally out of place, a clear indication of someone who would be given the opportunity to scale to the highest pinnacle of success and then be dashed down to reality.

He is fifty-six when his Jupiter-ruled septenary starts. Jupiter is extremely weak in Capricorn, conjunct an equally afflicted Moon. Within a few days he has married Eva Braun and the pair have committed suicide.

As they did with Eva Peron, the septenary rulers clearly describe in general terms the nature of Hitler's life in each of these seven-year periods.

* * *

Having arrived at the ascendant the septenary ruler, in a process similar to that previously described for the decan ruler, proceeds in a clockwise fashion to meet each of the other classical bodies, spending a year with each of them. And within each seven-year period each of the separate years has a specific nature.

Generalized Meanings of Each of the Septenary Years

The initial year of each set of seven is entirely of the nature, defined in terms of its inherent character, its Zodiac position, the House it occupies and the aspects it makes, of the planetary ruler of the septenary period. This year, the first of any set of seven, is invariably one of new beginnings, stimulated by and of the nature of the newly rising planet. It is inauguration day, the time when the new planetary governor takes office and begins to direct how the individual's life should be led. He will experience a new impulse that may at first occur internally, of which he is unaware consciously. As yet the new life direction exists only as a potential that has to be developed. Only later will the impetus for a change in life direction be seen to have occurred during this beginning year. There can be much emotional confusion now, the life direction seeming to be strangely elusive and uncertain as new possibilities flitter through the person's nightly dreaming. Much depends on the planet that has now come to rule the septenary. When this is the Sun the individual may become more impulsive than usual, more assertive, and there can be a new emotional intensity, a feeling of freedom and of new beginnings. Similar feelings often occur when Mars or Jupiter takes over the rulership of the septenary. This year should be considered the *Sunday* of any year-week, irrespective of which body has become the new septenary ruler. The astrologer will be greatly aided in his interpretation of the effect of any septenary ruler and the meaning of seven years of its rulership, by erecting a chart with the ruling body placed at the ascendant.

The second year within each set of seven has the ruling planet of the septenary coming, by direction, to the natal position of the first classical body it meets after rising above the eastern horizon, going in a clockwise direction around the natal chart. In the previous year the septenary ruler was brought from below the Earth to the horizon and now the rotation of the Earth lifts it yet further to the position of the classical planet that rose immediately before it.

The example of Adolf Hitler will make this clear. The Moon rising in the east characterized his first year of life. His second year has the Moon moving higher in the sky, coming to the position of his natal Saturn. The new impulse of the previous year that was triggered by the rising of Hitler's Moon now begins to express itself more completely. The second year of Hitler's life is therefore symbolized as the Moon coming, by direction, to meet the challenge that his natal Saturn poses: he will feel restricted in what he can and cannot do. Similarly, the twenty-second year of his life, which is the second year of his fourth seven-year period, is typified by the ruler of the fourth septenary, the Sun, the fourth of the classical seven to rise after birth, coming to the position of his natal Mercury, the first classical planet the Sun meets after it rises.

In each instance the new septenary ruler encounters the planet that ruled the previous 7-year period. In this second year the future is meeting up with the immediate past. Without that past there can be no future. Such an encounter, the new ruler meeting the ruler of the previous septenary, automatically occurs in the second year of each septenary. Irrespective of the nature of the planets involved, this second year of the seven is likely to be difficult. The world that was developed during the previous seven-year period may not be easily adapted to the direction in which the new life-impulse wishes to go. Expect therefore to observe *resistance from the past* at ages 1, 8, 15, 22, 29, 36, and so on. The nature and intensity of this conflict depends on the two bodies involved, how they are related in the birth chart, and the sign in which this directed conjunction occurs. The individual may become over cautious, even fearful, and try to avoid making the necessary changes in his life that the new impulse (begun the previous year) requires. He is still only vaguely aware of the new direction in his life. He may become overwhelmed by memories of the past, even paralyzed by them. Psychological conflicts and financial or social problems can arise. Think of this second year as the *Monday* of the year-week; irrespective of the planets involved, there will be some "Monday morning blues."

As the septenary ruler continues to rise in a counterclockwise direction it will encounter the next classical planet in **the third year** of each septenary period. When the Moon is the septenary ruler in Hitler's chart, the next personal body it encounters after Saturn is Venus. When Mercury is the septenary ruler it first comes to Jupiter and then moves on to meet the Moon. This third year can be thought of as the *Tuesday* of each of the septenary year-weeks. It is always of the nature of an archetypal Mars. The new trend that began two years earlier now takes on a definite form. How this happens is clearly defined by the directed conjunction that occurs this year. This should be an active time, the individual becoming more *outward*, yet this apparently positive approach to life may be accompanied by feelings of loneliness and inadequacy. The new direction the life wants to go may seem unrealizable; one's means may appear too few. This feeling of a lack of ability and resources can become very acute, yet with it there is often an intense internal pressure to go on, and opportunities to do so are likely to occur in the individual's immediate environment. Despite the feelings of inadequacy that are bound to be experienced in one way or another, it is in these twelve months that a clear definition is formed of the extent to which the septenary ruler will affect the life during this seven-year cycle. What is planned this year, what is imagined, and the clarity and detail of this preparation, sets the limits of what is possible. This Martian year is a karmic period; what is attended to in the third year of the seven will clearly bring a reaction in the sixth year of this same cycle.

The fourth year of the seven-year cycle is always of the nature of Mercury: a crossroad, a time of decision. During the year at least one major choice has to be made. If the native doesn't make it himself, others are likely to do so for him. This choice may be either conscious or unconscious, depending on the nature of the septenary ruler and the level of maturity of the individual. The ruler has now come to the third of the other six classical bodies it will encounter as it is directed around the wheel. For Hitler, at age three, this was the year the Moon came to Mars and the choices his father made that year, his plans to retire from the customs service and to move into the country to become a beekeeper, affected Hitler for the remainder of his life. Fourteen years later, when he was seventeen, Mercury, the directed ruler came to Saturn and Hitler decided that he would leave home and move to Vienna and become an artist. He had not yet applied to attend the Academy and had no job but he did have a vision of leading his people to freedom. At age 24, as the Sun, the ruler of his fourth septenary, came to his Moon, he left Vienna for Berlin and applied to join the German army.

Mercury is the planet of choices, and this fourth year should be considered the *Wednesday* of any year-week. It will probably be a year of mental struggle and conflict. Indeed, a fourth year without any obvious mental conflict is often an indication that the new impulse, the very purpose of this particular seven-year period, has been rejected, that the individual's growth has become stunted, that he has fruitlessly resigned himself to stay with the old, safe patterns. During this important year of choice, the individual may himself decide what to do, usually after much mental anguish, or circumstances will contrive to force the decision upon him.

The fifth year of Hitler's first septenary began on his fourth birthday, as the Moon reached the position of his natal Sun, the fourth of the other classical bodies that it meets as it circles the chart. This year is the *Thursday* of the year-week. It is always of a Jovian nature and can be the year of greatest self-expression in the cycle, when the keynote of the entire period reveals itself with great personal intensity. It is a year of *flowering* and conscious development within the limits of what was realized, planned or dreamed two years earlier during the Tuesday of this year-week. The manner of this flowering will be of the nature of the planets involved now, but whether this is a positive or negative experience also depends to a very great extent on how the previous year was tackled. If the appropriate choices were made then, there can now be a contact with one's highest potential. Sometimes a teacher or mentor appears, someone who can guide or help the individual attain his ambitions. For those who have allowed themselves to give up and sink into inertia, this fifth year can instead be a very negative experience. During it any remaining hopes and dreams can be utterly destroyed. In Hitler's Mars-ruled septenary, this occurs at age 32 and is symbolized as Mars coming to the Moon. That year, he gained control of the Nazi party, decided that he had to use force to increase his power in Germany, and was arrested for inciting a riot. It was while he was in prison however that he wrote *Mein Kampf*, a book that increased his popularity throughout Germany.

The sixth year within any seven-year cycle is of the nature of Venus. This is the *Friday* of the year-week, a time of *fruition and culmination*. However, don't be too quick to say "Thank goodness it's Friday." Like the second of the seven years, to which it is closely related, this sixth year is not always easy. There is often a need for some form of sacrifice; something may have to be given up—some cherished ideal from the past, an old personal contact perhaps. The individual may experience a restless sense of frustration and much dissatisfaction. There can be deep and tragic experiences. In this sixth year there is often the need to assess one's success or failure, to place oneself on Libran scales. The current seven-year cycle is winding down, what has been attained in it is close to completion; thoughts of a new state of being may fleetingly enter into the individual's dreams. He is being readied for future new growth. For Hitler in his Venus-ruled septenary this occurred when he was 40 years old when the directed Venus came to the position of his Moon. That year he first met Eva Braun, his future mistress and, for a brief few days, his wife.

Generalized Meanings of the Different Septenary Years

Year within Septenary	Generalized meaning
First	Feeling one's way to a new condition of being.
Second	Resistance from the past
Third	Attempting to exteriorize the new impulse in a definite form.
Fourth	Critical turning point. Can the pull of the past be overcome? Either growth or disintegration.
Fifth	The flower stage of the year-week. The year of greatest self-expression in which the keynote of the Septenary may be revealed.
Sixth	What is implied in the Septenary now bears fruit.
Seventh	Culmination and promise of a new start

Alexander Ruperti has called **the final year** of any seven-year cycle the seed year. The septenary ruler has come all around the chart to the position of its successor, the personal planet that next follows it in the Zodiac. The possibilities for growth inherent in the current septenary seem to be exhausted; nothing more can be achieved in the world the present time ruler has created. An entire part of life is ending and there is a need for newness. This seventh year contains the promise of a new beginning in the future. It should be a year of joyous fulfillment as the old phase of life closes, but all too often the need and hope for something better in the future predominates. Where there has been failure and frustration instead of fulfillment, a sense of inadequacy in the face of family or social pressure, there is the need and hope for another opportunity to start afresh. Irrespective of which planets are involved, this is always Saturn's year, the *Saturday* of the year-week, and it is either a period of culmination and illumination, or one of ending. Either way, this seventh year contains within it the substance of the next seven-year period, which will be ruled by the planet that is now challenging the old septenary ruler. When the Sun rules Hitler's septenary this is the year, 1916, when it comes to natal Mars, which will subsequently take over and rule the next seven years. Hitler is 27 years old, an army corporal running messages between trenches. This year he spends several weeks in hospital, having been wounded in the thigh, before returning to the Front. During this period, according to *Mein Kampf*, he first becomes aware of the activities of the German black market. He blames this undermining of his adopted country's war effort on Jewish profiteering.

Ages when each Septenary ruler is directed to each receiving planet

Rising sequence of septenary ruler	Rising sequence of Receiving Planet						
	1	**7**	**6**	**5**	**4**	**3**	**2**
1	**0**	1	2	3	4	5	6
2	8	9	10	11	12	13	7
3	16	17	18	19	20	**14**	15
4	24	25	26	27	**21**	22	23
5	32	33	34	**28**	29	30	31
6	40	41	**35**	36	37	38	39
7	48	**42**	43	44	45	46	47
1	**49**	50	51	52	53	54	55
2	57	58	59	60	61	62	**56**
3	65	66	67	68	69	**63**	64
4	73	74	75	76	**70**	71	72
5	81	82	83	**77**	78	79	80
6	89	90	**84**	85	86	87	88
7	97	**91**	92	93	94	95	96
1	**98**	99	100	101	102	103	104

In the above table the ages (0, 7, 14, 21, etc) when a septenary ruler comes to the ascendant are highlighted, the row and column having the same rising sequence value. For example, age 14, when the third ruler comes to the ascendant, is at the junction of row 3 and column 3.

The above descriptions can also be applied to each of the separate seven-year septenary periods. Thus the fourth septenary, commencing at age twenty-one, will be of a Mercury nature, and during it various decisions will need to be made, usually connected with the individual's career path. In the fourth year of these seven, the year starting with the twenty-fourth birthday, a key decision, one that will affect the rest of his life, may have to be made. Again, in the septenary commencing with the seventieth birthday, the other seven-year period related to Mercury, circumstances are likely to force the individual to make another major decision. Other seven-year periods similarly follow the general description given above for the individual years.

Each of the seven classical planets has ruled for a period of seven years when an individual attains his 49th birthday. The person has been drawn forward in turn by each of the seven time rulers from a state of potentiality to one in which he has attained full maturity. The inherent condition signified by the planets at the moment of birth has now become fully actualized: the acorn is an oak; the newborn babe has attained adulthood. He now possesses in full each of the attributes with which he was born. Growth is complete.

Thereafter the individual's abilities start to weaken. How this happens is very similar to what occurs each year following midsummer, the time when the length of daylight in a day is at its maximum. Before the solstice each day was becoming steadily longer. After midsummer a reverse occurs, the days gradually get shorter. The change is imperceptible at first but it is more and more apparent until, after the Autumnal Equinox, there is more darkness than light in a day. The change in the individual's abilities as he moves through his fifties is at first similarly imperceptible, but it becomes increasingly apparent in his sixties, and it is blatantly obvious that decay has set in by the time he reaches his seventies.

At age forty-nine the cycle of the seven planets begins again, but now one by one the different time rulers gradually remove the gifts with which they earlier endowed him. The planet that was the first to rise after birth governs this eighth septenary year-week, the planet that rose to the ascendant second after birth will rule the ninth, and so on. As before, the ruler coming to each appropriate planet (the receiving planets) signifies the individual years within each seven-year cycle.[1]

An explanation of how a septenary year may be split into different parts is provided in Appendix C.

---

[1] Initially, I believed there was a variation on the sequence after age 49; that a reversal of the septenary rulerships occurred when the initial seven cycles of seven years had been completed. It was only several years after I had published a description of the septenary, complete with my proposed variation, that I recognized my error. The extensive analyses carried out in preparation for this book confirm that I now have the method right.

Chapter 5

Applying the Decan & Septenary

I am more than ever convinced that persons are successively different persons,
according as each successive strand in their characters is brought uppermost by circumstances.

Thomas Hardy, *note written on 4th December 1890*

We are accustomed for moving planets, whether these move by transit, progression or direction, to stimulate a reaction from natal bodies. The reverse happens in the decan and septenary. The time ruler is the moving planet and it has a distinct intent, which is to create the world that it promised when it arose to the ascendant, and this proposed world can be very different from the one created by the preceding time ruler. To an extent the astrologer can deduce a planet's original intent by its inherent nature, the sign and house it occupies in the natal horoscope, the houses it rules, and its aspects. How strong or weak the time ruler is by sign is of primary importance in determining the nature of the years under its control.

Each of the natal planets that the time ruler comes to as it circles the chart represents an impulse that will help or hinder fulfillment of the ruler's aim. Natal Sun, Mars and Jupiter, also Uranus in the decan, will energize the ruler in their different ways, the Moon and Venus, also Neptune, are likely to distract, perhaps undermine, the direction of the ruler's impulse, while Saturn, also Pluto in the decan, and on occasion Mercury, is ever liable to cut short the ruler's ambitious plans. Each of the planets the ruler meets will modify the ruler's original intent, enhance or diminish it, and will do so in terms of that planet's inherent meaning and what it represents in the horoscope according to its sign, the house it occupies and those it rules relative to the time ruler, and the aspects it has to other bodies, especially those to the time ruler. The astrologer will be greatly assisted in his or her interpretation by erecting a series of charts that have each of the different time rulers at the ascendant; for this purpose whole-sign houses are recommended.

It is important also to recognize that time rulers which follow the planet that first rose to the ascendant will come into an environment that has already been created. The new impulse can only adapt and build on what was accomplished in the past. The earlier rulers have defined a world in which later rulers must operate, and the stronger the influence of these earlier rulers the more set the life is likely to be in their original terms. The world a particularly strong ruler creates is the one that may persist through all the years governed by later time rulers. Someone who has, for example, a prominent Saturn as time ruler early in life, especially one who has an afflicted Saturn as the first to rise, may continue to live in a cold and suspicious saturnine world irrespective of the strengths or weaknesses of the rulers that follow it. Indeed, the impulses, reactions and habits associated with the planet(s) that rules the first seven years of life tend to retain an underlying presence throughout an individual's later years—this is especially so if the first body to arrive at the ascendant is one of the classical seven, as the same planet will be the initial ruler in both the decan and septenary systems.

A year has a high likelihood of being positive and enjoyable when the ruler is directed to:

a. A planet occupying the sign in which the ruler is exalted. The year is likely to be strongly connected with honors, dignities, actions and changes of fortune. There can be a significant improvement in status, accomplished with only moderate difficulties. Should either planet be adversely aspected, especially by a malefic or debilitated planet, the improved changes of fortune may be associated with tumultuous changes in other areas of the life.

b. One of the signs that it rules. The year will then be a positive one that is representative of the individual's normal life, customary behavior and mentality.

c. The planet that is the ruler's dispositor.

A year is likely to be a difficult one when the ruler is directed to:

d. A sign in which it is exiled, in its detriment. The ruler will continue to act according to its own nature but will tend to do so in a depraved manner. An exiled benefic can bestow some good but much less than usual. If the ruler is in detriment in a sign ruled by a badly afflicted planet the individual's year is likely to be extremely difficult.

e. The sign in which the ruler is in its fall. The ruler will be weakened in its efforts to act according to its own positive nature. Instead, it will act in accord with its own negative nature, the sign it has come to, and the planet to which it has been directed.

The year will be less dramatic when the ruler is directed to:

f. One of the signs in which it is peregrine. The ruler will be weakened but not corrupted. When directed to a planet in a sign that is of the same positive or negative type, masculine or feminine, as the one the ruler occupies in the natal horoscope the ruling planet will suffer hardly any diminution in its power to act according to its own nature. The ruler directed to a planet in a dissimilar sign (positive to negative, masculine to feminine, and vice versa) can indicate a year of frustration: the individual being helpless to act for his or her own benefit.

The above indications apply in both the decan and the septenary. Having noted what is happening in one of these, the astrologer must also consider what is occurring coincidently in the other.

The decan, because it includes Uranus, Neptune and Pluto, tends to be more useful as a rectification tool than the septenary. However, the septenary should always be applied to confirm the decan's findings. The rectification of Bob Dole's time of birth is a good example. There is conflicting information of the actual time. One source quotes "soon after midnight" while two independent rectifications confirm each other with times that are some thirty-odd minutes after noon.

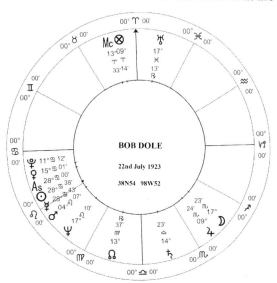

Nicholas Sutherland in *Considerations* XI: 3 (pp. 92-93) provides details of events in the life of the former Senate majority leader and presidential candidate.

Dole was first married at age 24 years 11 months. He had met his wife Phyllis Holden, an occupational therapist, several months earlier at the Battle Creek hospital in November 1947, at age 24 years 4 months. With Venus the next classical body following the Moon in the zodiac (we skip over Uranus and Pluto), the nature of the event at this age is appropriate for believing his birth was at night.

By contrast, no events are listed for Dole at age eighteen that would suggest he had been born during the daytime. In June 1941, when he was some six weeks shy of his eighteenth birthday, he graduated from high school. On December 2, 1942, aged nineteen years four months, he enlisted in the Army Reserve.

The following life-threatening events occurred when he was 21 and 22 years old:

Events in Bob Dole's Life at Ages 21 & 22

Date	Age	Event
Dec 1944	21	Embarked by troopship to Italy
Apr 14, 45	21	Wounded in right shoulder.
Apr 15, 45	21	Operation. Wound cleaned & examined for damage
Apr 18, 45	21	Transferred to Morocco. The damage is found to be severe, it includes spinal injury. He is paralyzed.
July 11, 45	21	His right kidney is removed
Nov, 45	22	Sent to Percy Jones Army Medical Center in Battle Creek, MI for physical therapy
Dec 21, 45	22	Pulmonary infarct. Treated with Dicumarol.
Feb 12, 46	22	Doctors stop Dicumaral. He nearly dies. Given Streptomycin. Sits up four days later.

Assuming Dole was born at night, only four planets could be the first to rise: the Sun, Venus, Pluto or Uranus.

For these, the ruler of Dole's twenties, when he experienced the above physical problems, was alternatively Mars, Mercury, the Sun or Venus.

Bob Dole's Alternative Decan Sequences

Nocturnal Birth				*Age*	*Diurnal birth*					
☉	♀	♇	♅	0 -	☿	♂	♆	♄	♃	☽
☿	☉	♀	♇	10 -	♂	♆	♄	♃	☽	♅
♂	**☿**	**☉**	**♀**	**20 -**	♆	♄	♃	☽	♅	♇
♆	♂	☿	☉	30 -	♄	♃	☽	♅	♇	♀
♄	♆	♂	☿	40 -	♃	☽	♅	♇	♀	☉
♃	♄	♆	♂	50 -	☽	♅	♇	♀	☉	☿
☽	♃	♄	♆	60 -	♅	♇	♀	☉	☿	♂
♅	☽	♃	♄	70 -	♇	♀	☉	☿	♂	♆
♇	♅	☽	♃	80 -	♀	☉	☿	♂	♆	♄
♀	♇	♅	☽	90 -	☉	☿	♂	♆	♄	♃

The nature of the events at ages 21 and 22 suggests Mars was ruling Dole's decan when he was in his twenties.

Does the septenary confirm this?

Bob Dole's Alternative Septenary Sequences

Nocturnal Birth		*Ages*	*Diurnal birth*				
☉	♀	0- 49-	☿	♂	♄	♃	☽
☿	☉	7- 56-	♂	♄	♃	☽	♀
♂	☿	14- 63-	♄	♃	☽	♀	☉
♄	♂	**21- 70-**	♃	☽	♀	☉	☿
♃	♄	28- 77-	☽	♀	☉	☿	♂
☽	♃	35- 84-	♀	☉	☿	♂	♄
♀	☽	42- 91-	☉	☿	♂	♄	♃

If the Sun is the first planet to rise following his birth, then at age 21 Saturn becomes Dole's septenary ruler. At the same time Mars rules his decan.

Age	*Decan*		*Septenary*	
	Ruler	*Directed to*	*Ruler*	*Directed to*
21	♂	☿	♄	As
22	♂	☉	♄	♂

Dole was wounded in the right shoulder and suffered serious spinal injuries that paralyzed him the year that Mars was ruling his decan and Saturn had come to his ascendant in the septenary. The following year he nearly died when the decan-ruler Mars was on his Sun and septenary-ruler Saturn on his Mars. These appear to be appropriate directions.

As further confirmation that the Sun was the first body to rise after Dole's birth:

	Decan		Septenary		
Age	*Ruler*	*Directed to*	*Ruler*	*Directed to*	*Events*
48	♄	☽	♀	☉	Divorces his first wife
60	☽	Aₛ	☿	♃	Mother dies

The two women who supported Dole when he was at his weakest went out of his life when the Moon was emphasized in the decan. Following his discharge from the army with a total and permanent disability, he was dependent on his first wife for very basic functions, just as he had been on his mother as a child—and he loathed it, as the nature of Saturn, his decan ruler at age 48, suggests.

The septenary directions are also meaningful. At the time of his divorce at age 48, Dole appears to have been utterly infatuated with another woman, also named Phyllis, and thus being strongly influenced by Venus his septenary ruler. Jupiter, the planet receiving the septenary ruler's direction when Dole was 60, is located in his fifth house, the eighth from the house associated with his mother, the tenth.

	Decan		Septenary		
Age	*Ruler*	*Directed to*	*Ruler*	*Directed to*	*Events*
24	♂	♀	♄	☉	Extensive physical therapy; marries.
57	♃	♀	☿	☉	Surgery: kidney stone removed
68	☽	♀	♂	♃	Surgery: prostate removed

Dole experienced surgery on many occasions, two of them when the decan ruler came to his natal Pluto. The only other year given by Sutherland for a ruler being directed to Pluto, when he was 24, also had Dole experiencing severe physical stress, and the transformation of his life that came with marriage.

The suggested time of birth has the Sun close to the ascendant. Thus septenary directions to the Sun at ages 24 and 57 may indicate Dole's consciousness of his physical weakness being apparent to others. Older persons often experience surgery when septenary Mars comes to Jupiter.

* * *

The decan and the septenary are independent of each other. Events in a year may be described by either approach. However, neither approach is complete in itself. Each needs the other to fill in the blanks. In that sense the two methods are complementary. Each separate, even contradictory, direction complements the other. Together the two offer a more complete view and understanding than either offers separately. The decan appears to emphasize happenings in the life that would appear in a person's biography, events in his outer world, those likely to be apparent to others around him. By contrast, the septenary tends to be more connected with the individual's growth, to his reactions and emotions, items that may be more private, ones he might confine to a private diary but not necessarily publicize. It should, however, be noted that this suggested difference between the decan and septenary is not a rigid one, every now and then the indications of the septenary are expressed publicly for all to see. The septenary gives the astrologer information that is additional to what the decan provides. However different the indications provided by the septenary and decan might appear at first sight it must be realized that taken together they describe what is happening in the life—in a sense the outer reaction and the inner response.

In any given year an individual can experience both difficult and pleasant experiences. The septenary for that year may suggest one kind, the decan the other. What may be a pleasant experience to one person may generate a negative reaction from another; all depends on the relationships within the natal horoscope. The two methods act in tandem. One provides what the other may lack.

When both decan and septenary indicate positive things, such as when both are ruled by benefics that are not afflicted in any way and in each instance the ruler applies to a planet located at birth in a sign where the ruler is welcomed, one it rules or where it is exalted, the astrologer can forecast a truly positive year. When the reverse happens, when bodies badly afflicted in the natus rule both decan and septenary and these are directed into unwelcoming signs or to planets with which they have difficult natal aspects, the astrologer must warn of severe problems in the coming year. Analyzing the natures of the respective planets involved, their natal positions and aspects, can determine the specifics of the positive or negative happenings to be expected in these years.

A personal example: in my horoscope three of the classical planets are in Taurus, which means that when Mars is the septenary ruler its directions to these three bodies bring a sequence of three difficult years. Any planet not just Mars will cause problems whenever it comes to a sign in which it is debilitated, but in the author's case the likelihood of difficulties is increased by Mars being natally in Scorpio and opposing the Taurus planets. Just how difficult the years are likely to be depends on the other time ruler. Mars has been the time ruler on three separate occasions in my life, twice in the septenary and once in the decan. The last of these three-year horrors occurred when I was in my early fifties, Mars ruled the septenary and the decan ruler was Venus.

First, in the septenary Mars came to my ascendant ruler, the Moon in Taurus. At the same time in the decan Venus joined Saturn in Aries. Both Mars and Venus were debilitated in the signs they had come to. Mars was attacking my family, and my father unexpectedly died.

The following year, as septenary Mars came to my Mercury, decan Venus came to Jupiter in Capricorn. Although Jupiter is in its fall in Capricorn, Venus is not. Events during the year would be less hurtful as those of the previous year. Even so, the Mars direction to Mercury brought financial problems (Mercury rules all forms of exchange, including money), and the involvement of Jupiter in Capricorn pointed to an unbending authority as the cause. A major event that year was a negative finding from an IRS audit, which resulted in the payment of a large fine. A very close friend also died that year (both Mercury and Venus are natally in my eleventh house).

In the third year, as Mars came to Venus in the septenary, the decan ruler Venus arrived at Mars in Scorpio. Mars had come to Venus at the same time that Venus arrived at Mars— ignoring all else, this emphasis on the same pair of planets had to be associated with an unforgettable year. As both Mars and Venus were in signs in which they are in exile, the year had be an extremely negative one. It was a year in which I faced many difficulties, among them the death of my mother.

Memorable years, whether pleasant or not, invariably occur when the same planet is involved in both the decan and septenary as the previous paragraph shows and the following examples will confirm:

Person	Age	Septenary		Decan		Major event in the year
		Ruler	Directed to	Ruler	Directed to	
Adolf Hitler	45	♄	☉♉	☉	♄♌	Becomes ruler of Germany
John F. Kennedy	45	☽	☉♊	☉	☽♍	Cuban crisis
Richard Nixon	37	♀	☉♑	☉	♀♓	First elected Senator
Prince Charles	32	♂	♄♍	♀	♄♍	Marries Diana
Albert Einstein	26	☉	♄♈	♂	♄♈	His great year: he publishes three major papers, including his Theory of Relativity.
Queen Elizabeth II	27	☿	☉♉	♀	☉♉	Coronation
Mao Zedung	55	♀	♃♉	♄	♃♉	Victory over the Nationalists. China becomes a Communist state.
Charles Lindbergh	25	☉	☿♓	♄	☿♓	Flies solo across the Atlantic
Winston Churchill	64	☿	♃♎	♆	☿♏	Becomes prime minister
Josef Stalin	61	☽	☉♐	☉	♂♏	Germany invades the USSR
Josef Stalin	62	☽	♂♏	☉	☽♎	Battle of Stalingrad
Josef Stalin	69	♂	☉♐	☉	♀♐	USSR first explodes an Atom Bomb
Hillary Rodham Clinton	23	♀	♄♌	♄	♅♊	First meets Bill Clinton, her future husband
President Dwight Eisenhower	52	♄	♀♐	♀	☽♎	Appointed Commander-in-Chief of Allied Forces in North Africa.
Abraham Lincoln	52	☉	♂♎	♂	♃♓	Civil War begins
Charles Lindbergh	30	♂	♃♑	♃	As♏	His son is kidnapped and murdered

As noted earlier, the signs to which the direction brings the time ruler must always be taken into account.

Einstein's Saturn is in Aries so the direction of his septenary ruler, the Sun, to Saturn brings it to the sign in which the Sun is exalted, and at the same time the Mars direction to Saturn in the decan takes it to the sign Mars rules. It is not so strange therefore that the year in which this occurred is known as his "great year".

Josef Stalin's armies did win the Battle of Stalingrad, but it was not immediately obvious that they would. Both rulers have come to signs where they are in their fall.

Without knowing that Prince Charles' mistress was a continuing presence in his marriage to Diana the directions of both the septenary and decan rulers to his Saturn in Virgo might be puzzling; but she was, and the later vagaries of the marriage of the heir to the British throne to his virgin bride were surely heralded by the directions of the septenary and decan rulers that year.

It is not necessary to discuss each of the other examples in the preceding table.

Only a quick glance at a birth chart is necessary for the astrologer to instantly identify whether years such as these will occur in the life and the age when this happens.

One needs to also examine the aspects (including antiscions), houses and other strengths or weaknesses of the different planets in the natal horoscopes in order to explain the full meaning of each of the above examples. Even so, it should be obvious that a planet that is repeated in these septenary-decan pairings acquires undue emphasis.

* * *

In order to better understand how the decan and septenary work, and indeed to confirm that they actually do and that I was not mistakenly seeing connections where none really existed—something astrologers are often accused of doing—I have since the late 1970s studied the biographies of people for whom I have an interest and related the events in their lives, on a year by year basis, to the associated decan and septenary. It takes time to gather data of this sort from a biography (a detailed year by year comparison can take some weeks, especially when the subject of the biography is a fascinating character, someone who led an eventful life), so in order to increase the amount of information available I have also made use of the abbreviated dated information provided in the books on rectification by Alexander Marr, the writings of Paul Wright, and other similar sources. Adding to my original database in this manner has enabled these comparisons to more quickly accumulate so that there is now a sufficiently large enough data set on which statistical testing can be made to see whether or not these septenary and decan methods are in fact meaningful.

In the database an individual's year (a year being from birthday to birthday) has been classified in one of three ways:

Positive: those years in which predominately positive or pleasant events occurred to the individual;

Negative: years in which negative events predominated, the years being difficult and generally unsuccessful; and

Don't Know: these were years that contain such a mix of positive and negative events that the year cannot confidently be said to have been either predominately one or the other. The 61st year of President Andrew Jackson falls into this Don't Know category. That year he became president but his wife also died.

When it came to testing the data for statistical significance the Don't Know years were omitted from the sample. That decision may concern those purists who believe no information should ever be excluded, and indeed there are good astrological grounds for retaining this set—a decan indicating positive times when combined with a septenary indicative of a difficult period, or vice versa, could be expected to be associated with such a Don't Know year. The decision to omit the Don't Knows was taken for two reasons: most years could be classified as either Positive or Negative and the remaining Don't Knows were relatively few in number,[1] and by retaining just the two categories the statistical testing and tabulated results become simpler and easier to understand.

Where it is stated in what follows the *% Positive* value is the number of positive years expressed as a percentage of both positive and negative years in that category,

% Positive = (# positive years * 100)/(# positive years + # negative years).

Before an astrologer examines a horoscope to predict whether an upcoming year will be a positive or negative one the assumption must be that there is an equal chance that the year can be either, that there is a 50% probability that a year will be positive and the same 50% probability that it will be negative. In the overall sample 55.3% of the years were positive, which above-50%-value is doubtless due to the fact that most of the people in the sample enjoyed successful lives—it is rare to find a published biography written about someone who failed to make a mark in the world. As this observed value is significantly greater than the expected 50%, all of the observed probability percentages have been adjusted to ensure that the stated results overall total to 50%.

Adjusted % Positive values that differ meaningfully from the expected 50% are highlighted in the tables that follow and shown with 1, 2 or 3 stars.

---

[1] This may surprise some. We invariably experience both positive and negative happenings most years, good and bad days, so one might expect such a year to be fall into the "Don't Know" category. However, the key word in deciding whether a year is predominantly positive or negative is "predominantly". Anyone who has examined a graph of the daily or weekly fluctuations of the price of a stock in a financial market will know the ups and downs of the price throughout the year. It is the overall trend that matters. Overall, is the line heading up, down or sideways? In my sample very few individuals experienced years that went nowhere, were directionless, going neither up nor down. Most members of my sample usually accomplished something in their lifetimes that justified someone writing their biography. These were not inert beings.

% Positive for each of the directions of the Time Ruler

Time Ruler	Receiving the direction											
	A$_{SC}$	☉	☽	☿	♀	♂	♃	♄	♅	♆	♇	All
☉	43.9	-	42.2	46.6	51.3	50.3	50.3	44.8	50.3	50.3	36.2	47.5
☽	44.1	44.2	-	54.4	53.5	48.9	51.8	44.5	60.3	50.3	47.4	49.2
☿	48.4	50.1	50.3	-	49.4	49.6	46.9	48.9	50.5	53.9	57.1	50.1
♀	52.3	56.5	54.3	54.9	-	53.4	51.8	47.1	58.7	60.3	57.1	**53.5** **
♂	49.3	45.9	50.3	**57.3** *	55.9	-	53.9	55.6	52.7	48.1	37.0	51.9
♃	56.1	54.4	**66.0** ***	**60.7** **	**61.1** ***	51.8	-	47.4	53.2	59.0	38.2	**56.1** ***
♄	**37.7** ***	44.9	48.3	45.2	48.5	52.7	51.1	-	**64.8** **	58.4	44.3	48.1
♅	40.6	39.2	43.2	40.4	**35.8**	45.2	49.5	45.2	-	52.7	49.0	44.2
♆	53.2	41.7	48.6	54.2	46.2	**27.8** ***	48.2	38.7	45.2	-	41.3	44.2
♇	49.1	41.4	51.9	37.5	42.1	50.4	54.2	**32.4** **	59.0	47.2	-	46.4
All	**47.4** *	48.1	51.6	51.8	51.6	50.2	51.5	**46.6** **	**55.3** **	53.5	**45.1** *	50.0

*   One star indicates that there is only a 1-in-10 chance that the observed percentage is the same as the expected 50%. Although this is an interesting result, it is not different enough from 50% to be considered statistically significant. The observation is highlighted because it is interesting even though it is unreliable; more observations will be needed to confirm the observed value before the observed value can be accepted as real.

**   Two stars says that the likelihood of actually being 50% is just 1-in-20. This is the 95% standard commonly used in science. It indicates that the observed variation from 50% is probably a true difference, one that is likely to be repeated when applied to the charts of people who were not members of the sample. It is a statistically significant result.

***   Three stars tells us there is only a 1-in-100 likelihood that the observed value is really the expected 50%. This should be taken to mean that there is a real difference between the observed value and the expected 50%, and that the astrologer can confidently apply it in his practice. It is a very significant result.

The absence of any stars indicates that the observed value is not really different from the expected 50%. Any variation the value has from 50% is likely to have occurred simply by chance. The lack of statistical significance may also be due to insufficient observations having been available.

Whether an observed % Positive value differs meaningfully from the expected 50% or not is always a function of the number of observations (N), as well as the observed % Positive. Values above 50% that are highlighted and starred in this manner inform us that the period ruled by the associated planetary combination has an above-average probability of being a pleasant and successful one for the individual concerned. Values below 50% that are highlighted and starred indicate planetary combinations that can be associated with difficult and unpleasant periods for the individual.

Where % Positive totals are provided these are weighted totals, the type readers usually expect to see. However, there is really no reason for the number of observations, N, to vary as they do. That they do vary is due to the sample being extremely biased, subject entirely to my moods and interests. It is more correct to use simple unweighted averages, and assume the values of N are constant and equal. This correction is something that those readers who wish to apply the results included in this book can and should easily calculate for themselves.

An explanation of the method used to identify these highlighted and starred results is provided in Appendix D.

In the sample the directions of Jupiter to the Moon were the most positive years in terms of percentages. The least positive were the years when Neptune as time ruler came to the place of natal Mars.

The directions of Jupiter and Venus, the two traditional benefics, were associated with the greatest probability of the year being successful. Pluto, Saturn and the ascendant are the places where the time ruler, whichever planet this was, had the most difficulties, Uranus the least.

For each of the different time rulers, counts of positive and negative years were taken for each of the ruler's directions. These were split by whether the person's chart was diurnal or nocturnal, whether the ruler or the receiving body was oriental or occidental from the Sun, and the zodiacal sign and whole-sign house each of the bodies were in at birth. This information is reported in the following pages.

By oriental I mean that the planet is behind the Sun in the zodiac and rising before it. As such the planet would have been above the horizon at sunrise. Occidental, by contrast, identifies the planet as having been below the horizon at sunrise, ahead of it in the zodiac, and rising after it.

Thirteen directions qualify for significance-indicating stars when these directions are split by whether the birth was diurnal or nocturnal:

Time Ruler	Directed to	% Positive	Significance	Day/Night
Jupiter	Moon	68.8	***	Day
Mars	Mercury	65.7	**	Day
Jupiter	Mercury	64.0	**	Day
Jupiter	Ascendant	63.3	**	Night
Jupiter	Venus	63.2	**	Day
Moon	Mercury	63.1	**	Night
Neptune	Mars	21.7	**	Day
Pluto	Saturn	24.7	**	Night
Uranus	Sun	25.8	**	Day
Sun	Pluto	29.0	**	Night
Sun	Moon	36.4	**	Night
Saturn	Ascendant	37.5	**	Day
Saturn	Ascendant	37.9	**	Night

In addition to the statistical information, examples are provided of a selection of the various events that occurred to people in the sample who experienced each of the planetary pairs. Readers will notice that described events often occur twice, although never for the same direction; the same event may be related once to the septenary and again to the coincident decan.

Also included are descriptions of the happenings in the lives of representative people who experienced each of the time rulers, both in their septenary and in their decan. The majority of these representative people are not of the modern era, a fact for which I may be criticized. My excuse for using figures from the past is two-fold: they are fascinating characters who led intriguing lives irrespective of when they lived, and their biographies have been written and are available for study, something that hasn't yet happened for many of the today's crop of notables. Explanations of how the appropriate decan or septenary combinations are appropriate for each of the described years' happenings have been kept to a minimum, and are frequently entirely absent. Those able to converse in astrologese will easily see the relevance of these associations.

Details of each of the different directions follow:

Chapter 6

The Sun as the Time Ruler

"The dust of many crumbled cities settles over us like a forgetful doze, but we are older than those cities. We began as a mineral. We emerged into plant life and into the animal state, and then into being human, and always we have forgotten our former states, except in early spring when we slightly recall being green again. That's how a young person turns toward a teacher. That's how a baby leans toward the breast, without knowing the secret of its desire, yet turning instinctively. Humankind is being led along an evolving course, through this migration of intelligences, and though we seem to be sleeping, there is an inner wakefulness that directs the dream, and that will eventually startle us back to the truth of who we are."

Jalal-uddin Rumi, *The Dream That Must Be Interpreted*

You are the hero of this story in which you are living, the star of this movie of your life. Everyone else: your mother, your father, your brothers and sisters, your husband or wife, your children, your boyfriend or girlfriend, the people living next door and those down the road, the people at work, the people you see every day and those you only see on rare occasions, even those people you will meet just once in your lifetime, they are all bit players, the supporting cast in your story. It's all about you. And you are not even asked to act. All you have to do is to be yourself. No false posturing, no pretence, just you as you are, warts and all. By just being yourself you will find out Who and What you truly are, the essential self with which you were born. Only then can you enjoy complete freedom and voluntarily live out your fate.

The Sun signifies both you and the one true God of this solar system. It is the source of life, the star around which each of the planets revolves, the heart from which everything emanates. It pours out warmth, creativity and love. It is the Self, the Universal Will, and the source of all action. It is pure energy, pure being, and represents the Divinity that stirs within us, our true character, who it is we truly are, all private and selfish actions, our pursuit of dominance, praise and recognition. It gives us our desire to live and to go on living even when times are hard, or we are sick, or our relationships have gone wrong. It shows how we relate to authority figures, particularly the father, and stimulates us to improve our lives and become self-reliant.

In the oldest texts known to us the Sun is associated with life and activity. By tradition the Sun is strongest when above the horizon in Aries, Leo or the 9th house. It is weakest when found in Libra, Aquarius, or in a nocturnal horoscope. The Sun directed to a planet in Libra or Aquarius can cause the native to lose his confidence or dignity.

The Sun symbolizes the affirmation of things as they are, including the mistakes one makes: it is an affirmative "yes" to that which is, without subjective protests—an acceptance of the conditions of existence as they are met with and assimilated, including the acceptance of one's own nature. Each individual needs to affirm his or her own destiny. In the process an ego will be forged that does not break down when incomprehensible things happen, an ego that will endure and be capable of coping with the world and with fate. How this is to be accomplished is seen by the zodiacal sign occupied by the Sun at birth, the angular relationship each of the other planets have to the Sun, and the Sun's position relative to the eastern horizon.

Depending on the level of self-reliance the individual has assimilated prior to these Sun-ruled years, there will now be opportunities for him to become more true to his essential self than he was in the past. If grasped these can lead to even greater invitations to shine, to become even more creative, to be all he is and should be, and in doing so become a single, coherent person. The Sun's sign, house and aspects identify both the type of achievements that are possible and the difficulties likely to be encountered on the way to their attainment.

Table ☉-1: **% Positive Years when the ☉ is Time Lord**

☉ directed to	Diurnal birth		Nocturnal birth	
	N	% Positive	N	% Positive
☉ rises	61	57.8	73	**32.2****
☽	53	49.5	67	**36.4***
☿	59	42.9	77	49.3
♀	53	49.5	74	52.5
♂	52	53.9	81	48.0
♃	58	54.5	67	55.3
♄	50	52.4	79	40.1
♅	16	39.6	20	58.8
♆	16	39.6	19	57.1
♇	12	52.7	28	**29.0***
All	430	50.9	585	**44.9****

In Table ☉-1 we see a difference in % Positive for the years when the Sun is rising. For a diurnal birth the % Positive value is 57.8%, while in a nocturnal chart the value for the same Sun rising direction is just 32.2%, which is significantly below the expected 50%. The directions of the nocturnal Sun to the Moon and to Pluto are also statistically significant, and again are associated with values that are markedly below 50%. These three directions of the nocturnal Sun, together with its direction to Saturn, were each associated in the sample with difficult years.

Indeed, nocturnal births in general tend to experience stress and discomfort in those years in which the Sun rules their lives. Exceptions to this are the Sun's directions to the benefics

Jupiter and Venus (the above-50% values for Uranus and Neptune must be treated with caution due to the small N involved in each case). Individuals born during daylight hours usually find the Sun-ruled years much easier to cope with, they are provided with better opportunities to be successful and pursue their goals in life.

Table ☉-2:

% Positive years when ☉ is the Time Lord, by ☉'s natal sign

☉ sign	Diurnal birth		Nocturnal birth	
	N	% Positive	N	% Positive
♈	10	72.3	43	60.9
♉	97	54.1	49	42.4
♊	36	60.3	16	33.9
♋	28	38.8	29	56.1
♌	42	40.9	40	31.6
♍	30	45.2	24	37.7
♎	42	49.6	42	29.4**
♏	29	68.6	64	53.7
♐	9	60.3	81	42.4
♑	25	54.2	73	61.9*
♒	45	36.2*	85	39.3*
♓	37	53.8	39	34.8*
All	430	50.9	585	44.9**

Table ☉-2 splits the years when the Sun was the time lord by the sign the Sun occupied at birth, separating the diurnal and nocturnal births.

Because the numbers in my sample fluctuate wildly—in Table ☉-2 there are only nine Sagittarian diurnal births while there were ninety-seven Taurean diurnal births—care needs to be taken in how these % Positive values are used. The sample is not balanced; it is undoubtedly biased. It only contains details of what happened in the years of people I know and what has been obtained from biographies of people in whom I have an interest. The vast majority of people are not the subjects of biographies. I do not know most of them.

Although only the starred values in bold face, the statistically significant values, can safely be considered to differ from 50%, the reader may wish to infer that %Positive values that are over 50% indicate years in which there is a better than average probability that the year will provide a pleasant outcome, and those %Positive values that are below 50% are associated with years in which a person will encounter more than his share of difficulties. The author's personal inclination is to bet on the starred boldface indications, and otherwise lean very tentatively in the appropriate direction.

The Sun is associated with the most positive events in a year when it is located at birth in Aries, Scorpio and Capricorn, signs in which Mars is traditionally strong. Aries is of course the sign of the Sun's greatest strength, in which it is exalted.

Both day and night births with the Sun in Aquarius, the sign in which it is traditionally in its detriment, are associated with difficult years.

A night birth with the Sun in Libra, the sign of the Sun's fall, is highly likely to experience a difficult year when the Sun is the time ruler. So too are night births with the Sun in Pisces. A night birth with the Sun in Capricorn is associated with a significant above-average proportion of positive years.

In Table ☉-3 we examine how well the Sun does by the sign to which it is directed and find that Leo and the two other Fire signs are associated with the greatest probability that the year will be positive, see Table ☉-4. As we will find confirmed throughout the data we examine, this suggests that it is not so much the natal position of the Sun that is important in determining whether the year will be a positive one or not, but the sign occupied by the planet to which it is directed.

Table ☉-3:

% Positive Years when ☉ is Time Lord, by the sign to which it is directed

Sign to which ☉ is directed	Diurnal birth		Nocturnal birth	
	N	% Positive	N	% Positive
♈	30	57.3	27	50.2
♉	53	51.2	52	**34.8****
♊	38	45.2	38	47.6
♋	35	41.3	34	47.9
♌	25	61.5	39	53.3
♍	23	43.2	42	36.6
♎	38	57.1	35	51.7
♏	26	41.7	50	56.1
♐	16	67.8	43	46.3
♑	30	39.2	51	51.4
♒	32	50.9	46	43.2
♓	23	47.2	55	46.0
All	*369*	*49.7*	*512*	*46.8*

The reduced N in Table ☉-3 is due to the exclusion of the Sun's sign when it is rising.

The direction of the Sun to Taurus in a nocturnal chart, and to a lesser degree to Virgo, is a strong indication that the year will be a difficult one.

54

These Sun-ruled years usually enhance a person's popularity and provide him with the opportunity to advance his career. Assuming the Sun is not badly afflicted, his father's life is likely to improve. This success will be magnified in those years in which the Sun directed to a planet located in Aries or Leo, signs in which the Sun is always well received. There are then likely to be sudden gains in wealth, much travel, time spent in foreign countries, quarrels with friends and relations, and the enjoyment of pleasure, parties and the company of attractive members of the opposite sex. Children may be born in these years, and the individual will attain success and become respected by his superiors.

However, the years are likely to be the opposite of the above when the time-ruling Sun comes to a planet located in Libra or Aquarius, or to one that closely afflicts it in the natal chart. Instead these can be miserable and complicated years, during which the individual can expect to experience failure in just about everything he attempts. He will lose money, be troubled by enemies, and mourn the deaths of others. It will be a time of mental worries, during which he may lose his wife or she may become sick, and he may then become depressed and lose his love of life.

Table ☉-4: **Element to which the ☉ is directed**

	Diurnal birth		Nocturnal birth	
Element	*N*	*% Positive*	*N*	*% Positive*
Fire	71	**61.1***	111	50.5
Earth	106	46.1	145	**41.2****
Air	108	51.1	119	47.1
Water	84	43.1	139	50.1

When the Sun is directed to a body located in a Fire sign, the element traditionally associated with the Sun, the year is more likely to be positive than when it is directed to any other type of sign. By contrast, the direction of the Sun to a planet in an Earth sign indicates likely problems. This is seen in Table ☉-4. The element to which the Sun is directed is a very important factor in the interpretation of this type of direction.

Table ☉-5 provides similar information by the houses occupied by the Sun. Note that, with the whole sign house system being used here, a previously risen Sun can still remain in the first house.

The low values in houses I-V in Table ☉-5 for the Sun's natal house position confirm the weakness of the Sun in a nocturnal chart. The relatively high values in houses VI, VIII and XII may surprise some. These are the three houses, tradition tells us, that are the most difficult of all twelve placements. William Lilly, for example, in his *Christian Astrology*, a book that many advocates of the Western tradition consider their bible, states that a planet (as I do, Lilly includes the Sun as one of the planets) located in any one of these three houses should be classified as having an Accidental Debility. Lilly does not say this about any of the other houses. As with all that is presented in this book: the findings have not been adjusted to prove or disprove any theory, traditional or modern.

Table ☉-5: **% Positive Years when the ☉ is Time Lord, by the ☉'s Natal & Directed House**

☉ Natal House				House	House to which ☉ is directed			
Diurnal birth		Nocturnal birth			Diurnal birth		Nocturnal birth	
N	% Positive	N	% Positive		N	% Positive	N	% Positive
34	47.9	121	**36.5***	I	34	50.5	54	40.1
-	-	133	44.2	II	17	47.8	78	48.6
-	-	117	**41.8***	III	29	46.7	69	53.7
-	-	62	46.7	IV	20	49.7	45	48.9
-	-	46	45.2	V	15	60.3	58	49.9
-	-	96	55.6	VI	19	52.4	36	**67.8****
75	50.6	-	-	VII	32	53.7	34	58.2
57	53.9	-	-	VIII	46	57.0	30	39.2
90	55.2	-	-	IX	29	46.7	27	33.5
40	49.7	-	-	X	36	40.1	25	39.8
81	40.1	-	-	XI	53	51.2	26	38.2
63	56.0	-	-	XII	39	44.0	30	36.2
430	50.9	585	**44.9***	*All*	369	49.7	*512*	*46.8*

The reduction in the above total N, the number of observations, for the directed Sun from those recorded in the previous tables is due to the exclusion of directions of the Sun to the ascendant.

The nocturnal Sun being directed to a planet in the natal 6th house is associated with an improvement in the individual's life. The emphasis on the 6th house in this table appears to be due to extremely positive years observed in the sample that are associated with the Sun being directed to Mercury, when either the Sun or Mercury occupies the natal 6th house. Particularly striking are those difficult years when a nocturnal Sun is directed to a planet located in one of the six contiguous natal houses that extend from the 8th to the 1st (proceeding anticlockwise). The 192 years covered by these 8th-to-1st houses are associated with just 38.2% positive years, a value that is significantly fewer than the 52.0% positive associated with the 320 years when the nocturnal Sun is directed to a planet in the 2nd to 7th houses. These observed percentages differ statistically both from the expected 50% and from each other. The reason for the high incidence of these difficult years is that planets occupying these houses will be encountered by the nocturnal Sun after it crosses over the ascendant earlier in life than will those occupying houses VII through II (counting in the same clockwise direction that the Sun takes).

Table ☉-6:

**% Positive when Sun is the Ruler
by its place in the Septenary sequence**

Place of Sun in septenary	Day		Night	
	N	% Positive	N	% Positive
1	0	-	90	**37.0****
2	1	90.8	80	51.6
3	33	51.1	80	**39.4***
4	50	57.4	55	61.2
5	66	54.5	25	50.9
6	72	50.6	10	27.3
7	56	56.1	0	-
Sum	278	54.1	340	**45.6***

The Sun is rarely the first planet to rise in a day chart—it can be so if all bodies are above the horizon and the Sun is the first that will set, but no-one in my sample had this rare configuration—which is why N is 0 for the first place in the column headed 'Day' in Table ☉-6. Similarly, as a night birth is someone born with their Sun below the horizon it is unusual for the Sun to be the last of the seven to rise to the ascendant after birth—it can occur, but it did not for anyone in my sample—which is why N is 0 for the seventh place in the column headed 'Night'.

In the sample the Sun was most helpful when it was placed fourth of the seven classical planets, which means that the Sun was the septenary ruler when sample members were aged between 21 and 27. This was so for both diurnal and nocturnal births.

Table ☉-7:

**% Positive when Sun is the Ruler
by its place in the Decan sequence**

Place of Sun in decan	Day		Night	
	N	% Positive	N	% Positive
1	0	-	34	**22.0*****
2	0	-	55	47.1
3	0	-	51	61.3
4	11	41.3	56	**33.5****
5	44	61.2	38	47.9
6	31	42.4	7	52.0
7	38	39.3	4	45.5
8	6	15.1	0	-
9	22	37.1	0	-
10	0	0.0	0	-
Sum	152	45.1	245	**43.9****

As we saw earlier, the Sun first to rise at night is associated with years that are frequently unpleasant. Sample members experienced difficult years in their thirties, which is associated in Table ☉-7 with the Sun being the fourth of the ten bodies to rise after birth.

The values of zero for N in the above table make sense when we remember that each of the Sun's places in the decan sequence is associated with the Sun ruling ten years of life, and combine this with the fact that the Sun is unlikely to be among the first of the ten bodies to rise in a daytime chart.

Those sample members born during the day experienced the most positive years when the Sun was the fifth body to come to the ascendant following the birth. This occurred when the individuals were in their forties. Persons born in the night experienced their best Sun-ruled decans when they were in their twenties, the Sun being the third body to rise to the ascendant following the birth.

As we have seen earlier, the Sun first to rise at night is associated with years that are frequently unpleasant.

Sample members, especially those born at night, experienced an above-expected incidence of difficult years in their thirties. This is associated in the above table with the Sun being the fourth body to rise after birth.

We will now consider each of the different directions of the Sun and provide some information on the type of experiences individuals in my sample had with each of them.

The Sun Rises

(44% positive years)

...You have no choice but to be who you are. Your choice is to be who you are at the highest possible level or not. And I would go so far as to say that who you really are preexists whom you are at the present moment, and it is pulling you forward to itself, and that pull is inevitable. Your getting all the way there, becoming a fully realized being, is not inevitable. Circumstances, accidents and of course the ever-present stupidity, or unconsciousness—whatever you call it—will all in varying degrees prevent us from getting to that perfect self-realization. But it is not written in the stars whether we will, or will not, ever be fully realized. What is written in the stars is how to do it—could we but read the chart from that point of view.

Robert Hand, *Towards a Post-Modern Astrology*
2005 lecture given in York, England

The year when the Sun rises to the ascendant begins an entirely new phase of life, one that was being increasingly hinted at as the previous year drew to a close. There is a major difference in ease between nocturnal and diurnal births that is quite startling. More than two thirds of the night births in my sample experienced a distinctly unpleasant year. They suffered most when their Sun was located at birth in any of the first five houses, or the ascendant was in Libra.

This year the Sun's influence will begin to predominate in the individual's life and increasingly compel him to become more self-reliant and independent, to be uncompromisingly himself, and to bring that self out into the public eye; to initiate action and take control of whatever situation he is in, to break away from the past, whether it was comfortable and nurturing or not, and to stand responsibly on his own two feet. This year is the first of a series of several years in which the individual can attain to something better than he has been heretofore in his life, to become something more true to who he really is and can eventually become. He will have a positive outlook on life, be filled with energy and increasingly will want to express his creative and organizing impulses.

Table ☉-8:   ☉ **to Ascendant: % Positive Years**

Day/Night	N	% Positive
Day birth	61	57.8
Night birth	73	**32.2***
All	134	43.9

Because a nocturnal birth experiences the Sun rising earlier in life than does a diurnal birth, the nocturnal Sun must be considered to act as a powerful malefic. This loss of nurturing and the insistence on independence, when it occurs in early life, can be catastrophic, especially when, as frequently occurs, it is accompanied by the loss or forced absence, often the death, of a parent, sibling or close friend. It can be a year of separations or of feeling abandoned; those on whom the native had come to rely on are no longer available. This may especially relate to the father, whose support may no longer be depended on. If, because several planets separate the nocturnal Sun from its rising, this direction occurs later in the person's life, after he has attained adulthood, it may time the absence or loss of a spouse or a loved one on whom he was especially dependent. The nocturnal Sun rising can also herald a year of financial crisis, stress or defeat, the latter often occurring when the individual, having become accustomed to success coming without much effort, is not sufficiently cautious and protective of assets or position. It will certainly be a critical, unsettling year in which there are likely to be changes of dwelling and the loss of what was familiar and comforting; a young child may be sent away to boarding school; others may criticize the person's efforts; and depression, disappointment, frustration and illness can affect the individual and his family.

By contrast, the diurnal Sun usually provides its natives with a much easier time. Again the emphasis is to become more independent and self-sufficient, but a diurnal native is typically older, more mature, and more able psychologically to cope with the Sun's demands than is his younger nocturnal cousin. Here the Sun acts as a benefic and what is experienced in the life should be considered to be a golden opportunity. There will be more awareness, increased energy, an improvement in health, and the opportunity for great success in the fields signified by the natal Sun's house and sign position. Defeat is now much less likely. Marriage is possible. Illness is rare. Important work will often start this year. Opportunities to shine and impress others will occur, the chance to become someone greater than he was heretofore in his life, more the person he wants to be, more the person he really is, and others will be likely to acknowledge and honor him; if firmly grasped this opportunity will open the way for ambitions to be realized. The native will stand up for himself and have cause to feel proud and self-important; if he didn't before this year is when he will begin to question the authority of those placed above him, asking "What makes them better than Me?"

For both nocturnal and diurnal births the rising of the Sun will invariably prompt a person to want to better understand the intent of his life, which is the essential requirement to becoming self-responsible and ceasing to overly depend on others. Nocturnal births experience events and situations that are likely to force this self-reliance to happen; diurnal births are usually provided with easier opportunities to comprehend the same underlying message.

There can be trouble with relatives this year, and some quarreling and difficulties with those in authority over the native. He is likely to travel and be anxious. He may experience headaches, ear pain, and possibly urinary or kidney afflictions. If the ascendant is in Libra or Aquarius, or the Sun is badly afflicted, there can be some danger to the father.

In the sample statistically significant values were observed for this direction when the Sun came from Cancer or from the 2nd or 3rd house, or when it was directed to an ascendant in Libra. Each of these values was significantly below 50%.

Examples of happenings to people in my sample (the names and astrological details of whom are listed in Appendix G) when the Sun became their time ruler:

Examples of the Sun becoming the time ruler in the decan:
Diurnal Sun rises in the decan: *strained nerves; publishes astrological tables of houses; his father's death is a powerful impetus toward building the structure he now makes his life's work; international fame when his theory is confirmed; moves; marries; becomes an ambassador; elected president/vice-president; death.*
Nocturnal Sun rises in the decan: *father leaves & family is forced to move into a slum; she is starved for first six months as her mother cannot feed her; mother dies; his father has cancer/is found guilty of rape/dies; her husband is ill; brother has typhoid; brother has a complete physical collapse; he is criticized; passes exam; sent to WW1 front & immediately into battle; insecure in his job; in prison.*

Examples of the Sun becoming the time ruler in the septenary:
Diurnal Sun rises in the septenary: *he is an inmate in an insane asylum; guest of the king; his interest in politics begins; elected senator; receives a $1-million trust fund; passes exams; honors; coronation; arrested & exiled; fame; wins a contract; his discovery revolutionizes physics; preoccupied with survival; alone & melancholy; marries; mother/daughter/lover dies; attempt on his life; accidently shoots himself.*
Nocturnal Sun rises in the septenary: *desperate financial situation forces family to be split up; sent away to boarding school; sister has polio; his wife leaves him; mother/wife dies; frustration with the woman he loves; her kidneys are permanently damaged when her husband beats her; forced to move house; defeated in election; arrested for treason; "a thoroughly depressing time;" death.*

When reading the examples of happenings that occurred to members of my sample in the year that the Sun was rising in either the decan or the septenary it must be remembered that for any single year there are always two complementary influences, one in the septenary and the other in the decan. The Sun is rising by one of these methods, but not necessarily by the other. It may be the planetary influence of the other method that stimulated the noted happening. No attempt has been made to decide which were Sun-at-ascendant events and which were not. The same confounding applies to other example happenings that are provided throughout this book. Simply appreciate that when the Sun is rising, to take just the above example, events such as those listed above can and do occur.

As the Sun moves beyond the place of its rising it will encounter each of the planets that rose before it. Each planet in turn symbolizes the help or hindrance that the growing individual may receive as he attempts to proceed along his intended path. Just as in a transit or progression the moving body (the ruler here) will trigger a response in the natal body that it meets. The difference here is that it is the ruler of the decan or septenary that has the basic intent, not the planet it encounters, and the reaction it stimulates is likely to become incorporated within the subsequent happenings with which the ruler becomes associated. Think of it as a transit in reverse. In a transit or progression the reaction occurs in terms of the natal body receiving the transit or progression. In the decan or septenary, however, the reaction is in how the ruler responds and assimilates the natal body's inherent characteristics, as indicated by its sign, house and aspects. The Sun transiting natal Saturn, for example, brings energy and light into what may be a dark and restricted area of a person's life, whereas the Sun as decan or septenary ruler when directed to Saturn is meeting dour energy that can force the Sun to organize itself better and clear up loose ends if it is to attain to its aim of becoming fully creative and self responsible.

Planets located in Fire signs are likely to provide support and beneficial opportunities that will aid the Sun's growth in the intended direction, according to their nature; planets in Air signs may provide different forms of pressure that seek to divert the individual, to alter him into something he may not wish to be, or even to destroy him completely. Although planets in Earth or Water signs tend to be unhelpful they are not necessarily malefic. The relationship in the birth horoscope between the Sun and the planet to which it is directed, including the sign that planet occupies, invariably determines how positive the encounter will be.

The Sun directed to the Moon
(42% positive)

The Sun and Moon are opposites in every respect. The Sun is the true source of light, the Moon only a reflection of that source. The Sun is considered to be masculine, the Moon feminine. The Sun is the Self; the Moon represents the Other. The Sun is of the Fire element, hot and dry; the Moon is a Water body, cold and moist. And, especially important to remember when we are interpreting how these two lights will combine when one is directed to the natal position of the other, the Sun is strongest during daylight hours while the Moon is most powerful at night, when she is growing in size, moving away from the Sun, waxing in a sunless sky.

The year in which the Sun as ruler of the septenary or decan comes to the natal place of the Moon is usually a difficult one. The single most important purpose of the Sun during this seven or ten-year period is to turn the individual's attention away from anything that will distract and to concentrate instead on his key purpose in life as indicated by the sign the Sun occupied at birth, modified by its House and aspects.

There are often too many diversions this year for the Sun's purpose not to be in danger of becoming sidetracked. His opposite self stands before him. The archetypal male is meeting face to face with the eternal female—people will want to encroach into his space.

This year there will be distractions—marriages (invariably of others) and affairs, daughters born or marrying—and these will demand the person's full attention. Fundamental changes in his home are likely to take place. If he is male, events in the lives of his wife, mother, sisters, daughters or other closely related females, those who normally provide him with his emotional and nurturing support, will involve much of his time, and their health too may be a concern for him. This year's stress may also take its toll on the person's own health. Public humiliation, being accused of a past wrongdoing or a too close-for-comfort scandal, may distract him from his normal everyday affairs and weaken his self-confidence. He could become the victim of an intrigue, or be forced by others to do things he dislikes doing and experience much stress as a result. He may also have to suffer the demise of a friend or the loss of a family member.

On a positive side, this should be a happy and healthy year for those who do not have their Moon located in Libra or Aquarius. The individual will indulge himself in idle pastimes, enjoy good meals and obtain new clothes. He should feel good about himself. It is also an excellent time for artists to bring their work before the public. How it is received will depend on the sign and aspects of the individual's natal Moon.

There are several examples in my sample of this Sun-to-Moon year coinciding with one's parents being at odds with each other and the break up of their marriage. The resulting stress, possible humiliation and loss of self-confidence from this divorce may strongly affect a young child and perhaps cause him to feel rejected, lonely and unloved.

Table ☉-9:   **Sun to the Moon: % Positive Years**

Nature of the ☽	Day birth		Night birth		All	
	N	% Positive	N	% Positive	N	% Positive
Waxing ☽	31	49.5	39	44.0	70	46.5
Waning ☽	22	49.3	28	25.9**	50	36.2*
All	53	49.5	67	36.4**	120	42.2

Victories, promotions and honors are also possible this year, especially for those born in the daytime with well-placed Moons. There may be opportunities to travel, to publish ideas, to make a new start in life. The individual may be forced to absent himself from his home, from his family, perhaps to work away or to attend college.

The events occurring in a Sun-to-Moon year depend very much on the natal strengths of the Sun and the Moon, especially on their birth relationship. In the sample the year was particularly difficult for those persons born at night at the time of a waning Moon. Statistically significant values were observed when the Sun came from the 1st or 3rd house, or when it was directed to the Moon in Pisces. Each of these values was well below 50%.

Happenings in the sample when the Sun as time ruler comes to the Moon in the decan:

Diurnal Sun to Moon in the decan: *wins the Nobel Prize; honorary doctorate; attracted to a new approach to astrology; attains power; start of business partnership; war prevents him from returning home; his first book is published; writing; lecturing; loses election; suffers from anti-Semitism; concerned for the safety of his son in the army; tortured by sciatica.*

Nocturnal Sun to Moon in the decan: *has an economic theory that will solve the world's problems; buys a boat; court & tax problems; others are jealous of his book's success; graduates; almost expelled from school; accused of sedition; mother remarries; parents die; friend dies; grandfather is assassinated; he is duped; travels; moves; he is in love; quarrels with his girl friend; the opposition of his girl friend's parents is much publicized; marries; divorce; affairs; arrested; exiled but escapes; promoted; intensely dislikes being held by her father on a horse; bronchitis; tonsillitis.*

Happenings in the sample when the Sun as time ruler comes to the Moon in the septenary:

Diurnal Sun to Moon in the septenary: *loses election; company merger; fighting in Spanish Civil War; jealousy; graduates; promoted; loses her job; scandal; under extreme stress; others conspire against him; intense love affair; marries; son born; daughter goes away to school; his brother is executed; wife/mother dies; rejected for military service; excommunicated; travels; severe illness; decides to become "what I myself am"; death.*

Nocturnal Sun to Moon in the septenary: *sent away from home to avoid the plague; sister/daughter marries; affair; marries; her lover is banished; mother remarries; her illusions are dashed; nursemaid straps him to a chair in a dark room; accused of corruption; imprisoned in the Tower of London; banished; publicly humiliated; loses election; his success goes to his head; famous; brother born; in his first film; learns to say "No"; forced to admit he was blackmailed; poems are published; moves; death.*

The Sun directed to Mercury
(47% positive)

This should be a year in which one's thinking is stimulated, and this will help to make it a very active and busy twelve months. There will be much talking, speaking in public, correspondence and calculation. News will be received that can cause some worries, perhaps even fear and anxiety. The mind is awake and the individual is likely to become fascinated with new mental interests. He will stand up for his own point of view, which he'll not be shy in expressing. And these voiced opinions may cause others, even some of his friends, to oppose him. There should be more money available this year, and this will allow him to pay off his debts. Children may cause trouble and one of them may be injured. Unless either the Sun or Mercury is badly afflicted in the natal horoscope, the person's reputation should be enhanced. Much depends on the strength of Mercury and the Sun; if each is strong, expect success, improved finances, and prosperity in business. If either is afflicted, there are likely to be failures.

These Sun-to-Mercury years were invariably difficult for people in the sample. Those born during the daytime with Mercury rising after the Sun experienced the most problems.

People in the sample who were born at night often experienced deaths in their families.

Table ☉-10:   **Sun to Mercury: % Positive Years**

Phase of ☿	Day birth		Night birth		All	
	N	% Positive	N	% Positive	N	% Positive
Oriental ☿	33	46.6	37	46.5	70	46.5
Occidental ☿	26	38.2	40	52.0	66	46.6
All	59	42.9	77	49.3	136	46.6

Statistically significant values above 50% were observed when either the Sun or Mercury was located in the 6th house.

Examples of happenings in the sample when the Sun as time ruler comes to Mercury in the decan:

Diurnal Sun to Mercury in the decan: *international fame; election success/defeat; mother/brother dies; travels: information overload; dysentery; disagreement with the Church; concerned with the psychological nature of evil; suffering much in body and mind; financial worries; friend accuses him of wrongdoing; death.*

Nocturnal Sun to Mercury in the decan: *brother marries; on the dole; first speaks in public; brother is assassinated; father dies/remarries; she dresses as a man; change of school; studying; graduates; moves; socializing; cleared of wrongdoing; goes into the army; classified as unfit for the army; rejected as a conscientious objector; under extreme stress; first shows he is clairvoyant; changes his job; argues against free will; his discovery is a pioneering study of archeology; editing newspaper; book published; continuously writing; attains power; bullied; homesick; travels; nightmares; kicked in the head by a horse; death.*

Examples of happenings in the sample when the Sun as time ruler comes to Mercury in the septenary:

Diurnal Sun to Mercury in the septenary: *financial crisis; very poor; career concerns; graduates; changes his job; removed from command & reduced in rank for disobeying orders; sells his company; begins studying astrology; landlord difficulties; jailed; much writing; campaigning; buys first computer & learns to program it; successful astrological predictions; marries; daughter born; long-lasting affair ends; parents/friends die; indecisive & anxious; depressed; arthritic pain in his arms; hypochondria; epileptic fit; death.*

Nocturnal Sun to Mercury in the septenary: *achieves high office* (this is the most frequently observed direction associated with attaining leadership of a company or state*); promoted; a year in which everything seems to go wrong; arrested; fails exams; studying; travels; moves; marries; divorce; affairs; meets future spouse; father/mother/wife/sister/friend dies; her son remarries; sexually molested by her stepbrother; has a compulsion to write; decides he'll be a writer; lonely; withdraws into himself; solo flight across the Atlantic; accused of fraud; branded as an imposter & a spy; bullied; mental conflicts; has a mental breakdown; in poor health.*

The Sun directed to Venus
(51% positive)

This year our hero may assume the role of the lover. Unless natal Venus is poorly positioned, it will be a happy, creative year, one in which friends are made and pleasures enjoyed, a time when everything in the world will seem to be beautiful and feelings are expressed through the arts, through music, singing, writing poetry and sometimes simply through rather pointless discussions. Marriage is a possibility. The individual will feel affectionate and sociable, he may fall in love and will certainly be more conscious of his appearance and will want to entertain others. His health should be good even though he will prefer to be inactive and luxuriate rather than to go to the gym to exercise his body. Finances should improve, promotions are possible and he may be honored.

Table ☉-11:   **Sun to Venus: % Positive Years**

	Day birth		Night birth		*All*	
	N	% Positive	N	% Positive	*N*	*% Positive*
Oriental ♀	25	47.0	27	46.9	*52*	*46.9*
Occidental ♀	28	51.6	47	55.8	*75*	*54.5*
All	*53*	*49.5*	*74*	*52.5*	*127*	*51.3*

Members of the sample generally enjoyed a happy pleasant year when the Sun came to Venus. Exceptions mainly occurred in years when Saturn was also one of the time rulers. Several people developed an interest in herbalism. The year was more pleasant for those born with Venus to the west of the Sun (Venus in its Evening Star phase) than for those persons with Venus rising ahead of the Sun. Venus placed in a Jupiter term was associated with significantly positive years.

Examples of happenings in the sample when the Sun as time ruler comes to Venus in the decan:

Diurnal Sun to Venus in the decan: *persuaded that it is too dangerous for her to have children; his wife leaves him; marries; mother dies; immense fame; honorary doctorate; stimulated by lecture he hears; he has total power; realizing old ambitions; thrown from a horse; manias, in turn deeply depressed & violently excited; depression; visits his birthplace; attempts suicide; attempt on his life; death.*

Nocturnal Sun to Venus in the decan: *studies existentialism; his father pressures him to become an accountant; moves; grieving; nursing her father; father dies; affair; refuses a marriage proposal; first meets future wife; marries; son born; wife & sons are very ill; her daughter goes away to college; graduates; mostly relaxing; becomes musical director for life; fights his family for independence & wins; reading poetry; great fame; motorbike accident; peace making.*

Examples of happenings in the sample when the Sun as time ruler comes to Venus in the septenary:

Diurnal Sun to Venus in the septenary: *election loss; has two mistresses; marries; in love; his wife is manic depressive; duel 'because of a lady'; son/daughter born; alone; promoted; released from insane asylum; foot surgery; becomes serious about his faith; happy with his friends; poetry; builds a musical theater; studying the laws of harmony in music; brother dies in air crash; death in an air crash.*

Nocturnal Sun to Venus in the septenary: *marries; divorce; loses his shyness; reading poetry; siblings born; son/father/mother/sister/friend dies; at sea in a full gale; her father survives a shipwreck; loses election; travels; expelled; moves; investigating consciousness; portrays exploitation & humiliation of labor; organizes a workers' strike; joins a protest march; frees his slaves; becomes self-employed; in poor health; seething paranoia; wounded in his head; pneumonia.*

The Sun directed to Mars
(50% positive)

The arrival of the Sun at the place of natal Mars can turn the native into something of a warrior, it will make him more combative than usual and this can provoke anger and resentment in others. These are usually positive years when a person has great self-confidence, more energy than usual and discovers how to stand up for himself. Even so he needs to be tactful and take care to avoid getting into risky situations, as quarrels, accidents and falls are possible. This is particularly so for those born with the Sun in Taurus, Cancer or Libra.

How the year will manifest depends to a large extent on the individual's age and ability to accommodate the extra impulse of energy. Usually in the teens or twenties the positive outlet is in sporting activities, otherwise it can be a dangerous year, in which there is violence, anger, and the desire for revenge for any and all slights and insults. A person or virus may attack him. Much also depends on the relative strength of Venus and Mars in the birth chart. Situations will occur that are aimed to bring about the release of tension. Given a task the individual can now be expected to work long and hard to accomplish it.

Table ☉-12:   **Sun to Mars: % Positive Years**

Phase of ♂	Day birth		Night birth		All	
	N	% Positive	N	% Positive	N	% Positive
Oriental ♂	23	55.1	45	42.2	68	46.6
Occidental ♂	29	53.0	36	55.2	65	54.2
All	52	53.9	81	48.0	133	50.3

After the age of 49, when the direction occurs for the second time in the septenary, the raw, primitive energy of Mars is greatly changed and becoming increasingly absent. In those later years the individual may experience such afflictions as rheumatism, fever, influenza, dysentery or chicken pox. He may lose money by theft or wasteful expenses, and have mental worries. With this direction fire is always a danger.

Those people in the sample who were born with a nocturnal Sun and an oriental Mars experienced the most difficulties this year. Statistically significant values were observed for this direction when the Sun came from the 1st house, or when it was directed to a Mars located in the 8th house. Sun in 1st was significantly below 50%. Mars in 8th was significant above 50%.

Examples of happenings in the sample when the Sun comes to Mars in the decan:
Diurnal Sun to Mars in the decan: *little money; has no creative impulse; wins election; discovers Sidereal Astrology; has a lucky escape in a plane crash; treated as a freak; constantly on the move; his brother commits suicide; son born; sleeps in cellar during bombing; life is a strain & his health suffers; assassination attempt; her morality is attacked.*
Nocturnal Sun to Mars in the decan: *declares war; moves from passivity to activity; his wife leaves him; starts living with his future wife; son born; cutting trees for fuel; starts a publishing company; routs men shouting abuse by charging them with his walking stick; book published; his book is criticized; first full-time job; mother/sister/brother dies; father is ill; paralytic affliction takes away the use of his hands; unable to walk; his face is burnt by a firework.*

Examples of happenings in the sample when the Sun comes to Mars in the septenary:
Diurnal Sun to Mars in the septenary: *his only child dies in a railroad accident; marries; son born; sister dies; promoted; wins Nobel Prize; in a car accident; joins the navy; wins tennis championship; severely wounded; she wants revenge; wins fencing championship; interrogated by grand jury; vicious attacks on his character; defeats; threatened; loss of freedom; collapses & is no longer sane; death.*
Nocturnal Sun to Mars in the septenary: *declares war; promoted; refuses to feel inferior; stands up for himself; kills his brother in a gun accident; brother is bankrupt; no money; quarrels; election success; hits head diving into shallow water; marries; son born; father/mother/friend dies; angry; quarrels; falls from horse that runs away with him; works as a laborer; deep depression; injures his nose; bad bout of flu; fractures his shoulder.*

The Sun directed to Jupiter
(55% positive)

This should be the very best year of the Sun-ruled septenary or decan. Jupiter will protect and provide positive opportunities for the Sun and this can cause the individual to enjoy good health and be full of self-confidence, dignity and at ease. In turn this confident attitude should impress others and can only be favorable to ensure the year is successful—it could be the year of opportunities, when the seeds of future prosperity are sown and the individual's reputation is made, a time when he can initiate new projects and expand his activities in a manner that will positively influence his career, status and position in society. The possibility may now exist for him to escape from a harrowing and inhibiting situation that has restrained him from being truly who he is. He may marry, travel, and is likely to improve how he dresses. It is a year in which he can prosper just so long as he avoids living beyond his means.

Day births with an oriental Jupiter seem likely to enjoy a pleasant, gainful year in which there can be opportunities for success. Nocturnal births frequently experience others leaving. Significantly above-average values were observed when the Sun was directed to a Jupiter located in the 5th house, or when the Sun came from a Jupiter term.

Table ☉-13:   **Sun to Jupiter: % Positive Years**

Phase of ♂	Day birth		Night birth		All	
	N	% Positive	N	% Positive	N	% Positive
Oriental ♂	22	65.7	29	53.0	51	58.5
Occidental ♂	36	47.7	38	57.1	74	52.5
All	58	54.5	67	55.3	125	55.0

Examples of happenings in the sample when the Sun comes to Jupiter in the decan:
Diurnal Sun to Jupiter in the decan: *stops eating meat; starts a new business; lectures to large audiences; re-elected; a positive year; resigns; his son's horrible death at the hands of the Gestapo destroys his will to live; breaks his foot; peak mystical experiences; seriously ill; writes on the unification of opposites; elected; defeated for re-election; sells his house; facing the fact that his career is finished; death.*
Nocturnal Sun to Jupiter in the decan: *world tour; anger against the myth of patriotism; happy with her lover; criticized; a difficult year; marries; father dies; brother is assassinated; loses money in financial panic; financial anxieties; first public speech; re-elected; travels; goes away to college; living alone; measles; cerebral spinal meningitis; losing his hearing.*

Examples of happenings in the sample when the Sun comes to Jupiter in the septenary:

Diurnal Sun to Jupiter in the septenary: *brother dies; arrested; travels; enjoys a lively social life; finances improve; wins large prize money; marries; divorce; life is a social whirl; new job with large salary increase; life improves; in debt; sent into exile; election success; sees harmony everywhere; removed from his command; sees his invention work; becomes aware that disease is discord and lack of harmony; gains weight; lethargic; sciatica; told he has an incurable disease.*

Nocturnal Sun to Jupiter in the septenary: *marries a wealthy widow; remarries; son born; his wife leaves him; deaths in the family; coronation; travels; he is 'discovered'; goes to college; passes exams; moves; his speeches inspire his besieged nation; flush with money & fame; crosses the line from rebellious schoolboy to revolutionary; in constant trouble; in poor health; in extreme pain; many violent fits of anger; typhoid; commits suicide.*

The Sun directed to Saturn
(45% positive)

This can be a very difficult year, containing periods of hard work and restraint, during which a person may be restricted in what he can and cannot do. People often become fearful, lonely, over cautious and envious of the easy success of others, especially if they were born at night when both the Sun and Saturn are weakest. Some loss of property is likely, as are accidents, quarrels, mental worries, a lack of energy, loss of confidence, and becoming a victim of theft. Serious illnesses to the individual and to members of his family that require lengthy convalescence can occur. Financial loss and the need to borrow money is another frequent occurrence.

Those born in the daytime can expect an easier year. Ambitions may be awoken that can lead to the achievement of great power and authority; this is especially so for those born with Saturn in Aries or Leo, signs in which Saturn is uncomfortable and less able to destroy the person's creativity and self-confidence.

Results from the sample confirm the opinions of classical astrologers that Saturn is stronger and more positive in a daytime birth. Notwithstanding these indications however, persons born at night with an unafflicted Sun in Libra, Capricorn or Aquarius (the Saturn signs) or with an unafflicted Saturn in Aries or Leo (the Sun signs) usually enjoyed pleasant times under this direction. Several diurnal births in the sample with an occidental Saturn became very famous this year.

Table ☉-14:   **Sun to Saturn: % Positive Years**

Phase of ♄	Day birth		Night birth		All	
	N	% Positive	N	% Positive	N	% Positive
Oriental ♄	27	50.3	35	38.8	62	43.8
Occidental ♄	23	55.1	44	41.1	67	45.8
All	*50*	*52.4*	*79*	*40.1*	*129*	*44.8*

Examples of happenings in the sample when the Sun comes to Saturn in the decan:

Diurnal Sun to Saturn in the decan: *living in cramped conditions in an unfriendly environment; ostracized; excommunicated by the Church; the Church stirs up the people against him; speaks on the transformation symbolism in the Mass; his former love dies; separated from his family; her husband is ill; immensely popular; finds the people in Naples disgusting; honored; her hobby becomes a business; house hunting; heart dilation following exertion; death.*

Nocturnal Sun to Saturn in the decan: *earns her professional license; has a house built; she rejects a marriage offer; marries; children born; father/mother/grandmother dies; little money; brother born; his book is an overnight success; puts on weight; bickering with her best friend; coronation; becomes a vegetarian; on trial for sedition & assault; arthritis.*

Examples of happenings in the sample when the Sun comes to Saturn in the septenary:

Diurnal Sun to Saturn in the septenary: *his writings forever change man's view of the universe; he is Man of the Year; first publishes his magazine; buys his first new car; marries; he no longer loves his wife; divorce; his wife dies; repairs roof; great suffering; conscripted; successful astrological predictions; in fierce battles, miraculously escaping death; a year of cruel surprises; severely wounded; travels; humiliated; promoted; he is deceived; dieting & losing weight; retires due to ill health; typhoid fever; death.*

Nocturnal Sun to Saturn in the septenary: *authorizes atom bombings; becoming famous; great fame; the apogee of triumph; father is found guilty of rape; arrested; work problems; war disrupts his life; blackmailed; father/mother/uncle dies; re-elected; twice in prison; father has son from later marriage; alone; daughters marry; feels he is now being of some use; no life outside of his work; graduates; bullied; husband has large salary increase; his book describes his system of philosophy; wants a divorce; inflamed kidneys; teeth problems; death of his enemy; emergency operation; malaria; death.*

The Sun directed to Uranus
(50% positive)

This can be an inspired period, an exciting and exhilarating year. The individual will try new ways of asserting himself and perhaps succeed in becoming free from old patterns. It should be a revolutionary year of change, the individual being attracted to what is new and exciting. He may change his job. It is however the very nature of this direction that few things will happen exactly as planned, and the more relaxed and flexible one is the less stress and fewer annoyances there will be. One should be prepared to break from one's habitual life, to try new ways of self-expression and to look forward to experiencing the unexpected.

Table ☉-15: **Sun to Uranus: % Positive Years**

Phase of ♅	Day birth		Night birth		All	
	N	% Positive	N	% Positive	N	% Positive
Oriental ♅	6	60.3	12	45.2	18	50.3
Occidental ♅	10	27.1	8	79.1	18	50.3
All	16	39.6	20	58.8	36	50.3

Because of the few observations involved, the values in Table ☉-15 should be treated with caution.

Examples of happenings in the sample when the Sun as time ruler comes to Uranus in the decan:
Diurnal Sun to Uranus in decan: *pension for life relieves him of the drudgery of hackwork; receives the Nobel Prize; election success; moves; writes a book; recuperating from severe manic attacks; attends cookery school; criticized; his house is completely destroyed by bombs; he assumes total power; mountain climbing; he is the victim of a witch-hunt instigated by Catholics; full of ideas & plans but unable to make any physical effort; father/wife/brother dies; death.*
Nocturnal Sun to Uranus in decan: *decides that only the nomadic life is right for her; marries; captured but escapes; witnesses an execution; life on the run; very restless; causes sensation by postulating gravity; signs with Motown Records; battle for survival; away at school; miserable; first mystical experience; promoted; becomes addicted to hashish; kidney infection; malaria; son/father/brother/grandmother dies.*

The Sun directed to Neptune
(52% positive)

A person experiencing this direction may find it difficult to stay objective this year for his thinking can become rather muddled. He is likely to become unusually idealistic, be interested in spiritual matters, and get immersed in a state of heightened imagination; perhaps feel scorned and neglected, and be victimized and trapped by circumstances. Others may not take what he says or does too seriously; they are likely to ignore him and perhaps go so far as to ridicule his ideas. He will tend to have less energy than usual, and will often feel exhausted. At the same time he is likely to feel worthless, inadequate and be self-pitying. He will be extremely sensitive to outside influences. Others may deceive him and he in turn may be tempted to deceive others. Neptune appears to be most positive in a nocturnal chart.

Table ☉-16:   **Sun to Neptune: % Positive Years**

Phase of ♆	Day birth		Night birth		All	
	N	*% Positive*	*N*	*% Positive*	*N*	*% Positive*
Oriental ♆	8	33.9	9	60.3	17	47.9
Occidental ♆	8	56.5	10	54.2	18	55.3
All	16	45.2	19	57.1	35	51.7

Again, because of the few observations involved, values in Table ☉-16 should be treated with caution.

Examples of happenings in the sample when the Sun as time ruler comes to Neptune in the decan:

Diurnal Sun to Neptune in decan: *breaks with his best friend; feeling helpless as if in prison; increasingly indolent; loss of consciousness; his wife is honored; mother dies; son born; war starts; moves; teaches himself programming; studying; insomnia; vitamins improve his health; depressed; humiliated; teeth problems; assassinated.*

Nocturnal Sun to Neptune in decan: *daughter born; husband/father dies; falls in love; several wild crushes; marries; travels; bullied; financial panic; accused of stealing scientific results; erroneously reported dead; letter bomb is intended for him; happy when hunting & fishing; learns his friend is a traitor; hysterectomy; death by drowning.*

The Sun directed to Pluto
(36% positive)

This can be a very difficult year, by far the worst of the Sun's decan. During it the new is coming into existence and the old is passing away. It is an unsettling time with separations and deaths. An upheaval in the workplace may take place. The existing order is being broken up and the past comfort and security, which was familiar and therefore safe, is being lost. He may be forced to live among strangers, perhaps in surroundings that are alien to him, and can feel isolated and unwanted. A positive response is to be willing to work harder to fulfill his ambitions.

Table ☉-17: **Sun to Pluto: % Positive Years**

Phase of ♀	Day birth		Night birth		All	
	N	*% Positive*	*N*	*% Positive*	*N*	*% Positive*
Oriental ♀	8	56.5	10	**9.0****	18	30.1
Occidental ♀	4	45.2	18	40.1	22	45.5
All	12	52.7	28	**29.0****	40	36.2

Despite the few observations in Table ☉-17, because of the significant result for the Sun to oriental Pluto at night, we should pay attention to the values that are reported in it.

In the sample the nocturnal Sun coming to an oriental Pluto invariably resulted in a particularly difficult and statistically significant year, something of a shocker, in which the individual's health was seriously undermined and/or there was complete failure of an enterprise the success of which had previously been considered virtually certain.

Examples of happenings in the sample when the Sun as time ruler comes to Pluto in the decan:

Diurnal Sun to Pluto in decan: *systematic self-analysis; inactive; mother remarries; husband drowns; honored; writes on freedom and organization; studying; discovers the Oedipus complex; moves; receiving threatening letters; lecturing; travels; writes astrology book; death.*

Nocturnal Sun to Pluto in decan: *in trouble at school; goes away to school; moves; considers immigrating; a frightened, miserable little girl, she adopts the role of a healthy bouncy extrovert; nearly shoots woman by mistake; buys a company; father dies; lesbian love affair; loses in court; he is responsible for the drowning death of a young woman; arrested; shoots a wild turkey but suffers great remorse & never hunts game again; at the lowest ebb of his life so far; nervous breakdown; scarlet fever; malaria; bronchitis; near-fatal pneumonia.*

Isabelle Eberhardt's Sun-ruled Decan

Sun in Aquarius rises: The Swiss anarchist writer Isabelle Eberhardt's Sun-ruled decan begins in February 1897 when she celebrates her twentieth birthday. The Sun also rules her septenary but is now in the final year of its rule, meeting her occidental Saturn in Pisces. It is a nocturnal birth and her Sun, weak in Aquarius, is closely sextile Jupiter, opposes Uranus, squares Pluto, and its antiscion opposes Neptune. With the Sun rising the year should be one of new beginnings, but because it is a nocturnal Sun and there is the accompanying septenary direction to Saturn we cannot expect this new start in life to be easy or pleasant. She quits her job as secretary of a terrorist group in Geneva, and with her mother moves from France to Algiers to join her brother Augustin. The two women convert to Islam. Augustin becomes ill with typhoid, which so distresses her mother that she dies suddenly from heart failure. Shocked and angry, Isabelle concentrates on "know thyself." Her real self seems to her so unfathomable, and so different from everyone else's that she chooses to hide it behind a mask. She dresses as a man and makes friends with local Arab students, learning Algerian Arabic, and slipping into an easy familiarity with her new life.

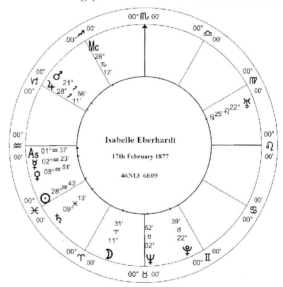

Sun directed to Venus in Aquarius: She is twenty-one years old in 1898, when her decan-ruler Sun, still in Aquarius, comes to her oriental Venus. The antiscion of Venus opposes Pluto, which in turn squares Uranus. This year the occidental Saturn in Pisces begins to rule her septenary. She is alone, grieving for her mother, and writes a fictionalized account of her mother's death. Her turmoil and despair give way to a numb state of shock. She is like a wounded animal. Everything seems pointless. She avoids people, going on solitary walks and making melancholy visits to her mother's grave. Inert and resigned, she is immobilized by her grief. She begins to write her first novel, at first called *Adrift*, which will be published as *Vagabond*. It becomes the key to a new state of mind: submission, a deliberate acquiescence in the workings of fate. She starts to exchange the European moral currency—hope, expectations, directed will—for that of a more ancient culture: submission, acceptance, living from day to day. Islam is the Arabic word for submission. She is present at a revolt of Arabs against the

French that galvanizes her out of her inertia. She enjoys a sensual pleasure in the physical violence and is intoxicated by the bloody battle. She returns to Geneva. Her brother Vladimir goes insane and commits suicide, putting his head inside a gas oven. Her father is very ill with cancer. She nurses him, waiting for him to die. She is forced to borrow money. She has an affair with a young Turkish diplomat but refuses to marry him. She is writing her novel *Rakhil*. We expect the second year of the decan to be difficult, the planet the ruler meets now should give shape to the ruler's raw potential. There were some Sun-on-Venus moments during the year, but the influences of the Sun remaining in Aquarius, the sign of its detriment, and Saturn coincidently arriving at her ascendant overshadow these.

Sun directed to Mercury in Aquarius: Eberhardt's Sun is still in Aquarius in 1899 when it comes to her oriental Mercury. The decan's third year is often the first in which the potential of the ten-year period starts to be actualized. She is twenty-two years old. Septenary Saturn has moved from Pisces into its own sign of Aquarius where it meets her Sun. She is nursing her father, who dies of throat cancer—there are rumors that she hastens his end with a dose of chloral. The sudden almost complete severing of the bonds to her past life bring an unforeseen elation; she feels a brimming, if guilty, sense of release of tensions, a deep sense of rebirth. "The farther behind I leave the past, the closer I am to

forging my own character." She leaves home, has sex with several sailors in Marseilles, then crosses the narrow sea to Tunis where she dresses as a man and calls herself Si Mahmoud Essadi. She is writing her novel. Fascinated with death, she visits Arab cemeteries, which she finds peaceful. She delights in sunrises. She is frequently with native lovers and lives as a nomad. In Tunis she travels with tax collectors, sleeping with them, meeting hostile receptions from those being taxed. She has a delicious sensation of liberty, peace and well being. She then discovers that she has no money and realizes that she has done no work but only wallowed in degrading debauchery. She goes to Paris to meet with her editors and writes *The Age of the Void*, an article that laments the joyless inanity of society as she sees it—its frantic pursuit of pleasure. Influenced by the Saturn direction to her Sun, she has become very pessimistic. She goes to Sardinia to be with Osman, a young Tunisian exile. Her brother Augustin marries.

Sun directed to Jupiter in Sagittarius: In February 1900, on her twenty-third birthday, Eberhardt's Sun finally leaves Aquarius and in this fourth year of the decan moves into Sagittarius, to her oriental Jupiter. This Sun direction to Jupiter should define not only what occurs this year but also what is possible in the decan. Septenary Saturn remains in Aquarius and has now arrived at her Venus. She is with Osman in Paris, but she soon leaves him to return to Africa. The more fragmented her life, the more she seeks the healing unity of a single idea, an absolute, whether it is the image of her mother's tomb, the idea of Allah, the simplicity of the desert, or the sun, the great monolithic healer and symbol of renaissance. She is trying to reduce her needs to a minimum: fulfillment through reduction, simplicity, and authenticity. Her interest in mysticism is growing. Her article *The Age of the Void* is published. She finally completes her novel. She makes contact with a secret Sufi brotherhood, the Qadiriyya, a sect heavily involved in helping the poor and needy while fighting against the injustices of French colonial rule, and becomes an initiate. She is happy in the desert with her new lover, Slimene, a young Arab army sergeant. She takes part in a two-day desert 'fantasia' for El Hachemi; she is the only European woman to have done so. She is accused of being dangerous and politically provocative, and is under surveillance by the army and police. There are anxieties over money and lack of food. By the end of the year she is too weak to write. Attempting to manipulate her out of the country, the army post Slimene to a distant garrison. She decides to follow him. During the year she becomes an aunt with the birth of a daughter to her brother Augustin.

Sun directed to Mars in Sagittarius: Her Sun comes to her oriental Mars in Sagittarius in February 1901 when Eberhardt is twenty-four years old. This is the fifth year of her decan and during it Pythagorean theory suggests the individual is likely to encounter new experiences. With Saturn on her Aquarian Mercury in the septenary these new experiences may teach her much discipline. Her arm is nearly severed when a religious fanatic wielding a sword attacks her. The arm heals badly; she is unable to bend it from the elbow. Released from hospital, she follows Slimene; making a seven-day journey by horse across the desert. The army refuses Slimene permission to marry her and she is expelled from Algeria. Feeling like a pitilessly hunted beast, she goes to Marseilles. In France she writes essays and a full description of the attempted assassination. Later in the year she returns to Algiers to attend the trial of her would-be assassin. At the trial her morality is attacked. Slimene is transferred to Marseilles and she marries him. She is now a French citizen.

Sun directed to Uranus in Leo: In 1902, in the sixth year of her decan, the Sun moves on to the sign it rules, Leo, where it finds a retrograde Uranus. This should be a fairly uneventful year during which the individual has the opportunity to settle down after the previous year's excitement. Eberhardt is twenty-five years old. Septenary Saturn has come to the Sagittarian Jupiter. She is in Algiers. Slimene is discharged from the army. She is refreshed and strengthened by a meeting with a woman mystic, who confirms that the nomadic life is the only one for Isabelle. She is now completely addicted to hashish. Her short story *The Magician* is published.

Sun directed to Pluto in Taurus: In 1903 she is twenty-six years old. It is the seventh year of her decan, often the most critical year of the ten. Her Sun is on Pluto in Taurus in the decan, and Saturn is on her Sagittarian Mars in the septenary. She is in Algiers where she becomes involved in local elections despite trying to avoid doing so. The antagonism and character assassination are debilitating to both Slimene and her. She has a vision that she will die soon. She becomes friends with a French general and he allows her to travel with the army as a war correspondent.

Sun directed to Neptune in Taurus: In 1904 Eberhardt is twenty-seven years old when the Sun comes to her Neptune in Taurus. This is the eighth year of the decan during which any previous instability should be balanced and the stage set for further development. It is the final year of her Saturn-ruled septenary. Saturn has moved into Aries, the sign of its fall, where it comes to her Moon. Both the Moon and Neptune are symbolically connected with deep running water, a rarity in the environment in which Eberhardt is living. She is a war correspondent in the Atlas Mountains as the French penetrate into Morocco. Disguised as an Arab man, she visits two brothels; they excite the voyeur in her. She stays in a Moroccan monastery, still in the guise of a man, spending her time writing. She is ill, suffering from syphilis. A bad bout of fever puts her into hospital. Slimene joins her on her release. The couple had been separated for the past eight months. They are together for just two hours when a flash flood hits the house. It carries Isabelle Eberhardt away and she is drowned.

Bertrand Russell's first Sun-ruled Septenary

The controversial British philosopher and mathematician Bertrand Russell, recipient of the Nobel Prize for Literature in 1950 and named "the greatest logician since Aristotle", whose autobiography is remarkable for its openness and objectivity, experienced the Sun as his time ruler three times in his long life. Two of these times had the Sun ruling his septenary.

Russell's was a diurnal birth—he went to Cambridge University a month after his eighteenth birthday and, within two months, influenced by the writings of John Stuart Mill, he had declared himself an atheist. The Sun is the seventh of the full set of ten bodies to arrive at the ascendant, and, skipping over Neptune and Pluto, the fifth of the classical seven. The Sun and Mars, both members of the five-body Taurus satellium, are closely conjunct in the 7th house. Their conjunction closely sextiles the Jupiter-Uranus pair in Cancer. As the Sun rules the MC, events involving his reputation and his relationships (it is located in the seventh) are likely to be emphasized during the years when it rules either his septenary or his decan.

Sun in Taurus rises: The septenary Sun rises in May 1900 when Russell is 28 years old. Mercury rules the decan and is being directed to its dispositor, Venus in Taurus—note that Venus follows Pluto in Russell's rising sequence. He is living in Cambridge where he is a Fellow of Trinity College. He describes this year as being one of "mathematical intoxication." He visits Paris where he first becomes aware of the work of Gottlob Frege and Giuseppe Peano, who had earlier failed in their attempt to derive, by means of symbolic logic, the whole of mathematics from certain logical constants. Meeting Peano was "a turning point in my intellectual life." Frege's and Peano's uncompleted work impresses Russell, helps him dispel an early infatuation with Hegelian idealism and prompts him to pose for himself the problem first raised by Kant—how to defend the objectivity of mathematics. He describes his excitement: "The time was one of intellectual intoxication. My sensations resembled those one has after climbing a mountain in a mist, when, on reaching the summit, the mist suddenly clears, and the country becomes visible for forty miles in every direction. For years I had been endeavoring to analyze the fundamental notions of mathematics, such as order and cardinal numbers. Suddenly, in the space of a few weeks, I discovered what appeared to be definitive answers to the problems that had baffled me for years. And in the course of discovering these answers, I was introducing a new mathematical technique, by which regions formerly abandoned by the vagueness of philosophers were conquered by the precision of exact formulae. Intellectually, the month of September 1900 was the highest point of my life." He is writing the *Principles of Mathematics* to introduce the new mathematical techniques.

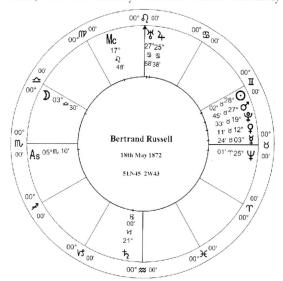

That same year Russell becomes a pacifist, which can be associated with Mercury coming to Venus in the decan, as can the following event. He and his wife attend a poetry reading, where he is "profoundly stirred by the beauty of the poetry." They return to where they were staying with friends to find their hostess "in an unusually severe bout of pain… Suddenly the ground seemed to give way beneath me, and I found myself in quite a different region. Within five minutes I went through some such reflections as the following: the loneliness of the human soul is unendurable; nothing can penetrate it except the highest intensity of the sort of love that religious teachers have preached; whatever does not spring from this motive is harmful, or at best useless; it follows that war is wrong, that a public school education is abominable, that the use of force is to be deprecated, and that in human relations one should penetrate to the core of loneliness in each person and speak to that… At the end of those five minutes, I had become a completely different person. For a time, a sort of mystic illumination possessed me. I felt that I knew the inmost thoughts of everybody I met in the street…" He is then, "…filled with semi-mystical feelings about beauty, an intense interest in children and a desire to find some philosophy that would make human life endurable".

The year is a major one in Russell's life. It is a new start, as one would expect when a new planet assumes rulership of either the septenary or the decan, and because it is the Sun in this role, it is an entry into an area of experience in which his thinking is bold and individual, and which will lead him during this same septenary to other epoch-making philosophical achievements, not least of which is to carry on the Fregian endeavor to its successful conclusion in the monumental *Principia Mathematica*.

Sun directed to Mars in Taurus: In 1901 Bertrand Russell is aged 29 when he experiences the Sun coming to Mars in the septenary. As it is the second year of the seven, Mars having been ruler of the previous septenary, some form of resistance from Russell's past can be expected. In the decan, Mercury has come to Pluto, the planet that will rule his next ten years. All four planets are in Taurus, the seventh sign from his Scorpio ascendant, and the Sun and Mars are closely conjunct at his birth. It is a difficult year. He first has an intellectual setback in his work, a contradiction he is unable to resolve. Then a more serious blow: "I went out bicycling one afternoon, and suddenly, as I was riding along a country

road, I realized that I no longer loved Alys..." He continues, "I told her that I no longer wished to share a room, and in the end I confessed that my love was dead. I justified this attitude to her, as well as to myself, by criticisms of her character." He later writes, "My self-righteousness at that time seems to me in retrospect repulsive..." They are living just outside Cambridge, in the village of Grantchester. "The most unhappy moments of my life are spent at Grantchester."

Sun directed to Venus in Taurus: In 1902, on May 23rd, a few days after his 30th birthday Russell finally completes his *Principles of Mathematics*. He has been working on it for five years and is now finally able to relax. In the septenary the Sun has come to its dispositor, and the same year the decan Pluto has arrived at the ascendant. The direction to Venus (its antiscion is conjunct the midheaven) in the septenary means that it should be a relaxed, pleasant year, one that can improve his reputation. As it is also the third year of the septenary we can also expect Russell to become more outgoing, which may cause a conflict with the direction Pluto wants him to go. He is elected a member of a small but elite dining club, *The Coefficients,* whose members dine together for the purpose of considering questions from a more or less Imperialist point of view. He soon resigns from the club when it becomes apparent that all of the other members disagree with his non-militant stance. Most of the year he lives an enjoyable social life in London and Florence. It is a however a period of complete intellectual deadlock, he cannot resolve several logical contradictions and continue his planned work on the *Principia Mathematica*.

Sun directed to Mercury in Taurus: Russell described this as a very painful year, extremely fruitful for his work but the difficulty and labor was too great for any pleasure. He is 31 years old. In the decan Pluto has also come to Mercury in Taurus. As this is the fourth year of the septenary a time of mental conflict is to be expected. Both rulers coming to Mercury places further emphasis on Mercury matters. He is writing *Principia Mathematica*, and tells a friend that he has "been working like a horse, and have achieved almost nothing. I discovered in succession seven brand-new difficulties, of which I solved the first six. When the seventh turned up, I became discouraged, and decided to take a holiday before going on. Each in turn required a reconstruction of my whole edifice." He goes off on a walking tour of Devon and Cornwall. This year his *Principles of Mathematics* is published and is well received. He makes his first public speeches, advocating Free Trade: "I had never before attempted public speaking, and was shy and nervous to such a degree as to make me at first wholly ineffective. Gradually, however, my nervousness got less."

Sun directed to Saturn in Capricorn: In 1904 Bertrand Russell is 32 when the septenary Sun finally leaves Taurus and moves on to his retrograde Saturn in Capricorn, a direction that could prompt the astrologer to forecast an difficult year. This is the fifth year of the septenary, the year in which the keynote of the whole seven-year period should reveal itself. The decan Pluto is on his Neptune in Aries. The year begins with Russell visiting Brittany and spending time walking in the countryside. He and Alys, his estranged wife, then move to Oxford, where they are building a house. Things began to improve in his life after a difficult two years during which he has been frustrated in his work by contradictions he was unable to resolve. He discovers his Theory of Types, which is a first step towards overcoming the problems that have baffled him for so long. However he describes the year as being very painful, extremely fruitful for his work on *Principia Mathematica* but the difficulty and labor are too great for any pleasure. In a letter to a friend, he writes, "I have fits of depression at times, but they don't last long. I have had a fair share of other people's tragedies lately; some in which intimate friends have behaved badly, which is always painful. Others, which vex me almost more, I only suspect and have to watch their disastrous effects in total impotence..."

Sun directed to the Moon in Libra: In 1905 at age 33 Bertrand Russell has the Sun directed to his waxing Moon in Libra by septenary, a direction that suggests Russell can be beset by distractions this year. Libra is a sign in which the Sun experiences discomfort. Pluto the decan ruler has arrived at Saturn in Capricorn. With the discovery of his Theory of Types, he has at last finally resolved all of his earlier problems, and it just remains to write out the *Principia Mathematic,* although he does not expect publication to occur for another four or five years. Even so it is a very painful year, one in which a close friend drowns, apparently by hitting his head against a rock in diving into a pool. He takes his late friend's son to Paris in the hope that the change of scenery might mollify his grief and prevent a complete collapse. "It has been, in a less degree, a rather terrible time for me too.

It made everything seem uncertain and subject to chance, so that it was hard to keep calm about all the goods whose loss one fears. And it brought up, as misfortunes do, all the memories of buried griefs which one had resolved to be done with. One after another, they burst their tombs, and wailed in the desert spaces of one's mind…"

Sun directed to Jupiter in Cancer: Bertrand Russell has the septenary Sun come to his exalted Jupiter in Cancer in 1906 at age 34. This is the final year of his septenary. Jupiter will rule the next seven years. An entire part of his life is ending and there is a need for something new. Pluto is on the Moon in Libra in his decan. He starts working on behalf of women's suffrage. He was still writing *Principia Mathematica* ten to twelve hours a day, persisting because he sees the difficulties in "the nature of a challenge that it would be pusillanimous not to meet and overcome".

Bertrand Russell's second Sun-Ruled Septenary

Sun in Taurus rises: This occurs for the second time in the septenary in 1949, the year the USSR first explodes an atomic bomb, when Russell is 77 years old. Jupiter, exalted in Cancer and conjunct Uranus, rules the decan, and it has come to Saturn in its own sign of Capricorn—the pair, both of them strong by sign, were opposite at his birth. In the twelve months beginning with his 1949 birthday, Russell's third marriage ends; he receives from the king the Order of Merit (OM), Britain's highest civilian honor; he publicly states his concern with the lessening of individual freedom that is so obviously accompanying the increase in industrialism; and he becomes a champion of nuclear disarmament.

The arrival of Russell's Sun at his ascendant at this time brings a new direction into his life: the cause of nuclear disarmament, how to best combat some maniacal Dr. Strangelove sitting with his gloved finger poised over a button, ready to thoughtlessly plunge the world into an all-consuming nuclear Armageddon, for which Russell will work tirelessly over the final two decades of his long life. The actual nature of this direction is described by the movement of the decan ruler, an exalted Jupiter coming from its natal conjunction with Uranus to the retrograde Saturn, the planet it had opposed at birth. His natal Jupiter, by reason of its position in Cancer, its closeness to Uranus, and its sextile to Mars and the Sun, is not likely to accept anything with which it disagrees no matter who says so. Saturn in Capricorn represents entrenched authority, together with our fears and all the reasons why something imposed by those in power should never be questioned. Jupiter, coupled with Uranus, wants freedom and equal rights for everyone; Saturn, especially when out of sect as it is here, below the horizon in a diurnal chart, represents those who possess the authority to make changes but who, perhaps because of their inertia and self-serving fears, are unwilling to do so.

Both in 1949 and previously in 1900, when Russell experienced the Sun rising at his ascendant, major beginnings occurred that become intensified over the later six years of the septenary. The Sun represents one's all-consuming purpose in life; what it is that makes one a true individual who will stand out in the crowd for what he thinks or how he acts; it symbolizes who one truly is. As Russell's Sun is conjunct Mars, his is the chart of someone who will always fight for whatever he believes is the truth.

Sun directed to Mars in Taurus: In 1950 the septenary Sun comes to Mars for the second time in his life. He is aged 78. Alys, Russell's first wife, whom he had rejected in the earlier Sun-to-Mars year, dies. The accompanying decan is, however, of a more pleasant nature, Jupiter the decan ruler has arrived at his Moon in Libra. There is much travel, he lectures in Australia and in the USA; he is awarded the Nobel Prize for Literature "in recognition of his varied and significant writings in which he champions humanitarian ideals and freedom of thought;" and he re-meets Lucy, an old friend, when he is lecturing in New York, at Columbia. She moves to London and the couple spends much happy time together. In addition to the death of Alys, Sun-to-Mars is apparent when a farm lorry smashes into Russell's car, but there are no injuries.

Sun directed to Venus in Taurus: Russell is 79 years old in 1951 when he again experiences septenary Sun on his Venus. In the same year the decan ruler Jupiter is on his 9th House Uranus in Cancer, where Jupiter is exalted. He and Lucy visit Greece. They are happy and in love.

Sun directed to Mercury in Taurus: In 1952 Bertrand Russell at age 80 again experiences septenary Sun on Mercury. This time it is accompanied by decan Uranus coming to the ascendant. He feels suddenly ill, turns blue and is expected to die within a few hours. "I was packed into an ambulance and whisked to hospital where they dosed me with oxygen and I survived." That same year he marries Lucy; it is his fourth marriage.

Sun directed to Saturn in Capricorn: In 1953, at age 81, Bertrand Russell again has septenary Sun conjunct Saturn; decan Uranus is on its conjunction partner Jupiter. The year begins with him and Lucy spending a carefree time in Scotland, but then Saturn starts to work his dreary wiles. His son and daughter-in-law, both of whom are beginning to show signs of mental illness, abandon their children for him and Lucy to look after— eventually they will become their legal guardians. There are major financial problems. Following the death of Stalin, whom he feels to be "as wicked as one man could be and to be the root evil of most of the misery and terror in, and threatened by, Russia", he condemns him on the radio and rejoices for the world in his departure from the scene, but the BBC refuse to air it. He has a serious operation and lengthy period of recuperation. He writes *Nightmares of Prominent Persons.*

Sun directed to the Moon in Libra: Russell is aged 82 years in 1954 when he experiences the septenary Sun on his Moon for the second time. Uranus in the decan has come to the Sun, so there is an emphasis this year on the Sun, which is closely conjunct Mars in Taurus natally. He gives a widely publicized talk on the radio, *Man's Peril*, which describes the likely affect of a nuclear attack. At other times he speaks in memory of the Jews killed in the Warsaw Uprising; gives several talks in Rome; lectures on History as an Art; and goes sightseeing in Paris. He attempts to get scientists to sign a statement against the bomb but other than from three of the world's senior scientists, Albert Einstein, Max Born and Linus Pauling, who have each achieved sufficient prominence that they can act independently of their governments, there is no interest. Russell is also writing essays that appear the following year entitled *Logic and Knowledge*. During the year he experiences what he describes as 'family troubles'.

Sun directed to Jupiter in Cancer: At age 83 in 1955 Russell again experiences the septenary Sun coming to his exalted Jupiter. Decan Uranus is on his Mars in Taurus. This brings together the planets in Russell's two key conjunctions: the Jupiter-Uranus and Sun-Mars pairings, which can be associated with so much in his long and distinguished life. It is a very active year, fully of the nature of these four planets. He has problems getting scientists to sign an anti-bomb statement (Uranus to Mars). He then holds a well-publicized press conference to launch the Nuclear Disarmament Manifesto. At the same time his eldest son is seriously ill, which causes much worry and heavy expenses (Jupiter rules the natal 2nd and 5th). He attends a World Government Conference in Paris; then another congress just outside of London, that is attended by three Russian scientists, the first time since the war that a Russian Communist has attended a conference in the West (Sun to Jupiter in 9th). He sells his London house and moves to Wales. He also campaigns unsuccessfully against the imprisonment of Morton Sobell in the United States. Sobell had been kidnapped by the US government from Mexico to be brought to trial in connection with the Rosenberg case. Rosenberg and his wife were condemned to death for spying on behalf of the Soviets, on the evidence of a known perjurer. Sobell was sentenced to thirty years imprisonment. Russell considered the Rosenberg executions were government-approved assassinations. However, fifty-three years later, in the summer of 2008, Sobell confessed to reporters that he and Rosenberg had indeed been spies.

This is the final year of the Sun's rulership. In 1956 Jupiter takes over Russell's septenary.

Bertrand Russell's Sun-ruled Decan

Sun in Taurus rises: The third instance of Russell's Sun rising is in the decan. This occurs in 1932. Russell is 60. In his septenary Mercury has arrived at the Sun in Taurus. The year starts with his separation from his second wife Dora—the marriage reaches a breaking point when Dora has two children with another man. For the previous five years he and Dora had run an experimental school, at which they put their innovative ideas, many of which have since been adapted, although some of them continue to be considered still ahead of their time even today, on how best to educate the young. Now he leaves the school to Dora, explains his ideas in *Education & the Social Order*, and begins an affair with his research assistant, Pat, who will later become his third wife. Six months after Russell's birthday Adolf Hitler becomes Chancellor of Germany and a gradual change in Russell's views over the next 7-8 years begins: he goes from being an ardent pacifist, a man who has several times been in prison for his non-resistance beliefs (Venus, the planet of harmony, rules the signs containing both Russell's Sun and his Moon), to someone who agrees that the Nazis had to be fought.

Sun directed to Mars in Taurus: In 1933 the Sun comes to Mars in his decan—he is 61 and Mars is also receiving the septenary ruler Mercury—Russell states that initially he is quite devoid of any creative impulse: "For about two months, purely to afford myself distraction, I worked on the problem of twenty-seven straight lines on a cubic surface. But this would never do, as it was totally useless." Having little money, he forces himself out of his creative inertia and begins writing *Power, a New Social Analysis*, an appropriately titled refutation of Marx for a Mercury-on-Mars year, and then *Which Way to Peace?* in which he maintains the pacifist position he had taken up during the First World War. Yet now, with Mars triggered in both his septenary and decan, his pacifist attitude is becoming unconsciously insincere. He "found the Nazis utterly revolting—cruel, bigoted, and stupid. Morally and intellectually they were alike odious to me. Although I clung to my pacifist convictions, I did so with increasing difficulty."

Sun directed to Venus in Taurus: In 1934 Bertrand Russell is 62 when his decan Sun comes to his Venus—because of Pluto's extreme latitude Venus is behind it in the rising sequence. Septenary Mercury is also conjunct Venus. The emphasis is on the dispositor of both the Sun and Mercury. It is the third year of his decan, often the first year that the potential of the decan ruler starts to become actualized. His book *Freedom and Organization 1814-1914* is published. In the same year he writes *The Amberley Papers*, a record of the brief life of his parents, which he describes as having "something of the ivory tower". He then starts work on *Power, a new social analysis*, a refutation of the fundamental assumptions shared by Marx and classical economists. In it he argues that power, rather than wealth, should be the basic concept in social theory.

Sun directed to Pluto in Taurus: Bertrand Russell has the Sun on Pluto by the decan in 1935 at age 63. Septenary Venus has come to the ascendant. It is a time of great happiness. He is in love with his research assistant, Pat.

Sun directed to Mercury in Taurus: In 1936 at age 64 Bertrand Russell marries for the third time, to his research assistant Pat Spense. The Sun is at Mercury in his decan, and Venus is on Mercury in his septenary. The emphasis on Mercury stimulates him to try to get an academic job at Cambridge. He wants to return to purely philosophic work, but is unable to do so.

Sun directed to Neptune in Aries: Bertrand Russell is 65 in 1937 when his decan Sun comes to his oriental Neptune in Aries, the sign of the Sun's exaltation. As the sixth of the decan's ten years it should be a time when conflicts are reconciled. However, septenary Venus is on his Saturn in Capricorn. Short of money, he is forced to sell the house where his school had been located, a sale he deeply regrets. "It represented continuity, of which,

apart from my work, my life has had far less than I could have wished. When I sold it, I could say, like the apothecary, 'my poverty but not my will consents'." His son Conrad is born.

Sun directed to Saturn in Capricorn: In 1938 Bertrand Russell at age 66 experiences Sun on Saturn in Capricorn in his decan and Venus on his Libran Moon in the septenary. He sells his house and lives with his wife and two children in a caravan in Wales; it rains practically the whole time and is "about as uncomfortable a time as I can remember." This year his former lover Ottoline dies. He goes to America, where he lectures in Chicago, and describes the weather as vile, the city as beastly. Then, he goes to Los Angeles where he becomes a professor at UCLA.

Sun directed to the Moon in Libra: In 1939 at age 67 he is a professor at UCLA, living in Santa Barbara. His son and daughter are with him and Pat. In the decan the Sun is on the Moon in Libra, the sign where the Sun experiences a fall. Septenary Venus is on his exalted Jupiter in Cancer. The onset of war stops them from returning to England. Russell injures his back and is tortured by sciatica, which forces him to lie flat on his back for a month. By now he is no longer a pacifist.

Sun directed to Uranus in Cancer: Bertrand Russell is invited to become a professor at the College of the City of New York in 1940. He is 68. He accepts and moves the family from Los Angeles to New York. Venus is on the Sun in his septenary, but in the decan the Sun is on his Uranus—the expect-the-unexpected direction. It is the ninth year of the decan, the year known as the Finishing Post—either the opportunities provided by the decan ruler have been accepted or they were ignored. The Sun is being emphasized—it rules the decan and is being triggered in the septenary—and this can indicate happenings this year that may force Russell to depend on his own resources. The mother of a student, who (as a female) is ineligible at that time to attend his graduate-level course in mathematical logic, protests that Russell's opinions, especially those relating to sexual morality, make him 'morally unfit' to teach at the college. A witch-hunt is instituted against him by Catholics, so that he is unable to lecture anywhere in the city. Many intellectuals protest this treatment but his appointment is annulled by a court judgment. He has no money and no opportunity for employment in NYC. Fortunately the Barnes Foundation of Philadelphia, who ask him to lecture on the history of philosophy, eventually save him and the family moves into a farmhouse near that city, where he writes *Inquiry into Meaning & Truth*. Later in the year he lectures at Harvard.

Sun directed to Jupiter in Cancer: In 1941 Bertrand Russell is aged 69 and the Sun is on his Jupiter in Cancer by decan. At the same time his septenary Venus is on Mars in Taurus. Unable to return to England because of the war, Russell and his family are living in a farmhouse near Philadelphia. There he writes his *History of Western Philosophy* and becomes a proponent of an international government (Sun to Jupiter).

After this year Jupiter rules Russell's decan and Mars rules his septenary.

...But I have no philosophy. I believe in universal turbulent acceptance.
which is no more than to say I live.
And I believe in the Aztec Emperors who held council, yearly,
to deliberate upon the movements of the sun,
and to question its power;
and to search into its meaning.
And, yearly, they allowed the sun to continue on its wonted course.

Dylan Thomas, 1914-53
"The Poet and his Critic"
Talk on BBC, 8th March 1947

Chapter 7

The Moon as the Time Ruler

One Nature. perfect and pervading. circulates in all natures.
One Reality, all comprehensive. contains within itself all realities.
The one Moon reflects itself wherever there is a sheet of water.
And all the moons in the waters are embraced within the one Moon.

Yung-chia Ta-shih, *665-713*

Although we call the Moon one of the two lights, it is of course simply a satellite of the Earth and the light it provides is just a reflection of the light it receives from the Sun. Even so, the Moon's effect on our lives is very great and should not be minimized.

While the Sun as Time Ruler wants the individual to understand who he really is and to become creative and self sufficient, the Moon when it assumes the rulership is concerned with society, with cooperation between people and with the family as a unit that is responsible for the continuing presence of people on the planet. The fertility of women, the making of a home, and the birth and rearing of children are prime concerns of the Moon. She is the archetypal Mother.

The shape-changing Moon also represents the ever-changing environment in which we live, our fluctuating moods, mannerisms and behavior. It shows our form and appearance; how we react to the outside world, the recognition we receive, our likes and dislikes, our emotions, sensitivities and appetites.

Old texts associate the Moon with a person's mind and status.

During the years the Moon has the role of the Time Lord, whether in the septenary or in the decan, the individual will experience situations aimed to increase his sensitivity, to make him become more caring, nurturing, responsive and sympathetic to the needs of others, and the Moon often does this by bringing him into new places or situations where he has to learn how to cope with people who have different customs and manners from those with which he was previously accustomed. The planets and signs the Moon comes to each year, and their relationship to the Moon in the natal horoscope, signify these varying challenges, all of which aim to enhance the individual's sense that despite the many apparent differences between people and places he is part of a world-wide community.

By tradition the Moon rules the night, is strongest when waxing, and most efficacious when placed in Taurus, Cancer or the third house. It is weakest at those times and places that are opposite of these, namely during the day, when waning, in Scorpio or in Capricorn. The

Moon coming to a planet in either of these signs can cause the native to be unsettled and act foolishly.

Table ☽-1 lists the different years in which people in the sample experienced the Moon as the time ruler. These years are split between day and night births, which in turn are divided by whether the natal Moon was waxing or waning. The waxing Moon is clearly associated with more positive years than is the waning Moon, especially at night.

Table ☽-1: **☽ as Time Ruler: % Positive Years**

Phase of the ☽	Day birth		Night birth		*All*	
	N	% Positive	N	% Positive	N	% Positive
Waxing ☽	284	50.6	306	53.8	590	52.3
Waning ☽	245	50.5	189	**37.8*****	434	**45.0****
All	529	50.6	495	47.6	1024	49.2

Table ☽-2 tells us how the Moon, in the years that it was time ruler, fared when directed to the different places in the horoscope. The Moon's directions to the ascendant, Sun and Saturn were associated with years that people in my sample usually found to be difficult.

Table ☽-2: **% Positive Years when the ☽ is the Time Lord**

☽ directed to	N	% Positive
☽ rises	121	44.1
☉	135	44.2
☿	128	54.4
♀	130	53.5
♂	135	48.9
♃	117	51.8
♄	132	44.5
♅	39	60.3
♆	45	50.3
♇	42	47.4
All	*1024*	*49.2*

In Table ☽-3 we see the sign that the Moon came from (its natal position) and the one to which it is directed in the years that it is the time ruler. Note how, like the Sun natally when located in its own sign of Leo, the Moon natally positioned in its own sign of Cancer is associated in the sample with a distinct below-average value for % Positive. Again, as we have seen for the Sun and as we now see in Table ☽-3, it is the nature of the sign to which the Moon is directed that my analysis of these directions in the sample finds most important. The Moon directed to a planet in Cancer is associated with an above-average likelihood that the year will be a positive one. By contrast, when the Moon is directed to a planet in Capricorn, the sign of its traditional detriment, it is unlikely that the year will be pleasant or successful. The direction of the Moon to a planet in Aquarius is also associated with an above-average % positive.

It is the welcome the ruler receives when it is directed to a planet, meaning whether or not the ruler is comfortable in the sign that planet occupies, that goes a long way to determining whether the year will be a positive one or not. Of course other factors, such as the nature of the planet to which the ruler is directed and the natal aspect between that planet and the ruler, need also to be taken into account, but in general the year in which a ruler is directed to a planet that it disposes either by rulership or exaltation has an above-average probability of being a pleasant, successful year. By contrast, the year in which the ruler is directed to a planet occupying a sign in which the ruler is in its detriment or fall can be a difficult year.

Table ☽-3: **% Positive Years when the ☽ is the Time Lord, by Sign**

☽'s natal sign	N	% Positive	Sign where Moon is directed	N	% Positive
♈	60	55.8	♈	59	52.1
♉	96	48.0	♉	107	51.5
♊	98	53.5	♊	66	52.1
♋	41	37.5	♋	72	**61.5***
♌	150	46.4	♌	65	52.9
♍	101	52.8	♍	72	47.7
♎	113	50.5	♎	93	48.6
♏	61	42.9	♏	73	42.1
♐	57	**36.5***	♐	79	43.5
♑	133	50.3	♑	95	**40.9***
♒	51	53.2	♒	75	59.1
♓	63	57.8	♓	58	42.1
All	*1024*	*49.2*	*All*	*903*	*49.9*

The years when the Moon comes to a planet in Taurus or Cancer, signs in which the Moon is most welcome, should be good times for working in the public eye and enhancing one's reputation. Finances should improve; there will be travel and success in legal matters, and he may marry.

The direction of the Moon to a planet in Scorpio or Capricorn, especially a Moon that is afflicted in the natal horoscope, indicates difficult years with much mental unease. The individual will be disappointed in every way, susceptible to accusations and slander, humiliations, being victimized by others and he can experience a personal downfall. In these years he may lose his perspective, have difficulty reasoning in a sensible manner, and be overwhelmed by unconscious forces, by his moods and feelings.

As most astrologers will attest, the Moon in the 1st house of a birth chart often indicates a lack of stability; something one initially learns in Electional and Horary astrology. This is confirmed in the sample where we see that the Moon in the 1st and in the 11th is associated with significantly few positive years. The Moon was associated with significant above-average positive years when located at birth in the 6th or 7th house.

Table ☽-4:

% **Positive Years when the ☽ is the Time Lord, by House**

Moon's natal house	N	% Positive	House to which Moon is directed	N	% Positive
I	92	**31.5*****	I	94	43.3
II	65	41.8	II	93	46.1
III	157	53.5	III	80	41.8
IV	98	54.4	IV	70	51.6
V	118	54.4	V	67	47.2
VI	50	**65.1****	VI	52	48.6
VII	43	**71.5*****	VII	79	53.8
VIII	116	48.9	VIII	70	46.5
IX	37	48.9	IX	59	53.6
X	86	45.2	X	62	40.9
XI	81	**36.8****	XI	94	53.9
XII	81	48.0	XII	83	**62.1****
All	*1024*	*49.2*	*All*	*903[1]*	*49.8*

The only other significant above-average result observed in Table ☽-4 occurs when the Moon, as the Time Ruler, is directed to a body located in the 12th natal house.

The Moon as either the first or second of the seven classical bodies to rise can be associated with a high likelihood of difficult years, see Table ☽-5. The absence of any of the night births in the sample in the second position is simply a chance happening, I have checked this against each of the nocturnal charts included in the sample and can confirm that, for some unknown reason, I appear to have an unconscious bias against selecting people born with this feature.

---

[1] The reduced N results from omitting the years when the Moon is directed to the ascendant.

Table ☾-5: **% Positive when Moon is the Ruler
by its place in the septenary sequence**

Place of Moon in septenary	Day		Night	
	N	% Positive	N	% Positive
1	61	40.3	45	**26.2*****
2	48	39.9	0	-
3	45	54.6	53	45.4
4	36	53.1	53	**68.9*****
5	45	62.8	26	55.8
6	18	45.6	83	48.6
7	32	34.2	50	49.0
Sum	285	47.4	310	49.0

Individuals in my sample who were born during the day with the Moon rising as the third, fourth or fifth of the classical seven planets experienced slightly above-average positive years when the Moon ruled their septenary. These were the years when the individuals were aged from fourteen to thirty-four. Those born during the night did best when the Moon was the fourth body to rise, her rulership occurring from the ages of twenty-one to twenty-seven. The observed % Positive in this period differs from the expected 50% by a highly significant amount. The following seven-year period, from twenty-eight to thirty-four, was also above 50% but not significantly so.

Table ☾-6: **% Positive when Moon is the Ruler
by its place in the decan sequence**

Place of Moon in decan	Day		Night	
	N	% Positive	N	% Positive
1	13	28.0	7	12.9
2	33	55.2	17	42.7
3	72	**62.4****	40	63.6
4	19	67.1	22	57.7
5	38	48.0	23	55.2
6	34	50.9	32	51.1
7	15	48.6	11	49.5
8	12	53.1	21	**12.9*****
9	1	0.0	11	0.0
10	7	52.1	1	0.0
Sum	244	54.3	185	45.2

Those individuals with the Moon as the first of the ten to rise experienced a high proportion of difficult years when the Moon was their decan ruler. So too did those people who were born at night with the Moon at the rear of the rising planets. Those born with the Moon occupying the third or fourth place among the ten had the least problematic years. These positive years were experienced when the individuals were in their twenties and thirties.

The Moon Rises

(44% positive years)

This year, more than usual, the individual will want to belong and to relate to others, to be a member of the family or group, to be supported in whatever he is doing. Most of the time therefore, in order to retain his place within the group, he will go along with whatever its direction may be. However, because he is particularly sensitive now to the moods and feelings of others, he will react quickly, often without forethought, if he suspects that his place within the group is being threatened in any way. Should he allow this emotional reaction to go unchecked it will only be later, after he has calmed down and is objectively able to see the damage he has done, that he will realize that perhaps he did overreact. Such moments of spontaneous insanity invariably come to those who were born with a Moon afflicted by Mars.

There can be emotional tension now and the individual is likely to be in constant need of stimulants; he may be restless and want a change of scenery, to move about, to travel and see more of the world, perhaps to change his residence. This is a time of transition, a year of change, of readjustments that can become permanent. Females in the family, his mother, sister or daughter will be a concern, although events involving a weakness of his father can also occur now. The person experiencing the Moon on his ascendant is also likely to become more aware of injustice, to be more sympathetic to those who are less fortunate than he is, those of a lower status in life, the weak, the poor, and the ethically shunned. However, he will probably lack the initiative to do much about the problems he observes. Instead he is likely to be over dependent on the constantly changing world of phenomena—a sympathetic observer but not someone likely to rectify the problems he sees. At the same time he will encounter emotional tensions and may come before the public in some way.

This year the individual needs to be objective, to cease being a blindly involved participant and to become a calm, still center amid the changing, unstable and volatile world in which he lives. He needs to become aware how transient needs and desires so often distract those about him—having the Moon come to his ascendant will bring him many opportunities to observe this state of flux in which most people live—and how, like those with whom he lives, he too is often a victim of ever-changing moods. Once he becomes aware of and is able to restrain his own immediate reactions, the only problem then is to avoid being sucked back into that ditzy, superficial world.

This Moon-rising year need not be unpleasant. The native will enjoy listening to music and improve his dress and appearance; he may study, perhaps marry, possibly have a child, move into more salubrious surroundings, and can expect to enjoy a fortunate time. Any mediumistic talent will be increased this year.

Table ☽-7:   ☽ **Rises: % Positive Years**

Phase of the ☽	Day birth		Night		All	
	N	% Positive	N	% Positive	N	% Positive
Waxing ☽	33	43.8	37	48.9	70	46.5
Waning ☽	29	49.9	22	**28.8***	51	40.8
All	62	46.7	59	41.4	121	44.1

However, those persons in my sample with this direction generally experienced a difficult year; only 44.1% of them had positive times. Those born with a waxing Moon in the daytime were associated with a below-average number of positive years, while a waning Moon at night was not seem much good for anything.

Whether the year will be positive or negative depends very much on the state of the person's natal Moon, its sign, house and aspects, and also to some extent on how the two rulers, those of the septenary and the decan, relate one to the other.

The natal Moon's placement in Leo had two contrasting results in the sample, both statistically significant: in a diurnal chart the waning Moon was associated with a high likelihood that the upcoming year would be positive, and in a nocturnal chart the waxing Moon must be considered a strong harbinger of difficulties.

Examples of happenings in the sample when the Moon is the time ruler in the decan:
Waxing diurnal Moon rises in decan: *election success; depressed; daughter publishes her first book; father/mother dies; leaves his wife; affair; lonely; many honors; writes on inhibitions and anxiety.*
Waning diurnal Moon rises in decan: *falls in love; meets his future wife; drives alone across USA; father/brother dies; fascinated by psychic phenomena; criticized as heartless; business success; defeated & forced to flee.*
Waxing nocturnal Moon rises in decan: *robbed by highwaymen; meets his future wife; divorces in the family; mother/son dies; in a sordid and impermanent environment; wounded & believed dead; resigns; very unpopular; promised a future promotion; feels she is being tortured by public opinion; death.*
Waning nocturnal Moon rises in decan: *mugged; his home is burglarized; vertigo; father dies; his father loses his shop; daughter born; sadly resigns her position; death.*

Examples of happenings in the sample when the Moon is the time ruler in the septenary:

Waxing diurnal Moon rises in septenary: *multiple injuries from a motorcycle accident; divorce; writing love letters daily; several love affairs; her engagement is called off; taking cocaine as a stimulant; his books are publicly burned; abstains from alcohol; working for the release of political prisoners; daughter born; mother dies; his mother expels him from the house.*

Waning diurnal Moon rises in septenary: *loses election; husband dies; marries; son is born; creates a commune; concerned with handling of contradictions or dichotomies in society; experiments confirm his atomic theory; choking fits; cerebral hemorrhage.*

Waxing nocturnal Moon rises in septenary: *unpopular; utterly alienated; bullied; daughter has appendicitis; son dies; emotional crisis; knighted; pleurisy; organizes mutual aid society; marries; his wife is jealous; sex makes itself apparent; he explains the tides; he halts the export of silver.*

Waning nocturnal Moon rises in septenary: *demands equal train seats for blacks; her book is the bible of the Women's Movement; assaulted by suffragettes; his wife leaves him; marries; abortion; flees the country; says that dividing consciousness into different layers causes friction & conflict; isolated; grain crisis; election success; resigns from the priesthood.*

The Moon comes to the Sun
(44% positive)

This year may not be the easiest of times. The Moon has come to a place that is strange to her. It may seem to be completely alien if the Sun is in Scorpio or Capricorn. Fundamental changes can occur, both in the home and even in the individual's physical appearance. A person experiencing the Moon coming to his Sun is likely to become more self-conscious, especially in his relationship with the opposite sex, and this can make him uncomfortable, especially if he is afraid of showing his feelings. A series of events may occur that will have lasting psychological overtones. Relationships should however be good. Often a person will meet his future spouse or someone who will be his partner in an important activity. Sexual unions are likely, affairs being more common than marriage. There can be health problems: pains in the eyes, stomach and feverish complaints. The emphasis this year is on the domestic and emotional life. Depending on the Sun's sign and its natal aspect from the Moon, there can be success or failure, a happy and prosperous time or one in which there are financial problems. Danger to the individual's parents and the loss of children and friends was observed with this direction.

In the sample people born with either the Sun or Moon in Sagittarius had difficult years under this direction. The Moon is often uncomfortable in fire signs.

The waxing Moon provides an easier time than does the waning Moon, and this was especially so in my sample for those individuals with their Sun at birth in the 1st or 12th houses.

Table ☽-8:   ☽ **to the** ☉**: % Positive Years**

Phase of the ☽	Day birth		Night birth		All	
	N	% Positive	N	% Positive	N	% Positive
Waxing ☽	38	50.0	35	49.1	73	49.5
Waning ☽	33	41.1	29	34.3	62	**37.9***
All	71	45.8	64	42.4	135	44.2

As we saw for the Moon's direction to the ascendant, the waning Moon in a nocturnal chart is associated with relatively few positive years. This result is repeated for the Moon's direction to the Sun.

Some observed happenings in the sample when the Moon comes to the Sun in the decan:
Waxing Moon to the diurnal Sun in the decan: *an empty, horrid time; hostile criticism; uneasiness & malaise; in very poor health; recurring headaches; marries; siblings born; gives up smoking; writes about discontent, defeated; arrested; lively social life; awarded a medal.*
Waning Moon comes to the diurnal Sun in the decan: *father/son dies; dislikes being alone; marries; in love; divorce; becoming increasingly unpopular; closes magazine; successfully defends himself in court; robbed & beaten up; unemployed; cataracts are removed; has lung cancer.*
Waxing Moon comes to the nocturnal Sun in the decan: *divorce; marries; meets future spouse; first sex; depressed; helping a friend; travels; accused of causing a fatal burning.*
Waning Moon to the nocturnal Sun in the decan: *daughter's letter upsets him; daughter is born; he is caught reading banned books; improved finances; arrested; in prison the whole year.*

Some observed happenings in the sample when the Moon comes to the Sun in the septenary:
Waxing Moon to the diurnal Sun in the septenary: *children born; marries; affair; meets future wife; mother/daughter dies; moves; persecuted & convicted for pacifism; financial worries; insomnia; honors; buys a farm; increasingly indolent; becomes paralyzed; fails all exams; much criticized.*
Waning Moon comes to the diurnal Sun in the septenary: *engaged; siblings born; mourning the death of her husband; wife/son dies; meets future wife; divorce; writes on the position of women; attains enormous power; paranoid; circumstances improve; death.*
Waxing Moon comes to the nocturnal Sun in the septenary: *improved self-confidence; a series of catastrophes; considers immigrating; publicly admits he has committed adultery; divorce; his marriage proposal is rejected; resigns; his house is destroyed by fire; hemorrhage; paranoia; prostatectomy.*
Waning Moon to the nocturnal Sun in the septenary: *loss of work; shot in the chest; resigns; his parents separate; mother/sister/spouse die; poor health (bronchitis, pneumonia, thrombosis, jaundice, smallpox, diphtheria); learns calligraphy.*

The Moon comes to Mercury
(54% positive)

By coming to Mercury the Moon has entered a noisy area in which information is being continually bandied about. The individual may learn new information about his family, which could prompt him to react emotionally. The new information will stimulate and excite him if Mercury is in Taurus or Cancer, but it is likely to cause depression should Mercury be in Scorpio or Capricorn. The individual will want to learn more and will be in a searching, inquiring and studious mood. He will want to share his news with others. However, as his thinking is strongly influenced by his moods now, he may not be as objective as he should be; he can become indecisive, and then have difficulty expressing all he wants to say. As he becomes increasingly aware of how rapidly having extra information causes his moods to change, he may concentrate more than usual on his feelings, especially as they relate to himself, and to his family and home.

Table ☽-9:

☽ to ☿: % Positive Years

Phase of the ☽	Day birth		Night birth		All	
	N	% Positive	N	% Positive	N	% Positive
Waxing ☽	33	57.5	39	58.0	72	57.8
Waning ☽	28	54.9	28	45.2	56	50.1
Total	*61*	*56.3*	*67*	*52.6*	*128*	*54.4*
Oriental ☿	31	49.5	34	42.6	65	45.9
Occidental ☿	30	63.3	33	63.0	63	**63.1****

Pre-existing disputes are likely to be settled this year. Children or love affairs should provide pleasure. Finances should improve, and the individual will accom-plish much of what he sets out to do, perhaps be honored, and have general happiness this year. Travel is likely, and he will have the opportunity to present his ideas to others. Gambling and the excessive use of alcohol or drugs can be potential problems.

The best results observed in the sample occurred when Mercury was occidental, while the waxing Moon provided more positive results than did the waning Moon. However, the waxing Moon *and* occidental Mercury do not combine together well. Instead, as Table ☽-10 shows, it is the waning Moon that combines best with occidental Mercury. The waning Moon *and* oriental Mercury were associated with a difficult year.

Table ☽-10:   ☽ - ☿ interaction

☽☿ interaction	Oriental ☿		Occidental ☿		All	
	N	*% Positive*	*N*	*% Positive*	*N*	*% Positive*
Waxing ☽	35	56.9	37	58.7	72	57.8
Waning ☽	30	**33.2***	26	**69.5***	56	50.1
All	65	45.9	63	**63.1****	128	54.4

In the sample the Moon coming to Mercury in Taurus, where the Moon is exalted, was a statistically significant indicator of a positive year. Significantly positive results were also observed when the Moon came from a Mars term to Mercury located in a Venus term.

Some observed happenings in the sample when the Moon comes to Mercury in the decan:
Waxing Moon to Mercury by day in decan: *conscripted into army; makes propaganda films; promoted; graduates; mother dies; becomes a hero overnight; criticized; accidents; studying; demolishes religion with psychoanalytic weapons; war correspondent; his marriage is over; marries; death.*
Waning Moon to Mercury by day in decan: *carpentry; mother dies; son born; interest in architecture; rejected; unable to succeed in anything; honors; book published; thrilled by statue of Athena; psychological crisis; breakdown; intensive data analysis; starts a youth group; in mental & physical agony; grief; appendectomy; death in air crash.*
Waxing Moon to Mercury by night in decan: *promoted; election success; shell-shocked; goes to college; writing poetry; loses touch with public opinion; marries; divorce; wife/son/mother/father die; travels; new job; increasingly bored; obtains funding for public transportation system.*
Waning Moon to Mercury by night in decan: *election defeats; speech writing; new job; much reading; openly disliked by his superior; less alert; marries; daughter born; fails correspondence course; her poems are published; studying; tries to obtain a full scholarship; death.*

Some observed happenings in the sample when the Moon comes to Mercury in the septenary:
Waxing Moon to Mercury by night in septenary: *publishes a magazine; starts a newspaper; creates propaganda; boxing; on trial; problems with authorities; legal success; violent struggle of wills; father dies; children born; paternity suit; gets lead billing; campaigning; coronation; explains calculus; flash of intuition; finds he is naturally a gifted mathematician; mental breakdown; attempts suicide.*
Waning Moon to Mercury by day in septenary: *information overload; dysentery; concerned with the psychological nature of evil; first book published; marries; proposes marriage by letter; son born; lecturing; international trips; espouses pacifism; studying; tonsillectomy; wins election; living in a commune; bitterly disappointed; death.*

Waxing Moon to Mercury by day in septenary: *quarrels; stage fright; much indecision; rejected; feelings of defeat; victory; excited intellectually; important discovery; graduates; divorce; remarries; writing love letters; honors; inheritance; cartooning; cybernetics; father dies; attempt on her life.*

Waning Moon to Mercury by night in septenary: *loses a finger; in prison; on trial; mother dies; his wife is sick; marries; election loss; travels; in a terrible emotional state; awarded a scholarship; moves; publishes journal; a difficult year; writing; buys a car; campaigning.*

The Moon comes to Venus
(54% positive)

This pairing is frequently associated with love, marriage and socializing, the birth of daughters and the desire to present one's best side to the world, which is shown in the sample by the Moon being most positive when in the third, fifth or seventh houses—the Moon joys in the third, Venus joys in the fifth, and the seventh is, of course, associated with one's spouse. Venus was most positive when located in the first house.

These should be pleasant years when a person is relieved of pressure, anxiety and drudgery. He will enjoy nature and good meals, become better dressed, and be at ease with himself and with the world, as one would expect for the time the Moon comes to the planet that rules the sign in which she is exalted. The spouse may receive unexpected gains this year. Several members of the sample had affairs. Daughters are often born now, but it can be harmful for other members of the individual's family, especially if Venus is afflicted by a malefic. These years are not always pleasant for male members of one's family. Indeed, should Venus be afflicted or in Scorpio or Capricorn, the native may suffer sickness or pains from a disease inherited from his mother, and lose property at the hands of enemies.

Table ☽-11:

☽ to ♀:
% Positive Years

Phase of the ☽	Day birth		Night birth		All	
	N	% Positive	N	% Positive	N	% Positive
Waxing ☽	39	46.4	38	66.6	77	56.3
Waning ☽	34	50.5	19	47.6	53	49.5
Total	*73*	*48.3*	*57*	*60.3*	*130*	*53.5*
Oriental ♀	43	48.4	22	49.3	65	48.6
Occidental ♀	30	48.2	35	67.2	65	58.4

We expect both the Moon and Venus to be strongest in nocturnal charts, and this was observed in the sample. Venus is more positive in her evening star role, in the west setting after the Sun, especially in a nighttime chart. The Moon is most positive when waxing at night.

Some observed happenings in the sample when the Moon comes to Venus in the decan:

Waxing Moon to Venus by day in decan: *ends an affair; wife has an affair; daughter born; writes on female sexuality; studying; bad cut on lip leaves a permanent scar; wife/father/editor dies; a happy, creative period; campaigning; overseas touring; successful applications of her theory.*

Waning Moon to Venus by day in decan: *daughter born; marries; affair; improved finances; first real professional opportunity; survives an air crash; difficulties with the authorities; resigns; cat/ex-wife dies; travels; confirmed; fails exams; honored.*

Waxing Moon to Venus by night in decan: *marries; sister dies; involved with an evangelist; reports on government toleration of drug smuggling; mother is diagnosed as a lunatic; touring; promoted; graduates; has a show dog.*

Waning Moon to Venus by night in decan: *father hospitalized; loss of consciousness; studying; electioneering; loses interest in poetry; uncle killed is by the police.*

Some observed happenings in the sample when the Moon comes to Venus in the septenary:

Waxing Moon to Venus by day in septenary: *very little money; his novel is a success; buys expensive clothes; receives a lifetime pension; father is sentenced to death; imprisoned; mother on trial as a witch is acquitted; wife/father/mother dies; daughter born; affair; marries; receives pilot's wings; moody; cancer.*

Waning Moon to Venus by day in septenary: *in love; unhappy marriage; engaged; first meets future husband; wife/father dies; son born; son has a mental breakdown; honorary degree; editing; discharged from army; captured but then rescued; holidays overseas; launches Playboy magazine; victories; agitating; in prison; accepts responsibility for failures; small pox; fainting fits;*

Waxing Moon to Venus by night in septenary: *son is in bad health; daughter born; in love; meets future spouse; marriage is cancelled; marries; family is reunited; divorce; suicidal; avoids death threat; first public speech; cross-USA drive; writing poetry; legal victory over IRS; awarded a medal; his portrait is painted; receives a bequest.*

Waning Moon to Venus by night in septenary: *an idyllic period; in love; marries; wife's suicide; dresses like a dandy; studies Hatha Yoga; first public speech; speaks against war; father is ill; missing his absent father; defends his mother against his father; very happy.*

The Moon comes to Mars

(49% positive)

Emotions may become heated this year, which can make a person feel intensely alive and active. He is likely to resent any interference in his personal affairs; anyone who tries to hold him back will find that he can stand up for himself and fight for his rights. This can result in useless disputes with his lovers, friends and relatives, and quarrels between husband and wife. If in direct contact with the public he should be diplomatic and keep his opinions to himself. This can be a time for changing where he lives, moving away from a place that has become too restrictive, too narrow to contain his energies. Accidents can occur, and the year may be dangerous for those with heart problems. Both accidents and

100

heart trouble are likely to result from impulsive actions, calmness being temporarily disturbed by anger or jealousy. In addition to emotional petulance, this direction can bring financial losses; danger from fever, fire and physical attack; pain and loss of blood; and car problems. It is not the best of times for the females of the family. Several members of my sample were in the military this year, some at war. As always, the natal state of either body, especially the sign occupied by Mars, influences the nature of the year.

In a diurnal nativity (both the Moon and Mars being nocturnal planets) the waxing Moon can be particularly difficult. The waning Moon in a nocturnal chart was associated with demanding years. Dangerous times, the individual being under threat and in potentially harmful situations, were often observed for this direction in the sample. Three results that had significant % Positive values that were below 50% were the Moon coming from the 1st or 9th houses, and the Moon coming to a Mars in Taurus—this last was unexpected.

Table ☽-12:   **☽ to ♂ : % Positive Years**

Phase of the ☽	Day birth		Night birth		All	
	N	*% Positive*	*N*	*% Positive*	*N*	*% Positive*
Waxing ☽	44	45.2	44	53.4	88	49.3
Waning ☽	26	52.2	21	43.0	47	48.1
All	*70*	*47.8*	*65*	*50.1*	*135*	*48.9*
Oriental ♂	35	49.1	28	42.0	63	45.9
Occidental ♂	35	46.5	37	56.2	72	51.4

Some observed happenings in the sample when the Moon comes to Mars in the decan:
Waxing Moon to Mars by day in decan: *exhausted; angry & jealous; depressed; dreads falling when on stage; head concussion; says US conduct in Vietnam is indefensible; war correspondent; entertaining the troops; fighting Indians; sees mob slaughter guards; failed invasion; marries; nephew is killed in war; daughter dies in childbirth; brother dies; writes on the nature of light; loses house & income; exiled; learns to pick pockets; graduates.*
Waning Moon to Mars by day in decan: *studying; seizes power; coronation; honored; recommends an absence of secrecy in nuclear discoveries; making his discoveries known; owes taxes; lung infection; unemployed; decides to specialize in surgery; music interests; cancerous tumor removed.*
Waxing Moon to Mars by night in decan: *promoted; criticized; undercuts a rival; out of work; his office is destroyed by fire; first car; graduates; travels; knee operations; bronchitis; reads his own obituary; death.*
Waning Moon to Mars by night in decan: *chronic fatigue; anger; dizzy spells; daughter commits suicide; makes a public confession; marries; escapes from prison.*

Some observed happenings in the sample when the Moon comes to Mars in the decan:

Waxing Moon to Mars by day in septenary: *attacked by a mob; angry & aggressive; resentful & jealous; wretched & restless; ostracized; affair; meets her future husband; son born; mother dies; his father is sentenced to death; caught up in the sexual imagery of bullfighting; promoted; moves; graduates; to military school; car accident; major operation.*

Waning Moon to Mars by day in septenary: *insomnia & headaches; a series of strokes; weary & overworked; in a rage; burns registration cards in protest; imprisoned; ends love affair; has twins; yachting; declares war; commands border patrol; father is promoted; works in a foundry; car dies; her writings are anti-Semitic; moves.*

Waxing Moon to Mars by night in septenary: *argues his first case in court; testifies before grand jury; son/father/uncle dies; son born; mother has no means of support; marries; joins the Freemasons; fire devours most of city; feels unwanted; argues; prostate surgery; bad fall from a horse; angry; jealousy; moves; survives ship sinking; buys computer; raises a private army; on active duty in navy.*

Waning Moon to Mars by night in septenary: *becomes a judge; forced to sell his house; lonely; in a battle; meets future wife; son/daughter/sister born; two sisters die by burning; she & her husband start a new business; war starts; damages his arm; asthma deprives him of sleep; long-lasting terror of the color purple; on safari; converts her religion.*

The Moon comes to Jupiter
(52% positive)

The Moon and Jupiter have a somewhat ambiguous relationship. Despite Jupiter being exalted in the Moon's sign of Cancer, these two bodies are not truly sympathetic at all times. The Moon being a nocturnal body while Jupiter is diurnal may perhaps explains this. In the sample oriental Jupiter positively embraces a waxing Moon, especially those people born during the night, but does not seem to care at all for the waning Moon, for then the times are unpleasant and rarely successful. Those born with other combinations—always of course depending on the natal state of both the Moon and Jupiter—can expect a general improvement in their financial condition and health this year.

In general Jupiter puts out a warm welcoming mat for the Moon: the individual has entered a period in which he will feel secure and protected and in which he has the opportunity to expand his world, be successful and improve his standard of living. This should be an enjoyable year. What may have been foreign and beyond his means before now can enter into his life—gaining weight is one possible result as plenty of food and comfort should be available. A person experiencing this direction can expect changes as he enters into a world of new experiences that could be the foundation for his long-term success or failure. Opportunities for promotion or the enhancement of his standing will occur. He will feel emotionally secure and in touch with his feelings. A child may be born. The native seems to be protected this year (females can be particularly helpful to him), able to avoid or escape unharmed from accidents, and kept out of harm's way, although others in his life may be less fortunate.

Table ☽-13:   ☽ - ♃ **Interaction**

☽♃ interaction	Oriental ♃		Occidental ♃		All	
	N	*% Positive*	*N*	*% Positive*	*N*	*% Positive*
Waxing ☽	31	**72.9****	21	48.9	52	59.9
Waning ☽	37	**25.9*****	28	51.7	65	40.6
All	68	*53.9*	49	*50.1*	*117*	*51.8*

People born with a waning Moon and an oriental Jupiter, or those with their natal Jupiter in Capricorn, the sign in which both the Moon and Jupiter are traditionally in detriment, may have problems with authorities and be forced to borrow money to pay for past extravagances. In the sample the Moon arriving at Jupiter in Capricorn had a % positive value significantly below 50%. In several cases the native became aware only several years later that others were plotting against him at this time.

Table ☽-14:   ☽ to ♃: **% Positive Years**

Phase of the ☽	Day birth		Night birth		All	
	N	*% Positive*	*N*	*% Positive*	*N*	*% Positive*
Waxing ☽	32	53.7	36	**65.3***	68	59.9
Waning ☽	26	52.2	23	**27.5***	49	40.6
All	58	*53.0*	59	*50.5*	*117*	*51.8*
Oriental ♃	22	49.3	30	57.2	52	59.6
Occidental ♃	36	55.2	29	43.7	65	55.4

The waxing Moon at night was helpful under this direction, but the waning Moon at night was decidedly less so. Those born with Jupiter in Cancer, especially when Jupiter is in the 11th house, were also associated with a statistically high % positive value.

Some observed happenings in the sample when the Moon comes to Jupiter in the decan:
Waxing Moon to Jupiter by day in decan: *theater; first meets future love; fails to be elected; husband is re-elected; power struggle; war begins/ends; chooses his future career; little money; great gambling losses; cuts himself off from his friends; tortured by noise & crowds; moves; bronchitis.*
Waning Moon to Jupiter by day in decan: *sons emigrate; writes on the nature of war & how to prevent it; overseas travel; becomes famous; fails exams; fails leading a rebellion; gets a dog; persuaded not to retire as he had planned; his wife is given a dreamed-of role.*
Waxing Moon to Jupiter by night in decan: *leaves airforce/army; marries; in love; children born; has a horror of drink; lives like a monk; dour & unsociable; autobiography is published; promoted; promised a promotion; shell shock; close to death; death.*

Waning Moon to Jupiter by night in decan: his mentor & protector dies; retires; defeated for re-election; having writing difficulties; in prison; depressed; noisy neighbors; loss of freedom; daughter/brother born; changes her therapist.

Some observed happenings in the sample when the Moon comes to Jupiter in the decan:

Waxing Moon to Jupiter by day in septenary: switches from being a potential bum to a success; fired from her job; re-elected; marries to help husband stay in USA; son & daughter are arrested; siblings die; his father's advice saves his life; affairs; learns the facts of life; bitterly cynical; publishes journal; his successful book lays the foundation for all future earnings; feels impotent; attacks the government's perfidy; to college; assassinated.

Waning Moon to Jupiter by day in septenary: nursing; vows permanent celibacy; passive resistance; father retires; daughter dies; starts school; borrows money; retires; moves; travels; deep depression; abdicates; engaged; working in a factory; organizing communes; book is published; has new writing space; fears for her life; avoids assassination; death.

Waxing Moon to Jupiter by night in septenary: frightened by girl who tries to seduce him; marries; children born; father/wife/daughter/friend dies; travels overseas; climbing; fame; rejects honors; publishes newspaper; negotiating peace; leaves navy; sells his estate; vivid dreams; starts magazine; studying; motorbike accident; defends herself against accusations.

Waning Moon to Jupiter by night in septenary: his reputation is irreparably damaged; happy in his job & in love; a dreary time; in prison; depressed; in a shattered emotional state; under much pressure; "the most difficult time of my life"; melancholia; unjustly vilified; failures; he resigns; circulatory problems; foot injury; mother arrested; wife leaves him; daughter's suicide; children born; abuses his son; on safari; wins scholarship;

The Moon comes to Saturn

(44% positive)

This can be a very unfortunate year with little peace of mind. The Moon has arrived at a sad, cold, unfeeling and harsh place. There will be failure and defeats. The individual experiencing this direction is likely to experience frustration, be depressed, despondent, gloomy, melancholy, anxious and unpopular. Others may harass him. He and his spouse or lover may become separated. He may live and travel alone, be isolated, separated from his family and friends, and away from society. He may lose his property, be forced to practice restraint, and his reputation could be harmed. Something from his past may come back to haunt him, and that past memory can cause him to have feelings of guilt and self-doubt. Much mental anguish can result. Self-analysis and introspection are often necessary this year. He is likely to reject honors or something will occur to cause him not to accept them. Besides problems with his own health, females in the native's family may experience ill health this year.

Table ☽-15:

☽ to ♄: % Positive Years

Phase of the ☽	Day birth		Night birth		All	
	N	% Positive	N	% Positive	N	% Positive
Waxing ☽	36	50.3	42	40.9	78	46.7
Waning ☽	26	41.8	28	46.7	54	43.5
All	*62*	*46.7*	*70*	*42.6*	*132*	*44.5*
Oriental ♄	28	45.2	36	46.7	64	46.7
Occidental ♄	34	47.8	34	39.9	68	43.9

The relatively low value observed in the sample for occidental Saturn in a night birth may be a back-handed confirmation of the tradition that says Saturn is strongest in the daytime and when oriental to the Sun.

Those sample members with their natal Moons in Leo found this a particularly difficult year, as did those with a 1st house Moon; both results are statistically significant. Individuals with Capricorn Moons usually had easier, less annoying times.

Some observed happenings in the sample when the Moon comes to Saturn in the decan:
Waxing Moon to Saturn by day in decan: *becomes aware that disease is discord & lack of harmony; war starts; marries; engaged; founds a newspaper; father's suicide; quits school; renounces his citizenship & religion; moves; election success; avoids attempted assassination; suicide.*
Waning Moon to Saturn by day in decan: *father dies; father is given death sentence; brother is executed; leaves husband; children born; his wife is sick; forced into an arranged marriage; affairs; jealous; sleepless; frenzy of excitement & activity; paranoid; war ends; at peak of fame but visibly miserable; honored; poor press notices; success; wins immense wealth; loses weight; alone; begins weekly spiritual gathering.*
Waxing Moon to Saturn by night in decan: *she changes from being a warm girl to one who rarely smiles; war of words; father dies; son born; son remarries; accused of fraud; edits magazine that fails; improved living conditions; diphtheria epidemic; in great pain; wound breaks open; hurts her knee; death.*
Waning Moon to Saturn by night in decan: *defends liberty of press; having problems with noise; moves; passes exams; taking a correspondence course; his wife has shingles; death in a duel; death.*

Some observed happenings in the sample when the Moon comes to Saturn in the septenary:
Waxing Moon to Saturn by day in septenary: *he feels cruelty, poverty, suspicion & persecution from the air he breathes; fails audition; honorary doctorate; his father's death sentence is commuted to 10 years; mother dies; father's suicide; son born; he fears for his sanity; not allowed to take communion; feels old & tired; in prison; not elected; very poor; moves; invasion fails; death.*

Vaning Moon to Saturn by day in septenary: *son born; mental & emotional conflict; his wife is very ill; leaves his pregnant wife; affair; loses election; starts a war; hospitalized in extreme pain; restricts his diet; has a growing sense of desolation; great creative period; studies; escapes plot against him.*

Vaxing Moon to Saturn by night in septenary: *divorce; husband/father ill; his son/daughter dies; son born; severe famine; working long hours; intense work; legal victory; rejects honors; loss on stock market; struck by lightning; in trenches & under fire; political/religious crisis; left a legacy; unhappy & lonely; melancholy; foils plan to be robbed & killed; near-fatal pneumonia; death.*

Vaning Moon to Saturn by night in septenary: *liver disease; tired; in low spirits; separated from her sick husband; remarries; son born; wife/friend dies; orders invasion; buys house/car; wins a prize; honored; narrowly avoids foreclosure of his ranch; he is now stone deaf; his health is permanently weakened; obsessed.*

The Moon comes to Uranus
(60% positive)

Thiſ year the inðiviðual will be tempteð to do things he has never done before. The Moon has come to an exciting place, where thrills, adventure, novelty, freshness and change will be experienced. Old habits will be left by the wayside. It is a year of great psychological change and some emotional confusion during which the native will need to retain a sense of balance. He may alter his daily routine; perhaps move into a new house. Sudden events involving females, his family and his home are likely to occur. If his natal Moon is not afflicted or weak, these changes in his life can be to his advantage. On the other hand, those born with an afflicted Moon should expect changes that end unhappily.

Table ☽-16:   ☽ to ♅: % **Positive Years**

Phase of the ☽	Day birth		Night birth		All	
	N	% Positive	N	% Positive	N	% Positive
Waxing ☽	8	56.5	11	**82.2***	19	71.3
Waning ☽	12	67.8	8	22.6	20	49.7
All	*20*	*63.3*	*19*	*57.1*	*39*	*60.3*
Oriental ♅	9	60.3	10	45.2	19	52.4
Occidental ♅	11	65.7	9	70.3	20	67.8

Despite the small number of observations involved, in the sample the Moon and Uranus appear to combine best when both are west of the Sun, especially at night.

Some observed happenings in the sample when the Moon comes to Uranus in the decan:

Waxing Moon to Uranus by day: *she is afraid of being ridiculed; loses weight; incapacitating headaches; death of her coach; has a sense of guilt; resigns; graduates; military training; moves; first job; rebels; his life is all intention, consciousness, duty & responsibility; advertising his work; in trouble with authorities; tries to run away from home.*

Waning Moon to Uranus by day: *graduates; promoted; in love; marries; honors; feels he has everything he has ever wanted; re-elected; marooned; total failure; greatly disillusioned; indifferent to religion; sends in false reports; organizes a fight against the arms race, war & injustice against individuals; conceives of the idea of a helicopter.*

Waxing Moon to Uranus by night: *attempt on his life; poor health; sponsors others; elected; promoted; children born; publishes books; depression; investigates gun running & drug trafficking; father retires.*

Waning Moon to Uranus by night: *moves; war starts; he is run over; kidnapped by his father; pneumonia; asthma deprives him of sleep; daughter born; his son rejects him; his son is killed in a duel; his daughter goes mad.*

The Moon comes to Neptune
(50% positive)

A person experiencing this direction is likely to be haunted by strange fears, and he may suspect that others are deceiving him. Although he will not want to be alone, he is likely to take steps to avoid others. He is likely to have difficulty dealing with the everyday world, going to and from his place of work, paying bills, and being a responsible member of a family. Instead he will want to escape to a place where he can feel secure, where he can avoid coming into contact with the mundane world. He is more sensitive than usual and may find his emotions confusing. He may become involved in a relationship with someone who is completely wrong for him. The arts, especially music, may attract him now, and this is a period when he can benefit from quiet meditation, self-reflection, study and research, activities in which he can be secluded and alone.

Table ☾-17: ☾ to ♆: **% Positive Years**

Phase of the ☾	Day birth		Night birth		All	
	N	% Positive	N	% Positive	N	% Positive
Waxing ☾	10	72.3	14	38.8	24	52.7
Waning ☾	14	51.6	7	38.8	21	47.4
All	24	60.3	21	38.8	45	50.3
Oriental ♆	11	49.3	13	48.6	24	49.0
Occidental ♆	13	69.5	8	22.6	21	51.6

In the sample those born in the daytime experienced a much better time this year than did those born at night.

Some observed happenings in the sample when the Moon comes to Neptune in the decan:

Waxing Moon to Neptune by day: *first sees his future wife; first sex; marries; election success; education reforms; makes a suicide pact; the beauty of music is awoken in him; alone; reinstated; buys antique car; starts school; fails exams.*

Waning Moon to Neptune by day: *graduates; his books are publicly burned; marriage ends; his son is killed in the war; high blood pressure; loses weight; distressed; stops paying alimony; defeated for nomination; decides that God does not exist; attends a hanging; loses his job; sells company at a profit; promoted; success; retires from all professional work.*

Waxing Moon to Neptune by night: *election success; poor, in debt; shop fails; taking part-time jobs; works as part-time photographer; sleeplessness; bronchitis; can't go out of doors; first house; leaves air force; loses sea battle; humiliating defeat; to college; books published; mother goes insane; father dies; describes his system of philosophy; death.*

Waning Moon to Neptune by night: *unemployed; refuses money offer; very lonely; his wife has shingles; rejected; resigns; promoted.*

The Moon comes to Pluto
(47% positive)

For most people this will be a very difficult year in which powerful emotional changes occur. Sudden separations are likely, which will be welcomed if the Moon is directed to a place where she is strong, but they can be sorrowful and tear-laden otherwise. Shocks and crises can happen throughout the year, as the native, an apparent victim of urgent feelings, is likely to feel antisocial and rebellious, determined to have his own way in a world that is unlikely to want to indulge him. Power struggles with females can occur. He may feel the need to distance himself from others, especially from those ties that seem to bind; those that he believes hold him prisoner and keep him from acting as he wishes. Disruption of the family and relationships is the obvious result. Should this happen, he will feel isolated, abandoned and very much alone.

Table ☽-18:   ☽ **to the ♇: % Positive Years**

Phase of the ☽	Day birth		Night birth		All	
	N	% Positive	N	% Positive	N	% Positive
Waxing ☽	11	57.5	10	27.1	21	43.0
Waning ☽	17	58.5	4	22.6	21	51.6
All	*28*	*58.1*	*14*	*25.8*	*42*	*47.4*
Oriental ♀	15	60.3	6	30.1	21	51.6
Occidental ♀	13	55.6	8	22.6	21	43.0

In the sample this clearly was a more comfortable direction for diurnal births than for those born at night.

Some observed happenings in the sample when the Moon comes to Pluto in the decan:

Waxing Moon to Pluto by day: *daughter born; marries; son marries; father/friend die; loses his job; elected; concerned about the growing menace of war.*

Waning Moon to Pluto by day: *mother dies; children born; marries; his son is a POW; brother dies; graduates; starts his first job; painful operation; pneumonia; anxious; honored; son earns PhD; expelled from France; becoming increasingly rebellious; cataracts; accused of child sexual abuse.*

Waxing Moon to Pluto by night: *daughter born; honors; both of his arms are badly crushed; change of sleeping habits damages his health; moves; confused; changes his college major; graduates; writing; promoted; imprisoned; criticized for appearing cold and unfeeling, prostatectomy.*

Waning Moon to Pluto by night: *sells house at a loss; swelling in the leg; he has two strokes; he gives away most of his belongings; living alone; he is having difficulty coping.*

Oscar Wilde's Moon-ruled Septenary

> *There is no man who is not, at each moment,*
> *all that he has been and will be.*
> Oscar Wilde. *De Profundis.*

The Moon in Leo rises: The brilliant Irish dramatist Oscar Wilde was a nocturnal birth with a waning 12th house Moon in Leo that is part of a tight T-cross with a Mercury-Uranus opposition, the Moon's antiscion being conjunct Uranus. The Moon is also applying to sextile the 10th house oriental Saturn retrograde in Gemini. His Moon-ruled septenary begins in October 1896 when he is forty-two years old. He is a prisoner in Reading jail, having been sentenced the previous year (the final year of his Saturn-ruled septenary) to two years' hard labor. His imprisonment is the result of a conviction for gross indecency—in British law of the time this term implies "homosexual acts not amounting to buggery". During the year he is released from prison and goes immediately to Dieppe in France. He had asked the Jesuits for a six-month retreat but this was refused. He experiences nature and life as if for the first time, rejoicing in all he can see, smell, hear, taste and touch. His decan ruler Jupiter has arrived at Mercury in Scorpio. He writes the poem *The Ballad of Reading Gaol,* and sends pleading letters to his wife, asking to see her and the children. His wife, who is in poor health with spinal paralysis, puts him off. In Dieppe he is snubbed by the many English she meets. He has sexual relations with a woman, a Dieppe prostitute; it is the first such experience in ten years and he describes it as "Like chewing cold mutton." He meets his old lover Lord Alfred Douglas, a psychologically inevitable meeting, and the pair go to Naples together.

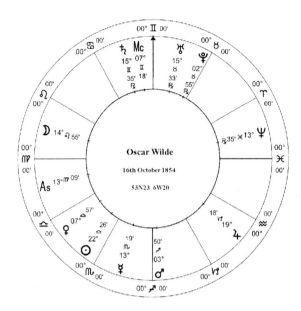

Moon directed to Saturn in Gemini: Wilde's septenary Moon comes to his retrograde Saturn in Gemini the following year, in October 1897 when he is forty-three years old. Decan ruler Jupiter has come to his Sun in Libra. He lives with Douglas in Naples for three months. His wife stops his weekly allowance because "he is living with a disreputable person." He has no money, is unable to concentrate, and senses that his literary life is over. He and Douglas separate. Wilde is slighted daily, wherever he goes, which never ceases to hurt. He has a constant uncertainty over whether people will acknowledge his existence or not. He is beginning to believe his life has been a failure rather than the creative success it truly was. A servant steals his clothing. *The Ballad of Reading Gaol* is published and enjoys phenomenal sales, selling as no poem has sold for years. He moves to Paris where he proofs his plays *The Importance of Being Earnest* and *An Ideal Husband* for their book publication. He is very lonely. His wife dies, the result of a botched operation on her spine. He is still not allowed to see his sons. He has an operation on his throat. It is an extremely difficult year as one would expect with the Moon coming to Saturn, a year of humiliations and of being ostracized.

Moon directed to Jupiter in Capricorn: In October 1898 Wilde's septenary ruler the Moon has arrived at his Jupiter in Capricorn. Both the Moon and Jupiter are unwelcome in Capricorn. Decan Jupiter is on Venus in Libra. He is forty-four years old. He is in Paris, living in "squalid lodgings", very lonely and he has no money. He begs from old acquaintances he meets on the street, and writes to others for money. His brother dies. He visits his wife's grave and finds that he isn't mentioned on her tombstone—it is as if he never existed. He is seen in a restaurant with his front teeth gone, and no denture plate. It is a gloomy time; many old friends on the street or in restaurants reject him. He gets a skin rash, which he calls "mussel poisoning," that brings great red splotches onto his arms, chest and back. Again it is a year of humiliations and being ostracized.

Moon directed to Mars in Sagittarius: He is forty-five years old in October 1899 when the septenary Moon arrives at Mars in Sagittarius. Jupiter, the decan ruler, is on his Leo Moon. The Moon is involved in both his septenary and decan. He is living in a Paris hotel, there by the owner's invitation and expense—a fortunate experience that can be associated with Jupiter coming to his Moon in the decan. He visits Palermo and Rome. His skin rash is persisting, and he finds it impossible not to scratch himself. He returns to Paris and the continued ostracism and humiliations. The death occurs of the Marquis of Queensbury, the man who brought him to his downfall, father of his homosexual lover Douglas. Douglas inherits a fortune. Oscar asks for an allowance, he had spent thousands on Douglas in earlier years, but he is rejected and accused of "wheedling like an old whore." He has a constant sense of ill being, which is checked but never eliminated by absinthe and brandy. He is staying in bed longer and longer until he eventually discovers that he is bedridden. He has an operation on his ear.

Moon directed to Mercury in Scorpio: Oscar Wilde's septenary Moon comes to his Mercury in Scorpio on his forty-sixth birthday in October 1900. Decan Jupiter has arrived on his Saturn in Gemini—the pair are widely opposite by antiscion. Both time rulers have been directed to planets occupying signs where the ruler is in its detriment. He is in Paris, bedridden. There is a discharge from his ear, and great pain from it. Encephalitic meningitis is diagnosed. It is the legacy of tertiary syphilis, an infection he contacted at age twenty—that year, 1874, his Mercury decan began, and septenary Mercury was on his Mars in Sagittarius. Now, as the Moon comes to Mercury in the septenary, the full consequences of that earlier Mercury-emphasized year become apparent—Mercury and the Moon are part of a T-square with Uranus. He has periods  of delirium, is baptized by a Catholic priest, and dies on the last day of November 1900. His remains are in the Pere Lachaise, Paris, under the famous funerary monument created by the sculptor Jacob Epstein.

Ernest Hemingway's Moon-ruled Septenary

Moon in Capricorn rises: The writer Ernest Hemingway is a diurnal birth with a waxing Moon in Capricorn, opposite Venus and sesquiquadrate Mercury. His septenary Moon comes to the ascendant in 1920 when he is 21 years old. The same year, decan Uranus arrives at its dispositor, Jupiter in Scorpio. Both the Moon and Uranus can be extremely volatile and Hemingway's smoldering ill will toward his mother explodes into open warfare and he is expelled from their Chicago suburban home. He moves into a down-at-heels boarding house, earning money by doing odd jobs. While there he hurts his stomach, has an affair, and is converted to Catholicism. He moves to Boyne City, Michigan but finds life alone so rough that he quickly returns to Chicago. This is when he meets Hadley Richardson, his future wife, who falls in love with him. He eventually finds work as a writer for an investment magazine. He begins and abandons work on a novel, writes poetry, and reads a great deal about the war. He also experiences frequent depressions; he soon becomes increasingly fearful of his impending marriage to Hadley.

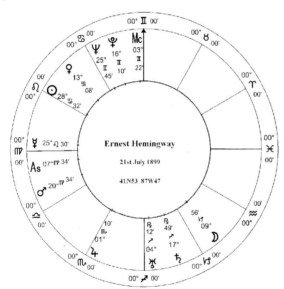

Ernest Hemingway
21st July 1899
41N53 87W47

Moon directed to Saturn in Sagittarius: The septenary Moon has arrived at her dispositor, the occidental Saturn in Sagittarius. He is aged 22. The decan ruler Uranus is on Mars in Virgo. His fiancée Hadley gives him a typewriter for his birthday and he writes a short story, *Up Michigan*. He meets Sherwood Anderson, who becomes his literary mentor and who, as a father figure, has a great influence on him. He and Hadley marry and move into a rented apartment in a rundown Chicago building. He is not working and lives off her wife's income. They move to Paris, where the *Toronto Star* employs him as a foreign correspondent. In Paris, due to the excellent dollar-franc exchange, he and Hadley are able to live fairly well—they are poor and happy, living in a Paris slum. They are excited to be in Europe and holiday in Switzerland, where he learns to ski and goes climbing in the Alps. Ernest is very competitive; ever out to demonstrate his masculine superiority. He regularly goes to horseraces in Paris and becomes addicted to gambling. He writes steadily and meets James Joyce, Ezra Pound, Gertrude Stein and Alice B. Toklas. As a reporter, he visits Milan, and interviews Mussolini.

Moon directed to Jupiter in Scorpio: It is 1922 and Hemingway is 23 years old. Occidental Jupiter is in Scorpio, the sign of the Moon's detriment. Decan Uranus is on Mercury in Leo. With both rulers in signs where they are in detriment the year can be expected to contain problems. Ernest and Hadley are living in Paris. During a hiking and fishing trip in the Black Forest, which he doesn't enjoy, he grows a mustache. He has his first flight in an airplane, and is thrilled by it, when he travels to Constantinople to report on the consequences of the Turkish-Greek war, but he is lonely there without Hadley, who has stayed in Paris. He catches malaria while in Turkey, and shaves his head to rid himself of lice. Although the *Toronto Star* has exclusive rights to his reporting work, he duplicates dispatches to Hearst's news service (INS). This is discovered and he has to squirm out of trouble. Even though his reporting is superb, his relations with the *Toronto Star* will never be the same again. Decan Uranus on his Mercury isn't finished with just that episode: Hadley loses all of his manuscript writings including carbons on a train, and then (the Moon's direction to Jupiter getting into the act) announces she is pregnant. Ernest reacts by becoming angry and depressed. He believes the pregnancy is to bind him to her, and feels he is too young to be a father. He visits Spain and sees his first bull fight, and is thrilled by it. He also visits the Ruhr, to report on the French occupation. Throughout much of the year he is writing miniature studies of violence.

Moon directed to Mars in Virgo: Ernest is 24 years old when his septenary Moon comes to Mars in Virgo in 1923. Decan Uranus is on his Cancer Sun. He and Hadley are living in Paris, where the *Toronto Star* employs him as a foreign correspondent. With Hadley he visits Pamplona in Spain for the bull fights. He is writing, caught up in the sexual imagery of bullfighting. His first book, *Three Stories and Ten Poems,* is published in Paris. He and Hadley sail to Toronto, where his first child, John, is born. This fourth year of the seven-year cycle is often a cross road at which major choices are made. Accordingly, fed up with newspaper work, Ernest quits his job. The young family then return to Paris, where he begins working as a sub-editor for Ford Maddox Ford on *The Transatlantic Review.* He also hires herself out as a sparring partner for professional boxers. He is feeling sorry for himself. He is unable to get his short stories published in any large-circulation or prestigious magazine, and—true to Moon-on-Mars—he is resentful of anyone who is in any way successful.

Moon directed to Mercury in Leo: The septenary Moon comes to Hemingway's Mercury in Leo in 1924 when he is 25. Decan Uranus is on Venus in Cancer. He writes a fish story, trying to recreate landscapes as if a series of pictures by Cezanne, aiming to endow a story in which 'nothing happens' with an inner drama of terrific intensity. He is living in Paris with Hadley and their newborn son. There is little money, and the family has to economize. Even so he finds a way to visit Pamplona in Spain to watch bullfighting. He becomes obsessed with watching bike racing, and enjoys having a kitten as a pet. He is falling out of love with Hadley, and looking for a way out of the marriage. He is writing a lot: angry, bitter thoughts about his mother come out in his short stories. Frequently depressed and frustrated, with feelings of defeat, he is delighted when told that his second book, *In Our Time*, is to be published. This fifth year of the septenary is often when a teacher appears, someone who will guide and help. He meets Scott Fitzgerald, and with him drives from Lyon to Paris. On another trip to Pamplona, with Hadley present, he has a romantic involvement with Duff Twysden; then, just with Hadley, he goes to Madrid to see more bullfighting.

Moon directed to the Sun in Cancer: The septenary Moon coming to Ernest's Cancer Sun in 1925 when he is 26 should be a positive direction. This sixth year of his septenary is often when what is implied in the seven-year period bears fruit. Decan Uranus has come to his 10th house Neptune in Gemini. While visiting Spain he begins to write his first novel; at first he calls it *Fiesta*. He and Hadley return to Paris, where they face a marital crisis—he becomes sexually involved with Pauline Pfeiffer. Feeling guilty for betraying Hadley with Pauline, he gives a painting by Joan Miro to Hadley for her birthday. He won the right to buy it in a game of dice. *In Our Time*, his second book, is published—his appalled parents throw it out of their home. He writes a parody of Sherwood Anderson, who has helped him very much over the years, with which Hadley disagrees. He is having bouts of depression and insomnia. There are financial worries. He is working to ensure his publisher will reject his next book and so allow him to break his contract and move to another publisher—that is, double-crossing the publisher who had helped him get started. To avoid feeling guilty about this, he manufactures a self-induced anger, a self-pitying sense of victimization and a convenient anti-Semitism. He becomes a Catholic and begins calling himself "Papa".

Moon directed to Venus in Cancer: The septenary Moon remains in Cancer in 1926 when he is 27. As the final year of the septenary it should be a time of fulfillment. Decan Uranus is on his Pluto in Gemini. His first novel *The Sun Also Rises* is published. It receives excellent reviews and is a great success. At the time he is in Paris alone, writing short stories. He hates living alone. His wife Hadley divorces him. He marries a second wife, Pauline, and they honeymoon in the Rhone delta, where he cuts his foot on a rock: anthrax infection sets in, his foot swells up and he spends ten days in bed. Appropriately for a Moon-on-Venus period, he purchases a hand-made suit, fedora and overcoat. He is preparing *Men Without Women*, a collection of short stories. The sales of his book are doing well; his apartment rent is being paid for by Pauline's uncle—all combine to make him very optimistic.

Ernest Hemingway's Moon-ruled Decan

The Moon rises in Capricorn: In 1939 Hemingway is 40 years old. His septenary Sun is on his Mars in Virgo as the Moon decan begins. He drives his latest love Martha Gelhorn from Key West to St. Louis, and then continues alone to Wyoming where he meets Pauline his second wife and his three sons. He makes the decision to leave Pauline once and for all—her sobbing is driving him to distraction. He goes to Montana, where Martha meets him, and then to Idaho for bird shooting. Martha leaves to cover the Russo-Finnish war as a journalist, and Ernest is lonely during the three months she is away. He and Martha are sexually incompatible. He lets his hair grow to conceal its increasing thinness. He works continuously on *For Whom the Bell Tolls*, the manuscript of which he completes just before his next birthday.

Moon directed to Saturn in Sagittarius: Hemingway is 41 years old in 1941 when the decan Moon comes to Saturn. His septenary Sun arriving at his Mercury in Leo, the sign the Sun rules, suggests that, with the Moon coming to its dispositor, this will be a very successful year for him. *For Whom the Bell Tolls* is published and it is the biggest seller in American fiction since *Gone With the Wind*. He buys *Finca Vigia*, a one-story sprawling farmhouse in Cuba. The affect of the Moon coming to Saturn plays out with his divorce from Pauline becoming final and he marries his third wife, Martha. His friend Scott Fitzgerald dies.

Moon directed to Uranus in Sagittarius: Hemingway is 42 in 1941 when the Moon comes to Uranus in his decan. His septenary Mercury is rising in Leo. His year begins when he and his new wife Martha meet his three sons in Idaho, and the five go antelope hunting on horseback. In Cuba he sets up a counter-intelligence group aimed at ferreting out Nazi spies in Havana, and uses his boat for hunting U-boats.

Moon directed to Jupiter in Scorpio: The direction to the sign where the Moon is in its fall occurs when Hemingway is 43 in 1942. Septenary Mercury has come to his Sun in Cancer. His youngest son, Gregory, becomes ill, and polio is feared. After Gregory recovers, Ernest talks about it as if he believes himself responsible for the cure. That same year he certainly does save Gregory from sharks.

Moon directed to Mars in Virgo: The decan Moon gets to Mars in 1943. Hemingway is 44 years old. In this fifth year of the decan we expect an individual to encounter new experiences. Septenary Mercury is on his Venus in Cancer. Ernest is starting to treat his wife Martha viciously. Martha goes to London as a war correspondent. He is angry that she is at war and he is not, although she pleads with him to join her. He grows a huge beard as a response to the hair on his head receding and thinning. He then goes to London himself as a war correspondent. There he meets Mary Welsh, his future fourth wife, and proposes to her despite both he and she being married. He injures his head in a car accident and has concussion. Martha says she is through with him.

Moon directed to Mercury in Leo: In 1944 Hemingway at age 45 is with the invading US army in France as a war correspondent. Decan Moon is on his Mercury in Leo and septenary Mercury is on his Moon in Capricorn, an interchange that should signify a memorable year. He injures his head and kidneys in a motor cycle accident, a second concussion just two to three months after the earlier one in London: for months after he suffers from double vision, slowness of speech, loss of verbal memory, a tendency to write backwards, dull headaches, ringing in the ears, and sexual impotence. He is present at the liberation of Paris, and at several battles. He is in his third major war and he acquits himself with bravery bordering on the lunatic. He has a cracked forehead from a car crash, four broken ribs, and a damaged left knee. He accepts that his marriage to Martha is over. He casts off what he decides was an unsuitable wife (Martha) and is about to take another (Mary Welsh), who might more closely correspond to his sexual fantasies.

Moon directed to the Sun in Cancer: Hemingway marries Mary Welsh, his fourth wife in 1945. He is 46 years old. The decan Moon has come to the sign it rules. Septenary Mercury is on his retrograde Saturn in Sagittarius. He starts writing *The Garden of Eden*, writing as if possessed, fearing he will die within the year. Saturn's location in the 4th house, from where it opposes Pluto and squares Mars, may have influenced such thinking.

Moon directed to Venus in Cancer: Hemingway's decan Moon is still in its own sign of Cancer and comes to Venus when he is 47 years old in July 1946. Septenary Mercury is on his Jupiter in Scorpio. He is writing *The Garden of Eden*, on which he has worked feverishly for the past year, which he stops to write the story *The Sea When Young*. He is shaken when he learns of the death of his editor Max Perkins. His sons Patrick and Gregory are in a car accident.

Moon directed to Neptune in Gemini: In 1947 at age 48 Ernest experiences the decan Moon coming to his Neptune in Gemini at the same time that his septenary Mercury arrives at his 1st house Mars in Virgo. He experiences high blood pressure, hears strange buzzing and humming inside his head like the sound of telephone wires along country roadsides. He cuts back on his drinking and begins to watch his diet, reducing his blood pressure and losing weight.

Moon directed to Pluto in Gemini: Ernest Hemingway has the decan Moon come to his Pluto in Gemini in 1950 at age 49. Mars has taken over the septenary and is at the ascendant. This is the final year of his decan. He has an eye infection that spreads to cover his entire face. Doctors fear it will end in blindness. When he eventually recovers he spends a happy time with her wife Mary in Torcello. He then meets and courts Adriana Ivancich. He is living a happy life in Cuba, although an article about him by Malcolm Cowley in *Life* magazine has many negative consequences. *Pluto rules his next decan.*

Chapter 8

Mercury as the Time Ruler

To be, or not to be—that is the question—
Whether 'tis nobler in the mind to suffer
The slings and arrows of outrageous fortune,
Or to take arms against a sea of troubles,
And by opposing end them?

William Shakespeare,
Hamlet, Prince of Denmark

Mercury represents our thoughts and reasoning ability. This tends to manifest in three ways. *Exchange* is the most obvious of the three. This includes the exchange of words, thoughts and ideas that we term communication and the methods we use for this exchange: paper and printing, words and language, radio, phone and the worldwide web. It also includes the exchange of goods, materials and possessions that we call trading, buying and selling, marketing and bartering, and equally it represents the money we use to enable this exchange to take place, whether it is coin, banknote or credit card. Mercury does not however represent wealth, which is the domain of Jupiter and to a lesser extent of Venus. When Mercury is well placed and has positive aspects the values of shares and commodities offered for sale in stock exchanges and markets tend to rise, when Mercury is ill placed or afflicted (particularly by Mars) the same prices invariably fall. The stock market crash that began in September-October 2008 had a stationary-retrograde Mercury conjunct a slow-moving Mars in Libra.

The association of Mercury with trading and exchange is well evidenced in our language. There are ninety-two words in the *Oxford English Dictionary* that begin with the letters MERC. Fifty-two of these words relate to trading and commerce: doing something for profit, reward or self-interest. These include such as Merchant, Mercenary, Mercantile, Mercer and Merchandise. One can include the archaic Merchet: "a fine paid by a tenant or bondsman to his overlord for liberty to give his daughter in marriage." A frequent modern meaning of Merc-words involves the chemical substitution (or trading) of one element for another.

Mercury is also *Connection*: how things relate one to another, how they couple and link up together. It is not just by chance that most weddings occur when the Sun is passing through Mercury's sign of Gemini. Mercury is also associated with children, the result of coupling and our connection with the future.

The third manifestation of our reasoning ability symbolized by Mercury is *Choice*. To be or not to be? Should I do this or that? Which is the larger? Which is more valuable? Should I go to the left or to the right? Mercury is the planet of "Either …Or", the planet of the crossroads. In earlier times a statue of Hermes (the Greek name for Mercury) stood at major crossings.

To the Greeks Hermes was the messenger of Olympus, the god of eloquence and self-expression, the guide of travelers and the patron of merchants and thieves. He was also the deceitful, unscrupulous divinity who conducted the souls of the dead to hell. The name Hermes gave rise to Hermeticism, the symbol of all that is inaccessible. Mercury's connection with death became very apparent in those years that members of the sample had the planet emphasized in either the decan or the septenary. Indeed, when Mercury was the ruler of either of these two methods, events in the lives of the people in my sample clearly showed that the planet was different—considerably more stronger—than the mere celestial messenger it is often depicted as in modern day astrology.

Mercury is the planetary ruler of astrology and always has been. Only in recent times has Uranus erroneously been given that rulership. In Greek myth the goddess Urania had rulership of the skies but that never gave Uranus rulership over astrology.

Indian astrologers know Mercury as Buddha. Giving the planet the same name as the enlightened spiritual teacher Siddharta Gautama is no coincidence.

By tradition Mercury is associated with speech and intelligence. It is strongest in Gemini, Virgo and the 1st house. It experiences problems in Sagittarius and Pisces.

Table ☿-1:

☿ as Time Ruler
% Positive Years

☿ relative to the ☉	Day birth		Night birth		All	
	N	% Positive	N	% Positive	N	% Positive
Oriental ☿	310	54.8	305	47.5	615	51.2
Occidental ☿	186	44.8	304	51.2	490	48.7
All	496	51.1	609	49.3	1105	50.1

In the sample Mercury was most positive when oriental of the Sun in a daytime chart or occidental of the Sun at night. These positions relative to the Sun describe Mercury as a morning or evening star, visible to sharp eyes in the sky before dawn and after sunset. This does not agree with tradition, which says Mercury is strongest when occidental. Even so, this unexpected finding is intuitively satisfying. It seems to make very good sense.

In the years that Mercury is an individual's time ruler there is likely to be an emphasis on exchange, connection and choice; on learning, writing, speaking and all intellectual efforts. There may be an increased involvement in business, especially if this involves communication. In these seven or ten years the individual is discovering trust, the underlying factor in any exchange, connection or choice. As Mercury is directed around the zodiacal circle each of the planets it encounters will enhance this knowledge by providing stimuli appropriate to that planet's position within the natal horoscope.

The years in which Mercury is directed to a planet in Gemini or Virgo should be happy and prosperous. During them the individual can increase his knowledge, successfully complete his studies, advance in his career and be favored by his superiors. His income should increase and he may enjoy unexpected windfalls. He will experience a happy family life with his wife and children, and his health will be good. It can be one of the most auspicious periods of his life.

Table ☿-2:

**% Positive Years
when ☿ is Time Lord**

☿ directed to	N	% positive
☿ rises	144	48.4
☉	139	50.1
☽	142	50.3
♀	141	49.4
♂	142	49.6
♃	133	46.9
♄	146	48.9
♅	43	50.5
♆	47	53.9
♇	38	57.1
All	1105	50.1

By contrast, the years when Mercury applies to a planet in Sagittarius or Pisces, or to a planet with which it is in sharp conflict in the natal chart, mental troubles, depression and instability are possible. His reasoning ability may become flawed, his interests scattered and his moral values weakened. He may then talk simply for the sake of talking, without any belief or reliability in whatever he is saying. There can be financial failure and loss from theft. He can become increasingly skeptical and materialistic in his outlook. Friends may be lost and he is likely to have trouble with his relatives.

None of the values in Table ☿-2 differ significantly from 50%. In general the year in which Mercury is directed to the ascendant or to any of the planets has a fifty-fifty likelihood of being a positive one. There were too few directions of Mercury to Neptune and Pluto in the sample for their above-average values to be relied upon.

119

Table ☿-3: **% Positive Years when ☿ is the Time Lord**
by Signs, natal & to where it is directed

☿'s natal Sign		Sign	Sign to where ☿ is directed	
N	% Positive years		N	% Positive years
123	53.6	♈	58	56.1
125	49.9	♉	112	53.3
57	39.7	♊	80	49.7
61	45.9	♋	87	55.1
58	49.9	♌	86	50.5
93	46.7	♍	65	47.3
38	64.3	♎	90	47.2
172	**41.5****	♏	69	48.5
84	50.6	♐	71	52.2
105	56.9	♑	96	51.8
134	56.7	♒	65	45.9
55	51.0	♓	78	47.5
1105	50.1	*All*	961	50.3

Mercury natally in Scorpio was associated with a statistically significant percentage of difficult years. Difficult years were also observed in the sample when the planet was in its own signs of Gemini and Virgo. This indication that the placement of the time ruler in its own signs indicates difficult years agrees with similar below-50% results noted previously for the Sun in Leo and the Moon in Cancer. None of the signs occupied by a planet to which Mercury, as time ruler, is directed differ meaningfully from the expected 50%.

In Table ☿-4 we see that Mercury natally placed in the 8th house was associated in the sample with a value that is significantly higher than 50%. Values significantly under 50% were observed for Mercury at birth in the 12th house and when directed to a planet in the 11th house.

Table ☿-4:

% Positive Years when ☿ is the Time Lord, by House, natal & to where it is directed

☿'s natal house		House	House to where ☿ is directed	
N	% Positive Years		N	% Positive Years
78	52.2	I	109	49.7
210	53.8	II	87	56.1
83	47.6	III	94	54.8
97	49.5	IV	72	51.4
53	46.7	V	74	42.8
120	51.6	VI	59	47.5
91	60.3	VII	76	46.4
39	**66.7***	VIII	79	56.1
82	52.9	IX	69	51.1
86	57.9	X	73	53.3
55	47.6	XI	94	**40.0***
111	**37.4****	XII	75	54.2
1105	50.1	All	961	50.3

In Table ☿-5, although there are few observations involved, Mercury in the 6th place in a night chart is a significant indicator of difficult years. The low value for Mercury in the 5th place at night, although not significant, can probably be relied upon.

Table ☿-5:

% Positive when Mercury is the Ruler by its place in the septenary sequence

Place of Mercury in septenary	Day		Night	
	N	% Positive	N	% Positive
1	22	49.2	47	49.5
2	26	48.6	99	47.0
3	43	52.5	99	57.3
4	72	52.6	43	58.5
5	61	56.2	36	36.2
6	69	47.1	10	**9.3****
7	31	46.6	18	51.7
Sum	324	51.0	352	49.7

Table ☿-6:   **% Positive when Mercury is the Ruler
by its place in the decan sequence**

Place of Mercury in decan	Day		Night	
	N	% Positive	N	% Positive
1	2	45.1	10	**18.6***
2	2	45.1	53	49.2
3	18	70.2	78	**65.7****
4	46	62.8	47	45.5
5	31	43.6	36	38.8
6	26	52.1	19	29.4
7	39	41.6	4	46.5
8	4	45.1	7	53.2
9	4	0.0	6	15.5
10	0	0.0	0	0.0
Sum	172	51.4	260	48.7

Mercury's close proximity to the Sun may explain the low value observed when it is the first of the ten to rise at night. Mercury would then be just ahead of an about-to-rise Sun.

The planet produces the most positive years when it rules an individual's third decan, which occurs when a person is in his twenties, years in which he may graduate from college and start his first job.

Mercury Rises
(48% positive years)

This should be the start of a busy period of years when the native can expect to be mentally brighter and more objective than he may have been for some time. The mind should be clearer and much sharper. He will want to express his point of view now that he is aware that his ability to communicate his thoughts is so much more fluent. The only problem this can represent is that his mind can easily become over stimulated, there is so much he wants to explain, that his thoughts can jump from subject to subject. This can confuse those to whom he is talking. No matter the individual's age and circumstances, young or old, rich or poor, he will feel alive and alert and will want to expand his knowledge in all and every way possible now, by reading, attending classes and studying, traveling, being involved in thoughtful conversations and by the exchange of writings. Academic or business success can occur now.

This year the possibility of an increase in the person's family is indicated, either by marriage or by a birth. The individual may relocate and improve the standard of his housing. There should be financial gains. He will probably make plans for the future that aim to improve his status in life. He may be promoted, and is likely to improve his appearance. He is also likely to be concerned for the welfare of his children.

In the sample Mercury rising was strongest when it rose before the Sun during the day and when it set after the Sun in a night birth—these are the times when Mercury is the morning and evening star. Oriental Mercury at night is associated with a % Positive that is significantly below 50%. Mercury was significantly above expectation when coming to the ascendant from Taurus.

Table ☿-7:

☿ **to Ascendant:**
% Positive Years

☿ relative to the ☉	Day birth		Night birth		All	
	N	% Positive	N	% Positive	N	% Positive
Oriental ☿	43	56.8	36	**30.1***	79	44.7
Occidental ☿	20	49.7	45	54.2	65	52.9
All	*63*	*54.5*	*74*	*43.5*	*144*	*48.3*

Some examples in my sample of Mercury coming to the ascendant in the decan:
Diurnal Oriental Mercury rises in decan: *learning oratory; leaves the army; has many quaint, ingenious ideas; his article is published; writing his first book; he is the victim of sales fraud; living in a revolutionary atmosphere; intensely preoccupied with images of his own unconscious; learning wood carving; promoted.*
Diurnal Occidental Mercury rises in decan: *his son has a mental breakdown; summarizing & popularizing his theories; dismayed by world events; husband loses election; poor health; lung operation.*
Nocturnal Oriental Mercury rises in decan: *angered by the media's coverage of his divorce; his marriage proposal is rejected; very popular; in prison; depressed; poor health.*
Nocturnal Occidental Mercury rises in decan: *has her first great record success; mother dies; marries; father remarries; campaigning; in prison for refusing military service; leaves army.*

Some examples in my sample of Mercury coming to the ascendant in the septenary:
Diurnal Oriental Mercury rises in septenary: *acts in propaganda films; studying; indecisive; father is declared insane; discovers wireless radio; marooned; rejected by military; loses fight.*
Diurnal Occidental Mercury rises in septenary: *his work is terminated; divorce; his son is a POW; psycho analyzed; writes on inhibitions & anxiety; searching for Nazi spies; starts studying astrology; unexploded bomb left on his porch; depressed; dream analysis.*
Nocturnal Oriental Mercury rises in septenary: *studying; promoted on death of his predecessor; separated from mother/wife; persecuted; on trial; poor health.*
Nocturnal Occidental Mercury rises in septenary: *wife/mother dies; knocked down by a car; defeated; his book is a great success; travels; works as a copywriter; death.*

Mercury comes to the Sun
(50% positive)

A person's thinking should be vitalized and clear this year. He may become introspective and indulge in some self-analysis, perhaps start keeping a diary. Although he may spend time alone, perhaps feel some remorse for past actions, even some humiliation, his correspondence is likely to increase now, and he will probably spend time studying and planning for the future. Others may lose their respect for him, his spouse may be sick, there can be troubles from rivals and superiors, and he is likely to meet with many obstacles. Those born in the daytime may travel. Fire can be a danger this year. The native may experience pains in his head or stomach.

If Mercury is combust the Sun, it can be an unhappy year with many worries, during which he may experience rejection and defeat—this is worse in a nocturnal chart. Mercury coming to the Sun in Pisces can cause the individual to act strangely.

The finances of those born with the Sun in Gemini or Virgo should improve this year, and he may unexpectedly find himself buying a house or a new car.

Table ☿-8: ☿ to ☉: % Positive Years

☿ relative to the ☉	Day birth		Night birth		All	
	N	% Positive	N	% Positive	N	% Positive
Oriental ☿	35	59.4	44	45.2	79	51.5
Occidental ☿	26	38.2	34	55.9	60	48.2
All	*61*	*51.5*	*78*	*49.8*	*139*	*50.1*

In the sample Mercury coming to the Sun from the 5th house was associated with a difficult year.

Some examples in my sample of Mercury coming to the Sun in the decan:
Diurnal Oriental Mercury to the Sun in decan: *rheumatism in hands & feet; changes his philosophy; writes on optics; worries; studying; spending time alone; promoted.*
Diurnal Occidental Mercury to the Sun in decan: *starvation diets; preoccupied with survival; travels; his son is a POW; destroys unpublished papers; wife dies.*
Nocturnal Oriental Mercury to the Sun in decan: *mother/wife/brother dies; daughter born; anxious; studying religion; loss of self-confidence; in a neurotic state; sells his stocks; angry exchange of letters; breaks his father's watch; military call-up; writes on light and color.*
Nocturnal Occidental Mercury to the Sun in decan: *protests government changes; to school; starts new business; receives much publicity; travels; lonely; anxious; has a new job.*

Some examples in my sample of Mercury coming to the Sun in the septenary:

Diurnal Oriental Mercury to the Sun in septenary: *cheated; has his first car; humiliated; making post cards; buys his first house; introspection & self-analysis; arrested; goes to college; has the idea for* Peter Pan; *discovers complementarity; starts a diary; her writings are published; writes on education.*

Diurnal Occidental Mercury to the Sun in septenary: *unemployed all year; very poor; sells his business at a profit; demolishing religion with psychoanalytic weapons; challenges the appeal of consensus; stabbed in his chest; immigrates to USA; his son is killed in the war; loss of job.*

Nocturnal Oriental Mercury to the Sun in septenary: *mother/brother/cousin dies; writes many articles; fights a duel; negotiates a higher salary; immense success; has to pay back taxes; studying; wins prize for memorizing; starts a long-lasting astrology association.*

Nocturnal Occidental Mercury to the Sun in septenary: *nightmares; witch hunt for traitors; receives occult training; negotiates contract extension; paranoia; wins prize; he dresses as a woman in private; forced to pay increased child support; breathing exercises; burglarized.*

Mercury comes to the Moon
(50% positive)

This will be an unusually busy year, one in which moods influence the native's rational mind. These moods may change very rapidly. He will be active, restless and talkative, on the go all the time; there is so much to be done, so much information to be gathered. Reading and conversation will be stimulating. He will want to expand his knowledge and is eager to teach others, who in turn will want to learn from him. He is likely to travel, and may marry.

If the Moon is in Sagittarius or Pisces, signs in which Mercury is unwelcome, the year will probably be difficult. His health may be poor: his arms and legs can become swollen and painful. Disputes with females and friends are also possible. He may act strangely and his actions may be criticized, as a result he may meet with many difficulties, including the ill will of his superiors or colleagues.

Females and friends are more likely to be helpful should the Moon be found in Gemini or Virgo. Then his business will increase, his past achievements be recognized and he may be honored for them. This could tempt him to return home for others to share in his triumph.

In the sample occidental Mercury at night was associated with difficult years. This was unexpected as usually Mercury when setting after the Sun at night indicates positive years.

☿ to ☽: % Positive Years

Planets relative to the ☉	Day birth		Night birth		All	
	N	% Positive	N	% Positive	N	% Positive
Oriental ☿	37	53.8	45	60.3	82	57.3
Occidental ☿	27	50.3	33	**32.9***	60	40.7
All	64	52.3	78	48.6	142	50.3
Waxing ☽	35	43.9	41	48.5	76	46.4
Waning ☽	29	62.4	37	48.9	66	54.8

Some examples in my sample of Mercury coming to the Moon in the decan:

Oriental Mercury to the Moon by day in decan: *mother dies; fascinated by harmonics; promoted; lecturing; his writing is an outstanding success; publishers reject his book; graduates; very happy; honors; gains control of the party; pneumonia; research; studying; proclaims neutrality; arrested.*

Occidental Mercury to the Moon by day in decan: *anxious; indecisive; hurts arm in a machine; job ends; friend dies; changes her appearance; passes exams; her book is a success; fears for his life; immigrates; marries; deaths in the family.*

Oriental Mercury to the Moon at night in decan: *lectures; writing; being tutored; graduates; searching for his past; has a compulsion to write; marries; mother is paralyzed; travels; castigated by the press; writing her autobiography.*

Occidental Mercury to the Moon at night in decan: *attacked by the press; siblings die; teaching; writing his autobiography; mental breakdown; graduates; father retires; assassination attempt; involved in his friend's murder.*

Some examples in my sample of Mercury coming to the Moon in the septenary:

Oriental Mercury to the Moon by day in septenary: *awarded Nobel Prize; knighted; conceives of the universal brotherhood of men; his ambitions are checked; friends help him repair his house; honors; teaching; book success; lectures; visions; poetry; seizes power; drunk; unable to write; her husband stops talking to her; promoted; graduates; death.*

Occidental Mercury to the Moon by day in septenary: *wins Nobel Prize; conscripted; war correspondent; writes against slavery & for independence; loss of speech; writes on prevention of war; magazine editor; campaigning; advocating self-sufficiency; cutting expenses; attends conferences; saves daughter from drowning; travels.*

Oriental Mercury to the Moon at night in septenary: *mental breakdown; depressed; his papers are destroyed; acquitted of wrong doing; unemployed; studying; travels; promoted; she is discovered; honored; much writing; marries; passes exams; children born.*

Occidental Mercury to the Moon at night in septenary: *mind training; graduates; busy on various committees; paralyzed; quarrels; record success; military training; son born; arrested; mother/wife/sister dies; passes exams; promoted; editing; travels; teaching; noise deprives him of sleep.*

Mercury comes to Venus
(49% positive)

This should be a happy, tranquil year in which the mind is usually clear and free from conflict. The individual's employment should go well, losing its irksomeness. He can acquire wealth and possessions. Children may be born and he should be happy in his marriage. The native will have little inclination to become involved in serious or heavy subjects but will instead be more interested in making friends, expressing his love and affection for others, vacationing and enjoying sightseeing trips. He is at his most creative now and may take an interest in poetry. He could be promoted, and/or work with young people.

News he receives can bring joy or grief, disappointment or pleasure, depending on how comfortable Mercury is in the sign Venus occupies. If Mercury is combust or tightly aspected by malefics, the news he receives is likely to be sad and depressing and involve a loved one.

This could be the year when those born with Venus in Gemini or Virgo are able to return home after a long absence.

Table ☿-10:

☿ to ♀: % Positive Years

Planets relative to the ☉	Day birth		Night birth		All	
	N	% Positive	N	% Positive	N	% Positive
Oriental ☿	37	53.8	39	51.0	76	52.4
Occidental ☿	26	45.2	39	46.4	65	45.9
All	63	50.3	78	48.6	141	49.4
Oriental ♀	29	43.7	28	51.6	57	47.6
Occidental ♀	34	55.9	50	47.0	84	50.6

In the sample those individuals with Venus in Aries had a significantly greater proportion of positive years than the expected 50%. Also in the sample, Venus in a Mercury-ruled sign or term was often associated with unpleasant years. Both of these observations were very much a reversal of what was expected. It was also noted that when this direction occurred in the septenary the planetary combination in the decan, whatever that was, tended to dominate the individual's year.

Some examples in my sample of Mercury coming to Venus in the decan:
Oriental Mercury to Venus by day in decan: *his wife dies; decides he no longer loves his wife; daughter marries; brother is killed; throat cancer is diagnosed; wins a large contract; unhappy unless working; attains great power; removed from his command; publishes book; has difficulties with her landlord.*

Occidental Mercury to Venus by day in decan: *financial losses; moves; writing; his work is being accepted; attends conference; friends visit.*

Oriental Mercury to Venus at night in decan: *in prison; father dies; her sister is in love; marries; demeaning & humiliating divorce; dangerous accident; fails exams; family is forced to split up; financial losses.*

Occidental Mercury to Venus at night in decan: *she is given lead billing; graduates; elected; she is one of sixteen who survive shipwreck in which 472 die; father is ill; starts a newspaper; leaves home; involved in quarrels & court battles; declares her independence; under much pressure; exhausted.*

Some examples in my sample of Mercury coming to Venus in the septenary:

Oriental Mercury to Venus by day in septenary: *attains power; earns his doctorate; promoted; wins championship; a happy, creative period; in love; marries; falsely accused; conscripted; betrayed & abandoned; buys a sailboat; frustrated; rejected by art academy; moves; jaundice*

Occidental Mercury to Venus by day in septenary: *military service; head concussion; mother dies; his wife says she is through with him; studying astrology; in prison; teaching; poor health; realizes his career is over; making speeches; country is attacked; personal worries.*

Oriental Mercury to Venus at night in septenary: *becomes a vegetarian; returns home after long absence; danger to his daughter; son/brother born; daughter elopes; he is an overnight success; criticized; has a great sense of triumph; article is published; career worries; expelled for cheating.*

Occidental Mercury to Venus at night in septenary: *becomes a vegetarian; writing; defeated; studying; offered a job; graduates; religious conversion; arrested; studying; beaten up; exiled; has no money; crisis in relationship; parents divorce; father retires.*

Mercury comes to Mars
(53% positive)

This year the native will probably be fully occupied with his work. There may be the need for much writing, lecturing and communication, during which he can become involved in disputes and have to defend his ideas. He may be torn between conflicting opinions, becoming impatient, touchy and irritable, unwilling to consider the long-term implications of his actions. Even so, although his ideas may initially receive a hostile reaction he should be able to persuade others to go along with them and to do what he wants, even if that means that he must take risks to do so. He may be forced to study, to learn in a Spartan, disciplined and regimented environment in order to obtain the qualifications he needs. He is reckless now, and may push his luck a bit too often. There are likely to be some trouble with his neighbors and in his marriage. Divorce or separation can occur. He may emigrate. Alcohol and drug addiction are potential dangers, and so too is gambling. Severe headaches and neuralgia are possible, as are blood afflictions. If either planet is badly afflicted death is likely to visit the family.

In the sample Mercury in Cancer and Mars in Pisces, the latter unexpectedly, were significantly above 50%. Mercury as morning and evening star was again associated with above-average positive years. Occidental Mercury directed to Mars for a day birth was particularly difficult.

Table ☿-11: **☿ to ♂: % Positive Years**

Planets relative to the ☉	Day birth		Night birth		All	
	N	% Positive	N	% Positive	N	% Positive
Oriental ☿	36	62.7	36	45.2	72	54.0
Occidental ☿	27	36.8	33	65.7	60	52.7
All	63	51.6	69	55.1	132	53.4
Oriental ♂	29	56.1	37	58.7	66	57.5
Occidental ♂	34	47.8	32	50.8	66	47.5

As was observed when Mercury came to Venus, in the sample when Mercury was directed to Mars in the septenary the planetary combination in the decan, whatever that was, tended to dominate the individual's year.

Some examples in my sample of Mercury coming to Mars in the decan:
Oriental Mercury to Mars by day in decan: *receives a trust fund; war starts; travels; daughter dies; friend is drowned; surgery removes cancerous tumor; released from prison; his girl friend attempts suicide; writing.*
Occidental Mercury to Mars by day in decan: *cancer found; year of cruel surprises; severe depression; writing; badly defeated; sister dies; irritable; husband resigns his job; her lover is away; exhausted; denies he is an atheist.*
Oriental Mercury to Mars at night in decan: *father makes wrong career decision; completes his apprenticeship; in prison; elected; moves; mother arrested; sister marries; sister dies; depressed & weary; writing; divorce; large cash settlement to ex-wife; pays back taxes; racked with guilt; wins trial; writings published.*
Occidental Mercury to Mars at night in decan: *honored; travels; writing adverts; wife's suicide; joins Rosicrucians; under much pressure; a difficult year; a happy year; quarreling; fails exams; poetry; marries; tries to find the secret of life by dissecting animals; moves; attacked as an atheist.*

Some examples in my sample of Mercury coming to Mars in the septenary:
Oriental Mercury to Mars by day in septenary: *in extreme pain; cuts the Gordian Knot; learns about sex; meets future wife; his sister & wife are executed; her husband is assassinated; divorce; honorary degrees; tours USA; buys a second house; defeated; quarrels; working long hours; defeated; exhausted; arrested for assaulting a policeman; escapes from prison; immigrates; earns professional qualifications; resigns from his job; cuts himself off from his friends.*

Occidental Mercury to Mars by day in septenary: father dies; defeated; disasters; believes he is destined for a terrible trial; working again after long spell unemployed; high blood pressure; in prison; war starts; painful operation; intensive dental work; death;
Oriental Mercury to Mars at night in septenary: kills a child who runs under her car; his wife is executed; war is lost; violence; reunited with her mother after a four-year separation; eye surgery; son/daughter marries; book published; catches his wife with another man; mother dies; has a horror of drink; saving his salary; first plays the role that will establish his fame; boxing; rioting; starts investigating astrology.
 Occidental Mercury to Mars at night in septenary: defeated; planting trees; reading frantically; frees his slaves; moves; founds a shipyard; editing crime novels; his energetic persistence & organizing talent are recognized; quits his job; immigrates; children born; crosses the Rockies in a covered wagon; discharged from army; angers a friend; goes to college; bronchitis.

Mercury comes to Jupiter
(47% positive)

The ease with which a person expresses his thoughts in speech or writing is likely to improve this year. As a result his ideas can become more widely known. He may travel. Business is likely to improve, studies should be successful and exams passed. The individual will want to expand his knowledge and skills, and he may decide to attend evening classes or take a correspondence course. He is likely to become interested in religious, spiritual and philosophical matters. Children are born or he marries. Some difficulties with those in authority may occur. All Mercury matters should do well this year. Failures, if any, will come from his over optimism, negligence or clumsiness. There may also be concern over the education of children.

Even so, the years when Mercury comes to Jupiter were not particularly positive ones for many of the people in the sample. But then Mercury and Jupiter have never been bosom chums. As planets they rule opposing signs and as gods they opposed each other, apparently dividing pre-Christian Europe into two opposing factions: Jupiter as Zeus was the chief god in lands around the Mediterranean, while Mercury as Woden held sway in the northern countries. Perhaps this is why the native may have more than usual problems with his friends this year.

Table ☿-13:   ☿ – ♃ **Interaction**

Mercury-Jupiter Interaction	Oriental ♃		Occidental ♃		All	
	N	% Positive	N	% Positive	N	% Positive
Oriental ☿	37	46.5	37	53.8	74	50.1
Occidental ☿	23	55.1	36	35.2	59	42.9
All	*60*	*49.7*	*73*	*44.6*	*133*	*46.9*

Persons in the sample born with both Mercury and Jupiter occidental at the same time had difficulties this year, especially when born at night.

Table ☿-12: **☿ to ♃: % Positive Years**

Planets relative to the ☉	Day birth		Night birth		All	
	N	% Positive	N	% Positive	N	% Positive
Oriental ☿	42	51.6	32	48.0	74	50.1
Occidental ☿	23	47.2	36	40.1	59	42.9
All	65	50.1	68	43.9	133	46.9
Oriental ♃	26	52.2	34	47.8	60	49.7
Occidental ♃	39	48.6	34	39.9	73	44.6

Some examples in my sample of Mercury coming to Jupiter in the decan:

Oriental Mercury to Jupiter by day in decan: *wins Nobel Prize; reduced in rank for disobeying orders; astronomy interest; retires; moves; announces that he has AIDS; book published; buys an Arabian horse; death.*

Occidental Mercury to Jupiter by day in decan: *espousing pacifism; improved finances; deep depression; her book wins a prize.*

Oriental Mercury to Jupiter at night in decan: *negotiating divorce settlement; hurt when he is ignored; double pneumonia; brings mother to USA; his horse wins the Grand National; lectures; sister born; son born.*

Occidental Mercury to Jupiter at night in decan: *works as a nursemaid; sells her first articles; sister dies; stops attending church; promoted; leaves home; decides his marriage was a serious spiritual mistake; passes exams; passes her driving test; his work is criticized; publishes almanac; death.*

Some examples in my sample of Mercury coming to Jupiter in the septenary:

Oriental Mercury to Jupiter by day in septenary: *working shorter hours; tells press of prison brutality; captures all of his opponent's treasure; his visa to go to South Africa is denied because of his skin color; rejected for jobs because of his prison record; attends Sufi retreat; reprimanded for willful behavior & disrupting a school outing.*

Occidental Mercury to Jupiter by day in septenary: *fascinated by magic; his ship hits a rock, forced to abandon it in a lifeboat; writes on the preordained failure of man's quest for happiness; she is 'The Lady Nobody Loves'; his feet & thighs are swollen with water-dropsy; emigrates to USA; lobbies for better pay & working conditions; rejected for Nobel Prize.*

Oriental Mercury to Jupiter at night in septenary: *studying; unhappy at school; graduates; meets future wife; elopes; hit by taxi; in prison; retires; tax problems; in a black depression; shows himself to be a 'born snob'; makes persuasive speeches; father has two operations.*

Occidental Mercury to Jupiter at night in septenary: *gets a recording contract; unpleasant evenings in society; loses libel trial; living in the house of a malevolent witch; his employer goes bankrupt; wins prize for musical composition; receiving occult training; her father flees the country; publishes satires.*

Mercury comes to Saturn
(49% positive)

This is likely to be a serious year in which the individual's luck can appear to have deserted him. It is as if a black cloud hangs permanently over his head. There are likely to be few successes and little happiness. His intellect is narrowed now, concentrated on only a few specific subjects, his mind filled with forebodings and grief. There can be separations, the family may be broken up, and he may live alone and be separated from his children. His parents may become sick and needy; his siblings may be disgraced. Others will criticize his beliefs and he may come to doubt himself and become pessimistic. There can be troubles with foreigners. He may pass or fail exams or interviews; it depends on whether or not he is prepared, ready for them. If unprepared, he may be humiliated. He may change his job and be taught an older way of doing things. This is a year in which a person is likely to experience Saturn matters whether these are pleasant like ice skating or skiing, or more soul-searing experiences such as loneliness, abandonment or death. It is unlikely to be a period in which his wealth, his income or his investments prosper. Instead, his very survival may depend on the charity of others.

Table ☿-14:   ☿ to ♄: % Positive Years

Planets relative to the ☉	Day birth		Night birth		All	
	N	% Positive	N	% Positive	N	% Positive
Oriental ☿	46	47.2	38	55.2	84	49.5
Occidental ☿	23	47.2	39	48.6	62	48.1
All	69	47.2	77	50.5	146	48.9
Oriental ♄	40	42.9	39	48.6	79	45.8
Occidental ♄	29	53.0	38	55.2	67	52.6

By tradition Saturn is more beneficial when located to the west of the Sun. This happened in the sample. The most difficult years occurred when occidental Mercury came to an oriental Saturn.

Table ☿-15:   ☿ –♄ Interaction

Mercury-Saturn Interaction	Oriental ♄		Occidental ♄		All	
	N	% Positive	N	% Positive	N	% Positive
Oriental ☿	50	52.4	34	45.2	84	49.5
Occidental ☿	29	34.3	33	60.3	62	48.1
All	79	45.8	67	52.6	146	48.9

Some examples in my sample of Mercury coming to Saturn in the decan:

Oriental Mercury to Saturn by day in decan: *seriously ill; arrested; wounded in the arm; marries; daughter born; quarrels; becomes a professor; estranged from his father; his wife dies; death.*

Occidental Mercury to Saturn by day in decan: *his ideas are now fashionable; travels; forced to reduce the size of her printing business; his writings are being translated; happy.*

Oriental Mercury to Saturn at night in decan: *marries; his wife is ill; he & his wife separate; brother dies; financial problems; elected; accused of corruption, but vindicated; writing his autobiography; becomes a professor.*

Occidental Mercury to Saturn at night in decan: *fights with her mother; mother dies; always tired; studying for the priesthood; records his personal faults; fantasizing; graduates.*

Some examples in my sample of Mercury coming to Saturn in the septenary:

Oriental Mercury to Saturn by day in septenary: *beaten by drunken nurse; moves; concentrated studies; runs a youth club; founds a science think tank; his vaccines save many lives in epidemic; patents his invention; has a feeling of grievance all year; buys new home; in a love triangle; profound religious experience; submits false reports; disillusioned; inherits title; learns to skate.*

Occidental Mercury to Saturn by day in septenary: *his dream of wealth is shattered; rethinks her policies; writing as if possessed; writes daily love letters; edits magazine; fears he will die within a year; in solitary confinement; when symptoms are talked out, his patient is cured; resigns as pastor; resolves never to back down again; rheumatoid arthritis; lead poisoning; assassinated.*

Oriental Mercury to Saturn at night in septenary: *abandoned by his mother; returns home after long stay abroad; sister dies in air crash; his brother dies; marries; his wife has an affair; never idle; studying; publishes architecture magazine; depressed; absconds to avoid arrest; shocked to see how the poor live; wins fencing championship.*

Occidental Mercury to Saturn at night in septenary: *wife/daughter/aunt dies; denunciations; husband is drowned; she is cursed by her father; fails interview; argues against free will; exiled; life on the run; very sick; climbing in Himalayas; large gains in commodity market; becomes very anxious; conscripted into army.*

Mercury comes to Uranus
(50% positive)

A sudden inspiration may awaken the individual's mind this year, and his ability to think and to assimilate will be transformed by new ideas, new discoveries, trips and exciting new knowledge. He will want to share these new discoveries and ideas, and to do so he will spend much time talking and writing. There is a danger that all this fresh and exciting new stimuli will overwhelm him and that he will experience difficulty consolidating the sudden spurt of new ideas into an objective whole. For the year to be fully successful, the individual needs to relax and be patient and flexible.

Accidents and other unexpected problems can occur while traveling. Children may leave home or otherwise display their independence. The individual's financial situation is likely to become extremely volatile, and this can cause much worry. Problems will be encountered if he attempts to do too much in too great a hurry. In the sample occidental Mercury was associated with a high percent of positive years.

Table ☿-16: ☿ to ♅: **% Positive Years**

Planets relative to the ☉	Day birth		Night birth		All	
	N	% Positive	N	% Positive	N	% Positive
Oriental ☿	13	48.6	13	34.8	26	41.8
Occidental ☿	5	54.2	12	67.8	17	63.8
All	*18*	*50.3*	*25*	*50.6*	*43*	*50.5*
Oriental ♅	10	45.2	14	45.2	24	45.2
Occidental ♅	8	56.5	11	57.5	19	57.1

Some examples in my sample of Mercury coming to Uranus in the decan:
Oriental Mercury to Uranus by day: *becomes president/CIA director; first book is published; threatened by lover's husband; surrounded by turbulence & war; initiated into a secret revolutionary society; places all 23 years of published magazines on web to be freely downloaded; malignant melanoma removed; emphysema; tonsillectomy; stops smoking; death.*
Occidental Mercury to Uranus by day: *starts a lesbian love affair; German measles; yachting; studies thermodynamics; death of pen friend.*
Oriental Mercury to Uranus by night: *self-conceited, his success goes to his head; concussion; unfortunate attachment to a girl who turns out to be completely selfish & an unscrupulous liar; first bicycle; publicly admits to adultery; arrested; makes several mathematical discoveries; graduates; builds a house; argues for a national bank; marries.*
Occidental Mercury to Uranus by night: *thought to be stupid & punished for being unable to learn; she is matured by accepting a demanding acting role in the face of much hostility; promoted; said to have a remarkable aura; becomes a Freemason; lonely; marries an older man; works as a laborer; father is permanently ill; studying for the priesthood; moves to New Zealand & joins orchestra; first learns astrology; one of the best years of his life.*

Mercury comes to Neptune
(54% positive)

Fantasy and make belief can take over the life now, which can make the year positive for actors, poets, musicians and those involved in spiritual or psychic matters, but is unlikely to be helpful for people in more down-to-earth situations, who may simply become confused and lack clarity. There is the danger that the native by overindulging in mythologizing will lose his sense of reality, deceive himself and neglect his work. His schemes may be fanciful, his ideas and conversation unpopular, and his friends are likely to avoid any discussion of these ideas, and perhaps even ridicule him behind his back. It is not a good time for making important decisions that could alter his life.

Table ☿-17:   **☿ to ♆: % Positive Years**

Planets relative to the ☉	Day birth		Night birth		All	
	N	% Positive	N	% Positive	N	% Positive
Oriental ☿	12	67.8	11	49.3	23	59.0
Occidental ☿	5	36.2	19	52.4	24	49.0
All	17	58.5	30	51.3	47	53.9
Oriental ♆	8	67.8	15	42.2	23	51.1
Occidental ♆	9	50.3	15	60.3	24	56.5

The observations in Table ☿-17 are too few for the values in it to be relied upon.

Some examples in my sample of Mercury coming to Neptune in the decan:
Oriental Mercury to Neptune by day: *divorce; financially independent; writing his memoirs; joins the navy; promoted; becomes a Hegalian; passes exams; solves astronomical problem; brain surgery; found to have AIDS.*
Occidental Mercury to Neptune by day: *honorary doctorate; his wide dies; first speaks on radio; cancer of the palate; ill from seasickness pills; botched operation.*
Oriental Mercury to Neptune by night: *experiences an extraordinary physical & spiritual transformation; preoccupied by the past; first exhibits his paintings; wins scholarship; unsure of his future; falls in love; caught up in a riot; feels trapped; marries; brother dies; has a wretched home life; depressed; acute insomnia & paranoia; fractures shoulder; smashes left arm in a fall*
Occidental Mercury to Neptune by night: *he is a prisoner of war; his system of philosophy is publicly condemned; re-elected to senate; becomes president; heart attack; solitary; studying history; she is rejected as a nurse & then by a man; inherits property on death of uncle; declares his independence; reading poetry; elected a Masonic Grand Master; erotic longings; has a loving relationship with a substitute mother; goes to Tibet.*

Mercury comes to Pluto
(57% positive)

New ways to understanding will be explored now. The individual experiencing this direction may become something of a maverick, rather antisocial, rebelling against the usual way that things get done. As his perceptions are likely to be sharpened and he is concerned with discovering the correct facts about whatever fascinates him, this it is a good year for undertaking any form of research that attempts to get at the truth. A career change is possible. Unless Pluto is afflicted or located in Pisces or Sagittarius the native should be able to influence others and get them to see his point of view.

This can also be a time of opposing proselytizing, at the same time that the individual is trying to persuade others, they may be attempting to get him to convert to their way of seeing things. Those employed in any form of advertising can be very successful now. Nervous troubles and a tendency to be obsessive are potential dangers. The individual needs to be receptive to other viewpoints without becoming too impressionable and pliant.

Table ☿-18: ☿ to ♇: % Positive Years

Planets relative to the ☉	Day birth		Night birth		All	
	N	% Positive	N	% Positive	N	% Positive
Oriental ☿	9	50.3	11	49.3	20	49.7
Occidental ☿	4	45.2	14	71.1	18	65.3
All	*13*	*43.6*	*25*	*61.5*	*38*	*57.1*
Oriental ♇	5	54.2	13	55.6	18	55.2
Occidental ♇	8	45.2	12	67.8	20	58.8

Mercury to occidental Pluto for a night birth stands out as looking quite promising, but the number of observations is far too few for it to be considered meaningful.

Some examples in my sample of Mercury coming to Pluto in the decan:
Oriental Mercury to Pluto by day: *becomes a pacifist; discovers function that mediates between consciousness & the unconscious; in prison; banned from public speaking; his theory that the sun rotates is confirmed; surgery for cancer; great financial panic;*
Occidental Mercury to Pluto by day: *daughter dies; preoccupied with not starving; son released from POW; his mind is unsettled & his memory confused;*
Oriental Mercury to Pluto at night: *his wife & mother both die on the same day; sister divorces & remarries; newspapers obtain taped phone conversations he had with his mistress; sets up a printing shop; fails to persuade people to act as he wants; incompatible marriage; becomes self-employed; hyperactive; wins law suit; death.*

Occidental Mercury to Pluto at night*: loses presidential election; extensive travels; hitchhiking about Europe; in his first battles; works in telephone exchange; becomes state's official printer; studies languages; founds a debating society; buys a motorbike; lonely, unhappy & bored; works as a laborer; avoids military service; learns to say "No"; fights off a robbery attack; has his first girl friend; parents divorce; attends a slave auction; eradicating his enemies.*

Carl Jung's first Mercury-ruled Septenary

Mercury in Cancer rises: The psychologist Carl Jung is a diurnal birth, with Mercury to the east of his Sun. Mercury is in the sixth house, conjunct Venus, sextile the exalted Moon, exactly sesquiquadrate the midheaven and semisextile Uranus. His Mercury-ruled septenary begins in 1889 when he is 14. Decan Neptune is on his Uranus in Leo. His father, as if giving all in his power to give, gives Carl the money to ride the train up the Rigi mountain. On top of the mountain there is a moment of initiation in a great natural temple.

Mercury directed to the Moon in Taurus: Septenary Mercury is on its dispositor in 1890 when he is 15 years old. As the second year of the septenary, this is a time when he can expect resistance from the past. Decan Neptune has come to his Sun in Leo, which it tightly squares. His parents try to discover the profession he intends to pursue. The strong family tradition is the priesthood, but he does not want to do this. His father agrees that he shouldn't. The same year he has his first communion and is disappointed when nothing startling happens; he feels it is a hollow event. He is reading books to find out what is known about God, and feels all that he reads is nonsense. He feels pity for his parson father, who has fallen victim of the mumbo-jumbo. At his mother's suggestion he reads Goethe's *Faust*. In it he finds "confirmation that there were or had

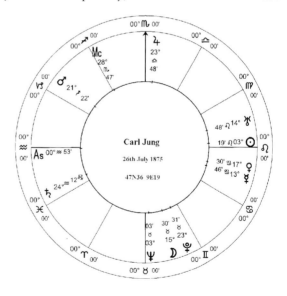

been people who saw evil and its universal power and—more important—the mysterious role in delivering man from darkness and suffering." The book has a great and lasting influence on him. At school he is nicknamed "Father Abraham." On one occasion seven boys ambush him. "I suddenly saw red, seized one of the boys by both arms, swung him around me and with his legs knocked several of the others to the ground." When he is accused of cheating in class, he becomes furious. He is happiest in the country, especially in the woods, away from the town.

Mercury directed to Saturn in Aquarius: Carl Jung is sixteen years old in 1891 when septenary Mercury comes to his Saturn. It is the third year of the septenary. During it some feelings of inadequacy are often felt. Decan Neptune is on his Venus. He is systematically reading philosophy, a subject not taught at his school. He then writes a brief introduction of the history of philosophy, which enables him to gain a bird's eye view of the subject.

Mercury directed to Mars in Sagittarius: Septenary Mercury is on Jung's Mars in 1892 when he is 17. This is the fourth year of the septenary, a time when choices often need to be made. The decan ruler Neptune is on his Mercury in Cancer. There is an emphasis on Mercury in both septenary and decan, with Mercury being directed to a sign where it is unwelcome. He changes from being timid to knowing what he wants and going after it. He becomes more accessible and communicative, and makes more and better friends. However, when he begins speaking openly about his ideas, this meets with hostile rejection. There is much fantasizing this year. His father, who is suffering from religious doubts, has become irritable and discontented. He and Carl have a number of rather vehement and fruitless discussions.

Mercury directed to Jupiter in Libra: Carl Jung has septenary Mercury on his Jupiter in 1893 when he is 18, in the fifth year of the septenary. In this year the keynote of the septenary is often revealed. Decan Neptune is on Pluto in Taurus. At school he is reprimanded for willful behavior and participating in the disruption of a school outing. He tries to help his parson father directly reach God but finds him to be hopelessly entrapped by the Church and its theological thinking. He dreams that he holds a tiny light cupped in

his hands, and he is going slowly forward against a mighty wind. Behind him is a gigantic black figure. He goes on. He recognizes the light as his consciousness and the black figure as his shadow, personality number Two. A schism takes place between him and his number Two, the "I" becoming assigned to personality number One. As a result of this dream, he decides that at university he would study science (medicine) rather than his natural interests of philosophy or history. He thus forsakes the strong family tradition of priesthood.

Mercury directed to the Sun in Leo: Carl Jung's septenary Mercury comes to his Sun when he is 19 in 1894. It is the sixth year of the seven; the time when what is implied in the septenary is expected to bear fruit. Decan Neptune is on his Moon in Taurus. He passes his university entrance exams and enrolls in the medical faculty at Basel University, where he becomes an enthusiastic student, joining the student fraternity and attending their weekly meetings. He is humiliated when his father is forced to apply to the university for a stipend to pay for the education. His father is unwell, complaining of having 'stones in his abdomen'.

Mercury directed to Venus in Cancer: Carl Jung is 20 when his father dies. Septenary Mercury has come to his Venus in this final year of the seven; Mercury and Venus are conjunct in Cancer in the 6th house at his birth. The decan Moon in Taurus is rising. It is a gloomy and painful time. Twice, soon after the death, Carl dreams of his father coming home after having been away on holiday. There are financial problems, and the family is forced to vacate the parsonage and move. He obtains loans to continue his studies at the university, and earns some money from being appointed a junior assistant in anatomy. He becomes fascinated by psychic phenomena and attends séances. He is reading Nietzsche.

Carl Jung's second Mercury-Ruled Septenary

Mercury in Cancer rises: In 1938 septenary Mercury rises for the second time in Jung's life. He is now 63 years old. The decan Sun is on his Pluto in Taurus. In a magazine interview that year he depicts Hitler as a kind of medicine man or shaman, who reflects the unconscious of the Germans. The same year he receives an honorary doctorate at Oxford University; is the editor of a psychological journal; and studies alchemical texts.

Mercury directed to the Moon in Taurus: In 1939 Jung's septenary Mercury again comes to his Moon. He is now 64. Decan Sun is also on his Moon; the double emphasis on the exalted Moon indicating that this will be a memorable year. His old colleague and rival Sigmund Freud dies; Jung writes an obituary. The Second World War begins and he moves his family and grandchildren into the mountains. His son Franz is away from home in the army. He resigns from the chair of the International Society for Psychotherapy and stands as a candidate for the Swiss national assembly, but is not elected. He has a vision of Christ with a body of greenish gold, which he understands to show the analogy of Christ with the philosopher's gold of alchemy.

Mercury directed to Saturn in Aquarius: Jung is 65 in 1940 when the septenary Mercury comes for the second time to his Saturn. The Sun is on Neptune in his decan. As the Sun and Neptune were in a close square at Jung's birth, events in this year can be expected to bring out much of what this aspect symbolizes in his life. The world is at war and Jung feels as helpless as if living in a prison. Throughout the year the religious aspect is magnified in life and, appropriate for septenary Mercury being on his Saturn, he writes about it even though much that he has to say proves to be unpopular. His book *Psychology and Religion* is published; it irritates many who read it. He decides that the Trinity needs a fourth principle—either the feminine or one of darkness or evil—for totality; and he writes *A*

Psychological Approach to the Dogma of the Trinity. This year he also writes *Essays on a Science of Mythology*. Finally, excited by an essay on the Aegean Festival in Goethe's Faust, he starts work on *Mysterium Coniunctionis*, which will be his last great work.

Mercury directed to Mars in Sagittarius: Septenary Mercury again came to Mars in 1941 when Jung was 66. Europe is at war. He lectures on the *Transformation Symbolism in the Mass*, and for the 400th anniversary of the death of Paracelsus gives a paper on *Paracelsus the Physician*. He discusses alchemy as a form of religious philosophy. Decan Sun is on Jung's Saturn in Aquarius. Both Mercury and the Sun have come to signs in which they are in detriment.

Mercury directed to Jupiter in Libra: In 1942 septenary Mercury again comes to Jupiter. Jung is 67 and the decan Sun is on his Mars in Sagittarius. Europe is at war. He is forced into cutting down trees for fuel, and has dug a large potato patch to supplement the family food supply. He is also studying alchemy and writing *Psychology and Alchemy*. He is no doubt feeling the affect of his septenary ruler, as for his annual Eranos lecture he chooses as his subject *The Spirit Mercurios*. Prior to delivering this lecture he has several dreams concerning Mercury. He feels his anima is moved and "seized by Mercury, the spirit of life."

Mercury directed to the Sun in Leo: Mercury again comes to Jung's Sun in 1943 when he is 68. The decan Sun is on his Jupiter in Libra. By its involvement in both septenary and decan, the emphasis this year is on Jung's Sun, and this could be difficult, as the decan Sun has come to the sign of its fall. Europe is at war. He is named Professor-in-ordinary of psychology at Basel University. He is having difficulty writing *Mysterium Coniunctionis*, which concerns the unification of opposites, the problem of the masculine and feminine halves of the self, of psychic integration and maturity. It will become the most important work of his later years. He slips on the snow, falls and breaks his foot. A heart attack follows and he is on the edge of death for several weeks. In his autobiography he describes having peak mystical experiences while in a state of deep unconsciousness, deliriums and unexpectedly grandiose visions. His doctor dies shortly before he recovers; in his vision the same doctor requested that Jung not die and offers his own life in exchange. Only after this illness does he understand how important it is to affirm one's destiny. "Only then is an ego forged that will endure, that can cope with the world and fate." He abandons his university teaching duties after this heart attack. We see the inherent meaning of the Sun here in Jung's words.

Mercury directed to Venus in Cancer: In 1944 Jung is aged 69 when septenary Mercury comes to Venus for the second time. It is the final year of the Mercury-ruled septenary. Decan Sun is on his Uranus in Leo, which should produce a positive year. He is recovering his health after the serious heart attack of the previous year, full of ideas and plans but unable to make much physical effort and only able to work two hours daily at his desk. He is writing *Mysterium Coniunctionis*, which will establish the historical foundation of his psychology. Basel University names him professor of Medical Psychology. He publishes *Psychology and Alchemy*, which describes alchemy as a form of religious philosophy.

Carl Jung's Mercury-ruled Decan

Mercury in Cancer rises: In the decan Jung's Mercury rises in 1915 when he is 40. Septenary Jupiter is at Saturn in Aquarius—the two are in an exact trine at his birth. The First World War began a few months earlier. Jung is experiencing a midlife crisis. He cannot read a scientific book and is instead intensely preoccupied with the images of his own unconscious. He feels suspended in mid air, without a footing, humiliated and completely helpless. These trials of his unconscious will continue for several years.

Mercury directed to Pluto in Taurus: In 1916 Jung is 41 when decan Mercury comes to his Pluto. This is the second year of the decan, a time when interests are often redirected. Septenary Jupiter has come to Sagittarius, a sign it rules, to the place of his Mars. The senseless slaughter known as World War One is happening in the world outside Switzerland. He is restless. In his house he feels an ominous atmosphere all around him, a strong feeling of oppression. A regular haunting begins, his daughters independently see ghosts. "The whole house was filled as if there were a crowd present, crammed full of spirits. They were packed deep right up to the door and the air was so thick it was scarcely possible to breathe" He feels an inner need to put the flood of images and thoughts into literary and artistic form and starts writing *Seven Sermons to the Dead*. As soon as he "took up the pen the whole ghostly assemblage evaporated." He has an inner urge to sketch and paint mandalas and is intensely preoccupied with the images of his own unconscious. The stream of fantasies he has been experiencing begin to die down. He is now able to view them objectively, to reflect on the whole experience, and begins to discern the  workings of a function that serves to mediate between consciousness and the unconscious, the so-called transcendent function, which forms a bridge between the rational and the irrational. It is an energy that springs from the tensions of opposites. In the same year he forms the Psychological Club of Zurich; writes *The Transcendent Function*, in which he first mentions the method of active imagination; writes an article on the relations between the ego and the unconscious; writes *The Structure of the Unconscious*; writes the preface to his *Collected Papers on Analytical Psychology*; and becomes a Medical Corps doctor and the commandant of an internment camp for British troops.

Mercury directed to the Moon in Taurus: Mercury gets to its dispositor in 1917, in the third year of the decan. He is 42. Septenary Mars is rising. He is serving as a Medical Corps doctor and the commandant of an internment camp for British troops. He sketches mandalas every morning.

Mercury directed to Neptune in Taurus: Jung is 43 when decan Mercury comes to Neptune in 1918. This fourth year of the decan is very important as all that follows in the remaining years of the decan tends to depend on how the two planets involved in the decan now combine and what is manifested this year. Septenary Mars is on his Jupiter in Libra, a sign in which Mars is weakened. He is serving as a Medical Corps doctor and the commandant of an internment camp for British troops. He sketches mandalas every morning. After the peace treaty that ends the war, in a dream he sees Germany consumed in a rain of fire, with this connected to "the key year of 1940". He starts studying Gnostic writings, a study that will continue for many years.

Mercury directed to Saturn in Aquarius: Decan Mercury comes to Jung's Saturn in 1919, when he is 44. This fifth year of the decan is often one in which the individual goes off in an entirely new direction and encounters new experiences. Septenary Mars has arrived at his Sun in Leo. He visits London and then goes to Tunisia. He is briefly in the desert. His encounter with Arabic culture strikes him with overwhelming force. He feels the Arabs have had a static, age-old existence, and that their eternity will inevitably be chopped by the god of time into the bits and pieces of hours, minutes and seconds, their life tempo becoming accelerated, just as the European's is already. Jung is ill for several days from infectious enteritis, and then continues his studies of Gnostic writings.

Mercury directed to Mars in Sagittarius: Decan Mercury comes to Mars, his septenary ruler, when Jung is 45 in 1920, in the sixth year of the decan, the year in which an entirely new impulse often appears. Septenary Mars is on his Venus in Cancer. Both rulers are in signs in which they are unwelcome, and Mars is emphasized by the two methods. He writes *Psychological Types*—his first writing in seven years—in which he differentiates between the introvert and the extrovert, saying there are two rational types, the thinking and the feeling, and two irrational ones, sensation and intuition. He writes that every judgment an individual makes is conditioned by his personality type and that every point of view is necessarily relative—astrologers will understand that Jung was groping his way to an ancient truth.

Mercury directed to Jupiter in Libra: In 1921 when Jung is 46 his book *Psychological Types* is published. His decan Mercury is on his Jupiter, and his septenary Mars is on his Mercury in Cancer. This time it is the septenary ruler that comes to his decan ruler, with Jung's Mercury emphasized by the two methods. The seventh year of the decan often rebalances any instability that may have occurred in the previous year. Throughout the year he studies Gnostic writings.

Mercury directed to Uranus in Leo: In 1922 Jung is 47. In the eighth year of his decan, which should contain a new beginning, Mercury arrives at his Uranus. Septenary Mars is on his Moon in Taurus, a sign in which Mars is harmed. His mother dies. He purchases land at Bollingen on upper Lake Zurich, and with two assistants starts to build a simple house with a tower. This house will grow as he grows. He continues his studies of Gnostic writings.

Mercury directed to the Sun in Leo: Decan Mercury comes to Jung's Sun in 1923 when he is aged 48. It is the ninth year of the decan and should contain all that has been accomplished in the decan. Septenary Mars is on his Saturn in Aquarius. He completes building his tower at Bollingen and spends much time there alone. He feels an intense feeling of repose and renewal when he is there. It represents to him the maternal hearth. He continues to study Gnostic writings throughout this year.

Mercury directed to Venus in Cancer: Jung's decan Mercury comes to Venus in 1924 when he is 49. It is the final year of his decan. Septenary Saturn has arrived at the ascendant. He goes to the USA, visiting Chicago and the Grand Canyon, and then Taos in New Mexico, where he visits the settlements of the Pueblo Indians. The Indians' criticism of white men in general—they think with their heads and not with their hearts—startles him, and opens up a new understanding. He realizes that what Europeans had called the spread of civilization, colonization, the many missions to the heathen, and so on, has another face, the face of a bird of prey seeking with cruel intentness for distant quarry. All the eagles and the other predatory creatures that adorn our coats of arms are apt psychological representatives of the white man's true nature. He is also impressed by the Indians' natural mysticism. He has never before encountered such an atmosphere of secrecy about religion. For the Indians, their religious concepts are not theories but facts. To them the sun *is* God. Jung "...recognized on what the 'dignity,' the tranquil composure of the individual Indian, was founded. It springs from his being a son of the sun; his life is cosmologically meaningful, for he helps the father and preserver of all life in his daily rise and descent. If we set against this our own self-justifications, the meaning of our own lives as it is formulated by our reason, we cannot help but see our poverty. Out of sheer envy we are obliged to smile at the Indians' naïveté and to plume ourselves on our cleverness; for otherwise we would discover how impoverished and down at heels we are. Knowledge does not enrich us; it removes us more and more from the mythic world in which we were once at home by right of birth." Returning to Zurich he holds a seminar in which, for the first time, he uses autobiographical material. He continues his study of Gnostic writings, and has a series of dreams about an unknown wing of his house that contains a wonderful library of volumes.

Thomas Paine's Mercury-ruled Septenary

Here lies the body of John Crow.
Who once was high but now is low.
Ye brother Crows take warning all
For as you rise, so must you fall.

With the above words, written when he was just eight years old, Paine gave warning of his lifelong contempt for hubris and disdain for servility; in an age of corrupt governments manned by sycophants, he pointedly called George III "Mad-jesty". In scornful style, Paine satirized corruption caused by unaccounted power. He aimed his quill at the indignity of poverty, the ugliness of war, uncurbed markets and greedy banks; and did all he could to prevent governments from abusing the rights of citizens. He rejected all examples of hereditary elitism and was horrified at any form of racial or ethnic segregation. From the principle that the earth is common to all he concluded that the most vulnerable in society, especially the very young and the very old, should have a guaranteed right to a fair share of its wealth.

The author of the three best-selling books of the 18th and early 19th centuries, Paine championed clean, open and humble government. His lifelong devotion to the cause of liberty for all, his brave and unshrinking advocacy of truth in politics, and his deep-seated dislike of kingship and priestly tyranny, all guarantee that he should be forever remembered. That underlines his scandalous treatment; especially by political and religious bigots who dreamed of dangling him from a gibbet, had him publicly burned in effigy, and only failed in their efforts for him to die at the guillotine when his sentence was mistakenly chalked on the wrong side of his cell door. Since his death the supporters of the mad king's descendants and mindless Christian sectarians have continued to damn him; to accuse him of seditious libel and to condemn him as a "filthy little atheist" (Teddy Roosevelt's infamous words). Paine's bones are lost, but memories of his brilliant achievements survive.

During Carl Jung's long life he experienced the Mercury-ruled septenary twice and also the affect of its decan. By contrast, Thomas Paine experienced Mercury ruling his septenary just the one time and he never did feel the affect of Mercury as the ruler of a decan. Yet what occurred in his Mercury septenary had a major effect on his life and it was directly instrumental in changing history on two continents.

Mercury in Pisces rises: The same year that Mercury assumes rulership of Paine's septenary the decan ruler Neptune comes to the place of natal Mercury. This is an important indication that his Mercury-ruled septenary will be especially important in his life. Neptune in Gemini is close to the IC, and connects a grand trine to a T-cross. It forms the grand trine with Jupiter in Aquarius and Pluto retrograding at the start of Scorpio. The T-cross is made up of Venus in Aries squaring the Neptune-Uranus opposition. Mercury is in

Paine's 12th house, in Pisces, exactly sextile to the Midheaven and square to the Moon-Saturn conjunction in Gemini in the 3rd house.

The emphasis on Mercury this year can be expected to prompt matters indicated by its house to become emphasized in the life. The 12th house relates primarily to the services we provide for others, or, if you prefer, what occurs when we are subservient to the whims of others (serving time in prison, detained in hospital, acting as a public servant). As the houses above the horizon correspond in the outside world to the more self-regarding and private nature of houses below the horizon, so the inherent meaning of the 12th house is to externally complement the 6th house, which in turn relates to the services others (our servants, our employees, even our bodies) provide for us. In a basic sense Mercury means the exchange of information and the planet's location in the 12th house tells us that this communication is likely to occur in the service of or for the benefit of the public.

In 1772, when Mercury becomes septenary ruler at the same time that Neptune has come to Mercury in the decan, Paine is a 35-year-old Excise Officer stationed in Lewes a country town eight miles from the south coast of England. It is not an easy assignment, for the southeast beaches are popular with tobacco, tea, gin, brandy, and silk smugglers. The previous year he had married and he and his wife are managing a grocery shop. He is also a member of the local Headstrong Club, the members of which meet regularly to argue over local and national affairs. It is there that Paine has discovered a love for debating and he is a popular figure in the town.

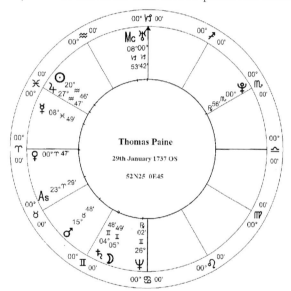

Thomas Paine
29th January 1737 OS
52N25 0E45

That year excise men, who are treated with contempt by every level of British society, decide that their financial condition has become unbearable. They resolve to act and choose Paine to represent them, to ask for some addition to their salaries. He drafts a petition *The Case of the Officers of Excise* that his fellows accept as well presenting their case. Each taxman throughout the country is persuaded to contribute enough to print four thousand copies of the petition and to cover Paine's costs of traveling to London to present their case.

Mercury directed to Jupiter in Aquarius: The following year 1773 Paine is in London waiting for a final decision from the government on the case, having to take jobs as a private tutor after the money from his fellow taxmen is exhausted. His Mercury is now on its dispositor, the 11th house Jupiter in Aquarius, and the decan ruler Neptune has also arrived at Jupiter. The emphasis on Jupiter suggests Paine will come into contact with persons of a higher social status. Paine sends a copy of his petition to the playwright Oliver Goldsmith, and meets with and befriends the historian Edward Gibbon, author Samuel Johnson, and the agent for the colonies, Benjamin Franklin, all of whom are strong believers in meritocracy and willing to ignore Paine's low social status when he proves to them that his opinions are worth hearing. Back in Lewes the grocery business, run by his wife in his absence, is going bankrupt.

Mercury directed to the Sun in Aquarius: Paine is 37 years old in 1774 the year that both of Paine's time rulers, Mercury and Neptune, are directed to his Sun in Aquarius One of the basic meanings of the Sun is the king—and a Sun that is weakened in Aquarius says this is a needful king. Sure enough, the king of England asks Parliament to increase his own annual stipend by another hundred thousand pounds, and Paine's efforts on behalf of the poor taxmen, like much else, are rejected as the inept government scrambles to keep the

monarch happy. Paine's long absence from his post without official leave has the Board of Excise relieve him of his duties. He is in danger of arrest for debt. His household furniture and the shop's stock are auctioned off to pay his debts. Paine and his wife separate—the Sun's primary demand is that the native should become independent in order to follow his destiny. Benjamin Franklin suggests he leave England and go to America, writing letters of introduction for him. By the end of the year Paine is several thousand miles away from the scenes of his year's utter failure; he has arrived in Philadelphia.

Mercury directed to the Moon in Gemini: With Paine's Moon in Mercury's own sign of Gemini, Mercury's direction to it in 1775 should produce a positive year. In the decan Neptune has come to Uranus in Capricorn. The position of Uranus close to his Midheaven suggests it could bring him to prominence. In Philadelphia Paine quickly befriends a printer, Robert Aitken, who likes him enough to give him a job as editor of the about-to-appear *Pennsylvania Magazine*. It is the perfect job for him and he is an immediate success. The magazine thrives. It quickly becomes important at the heart of colonial life. People pay attention to what Paine writes. His article attacking slavery inspires the founding of the first abolitionist organization in the Americas. Another article, "Thoughts on Defensive War" responds to the Quakers who do not support any revolt against the British throne. Then Paine sits down and writes his stirring *Common Sense*. The pro-independence pamphlet will have the greatest impact on American history of any piece of writing, more so even than *Uncle Tom's Cabin*, and make him the bestselling author of the 18ᵗʰ century. The initial copies are printed two weeks before his next birthday.

Mercury directed to Saturn in Gemini: It is 1776 and *Common Sense* is read everywhere. In it Paine proclaims the benefits of American independence before anyone else is brave enough to speak of such matters in public. He will donate all income from this best seller to the war effort. Suddenly he is internationally famous. Mercury is now on Saturn but still in its own sign of Gemini. In Paine's decan Neptune has come to Pluto in Scorpio. He is 39 years old and overnight he is recognized as a sage. Sadly he fails in his attempt to have an anti-slavery clause included in that summer's Declaration of Independence that his pamphlet inspired. He enlists in the rebel army, helps frame the constitution of Pennsylvania, and, at a time when the rebels are regularly being defeated by the better equipped and trained British army, inspires them to continue their fight by writing the first of his sixteen pamphlets entitled *The American Crisis*: "These are times that try man's souls. The summer soldier and the sunshine patriot will, in this crisis, shrink from the service of their country…" The pamphlet is read aloud to the troops during one of America's darkest hours.

Mercury directed to Mars in Taurus: The following year, 1777, Mercury comes to Mars in Taurus in the septenary, and Pluto becomes the decan ruler and moves to the ascendant. He is appointed secretary to a commission sent by Congress to treat with Indians. He coins the name United States of America for the country in his second *Crisis*. An oath of support for the United States is proposed in his third *Crisis*. A grateful Congress appoints him secretary to its Committee of Foreign Affairs, the most important congressional secretaryship, and forerunner of today's Secretary of State. He is at the nexus of power, the Mercury who communicates between George Washington on the battlefield and Ben Franklin in Paris raising money and support for the revolution.

Mercury directed to Venus in Aries: The final year of Thomas Paine's Mercury-ruled septenary occurs in 1778, when it comes to Venus in Aries. In the decan Pluto has come to Neptune, ruler of the previous decan. Paine writes his fourth and fifth *Crisis*, the latter at Valley Forge in which he defends General Washington against the attacks of John Adams and others. His writings continue to inspire the rebels in their fight for independence. But then Congress sacks him for writing that France was helping the rebels, an open secret that just about everyone knows. This loss of position is a severe blow. The United States government will never again employ him, and, while others who had much less to do with the country's independence enjoy lasting fame, Tom Paine tends to disappear into the shadows. That he was later also an important figure in the French Revolution, the one man who was a leading protagonist (he sent the key of the Bastille to George Washington) in both of these successful revolutionary victories, makes him unique in history.

The following year, although Paine's Pluto-ruled decan continues,
his Mercury-ruled septenary has ended.

Chapter 9

Venus as the Time Ruler

The sect of lovers is distinct from all others:
Lovers have a religion and a faith all their own.
Jalal-uddin Rumi

Love is infallible; it has no errors, for all errors are the want of love.
William Law

Venus represents Life in all of its forms. It also signifies the love one feels for another. Venus is peace, agreement, harmony, tranquility and accord. The planet is also our love of life and nature, for the flora, fauna and features of our planet, the simple growth and propagation of all that is present around us, there for our delight, enjoyment and guidance. The love felt between members of the opposite sex is the necessary stimulation for the propagation of our species. In these years ruled by Venus the individual can expect to become involved in various relationships as he learns how to love another person and how to relate harmoniously with other people in friendship. As she moves among the planets Venus gives affection to each planet in turn, enabling each one to act in its own way to remove the imbalances that have crept into our lives.

In the years that Venus rules the septenary or decan the individual has the opportunity to discover and express the joy of being alive. People fall in love, marry, give birth to children, improve their dress, enjoy a social life, appreciate the woods, streams and flowers of this world, and get aesthetic pleasure from music, poetry and all forms of the arts. Love may seem a frail defense against the horrors of the world, but during these Venus years the individual learns to hold fast and believe in it, for it is often all that he has. In general in these times we experience periods of harmony that are free of unwelcome disturbance.

Table ♀-1:   ♀: **% Positive Years**

Position relative to the ☉	Day birth		Night birth		All	
	N	% Positive	N	% Positive	N	% Positive
Oriental ♀	266	**58.1***	198	48.4	464	54.0
Occidental ♀	217	48.7	403	**55.6***	620	53.3
All	483	53.9	601	53.3	1084	**53.5**

Venus in the sample was most positive when oriental of the Sun in a daytime chart or when occidental of the Sun in a nocturnal chart. These positions relative to the Sun denote Venus as a morning or evening star, visible prior to dawn and after sunset. This is contrary to all tradition, which states that Venus is strongest when occidental. These results are statistically significant and this finding confirms the empirical results earlier observed for

Mercury. These observed results for Venus and Mercury, although contrary to standard astrological lore, make very good sense.

Older astrologers associated Venus with love and sexual intercourse. The planet can combine the incestuous habits of the Borgia popes with the Renaissance painting and sculpture they financed: sex and art.

In these Venusian years an individual should enjoy nature, luxuries, comforts, romance and the joys of married life. If Venus is unafflicted and the planet to which it is directed is in one of the signs in which Venus is welcome (Taurus, Libra or Pisces) life should be happy, with ease and indulgence. Artistic endeavors will be successful, business will be favorable, reputations gained and ambitions realized. It can be a sensual period, one that is smooth sailing in just about everything.

Table ♀-2

% Positive Years
when ♀ is Time Lord

♀ directed to	N	% Positive
♀ rises	128	52.3
☉	136	56.5
☽	153	54.3
☿	140	54.9
♂	132	53.4
♃	131	51.8
♄	144	47.1
♅	37	58.7
♆	42	60.3
♇	41	57.1
All	*1084*	**53.5****

A badly afflicted Venus or one applying to a planet in Aries, Virgo or Scorpio often indicates an individual who that year becomes promiscuous, self-indulgent and indolent. He may experience some mental unrest. He can quarrel with his lover or partner, and there may be a separation. During these periods of imbalance he is likely to encounter much misery and trouble. He may be hospitalized and perhaps have financial problems that force him to take out loans or mortgage his home. Venus afflictions often correlate with financial problems. The years that Venus rules the septenary or decan can improve or reduce a person's financial position, depending the planet to which it is directed and the sign that planet occupies.

The rising of Venus and the planet's direction to each of the planets, with the exception of its arrival at the place of Saturn, is seen in Table ♀-2 to be more likely to be associated with a positive year than with a negative one. Indeed, the overall % positive for the years when

Venus is the ruler of time is itself statistically significant, higher than the expected 50%. Had tradition not told us so already, Venus would be designated as a benefic based purely on the evidence provided here.

Table ♀-3   **% Positive Years, Venus by Natal & Directed Sign**

♀'s natal sign		Sign	♀'s directed sign	
N	% Positive Years		N	% Positive Years
121	55.3	♈	43	46.3
161	52.8	♉	125	**65.8***
71	57.3	♊	72	56.5
88	44.2	♋	85	56.4
27	50.3	♌	99	51.1
66	43.9	♍	73	50.8
125	55.0	♎	87	52.0
79	59.5	♏	88	55.5
121	56.8	♐	71	43.3
92	52.6	♑	87	53.0
72	56.5	♒	78	40.6
61	54.9	♓	58	56.1
1084	**53.5****	*All*	956	**53.7***

Venus directed to a planet occupying Taurus, one of the signs the planet rules, is a strong indication that the following year will be positive.

Table ♀-4   **% Positive Years, Venus by Natal & Directed House**

♀'s natal house		House	♀'s directed house	
N	% Positive Years		N	% Positive Years
84	48.5	I	90	52.3
165	50.5	II	107	**62.6***
144	58.4	III	95	57.1
99	**62.1***	IV	72	54.0
99	43.9	V	70	54.2
84	58.1	VI	56	40.3
75	51.8	VII	74	56.2
41	44.1	VIII	72	47.7
48	45.2	IX	65	45.9
70	45.2	X	81	54.7
128	**65.0***	XI	78	52.2
47	53.9	XII	96	57.4

Natal Venus placed in the 4th and 11th houses indicates years that have a strong likelihood of being positive. Those people born with Venus in the 5th, 8th, 9th or 10th have the planet in the least positive places.

Venus directed to a planet the 2nd house is a strong indication that the year will be positive.

Compare the difference in the % Positive Years for the direction of Venus to the 2nd and 8th houses, and between the 3rd and the 9th, and again between the 12th and the 6th. These differences between opposing houses appear to be meaningful.

Table 9-5

**% Positive when Venus is the Ruler
by its place in the septenary sequence**

Place of Venus in septenary	Day		Night	
	N	% Positive	N	% Positive
1	27	56.7	42	49.2
2	37	51.1	30	**28.5****
3	33	57.3	83	54.4
4	78	47.3	88	55.5
5	64	**63.4****	46	53.0
6	36	**65.1***	34	39.0
7	35	46.3	40	51.8
Sum	310	**54.9***	363	50.1

In the septenary Venus is associated with a significant likelihood of difficult years when it is placed second of the seven in a nocturnal chart, which relates to ages 7 to 13. This might be related to hormonal growth, to the advent of sexual urges, but there is no obvious reason why it should apply only to nocturnal births. There is a high incidence of positive years when Venus is located in a diurnal chart and placed in the fifth or sixth place, which corresponds to the years between ages 28 and 42.

Table ♀-6

% Positive when Venus is the Ruler
by its place in the decan sequence

Place of Venus in decan	Day		Night	
	N	% Positive	N	% Positive
1	5	90.1	2	0.0
2	21	42.9	18	51.0
3	21	68.6	46	77.9***
4	13	62.4	68	51.3
5	30	45.0	57	64.4**
6	35	41.1	37	42.1
7	18	45.0	1	0.0
8	29	59.0	0	-
9	1	90.1	3	91.8
10	0	-	0	-
Sum	173	52.1	232	58.2

Venus in the third place of the ten, ruling the decan when individuals are in their twenties, is associated with years that are usually very positive. As it is Venus that is involved we can assume these years involved love relationships. The difference between Venus at night and day, although apparently quite large, is not significant.

Venus Rises
(52% positive years)

Meaningful firsts will probably happen this year. Usually these will involve a member of the opposite sex. Relationships start, they go through difficult times, they may break up. A person may fall in love and may marry. He will be naturally affectionate now and want to relate to others; to do so he will be willing to make compromises. His appearance becomes important and he will want to improve it to impress others, making himself more attractive, especially to members of the opposite sex. Ample funds should become available for this. He will also be more aware of natural beauty now, and prefer pleasure to work. This should be a pleasant year, one in which past enemies and problems disappear, children are born, and an interest is taken in arts and crafts.

Table ♀-7:

♀ to Ascendant:
% Positive Years

♀ relative to the ☉	Day birth		Night birth		All	
	N	% Positive	N	% Positive	N	% Positive
Oriental ♀	28	51.6	26	55.6	54	53.6
Occidental ♀	27	43.5	47	55.8	74	51.4
All	55	47.6	73	55.7	128	52.3

If Venus is afflicted, especially by Saturn, relationships may break up and there can be feelings of guilt. Family members may go into hospital or a nursing home.

In the sample we found Venus is most positive for those born at night. It is not a pleasant year for day births who have an occidental Venus, for then problems involving females occur. People in the sample born with their ascendant in Cancer were significantly below 50%.

Some happenings in the sample when Venus begins ruling the decan:
Oriental Venus rises by day in decan: *first meets his future wife; son born; in battle; very poor; loss of home & children; captured then rescued; living in friend's attic; resigns from being Chancellor; kidney surgery; his illness postpones his coronation; death.*
Occidental Venus rises by day in decan: *alone & melancholy; engaged; divorce; remarries; lengthy honeymoon; wins prize for poetry recitation; speaks against USA's indoctrination of its people; arrested for theft; lethargic; gaining weight; epileptic fit.*
Oriental Venus rises at night in decan: *joins army; leaves RAF; discusses non-violence with Gandhi; her book is nominated for a prize; divorce; mountaineering; the last semblance of order & tidiness in the family goes when sister runs away; cystitis.*
Occidental Venus rises at night in decan: *lied to by her husband; marries; working long hours; becomes stone deaf; "My hour of darkness"; twenty-year-long friendship ends; wins election; success in new radio soap opera; gets a dog; high heels cause a blood clot behind her knee; skiing; overseas travel; son dies.*

Some happenings in the sample when Venus begins ruling the decan:
Oriental Venus rises by day in septenary: *children born; first sees future spouse; marries; marriage ends abruptly; loss of house and children; researching guilt; self-imposed retirement; leaves navy to run family's peanut farm; alone & very poor; cystitis; death.*
Occidental Venus rises by day in septenary: *awarded Nobel Peace Prize; discovers wife's infidelity; unhappy with her marriage & her job; discovers yoga & has a Tibetan teacher; feted but also treated as a freak; meets the Pope; buys house & a new car; friends die; her son is lost in the desert for days.*
Oriental Venus rises at night in septenary: *has her hair curled; marries his long-time mistress; jealous; loses his shyness; her lover leaves her; physically & morally exhausted; pays off house mortgage; his son is badly hurt; promoted; wins an award; sad & self-pitying when father dies.*
Occidental Venus rises at night in septenary: *incompatible marriage; first sex; friends quarrel among themselves; divorces of children; publicly confesses to an affair; has a suit tailored for a friend; comes into a fortune; financial losses; unhappy in sordid surroundings.*

Venus comes to the Sun
(56% positive)

This year an individual will want friendship and close relationships with others. He wants to be popular and receive attention, and if this is not forthcoming he may travel and even relocate his home to find it. He may express his feelings through his relationships and in music, poetry and other forms of creativity. There is likely to be much social activity.

Most people experience this as a happy year. However, if either Venus or the Sun is afflicted, the individual may become involved in an unfortunate love attach-ment, which can cause humiliation. He may then reject friends or lovers, or be rejected by them. An affair is possible. There can simply be too much indulgence. He may make impulse purchases, spending more than he can afford. His prosperity may collapse and there can be troubles with the partner and with children, disputes and quarrels involving land and property. A child may be injured. Injuries and diseases affecting the head, belly and eyes can occur. His appearance may be altered.

In my sample, diurnal births in the septenary had an easier time before the age of 49 years, while for nocturnal births the year was usually more pleasant after that age. A Venus-to-Sun septenary year tends to be mostly influenced for better or worse by the coincident planetary combination in the decan, whichever that is.

Oriental Venus was associated with positive happenings in these years, more so than occidental Venus. Positive values significantly above 50% were noted when Venus was directed to the Sun in the 2nd or 3rd houses. These values were also significantly high when Venus was in Sagittarius or the 11th house. Significantly low values were noted in the sample when Venus was in the 7th house, or when directed to a Sun in the 6th or 8th houses.

Table ♀-7 :

♀ to ☉:
% Positive Years

♀ relative to the ☉	Day birth		Night birth		All	
	N	% Positive	N	% Positive	N	% Positive
Oriental ♀	40	61.0	28	61.4	68	**61.1***
Occidental ♀	22	53.4	46	51.1	68	51.9
All	*62*	*58.3*	*74*	*55.0*	*136*	*56.5*

Some happenings in the sample when Venus comes to the Sun in the decan:
Oriental Venus to Sun by day in decan: *writing daily love letters; promoted; fired from her job; loses election; writing his autobiography; awarded Nobel Peace Prize; begins publishing a quarterly magazine; buys his first new car; taking cocaine; death.*
Occidental Venus to Sun by day in decan: *a friend betrays him; father loses election; graduates; rejected by law school; his dream of wealth is shattered.*

Oriental Venus to Sun at night in decan: *coronation; beaten up by police; peace after lengthy war; depression; makes angry speeches; writes the lyrics for a successful musical; tours overseas.*

Occidental Venus to Sun at night in decan: *children born; experiences horror; husband dies; lonely & dispirited; affair; marries; the turning point of his life; appointed Supreme Commander; first time on TV & radio; told to stop wearing high heels; buys house; quadruples his fortune.*

Some happenings in the sample when Venus comes to the Sun in the septenary:

Oriental Venus to Sun by day in septenary: *repairs the roof; loses money in mutual funds; debts; elected to an elite club; dysentery; buys large power boat; researching historical symbolism; her husband loses his professional license; engaged; preoccupied with survival; commissioned as a pilot; he becomes an inmate in an insane asylum.*

Occidental Venus to Sun by day in septenary: *serious financial problems; his wife is obsessed with her inheritance; folding leaflets for election campaign; shell shocked; leads protest marches; reshuffles her cabinet to cure malaise; bitterly disappointed when rejected; receives threatening letters; travels; nursing others back to health; sees a murderer hanged.*

Oriental Venus to Sun at night in septenary: *now she is wealthy; a society is formed to sponsor his work; discovers penicillin; she is a love junky; marries; divorce; authorities cancel his play's performance; convalescence; promoted; meditating; attends coronation; re-elected to the Senate; heart attack.*

Occidental Venus to Sun at night in septenary: *he has two jobs; money wrangling; sells his company; cuts his wife out of his will; tries but fails to divorce her husband; his hair goes white overnight; writing poems; frequently falling in love; peace making; unable to walk.*

Venus comes to the Moon
(54% positive)

Always depending on the natal state of Venus and the sign occupied by the Moon, the necessary love and harmony Venus brings should be enhanced now through the individual's interaction with his family and other Moon-related areas. It should be a pleasant year, one in which the bluebird of happiness may rest awhile on the individual's shoulder, prompting the native to feel especially cheerful and gregarious. He may fall in love, and want to express how he feels to another. He is likely to be invited to attend social gatherings. He may want to refurnish his home and entertain others there, paying attention to his appearance and wanting to appear at his best; in doing so he may spend more than he can afford, with money problems as a result. Education should progress well, knowledge is easily gained, and exams are there to be passed. Females will be helpful. Any matrimonial troubles that arise can be resolved during the year. Interest in meditation and poetry has been frequently observed, the native becoming tranquil and at peace, unruffled by anxiety. Flashes of inspiration are not unknown.

An afflicted Moon or Venus is often associated with moodiness and irritability.

A large difference was observed in the sample for those born at night with their natal Venus rising before or after the Sun. The higher positive value observed for the occidental Venus agrees with traditional statements. Positive values significantly higher than 50% were also observed when either Venus or the Moon was in the 4th house.

Table ♀-8:   **♀ to ☽: % Positive Years**

Planets relative to the ☉	Day birth		Night birth		All	
	N	% Positive	N	% Positive	N	% Positive
Oriental ♀	39	53.3	27	43.5	66	49.3
Occidental ♀	33	54.8	54	60.3	87	58.2
All	*72*	*54.0*	*81*	*54.7*	*153*	*54.3*
waxing ☽	41	52.9	46	57.0	87	55.1
waning ☽	31	55.4	35	51.6	66	53.4

Some happenings in the sample when Venus comes to the Moon in the decan:
Oriental Venus to the Moon by day in decan: *meets his future wife; engaged; begins working for women's suffrage; wins election; writes on psychic energy; says "Galaxies are little orchards, planetary systems are trees, and fruit is consciousness;" son born; chickenpox.*
Occidental Venus to the Moon by day in decan: *he has great personal authority; captures the Pope; her town is bombed; graduates; husband has heart surgery; marries; in a deep depression; assassination attempt; in an accident; death.*
Oriental Venus to the Moon at night in decan: *two daughters have smallpox; daughter marries; son commits suicide; disinherits his son; her brother runs away; mother is ill; husband's salary is increased; first & only flight; spiritual experience; typhoid; nearly dies.*
Occidental Venus to the Moon at night in decan: *affair; wife dies; marries; leaves his wife; husband has lung surgery; children born; nephew attempts suicide; loses paternity trial; his reputation is irreparably damaged; builds an addition to his house; assaulted by suffragettes.*

Some happenings in the sample when Venus comes to the Moon in the septenary:
Oriental Venus to the Moon by day in septenary: *his wife is assassinated; marries; living with his new love; living as a house husband; in a manic high; being impeached; experiences prana; wins scholarship; declared legally insane; sciatica.*
Occidental Venus to the Moon by day in septenary: *becomes famous overnight; getting fatter; helps a friend who had publicly rejected the war; peace treaty; poetry; first meets his future wife; affair; promoted; his daughter refuses a marriage proposal; heart dilation following exertion.*
Oriental Venus to the Moon at night in septenary: *ends an affair; in great debt; pays off debts; terrified, he is forced to flee; feels alone & empty; refuses honors; takes LSD; first published prose; experiences a spiritual watershed; buys his first car; very depressed; touring.*
Occidental Venus to the Moon at night in septenary: *puts on weight; extensive travels; happy; resigns; feels the need to make a transition, to transform the direction of her life; no money, heavy debts, bankrupt; first performance of his symphony; promoted; buys house.*

Venus comes to Mercury
(55% positive)

This year communication and other Mercury-signified abilities should enhance the necessary balance and harmony the person is trying to attain. There are likely to be financial gains, sound health and improved knowledge. However, the individual may also be more sensitive than usual and can experience illness, worries and loneliness. He will have an intellectual appreciation of beauty, music, poetry, drama and the arts in general. Friends are likely to visit or to ask him out. There will be news of a loved one and he will communicate his feelings to others and want to discuss his relationships with them. The loss of someone or an object with which he is identified or greatly attached can also occur this year.

Table ♀-9:   ♀ to ☿: % Positive Years

Planets relative to the ☉	Day birth		Night birth		All	
	N	% Positive	N	% Positive	N	% Positive
Oriental ♀	37	56.2	23	59.0	60	57.2
Occidental ♀	28	54.9	52	52.2	80	53.2
All	*65*	*55.6*	*75*	*54.2*	*140*	*54.9*
Oriental ☿	37	56.2	40	49.7	77	52.8
Occidental ☿	28	54.9	35	59.4	63	57.4

Travel is indicated this year; business or relocation may separate him from his home, spouse and children for a short period. This can cause the spouse to be unhappy. The year should be good for business, learning and legal matters: he may pay or receive large sums of money.

Statistically significant values above 50% occurred in the sample when either Venus or Mercury was in Taurus.

Some happenings in the sample when Venus comes to Mercury in the decan:
Oriental Venus to Mercury by day in decan: *a dream anticipates his study of alchemy; book published; parents die; son born; writing daily love letters; receives a major pay increase; learns how when a patient's symptoms are talked out, she is cured; marries; sciatica; one of his helicopters is exhibited at MOMA.*
Occidental Venus to Mercury by day in decan: *extreme rages; paranoid; ignoring advice; moves; sister dies; completes his* Lives of the Poets; *re-elected.*
Oriental Venus to Mercury at night in decan: *divorce; overseas touring; mother is ill; screenwriting; her brother runs away from home.*
Occidental Venus to Mercury at night in decan: *nightmares; Wall Street crash; financial problems; girl friend rejects him; promoted; slowly grasps the principle of universal gravity;*

loses election; travels alone for the first time; forbidden to drink coffee or wine.

Some happenings in the sample when Venus comes to Mercury in the septenary:

Oriental Venus to Mercury by day in septenary: *he argues that one should follow reason not emotion; brief art interest; regularly recurring periods of exhaustion; told he has AIDS; writing becomes his obsession; recording his ideas, dreams & experiences; not enough to eat; discovers principles governing helicopter flight; first bank account; writing a play; third marriage.*

Occidental Venus to Mercury by day in septenary: *confused; writing criticism; first substantial poem is published; mother dies; daughter born; his girl friend attempts suicide; giddiness; travels; peace treaty; gives popular lectures; becoming increasingly unpopular; learns to handle people as individuals & in groups.*

Oriental Venus to Mercury at night in septenary: *breaks with her lover; meditation convinces him he is inwardly a woman; afraid her writing will be ridiculed; forced to move; first book of poems; his wife has an affair; writes book with his son; living on a ferry boat; has psychosomatic anxiety symptoms; his playing is criticized; lectures for high fees; little money.*

Occidental Venus to Mercury at night in septenary: *criticized; fined for letting his sheep loose; increasing deafness; getting parts in theater by sleeping with producers; insecure in his job; his book is a best seller; marries; separated from his wife; son born; deaths in the family.*

Venus comes to Mars
(53% positive)

Participation in sport, increased physical effort and other Mars-related abilities should now enhance the necessary balance and harmony the individual is attempting to achieve. A preference for being with those who are younger than himself is likely. His love nature can become inflamed, causing him to strongly desire physical love. Duties may be neglected if he is overly tempted by passion and pleasure. He may marry. Some form of tension between activity and passivity will certainly occur during the year. He will be more active than he has been in the past; stimulated to act by criticism, anger or violence. If either body is afflicted or if Mars is located in a sign that doesn't welcome Venus, difficulties with the spouse or friends are possible; he may break with them. Several members of my sample experienced financial losses this year. Deaths in the family were also observed on several occasions.

Occidental Venus in the daytime was particularly negative in the sample. Again, as we have observed on several other occasions, Venus as morning or evening star was associated with above-average positive years. Significantly high positive values were noted when Venus was in the 4th or 11th houses, or when directed to Mars in the 2nd house or in Taurus.

Table ♀-10 :   **♀ to ♂ : % Positive Years**

Planets relative to the ☉	Day birth		Night birth		All	
	N	% Positive	N	% Positive	N	% Positive
Oriental ♀	33	65.7	26	48.6	59	58.2
Occidental ♀	29	37.4	44	57.5	73	49.5
All	*62*	*49.9*	*70*	*54.2*	*132*	*53.4*
Oriental ♂	24	60.3	35	51.6	59	55.2
Occidental ♂	38	47.6	35	56.9	71	52.0

Some happenings in the sample when Venus comes to Mars in the decan:

Oriental Venus to Mars by day in decan: *falls in love; conscripted into the army; builds a place where he can exist for himself alone; daughter born; finances improve.*

Occidental Venus to Mars by day in decan: *believes himself 'above the law'; war starts; escapes from exile; husband dies; defeated; becomes a convinced vegetarian; travels overseas to study law.*

Oriental Venus to Mars at night in decan: *quits his job to become a freelance poet; children born; son dies in battle; victory in battle; arrested; lonely; very ill; unhappy.*

Occidental Venus to Mars at night in decan: *becomes a barrister; legal victory; writes book; attacked by women; buys a house; his wife is ill; marries; separated from his wife; stops giving talks; works as a drummer in music halls; job hunting; in a car accident.*

Some happenings in the sample when Venus comes to Mars in the septenary:

Oriental Venus to Mars by day in septenary: *his affair breaks up two marriages; she leaves her husband & quits her job; has a second job working nights in a bakery; graduates; first job; son born; hopeful & optimistic; struggles to control his own emotions; stimulated by lecture he hears; has anxiety dreams; becomes World Champion; teaching; moves.*

Occidental Venus to Mars by day in septenary: *being harassed by a former lover; criticized as heartless; children born; his wife becomes a feminist; large gambling losses; journalism; has a love for poetry; attains great fame; friend dies; living in Nazi-occupied country; marries; writes on the nature of light.*

Oriental Venus to Mars at night in septenary: *loss of self confidence; hatred of tyranny; faints from heat; learns sailing; tension; writes his first play as an answer to complaints of his idleness; book is published; graduates; planning his daughter's marriage; parents divorce; friend's suicide; meditating; studies the Cabbala.*

Occidental Venus to Mars at night in septenary: *campaigning; paranoid & angry; his mother remarries; his son's murderer is executed; wretched home life; severe depression; insomnia; impatient; much writing; loses money in financial panic; bickering with her best friend; gets a motorbike; wanting to become an actress; wants to be with young people.*

Venus comes to Jupiter
(52% positive)

This year good fortune associated with Jupiter should enhance the balance and harmony Venus is trying to achieve. It could mark the end of dependence with the means of the individual's future livelihood being now decided. His employers are likely to benefit him and his finances should improve, although some anxiety and disputes with religious people are likely. It should be a happy time for the individual with admirers showing their affection. He is popular now and likely to be asked out socially. He may visit foreign countries, usually for pleasure on vacation. Both his appearance and his relationships should improve. He may fall in love. Venus coming to Jupiter can also signify another form of rest and relaxation, for the individual may be forced to spend a lengthy time in bed, recovering his strength after a severe illness.

Table ♀-11: ♀ to ♃: **% Positive Years**

Planets relative to the ☉	Day birth		Night birth		All	
	N	% Positive	N	% Positive	N	% Positive
Oriental ♀	34	61.1	24	33.9	58	49.9
Occidental ♀	29	53.0	44	53.4	73	53.3
All	*63*	*57.4*	*68*	*46.6*	*131*	*51.8*
Oriental ♃	29	49.9	26	59.1	55	54.2
Occidental ♃	34	63.8	42	38.8	76	50.0

There are a couple of unexpected values in Table ♀-11: 34% for oriental Venus at night, and 39% for occidental Jupiter at night. This combination is not automatically positive. Should Venus be combust, oriental in a nocturnal nativity, directed to an afflicted Jupiter, or to a Jupiter that is in a sign in which Venus is uncomfortable, there can be grief over the loss of a loved one, business loss or problems with the authorities. Jupiter in the 11th house was associated with a significantly high percentage of positive years.

Some happenings in the sample when Venus comes to Jupiter in the decan:
Oriental Venus to Jupiter by day in decan: *receives an honorary doctorate; honored; son born; friends die; international business trips; his only child is killed; death.*
Occidental Venus to Jupiter by day in decan: *suffering defeats; confesses to theft; wife & son leave him; attempts suicide; rejects peace offers; exiled; father is promoted.*
Oriental Venus to Jupiter at night in decan: *marries; ends her marriage; forced out of the organization she founded; has his son arrested & tortured—choosing his life's work over his parental feelings; in poor health; his wife is very ill.*
Occidental Venus to Jupiter at night in decan: *found Not Guilty in paternity suit; father dies; marries; son born; his autobiography loses him friends; loses all of his belongings in a fire; moves overseas; becomes a U.S. citizen; exhausting overseas tour; promoted; gives first public talk in five years; conscripted into army.*

Some happenings in the sample when Venus comes to Jupiter in the decan:

Oriental Venus to Jupiter by day in septenary: *buys a dairy farm; his throat is slashed; moves in with her lover; buys a convertible car; motorbike accident, he is unhurt but his sister dies; learns to fly; becomes an atheist; honors; introduced to astrology; sees a woman hanged; emigrates; his fourth marriage; writing his doctoral dissertation; syphilis; sets up trust fund for his mother.*

Occidental Venus to Jupiter by day in septenary: *starts civil disobedience campaign; his wife's mishandling causes their business to collapse; frustrated love life; achieves his greatest ambition; depressed; marries; his invention saves many lives; cataloguing a library; exhausted from political infighting; shop fails; university buys his love letters.*

Oriental Venus to Jupiter at night in septenary: *theater & party going; sprains his ankle; falls from a horse; writes on art; period of confusion; obtains federal funding; father's company is bankrupt; promoted; negotiating; learns Italian; idleness; joins a Gnostic group; travels; escapes suburbia.*

Occidental Venus to Jupiter at night in septenary: *goes to expensive tailors; changes his major at college; severe bronchitis; traveling; promised a promotion; teaching; large pay increase; has a house built; peace negotiations; barred from going to France; lengthy illness; death.*

Venus comes to Saturn
(47 % positive)

This is often the most difficult of the years ruled by Venus. During it there are likely to be austerities and the individual will be forced to practice constraint or to act in some other manner, as indicated by his natal Saturn, aimed at better defining the balance and harmony required in his life. An affair or even marriage with a much older partner is possible. Money will be more scarce than usual and debts can increase. There is a distinct danger that, unable to cope with the discipline Saturn imposes, the individual will fall into bad company, be tempted to gamble or become addicted to drugs. He may doubt his own abilities now, especially if he was born at night. He may lose the accustomed support of his spouse, father or a mentor, people on whom he has come to rely, and may feel unloved and lonely; feel deserted and want to withdraw from others. He will become particularly upset if others claim credit for work that he did. During the year he may become ill, be easily exhausted, depressed, lose his appetite, and allow himself to get into a poor physical condition. He will need to conserve his energy. These troubles are less in a diurnal nativity.

Day births had an easier time in the sample than did those born at night. This was most apparent for those diurnal births with either an oriental Venus or an occidental Saturn. Saturn in the 8th house was significantly lower than 50%.

Table ♀-12:   **♀ to ♄: % Positive Years**

Planets relative to the ☉	Day birth		Night birth		All	
	N	% Positive	N	% Positive	N	% Positive
Oriental ♀	30	60.3	26	34.8	56	48.5
Occidental ♀	30	48.2	58	45.2	88	46.2
All	*60*	*54.2*	*84*	*42.0*	*144*	*47.1*
Oriental ♄	29	46.7	39	39.4	68	42.6
Occidental ♄	31	61.2	45	44.2	76	51.2

Some happenings in the sample when Venus comes to Saturn in the decan:

Oriental Venus to Saturn by day in decan: *discovers his Theory of Types; father/friend dies; graduates; studies Greek & Latin; living alone in the woods.*

Occidental Venus to Saturn by day in decan: *exiled; wins election; others find his theory is untenable; authorizes atom bombing of Japan; receives his pilot's wings; son born; he is a religious outcast; death.*

Oriental Venus to Saturn at night in decan: *husband leaves her, then returns; son has TB; children born; revises inheritance laws; in several battles; war ends; her first story is published; she is secretary for a terrorist group; her plans are thwarted & she wants revenge.*

Occidental Venus to Saturn at night in decan: *mother dies; mother remarries; mother's marriage ends; his brother is charged with sodomy; daughter born; reduced income; eye troubles; malaria; marries; studies public speaking; mentor's death leaves him wealthy; stops buffalo becoming extinct; accused of being a communist sympathizer; much time alone; hunted by the army; first buys a house; death.*

Some happenings in the sample when Venus comes to Saturn in the septenary:

Oriental Venus to Saturn by day in septenary: *unsought & unwelcome leisure; almost loses sight in his left eye in a bar fight; buys old farmhouse; sells house, turning out his ex-wife; enjoys the beauty of nature & of poetry; doubts his past beliefs; mad love affair; large financial losses in the stock market; convicted for fraud; her therapist dies; his son is wounded; very large book sales; pessimism; unhappy, pneumonia; contemplates suicide.*

Occidental Venus to Saturn by day in septenary: *father/mother/friend/protector dies; graduates; convalescing; "The substance has gone out of everything"; deserted by her lover; sense of guilt, doubt & self-denigration; family squabbles over father's will; furious; feels old-fashioned; honors; reduced income; often alone; eye troubles.*

Oriental Venus to Saturn at night in septenary: *parents separate; sees her son for the first time in nine years; her daughter starts school; troubles in marriage & at work; she has a new lover; divorces & then remarries; his sweetheart marries another; learning how things work; in debt; wins a prize; has eyesight problems.*

Occidental Venus to Saturn at night in septenary: *son has a serious accident; a love for poetry; exiled; lucky escape in plane crash; at the apex of his public career; badly injured in car accident; reelected by a landslide; anarchy; international fame; eye/nose/hernia operation; depression; psychological crisis.*

Venus comes to Uranus
(59% positive)

Unexpected changes, innovations or other Uranus-related events can now disturb the balance and harmony that Venus is aiming for. The native can become extremely restless, have a sense of delay, and feel that he is unable to accomplish all that he wants to achieve. Unexpected events may occur in the home. He'll want excitement in his relationships. Those that have become boring will be either revitalized and renewed or finished completely. Artists should find this is a very creative period.

We already know from tradition and also from previous examples that Venus is strong at night when occidental from the Sun, and this was confirmed in the sample. We might tentatively consider Uranus to be also most positive at night, but differing from Venus in that it is stronger when it rises before the Sun.

Night births had a much easier time this year than did day births. Oriental Uranus appears to respond very positively to Venus' direction.

Table ♀-13:   ♀ to ♅: % Positive Years

Planets relative to the ☉	Day birth		Night birth		All	
	N	% Positive	N	% Positive	N	% Positive
Oriental ♀	8	45.2	5	54.2	13	48.6
Occidental ♀	6	45.2	18	70.3	24	64.0
All	*14*	*45.2*	*23*	*66.8*	*37*	*58.7*
Oriental ♅	6	45.2	19	**71.4***	25	65.1
Occidental ♅	8	45.2	4	45.2	12	45.2

Some happenings in the sample when Venus comes to Uranus in the decan:

Oriental Venus to Uranus by day: *promoted to command all armies; writing his autobiography; elected FRS; in-depth study of the astrology of his own life; a difficult year; considers himself a failure; heavy workload; burglary; buys a new house; his writings are said to be anti-Semitic; using cocaine; death.*

Occidental Venus to Uranus by day: *marries; son born; goes to university; steals money; sheds recent lethargy; feet & thighs are swollen with water-dropsy; attempt on his life; defeated; death by suicide.*

Oriental Venus to Uranus by night: *husband leaves her when she is pregnant; father dies; making peace; in his first battles.*

Occidental Venus to Uranus by night: *appointed commanding general; wife/father dies; husband has heart surgery; son born; defends himself against accusations; speaks against war; obsessed with security; meets future husband; gets large contract; his book of verse & erotica is published; interest in magic; his rite of passage into adulthood; elected president/vice-president; fails in his attempt to get an official position; his book that will revolutionize physics is published; repelled & exhausted; rheumatism.*

Venus comes to Neptune

(60% positive)

Being receptive or acting in some other Neptune-related manner this year will enhance the balance and harmony that Venus requires. The native may start to see beauty is everything. Art, music and poetry are likely to come into his life and they will certainly stimulate him. He may fall in love but he can be easily deceived, so this is not the time for him to renounce his everyday responsibilities and drastically change his life. Indeed, this is a period in which he is apt to fall for the impossible. It can be an inspirational and successful year for artists, musicians, poets, and those involved in the theater and other forms of make-believe. He will probably be defeated if he becomes involved in any legal action.

Table ♀-14 : ♀ to ♆: % Positive Years

Planets relative to the ☉	Day birth		Night birth		All	
	N	% Positive	N	% Positive	N	% Positive
Oriental ♀	9	60.3	7	38.8	16	50.8
Occidental ♀	6	45.2	20	**72.3***	26	66.1
All	*15*	*54.2*	*27*	*63.7*	*42*	*60.3*
Oriental ♆	8	67.8	16	50.8	24	56.5
Occidental ♆	7	38.8	11	**82.2***	18	65.3

The numbers are small, but night births in the sample clearly had an easier time than did day births. Above-average positive years were associated with either planet being oriental for day births, or occidental at night.

Some happenings in the sample when Venus comes to Neptune in the decan:
Oriental Venus to Neptune by day: *very happy; studying alchemy; receives his opponent's surrender; his autobiography is published; starts keeping a diary; her sister marries & then dies; loses election; she is in love with her girl friend; gets his first computer; sponsors Science & Mysticism seminar; writes on astrology; Wicca interest.*
Occidental Venus to Neptune by day: *moves; unauthorized nude photos of her are published; in exile; re-elected president; father dies.*
Oriental Venus to Neptune at night: *onset of a grievous ague that will last seven years; marries; organizes a conference; keeping goats; avoids arrest; father dies; becomes queen.*
Occidental Venus to Neptune at night: *awarded Nobel Peace Prize; fears he is going blind; meets future wife; he is in a love triangle; his wife discovers him fondling their servant girl; angry when accused of plagiarism; finds an ideal home; buys house; husband becomes president; promoted; FBI say he is a major security risk; denounces segregation; grandfather is assassinated; malaria; exhausted.*

Venus comes to Pluto
(57% positive)

The individual may now find that he needs to transform his life in some way to provide the balance and harmony that Venus requires in his life. He may change his appearance, the style of car he drives, change his job or relocate his home, perhaps even separate from his family, all in an attempt to fill a void, to escape from his loneliness and the feeling of being unwanted. This can be a period of disillusionment. Loved ones and friends may be lost.

Table ♀-13:   **♀ to ♇: % Positive Years**

Planets relative to the ☉	Day birth		Night birth		All	
	N	% Positive	N	% Positive	N	% Positive
Oriental ♀	8	56.5	6	60.3	14	58.1
Occidental ♀	7	38.8	20	63.3	27	57.0
All	*15*	*48.2*	*26*	*62.6*	*41*	*57.3*
Oriental ♇	10	54.2	12	67.8	22	61.7
Occidental ♇	5	36.2	14	58.1	19	52.4

The numbers in the above table are too few for any conclusions.

Some happenings in the sample when Venus comes to Pluto in the decan:
Oriental Venus to Pluto by day: *writing love letters; rioting; excited by hypnotism; separates from his wife; studying alchemy; edits book drawn from his diary; loses election; mother dies; sexually molested by her stepbrother; severe headache; promoted; gives property to his lover; planning publication of new magazine; mental breakdown.*
Occidental Venus to Pluto by day: *working as an editor; graduates; thrown from his horse; engagement is called off; paralytic stroke; loss of speech; inflamed prostate; father dies;*
Oriental Venus to Pluto at night: *in several battles; halts cathedral service; working long hours; her book is short listed for a prize; son dies; wants to get away from the vices of civilization; wounded in the head.*
Occidental Venus to Pluto at night: *in first films; son born; son/daughter marries; taxes large fortunes; mother dies; starts publishing scientific research papers; refuses to be intimidated or silenced; dines with the king; dog is killed; defamed as a communist & liar; investigated by FBI; challenges the concept of the subconscious mind; rising socially; many passionate speeches; removes inequality in health care; becomes self-employed; pleurisy; rheumatism.*

Jeddu Krishnamurti's first Venus-ruled Septenary

Although many believed Krishnamurti was the "vehicle" for an expected World Teacher, he disavowed this idea and dissolved the worldwide organization others had established to support it. He claimed allegiance to no nationality, caste, religion, or philosophy, and spent the rest of his life traveling the world as an individual speaker, speaking to large and small groups, as well as with interested individuals.

Jeddu Krishnamurti
12th May 1895
13N34 78E28

Venus in Gemini rises: Jeddu Krishnamurti is a night birth with an occidental Venus located in the fifth house in Gemini. He is fourteen in May 1909 when Venus becomes the septenary ruler. Mercury, his decan ruler, has come to Saturn in Scorpio. The two rulers are in mutual reception: Mercury in late Taurus, closely opposing his Midheaven, and Venus in late Gemini, about to be opposed by the Moon. This is the year the world discovers him. The clairvoyant Charles Webster Leadbeater sees him among a group of boys playing on the beach by the wide Adyar river, just south of Madras, India, and in a letter to Annie Besant the leader of the Theosophical Society describes the boy's aura as the most wonderful he has ever seen, without a particle of selfishness in it. Mrs. Besant comes to Adyar, meets Krishnaji and takes him into her care. Shortly after he experiences a spiritual initiation in his astral body: *"So this boy was prepared, properly dressed and all the rest of it and taken to Dr. Besant's room and went to sleep or became un-conscious—it is not clear, for me, for twenty-four hours or more. And when he came out of this state, all of them… saw an astonishing change in the face of this boy and some of them fell on their feet and touched his feet."*

Venus directed to Mercury in Taurus: Venus comes to its dispositor in Krishnamurti's septenary in 1910. He is fifteen years old. This second year of the septenary is often difficult. In his decan Mercury has arrived at Mars in Cancer. There is an emphasis this year on Mercury, which receives Venus in the septenary and is itself the decan ruler. Mercury closely opposes the midheaven and occupies Taurus, the sign ruled by the septenary ruler. Mrs. Besant takes Krishnaji and his younger brother, Nitya, to Benares. The 15-years-old boy begins teaching his elders the four qualifications for discipleship—Discrimination, Desirelessness, Good Conduct and Love. Every afternoon there are strenuous tennis

166

matches. *At the Feet of the Master* is published. The book is supposedly written by Krishnaji and revised by Leadbeater. An international organization, the Order of the Star in the East, is formed, its purpose being to prepare public opinion to receive Krishnamurti as a great spiritual teacher. Mrs. Besant brings the two boys to London, where a great crowd meets them.

Venus directed to the Sun in Taurus: Venus remains in Taurus and comes to Krishnamurti's Sun in 1911. He is sixteen years old. It is the third year of the septenary, the time when the new trend that began two years earlier now takes on a definite form. The decan ruler Mercury has arrived at his exalted Jupiter in Cancer. He is living in London and is taken by Mrs. Besant to briefly visit Paris. He attends her lectures on "The Coming of the World Teacher" and makes his own first speech in public. He suffers from painful indigestion, and then returns to India. An event of transcendent importance takes place on December 28, 1911, of the nature of Venus coming to his Sun in Taurus, at the Theosophical conference in Benares, when some four hundred people witness tremendous Pentecostal power flowing from Krishnaji. The boys' father is becoming concerned about the continued proximity of the boys to Leadbeater, who he now learns has been accused in the past of homosexuality.

Venus directed to the Moon in Sagittarius: In 1912 Krishnamurti's Venus comes to his waning Moon in Sagittarius. He is seventeen years old and this is the fourth year of the septenary, one in which there is often some mental conflict. Mercury is on his Venus in Gemini in his decan, Mercury and Venus being in mutual reception. Mrs. Besant moves the boys from India back to England. The boys' father takes legal steps to recover them from Mrs. Besant's custody, and the case is heard in the Madras High Court. The judge directs Mrs. Besant to return the custody of the two boys to their father.

Venus directed to Saturn in Scorpio: In 1913 Krishnamurti is eighteen. Occidental Venus comes to the position of his occidental Saturn in Scorpio in the fifth year of the septenary. Decan Mercury has arrived at Neptune in Gemini. There are conflicting influences: the septenary ruler has come to a sign where it is in its detriment, while the decan ruler has arrived at a sign that it rules. Krishnaji and his brother are back in England. The Madras High Court has found against Mrs. Besant and she is ordered to return custody of Krishnaji and his brother to their father. Mrs. Besant asks for a stay of execution pending her appeal. They spend several months in France. A sixty-four-page glossy magazine is published, with Krishnaji as the nominal editor. The brothers learn to play golf. When Mrs. Besant's appeal is rejected she appeals to the Privy Council in England.

Fearing kidnapping, the two boys are briefly hidden in Sicily. Mrs. Besant wins her appeal at the Privy Council. Krishnaji gets a motorbike.

Venus directed to Mars in Cancer: In 1914 septenary Venus comes to Krishnamurti's Mars. Natal Mars is in Cancer, the sign of its fall. He is now nineteen years old and this is the sixth year of the septenary, the time when old contacts are often lost. That same year the decan ruler Mercury is on Pluto in Gemini, the planet that will rule his twenties. He spends time playing golf and riding, polishing and tinkering with his motorbike. He is becoming a first-class mechanic, but he is lonely and bored. War begins. Not allowed to go to France, he briefly scrubs floors in a London hospital, but then is told to give up all ideas of war work and to concentrate on his studies.

Venus directed to Jupiter in Cancer: In 1915 Krishnamurti is twenty years old. In this final year of his septenary the ruler Venus has arrived on his Jupiter in Cancer. Pluto in Gemini now assumes rulership of the decan. He is living in London, bored and lonely. A new friend installs into Krishnaji and Nitya a love of good clothes. Whenever they can escape from the holy atmosphere of Theosophy the brothers go shopping or to cinemas.

Jeddu Krishnamurti's second Venus-Ruled Septenary

Venus in Gemini rises: In 1958 Venus again begins to rule his septenary. He is now sixty-three years old and it is twenty years since he publicly rejected the role of Messiah that Besant, Leadbeater and the other Theosophists expected him to accept, and dissolved the worldwide organization they had formed around him. He is in India, staying there for the longest time since he left in 1912, living in retirement in Poona, studying Sanskrit, communing with trees and enjoying good walks, plenty of solitude, and stupendous views of the Himalayas. Undoubtedly under the influence of Mars, his decan ruler, coming to Neptune in Gemini, he signs away the copyright of all of his books and articles, past and future; an act he will later deeply regret.

Venus directed to Mercury in Taurus: Venus comes to Mercury for the second time in 1959. Krishnaji is now sixty-four years old. Decan Mars has come to Pluto in Gemini. He is in India and falls ill with a painful kidney infection, for which he receives antibiotics that temporarily paralyze his legs and he is so weak that he must be fed like a baby. Six months of relative solitude recharge his mind. On recovery he flies to Zurich for a full check up.

Venus directed to the Sun in Taurus: Venus again comes to the Sun in 1960 when Krishnaji is sixty-five years old. Mars is at Mercury in Taurus in his decan—with Mars uncomfortable in Taurus some physical weakness may be expected. He has just returned from Europe to California, where his lack of energy had forced him to cut short a planned series of talks in order to recuperate and regain his strength. Once he recovers he goes to India, where he discusses Time and explores the nature of the observer and the observed. He goes on to visit Rome.

Venus directed to the Moon in Sagittarius: In 1961 Venus has once more come to Krishnaji's Moon. He is now sixty-six years old. In his decan Mars is at the place of his Sun in Taurus, a sign in which Mars is not welcome. It is a frenetic year that begins with much flying from place to place. He has several fainting spells. He goes home to Ojai, California for first time in several years. Then he travels to Europe, where he spends time writing and giving talks at the first Saanen gathering; then it is on to India, where he gives more public talks. He returns to Europe, to Rome, where he has a recurrence of an earlier kidney trouble, complicated by a severe attack of mumps, then to England. His fragile relationship with Rajagopal, his "travel agent", reaches a breaking point. He is exhausted.

Venus directed to Saturn in Scorpio: In 1962 Venus is on Saturn in the septenary, and Mars is on the Sagittarian Moon in the decan. He is sixty-seven. He spends all year in Europe. He decides that to avoid the incessant travel there should be a center in Europe where yearly gatherings are held. These annual gatherings at Saanen in Switzerland continue for the next twenty-five years.

Venus directed to Mars in Cancer: In 1963 Venus is again on his Mars in the septenary. Mars is on Uranus in Scorpio in the decan. This year the emphasis is on Mars, ruler of his 3rd house and his MC. He is in Europe and his health has improved. He then goes to India, where he learns of the death of "Mum", an English woman who has been his beloved substitute mother for the past fifty-two years. He is 68 years old and questions the fact of himself—how did it happen? Why was the vacant, stupid boy not conditioned by the Theosophists and their rituals, or by life in the West? He expresses a general dissatisfaction with the reaction in India to his talks; despite speaking there for thirty years nothing has happened. "There is not one person who is living the teaching."

Venus directed to Jupiter in Cancer: He is sixty-nine in 1964. Both of the rulers of the septenary and decan are on the planets that will govern the next phase of his life. Venus is on the exalted Jupiter in the septenary, and Mars has come to Saturn in Virgo in the decan. There is much travel between Europe and India. He has a new traveling companion, Alain Naudé, a South African concert pianist.

Jeddu Krishnamurti's Venus-ruled Decan

Venus in Gemini rises: Krishnamurti's Venus-ruled decan begins with his fortieth birthday, in 1935. His 9th house Saturn is the ruler of his septenary and it is on his Sun in Taurus. He tours South America for an arduous eight months, giving talks in Brazil, Uruguay, Argentina, Chile and Mexico. In each new place he prefaces his talks by a declaration that he does not belong to any religion, sect or political party, *"for organized belief is a great impediment, dividing man against man and destroying his intelligence…"* At one of his talks men belonging to a Roman Catholic organization come with tear-gas bombs intending to break up the meeting, but fail to throw the bombs—they later say they do not why exactly. That same year he flies to London to buy clothes, staying with old friends.

Venus directed to Neptune in Gemini: In 1936 Krishnamurti's Venus comes to Neptune in Gemini in the second year of his decan, a time when it should be apparent that he is changing. The same year his septenary ruler Saturn has arrived at his Moon in Sagittarius. He is forty-one years old. He flies from California to Europe, and then on to India. He is appalled by conditions in India, where it is believed that the problems of starvation, disease and unemployment can be solved by nationalism. In his view, no kind of social reform can ever be the answer to the fundamental question of human misery; until man changes radically all other change is useless and irrelevant. He is 'dead tired', having been on the move for seven months.

Venus directed to Pluto in Gemini: Krishnamurti's Venus arrived at his Pluto in Gemini in 1937. The same year the Moon in Sagittarius assumes rulership of his septenary. He is forty-two years old. This third year of the decan is often the first in which the potential of the decan ruler, here Venus, starts to become actualized. His year begins in Switzerland where he is suffers from hay fever and bronchitis. Appropriately for the Venus direction to Pluto in Gemini, he challenges the whole concept of the subconscious mind, maintaining that there is only one consciousness: dividing the consciousness into different layers only causes friction and conflict. He then returns to California, where he holds no meetings and gives no interviews.

Venus directed to Mercury in Taurus: Venus comes to Mercury in Krishnamurti's decan in 1938 when he was forty-three. Venus and Mercury are in mutual reception. The fourth year of the decan usually defines what is possible during the decan. His septenary Moon is on Saturn in Scorpio, a sign in which the Moon is ever uncomfortable. He travels alone for the first time, from New York to Rotterdam by ship. After attending a gathering he sails on (now with a companion) to India, then to Australia and New Zealand before returning to California longing for a complete rest.

Venus directed to the Sun in Taurus: In 1939 Venus came to the Sun in Krishnamurti's decan. He was forty-four and the septenary Moon is on his Mars in Cancer. Both rulers, Venus and the Moon, have come to bodies located in signs in which the rulers are strong.

He has returned from Australia to California, arriving there just before war breaks out in Europe. He reiterates his pacifism.

Venus directed to the Moon in Sagittarius: In 1940 when Krishnamurti is forty-five Venus is on his Moon in Sagittarius in the decan. This sixth year of the decan is usually one of settling down again after earlier distractions. Septenary Moon is on his Jupiter in Cancer. Europe is at war. He is living quietly in Ojai, taking long solitary walks every day. Because of his anti-war propaganda the US authorities are hesitant about extending his visa.

Venus directed to Uranus in Scorpio: Krishnamurti experiences Venus on Uranus in Scorpio in 1941 when he is forty-six. The Moon is on Venus in Gemini in his septenary. He visits the Sequoia National Park. His visa to stay in the USA is granted. He takes long solitary walks every day. His friends in England criticize his statements against the war. He gives no public talks.

Venus directed to Saturn in Scorpio: In 1942 Venus comes to Saturn in the decan. The Moon is on his Mercury in Taurus in the septenary. There are conflicting influences: the Moon is exalted in Taurus but Venus has problems in Scorpio. He is aged forty-seven. He is looking after a vegetable garden and two cows, writing each morning, and meditating for at least two hours daily.

Venus directed to Mars in Cancer: Venus comes to Krishnamurti's Mars in 1943. In the same year septenary Moon, still in Taurus, is on his Sun. He is forty-eight and somewhat isolated in California, separated from the war. He spends his time looking after his vegetable garden and cows, taking solitary walks, meditating and writing.

Venus directed to Jupiter in Cancer: In 1944 Krishnamurti is forty-nine. Decan Venus is on his Jupiter, and the Sun in Taurus has again become ruler of his septenary. He is in Ojai, California, somewhat isolated because of the war. After several years giving no talks, he begins doing so again. The candor with which he speaks against the war is almost unique in the USA at the time. His stated view is that if you resist evil you become evil.

The next year Jupiter will begin to rule Krishnamurti's decan.

Samuel Pepys' Venus-ruled Decan

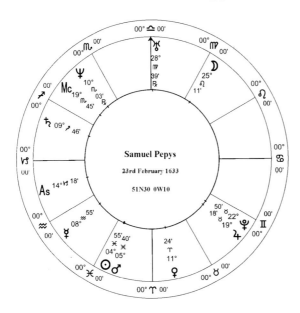

Samuel Pepys
23rd February 1633
51N30 0W10

Samuel Pepys was born in 17th Century London, the son of a tailor. He is famous nowadays for the diaries he kept between 1659 and 1668, and for his description of the Fire of London, but in his own time he was the man who reorganized England's navy, creating the force that would in later years control the oceans of the world and be instrumental in defending the most extensive empire the world has yet known.

Venus in Aries rises: Occidental Venus in its detriment in Aries begins ruling Pepys' decan in February 1663 when he is thirty years old. Venus is sextile Saturn in Sagittarius and in mutual reception with Mars. His Jupiter has come to his combust Mars in Pisces in the septenary. The combination of a weak Venus and a strong Jupiter suggests the year will contain conflicting events, both pleasant and difficult. He is a clerk employed by the Navy Board, and writes his diary nightly. Mary Ashwell, a new companion for his wife Elizabeth is employed in the household. Elizabeth is learning to dance and Sam, listening to the sound of prancing feet in the room above his study, becomes very jealous of her dancing instructor. Elizabeth and Ashwell quarrel and Sam has to tell Ashwell to leave. He writes to Lord Montagu, his mentor, informing him that Montagu's love relationships are causing people to gossip.

The period from 1663 to 1667 is a key one for Pepys. An unusual continuing trend between the septenary and decan occurs in these years. It is one that we will see appear again for Churchill in the critical years of the Second World War, and for the final years of Dr. Martin Luther King Jr. The decan ruler will come to the same planet that the septenary ruler had been directed to the previous year. This is repeated for four years, the period during which Pepys rose from being a middle-level admiralty clerk in 1663 to having attained sufficient status to be able to stand up in Parliament to defend the Navy Board.

Year	Septenary	Decan
1663	♃♂	♀♀
1664	♃☉	♀♂
1665	♃☿	♀☉
1666	♃♄	♀☿
1667	♃☽	♀♄

Venus directed to Mars in Pisces: Venus and Mars are in mutual reception. Jupiter is now on his Pisces Sun in the septenary. Both rulers have come to Pisces, a sign in which each is strong. He continues to write his diary. His brother Tom dies. Sam has several sexual adventures. He is elected a Fellow of the Royal Society and buys a microscope.

Venus directed to the Sun in Pisces: The next year, 1665, Venus remains in Pisces, and is now on Pepys' Sun. He is thirty-two years old. Jupiter is on his Mercury in Aquarius in the septenary. He continues with his diary, and is appointed treasurer of the Tangier Committee. He also becomes surveyor-general of victualling for the navy, a post he proposes for himself. He makes an alarming muddle of his personal accounts, and as a result reports that he is very confused, humiliated and dismayed. This is the year of the Great Plague in London when thousands die. There is also war with the Dutch. Sam is kept very busy and as a result is happy. His two new positions, treasurer and surveyor-general, help him quadruple his fortune—as undoubtedly does Jupiter directed to Mercury in the septenary. He spends time organizing a wedding. He gleefully reports that the king now knows him by name.

Venus directed to Mercury in Aquarius: 1666 is the year of the Great Fire of London. Sam's house escapes the flames. He is thirty-three years old and Venus is on his Mercury. Jupiter is on his Saturn in Taurus in the septenary. He has nightmares involving the fire for several months after it is finally extinguished. He is becoming very concerned that the king is making insufficient money available for the navy. His diary records the news that Jane Birch, his former servant, has agreed to return to work for him, which makes him very happy.

Venus directed to Saturn in Sagittarius: Venus comes to Pepys' Saturn in Sagittarius in 1667. Jupiter has come to his Moon in Leo in the septenary, and Sam's mother dies. Sam makes a speech before the king, warning him that failure to adequately fund the navy will lead to disaster. His gloomy prediction is soon proved correct for the Dutch attack ports on the River Medway. It is the worst humiliation England has suffered in 600 years. There is panic in London. Sam is concerned with safeguarding his money and devises many ways to do so. He fears that he will be among those blamed for the navy's defeat, and resigns his post as surveyor-general of victualling for the navy, losing the income that went with the job. As a demonstration of his continued faith in Sam, the king grants him a small prize ship that was captured in an encounter with the Dutch. Deborah Willet joins the household as Elizabeth's companion. Sam's eyes are beginning to trouble him.

Venus directed to Neptune in Scorpio: 1668 is the final year of Pepys' diary. He is thirty-five years old. Venus is on his Neptune in Scorpio. The Moon in Leo is commencing its rule of his septenary. The Navy Board is attacked for mismanagement in the House of Commons. At the culminating point of his career so far Sam defends the Navy Board, addressing the full House for three hours to the admiration of all who hear him. The king praises him for his speech. Sam writes a report on the state of the navy, recommending how it can be improved. His eyes continue to give him trouble. The direction of Venus to the sign of its detriment plays out in typical fashion. He has fallen in love with Deborah Willet, and Elizabeth discovers him with his hand up Deborah's dress, fondling her. Elizabeth is furious. The diary describes scenes of marital rage and jealousy. Deborah leaves. Elizabeth flirts with Henry Sheeres. Pepys closes his diary, writing that ending it is like a form of death. He believes he is going blind.

Venus directed to Uranus in Virgo: Venus comes to Pepys' Uranus in Virgo in 1669 when he is thirty-six years old. Venus is in her fall in Virgo and this sixth year of the decan is often the most critical time of the whole ten-year period. However, the Moon is on Jupiter in Taurus in the septenary, which should be a strong positive indicator. The year is certainly a critical one, combining the unexpected shock one expects from Venus coming to Uranus in Virgo with the positive opportunities usually associated with the Moon coming to Jupiter in the sign in which the Moon is exalted. The year begins with Sam being upset when his servant Jane Birch and his clerk Tom Edwards marry. He and Elizabeth then go on holiday to France. It is Elizabeth's first time out of the country. On their return to London Elizabeth becomes immediately ill and dies. Parliament is investigating the Navy Office for the loss of the Dutch War. Sam defends himself and the office by making a powerful counterattack—saying that the navy couldn't function well in the absence of sufficient money. Despite this public criticism of the king's parsimony, he has become one of the king's favorites. The king's brother, the Duke of York, recommends Sam for a seat in parliament.

Venus directed to the Moon in Leo: Venus is on the Moon in Leo in Samuel Pepys' decan, and at the same time the Moon is on Venus in Aries in the septenary—the emphasis on this same pair is a clear indication that the year would be of their combined nature, and an important one. The year certainly doesn't begin that way. Thirty-seven years old Sam fails to win election to parliament. He then spends much time preparing a summary of the financial state of the navy for the king. But then he meets Mary Skinner, falls in love with her, and the pair begins a relationship that will last for thirty-three years.

Venus directed to Pluto in Taurus: Little is known about Pepys' doings the next year, 1671, which is often the way when Pluto is involved. He is thirty-eight years old and the Moon is on Mars in Pisces in his septenary. He dines with John Evelyn, another famous diarist but who is unlike Sam in that he comes from an aristocratic background—Sam is rising socially.

Venus directed to Jupiter in Taurus: 1670 brings news of the death of Sam's mentor Montagu in a naval battle with the Dutch. Pepys is now thirty-nine years old and this is the final year that Venus will rule his decan. It is on his Jupiter in Taurus, the planet that will rule his next ten years. In the septenary the Moon is on his Sun in Pisces. He is elected to the council of the Royal Society, both then and now the world's leading scientific assembly—he will remain a member of the society's council for the next 27 years, in time becoming its president. Fire destroys the Naval Office. His nearby house is destroyed, but Sam escapes. He does however lose his goods, clothes, pictures and memories of the house where he and Elizabeth lived. The ending of the decan is truly the ending of an era in the life of Samuel Pepys.

* * *

Chapter 10

Mars as the Time Ruler

Before the gates of excellence the high gods have placed sweat:
long is the road thereto and rough and steep at first:
but when the heights are reached, then there is ease.
though grievously hard in the winning.

Hesiod, *Works and Days*

Mars signifies violence, contention, war, vulgarity and the muscular energy a person uses when trying to make something happen. During the years that Mars rules the septenary or the decan the individual will challenge the world in which he finds himself, discover what it is he needs to accomplish to assert his identity, what he needs to do to stand up for himself against others, and what it is he must achieve in order to survive and defeat Death. It is only by procreation that an individual can attain never-ending life, to ensure his genes live on in his children and their descendants long after his own life span is complete. Mars signifies those biological urges responsible for procreation. Venus attracts but it is Mars that acts. It is only when these impetuous biological instincts are frustrated that Mars takes on the character of a violent, killing malefic.

To the ancients Mars symbolized truthfulness and strength.

In today's world, in addition to those competitive souls involved in sporting activities or military action, Mars also signifies lawyers, barristers and attorneys; in court these advocates are the champions that represent opposing and contentious sides. Mars does not represent the law, however, for that is Jupiter's province. Even so legal training tends to be an essential qualification for a career in politics and a leadership role in public life.

When Mars is the time ruler an individual will usually have sufficient energy for whatever he wishes to accomplish. The planets it connects with as it circles the chart will provide different situations in which the individual will be given the opportunity to better enhance his ability to stand up for himself. Unless Mars is badly afflicted, rapid advancement and success are now possible. Sons may be born, property acquired, sexual passions heightened, and surgery experienced during these years. The greatest success is likely to be achieved if the individual is involved in mechanical or technical work, in the military, the police or the legal profession.

Increases in both income and the respect of others are to be expected in the years that Mars is directed to a planet in Aries or Scorpio. Promotions and victory in all his struggles are likely to occur when Mars comes to a planet in Capricorn, for he can then destroy any competition or opposition.

If Mars is badly afflicted or in those years in which it is directed to a planet in Taurus, Cancer or Libra there is danger of accidents, violence, cuts and burns. An individual is then likely to become involved in arguments, to display a rash temper, to be in danger from enemies, to be reckless and over hasty in everything he does, and to have financial difficulties. He will want to boss everyone else about, to place his own desires above those of others. Domestic disharmony can result, and the loss of his wife and children is a distinct possibility. His life can become miserable and his reputation is likely to suffer. Diseases of the blood and muscular system are also possible at these times.

Table ♂-1:

Mars as time ruler: % Positive Years

Position relative to the ☉	Day birth		Night birth		All	
	N	*% Positive*	*N*	*% Positive*	*N*	*% Positive*
Oriental ♂	292	**59.5***	277	50.6	569	**55.2**
Occidental ♂	206	54.0	285	**43.8****	491	48.1
All	*498*	*57.2****	*555*	*47.7*	*1060*	*51.9*

Tradition has Mars as a nocturnal planet but this is not confirmed in the sample. Besides observing that day births are associated with a significant percent of positive years, we also see that Mars is more helpful when oriental to the Sun. The red planet is least beneficial when occidental in a nocturnal horoscope. The differences day vs. night, and east vs. west are statistically significant.

Table ♂-2:

**% Positive Years
when ♂ is Time Lord**

♂ directed to	N	% Positive
♂ rises	132	49.3
☉	126	45.9
☽	124	50.3
☿	142	**57.3***
♀	136	55.9
♃	151	53.9
♄	122	55.6
♅	36	52.7
♆	47	48.1
♇	44	37.0
All	*1060*	*51.9*

Overall, the years when Mars rules the life tend to be marginally positive, with the direction to Mercury being the most positive. Exceptions are those years when Mars is directed to the Sun or Pluto, which are more often negative than not.

Mars is associated with the greatest likelihood of positive years when natally located in Aries, the least when located in Pisces (see Table ♂-3). The apparent negativity of Mars in Pisces, and to a lesser degree of Mars in Scorpio and Capricorn, may be unexpected to some. Mars, after all, is said to rule Scorpio (and Aries) and to be exalted when in Capricorn. When examined by element (see Table ♂-4) Mars in a Water sign, the element the planet rules according to Ptolemy, Lilly and other authorities, stands out for its negativity.[1]

Table ♂-3

Mars % Positive Years by Sign

♂ natal sign		Sign	Sign to where ♂ is directed	
N	%		N	%
62	**61.2**	♈	59	**62.8***
148	55.0	♉	112	**41.2***
50	56.1	♊	77	44.6
51	49.6	♋	98	56.3
88	51.4	♌	65	52.9
88	53.4	♍	74	55.0
107	56.6	♎	72	50.2
107	43.1	♏	85	50.0
76	54.7	♐	74	**61.1***
119	43.3	♑	81	54.7
77	58.7	♒	66	54.8
87	**35.4***	♓	65	50.1
1060	*51.9*	*All*	*928*	*52.3*

Table ♂-4:

Element of the sign containing Mars, natal & to where directed

Element	Natal ♂		Directed ♂	
	N	% positive years	N	% positive years
Fire	226	55.2	198	**58.9**
Earth	355	53.3	267	49.1
Air	234	57.1	215	49.6
Water	245	**41.7**	248	52.5

---

[1]   It has always appeared more logical to me that Jupiter should rule the Water signs. It rules Pisces and is exalted in Cancer. By contrast, Mars, while ruling Scorpio, has a Water sign, Cancer, as its Fall. The traditional rulerships of the elements are simply allocated to the planet ruling the fixed sign within each element, and this makes little sense when dealing with the Water element.

The low % Positive observed when Mars is directed to a planet in Taurus agrees with traditional statements.

The Fire and Air signs are of course the positive, male signs, while the Earth and Water signs are negative and feminine. All of the data from the sample shows that Mars is associated with a significant above-average number of positive years when directed to a planet in a fire sign, especially to one in Aries or Sagittarius.

Table ♂-5

**Mars % Positive by house,
natal & to where it is directed**

Natal house of ♂		House	House to where ♂ is directed	
N	%		N	%
75	44.6	I	94	**61.6****
118	56.0	II	108	53.6
62	54.0	III	105	55.2
126	49.5	IV	63	45.9
86	41.0	V	66	46.6
61	48.9	VI	59	49.0
96	**63.1****	VII	53	61.4
100	42.5	VIII	62	42.3
101	49.3	IX	68	45.2
74	59.9	X	77	52.8
76	51.2	XI	94	49.1
85	**62.7****	XII	79	58.4
1060	*51.9*	*All*	*928*	*52.3*

Three of the values listed in Table ♂-5 are statistically significant at the 95% level: Mars coming from the 7th or 12th houses, and when it is being directed to a planet in the 1st house.

The lower quantity in Table ♂-5 for N under the 'House to where ♂ is directed' is due to the exclusion of its direction to the ascendant.

Table ♂-6:

% Positive when Mars is the Ruler
by its place in the septenary sequence

Place of Mars in septenary	Day		Night	
	N	% Positive	N	% Positive
1	64	43.6	29	45.0
2	48	60.1	49	45.9
3	69	56.8	21	49.0
4	44	**73.0***	31	61.9
5	64	51.1	89	46.5
6	30	**67.6***	34	52.4
7	29	43.4	53	53.9
Sum	346	**55.7**	306	49.9

Mars is significantly greater than 50% when it rises fourth in a daytime chart, which corresponds to Mars ruling the decan when an individual in his thirties.

Table ♂-7:

% Positive when Mars is the Ruler
by its place in the decan sequence

Place of Mars in decan	Day		Night	
	N	% Positive	N	% Positive
1	8	78.9	12	20.8
2	21	63.1	47	56.9
3	43	66.0	44	52.8
4	15	70.8	26	33.3
5	26	50.5	31	61.9
6	30	48.3	40	**27.9***
7	6	75.1	38	40.5
8	2	0.0	9	60.0
9	1	0.0	1	0.0
10	0	0.0	1	0.0
Sum	152	**60.5**	249	45.0

Mars is associated with above-average positive years when it is one the first four planets to rise in a daytime chart. In the sample individuals born at night with Mars in the sixth place experienced an unusual amount of difficulties in their fifties. The difference between day and night births when Mars is the decan ruler is statistically significant.

Mars Rises

(49% positive years)

The year when Mars assumes rulership over a person's life, either in the decan or the septenary, can be unpleasant. The individual is likely to have more energy than usual and to get into situations where he must be more assertive, which can bring out his inherent combative, competitive nature. This often occurs in times of war. The individual may be forced to defend himself against attacks from others, and he could become involved in quarrels, conflicts, and disputes. Many upsets and much frustration can result, and because of his increased arrogance his siblings and friends may reject him. He may be attacked on the street or his house may be burgled. The sexual urge will be strong. Sports or activities in which he is physically active are often necessary to use up the sudden burst of high energy he experiences this year. When these activities are either unavailable or hampered he is likely to behave in a confrontational manner, be reckless and become accident-prone. He will tend to become wholly involved in whatever it is he is doing; push himself to the limit and demand that others too fulfill their part. He will want everything now, instantly. Should he believe his efforts are being blocked he is likely to become angry and resentful. Financial problems are possible and he may be deprived of an expected inheritance at this time. Car problems frequently occur. Several members of my sample spent all or part of the year studying law. Others had to defend themselves in court.

Table ♂-8:   **♂ to Ascendant: % Positive Years**

♂ relative to the ☉	Day birth		Night birth		All	
	N	% Positive	N	% Positive	N	% Positive
Oriental ♂	32	62.2	33	43.9	65	52.9
Occidental ♂	31	49.6	36	42.7	67	45.8
All	*63*	*56.0*	*69*	*43.2*	*132*	*49.3*

Should the ascendant be in Aries, Scorpio or Capricorn the individual may open an independent business, buy a house or win out in a tense legal situation. He will experience the need to impress and wield power over others.

Those with an ascendant in Taurus, Cancer or Libra may become involved in a scandal, experience surgery, and lose both friends and money. For them it can be a year when everything appears to go wrong. He will need to slow down, not be so hasty in whatever he is doing, and ensure that whatever he does or says is accurate.

Although tradition teaches that Mars is strongest in a nocturnal horoscope, the values observed in the sample deny this. Members in the sample who were born during the day had a much easier time than did night births. The clear difference between oriental and occidental Mars agrees with traditional teachings.

In the sample Mars natally in the 10th house or the ascendant in Sagittarius indicated significantly positive years.

Some happenings in the decan when Mars assumes the rulership:
Oriental Mars rises in daytime in decan: *he is healthier & stronger; furious; forced to avoid war as he is unready; resolves never to back down again; writes* Description of a Struggle*; fails to be elected; awarded the Nobel Prize for Physics; studying law; admitted to the New York Bar; his father remarries; first sex; much sexual activity; knee injury; wife's health is bad; his marriage is ending.*
Occidental Mars rises in daytime in decan: *angry; studying law; escapes assassination attempts; profoundly impressed by* Bhagava Gita *&* New Testament*; starts a war; arrested for drunk driving; passes exams.*
Oriental Mars rises at night in decan: *death of his heir; her ex-husband is murdered; parents die; divorced; learns to swim; stops meditating; interest in war; with friends forms a militia.*
Occidental Mars rises at night in decan: *angry; arguments; studying law; an old friend is angry at him; admonished for being drunk; estranged from his wife; embarrassed by girls; intense work.*

Some happenings in the septenary when Mars assumes the rulership:
Oriental Mars rises in daytime in septenary*: passes her law exams; wins in court; her husband dies; he becomes a Hegelian; concerned about the intense nationalism in the US; states his desire to live through the war; difficulties with his superiors; his book attacks German culture; surgery; thrombosis; tonsillitis; operation for slipped disk.*
Occidental Mars rises in daytime in septenary: *in trouble with his superiors; his first prose work captivates the public; invades Russia; in battle; arrested; steals money; he is an immense success; he is an undercover agent investigating opium dens; awarded the Iron Cross; burglarized; car problems; double pneumonia; catches an eye infection that spreads over his whole face; nearly dies from excessive bleeding.*
Oriental Mars rises at night in septenary: *making angry speeches; acquires his first slaves; war starts; peace after 21 years of war; her brother's ship is sunk; she is hated; falls from a horse; many debts; faints; very lonely.*
Occidental Mars rises at night in septenary: *saves girl from drowning; jealousy; witnesses an execution; writes* Encyclopedia of Murder*; in prison; death of siblings; investigates primeval fear; in a fire; very sad; nervous breakdown; paranoid; snubbed; breaks his ankle; much pain; stroke; death.*

Mars comes to the Sun
(46% positive)

This is usually a difficult year. The individual should expect to have to fight to be himself now, perhaps even for his right to live. Circumstances will evolve in which he will discover that in order to overcome difficulties and dangers, and to stand up to the attacks of others, he needs to stop pretending to be anyone other than himself. Others may accuse him of some misdeed and he will need to defend himself against these accusations. In doing so he will be tempted to dominate others and, possessing extra energy this year, he may find that this is something he can do quite easily. As a result he is likely to become less respectful to others.

He may show an interest this year in how things work, and want to gain a better understanding of mechanical things. Power will attract him. This can manifest in many ways, such as the desire to drive a faster car or to upgrade his computer. There is danger from fire. He may have nightmares. Sickness may be wrongly diagnosed. Members of his family may be hospitalized or go into nursing homes, and friends may disappear from his life. Several members of the sample had cardiac troubles, heightened blood pressure, or their homes were burgled during the year—the attacks associated with this direction can come in many different ways.

Table ♂-9:

♂ to ☉: % Positive Years

♂ relative to the ☉	Day birth		Night birth		All	
	N	% Positive	N	% Positive	N	% Positive
Oriental ♂	37	46.5	33	52.1	70	49.1
Occidental ♂	28	48.5	28	35.5	56	42.0
All	*65*	*47.3*	*61*	*44.5*	*126*	*45.9*

In Table ♂-9 we again see that Mars is associated with more positive years when it is oriental than when occidental. The combination of a nocturnal Sun and an occidental Mars frequently indicates a difficult year.

Another indication of a positive year is observed when Mars is directed to a 1st house Sun. This may be unexpected. We have seen previously that the Sun below the horizon in the 1st house is a strong indicator of difficult years. These difficulties appear to be due to the Sun coming to the ascendant when the individual is still very young and an easy victim of circumstances. The arrival of Mars at the position of a 1st house Sun is not at all the same. It does not necessarily occur at a young age.

In the sample Mars coming from the 12th house can be associated with above-average positive years. When Mars comes to the Sun from the opposite house, the 6th, the years tend to be difficult.

Some examples of happenings when Mars comes to the Sun in the decan:

Oriental Mars to the Sun in decan by day: *war; close to a nervous collapse; annoys publisher who stops his article being published; working long hours; her son is sentenced to prison; arrested; abstains from alcohol; his wife is hated; first publication; new job; feels his life has no purpose; voted into NFL Hall of Fame.*

Occidental Mars to the Sun in decan by day: *learns that his father, whom he had thought executed, is still alive; bike crash; his watch is stolen; failed attempt to emigrate; overcomes his natural shyness; takes his company public; fascinated by radio.*

Oriental Mars to the Sun in decan at night: *a year in which everything seems to go wrong; resigns as president's ADC; apprenticed to an engraver; marries; poems published; learns sailing; blood in urine, gallstones removed.*

Occidental Mars to the Sun in decan at night: *graduates; promoted; starts a new job; says "totally destroy all yesterdays in order to meet the new"; heart attack, bowel bleeding, pulmonary infarction; deaths in the family.*

Some examples of happenings when Mars comes to the Sun in the septenary:

Oriental Mars to the Sun in septenary by day: *excommunicated; seaplane sinks, swims in icy water to rescue; he is coshed from behind and loses the sight in his right eye; parents divorce; appendectomy; war starts; founds company; he and his mother flee; begins studying astrology; visits USA.*

Occidental Mars to the Sun in septenary by day: *introduced to astrology; husband dies in an accident; finds the people in Naples disgusting; furious when his work is savagely criticized; learns how to pick pockets; car broken into; appendectomy (wrongly diagnosed); barely escapes choking death from poison gas & is blind for several weeks; wounded; head concussion; cuts artery in his leg; severe pain.*

Oriental Mars to the Sun in septenary at night: *she & her husband buy a company; father abandons the family; his theories are disputed; "Life is hell"; studying law; his wife is nagging & moaning; declares war; avoids arrest; writes on electricity; brother dies in air crash.*

Occidental Mars to the Sun in septenary at night: *fighting to survive; "Life is strife"; several public rows; bad temper; ostracized; fire destroys palace; rioting; sent into battle; granted a pension for life; builds addition to his house; "the violence all around is crazy"; travels; extensive dental treatment; infantile paralysis.*

Mars comes to the Moon

(50% positive)

Although the direction of Mars to the Moon has a difficult reputation members of the sample usually experienced fewer problems than one might expect. This is certainly a year during which the individual is kept very busy, one that contains more work for him to accomplish than in other years. It can be a profitable period, one in which the individual sleeps well and has few worries. Property may be gained, or perhaps he will decide to renovate his home. However, there can also be unpleasant surprises. Problems with his parents can occur, and these may cause him grief. He may be attacked physically. Several members of the sample were involved in the military this year, some at a time of war. Tempers are easily lost, and the individual can become quite belligerent and act impulsively. Persons with their Moon in Aries, Scorpio or Capricorn are likely to feel intensely alive and active. Those with the Moon in Taurus, Cancer or Libra may experience of a loss of energy, and often may display a lack of will or courage. Contagious and inflammatory complaints, bladder infections, pain and surgery are also possible this year.

Table ♂-10   ♂ to ☽: **% Positive Years**

Planets relative to the ☉	Day birth		Night birth		All	
	N	% Positive	N	% Positive	N	% Positive
Oriental ♂	34	50.5	29	46.7	63	48.8
Occidental ♂	25	61.5	36	45.2	61	51.9
All	59	55.2	65	45.9	124	50.3
Waxing ☽	29	53.0	36	47.7	65	50.1
Waning ☽	30	57.3	29	43.6	59	50.6

In the sample Mars coming to the Moon in the 1st or 3rd houses indicates the upcoming year has a good chance of being positive; the direction of Mars to a Moon located in the 4th house indicates the reverse. Other significant indicators of a negative year occur when Mars is in the 8th house or in Pisces or it is directed to a Moon located in Taurus, one of the signs in which Mars has its detriment.

Table ♂-11   ♂ - ☽ **Interaction**

☽ relative to the ☉	Oriental ♂		Occidental ♂		All	
	N	% Positive	N	% Positive	N	% Positive
waxing ☽	27	40.1	38	57.1	65	50.1
waning ☽	36	55.2	23	43.2	59	50.6
All	63	48.8	61	51.9	124	50.3

Day births in the sample were associated with above-average positive years, especially so when Mars is occidental and the Moon is waning (that is, oriental). However, this pairing apparently does not combine well together. Instead the waning Moon combines best with an oriental Mars, and the waxing Moon best with occidental Mars—meaning that these two bodies produce positive years when both are on the same side of the Sun, and are associated with difficult years when they are located on a different side of the Sun. This interaction, which is statistically significant at the 90% level, is seen in Table σ-11.

Some happenings when Mars comes to the Moon in the decan:

Oriental Mars to the Moon in decan in the daytime: *his brother is executed; conscripted into army; graduates; females in the family die; separated from his wife; travels for his company; experiences an emotional nadir.*

Occidental Mars to the Moon in decan in the daytime: *qualifies at the bar; fights for national self-respect; sports success; begins studying mathematics; father dies; leaves school.*

Oriental Mars to the Moon in decan at night: *masters carpentry; angry; frustrated; forced to become king by his brother's abdication; starts a law practice; assassinated.*

Occidental Mars to the Moon in decan at night: *hit by lightning; in battle; boxing; fears shipwreck; females die; bombing damages his apartment; unhurt when boat is damaged on rapids; bankrupt; a disciple commits suicide.*

Some happenings when Mars comes to the Moon in the septenary:

Oriental Mars to the Moon in septenary in the daytime: *wins his first battles; bladder infection; studies black-body radiation; climbing; his house is completely destroyed by bombs; has a scarred forehead from attempted assassination; wife dies; political victory; loss of money from a bad deal; in jail after a gang fight; frequently beaten by sadistic teacher.*

Occidental Mars to the Moon in septenary in the daytime: *wins Pulitzer Prize; arrested for theft/inciting a riot; violent quarrel with his best friend; converts Rolls Royce into a pick-up truck; realizes he must use force to attain his ambitions; building a house; father dies; complete exhaustion.*

Oriental Mars to the Moon in septenary at night: *mother dies; his writings are published; hospital is founded; husband's affair causes scandal; joins RAF; friend's death ends an era; repairs old house; elected; works in mother's store; father's quarrel almost ends in a duel; father has two operations.*

Occidental Mars to the Moon in septenary at night: *old wound breaks open, requiring surgery; miscarriage; mother/sister/daughter/first love dies; son born; elected; stimulated to write describing his discoveries, the turning point of his life; her first one-woman show is a success; lectures; travels; death.*

Mars comes to Mercury
(57% positive)

News is likely to be received that causes the individual to become annoyed. His ideas may be criticized, he'll be contradicted, and he may be forced to fight to defend his integrity. His financial situation may be threatened and cause him worry; he will need to use all of his skills in order to avoid losses becoming irreparable. If employed his job may be endangered, perhaps due to malicious gossip. He will need to be discreet now. He should relax, take things as easy as possible, and avoid getting into a war of words. Even so, this is a year in which the individual should be able to accomplish much mental work.

In the sample these were the most positive of the years with Mars as time ruler. Day births had a much greater likelihood of positive years than did nocturnal births, a difference that is statistically significant. People with an oriental Mars in the daytime had a significantly high likelihood of a positive year. Mercury in a sign where Mars is unwelcome was frequently associated with the deaths of friends and tax problems.

Table ♂-12:   ♂ to ☿: **% Positive Years**

Planets relative to the ☉	Day birth		Night birth		All	
	N	% Positive	N	% Positive	N	% Positive
Oriental ♂	41	**70.5****	38	45.2	79	58.4
Occidental ♂	25	57.9	38	54.7	63	56.0
All	*66*	**65.7****	*76*	*50.0*	*142*	***57.3***
Oriental ☿	41	63.9	36	50.3	77	57.5
Occidental ☿	25	**68.7***	40	49.7	65	57.1

Mars natally in the 1st house was associated with difficult years. By contrast, Mars directed to Mercury in the 1st house was significantly above 50%. This is yet one more indication that it is not where the time ruler comes from but to where it is directed that matters.

Some examples of happenings when Mars comes to Mercury in the decan:
Oriental Mars to Mercury in a diurnal chart in decan: *renounces his wealth & family; his adolescent shyness becomes existential loneliness; training his voice; laying of Atlantic Cable is completed; police strike; cannot write anything that satisfies him; first sees an airplane; experiences sudden fear before an audience.*
Occidental Mars to Mercury in a diurnal chart in decan: *his father is arrested for assault; leaves school; convalescence; becomes more thoughtful & more speculative; sails between West Indies & the Canaries; sports success; learns the facts of life.*
Oriental Mars to Mercury in a nocturnal chart in decan: *his war games are cancelled; civil war; argues her first legal case; enlists in the army; suspended for cheating; studying; starts at new school/college; researching UFOs.*

Occidental Mars to Mercury in a nocturnal chart in decan: *escapes from an unconsummated marriage; finds his pregnant wife is no longer attractive; emergency operation; law degree; friction; re-elected; falls from horse, unhurt; severely wounded; paralyzed; kidney removed; promoted.*

Some examples of happenings when Mars comes to Mercury in the septenary:

Oriental Mars to Mercury in a diurnal chart in septenary: *becomes king/tsar following the assassination of his father; son born; has her first garden; enters military academy; drugs briefly send him out of his mind; evacuated because of war; his letter starts atomic bomb research; has the worst & most protracted attack of migraine.*

Occidental Mars to Mercury in a diurnal chart in septenary: *much public speaking; suicidal; father dies; loses battle; routs men by charging them with his stick; his literary career is suspended during Jacobite uprising; harmful article about him; IRS audit; improved pay; moves from passivity to activity; skin infection; very busy.*

Oriental Mars to Mercury in a nocturnal chart in septenary: *deaths in the family; her friend is murdered; his wife returns after 16-months absence; elected; breaks off his engagement; proves that lightning is electrical; unable to meditate; arrested & interrogated; severely ill, nearly dies.*

Occidental Mars to Mercury in a nocturnal chart in septenary: *accused of mental cruelty; throat operation; leader of a failed climb; he is an intellectual about to go into hiding; explains his theory of the tides; planning invasion; mental depression; starts a debating society; her book resolves financial anxieties & wins a prize.*

Mars comes to Venus
(56% positive)

If neither planet is afflicted this can be a pleasant year in which finances improve, new clothes are bought, property is acquired, knowledge is increased, and domestic happiness enjoyed. The native will be strongly attracted to the opposite sex and may fall in love. Marriages occur. Travel can be enjoyed and the means to do so should become available. It can also be a good time for artistic activity.

Table ♂-13:   **♂ to ♀: % Positive Years**

Planets relative to the ☉	Day birth		Night birth		All	
	N	% Positive	N	% Positive	N	% Positive
Oriental ♂	38	**66.6***	33	52.1	71	59.9
Occidental ♂	25	50.6	40	52.0	65	51.4
All	*63*	*60.3*	*73*	*52.0*	*136*	*55.9*
Oriental ♀	25	47.0	28	48.5	53	47.7
Occidental ♀	38	**69.0****	45	54.2	83	**61.0***

If either planet is afflicted, his friends may become angry with him, and his parents may be endangered. He may succumb to temptation, and forget other commitments in his pursuit of pleasure. Infidelity may cause his marriage to break down. The health of females and of children can be a worry.

In the sample oriental Mars was associated with significantly more positive years than occidental Mars, especially in a daytime chart. Oriental Mars combines well with occidental Venus.

Either Mars or Venus in the 7th house was associated with a value significantly above the expected 50%. Mars coming from a Saturn term to Venus located in a Mercury term was another indication of a significantly positive year.

Table ♂-14   **Mars-Venus Interaction**

Mars-Venus Interaction	Oriental ♂		Occidental ♂		All	
	N	% Positive	N	% Positive	N	% Positive
Oriental ♀	32	50.8	21	43.0	53	47.7
Occidental ♀	39	**67.3****	44	55.5	83	**61.0***
All	*71*	*59.9*	*65*	*51.4*	*136*	*55.9*

Some examples of happenings when Mars comes to Venus in the decan:
Oriental Mars to Venus by day in decan: *a series of small strokes; marriages in the family; children born; outbreak of boils; happy with his friends; promoted; hopeful & optimistic; cuts back on her public activities.*
Occidental Mars to Venus by day in decan: *parents die; marries; first girl friend; conscripted; passes bar exams; feels unqualified.*
Oriental Mars to Venus at night in decan: *dresses as a woman in private; terrified & forced to flee; creates his first original engraving; falls in love; children born; extends his contract; paying increased maintenance; elected.*
Occidental Mars to Venus at night in decan: *marries; men try to seduce his wife; deserted by her lover; affairs; angry; skiing; boxing; climbing; increased salary; mother is hospitalized; discharged from military; promoted.*

Some examples of happenings when Mars comes to Venus in the septenary:
Oriental Mars to Venus by day in septenary: *obsessed by thoughts of sex; marries; financial panic; engaged; living with his daughter; studies efficiency of light bulbs; elected; her acting coach dies; daughter born.*
Occidental Mars to Venus by day in septenary: *father is away in the army; mother dies; son is arrested; wounded; recovers his confidence; books published; reduced salary; his violin concerto is performed; wins prize; refuses honors.*
Oriental Mars to Venus at night in septenary: *remarries; meets his future wife; affair; has an uncongenial job & a nagging wife; daughter marries; in several battles; hysterectomy; son's murderer is arrested; nursing her son; his defense plan is rejected; returns to her roots; honors.*

Occidental Mars to Venus at night in septenary: grandfather is assassinated; drunk; has a show dog; his bank fails; ends his engagement; brother dies; loved by older lesbian; throat cancer; crippled by a fall & has to use crutches.

Mars comes to Jupiter
(54% positive)

Tʜᴇʀᴇ sʜᴏᴜʟᴅ ʙᴇ ʟᴇss ɴᴇᴇᴅ ɴᴏᴡ for the individual's defenses against the world to be a necessary top priority in his life. Others will be on hand to share some of this burden. An unfortunate period should now be ending and this can be a successful year. The individual's efforts can now be given a wider canvas, and he will have the freedom and confidence to seize the opportunities that present themselves and improve his position in the world. His reputation is likely to expand and his superiors will see his best side. Children may be born. He will probably have plenty of energy and enjoy good health now. Members of the military or legal professions can expect to enjoy success in their work. So too should the individual's father, who is likely to be signified by Jupiter.

If Jupiter is afflicted or occupies a sign that does not welcome Mars the year will be less easy and there is a danger of insect bites, severe headaches, accidents due to taking foolish risks, fire, attempts by others to undermine the person's status, and spending more money than he can afford.

In the sample Mars in the 5th is associated with a significantly low % positive. By contrast, Mars in the 7th is associated with a value that is significantly above 50%.

Table ♂-15:   **♂ to ♃: % Positive Years**

Planets relative to the ☉	Day birth		Night birth		All	
	N	% Positive	N	% Positive	N	% Positive
Oriental ♂	43	**65.2***	39	53.3	82	59.6
Occidental ♂	30	57.2	39	39.4	69	47.2
All	*73*	***61.9****	*78*	*46.4*	*151*	*53.9*
Oriental ♃	29	59.2	34	50.5	63	54.5
Occidental ♃	44	**63.7***	44	43.1	88	53.4

Mars is again most positive when oriental in a daytime chart, and the planet to which Mars is directed is most positive when occidental in the day.

Some examples of happenings when Mars comes to Jupiter in the decan:
Oriental Mars to Jupiter in a diurnal chart in decan: *elected; starts working at a law firm; travel, which he enjoys; runs an experimental school; building a theater; happy; father creates independent consultancy; his company builds world's largest oil rig; interest in rock-&-roll music; daughter drowns in the family pool.*

Occidental Mars to Jupiter in a diurnal chart in decan: *father is transferred from Sing Sing prison to an insane asylum; starts playing the piano; company merger, he is CEO of the new company; father is absent on a course; boxing; in prison.*

Oriental Mars to Jupiter in a nocturnal chart in decan: *in several defeats on battlefield; unhappy at boarding school; plays soldiers with adolescent friends; repairing house; inaugurated as president & Civil War starts; goes abroad to school; quells riots; grandfather dies.*

Occidental Mars to Jupiter in a nocturnal chart in decan: *her lover dies in a motorcycle crash; defeated in war; sells his estate; marries a prince; death of his rival; his plays fail & are mocked; receives an inheritance; his offices are destroyed in the blitz; plays a nurse ministering to a man dying of syphilis; stops drinking.*

Some examples of happenings when Mars comes to Jupiter in the septenary:

Oriental Mars to Jupiter in a diurnal chart in septenary: *affairs; children born; learns to play the violin; sells fifteen paintings; lectures overseas; elected/inaugurated; expelled from school; key partnership begins; marries; sister moves in to care for him; travels; admitted to the Bar; bullied at school; makes commercials.*

Occidental Mars to Jupiter in a diurnal chart in septenary: *twice breaks his arm; divorce—a great release, she feels reborn; becomes a vegetarian; first recognized as a political force; severe headaches; learns to depend on his own intuition; father takes him to court; father away in army; first skiing; awarded Nobel Prize.*

Oriental Mars to Jupiter in a nocturnal chart in septenary: *his son is kidnapped & murdered; death of his son, mother & then his wife; she & her whole family are murdered; learns to swim; victory in largest-ever battle on British soil; sells house at a loss; becomes wealthy; severe urethra pains; prostatectomy; inflammation of temporal arteries.*

Occidental Mars to Jupiter in a nocturnal chart in septenary: *sister/daughter dies; daughter/son born; campaigning; loses his sanity; first time on a plane; very sociable life; brings his mother to USA; collapses; his daughter elopes; his legs are swollen; painful bladder problems; his aging body is deteriorating but his brain is untouched; death.*

191

Mars comes to Saturn
(56% positive)

Saturn and Mars have an ambivalent relationship. Saturn tends to welcome Mars, exalting Mars in Saturn's sign of Capricorn; but there is no reciprocity for Saturn is in its fall when in Mars' sign of Aries. Here, however, we are concerned with the former case, with the welcoming reception that Saturn can provide to Mars when it arrives at the position of Saturn in the natal horoscope. This year Saturn should direct the individual's attention away from himself and involve him instead with the needs and actions of others. Energy needs to become concentrated, instant reactions to become muted and more disciplined.

Table ♂-16: ♂ to ♄: % Positive Years

Planets relative to the ☉	Day birth		Night birth		All	
	N	% Positive	N	% Positive	N	% Positive
Oriental ♂	34	55.9	31	55.4	65	55.6
Occidental ♂	25	50.6	32	59.3	57	55.5
All	*59*	*53.6*	*63*	*57.4*	*122*	*55.6*
Oriental ♄	34	50.5	33	60.3	67	55.3
Occidental ♄	25	57.9	30	54.2	55	55.9

This year the individual's energies are being curbed and directed along lines that should benefit the individual in the long run. There can be a certain amount of frustration and anxiety, periods of impotence and weakness that need to be patiently worked through.

If Saturn is in Taurus, Cancer or Libra there is a danger of financial and property loss. He may suffer defeats. He can lose his position, be the victim of bullies and become unpopular. There is the danger of a nasty fall. Surgery may be necessary. Sleep can become erratic. There is a danger from weapons and he may have to appear in court. Deaths occur, and members of his family may be ill or their actions upset him, and he may separate from his wife. As a result he can become bitter and angry about his fate. Even so, people in the sample generally experienced a fairly pleasant year.

In the sample Mars coming from the 7th house was significantly above the expected 50%, as was Mars directed to Saturn located in its own (Saturn's) term.

Some happenings when Mars comes to Saturn in the decan:
Oriental Mars to Saturn by day in decan: *his great year, writes four papers that forever change man's view of the universe; attempt on his life; orders the Cultural Revolution; studies history; marries; husband dies; depressed; has difficulty sleeping; stage fright; death from chronic diarrhea.*

Occidental Mars to Saturn by day in decan: *caught in act of picking a pocket; boxing; conscripted into the military; victory by a bluff; nursing during war; digging graves; in gym team; hiking; his life changes when his father is promoted; overseas for the first time.*

Oriental Mars to Saturn at night in decan: *studies the law; graduates; "everything seems to be collapsing"; births in the family; daughter marries; starts a seven-year apprenticeship; his face is burnt; overseas travel.*

Occidental Mars to Saturn at night in decan: *leaves home; marries/separates; re-elected/loses election; in love with younger boy; climbing; bad fall from a horse; traveling; joins RAF; shot; kidnap threats.*

Some happenings when Mars comes to Saturn in the septenary:

Oriental Mars to Saturn by day in septenary: *his will to live is destroyed when the Gestapo kill his son; imprisoned; tension; money & fame, but insecurity; passes his driving test; wins Nobel Peace Prize; his marriage proposal is rejected; former lover dies; first sexual experience; starts school; feels estranged.*

Occidental Mars to Saturn by day in septenary: *feeling repose & renewal when alone; studying law; loses in court; defeated; his One Hundred Days; enjoying his fame; defiant; many acts of self-degradation; infatuated; he is diminished; erratic sleep; exiled; frustrations; publishes his greatest poem.*

Oriental Mars to Saturn at night in septenary: *orders complete cessation of Vietnam war; Civil War starts; WW1 ends; son is born; parents separate; divorce; proves lightning is a form of electricity; first attack of gout; writes on educational reform; publishes her first novel in seven years; her brother is home from the war.*

Occidental Mars to Saturn at night in septenary: *concentrated effort brings peak experiences out of boredom & misery; revels in war, victory and gore; immense fame; honors; graduates from law school; she has two miscarriages; refuses to be the Theosophists' guru; given freedom of the City of London.*

Mars comes to Uranus
(53% positive)

This can be an uncomfortable year. An individual will have to maintain his individuality in the face of the pressures that can threaten him. He will possess great energy, have more self-confidence than usual, and as a result may behave impulsively, taking risks where they are not really necessary. Accidents can result. There may be outbursts of anger, and he is likely to encounter violent people. Unpleasant events can occur without any warning, from unexpected sources.

The problems are usually less if Uranus is in a sign where Mars is welcomed and the nature of the planets involved in the coincident septenary is important in determining the likely nature of the coming year. Some of those sample members involved in a contemplative life report experiencing kundalini rising through their bodies this year.

Table ♂-17:   ♂ to ♅: % Positive Years

Planets relative to the ☉	Day birth		Night birth		All	
	N	% Positive	N	% Positive	N	% Positive
Oriental ♂	11	49.3	13	62.6	24	56.5
Occidental ♂	4	67.8	8	33.9	12	45.2
All	*15*	*54.2*	*21*	*51.6*	*36*	*52.7*
Oriental ♅	8	56.5	9	50.3	17	53.2
Occidental ♅	7	51.6	12	52.7	19	52.4

There are too few observations here for the results to be counted on.

Some happenings when Mars comes to Uranus in the decan:
Oriental Mars to Uranus by day: *war starts; passes law exams; inherits title; marries; separated from his wife; meets future husband; long-lasting affair ends; plays violin duets with his friends; loses election; daughter refuses marriage offer; wins a sweepstakes; writes on morals.*
Occidental Mars to Uranus by day: *starts weekly newspaper; loses election/his job; organizing others; hospitalized, in a coma; immersed in religious studies.*
Oriental Mars to Uranus at night: *seen as an outsider, an alien; sister dies in plane crash; nearly driven insane by noise; passes exam; travels; goes to a new school; his book is published.*
Occidental Mars to Uranus at night: *lengthy convalescence; pay increases; studying law; religious doubts; rejected; substitute mother dies; his wife leaves him.*

Mars comes to Neptune
(48% positive)

Self-discipline will be needed to face the difficulties imposed by this year's encounter with unreality. It can be a time of defeat. The individual may lose his dignity and prestige and be mortified. Scandals can occur. Others may defeat him unfairly, using tricks. He may be powerless to fight, and may believe himself surrounded by enemies, threatened from all directions. Few escape this year without feelings some sense of paranoia. The individual should avoid involvement in any scheme that has the faintest possibility of being dishonest. When at all possible he should avoid using drugs, prescribed or not. His energy is low and his physical defenses are weak now, as a result he can easily catch infections.

Table ♂-17: ♂ to ♆: % Positive Years

Planets relative to the ☉	Day birth		Night birth		All	
	N	% Positive	N	% Positive	N	% Positive
Oriental ♂	11	74.0	14	51.6	25	61.5
Occidental ♂	7	64.6	15	**18.1****	22	32.9
All	*18*	*70.3*	*29*	*34.3*	*47*	*48.1*
Oriental ♆	9	70.3	20	40.7	29	49.9
Occidental ♆	9	70.3	9	20.1	18	45.2

There is further evidence in the above table that Mars is most positive when oriental in a daytime chart, although here that evidence comes from the opposite side: a significantly low value associated with occidental Mars in a nighttime birth. This was an important year for individuals starting a legal practice.

Some happenings when Mars comes to Neptune in the decan:
Oriental Mars to Neptune by day: *final year of legal studies; endows a university chair; retires; elected; says religion is based mainly on fear of the unknown; prostate operation; reviews the navy; discovers his wife's infidelity; marriage ends.*
Occidental Mars to Neptune by day: *becomes serious about his faith; released from prison; forms ambulance corps during war; fails exams; elected; called to the Bar; goes into the army; father is released from insane asylum.*
Oriental Mars to Neptune at night: *joins the navy; brother dies in plane crash; sees those he loves cut to pieces; father has two operations; stroke; paralysis.*
Occidental Mars to Neptune at night: *opens a private law practice; sells his estate; mother dies; he is utterly alienated; world tour; a wretched year; works as a maid; accused of corruption; told his son has cancer; has to flee from his country.*

Mars comes to Pluto
(37% positive)

This can be a very stressful year, as the value of 37% indicates. To help him better to face the future, an aspect of the individual's life will probably pass away now, making way for something new. Whether this will be for the better or not depends very much on the sign Pluto occupies: the change is usually positive if Pluto is in a sign where Mars is welcomed, but it is likely to be negative when Pluto is occupying one of the signs in which Mars is uncomfortable. Those on whom the individual has depended in the past may leave him. Parents die, wives leave, children run away, friends depart. He may feel that he is completely alone, with no one there to fight in his corner. Violent conflicts may occur when the individual finds himself in a situation in which he needs to escape the domination of another.

Table ♂-18: **♂ to ♀: % Positive Years**

Planets relative to the ☉	Day birth		Night birth		All	
	N	% Positive	N	% Positive	N	% Positive
Oriental ♂	11	41.1	14	51.6	25	47.0
Occidental ♂	6	45.2	13	**13.9****	19	**23.8****
All	*17*	*42.6*	*27*	*33.5*	*44*	*37.0*
Oriental ♀	11	49.3	15	36.2	26	41.8
Occidental ♀	6	30.1	12	30.1	18	30.1

Again a statistically significant low value associated with occidental Mars in a nighttime birth.

Some happenings when Mars comes to Pluto in the decan:
Oriental Mars to Pluto by day: *her son is severely ill; loses election; father dies; imprisoned; found not guilty of child molestation charges; admires the harmony of nature; hires an old enemy; avoiding alcohol; lumbago.*
Occidental Mars to Pluto by day: *ordained as a minister; bullet wound in the stomach; marries; legal work; he is badly beaten up in prison/by racist mob; begins listening to opera; enters seminary; graduates from submarine school; starts getting into trouble at school.*
Oriental Mars to Pluto at night: *writes book under a pseudonym; becomes a theosophist; fascinated by the Sphinx; writes on charlatan messiahs; a thoroughly depressing year; legal battle over child support; studies artillery; delivers the Gettysburg Address.*
Occidental Mars to Pluto at night: *pretends insanity; son/father dies; start of homosexual affair that will end in his total disgrace; feels unwanted; reelected prime minister; interest in theosophy; rejected for war service; large pay increase; extensive physical therapy; mild stroke; tired & haggard, he is a very sick man.*

Abraham Lincoln's Mars-ruled Decan

Mars in Libra rises: Abraham Lincoln is fifty years old in February 1859 when Mars rises and takes over the rulership of his decan. Oriental Mars is in the 9th House, close to the start of the 10th, and is trined by the nocturnal rising Sun, both bodies being located at his birth in signs of their detriment, Mars in Libra and the Sun in Aquarius. The weakness of Mars warns that much unpleasantness of a martial nature can occur over the coming decade. The Sun has come to his Capricorn Moon in the septenary. The Illinois legislature chooses his rival Stephen A. Douglas for the U.S. Senate over Lincoln. He makes his last trip through the 8th Judicial Circuit, and writes a short autobiography.

Mars directed to Venus in Aries: In February 1860 Mars comes to Lincoln's 3rd house Venus. Mars has come to one of the signs that it rules. As Venus and Mars are in a positive mutual reception the year should be a positive one. In the septenary the Sun is on Saturn in Sagittarius. Lincoln is now fifty-one years old. He delivers an impassioned political speech against slavery in New Haven, Connecticut. The *Lincoln-Douglas Speeches* are published. He is nominated as the Republican candidate for President of the United States, and writes a longer autobiography. He is then elected the 16th U.S. president, the first Republican to gain the office. South Carolina immediately secedes from the Union. This act is followed by the secession of Mississippi, Florida, Alabama, Georgia, Louisiana and Texas.

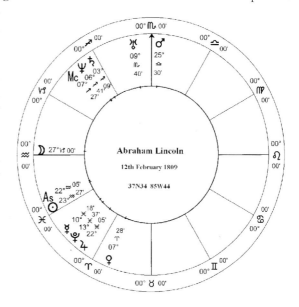

Mars directed to Jupiter in Pisces: Mars has come to Jupiter in Pisces, while septenary Sun has arrived at Mars in Libra. The emphasis on Mars is appropriate for the start of the Civil War this year, and so is the weakness of the septenary Sun in the sign Mars occupies. Lincoln as president authorizes the suspension of the Writ of Habeas Corpus. His political rival Stephen A. Douglas unexpectedly dies of acute rheumatism. The Union army is defeated at Bull Run, close to Washington. Lincoln frees the slaves being used by the Confederates in their war effort.

Mars directed to Pluto in Pisces: Lincoln is fifty-three years in 1862. Mars comes to Pluto in the decan. This direction points to the year being one that could include many deaths. In the septenary the Sun comes to Venus in Aries, where the Sun is exalted. Lincoln's eleven-year-old son Willie dies. Mary, his wife, is emotionally devastated and never fully recovers. Lincoln takes direct command of the Union armies. He announces that the government will give 160 acres of publicly owned land to anyone who will claim and then work the property for five years. The Union army is defeated at the second Battle of Bull Run in northern Virginia. The Confederates are halted at Antietam on the bloodiest day in U.S. military history. Lincoln issues an Emancipation Proclamation freeing all slaves. The Union is defeated at Fredericksburg.

Mars directed to Mercury in Pisces: In 1864, with Mars on his Mercury in the decan and the Sun on Jupiter in Pisces in the septenary, Lincoln creates a national banking system and introduces military conscription. The Union army is defeated at Chancellorsville but then wins the Battle of Gettysburg. He meets with the abolitionist Frederick Douglass who pushes for full equality for Union 'Negro troops'. Lincoln delivers the Gettysburg Address, and issues the Proclamation of Amnesty and Reconstruction for the restoration of the Union.

Mars directed to the Sun in Aquarius: Abe Lincoln is fifty-five years old in 1864. Mars is on the Sun in the decan as the septenary Sun has comes to Mercury. The emphasis on the Sun speaks of matters involving leadership. Lincoln appoints Ulysses Grant as general-in-chief of all the Federal armies. A coalition of Republicans and War Democrats nominates him for a second presidential term. He calls for volunteers for military service. Atlanta is captured. He approves Sherman's march to the sea. Lincoln is then re-elected president.

Mars directed to the Moon in Capricorn: The decan ruler Mars comes to Lincoln's waning Moon in Capricorn in 1865. This is the year that the weak Mercury in Pisces (ruler of his natal 8th house) takes over his septenary. Lincoln is fifty-six years old. The commander of the Confederate armies Robert E. Lee surrenders to Grant in Virginia. The war has ended. Lincoln speaks on the problems of reconstruction. He is then killed, assassinated by gunshot in a theater.

Adolf Hitler's Mars-ruled Septenary

Mars in Taurus rises: Hitler is 28 years old in April 1917 when Mars assumes control of his septenary. Mars is in the 8th house, conjunct Venus and square to Saturn; the Saturn antiscion is conjunct Mars and Venus. Jupiter is the ruler of his decan and this year it is on the Sun in Taurus. He is a corporal in the German army and had been wounded late the previous year at the Battle of the Somme. After a period in hospital he returns to his unit, the 16th Regiment, and resumes his duties as a runner. Waiting to go into battle he spends time painting. He then participates in the battle of Ypres and is awarded the Military Cross, 3rd Class, with swords. On leave he visits Leipzig and Dresden. He is reading history and philosophy. He loses his dog and his paintings are stolen. There is a lack of food during the bitterly cold winter, and he is famished.

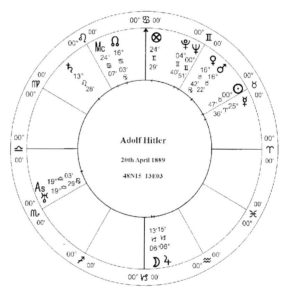

Mars is directed to the Sun in Taurus: Single-handed he captures four French prisoners. For previous achievements he is awarded the Iron Cross, 1st Class—"For personal bravery and general merit". That same year he is awarded three other decorations: the *Regimentsdiplom* for outstanding bravery; the *Verwundetenabzeichen* (medal for wounded); and the *Dienstauszeichung* (Service medal), 3rd Class. Hitler is 29 years old. Jupiter the decan ruler has come to Mercury in Aries. With Mars weak in Taurus, he barely escapes a choking death from mustard gas and is blind for several weeks. He is also wounded. Germany is defeated; he is ashamed by Germany's defeat—demoralized, in a black despair. He hears voices and sees a vision. He recovers his sight, but then has a second, hysterical blindness. Anarchy extends throughout Germany.

Mars is directed to Mercury in Aries: Hitler is 30 years old in 1919 the year that Mars comes to its own sign. Mercury has become the ruler of Hitler's decan. The emphasis on Mercury in both decan and septenary is played out in several events this year. Hitler goes to Munich where he attends lectures at the university. There is bitter fighting in Munich, the Free Corps defeating the Communists—dead bodies litter the streets. He is discovered to be a natural orator, and gives many speeches as a member of a military propaganda team—
"Herr Hitler is a born people's speaker, and by his fanaticism and his crowd appeal he clearly compels the

attention of his listeners, and makes them think his way." He leaves the army. He joins the German Workers Party, impresses the leaders by his speaking ability, and quickly becomes one of its leaders, reorganizing the Party and rapidly increasing its membership. He is living in a revolutionary atmosphere, and everywhere sees a conspiracy of Jews and Marxists aimed against the German workingman.

Mars is directed to Jupiter in Capricorn: Hitler is 31 years old in 1920. Both his decan ruler Mercury and the septenary ruler are on his Jupiter, with Mars coming to the sign where it is exalted. The year is a turning point in his life. He gives his first speeches before large audiences, and takes his first flight. Almost singlehandedly he broadens the base of the party, which is renamed *Nationalsozialistische Deutsche Arbeiterpartei* (NSDAP). It is a name Hitler hopes would inspire and incite, that will scare off the timid and attract those willing to bleed for their dreams. He adopts the swastika as the party's symbol; for millennia it had represented the wheel of the sun or the cycle of life, from now on it will have a more sinister connotation. With General Ludendorff he becomes the joint leader of the party. The party buys a newspaper, and the first national congress occurs. In less than a year his magnetic personality, crowd appeal and obsessive drive make him a political force in Bavaria.

Mars is directed to the Moon in Capricorn: Mars is still in the sign of its exaltation. Mercury is also on the Moon in the decan. The emphasis is on his Moon. He is 32 years old. He is elected chairman of the NSDAP and is now in absolute control of the party. A private army, *Sturmabteilung* (SA) is created. He realizes that he must use force if he wants things to go his way. He spends five weeks in jail for inciting a riot.

Mars is directed to Saturn in Leo: Hitler is 33 years old in 1922 when Mercury comes to Uranus in Libra in his decan. Membership of the Party has increased. He leads his party and invades Coburg ending the Communist domination of the town. Hermann Goring and Rudolf Hess join him. The United States begins to take an interest in Hitler, and has military officers attend and report on his speeches.

Mars is directed to Venus in Taurus: He is 34 years old. Mars has come to its dispositor, and Mercury has arrived at Saturn in Leo in the decan. There is a pressing need for money and he sets off on a series of tours to raise funds for the party. In his obsessive hatred of Jews, he goes over the edge of reality. He is becoming paranoid. There is massive inflation throughout Germany, and he becomes convinced that people are now ready for revolution. He orders a Putsch, which after three days of fighting the government forces fails and he is wounded in his arm. He ends up in prison, where initially he broods and refuses to eat. His party is disbanded by law. Sentenced to five years in prison, he recovers his confidence and starts writing *Mein Kampf.*

Adolf Hitler's Mars-ruled Decan

Mars in Taurus rises: Hitler is 50 years old in April 1939. The previous decan ruled by his Sun brought him to power, provided his bloodless takeover of Austria, and ended with his unopposed invasion of Czechoslovakia. Now, with his septenary Moon directed to the elevated Saturn in Leo, he signs a secret pact with Russia to divide Eastern Europe. He then starts the Second World War by invading Poland, where he has Polish Jews and intellectuals killed. He tries to make peace with Britain and France. There are several attempts on his life.

Mars is directed to the Sun in Taurus: The direction of Mars to a planet in Taurus usually suggests a difficult year, but Mars was already in Taurus at Hitler's birth. The septenary Moon is also in Taurus, where it is exalted, coming to Venus the sign's ruler, which is a powerful positive indicator that conflicts with the negativity we might associate with the decan's direction of Mars. He invades Denmark and Norway and follows this a month later by invading Belgium and Holland. His armies win several quick victories, ending with victory over France. The British army escapes capture at Dunkirk. He tours Paris in triumph, and signs a Tripartite Pact with Japan and Italy. He visits Franco in Spain but cannot persuade him to enter the war, and vacillates between whether to invade England or Russia. He is unaware that the British are decoding all his directives. He sanctions mass air raids on London but fails to wins the ensuing Battle of Britain. He invades Yugoslavia and Greece. Believing himself to be "more godlike than human", the first of a new race of supermen, the first and only mortal to have emerged into a 'superhuman state', he decides he is not bound by any human morality or convention and is 'above the law'. He is however self-conscious about his need to use glasses for reading.

Mars is directed to Mercury in Aries in 1941 when Hitler is 52 years old. At the same time the Moon, still in Taurus where it is exalted, comes to Mars in his septenary. This added emphasis on Mars indicates that it would be an important year, one strongly influenced by the red planet. Both time rulers have come to signs in which they are strong. In a rage when his deputy Hess flies to England on his astrologer's advice in an attempt to make peace, he has all astrologers arrested. He invades Russia and has several great victories. He is however sick, experiencing recurrent stomach pains, followed by dysentery. An incurable heart disease is discovered but he is not told of this. The German army's advance is stopped by the onset of the Russian winter. Following Pearl Harbor, he declares war on the USA. The extinction of the Jews begins.

Mars is directed to Jupiter in Capricorn: It is 1942 and Hitler is 53 years old. The septenary Moon continues to be directed to Taurus and has now come to the Sun. Each of the time rulers has arrived at a sign in which it is exalted. Appropriately, he now has more *de facto* power than anyone in history. His health improves and his spirits rise. The mass extinction of the Jews is accelerated. His armies are victorious in Northern Africa but his allies, the Japanese, suffer loses in the Pacific. He refuses to listen to anyone's advice, and goes into extreme rages, swinging from extreme optimism. Paranoid, convinced he is surrounded by traitors, he begins eating alone in his room. Then the war turns sour. He is defeated at Stalingrad, and in North Africa the German armies are in retreat. He vacations at Berchtesgaden.

Mars is directed to the Moon in Capricorn: He is 54 years old in 1943. The septenary Moon has come to Mercury in Aries. The Moon, weak in Capricorn, is being emphasized. Defeats continue. Plans to assassinate him fail. North Africa is lost. Anglo-American troops land in Sicily. Italy is defeated and Mussolini arrested. The allies' carpet-bombing of Hamburg creates a blazing mass of ruins. His health is failing, yet he categorically refuses to negotiate with Stalin. He has Mussolini rescued, and then has the Warsaw ghetto destroyed to speed up the destruction of the Jews. He has now become more open about this Final Solution.

Mars is directed to Uranus in Libra: Hitler is 55 years old in April 1944. Mars is directed to Libra where it is weak, and at the same time the septenary Moon has come Capricorn, a sign in which she is also weak, to his Jupiter. These are ominous indications for Hitler. His health is poor. The allies land at Normandy. He inaugurates V-1 rocket attacks on London, and then follows them with the even more frightening and destructive V-2s. He escapes assassination attempts. He is in a deep depression, losing allies and the war, facing total defeat from all sides. His enemy Roosevelt dies.

Mars is directed to Saturn in Leo: He is 56 years old and fully aware that his armies have been defeated. Jupiter in its fall in Capricorn takes over rulership of his septenary. Within days of his birthday, Hitler marries Eva Braun, and the two of them then commit suicide.

Oliver Cromwell's Mars-ruled Decan

Tradition says the never-defeated Puritan cavalry general who became the Lord Protector of England was born in the early hours of 25th April 1599 (old style), with Aries rising. A nocturnal birth should have prompted a notable life-direction change at age 24¼, but at that time nothing seems to have occurred; Cromwell was leading a quiet life in a country town with his wife and growing family. On 24th June 1617, however, when he was eighteen years and two months old, his father died and he was forced to abandon his studies at Sussex College, Cambridge and return home. He never resumed his studies at Cambridge. Instead he spent the next two years studying law at the Inns of Court in London. Accordingly I propose that England's greatest hero was born during the daytime, and suggest that his ascendant was in Cancer and that the exalted Jupiter was the first planet to rise following the birth.

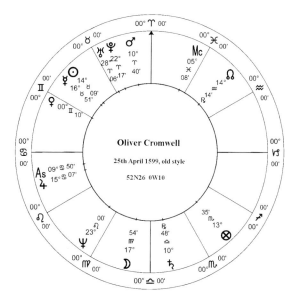

Oliver Cromwell
25th April 1599, old style
52N26 0W10

Cromwell's horoscope is extremely strong, as one would expect for a commoner who achieved the power of a king. The retrograde Saturn receives a tight opposition from Mars in Aries in the 10th house. These two bodies are part of a T-cross with Jupiter, which I place close to the ascendant. As two of the planets, Jupiter and Saturn, in this T-cross are in signs where they are exalted[2], and the other one, Mars, is in a sign it rules, this is a very powerful configuration. Mercury is also especially strong. It is with the Sun in Taurus, and in mutual reception with Venus in Gemini by rulership and with the Moon in Virgo by exaltation, and these two, Venus and the Moon, are in turn the dispositors of the Jupiter and Saturn, the two exalted planets. To add to the strength of this chart, the Sun closely squares the two lunar nodes; Pluto is in Aries, the sign in which it is most powerful, where it is conjunct Uranus and trined by Neptune; and the antiscion of the Moon falls close to Mars.

The placement of the planets in a bowl in the eastern half of the chart, enclosed by the Mars-Saturn opposition, shows Cromwell's inherent independence: this is a man who

---

[2] Jupiter and Saturn are simultaneously in their exaltation signs every 59 years. They were occupying them in July 1776 when the American colonies declared their independence from Great Britain.

thinks for himself. Jupiter, the planetary protector, is at the ascendant, and this deeply religious man would become England's Lord Protector, the champion of the common people and a strong advocate for the freedom of religion. Saturn retrograding in the northernmost part of the chart indicates how history, influenced by the clever propaganda of a restored royalty, would see him as a cruel traitor, a hypocritical regicide and a tyrannical usurper. The strong Mars applying to conjunct the midheaven says he would come to prominence in a time of war, and this happened in the decan described here.

Mars rises in Aries: Cromwell is forty years old when the new decan begins in May 1639. In the septenary Mercury is in the penultimate year of its rulership and has arrived at Jupiter in Cancer. In May Cromwell's eldest son Robert dies of an unknown fever. He experiences

a fierce grief, the memory of which will remain with him for the rest of his life. The following April he is elected Member of Parliament for Cambridge and attends the Short Parliament. It is the first time the King has summoned Parliament in eleven years, and he only does so to obtain money for his war with the Scots. He dissolved it after a few weeks, once these wishes are fulfilled.

Mars comes to Saturn in Libra: Cromwell is forty-one years old in 1640, the final year of Mercury's rulership of his decan, when it comes to Venus in Gemini. On 3rd November, the King's differences with the Scots not resolved, what has come to be known as the Long Parliament opens. It will continue sitting for thirteen years. Cromwell is again the Member for Cambridge. His first public speech brings him much attention when he indignantly questions the imprisonment of a man sentenced for the distribution of unlicensed literature.

Mars comes to the Moon in Virgo: He is forty-two years old in May 1641. Venus in Gemini becomes the septenary ruler. This is the year of the *Grand Remonstrance,* in which Parliament presents its grievances against the actions of the King. Cromwell's part in this is to identify instances of peers and bishops abusing their privileges at the king's request. The King reacts by entering Parliament to arrest the five members whom he considers are the ringleaders in these attacks on his royal authority. When he asks where they are, the Speaker responds, "May it pleasure your Majesty, I have neither eyes to see nor tongue to speak in this place but as the House is pleased to direct me, whose servant I am…" The five MPs escape and the King leaves London, never to return until the time of his death. Cromwell proposes there should be a committee for placing the kingdom in a posture of defense, and this is ordered. A month later he makes an angry speech opposing episcopacy.

Mars comes to Neptune in Leo: Oliver Cromwell is forty-three years old in 1642 and the septenary ruler Venus has come to Mercury in Taurus, the sign Venus rules. He learns that Cambridge University is about to send silver plate to the king and with volunteers he stops the treasure from leaving Cambridge. Two weeks later, on 22nd August, the anniversary of the birth in 1485 of monarchial authority as established by Henry VII at Bosworth Field, Charles I raises his standard at Nottingham, his challenge opening the Civil War. Cromwell's response is vigorous, effective and brisk: within a week he has mustered a troop of horse. On 23rd October, the first battle of the Civil War, that of Edgehill, takes place. Cromwell and his troop arrive late, after Prince Rupert's cavalry has defeated the parliamentary forces. In March, Cromwell becomes a colonel and expands his troop of volunteers into a full regiment, the Ironsides, having a special care to enlist religious men. The discipline of his men is in marked contrast to the general run of military custom—they are fined if they curse, set in the stocks if they get drunk. In time they will become the New Model army.

Mars comes to Jupiter in Cancer: He is forty-four years old in 1643 and the decan ruler has comes to the sign in which it is its fall. In the septenary Venus stays in Taurus and has come to the Sun. The first success of Cromwell's disciplined and godly force, who go into battle singing psalms, comes in a skirmish near Grantham in May, when his twelve troops rout twenty-five troops of Royalists; only two of his men are killed, to nearly one hundred of the enemy. In July he leads the successful siege of Burghley House, taking it with no loss of life and capturing two hundred Cavalier prisoners, and then relieves Gainsborough, hard pressed by a Royalist siege. He becomes Governor of the Isle of Ely. In October, he leads the first cavalry charge (against superior odds) at the Battle of Winceby. His horse is killed under him, but on another horse he leads a second charge that puts the enemy to flight. Most of the autumn he spends in Ely with his family. In January, despite himself being a passionate lover of music, he stops the service in Ely Cathedral because he finds the practice of a choir service "unedifying and offensive." In January, he is promoted to Lt-General. The siege of York begins in April but is withdrawn when news arrives of Prince Rupert coming with an overwhelming force to relieve the city.

Mars comes to Venus in Gemini: He is forty-five years old in May 1644. The decan ruler Venus is on Mars in Aries. The decan-septenary combination with its emphasis on Mars points to a memorable year. With Venus coming to Aries, where it is in detriment, the year is also likely to contain sadness. It begins with the death from smallpox of his twenty-one year old son, Oliver, "a civil young gentleman and the joy of his father". Then, in July the parliamentary army defeats the Royalists at the Battle of Marston Moor, the largest battle ever fought on British soil. Cromwell's cavalry dramatically routs Prince Rupert's cavalry, but then, going quite against the instincts of the time, he stops his men from pursuing the fleeing cavalry and instead goes to assist the rest of the parliamentary army that is in dire straits. His charge from the enemy's lines totally demoralizes his opponents. The victorious army sings a Psalm of thanksgiving and then sleeps unfed under a Harvest Moon. Four thousand Royalists and less than three hundred Roundheads are killed; at least fifteen hundred Royalists are taken prisoner. There is then dissention between the parliamentary generals concerning how to finally defeat the king's remaining forces, with Cromwell pleading his case before the House of Commons. In December, at Cromwell's instigation, Parliament began debating the Self-Denying Ordinance by which no Member of Parliament could hold office in the Army. Most of the army commanders resign their positions in order to stay in Parliament, but Cromwell retains his command. He is concerned with making the New Model army militarily efficient, as opposed to it being Parliament-controlled.

Mars comes to Mercury in Taurus: Cromwell is now forty-six years old. In his septenary Venus has arrived at Saturn in Libra. This is another year in which the two rulers have different strengths: Venus is strong in Libra but Mars has difficulties in Taurus. In a series of skirmishes and assaults near Oxford, he shows himself at his brilliant best and stops the King from leaving his stronghold at Oxford to go north to join Prince Rupert. He is then ordered to go to East Anglia and in his absence the King escapes from Oxford. In June the New Model Army overwhelm the King's army and capture the King's private papers at the Battle of Naseby, with Cromwell leading the cavalry charge that decides the battle. In July his army massacres Royalists at the Battle of Langport. In September Cromwell successfully captures Prince Rupert's stronghold, the city of Bristol. More successful sieges follow at Devizes, Winchester and the Catholic stronghold at Basingstoke. Now only Oxford, to where the King and Prince Rupert have returned, retains a significant Royalist center of defiance. The conflicting directions of the decan and septenary rulers are apparent in January when Cromwell's favorite daughter Bettie is married but he is unavoidably absent, on military duty.

Mars comes to the Sun in Taurus: In 1646 Cromwell is forty-seven years old. In the septenary Venus has come to his Moon in Virgo. This year both rulers are in signs in which they are weak. In April the King flees from Oxford to the Scottish Army, where he believes he will be safe—they make him a prisoner. Cromwell's eldest daughter Bridget marries his friend Henry Ireton. On 24th June, Oxford surrenders. The Civil War is finally over, and Cromwell is a hero recognized not only by those who served under him, but throughout England as Parliament's most glorious General. He leaves the army and experiences the obscurity of civilian life after his military glories of the previous four years, becoming extremely depressed. He brings his family from Ely to London. In February, the Scots hand the King over to Parliament, who imprison him in Oxford. In the same month Cromwell is severely ill from an infected abscess in the head—he says later that he nearly died. He complains about those in Parliament who are now squabbling over their newly found power. Internal problems are increasing among the Civil War's victors. Those who had fought the war have many grievances including not having been paid and they petition Parliament, while the civilian population resents that the army continues to exist under arms. Cromwell becomes increasingly unhappy that Parliament is not being sympathetic for the grievances of the soldiers, and starts to avoid the debates. He is dissatisfied with the whole progress of his life and considers leaving England, to serve in Germany in the cause of the Elector Palatine.

Mars comes to Uranus in Aries: Mars has arrived at the sign its rules. In the septenary Venus has come to Jupiter in Cancer. Cromwell is forty-eight years old and this year, 1647, is the final one of Venus' rulership of his septenary. In May he is one of the four Parliamentary commissioners who hears the complaints of the upset Army. The Presbyterians, who control Parliament, demand that the Army is disbanded, and the King returned to the Scots. On 1st June Cromwell has a troop of five hundred soldiers collect the King from Oxford and bring him to Cambridge. On 4th June, Cromwell leaves London to avoid being arrested by the Presbyterians, and goes to the Army at Newmarket. On 5th June the Army establishes a Council that includes Cromwell and denies that it wants to overthrow Presbyterianism, but it refuses to disband. At his own request the King is moved to Newmarket; he believes he can use the conflict between the Army and Parliament to his advantage. The Army calls for fresh elections to the House of Commons, which Parliament rejects. In July the citizens of London as a mob attack Parliament. In early August the Army, headed by Cromwell, marches into London to the cheers of the population, and becomes the authority in the land. The Army proposes complete manhood suffrage and a new system of government. On 11th November, the King flees, ending up on the Isle of Wight.

Mars comes to Pluto in Aries: In 1648 Mars continues to be in the sign it rules, and now it has arrived at the place of its co-ruler. Cromwell is forty-nine years old. The exalted Jupiter assumes control of the septenary. A Royalist uprising in Wales starts the second Civil War on 30th April. Cromwell leads the Army into Wales and captures the castles at Chepstow, Tenby and Pembroke, the last with twenty-foot thick walls requires a six-week siege. In August he defeats the Scots and their English Royalist allies at the Battle of Preston. In October he captures Pontefract Castle and ends the war. In December Cromwell returns to London and organizes the trial of the King. On 20th January 1649 the formal trial of the Charles I begins. On Friday 26th January the King is found guilty of having levied war against his people. He will be "put to death by the severing of his head from his body." At two o'clock in the afternoon of Tuesday, 30th January, in this the final year of Mars' rulership of Cromwell's decan, Charles I, the King of England, is executed.

Pluto will rule Cromwell's next decan. During it he becomes the ruler of England.

Chapter 11

Jupiter as the Time Ruler

Nature's great masterpiece, an elephant;
the only harmless great thing.
—John Donne

Nobody grows old merely by living a number of years.
We grow old by deserting our ideals.
Years may wrinkle the skin, but to give up enthusiasm wrinkles the soul.
—Samuel Ullman

Too much of a good thing is wonderful.
—Mae West

Jupiter is quality, luck, protection, growth and expansion. When Jupiter rules either the septenary or decan, unless it is badly afflicted, the individual will be optimistic about the future and enthusiastic about whatever he is doing. It should be a lucky period of prosperity and happiness, during which his standing in the world is likely to improve. Others will assist him and some of his dreams and ambitions will become reality. Jupiter opens doors and provides opportunities, which can improve a person's position in life and ensure his domestic life is harmonious. He can expect to be successful in just about everything he undertakes. The planets Jupiter meets as it moves around the horoscope symbolize the opportunities that can come his way. Marriage is likely in these Jovian years. Children are born, or they have an increased influence in the person's life. His wealth should increase, his standard of living is likely to improve and all manner of luxury and comfort should be there to be enjoyed. These pleasant times are usually enhanced in those years in which Jupiter is directed to planets in signs where it is welcome. Events involving the father are often important to the individual in a Jupiter-ruled period.

Jupiter provides us with our moral sense, our conscience. During the years that Jupiter rules the decan or septenary this sense will develop and be refined. We will learn to respect the dignity of others and not to violate their rights.

Hindu astrologers know Jupiter as Guru, the spiritual guide and teacher, and they also relate the planet to Ganesha—he of the elephant head—the one who overcomes material and spiritual obstacles, the god of good luck and wisdom, who is the patron of arts and science.

The earliest astrologers associated Jupiter with knowledge and happiness.

Jupiter is emphatic and it is enlargement. Ruling the septenary or decan, it can persuade the native to believe in himself as an instrument of noble purpose; a belief that others may find insufferable. Theodore Roosevelt became president the year his septenary Jupiter rose in the east. During the following seven years he "enlarged the powers of the president, enlarged the government's control of the nation's economic life, and enlarged America's part in world affairs." At the same time his ego became grossly enlarged.

Prier Wintle has suggested that to gain the most from a Jupiter period one should expect something wonderful and feel fully deserving of it. One needs to think big and leave being careful-and-practical behind, and just confidently allow chance and luck to take over.

Should natal Jupiter be badly afflicted all kinds of miseries are possible during the period that it governs the life. One's luck can become devastated, which is unfortunate as the individual will have become more materialistic in these years than at other times, and virtually everything he sets out to do can end in failure. He may become complacent, excessive, careless and dishonest, losing respect for the moral values he may have had in the past. His wife or sweetheart may go out of his life, children may be lost, and he may be forced to leave his home to avoid prosecution. In these years his health can suffer, his income decline and he may lose both his reputation and self-respect.

Table 4-1: **♃ as time ruler: % Positive Years**

Position relative to the ☉	Day birth		Night birth		All	
	N	% Positive	N	% Positive	N	% Positive
Oriental ♃	285	53.0	191	**60.1*****	476	**55.8****
Occidental ♃	277	**57.8****	372	**55.2****	649	**56.3*****
All	562	**55.3****	563	**56.9*****	1125	**56.1*****

Years ruled by Jupiter are often the very best of times. The opportunities they offer should be taken. These opportunities can become an entrance into positions the individual usually only dreamt of occupying.

Table 4-2:

Table 4-2:

**% Positive Years
when Jupiter is Time Lord**

♃ directed to	N	% Positive
♃ rises	137	56.1
☉	143	54.4
☽	141	**66.0*****
☿	134	**60.7****
♀	151	**61.1*****
♂	131	51.8
♄	143	47.4
♅	51	53.2
♆	49	59.0
♇	45	38.2
All	*1125*	*56.1****

According to what was observed in the sample, of all the hundred different types of direction in the septenary-decan system, the year Jupiter is directed to the Moon has the highest probability, 66.0%, of being positive. The year Jupiter comes to Pluto can provide shocks, more so because the other years ruled by Jupiter, except those when it is directed to Saturn, tend to be associated with positive times.

Table 4-3:

Jupiter by signs, natal & to where directed

♃'s natal sign		Sign	Sign where ♃ is directed	
N	% Positive Years		N	% Positive Years
59	52.1	♈	77	51.7
118	55.2	♉	125	55.0
68	**71.8*****	♊	80	56.5
172	**56.8***	♋	80	46.3
57	50.8	♌	81	56.9
44	**63.7***	♍	81	56.9
62	52.5	♎	102	**62.1****
84	48.4	♏	82	**61.7****
80	53.1	♐	81	51.3
153	52.0	♑	62	**62.7***
140	55.5	♒	68	59.8
88	**66.8*****	♓	67	51.3
1125	*56.1*	*All*	*988*	*56.1*

There are some unexpected results in Table 4-3. Years when Jupiter was directed to a planet occupying a sign in which Jupiter is traditionally strong, Cancer, Sagittarius and

Pisces, were years in which people in the sample experienced the least positive years. Instead, directions to planets in Capricorn (the sign of Jupiter's fall), Libra and Scorpio stand out as having been the most positive.

Jupiter's natal sign also provides unexpected results. Jupiter in Cancer (its exaltation) and Pisces (one of the signs it rules) are strong, but so too is Jupiter in Gemini and Virgo, signs in which the planet is traditionally in its detriment.

Table 4-4: **Jupiter by house, natal & to where directed**

N	% Positive Years	House	N	% Positive Years
	♃'s natal house	House	House where ♃ is directed	
53	58.0	I	101	51.0
100	53.3	II	110	**66.6***
172	55.7	III	91	57.6
126	51.7	IV	69	47.2
127	**62.7***	V	69	52.4
102	53.2	VI	60	54.2
120	53.5	VII	78	58.0
68	57.2	VIII	72	59.0
98	**61.8**	IX	72	59.0
41	48.5	X	87	53.0
78	56.8	XI	88	52.4
40	61.0	XII	91	58.6
1125	*56.1*	*All*	*988*	*56.1*

Jupiter was at its strongest in the sample when located natally in the 5th or 9th houses, the locations from where it trines the rising sign. Years when Jupiter was directed to a planet occupying the 2nd house value were significantly higher than 50%.

Table 4-5:

% Positive when Jupiter is the Ruler
by its place in the septenary sequence

Place of Jupiter in septenary	Day		Night	
	N	% Positive	N	% Positive
1	47	45.7	26	61.7
2	51	**33.4****	28	44.5
3	70	58.8	31	**69.0****
4	35	**79.3*****	101	**69.4*****
5	30	65.6	31	60.3
6	37	62.9	76	50.4
7	44	**69.2****	24	**74.2****
Sum	314	**57.6*****	317	**61.5*****

People born with Jupiter in the second place of the seven had difficulties in the years that Jupiter ruled their septenary, when they were in their teens. By contrast, those born with Jupiter rising later had a much easier time.

Table 4-6:

% Positive when Jupiter is the Ruler
by its place in the decan sequence

Place of Jupiter in decan	Day		Night	
	N	% Positive	N	% Positive
1	9	39.8	5	17.8
2	46	54.4	8	66.8
3	69	59.7	41	58.6
4	63	41.2	41	47.8
5	11	73.3	68	45.8
6	16	44.7	46	62.0
7	11	65.1	31	46.0
8	17	47.4	4	44.5
9	6	59.7	1	0.0
10	0	0.0	1	0.0
Sum	248	52.4	246	51.0

Compare the totals in Table 4-5 with those in Table 4-6. The years when Jupiter was the septenary ruler were much easier than those in which Jupiter ruled the decan.

Jupiter rising
(56% positive years)

What occurs this year should tell us much about what is possible in the following seven or ten years. It should be an excellent year, a lucky time, a year of domestic happiness, the best of all possible times. The individual should be fired with hope and promise; he will be energized, his reputation can be expected to increase, his finances should prosper and he will benefit both socially and from his occupation. He may be invited to speak at conferences and by doing so enjoy the favor of many. He should enjoy success in all he does.

If afflicted, the individual's income, prestige and honor may be at stake. He may spend more than he can afford, become pompous, and reject the spiritual values of others. There is the danger of high blood pressure and injuries to the legs and feet. Relatives may be injured, and some of them may die.

Table 4-7:   **♃ to Ascendant: % Positive Years**

♃ relative to the ☉	Day birth		Night birth		All	
	N	% Positive	N	% Positive	N	% Positive
Oriental ♃	32	53.7	26	62.6	58	57.7
Occidental ♃	35	43.9	44	**63.7***	79	54.9
All	*67*	*48.6*	*70*	*63.3***	*137*	*56.1*

In the sample night births had a distinctly easier time this year than did those born during the daytime. People in the sample who were born in the daytime with Jupiter rising after the Sun often had a difficult time.

Examples of happenings in the sample when Jupiter becomes the decan ruler:
Oriental Jupiter rises by day in decan: *becomes famous; arrested; sister dies in an air crash; switches from being a potential bum to a success; travels overseas; no money, no home—sleeping rough; friend killed in helicopter crash; first record released; marries; meets his future wife; paternity scandal; nose operation.*
Occidental Jupiter rises by day in decan: *passes exams; concerned about the intense nationalism in the US; decides that he should become "what I myself am"; his plane is shot down into the sea; marries; sister moves in to set up his home; her father becomes mayor; loses his job & is forced to borrow money; war ends.*
Oriental Jupiter rises at night in decan: *negotiates large pay increase; immense success; son is kidnapped & murdered; drawing Biblical emblems; honored; becomes recognized for his authority; travels abroad; her father becomes king; war ends; death.*
Occidental Jupiter rises at night in decan: *happy in his job & loving his home—an idyllic period; friend/brother/daughter dies; doing well financially; mental breakdown & derangement; travels overseas; his wife is an alcoholic; promoted; resigns his position; receives his doctorate.*

Examples of happenings when Jupiter becomes the septenary ruler:

Oriental Jupiter rises by day in septenary: *travels overseas; his life-long dream becomes a hideous nightmare; achieves his ambition; graduates; start of a meteoric rise to fame; threatened & gets police protection; receives enemy's surrender; starts at college; deaths in the family; moves; high blood pressure; arrested.*

Occidental Jupiter rises by day in septenary: *receives opponents' surrender; war starts; bored; moves; daughter born; deaths in the family; inflation; financial panic; he is owed money; his theory is confirmed; start of his new work; mythology studies; consulting overseas; travels; exiled; lengthy convalescence.*

Oriental Jupiter rises at night in septenary: *children born; promoted; repelled & exhausted; opens private law practice; away from home; publishes new magazine; begins seven-year apprenticeship; in a charitable institution; first attracts strong supporters; death.*

Occidental Jupiter rises at night in septenary: *a year of true grace; son born; marries; a positive year; his plays fail and are mocked; receives an inheritance; mugged; rejected by Scientology; wins scholarship; studies; law degree; solitary; involved with anarchists; first talks in public; demands people awaken from lethargy.*

Jupiter comes to the Sun
(54% positive)

Unless afflicted the individual should experience this as a most successful period during which wealth comes without too much effort and others think well of him. He will be confident about himself now, assured and at ease in most situations. His superiors and friends will be of great help, they will provide him with the opportunity to gain recognition. It is a time of victory, a period when he can enjoy some of life's rewards. What he does now can also blossom in the future. He may marry, or he may join a church or religious society that can later greatly benefit him. When Jupiter or the Sun is badly afflicted or the Sun occupies a sign in which Jupiter is unwelcome individuals often experience a loss of bodily strength.

Table 4-8:   **♃ to ☉: % Positive Years**

♃ relative to the ☉	Day birth		Night birth		All	
	N	% Positive	N	% Positive	N	% Positive
Oriental ♃	29	65.5	29	56.1	58	60.8
Occidental ♃	37	48.9	48	50.9	85	50.0
All	*66*	*56.2*	*77*	*52.8*	*143*	*54.4*

Jupiter is strongest when east of the Sun.

Happenings in the sample when Jupiter comes to the Sun in the decan:

Oriental Jupiter to the Sun in the day in decan: *money & fame; teaching; travels; starts working for the government; gall bladder surgery; famished; meets father for first time since he was five years old; drugs; passes his driving test; in battles; war ends; refuses to feel inferior; goes to college; grandmother dies; first rock climbing.*

Occidental Jupiter to the Sun in the day in decan: *becomes a lecturer; mother/sister dies; attacked by a homosexual; loses any respect for his father; starts a new company; much publicity; briefly in jail after a gang fight; studying law; writing; retires.*

Oriental Jupiter to the Sun at night in decan: *saves girl from drowning; fails exams; social life broadens; large contract; his father doesn't allow him any freedom; he resigns; single-minded he pursues the best.*

Occidental Jupiter to the Sun at night in decan: *travels; wants a life of action; publishes new magazine; restless; pays off his debts; in despair over his increasing deafness; considering whether to accept offered promotion; black depression; lecturing; takes LSD; advocates educational reform; re-elected; joins Theosophical Society.*

Happenings in the sample when Jupiter comes to the Sun in the septenary:

Oriental Jupiter to the Sun in the day in septenary: *meets his father for first time in fifteen years; imprisoned; abdominal operation; survives being shot in the stomach; retires; named Debutante of the Year; gives talks; his school work improves; goes to a new school; travels; problems with a colleague; buys an antique car.*

Occidental Jupiter to the Sun in the day in septenary: *his wife is ill; arrested for debt; great territorial expansion; travels; overindulgence; teaches himself programming; buys a house; his life changes when his father is promoted; book published; changes his profession; death.*

Oriental Jupiter to the Sun at night in septenary: *father dies; her parents are honored; elected; becomes a Buddhist; editing; improved living conditions; fiancée dies; interviewed on television; travels overseas; leaves home; unhurt in car accident; works as a nursemaid.*

Occidental Jupiter to the Sun at night in septenary: *daughter born; travels; meets future spouse; ends marriage; to new school; receives study grant; death of rival; sexual adventures; lectures; moves; graduates; forced out of group she founded; becomes financially independent.*

Jupiter comes to the Moon
(66% positive)

Jupiter has arrived at the ruler of the sign in which he is exalted. It should be a wonderful year, during which the individual may become enriched in every way. This could be a time of fame and fortune, as he can become extremely prosperous, acquire property, move into a better house, benefit from his children, and enjoy sexual pleasures. He will impress others wherever he goes. Welcome changes occur. He will dress well and in good taste, enjoy good meals and live in comfortable surroundings. His positive outlook will attract others. A daughter or sister may be born, and he will probably pass his exams. This can be a year of important firsts, new starts that will prove to be important in later life. Killjoys may take pleasure in reminding him that there is a danger of over indulgence, living too rich a life and having too much of a good thing, but this year is the same as any other, it only contains twelve months, and the individual should enjoy all of them while he can.

If afflicted there can be a sense of delay. He may lack ambition, not demanding enough of himself and then be forced to take out a large loan to keep from being submerged by his debts.

These are usually the very best of the whole series of excellent Jupiter-ruled years. As we might expect, the Moon is strongest when waxing (occidental); Jupiter strongest when occidental. Day births have the most pleasant and successful of times.

In the sample Jupiter coming from the 4th or 8th house and/or from Cancer was significantly higher than 50%, similar results also occurred when Jupiter was directed to a Moon located in the 6th house, in Virgo, or in a Venus term.

Table 4-9:

♃ to ☽: % Positive Years

Planets relative to the ☉	Day birth		Night birth		All	
	N	% Positive	N	% Positive	N	% Positive
Oriental ♃	36	62.8	27	67.0	63	**64.6****
Occidental ♃	35	**74.9*****	43	61.0	78	**67.2*****
All	*71*	**68.8*****	*70*	*63.3*	*141*	**66.0*****
Waxing ☽	33	**76.7*****	44	**65.8***	77	**70.5*****
Waning ☽	38	61.9	26	59.1	64	60.7

Some happenings in the sample when Jupiter comes to the Moon in the decan:
Oriental Jupiter to the Moon in the day in decan: *children born; affairs; frenetic period; he is disoriented; a year of important firsts, studying; new starts that will be important in the life; experiences a spiritual transformation.*
Occidental Jupiter to the Moon in the day in decan: *graduates; marries; saves trapped girls; improved finances; wins prize; important discovery; socializing.*

Oriental Jupiter to the Moon by night in decan: *honored; becomes famous; difficult time for mother/wife; travels overseas; book published; changes his occupation.*
Occidental Jupiter to the Moon by night in decan: *son born; marriage problems; opportunities for promotion; overseas travel; safely avoids dangerous attacks; retires; affair; complicated finances.*

Some happenings in the sample when Jupiter comes to the Moon in the septenary:
Oriental Jupiter to the Moon in the day in septenary: *sister born; studies paranoia & the source of guilt feelings; foreign travel; moves; wants to become a priest; divorce; changes son's school; in desert searching for legendary oasis; studies aerodynamics; founds a weekly journal; passes examinations.*
Occidental Jupiter to the Moon in the day in septenary: *starts his first job; war starts/ends; writes a book; avoids alcohol; it is a period of transition; hires an old enemy; honored; midlife crisis; father is promoted; his* Wanderjahr; *discovers new remedies; death.*
Oriental Jupiter to the Moon by night in septenary: *children born; parents die; success for father; travels abroad; denounces segregation; unhappy at school; attends lectures; works long hours.*
Occidental Jupiter to the Moon by night in septenary: *overseas travel; deaths in the family; buys larger house; a fairy tale year; marriage goes sour; affair; honors; bullied; one of the best years of his life; his writings are widely circulated; her printing press changes from a hobby to a business.*

Jupiter comes to Mercury
(61% positive)

This should be another good year. News will be received that recognizes the individual's achievements and social status. He should be happy now, increase his knowledge, add to his wealth by trade, be favored by his superiors, enjoy material comforts, and travel. Others will appreciate the value of what he says. He will be rewarded for his past efforts, and is likely to receive an increase in his pay. He is likely to have an increased interest in philosophical and religious subjects now.

If afflicted, the desire for money may tempt him to become dishonest. Losses from gambling are possible.

Day births in the sample experienced a greater proportion of positive years than did nocturnal ones. Both occidental Jupiter and occidental Mercury were associated with above-average positive years. Jupiter in the 5th house, Mercury in the 2nd house, and Jupiter coming from a Mercury term all had positive values that were significantly higher than 50%.

Table 4-10:   **♃ to ☿: % Positive Years**

Planets relative to the ☉	Day birth		Night birth		All	
	N	% Positive	N	% Positive	N	% Positive
Oriental ♃	33	60.3	23	55.0	56	58.1
Occidental ♃	32	**67.8***	46	59.0	78	**62.6****
All	65	**64.0****	69	57.7	134	**60.7****
Oriental ☿	37	58.6	31	58.3	68	58.5
Occidental ☿	28	**71.0****	38	57.1	66	**63.0***

Some happenings in the sample when Jupiter comes to Mercury in the decan:

Oriental Jupiter to Mercury by day in decan: *marries to allow husband to stay in the USA; travels; teaching; writes play & textbook, hails Russian revolution as the start of a society based on reason and science; has all teeth removed; released from prison.*

Occidental Jupiter to Mercury by day in decan: *writes on his foreign travels; has substantial money from selling his farm; in very poor health; book published; lectures overseas; in school play; honors.*

Oriental Jupiter to Mercury at night in decan: *talks to massive crowds; he is at the head of a mob; attends conference on Swedenborg; severe creative crisis; planning to form new company; problems with his father.*

Occidental Jupiter to Mercury at night in decan: *book published; psychosomatic anxiety symptoms; buys an apartment; studies the Tarot; leaves academia; constant worries; flees; investigating consciousness.*

Some happenings in the sample when Jupiter comes to Mercury in the septenary:

Oriental Jupiter to Mercury by day in septenary: *learns to read & write; insight into the roots of religion; a year of obsessions; receives bike as reward for passing exams; arrested; frenetic time; constant touring; travels overseas; receives an honorary doctorate; becomes a millionaire.*

Occidental Jupiter to Mercury by day in septenary: *starts making his discoveries known; wins/loses elections; father is absent on a course; owing taxes; separated from his wife; confronted with career choices; has his first telescope; protesting; very worried; arrested.*

Oriental Jupiter to Mercury at night in septenary: *children born; first engravings; given a typewriter; works as an advertising copywriter; very busy; studies economics; starts at a new school; scandal.*

Occidental Jupiter to Mercury at night in septenary: *writing book that will make him famous; quadruples his fortune; studies logic; now has permanent freedom to pursue his studies; travels; affair; births in the family; very busy.*

Jupiter comes to Venus
(61 % positive)

This year the individual should experience peace of mind, financial gains, business success, promotions, an enhanced reputation, the enjoyment of friends and social events, family reunions, and marital happiness. Others will be there to help him get ahead. He may fall in love, and children may be born. He is likely to buy new clothes, and may spend enjoyable times in the theater, visiting galleries or museums, and be very popular. He may return to a spiritual path after a long time having deviated from it.

If afflicted expect troubles from females, scandal, and the loss of the native' reputation, children and pets. His marriage may break up over an affair. He may get into trouble at school or at his place of employment. Jupiter coming to Venus in Capricorn may bring love problems and experiences of jealousy.

Table 4-11: **♃ to ♀: % Positive Years**

Planets relative to the ☉	Day birth		Night birth		All	
	N	% Positive	N	% Positive	N	% Positive
Oriental ♃	33	54.8	25	68.7*	58	60.8
Occidental ♃	40	70.1**	53	54.6	93	61.2**
All	*73*	*63.2***	*78*	*59.1*	*151*	*61.1****
Oriental ♀	36	67.8**	31	61.2	67	64.8**
Occidental ♀	37	58.6	47	57.7	84	58.1

In the sample occidental Jupiter for a day birth and oriental Jupiter for a night birth were strong; day births were more positive than night ones; oriental Venus was most positive during the day; and the combination of oriental Jupiter and oriental Venus combined especially strongly together.

Table 4-12: **Jupiter-Venus Interaction**

Jupiter-Venus Interaction	Oriental ♃		Occidental ♃		All	
	N	% Positive	N	% Positive	N	% Positive
Oriental ♀	26	76.5**	41	57.3	67	64.8**
Occidental ♀	32	48.0	52	64.3*	84	58.1
All	*58*	*60.8*	*93*	*61.2***	*151*	*61.1****

Jupiter located in the 5th, 9th or 12th natal house or in Gemini or Pisces had % positive values that are significantly higher than 50%. Highly significant positive results were observed when either Jupiter or Venus was located in a Mercury term.

Some happenings in the sample when Jupiter comes to Venus in the decan:

Oriental Jupiter to Venus in the day in decan: *travels overseas; affair; divorce; marries; meditating; heightened sensitivity; leading a charmed life in battles; poetry; mother is ill; discharged from army; thought to be crazy.*

Occidental Jupiter to Venus in the day in decan: *first/new job; entranced with being for the first time with others who believe as she does; presents his thesis; lectures abroad; graduates; he is against the evils of extreme nationalism; engrossed in working out his theory; betrayed & abandoned by his lover & friend.*

Oriental Jupiter to Venus by night in decan: *frees his slaves; affair; for the first time able to mix freely with common people; wins fencing championship; his film shows the exploitation & humiliation of labor; no one is caring for his mother; honors, increased salary.*

Occidental Jupiter to Venus by night in decan: *finds a wealthy (11 years old) maiden to marry; wanting to find a wife; in love; inherits land from his mother; granted a life pension; escapes suburbia; baptized; in a shipwreck; honors.*

Happenings in the sample when Jupiter comes to Venus in the septenary:

Oriental Jupiter to Venus in the day in septenary: *marries; studies/works overseas; retires; writes on incest; nurses his sick son; touring in an RV; sketching; studying to be a teacher; moves.*

Occidental Jupiter to Venus in the day in septenary: *elected; continuous travel & partying; arrested during anti-apartheid rally; wins money on horses; visits a brothel; his parents divorce; marriage problems; falls in love; incorporates his company; starts school; finds remedy for terror; honored.*

Oriental Jupiter to Venus by night in septenary: *appointed to Foreign Relations Committee; travels; much drinking, dancing & flirting; able to do her own work again; awarded prizes; has an interest in music; touring with a dance troupe; starts publishing research papers; sells company on death of husband;*

Occidental Jupiter to Venus by night in septenary: *his book is an overnight success; start of her maturity & fame; writes lyrics for a successful musical; brother is assassinated; attending literary parties; he is a victim of police brutality; baptized; new yoga breathing exercises; promoted; public speaking.*

Jupiter comes to Mars
(52% positive)

There can be all manner of disappointments and troubles this year: loss by fire or theft, financial loss or business failure, the deaths of near and dear relatives, separation from family, mental depression, inflammatory diseases and increased blood pressure. The native may be forced to take great risks, and wander far from his home. He may get into debt. Others may attack his competency and he may lose his job or be transferred.

Those persons with Mars in a sign where Jupiter is welcomed should have enhanced energy and confidence, they can acquire wealth and fame, survive adventures, and finally be able to return home after a lengthy time overseas, perhaps away at a war. They may be rewarded for passing exams and obtaining final qualifications; perhaps they will obtain long-term contracts that will start them towards future prosperity. This can be a successful time for athletes. Medical treatment for long-term ailments can be beneficial now.

Table 4-13:

♃ to ♂: % Positive Years

Planets relative to the ☉	Day birth		Night birth		All	
	N	% Positive	N	% Positive	N	% Positive
Oriental ♃	37	56.2	19	57.1	56	56.5
Occidental ♃	36	47.7	39	51.0	75	49.4
All	*73*	*52.0*	*58*	*53.0*	*131*	*52.5*
Oriental ♂	43	**65.8***	30	57.3	73	55.5
Occidental ♂	30	54.2	28	48.4	58	51.4

In the sample Jupiter directed to an oriental Mars in a diurnal chart was associated with a strong % positive value. When Jupiter is directed to Mars in the 2nd or 12th houses the observed percents are significantly higher than 50%. A similar positive result was observed when Jupiter came to a Mars located in a Mercury term.

Some happenings in the sample when Jupiter comes to Mars in the decan:
Oriental Jupiter to Mars by day in decan: *he is part of a confidence trickster gang; released from prison; travels overseas; moves; painting; upsets religionists; children born; thigh wound; has syphilis; appendectomy; small pox.*
Occidental Jupiter to Mars by day in decan: *obtains scholarship; great success; in extreme pain; buys house; studying; his compositions are performed; writing; returns home after lengthy absence overseas.*
Oriental Jupiter to Mars at night in decan: *calms seawaters with oil; quarrels; loses court case; publishes satires; called a coward for not joining army; in partnership; moves; injures his nose; double pneumonia.*
Occidental Jupiter to Mars at night in decan: *becomes wealthy; bankrupt; leaves the army; her husband saves daughter from drowning; his wife leaves him; first public speech; foils plan to rob & kill him; paralyzed; bladder troubles.*

Some happenings in the sample when Jupiter comes to Mars in the septenary:
Oriental Jupiter to Mars by day in septenary: *his son is killed in the war; grandfather killed by a bomb; fascinated by war; father is arrested for assault; father returns from army; bullied; in a state of continuous excitement; lively social life; rebels; travels; high blood pressure is diagnosed; he is murdered.*
Occidental Jupiter to Mars by day in septenary: *mistakenly given AIDS-tainted blood; arrested for drunk driving; concerned with military aspect of communist threat; at war; reduces his weight; great suffering; promoted; building a theater; son born; punished for inveterate lying; chronic diarrhea.*
Oriental Jupiter to Mars at night in septenary: *orders bombings; he is a soldier in the militia; army rejects her husband; sues the county; separates from his wife; teaches evenings to augment his income; has VD; unhappy away from home at school; graduates; forms a partnership.*

Occidental Jupiter to Mars at night in septenary: *aware of more active, suppressed energy about; legal problems; advocates execution of Mary, Queen of Scots; angers his therapist, who ends his treatment; jealous; in extreme pain; travels; fights his family for independence and wins; victory in war.*

Jupiter comes to Saturn
(47% positive)

This is often the year when the chickens come home to roost. Unless Saturn is located in a sign where Jupiter is welcomed it can be an unfortunate period, for it is likely to be a time of economic retrenchment, when the individual is forced to recognize that he has been living beyond his means and must now tighten his belt. Enjoyment will need to be drastically curtailed and there will probably be a more somber approach to life.

By contrast, those thrifty individuals with Saturn in Cancer, Sagittarius or Pisces should have a contented year. Their circumstances may even improve. They will enjoy happiness in and with their families, lead a comfortable life, be promoted in their work, and have their plans realized. Such people may relocate to places where their ambitions are likely to be further realized.

Both Jupiter and Saturn are most positive when they rise after the Sun.

In the sample oriental Jupiter coming to Saturn in a daytime birth was associated with values that are well below average—this is an indicator of future difficulties. Significant below 50% values were also observed when Jupiter was natally in Taurus or when Jupiter was directed to Saturn in Sagittarius. The latter result was unexpected.

Table 4-14: ♃ to ♄: **% Positive Years**

Planets relative to the ☉	Day birth		Night birth		All	
	N	% Positive	N	% Positive	N	% Positive
Oriental ♃	42	**34.4***	25	50.6	67	40.5
Occidental ♃	34	55.8	42	51.7	76	53.5
All	*76*	*44.0*	*67*	*51.3*	*143*	*47.4*
Oriental ♄	39	39.4	28	48.4	67	43.2
Occidental ♄	37	48.9	39	53.3	76	51.2

Some happenings in the sample when Jupiter comes to Saturn in the decan:
Oriental Jupiter to Saturn in the day in decan: *convicted for fraud; friends die; in a bar fight; husband is killed; divorce; meets future wife; finances improve; promoted; on safari in Kenya; seriously ill; moves overseas; returns home after years working overseas; successfully predicts epidemic; series of job interviews.*

Occidental Jupiter to Saturn in the day in decan: *on sick leave; leaves home; moves; living in a country occupied by the enemy; wounded; joins army; leaves navy; frequently beaten; increased industrialism brings a lessening of individual freedom; working in plastics factory; has a new job.*

Oriental Jupiter to Saturn by night in decan: *husband is ill; marriages in the family; campaigns against taxation; divorce; interrogated by grand jury; he is 'discovered'; caught trespassing.*

Occidental Jupiter to Saturn by night in decan: *daughter/wife/mother dies; others plot against him; depression; falls down mountain crevasse; financial difficulties; happy, an idyllic period; studies geometry; stops writing music for several months; reads biography about himself; nuclear disaster; promoted.*

Some happenings in the sample when Jupiter comes to Saturn in the septenary:

Oriental Jupiter to Saturn in the day in septenary: *starts to loathe school; graduates; pets die; released from prison; hospitalized; watch is stolen; wife in a coma, she then dies; marries; moves for economic reasons; immigration plans are cancelled; a very difficult year; in love & happy; wins a large contract; death.*

Occidental Jupiter to Saturn in the day in septenary: *surrounded by turbulence & war; defends his dissertation; retires; writes a book; deaths in the family; her music lessons stop; marriage ends; moves; describes the miseries of idleness; has shingles; the worst year of his life to date.*

Oriental Jupiter to Saturn by night in septenary: *wins/loses election; chickenpox; travels overseas; sells his estate; increased salary; becomes a US citizen; marries an older man; defamed as a communist & liar; inquisition; father is permanently ill; sponsors others; ends his schooling.*

Occidental Jupiter to Saturn by night in septenary: *defeated; financial success; little money; depressed; enemy dies; rock climbing; studying for the priesthood; studies history; rejected by his son; becomes a prisoner of war; in prison; father/brother is sick; others are jealous of his success; resigns; buys first house.*

Jupiter comes to Uranus
(53% positive)

Vnexpecteð events this year can utterly change the individual's status and way of life. Some clue to the nature of what can be a dramatic life-changing event can be obtained from the house and sign Uranus occupies. For example, with Uranus in the second house he may unexpectedly have a compelling reason to go abroad and this excursion can make or break him financially depending to a large extent on whether Uranus occupies one of the signs in which Jupiter is strong or not. As he changes his approach to life he may be tempted to take on risky ventures, perhaps to break the rules.

Table 4-15:   **♃ to ♅: % Positive Years**

Planets relative to the ☉	Day birth		Night birth		All	
	N	% Positive	N	% Positive	N	% Positive
Oriental ♃	15	42.2	5	72.3	20	49.7
Occidental ♃	11	49.3	20	58.8	31	55.4
All	*26*	*45.2*	*25*	*61.5*	*51*	*53.2*
Oriental ♅	10	36.2	16	67.8	26	55.6
Occidental ♅	16	50.9	9	50.2	25	50.6

Some happenings in the sample when Jupiter comes to Uranus in the decan;

Oriental Jupiter to Uranus in the day: *several attempts on his life; his throat is slashed; mother dies; war starts; goes overseas to work; constantly headline hunting; change of career; falls in love; feuding with past partners; finances improve; cheated out of his pay; first bank account.*

Occidental Jupiter to Uranus in the day: *patents his invention; father remarries/dies; romance; travels; rejected; writing; leaves Navy to run family farm.*

Oriental Jupiter to Uranus by night: *father's insurrection fails; wins a prize; extensive travels; book published; encouraging & organizing the war effort.*

Occidental Jupiter to Uranus by night: *unemployed; children born; marriage problems; proves himself innocent of charges; promoted; acute depression; his hearing is worse.*

Jupiter comes to Neptune
(59% positive)

Don't get too optimistic. Yes, this year is when a person may finally be given that hoped-for promotion or job change but a word of caution: it may not provide him with the gains he had hoped for. He may even be worse off now that he has it than he was before. Something changed and nobody told him.

This can be the time of a leap of faith, when the temptation to pursue a belief or dream becomes overwhelming. Should this happen, and the individual in order to follow his bliss drops everything and, for example, emigrates to a distant land, the success or otherwise of this drastic redirection of his life will depend very much on the strength of natal Jupiter and whether or not it is welcomed in the sign Neptune occupies. The change is likely to be a positive one if Neptune is in Cancer, Sagittarius or Pisces. It will probably be one that is later regretted should Neptune be located in Gemini, Virgo or Capricorn.

Table 4-16:
♃ to ♆: % Positive Years

Planets relative to the ☉	Day birth		Night birth		All	
	N	% Positive	N	% Positive	N	% Positive
Oriental ♃	14	51.7	7	77.5	21	60.3
Occidental ♃	10	54.2	18	60.3	28	58.1
All	*24*	*52.7*	*25*	*65.1*	*49*	*59.0*
Oriental ♆	13	48.7	13	69.6	26	59.1
Occidental ♆	11	57.5	12	60.3	23	59.0

Jupiter expands; Neptune exaggerates. Between the two of them they will blow up a virtual bubble of optimism that can eventually burst, usually with devastating effects. Excess is invariably punished, and this may be a year when dreams set themselves up to be shattered, when wealth is bogus and prosperity fictitious. It can too often be a time of enthusiasm without reason, one that only ends in disillusionment. An individual should avoid agreeing to anything that seems too good to be true—it probably isn't. He can be easily allured to exchange a good situation for promises of something better, only to end up much worse by doing so. This can be a time of scams and fraudulent misrepresentations. Perhaps the best way to cope with this year is to assume that nothing is as it appears, that nothing is truly real, and avoid becoming overly involved with whatever is supposed to be happening. One needs to avoid becoming either a victim or a cynic. Others are unlikely to believe everything the individual says this year; they will reject many of his ideas.

In the sample people born at night clearly had an easier time with this direction than did those born during the daytime.

Some happenings in the sample when Jupiter comes to Neptune in the decan:

Oriental Jupiter to Neptune in the day: sentenced to a year in solitary; decides the self has components related to powers represented by the planets; transcendental meditation; becomes a drug addict/vegetarian; testing helicopters; miraculously escapes death; borrows money; marries; moves; his mind is filled with thoughts of accelerated motion, gravity & space.

Occidental Jupiter to Neptune in the day: in seaplane that sinks; has twins; rejected; shocked & humiliated when his father loses his position; organizes exhibition; first date; estranged.

Oriental Jupiter to Neptune by night: enjoying great fame; measles; maps the Gulf Stream; her kidneys are permanently damaged from husband's beating; son's murderer is arrested; evacuated.

Occidental Jupiter to Neptune by night: accused of treason; homeless; meditating; solves challenge problems; hides his new discovery; high blood pressure; depressed; travels; feels totally free; has no income; gathering evidence to defend himself; occult studies.

Jupiter comes to Pluto
(38% positive)

The year that Jupiter comes to Pluto is often the most difficult of Jupiter's years as the decan ruler. Someone may leave and there may be a sense of relief at the departure. There can be a change in occupation and finances. The individual may receive an inheritance or find himself in a position where he has more control than formerly over his life. Jumping headlong into the fray can make this year one of rapid progress or one of dismal failure, much depends on the sign Pluto occupies. Resistance or inertia can be overcome if Pluto is in Cancer, Sagittarius or Pisces, but this is less likely to occur should Pluto be in Gemini, Virgo or Capricorn.

Table 4-16: ♃ to ♇: % Positive Years

Planets relative to the ☉	Day birth		Night birth		All	
	N	% Positive	N	% Positive	N	% Positive
Oriental ♃	14	38.7	5	36.2	19	38.1
Occidental ♃	7	51.7	19	33.3	26	38.3
All	*21*	*43.1*	*24*	*33.9*	*45*	*38.2*
Oriental ♇	13	48.7	10	27.1	23	39.3
Occidental ♇	8	33.9	14	38.7	22	37.0

Some happenings in the sample when Jupiter comes to Pluto in the decan:

Oriental Jupiter to Pluto in the day: *in prison; divorce; spinal operations; multiple injuries from motorcycle accident; facial wound from car accident; start of life-long study of astrology; moves; nightmares; attempts suicide; fined for drug possession; feted.*

Occidental Jupiter to Pluto in the day: *fined for hunting blue heron; exhausted; passes his law exams; marries; disappointment & self-contempt; reconciled with his sister; travels.*

Oriental Jupiter to Pluto by night: *writes about a middle-aged woman at a point of crisis; first bike/film; her father flees; daughter born; concussion; unsuccessful in his petitions; joins the army.*

Occidental Jupiter to Pluto by night: *receives Nobel Peace Prize; catches his wife with another man; writing crime stories; a pestering female fan complicates his life; joins a Gnostic group; retires; defeated; fights a duel over a woman; in extreme pain; promoted; war is declared.*

Arthur Young's Jupiter-ruled Decan

Arthur Young invented the helicopter. He first has the idea in his twenties, a decan ruled by his waxing Moon in Aquarius, and after much stumbling he determined the principles governing helicopter flight, discovered the stabilizing bar, and learned how to get a helicopter to hover. His remote-control model so impressed the Bell Aircraft Company that he was given the financial backing to produce a full-size commercial helicopter. This he did in his thirties, years ruled by Saturn in Aquarius, the first true helicopter being built in 1942 when he was thirty-seven years old—that year Saturn was on Neptune in his decan, the diurnal Sun on his Jupiter in his septenary. *Look* magazine proclaimed him Man of the Year for 1942.

Jupiter rises in Gemini: Jupiter takes over Arthur's decan in November 1945 on his fortieth birthday. At birth Jupiter is retrograde in Gemini, oriental to the Sun in the seventh sign from the ascendant, receiving an applying trine from the waxing Moon. The Sun rules his septenary and it has come to Mars in Capricorn. Arthur is still working at the Bell Aircraft plant in Buffalo, New York. The latest version of the helicopter, model 47, is produced on schedule, and he now faces the onerous requirements of mass production. The whole Bell operation has shifted to making helicopters. The first commercial helicopter license is issued, and the first long-distance flight, from Buffalo to Philadelphia and back, takes place. Arthur is busy diagnosing mistakes in helicopter design and with production problems. He is deeply troubled when a friend is killed in a helicopter crash, and takes up yoga and meditation. He is reading the writings of Helena Blavatsky and being introduced into a new world.

Jupiter directed to Saturn in Aquarius: In November 1946 Jupiter comes to Arthur's strong Saturn. In the septenary the Sun is on his Mercury in Scorpio. He experiences a series of precognitive dreams. His interest in the helicopter is phasing out after an intense involvement of seventeen years. He goes scuba diving for the first time. There is an intense pain in his arms, he is unable to lift them, and he goes from one specialist to another trying to find relief. He begins a relationship outside his marriage, with a woman named Ruth. There is trouble at Bell, two helicopter crashes occur. He experiences a psychic event, the first in his life, and enters psychoanalysis. He is first introduced to astrology. He moves, leaving both Buffalo and Bell.

Jupiter directed to the Moon in Aquarius: Arthur is forty-two years old in November 1947. Mercury in Scorpio, ruler of his 7th house, takes control of his septenary. He is undergoing psychoanalysis. He spends forty days in Reno, Nevada waiting to obtain a

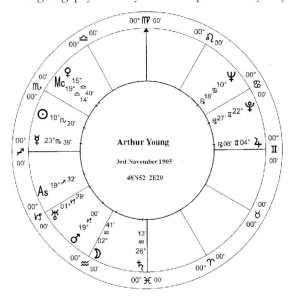

divorce, and has a brief affair. His parents are shocked that he is sleeping with Ruth when divorced and unmarried. He and Ruth marry. He is practicing yoga and undergoes dream analysis. Now that he is no longer at Bell he is disoriented. He decides that his new career is to be devoted to hunting for the psyche. He begins to seriously study astrology.

Jupiter directed to Mars in Capricorn: Starting in November 1948 Jupiter is on Arthur's Mars in Capricorn. Jupiter has its fall in Capricorn. He is now forty-three years old. Septenary Mercury is on his Sun in Scorpio. He takes a series of courses with Mary Benzenberg Meyer on symbolism and myth. She provides clues to the use of ancient teachings that help him with his theory of process. He is working on the meaning of his dreams. He goes to a medium to obtain the birth time of an old friend from college.

Jupiter directed to Uranus in Capricorn: Jupiter is still in Capricorn, its fall. Arthur is forty-four years old. Septenary Mercury has come to Venus in Libra, close to the midheaven. His mother dies. He has several important dreams, in one of which he dreams a prayer and receives an answer. He visits Mount Desert Island in Maine. He begins to sense how the Sabian Symbols of the zodiac degrees 'influence' the day, and breaks with Mary Benzenberg Meyer when she tells him he should not study astrology. He is getting private tutoring from the astrologer Marc Edmund Jones. He becomes interested in L. Ron Hubbard's *Dianetics*, and also in radionics.

Jupiter directed to Mercury in Scorpio: Arthur is forty-five years old in November 1950 when Jupiter comes to its dispositor. At the same time septenary ruler Mercury has come to Jupiter in Gemini. This interchange of the planetary pairs should produce important experiences. In his autobiography Arthur calls this his "Gee Whiz!" period, during which he is encountering, and seeking out, various far-out phenomena. He visits Honduras, Mexico and California. He has a series of remarkable experiences in the sleep state that convince him that he is in communication with Dr. Sharpe, who had brought his helicopter work to the attention of Bell Aircraft and who is now dead. Arthur believes Sharpe acts as his guiding spirit. He meets Dr. Oscar Brunler, who is attempting to measure a person's soul-age by the amount of radiation that emanates from that person's brain. Arthur is intrigued by radionics and by the work of Dr. Ruth Drown, the foremost radionics practitioner.

Jupiter directed to the Sun in Scorpio: It is November 1951 and Arthur is forty-six years old. Septenary Mercury is on Saturn in Aquarius. He establishes the Foundation for the Study of Consciousness, to sponsor research to bridge the gap between modern science and the esoteric tradition. He experiences the pains of rheumatoid arthritis, and suffers from lead poisoning. He works extensively with Frederick Marion, a sensitive able to psychometrize an object, to give its history by feeling it, to obtain his own birth time. He meets Andrija Puharich, who experiments with a Faraday cage to heighten the performance of sensitives. Dr. Brunler dies. He and Ruth go to England where they meet various radionics' investigators and obtain Brunler's list of measured brain radiations (age of the soul) of different subjects in order to compare Brunler's theory against the findings of astrology. In England he buys an antique Rolls Royce, which he will later convert into a pick-up truck. He has a crisis of self-awareness, and is concerned with a dread of evil, worrying that he may be misusing his powers.

Jupiter directed to Venus in Libra: In November 1952 Arthur becomes forty-seven. In his septenary Mercury is on his Aquarian Moon. Arthur and Ruth return to New York. He works with Andrija Puharich and again with the sensitive Frederick Marion. Influenced by the direction to Venus, he is writing poetry and buys a painting by Van Dyke. He and Ruth vacation in Honduras. He does extensive work with a Faraday cage. He is also working on mathematical meanings.

Jupiter directed to Neptune in Cancer: Jupiter has now come to the sign in which it is exalted. Arthur is forty-eight years old. Mercury is on his Capricorn Mars in the septenary. He hires a full-time research assistant, Jan Forman, a physicist with more than a dozen patents to his credit, who doesn't last more than a year. He meets Royal Rife, the creator of a microscope that is capable of very high magnification. He continues his work on mathematical meanings. He proposes thinking of the self as having components related to the powers represented by the planets. His investigations are interrupted when he is called back to Bell to make a device to test helicopters. He attends a conference on UFOs. A friend is trapped in an avalanche.

Jupiter directed to Pluto in Gemini: Pluto will rule his next ten years. Arthur is forty-nine years old in November 1954. His Capricorn Mars takes over rulership of his septenary. Frances Farrelly, one of Ruth Drown's students, joins the Foundation as its radionics researcher. Arthur begins writing *The Geometry of Meaning,* a book based on his understanding of the third derivative, or control. He first meets the astrologer Charles Jayne, who will become a very close friend.

Theodore Roosevelt's Jupiter-ruled Septenary

Jupiter rises in Gemini: The soon-to-be 26th president of the United States, Theodore Roosevelt, is forty-two years old in October 1990 when Jupiter begins to rule his septenary. Jupiter, retrograding in Gemini, had rising into the eastern sky at New York a few minutes

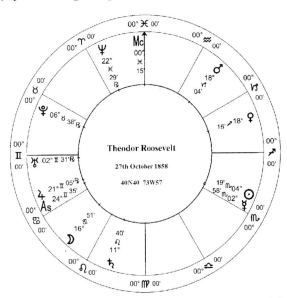

Theodor Roosevelt

27th October 1858

40N40 73W57

before he was born and is thus the last of the planets that will come to the ascendant following his birth. Oriental in a nocturnal chart, Jupiter is square to Neptune and opposed by Venus, both bodies in a sign it rules. That same year his decan ruler Venus has arrived at the place of Mercury in Scorpio. Both rulers are in signs in which they can expect to receive an unfriendly reception. Roosevelt is elected vice president a month after the year begins. Six weeks before his next birthday he becomes president when his predecessor William McKinley is assassinated. Before his year ends he is strongly criticized for being the first president to invite an African-American to diner at the White House. The nature of the year's events would seem to disagree with the idea that rulers coming to signs in which they are unwelcome correlate with difficult years. However, the rapid ascendancy of Teddy Roosevelt was not at all popular with the entrenched establishment of the time. Not everyone welcomed him to the position of president.

Jupiter directed to Mars in Capricorn: Teddy Roosevelt is forty-three years old in October 1901. He has been president for just six weeks. Venus has come to his Saturn in Leo in the decan. Mars may be exalted in Capricorn but it is how the ruler, Jupiter, fares there that will tell us whether the year is to be easy or difficult, and Jupiter has come to the sign of its fall. He makes a law to stop buffalo from becoming extinct and settles strikes by coal miners. His wife has a miscarriage. He discovers that the head of the US army is plotting against him. His horse-drawn carriage crashes into a tram and, as a result of injuries, he can only get about first in a wheelchair and later with crutches. He mediates in a conflict between labor and capital.

Jupiter directed to Venus in Sagittarius: Jupiter comes to one of the signs it rules in Roosevelt's septenary in October 1902. He is forty-four years old. Venus has come to the Moon in Cancer in the decan. The emphasis on Venus should come out during the year. As president he is trying to buy canal land in Panama. He arbitrates in a Venezuelan conflict. He spends time bear hunting and as a result toy teddy bears make their initial appearance in shops. His wife has another miscarriage. This year, responding to the influence of his septenary ruler, his actions and statements show him to be an expansionist.

Jupiter directed to the Sun in Scorpio: Teddy Roosevelt is forty-five years old in 1903. Jupiter has come to his nocturnal Sun in the septenary. Venus is on its dispositor, his Jupiter in Gemini, in the decan. Jupiter is being emphasized. A revolution in Panama, which some say he helped instigate, provides him with the opportunity to obtain the treaty to build the Panama Canal. His party nominates him to be president in his own right. He receives a bequest that makes him rich. His success appears to have gone to his head for he is becoming increasingly egotistic.

Jupiter directed to Mercury in Scorpio: Teddy Roosevelt is elected president of the United States in his own right when he is forty-six years old. Jupiter, his septenary ruler, has come to its dispositor. Venus, the decan ruler, is on his Uranus in Gemini. He starts building the Panama Canal. His diplomacy helps end the Sino-Russian war. He extends the Monroe Doctrine to include economics. He suffers injuries while boxing and riding, and is ill with a bout of malaria.

Jupiter directed to Saturn in Leo: Roosevelt is forty-seven years old in October 1905. In his decan Venus has come to Pluto in Taurus, a sign Venus rules. His daughter marries. There are problems with organized labor. He responds to Jupiter's direction to Saturn by attacking greed, by taxing large fortunes. He arranges peace between Russia and Japan. This is the year of the Food and Drug act. He coins the term 'muckraker'. His son almost dies from diphtheria. He spends much time attempting to simplify spelling.

Jupiter directed to the Moon in Cancer: 1906 is the final year of Jupiter's rulership of Teddy Roosevelt's septenary. It has come to the place of his waning Moon in Cancer, the body that will assume rulership of his next seven years. Venus is at his Neptune in Pisces in the decan. Both rulers are in signs where they are exalted, but it is not an easy year, as often happens when Neptune is involved. He punishes a black regiment in Texas by completely disbanding it for reasons that today appear inadequate. He visits Panama to inspect the construction of the canal. He is awarded the Nobel Peace Prize for his successful arbitration of the Sino-Russian conflict. There is financial panic on Wall Street. He denounces segregation.

The following year the Moon's decan begins.

Barack Obama and Jupiter

What is the astrological reason for Obama's election to the presidency in November 2008? It happened because of Jupiter. Jupiter was the final planet to rise over the eastern horizon after Obama was born. It is retrograding in the first degree of Aquarius, opposite Mercury and with a separating trine from the Moon in Gemini. Jupiter began ruling his septenary in August 2003, and five years later on Obama's 47th birthday it arrived at his Venus in Cancer. This is the sign in which Jupiter is exalted, and as one would expect his popularity increased throughout the year, sufficiently so that within three months, by November 2008, it had grown enough to ensure his election to the Oval Office.

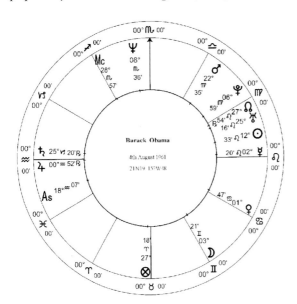

This high appreciation may not, however, continue at quite the same elevated level in the following year, beginning in August 2009, for Jupiter will move on to the Moon in Gemini. The Moon and Jupiter are connected by a trine, which is a most positive connection, but Jupiter is not as welcome in Gemini, where it is in detriment, not exalted as it was in Cancer.

After August 2010 the Moon takes over the rule of Obama's septenary and his popularity can be expected to begin to fluctuate. As Gemini is the twelfth sign from the Moon's sign of Cancer, it is not always a happy place for the Moon to be in; life there is often too unsettled. There is also the opposition by antiscion of the Moon with Saturn, and its applying square to Pluto. This combination suggests that the years beginning after Obama's 49th birthday will be very different from his first few months in office.

The table on the next page lists the septenary and decan rulers and their directions for the year containing Obama's great Jupiter-to-Venus-in-Cancer direction and for several years thereafter.

The appearance of Pluto in the decan listing after August 2010 warns of radical changes ahead for the president and the United States. Pluto is in Virgo and these changes may involve his plans to radically alter how Americans receive health care. The year in which the septenary Moon comes to Saturn in Capricorn, starting on his August 2012 birthday, could be particularly difficult. That is when he is due to stand for reelection. This direction, especially as Pluto then rules the decan, suggests he will be a one-term president.

Year	Age	Septenary	Decan
8/2008 - 7/2009	47	♃ to ♀ in ♋	♅ to ♇ in ♏
8/2009 - 7/2010	48	♃ to ☽ in ♊	♅ to ♂ in ♍
8/2010 - 7/2011	49	☽ rises in ♊	♅ to ♀ in ♍
8/2011 - 7/2012	50	☽ to ♃ in ♒	♀ rises in ♍
8/2012 - 7/2013	51	☽ to ♄ in ♑	♀ to ♅ in ♌
8/2013 - 7/2014	52	☽ to ♂ in ♍	♀ to ☉ in ♌
8/2014 - 7/2015	53	☽ to ☉ in ♌	♀ to ☿ in ♌
8/2015 - 7/2016	54	☽ to ☿ in ♌	♀ to ♀ in ♋

By contrast, the two years that start with his 53rd birthday on August 2014, when Pluto comes to Mercury in the decan, and then in the following year when the Moon comes to Mercury in the septenary, should be more pleasant as Mercury is the dispositor of both Pluto and the Moon. There is going to be a light at the end of a dark and dangerous tunnel, if Obama can reach it.

Written April 2009

* * *

Chapter 12

Saturn as the Time Ruler

"Behind these faces, every deep desire, every act of revolt, every impulse was hobbled by fear. Fear of rebuke, of time, of the news, of the collectivity that multiplied its forms of slavery. There was fear of one's own body, of the sanctions and pointing fingers of publicity: there was fear of the womb that opens to the seed, fear of the fruits and of the water; fear of the calendar, fear of the law, fear of slogans, fear of mistakes, fear of the sealed envelope, fear of what might happen"

Alejo Carpentier, *The Lost Steps.*

Saturn represents the whole frame of social and moral rules that keep individuals imprisoned, and during these years a person will discover the limits within which he must live and the responsibilities he needs to shoulder. It is time that makes one needy, wanting to have more, to become more, to be taller, greater, richer, healthier—becoming is the credo, to be better than one really is. Saturn is the hunger one has for what one does not possess, and at the same time it is the self-inflicted barriers that hold a person back from attaining what he wants out of life. The planet engenders discipline through respect and fear.

Saturn is also a person's concealed and least presentable side. Who it is he keeps hidden beneath his fancy clothes and fancy ways, who it is he becomes when there's no one to see him, when he is alone in the dark. The Sun asks that we be who we truly are; Saturn signifies how we view that person. It represents our weakness, our limitations, our anxieties and our inhibitions. Saturn is the planet of reality.

The earliest astrologers that we know of related Saturn to ignorance and old age.

A gloomy period of years usually begins as Saturn takes over as the time ruler. The world is dark and chilly; the sun rarely shines. There will be the need for sustained hard work if anything of value is to be accomplished in this dreary world. For far too long these will seem to be dull, dismal and disappointing years when everything goes wrong and there will be little or no evidence that any headway is being made. There will be little joy. Patience and discipline are required in order to build a solid base on which to set one's life, a firm foundation for one's career. Money will be scarce, the individual may no longer be popular, and he will feel unwanted and depressed. The individual is learning to be responsible, to be humble, and to possess integrity.

Over time, if Saturn is strong, gains in wealth, authority and responsibility may come. Money may arrive from inheritance, from real estate or as indicated by the planet's natal house. The planets around the celestial circle that Saturn meets during its periods of governance will help or hinder the individual's ability to place his feet on a sound footing. The years when Saturn is directed to a planet in Libra, Capricorn or Aquarius can be enjoyable and may involve travels abroad, friendship with great persons, successful litigations, and the acquiring of great wealth.

If Saturn is afflicted, the restrictions, delays, poverty, hardships, injuries and illnesses are likely to persist, turning these Saturn-ruled years into a nightmare. They can be at their worst when Saturn is directed to a planet in Aries, Cancer or Leo. The individual may then experience unexpected losses, disappointment in his undertakings, professional downfalls, and loss of honor. He will become anonymous in a cold, unfeeling world. There will be a continuing threat of failure, deficiency, and even more difficulties. He can experience the pains of rheumatism and the frustrations of paralysis. They can be miserable years.

Saturn is usually stronger in a day birth than it is at night.

Table ♄-1　　　　　**♄ as time ruler: % Positive Years**

Position relative to the ☉	Day birth		Night birth		*All*	
	N	% Positive	N	% Positive	*N*	*% Positive*
Oriental ♄	333	46.7	266	50.0	*599*	*48.2*
Occidental ♄	239	51.1	304	45.5	*543*	*48.0*
All	*572*	*48.5*	*570*	*47.6*	*1142*	*48.1*

Saturn appears to be most helpful when either occidental by day or oriental at night.

The year that begins Saturn's rulership of the septenary or decan, the year it rises into world, is often the worst of the series. The remaining Saturn-ruled years are often spent recovering from the difficulties of that initial year.

Table ♄-2　　　　　**% Positive Years
when ♄ is Time Lord**

♄ directed to	N	% Positive
♄ rises	144	**37.7***
☉	143	44.9
☽	144	48.3
☿	146	45.2
♀	136	48.5
♂	132	52.7
♃	145	51.1
♅	53	**64.8****
♆	48	58.4
♇	51	44.3

The high positive value observed in the sample when Saturn was directed to Uranus may relate to these two planets sharing rulership of Aquarius.

Table ♄-3:

Saturn by Sign, natal & to where directed

♄'s natal sign		Sign	Sign to which ♄ is directed	
N	% Positive Years		N	% Positive Years
68	50.5	♈	52	38.3
107	47.3	♉	136	49.2
97	49.4	♊	88	46.2
101	55.5	♋	83	46.8
114	53.1	♌	85	47.9
95	49.5	♍	87	50.9
82	47.4	♎	75	50.6
115	48.7	♏	71	53.3
82	40.8	♐	83	49.0
89	44.7	♑	88	51.4
115	46.4	♒	84	51.7
75	**39.8***	♓	58	56.1
1142	48.1	All	998	49.5

In Table ♄-3 we see that Saturn directed to a planet in Aries, where the planet is in its fall, is associated with difficult years, as one would expect. The values for Saturn coming to a planet in Libra, Capricorn or Aquarius, the three signs in which Saturn is traditionally strong, are each slightly above average, but not significantly so. Saturn coming from Pisces or Sagittarius was associated in the sample with difficult years. It is thought provoking to note that Saturn was strongest in the sample when found natally in two of the signs, Cancer and Leo, in which it is traditionally weak.

Table ♄-4: **Saturn by House, natal & to where directed**

♄'s natal house		House	House where ♄ is directed	
N	% Positive Years		N	% Positive Years
74	43.9	I	124	45.9
74	52.5	II	112	46.8
208	52.6	III	82	49.6
102	**33.7***	IV	77	45.8
100	49.7	V	70	50.4
40	54.2	VI	59	53.6
62	49.5	VII	86	52.5
95	44.8	VIII	69	56.3
125	48.5	IX	57	47.6
159	46.0	X	64	49.5
50	50.6	XI	107	50.7
53	56.3	XII	90	50.3
1142	*48.1*	*All*	*998*	*49.5*

Saturn in the natal 4th house, according to Reinhold Ebertin, is often an indicator of modest or aggravating circumstances caused by family ties. In the sample, the years when Saturn was natally in that house were particularly difficult.

Table ♄-5: **% Positive when Saturn is the Ruler by its place in the Septenary sequence**

Place of Saturn in septenary	Day		Night	
	N	% Positive	N	% Positive
1	69	53.1	29	43.6
2	54	45.1	30	48.2
3	45	56.2	28	35.5
4	82	46.8	39	54.2
5	34	**23.8***	104	52.9
6	23	54.9	45	39.3
7	18	65.1	57	51.4
Sum	325	48.3	332	48.3

Saturn was associated with significant number of difficult years when it was the fifth of the seven to rise in a daytime chart—ruling the septenary during the seven-year period that begins with the 28th birthday and again with age 77.

% Positive when Saturn is the Ruler
by its place in the Decan sequence

Place of Saturn in decan	Day		Night	
	N	% Positive	N	% Positive
1	17	37.1	7	12.9
2	32	56.4	28	45.2
3	47	46.1	32	81.9***
4	75	58.5	44	48.2
5	25	46.9	36	26.9***
6	23	54.9	38	44.0
7	21	30.0	14	45.2
8	3	0.0	26	45.2
9	4	0.0	13	41.7
10	0	0.0	0	0.0
Sum	247	48.8	238	46.5

Persons born during the night experienced a significant number of positive years in their twenties with Saturn as their decan ruler; those in their forties had a significant number of difficult years. Both day and night births experienced great difficulties when Saturn was the first of the ten to rise.

Saturn Rising
(38% positive years)

This year will probably be difficult. It can be a time of diseases, troubles and torments. There are likely to be failures: financial loss, much mental anguish, suffering, poor health, quarrels within the family, disputes with relatives and serious enmities. Fevers, blood complaints and mental derangement are possible. At this time the individual may be forced to rely on the help of others, which he will hate. He must face now the requirement that he acknowledges and lives within his own limitations.

If Saturn is strong and directed to an ascendant in Libra, Capricorn or Aquarius, events may occur that increase the individual's experience and add to his responsibilities. It can be a serious time in which relationships that are less than perfect may end.

An individual with an afflicted Saturn is likely to be particularly badly hit this year. Fears, psychological blocks and inhibitions can emerge as if from nowhere and take over his life. He may lose his home and family, and be forced to resign his position. There will be little or no money, and what he has he will be frightened to spend. He may lack the basic means of getting to and from his place of employment, and be forced to depend on others to provide him with lifts. Friends desert him or they die. To avoid facing his responsibilities drugs may be taken, and alcohol consumed in excess. Children are born out of wedlock. It can be a shameful year in which the individual loses his self-respect, and his lack of confidence can cause him to sink into a black depression. He is likely to doubt himself and want approval in everything he does. His standing in the world can disappear overnight, and he may be forced to descend into the lowest levels of society before he is able to find someone to welcome and provide him with comfort. He is likely to have great wants now, a hunger that cannot be appeased. His health may also be attacked, his natural functions and vitality slowed.

Table ♄-7: **Saturn Rising: % Positive Years**

♄ relative to the ☉	Day birth		Night birth		All	
	N	% Positive	N	% Positive	N	% Positive
Oriental ♄	38	**30.9****	35	**28.4****	73	**29.7*****
Occidental ♄	32	45.2	39	46.4	71	45.8
All	*70*	*37.5***	*74*	*37.9***	*144*	*37.7****

People in the sample found this a very difficult year. Those born with an oriental Saturn experienced the most problems. Even those with an occidental Saturn, a much more positive situation, had a less than a fifty-fifty chance that the year would be a positive experience. There is no obvious difference between day and night births; both usually experienced ghastly years.

Saturn in the 9th house was significantly below 50%, and so too was the ascendant in Leo. Either Saturn or the ascendant in a Venus term was also a significant negative.

Some happenings in the sample when Saturn becomes the decan ruler:
Oriental Saturn rises by day in decan: *marries; leaves RAF; concentrated studies; forced to retreat; evening classes; living alone; wounded; in poor health; hospitalized.*
Occidental Saturn rises by day in decan: *poor health; bleak outlook; maximizes the efficiency of light bulbs; believes his work has failed; her book has very large sales; buys old house; rebuilds barn.*
Oriental Saturn rises at night in decan: *she is starved of human warmth; attacked in the press; always hungry; arrested; refuses advice; his faculty of near total recall awakens; graduates; her hair goes grey; homesick.*
Occidental Saturn rises at night in decan: *working feverishly; little sleep; depressed; lonely & sad; displays strong anti-Semitic feelings; his daughter elopes; being bullied by his pregnant wife; resigns from his position; ill; failures; wants to awaken from lethargy.*

Some happenings in the sample when Saturn becomes the septenary ruler:
Oriental Saturn rises by day in septenary: *first sees poverty, sickness, old age & death; experiences a spare diet, thin clothing and hard exercise; shocked and humiliated; imprisoned; defeated; expelled; major crisis; surgery.*

Occidental Saturn rises by day in septenary: *feels helpless, fearful & unqualified; separated from his family; poor health; starts work; son born; passes exams; graduates; editing; moves; travels; resigns in protest.*

Oriental Saturn rises at night in septenary: *resigns his position; the worst time in her life; her mother dies at her birth; promoted; happy time; marries; defeated; frustrated; honored; travels away from home.*

Occidental Saturn rises at night in septenary: *marries; his work is criticized; mourning; depressed; death of father/brother/wife; matured by tackling a demanding role in the face of much hostility; spinal injury; paralyzed; kidney removed; exhausted; honored.*

Saturn directed to the Sun
(45% positive)

This can be another difficult year. It is likely to be a time of the empty nest during which the individual will be forced to spend much time on his own. Perhaps his child has gone off to college, or his wife is absent visiting her parents, or away on a cruise with friends from college. The individual himself may be forced to work away from the home. Perhaps there is a divorce or legal separation. However it happens this is a year when the family can become split. The individual is likely to become depressed; he misses his usual companionship and comforts.

Table ♄-8: **♄ to ☉: % Positive Years**

♄ relative to the ☉	Day birth		Night birth		All	
	N	% Positive	N	% Positive	N	% Positive
Oriental ♄	35	49.1	40	36.2	75	42.2
Occidental ♄	40	47.5	28	48.4	68	47.9
All	*75*	*48.2*	*68*	*41.2*	*143*	*44.9*

It can be a year of defeats, rejection and business failure. There can be trouble with superiors or from theft. The individual's dignity may be lost, his self-confidence endangered. His incapacities and weaknesses are likely to be apparent to others. He may lose his job or retire from the workplace. His body may experience pain and disorder; there is danger from blood poisoning and the eyes can become afflicted. There will be little excess energy, just enough to deal with what has to be done. There can be sickness in the family. Pets are in danger now and the health of the father-in-law may cause worry. The individual can become fearful and over cautious. Death can be close.

Those born with the Sun in Libra, Capricorn or Aquarius often escape these problems, as can those diurnal births with Saturn above the horizon and sextile, quintile or trine to the Sun. They may be promoted, negotiate successful deals, or conceive of timely business innovations. Some assistance can come to them from older friends.

In the sample there was further confirmation that Saturn is associated with more positive events when it is occidental of the Sun. Those persons in my sample born with an oriental Saturn and a nocturnal Sun experienced the most difficult years. Saturn in the 10th house was significantly below 50%.

Some happenings in the sample when Saturn comes to the Sun in the decan:
Oriental Saturn to the Sun by day in decan: *deaths in the family; desolate with grief; moves; intense study of music; improved finances; fights to avoid being cheated; forced to take out a large loan; lengthy hospitalization; honors.*
Occidental Saturn to the Sun by day in decan: *deaths in the family; poor health; drafted into army; starts violin lessons; nursing; wins a key contract.*
Oriental Saturn to the Sun at night in decan: *deaths in the family; kills child who runs under her car; nursing; joins the navy; thrashed; studying; very ill; opens a shop; honors.*
Occidental Saturn to the Sun at night in decan: *marries; "life is hell"; his wife is nagging & moaning; very sad; studying; has difficulty walking; extensive physical therapy; lonely; travels; fearful; honors.*

Some happenings in the sample when Saturn comes to the Sun in the septenary:
Oriental Saturn to the Sun by day in septenary: *mental & nervous breakdown; separated from wife; marries; mother dies/ill/is absent; in a coma; confused; feeling asphyxiated; success; retires; ordered to leave US.*
Occidental Saturn to the Sun by day in septenary: *wife dies; difficult year; preoccupied with the past; overworked; very ill; feels disdain for his father/mentor; out of prison; changes his life direction; wounded; organizes others.*
Oriental Saturn to the Sun at night in septenary: *daughter born; unemployed; very nervous & frightened; promoted; honored; travels; proves himself innocent of charges; considered a prude & a bore; new job.*
Occidental Saturn to the Sun at night in septenary: *travels; thrown from a horse; doctors lie to her; grief; defeated; his offices are destroyed in blitz; defeated; accused of libel; bi-polar mania; suicidal; insomnia; exhausted.*

Saturn directed to the Moon
(48% positive)

This can be a frustrating time, a depressing year when little of a positive nature happens. The individual may become unemployed. Money and property can be lost, he will be limited in what he can and can't do, and he may be reduced to great need. Long-term loans may need to be taken out, property mortgaged or sold. There can be family disputes in which the long simmering enmities of relations come out into the open. A close relative may die. Friends may turn their back on the native. He may feel lonely, be homesick, and believe that he is helpless. There may be problems with his eyesight, cataracts perhaps that prevent him from driving at night.

If the Moon is in a sign that welcomes Saturn the native may return to visit his old home after a lengthy absence, meeting again those loved ones he has not seen for many years. He may buy a new car, make repairs to his house, study history or mythology, and feel a renewed desire to be independent. If the Moon is in Aries intense emotional suffering can occur; he has been hurt and as a result may lack any sense of self-worth.

Table ♄-9:   **♄ to ☽: % Positive Years**

Planets relative to the ☉	Day birth		Night birth		All	
	N	% Positive	N	% Positive	N	% Positive
Oriental ♄	43	44.2	30	48.2	73	45.8
Occidental ♄	30	54.2	41	48.5	71	50.9
All	*73*	*48.3*	*71*	*48.4*	*144*	*48.3*
Waxing ☽	46	39.3	42	53.8	88	46.2
Waning ☽	27	63.6	29	40.5	56	51.7

Day births with occidental Saturn or waning Moon had the most positive years. Saturn directed to a Moon in Cancer, the sign the Moon rules but in which Saturn is never comfortable, was significantly below 50%.

Some happenings in the sample when Saturn comes to the Moon in the decan:
Oriental Saturn to the Moon by day in decan: *out of work; very poor; deaths in the family; successful astrological predictions; goes to new school; miserable; travels to see lunar standstill; difficulties with superiors; unhappy marriage; police confiscate his uninsured car.*
Occidental Saturn to the Moon by day in decan: *suicidal; worries; moves to a commune; finds errors in his work; rejects job offer; separated from his family; destroys his papers; on trial for double murder; transformation of his life.*
Oriental Saturn to the Moon at night in decan: *marries; starts going to a gym; unpopular; hated; homesick; interrogated; defeated; victory; appendectomy; her autobiography wins a prize; bitter; tries to make peace.*
Occidental Saturn to the Moon at night in decan: *moves; threatened & needs police protection; teeth problems; given wrong tax advice; invents damper for stoves & chimneys; autobiography; sells house; miserable; loses weight.*

Happenings in the sample when Saturn comes to the Moon in the septenary:
Oriental Saturn to the Moon by day in septenary: *mother dies; homesick; buys new house; loses his house & income; choking fits; starts/leaves school; exiled; public squabbles; conscripted; meets long-time love; sells RV; death.*
Occidental Saturn to the Moon by day in septenary: *sells his farm; reduced spending; poor; in a bad temper; negotiations fail; travels; tension with mother; affair ends; parents quarrel; deaths in the family.*
Oriental Saturn to the Moon at night in septenary: *births/deaths in the family; chaotic living conditions; bankrupt; on committee she hates; he is a broken man; declines honors; joins navy; promoted; leads invasion; assassinated.*

Occidental Saturn to the Moon at night in septenary: lung problems; births/deaths in the family; debts; travels; photography interest; unemployed; into psychiatric hospital; mocks pretensions; new job; marries; wants to go home.

Saturn directed to Mercury
(45% positive)

This is unlikely to be a happy year. News received can cause worry and doubt. Bill collectors may be on the phone or knocking at the door. The individual can be placed in a humiliating position and is forced to quickly do something about it. He may have to borrow money to keep his business and family afloat. He is likely to be under continual pressure and may have to defend himself against the accusations and threats of others, to take determined steps against those who would deprive him of all he possesses. A form of communication may become silenced, and there are likely to be worries concerning the health of family members. If in previous Saturn-ruled years the individual has become weakened physically, the direction to Mercury can bring death.

Mercury in Libra, Capricorn or Aquarius can indicate success in precise but cautious intellectual work.

Daytime births usually have a much easier year than do nocturnal ones. In the sample nocturnal births had very difficult periods when Saturn was occidental or Mercury oriental.

Table ♄-10:   ♄ to ☿: % Positive Years

Planets relative to the ☉	Day birth		Night birth		All	
	N	% Positive	N	% Positive	N	% Positive
Oriental ♄	37	56.2	39	44.0	76	50.0
Occidental ♄	29	59.2	41	**26.5***	70	40.0
All	*66*	*57.5*	*80*	*35.0*	*146*	*45.2*
Oriental ☿	36	55.3	39	**27.8***	75	41.0
Occidental ☿	30	60.3	41	41.9	71	49.7

Saturn coming from Cancer is a significant indicator of difficult years.

Some happenings in the sample when Saturn comes to Mercury in the decan:
Oriental Saturn to Mercury in the day in decan: loss of money to taxes; learns to skate; choking fits; ptomaine poisoning; fearing disgrace; editing; unhappy marriage; feeling out of place; studying; starts school; son born; fascinated by magic; reading avidly; editing magazine; lengthy commute; starts a school.
Occidental Saturn to Mercury in the day in decan: moves; homesick; goes to a new school; stories are published; religious studies; exiled; regrets letter he wrote in the previous year; buys a powerboat; has no strength.

Oriental Saturn to Mercury at night in decan: *concentrates on his studies; breaks his nose; grief; travels; marries; career worries; leaves college before graduating; refuses to promote her novel; death.*

Occidental Saturn to Mercury at night in decan: *unable to walk; exhausted; legal problems; buys house; unable to meditate; his marriage has gone sour; very sensitive; "empty the mind of all but facts"; his lecture is published.*

Some happenings in the sample when Saturn comes to Mercury in the septenary:

Oriental Saturn to Mercury in the day in septenary: *legal problems; FBI taps his phone; wins immense wealth; marries; closes magazine; studying alchemical texts; worries; ordained; graduates; moves; travels; defends himself in court against ex-wife's alimony claims; lecturing; boxing; depression; cataracts; rheumatism; health worries.*

Occidental Saturn to Mercury in the day in septenary: *her plane is lost in fog over mountains; graduates; in prison; anxiety; autobiography; husband retires; engrossed in his theories; travels; children marry; disagreement with his father; awarded Pulitzer Prize; hostages are taken; he fears throat cancer; teaching; negotiating.*

Oriental Saturn to Mercury at night in septenary: *deaths in the family; travels; sees those he loves cut to pieces; studying; honors; loss of position through hesitation; humiliated; learns taxidermy; has his first gun; death.*

Occidental Saturn to Mercury at night in septenary: *deaths of males in family; printing currency; "time only exists if thinking occurs"; signs treaty; she is sexually frigid; expelled; accused of corruption, but vindicated; suicidal; kidnap threats; negotiating; has strained nerves; buys new house; depression; exhausted; ill health; death.*

Saturn directed to Venus
(48% positive)

This may be a sad year. There can be mourning following the deaths of family members. The native may reject those who want to be his friends. There can be renewed interest in arts and crafts, and a connection to an older way of worship. A pension may be received. Financial restraints may occur and with them the need to economize. The individual needs to discover how to take pleasure in fulfilling his duties and responsibilities, how to love his work and live within his limitations.

Table ♄-11:   ♄ to ♀ % Positive Years

Planets relative to the ☉	Day birth		Night birth		All	
	N	% Positive	N	% Positive	N	% Positive
Oriental ♄	40	56.5	30	54.2	70	55.5
Occidental ♄	30	54.2	36	**30.1****	66	41.1
All	*70*	*55.5*	*66*	*41.1*	*136*	*48.5*
Oriental ♀	36	55.3	25	43.4	61	50.4
Occidental ♀	34	55.8	41	39.7	75	47.0

If Venus is in a sign that does not welcome Saturn, especially for a nocturnal birth, the year may contain much frustration and upset, perhaps even a degree of shame. Those born at night with an occidental Saturn had a particularly difficult year. So too did people in the sample with Saturn in the 4th house.

Saturn coming from its own term was a significant positive indicator.

Some happenings in the sample when Saturn comes to Venus in the decan:
Oriental Saturn to Venus by day in decan: *borrows money; son born; depressed; marriage problems; working again after long spell unemployed; fails all exams; leaves school; first meets relatives; becomes a bully; spends a night in jail; death.*
Occidental Saturn to Venus by day in decan: *deep depression when his work is criticized; loses; in a street fight; son arrested for assault with a knife; abdominal operation; parents separate; his wife divorces him; very bad time, much suffering; insomnia.*
Oriental Saturn to Venus at night in decan: *fear; uncertainty; plotted against; defeated; exhausted; falls from horse; becomes a "born snob"; marries; first goes on the web; ignored.*
Occidental Saturn to Venus at night in decan: *premonitions of disaster; wife and children leave him; many honors; sees his life until now has been wasted; discusses fear & freedom; knighted; in poor health; bored.*

Some happenings in the sample when Saturn comes to Venus in the septenary:
Oriental Saturn to Venus by day in septenary: *meets future wife; fails leading a rebellion; starts her diary; victory; studies psychic energy; seaside holiday; "religion is based mainly on fear of the unknown;" promoted.*
Occidental Saturn to Venus by day in septenary: *lover marries another; studies oriental art; lonely; elected; marries; swelling from blow completely closes his eyes; girl friend's suicide; overcomes his natural shyness; hunger strike; religious quest is awakened; father is dying; travels.*
Oriental Saturn to Venus at night in septenary: *lover dies in motorbike crash; thrashed; others plot against him; promoted; attacked as a catholic sympathizer; son born; has a foreign lover.*
Occidental Saturn to Venus at night in septenary: *deaths of females; devoting time & energy on abolition of slavery; at cookery school; leaves his mistress; sick with guilt; nuclear disaster; moves; suicidal; feeling of emptiness; has a defeatist attitude; depressed; high blood sugar; cancer of uterus.*

Saturn directed to Mars
(53% positive)

Although Mars is exalted in Saturn's sign of Capricorn, there is no reciprocity and Saturn is not considered welcome in any of the signs that Mars rules. Accordingly, this can be a bleak year in which the individual is made to feel un-wanted. He may feel old and out dated, cold and lonely, physically weak, tired and ill. His speech and hearing may be affected. He is likely to find other people irritating, and become bitter and angry. As a result he may meet with strife and serious enmity, and be attacked and injured. He may be disgraced, lose money by fraud or theft, be forced to leave his job, perhaps change where he lives and lead an unsettled life, wandering from place to place. He can become a distress to his family and friends. He may experience surgery, and have to cope with severe headaches, cancer or arthritis.

In the sample there was a distinct contrast here between whether Mars rises before or after the Sun, with the earlier rising more positive. Night births were more positive than day births.

Table ♄-12:   **♄ to ♂ % Positive Years**

Planets relative to the ☉	Day birth		Night birth		All	
	N	% Positive	N	% Positive	N	% Positive
Oriental ♄	37	46.4	32	56.5	69	51.1
Occidental ♄	29	49.9	34	58.5	63	54.5
All	*66*	*47.9*	*66*	*57.5*	*132*	*52.7*
Oriental ♂	32	59.3	33	**65.8***	65	**62.6***
Occidental ♂	34	37.2	33	49.3	67	43.2

Some happenings in the sample when Saturn comes to Mars in the decan:
Oriental Saturn to Mars by day in decan: *in a public controversy; yachting; becomes obstreperous; divorce; earns final professional qualifications; moves to USA; travels overseas.*
Occidental Saturn to Mars by day in decan: *motorbike accident; enlists in the navy; irritable & angry; pugnacious; trying for self-control; accused of murdering his ex-wife & her lover; very active.*
Oriental Saturn to Mars at night in decan: *liver disease; imprisoned; bedridden; studying hard; conspiracy against him; has increased authority; ostracized; has no money; humiliated.*
Occidental Saturn to Mars at night in decan: *learns new yoga breathing exercises; agitated; daughter born; returns home; honors.*

Some happenings in the sample when Saturn comes to Mars in the septenary:
Oriental Saturn to Mars by day in septenary: *tames a wild horse; surgery removes cancerous tumor in his bladder; ordered to leave USA; confused & angry; attempt on his life; loses his job; arrested; defeated.*

Occidental Saturn to Mars by day in septenary: *a complete failure, unable to succeed in anything; persistent headaches; criticized; no money; in poor health.*

Oriental Saturn to Mars at night in septenary: *deaths in the family; imprisoned; no income; headaches; homeless; elected; promoted.*

Occidental Saturn to Mars at night in septenary: *resigns; excessive work; lack of sleep; severe depression; pulmonary infarct; becomes a garrulous maniac; "allegiance to anything is the beginning of corruption"; tedious inertia; eating little.*

Saturn directed to Jupiter

(51% positive)

Life should start to improve this year. Financial problems may not yet be fully resolved but they are somewhat eased. There may be still more embarrassment and humiliation, but light is at last visible at the end of the tunnel. This can be a time for restrained, careful and cautious expansion, a year in which one's optimism and hopes for the future begin to increase as the months pass. The native's objectives have again become a possibility, and he should start to take the necessary steps to realize them. During the year methods and systems that were successful in the past should be carefully maintained and brought up to date as an investment for the future.

Table ♄-13:   **♄ to ♃ % Positive Years**

Planets relative to the ☉	Day birth		Night birth		All	
	N	% Positive	N	% Positive	N	% Positive
Oriental ♄	42	47.4	31	61.2	73	53.3
Occidental ♄	31	43.7	41	52.9	72	49.0
All	*73*	*45.8*	*72*	*56.5*	*145*	*51.1*
Oriental ♃	30	39.2	32	62.2	62	51.0
Occidental ♃	43	50.5	40	52.0	83	51.2

Unexpectedly, because both Jupiter and Saturn are traditionally said to be strongest during the day, day births in the sample experienced considerable difficulties in these years. Saturn coming to a Jupiter in its own (Jupiter's) term indicated a significantly positive year.

Some happenings in the sample when Saturn comes to Jupiter in the decan:

Oriental Saturn to Jupiter by day in decan: *father remarries; separates from his family & lives alone; fails audition; husband dies; under extreme stress; first lectures in public; restricted diet; emigrates; mother is ill.*

Occidental Saturn to Jupiter by day in decan: *engaged; marriage is breaking up; book published; death.*

Oriental Saturn to Jupiter at night in decan: *poor health; loss of self-confidence; resigns; very lonely; has no money & is forced to beg.*

Occidental Saturn to Jupiter at night in decan: *children born; solvent; first gets into Tibet; starts working as a lawyer; divorce.*

Some happenings in the sample when Saturn comes to Jupiter in the septenary:

Oriental Saturn to Jupiter by day in septenary: *renounces wealth & family; persuaded not to retire as he had planned; parents die; financial losses; becomes indifferent to religion; first job; much enforced idleness; changes his job; promoted; daughter born; astronomy interest.*

Occidental Saturn to Jupiter by day in septenary: *his protector is sent away; emigrates; accused of attempted murder; brother born/dies/catches syphilis; badly beaten by a mob; incorporates; loses his children; moves; depressed & believes his whole life has been a failure; starts piano lessons; presents his thesis.*

Oriental Saturn to Jupiter at night in septenary: *rejected for war service; her wedding reception & honeymoon are cancelled; discharged from navy; elected; domestic tension; living in a new environment; breaks her shoulder; bowel bleeding, told to slow down.*

Occidental Saturn to Jupiter at night in septenary: *marries; criticized for biased reporting; undercuts a rival magazine; proposes the abolition of slavery; leaves home to make his way in the world; ordered to rest; building nursing homes; attacked as an atheist; elected FRS; sued for debt; he is a patient in a psychiatric hospital.*

Saturn directed to Uranus
(65% positive)

This can be an erratic year, a disruptive one in which old conditions no longer seem to apply. Circumstances, usually outside the individual's control, may sud-denly alter and he, perhaps with many others, may find that rules have been changed and that he is forced to convert to a new ways of doing things. What previously had appeared fixed and dependable is now under threat. These changes may occur unexpectedly, without prior warning, and the individual has little choice but to accept them.

Table ♄-14:   **♄ to ⛢ % Positive Years**

Planets relative to the ☉	Day birth		Night birth		All	
	N	% Positive	N	% Positive	N	% Positive
Oriental ♄	17	63.8	12	67.8	29	**65.5**
Occidental ♄	14	64.6	10	63.3	24	64.0
All	*31*	*64.2*	*22*	*65.8*	*53*	*64.8*
Oriental ⛢	13	**76.6***	13	**76.6***	26	**76.6***
Occidental ⛢	18	55.3	9	50.2	27	53.6

The native is likely to break away now from situations that he has outgrown but which continue to stop him from progressing where he wants to go. The unexpected is to be expected. There is an element of surprise about much that happens to the individual this year.

Saturn directed to an oriental Uranus is an excellent predictor of a positive year. The relatively high values for this direction are perhaps not so surprising when we recall that following its discovery astrologers quickly related the planet to Aquarius, Saturn's daytime sign.

Some happenings in the sample when Saturn comes to Uranus in the decan:

Oriental Saturn to Uranus in the day: very poor; rejects his pregnant wife; buys a house; his job is terminated; first freelance jobs; parents separate; son born; separated from his mother; falls; wins a lottery.

Occidental Saturn to Uranus in the day: vows permanent celibacy; uses passive resistance; fails to prevent bombing; "Religion is a collective neurosis"; named an outstanding classical scholar; begins studying astrology; graduates; discovers the principles of helicopter flight; falls in love & begins a homosexual relationship.

Oriental Saturn to Uranus at night: founds a city; learns to fly; ends his marriage; returns to her roots; restores the Republic; her autobiography is published; humiliated.

Occidental Saturn to Uranus at night: quashes a riot; receiving occult training; heart attack; very happy; in love; vicious attacks on his character.

Saturn directed to Neptune
(58% positive)

This can be an unpleasant year. Fear is often a dominant feeling, which can drain away a person's energy. The individual may fear that his unsavory past is going to catch up with him, that the skeletons in his cupboard will become visible to others, that his weaknesses will be obvious to all. He feels betrayed, and may appear as if paralyzed, lacking the will needed to direct his own life. There is confusion and disappointments, too many worries and not enough joy. Drugs may be taken. The person's concept of reality is changing now as he discovers that many of the structures in his life that he believed to be permanent and indestructible only existed as such in his imagination.

Table ♄-15: ♄ to ♆ % Positive Years

Planets relative to the ☉	Day birth		Night birth		All	
	N	% Positive	N	% Positive	N	% Positive
Oriental ♄	16	56.5	11	74.0	27	63.6
Occidental ♄	9	50.2	12	52.7	21	51.7
All	*25*	*54.2*	*23*	*62.9*	*48*	*58.4*
Oriental ♆	16	50.9	15	60.3	31	55.4
Occidental ♆	9	60.3	8	67.8	17	63.8

Those members of the sample born with Saturn oriental to the Sun (or Neptune occidental therefrom) had a high percentage of positive years. Saturn coming to Neptune from Leo was also significantly over 50%, which is yet another indicator that the natal weakness of Saturn is no drawback to positive years.

Some happenings in the sample when Saturn comes to Neptune in the decan:
Oriental Saturn to Neptune in the day: *nose operation; leaves school/job/army; successful astrological predictions; several friends die; lampoons helpless victims; badly injured in car accident; gets his first car; lacking courage; lonely, buys an old, dilapidated house; mourning husband's death; drained of energy; exhausted.*
Occidental Saturn to Neptune in the day: *starts piano lessons; imprisoned; agitating; jealousy; promoted; affair ends; loses fight; first free flight; surgery on his nose causes breathing problems.*
Oriental Saturn to Neptune at night: *returns home after long absence; joins navy; no money; moves; very happy; his literary life is over.*
Occidental Saturn to Neptune at night: *very bitter when his son is killed in the war; many honors; travels overseas; uncongenial job; pneumonia; infantile paralysis.*

Saturn directed to Pluto
(44% positive)

This can be a year of loss and sorrow, disgrace and ruin, when the individual is forced to accept cold, hard truths. Showdowns, clashes or misunderstandings can lead him to a necessary understanding of reality. He may feel the need to go off alone and hide his grief or shame from others. There can be a loss of freedom. What has become weak and out of date will need to be replaced and strengthened now. Several similar examples of this need for renovation occurred in the sample: different people spent much time this year repairing old houses. Faced with the problems that only become apparent this year, the temptation is to give up, to run off and just leave the troubles behind. Whether the individual does just this or attempts to repair the damage depends very much on the strength of Saturn and the sign placement of Pluto. Should he fail to adequately update his defenses against the outside elements, the problems will only return magnified in the future.

Table ♄-16:   **♄ to ♀ % Positive Years**

Planets relative to the ☉	Day birth		Night birth		All	
	N	% Positive	N	% Positive	N	% Positive
Oriental ♄	23	43.2	11	41.1	34	42.5
Occidental ♄	7	38.7	10	54.2	17	47.9
All	*30*	*42.2*	*21*	*47.4*	*51*	*44.3*
Oriental ♀	21	34.4	12	45.2	33	38.4
Occidental ♀	9	60.3	9	50.2	18	55.3

In the sample occidental Pluto was associated with a higher proportion of positive years than was oriental Pluto.

Some happenings in the sample when Saturn comes to Pluto in the decan:

Oriental Saturn to Pluto in the day: *mother dies; marries; foot surgery; conscripted; children born; angry & aggressive; suffers in waterless desert; pays off old debt; repairing an old house; moves into a new house; told he was to die but miraculously recovers his health.*

Occidental Saturn to Pluto in the day: *imprisoned; fame; deceived; he is Man of the Year; given a new contract; father/friend dies; liver pain; knee reconstructive surgery following horseback riding accident.*

Oriental Saturn to Pluto at night: *discovers penicillin; snubbed on release from prison; his parents are overseas; poor health; death.*

Occidental Saturn to Pluto at night: *repairing old house; borrows money; in a shattered emotional state; furious; tension in the workplace; criticized; marriage disintegrates.*

Hitler's Saturn-ruled Septenary

Saturn in Leo rises: Adolf Hitler is forty-two years old in 1931 when his elevated Saturn, weakened by being located in Leo, assumes control of his septenary. In his decan the Sun, the ruler of Saturn's natal sign, has arrived at Jupiter in Capricorn. He renounces his Austrian citizenship and becomes a German citizen. His girl friend Geli Raubal commits suicide after she discovers that he is spending time with Eva Braun. He is in shock and stops eating meat, suffering from severe depression. He loses the election for president after a run-off with Hindenburg, partly due to a homosexual scandal involving one of his key followers, Ruehm. He is distressed to learn that he himself may be part Jewish. His book *Mein Kampf* is selling well.

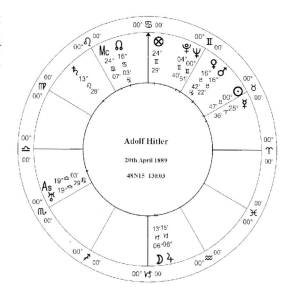

Saturn directed to Venus in Taurus: Saturn comes to Hitler's ascendant ruler Venus in the septenary in April 1932. He is forty-three years old. The two are in a square aspect and Saturn's antiscion is closely conjunct Venus. In his decan the Sun has come to his waning Moon in Capricorn. He is campaigning for elections to the Reichstag and is mobbed by adoring women wherever he goes—clearly the affect of the Sun coming to the Moon.

He is infuriated when Hindenburg only offers him the position of Vice-Chancellor. Eva Braun attempts suicide. His party loses seats in the Reichstag elections. He consults the astrologer Eric Jan Hanussen who predicts that Hitler's rise to power would begin on

January 30, 1933. On the specified day Hitler becomes Chancellor and assumes power. A Communist rebellion fails. The Reichstag fire, which he makes full use of as a propaganda tool, occurs. He orders a boycott of Jewish-owned businesses. This year the first concentration camp is opened.

Saturn directed to Mars in Taurus: Saturn arrives at Mars in Hitler's septenary in 1933. Saturn and Mars are in square aspect and Saturn's antiscion is conjunct Mars. In the decan, the Sun is on Uranus in Libra, the sign of the Sun's fall. Consummate politician that he is, Hitler assumes power gradually, ensuring he does so with the people's consent. He obtains financing from industrialists and uses it to blanket the nation with publicity. Organized labor is obliterated. He then expunges democracy and declares that the Nazi party is now

the only political party in Germany. A single party controls Germany and that party is controlled by a single man who, in turn, is possessed by a dream. He has Germany quit the League of Nations and trebles the size of the army. He holds a plebiscite and 95.1% of the voters approve his foreign policy. His mandate is overwhelming.

Saturn directed to the Sun in Taurus: In 1934 Hitler experiences an unusual combination of septenary and decan indicators. In the septenary Saturn is on his Sun, its dispositor, while in the decan the Sun has come to his elevated Saturn. Saturn is in Leo, the Sun-ruled sign, and the Sun is in Taurus, one of the earth signs, an element that Saturn rules. Hitler is now forty-five. Concerned that an agreement between France and the Soviet Union might be the start of an encirclement of the Reich, he looks for a strong ally and meets with and is humiliated by Mussolini. Believing Röhm, the head of the Brownshirts, is organizing a mutiny, Hitler has him and his associates executed; the event becomes known as The Night of the Long Knives. He has become immensely popular. Hindenburg dies and Hitler succeeds him as the ruler of Germany. He is now the Fuehrer and is moving from the lawful and legal to the illegal and unlawful. The first Nuremburg Rally takes place. Outwitting the leaders of other European countries, he enjoys a series of diplomatic successes. He is rearming Germany.

Saturn directed to Mercury in Aries: Saturn is at the sign of its fall in 1935. He is now forty-six years old. The Sun is on occidental Pluto in Gemini in the decan. The year begins with a widely heard speech in which he states his chief aim is peace and he has no dreams of conquest. His social life is expanding. A growth in his larynx revives a fear of throat cancer. Feeling abandoned, Eva Braun again attempts suicide. He attacks the Jews in a speech, and states that only those people of "German or related blood" can be citizens. He is upset when Mussolini invades Ethiopia. He reoccupies the Rhineland and in doing so discovers how easy it is to successfully bluff France and Britain, two countries that are terrified by the thought of another world war.

Saturn directed to Jupiter in Capricorn: Saturn has come to its own sign and is on Hitler's oriental Jupiter in 1936. He is forty-seven years old. The Sun is on his Neptune in Gemini in the decan. His chauffeur is killed in a car crash. He is having difficulty sleeping. He gives Franco support in the Spanish civil war, using it as a prelude to a genuine conflict. The Olympic Games are staged in Berlin, and he attends most track and field events—they are an almost unqualified Nazi triumph. He says the German army and its economy must be ready for war in four years. He is disappointed by the abdication of his ally Edward VIII from the British throne. His health has improved, and he has changed the face of Germany with a network of autobahns and has ordered the development of a "people's car," the Volkswagen.

Saturn directed to the Moon in Capricorn: Saturn is still in its own sign and in 1937, the final year of its rulership of the septenary, it comes to Hitler's waning Moon. He is forty-eight years old. In his decan the Sun has come to Venus, its dispositor and his ascendant ruler. He visits Mussolini in Rome. Carl Jung observes Hitler and notes that he is like a robot. "He seemed as if he might be a double of a real person, and that Hitler the man might perhaps be hiding inside…" He is planning over the next few years to invade first Czechoslovakia, then Poland and France, hoping England will remain neutral, so that by 1943 the way will be cleared to wage major warfare and knock out his primary enemy, Russia. He complains of loneliness. He is now the supreme dictator of the German Reich. He reorganizes the army and it occupies Austria, enabling him to make a triumphant entry into the land of his birth.

Sir Laurence Olivier's first Saturn-ruled Septenary

Saturn rises in Pisces: The actor Sir Laurence Olivier is a day birth, born shortly after dawn. Saturn becomes his septenary ruler in May 1928 on his 21st birthday. In his decan Neptune is on his Jupiter in Cancer. He is in several London plays, including his first leading West End role, the title part in *Beau Geste*. He meets and is smitten by Jill Esmond, a fellow cast member in the production of *Bird in the Hand*. Her cool indifference to him does nothing but further his ardor.

Saturn directed to Mars in Capricorn: In 1929 Saturn comes to its own sign, where it meets the exalted Mars. Neptune is on his Pluto in Gemini in the decan. He is twenty-two years old and in love with the actress Jill Esmond. She goes to New York and he, determined to be near her, follows her to New York City where he acts in *Murder on the Second Floor*. Esmond wins rave reviews for her performance but he is less successful. Being in Manhattan is very exciting and he enjoys it in careless extravagance. He returns to England and then goes to Berlin to appear in his first film, *The Temporary Widow*.

Saturn directed to the Moon in Virgo: Olivier experiences Saturn on his Moon in the septenary in 1930 when he is twenty-three years old. Neptune rules the decan and is on his Sun in Taurus. He plays the role of Victor in Noel Coward's *Private Lives* in London and New York. He appears in two films: *Too Many Crooks* and *Potiphar's Wife*. Having asked her several times and been rebuffed, Jill Esmond finally agrees to marry him. She is not however in love with him and he quickly becomes sexually frustrated. The couple attend many parties in Manhattan. Jill goes into a New York hospital for appendicitis.

Saturn directed to Jupiter in Cancer: Laurence Olivier's septenary ruler Saturn comes to Jupiter in Cancer in 1931. Jupiter is exalted and is Saturn's dispositor, but Saturn is unwelcome in Cancer. This combination can indicate a time of frustration. Neptune is on his Mercury in Taurus in his decan. He is twenty-four years old. He and Jill go to Hollywood for the first time, living in a house on top of Look-Out Mountain. He makes two films: *Friends and Lovers* and *The Yellow Passport*. He appropriately catches yellow jaundice and suffers from much enforced indolence.

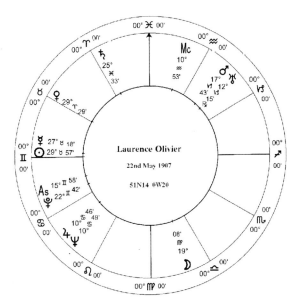

Saturn directed to the Sun in Taurus: In 1932 Saturn has come to his Sun. He is twenty-five years old. In the decan Neptune has arrived at his Venus in Aries. He is in Hollywood where he appears in *Westward Passage*. He returns to England where he films *Perfect Understanding* with Gloria Swanson. There is no stage work and he feels asphyxiated.

Saturn directed to Mercury in Taurus: In 1933 Laurence Olivier's septenary ruler Saturn comes to his Mercury. He is twenty-six years old. Decan ruler Neptune is on his Saturn in Pisces. Saturn is being emphasized by both systems. He acts in *Rats of Norway* with Gladys Cooper at the Playhouse, London. Being an actor in the theater again after lengthy spells in Hollywood is as if he has recovered from some kind of asphyxiation. He returns to Hollywood to film *Queen Christiana* with Greta Garbo but is fired, so instead has a vacation in Hawaii. In New York he acts in the successful *The Green Bay Tree,* but is angry and resentful towards his director Jed Harris—"the most loathsome man I ever met."

Saturn directed to Venus in Aries: Septenary ruler Saturn comes to Olivier's Venus in 1934. His decan ruler Neptune is on his Mars in Capricorn. He is twenty-seven years old. He is back in the London theater, where he is happiest. After appearing in a flop, *Biography*, he plays Boswell in *Queen of Scots*, a production in which he makes many long-lasting friendships.

Sir Laurence Olivier's Saturn-ruled Decan

Saturn rises in Pisces: Laurence Olivier is sixty years old in 1967 when his occidental Saturn begins to rule his decan. In his septenary the waxing Moon is on his oriental Venus in Aries. It is a very difficult year. He is the director of the Britain's National Theatre, which was launched four years earlier. This year his relations with the theater's chairman, Lord Chandos, begin to deteriorate. He is also violently at odds with the producer Peter Brook over the placing of a statue of a phallus on the stage in the play *Oedipus* and broods over his defeat. He is experiencing crippling stage fright due to the effect of labyrinthis. He is diagnosed as having cancer of the prostate gland and undergoes unpleasant but successful treatment for this. His ex-wife Vivien Leigh dies. He tours Canada. At different times this same year he suffers from appendicitis, pneumonia and gout. Not surprisingly, he is often moody and depressed.

Saturn directed to Mars in Capricorn: In 1968 Olivier is sixty-one years old. In his septenary the Moon has come to his Saturn in Pisces. Saturn is involved in both septenary and decan, and is also directed to its own sign of Capricorn. Although he has no theater parts, he makes three films, and wins a Tony award in New York for earlier work. He is offered a peerage, which he refuses. He then surprises many by involving himself in a public controversy and writing a letter to *The Times* in defense of Hochhuth's play *The Soldiers* and of Ken Tynan, a critic and director with whom he has had many disagreements in the past.

Saturn directed to Uranus in Capricorn: Sir Laurence Olivier's Saturn comes to Uranus in 1969. He is sixty-two years old. The Moon his septenary ruler is on Mars in Capricorn, a sign in which the Moon is unhappy. Capricorn is emphasized, with both rulers directed there, Mars and Uranus being conjunct in the sign. He spends time in hospital for a haemorrhoidectomy. At the National Theatre he directs a successful production of Hedda Gabler. He disagrees with his wife, Joan, about her going to the USA to make a film. The Queen honors Joan by awarding her the CBE (Commander of the British Empire) medal. He plays Sherlock to Joan's Portia in the *Merchant of Venice,* and this marks the end of five years of his paralyzing stage fright, which is a great relief for him. He directs Chekhov's *Three Sisters,* in which he plays the role of Chebutikin; critics agree it is among his best work.

Saturn directed to the Moon in Virgo: Olivier has Saturn on his Moon in his decan in 1970. He is sixty-three years old and the exalted Mars has become his septenary ruler. He accepts a peerage, becoming Baron Olivier of Brighton, and makes his maiden speech in the House of Lords. He is in hospital for surgery on thrombosis in his right leg, a delayed effect of the cancer treatment he experienced three years before. He continues to have difficulties with Lord Chandos, the chairman of the National Theatre, and has him removed by complaining to the prime minister. He tries to produce *Guys and Dolls* but his thrombosis forces him to postpone it.

Saturn directed to Neptune in Cancer: Laurence Olivier is sixty-four years old when his decan ruler Saturn comes to his Neptune in May 1971. Saturn will always create problems when directed to a planet in Cancer, a sign where it is in detriment. In his septenary Mars is on his Moon in Virgo. Several friends die this year: Lord Chandos, who had done so much for the National Theatre, Stephen Arlen, and the director Michel St Denis. He stars as James Tyrone in O'Neill's *Long Day's Journey into Night*, which is a success. He is badly hurt when the National Theatre committee cancel *Guys and Dolls* from all future plans—feeling drained and helplessly exhausted, he has lost his courage and gives up his hopes much too quickly; he is almost in a state of paralysis, will-less. He decides to end his directorship of the National Theatre and is upset when he isn't consulted about who is to be his successor.

Saturn directed to Jupiter in Cancer: Olivier's Saturn comes to its dispositor in his decan in 1972 when he is sixty-five years old. In his septenary Mars has also come to the place of Jupiter in Cancer. Both rulers have come to the same planet in a sign in which both are weak. He resigns as the director of Britain's National Theatre. He makes two films: *Sleuth*, with Michael Caine, and *Long Day's Journey into Night*. Needing money for his children's school fees, he shocks Britain's acting community by making advertisements, for Polaroid. His friends Noel Coward and Max Adrian die this year.

Saturn directed to Pluto in Gemini: Laurence Olivier's Saturn comes to the place of his Pluto in 1973. He is sixty-six years old. Septenary Mars has come to his Sun in Taurus, and this direction is harmful to Olivier. He is burgled twice; during the second he is hit on the head from behind, the blow causing him to lose the sight in his right eye. A close friend, Binkie Beaumont, dies. He acts on stage for the final time, playing John Tagg in *The Party* at the National Theatre. The play is concerned with the unsatisfactory state of the Communist Party in England. He experiences difficulty memorizing his lines and has to work particularly hard at it.

Saturn directed to the Sun in Taurus: Laurence Olivier's decan Saturn comes to his Sun in 1974 when he is sixty-seven years old. Septenary Mars remains in Taurus, where it is now on his Mercury. He acts in *Love Among the Ruins*, a television play with Katherine Hepburn, which he describes as being an unforgettable, memorable six weeks. His vacation in Italy is less pleasant the direction of Mars to bodies in Taurus continues to harm him physically: first he hurts his back while diving into the sea, then his face swells up with dermatopolymyocotis and he has to be hospitalized for the rare disease, needing to be fed large doses of steroids daily and, as a result, goes out of his mind, from which he needs six months to recover. He then experiences colds, flu, a wisdom tooth extraction, and quinsy on the tongue. A railway engine is named after him, and he is awarded his country's highest civilian honor, the Order of Merit.

Saturn directed to Mercury in Taurus: Olivier has his decan ruler Saturn come to his Mercury in 1975 when he is sixty-eight years old. He acts in two films: *The 7% Solution* and *The Marathon Man*. Septenary Mars has come to his Venus in Aries. It is a relief to have Mars directed to its own sign after the physical problems of the previous two years that had coincided with an unhappy Mars coming to Taurus.

Saturn directed to Venus in Aries: 1976, the final year of Laurence Olivier's Saturn-ruled decan, has it on his oriental Venus in Aries, which does not promise a pleasant year. He is sixty-nine years old. It is also the final year of his Mars-ruled septenary, with Mars coming to his Saturn in Pisces. He produces six plays for television, acting in five of them. The following year Venus will rule Olivier's decan.

The Saturn-ruled Septenary
of the Emperor Augustus Caesar

Originally named Gaius Octavius, he becomes Octavius Caesar, the adopted son of his uncle Julius Caesar, and his heir following Caesar's 45 BC assassination. It is not until he is 37 years old in 26 BC that he becomes known as Augustus, the Revered One. When Saturn begins to rule his septenary in 42 BC he is 21 years old, a member of the triumvirate, with Lepidus and Mark Anthony, that rules Rome. Saturn is conjunct Mars in Taurus, and it sextiles the Uranus-Neptune conjunction.

Saturn rises in Taurus: Although present, because he is sick with dropsy, Octavius is unable to participate in the Battle of Philippi, the largest battle ever to occur between two Roman armies, in which Mark Anthony defeats Brutus and Cassius, the murderers of Julius Caesar. After the battle, in icy anger Octavius has the prisoners his army captured put to death. In the decan the Moon has come to Venus in Scorpio, the sign in which both the Moon and Venus experience difficulties. He marries but this lasts only for a few months and, for political reasons, a new marriage is quickly arranged.

Saturn directed to the Moon in Capricorn: The Moon and Saturn are in mutual reception. It is 41 BC and he is 22 years old. The Moon, his decan ruler, is conjunct the Sun in Virgo. Octavius defeats Mark Anthony's brother, Lucius, in battle at Porusia, and follows this with a mass sacrifice of 300 prisoners to Julius Caesar. He marries Scribonia (she is in her mid thirties, which advanced age is appropriate with the emphasis this year in both decan and septenary on the Moon in Capricorn). Mark Anthony invades Italy, but he and Octavius make peace that is cemented by Mark Anthony marrying Octavia, Octavian's sister.

Saturn directed to Venus in Scorpio: Saturn has come to its dispositor. The Moon is on Mercury in Virgo in the decan. He divorces Scribonia. Rome suffers from inflation caused by pirates, led by Sextus, the son of Pompey the Great, blockading Italy. Octavius loses touch with public opinion, and there are demonstrations and riots against him. In an act of bloody-minded courage he stands up to face the rioters but is stoned by crowds. Mark Anthony intervenes and saves his life. He meets with Sextus and the pirates and makes peace.

Saturn directed to the Sun in Virgo: It is 39 BC and Octavius is 24 years old. In his decan the Moon has come to Jupiter in Cancer, one of the very best possible directions. He falls passionately in love with Livia Drusilla, and they marry. The couple will stay together until she poisons him fifty-two years later. A daughter is born. He first shaves.

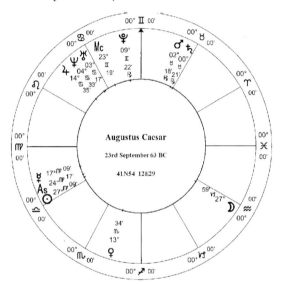

Augustus Caesar

23rd September 63 BC

41N54 12E29

Saturn directed to Mercury in Virgo: The ruling triumvirate of Rome, Octavius, Lepidus and Marc Anthony, is renewed for another five years. In the decan the Moon has come to Neptune in Cancer. The Moon is of course strong in her own sign of Cancer, but Neptune by its rulership of Octavian's 7th house will always represent a problem. He loses a sea battle near Sicily to the pirate Sextus; his fleet is destroyed, and he is in danger of losing his life. It is a humiliating defeat.

Saturn directed to Jupiter in Cancer: His general Agrippa trains a navy with which he invades Sicily but is initially repulsed by Sextus. There is an attempt on Octavius' life and he is forced to hide in the mountains. He and Agrippa finally defeat Sextus at the battle of Baulochus. The grateful Assembly votes for a house to be presented to Octavius at public expense. In the decan the Moon is on his Uranus in Cancer. Both rulers have come to Cancer, Saturn is debilitated there but the Moon is strong.

Saturn directed to Mars in Taurus: He returns to Rome where he is voted many honors. In the decan the Moon has come to Pluto in Gemini. He is angry when he learns that Mark Anthony has rejected his sister Octavia and is living with Cleopatra in Egypt. When campaigning in Illyricum he is wounded in the leg, and both of his arms are badly crushed. His Saturn-ruled septenary appropriately ends.

Chapter 13

Uranus as the Time Ruler

Fate is like a small sandstorm that keeps changing directions. You change direction but the sandstorm chases you. You turn again, but the storm adjusts. Over and over you play this out, like some ominous dance with death just before dawn. Why? Because this storm isn't something that blew in from far away, something that has nothing to do with you. This storm is you. Something inside of you. So all you can do is give in to it, step right inside the storm, closing your eyes and plugging up your ears so the sand doesn't get in, and walk through it, step by step.

—Haruki Murakami, *Kafka on the Shore*

Uranus can be disruptive and chaotic; the planet represents independence and freedom, and is always pragmatic and rational. It wants to control the objective material world through the exercise of pure reason unimpeded by any form of check or control. It is enthusiastic about whatever is new and modern, by all forms of technology and science.

When Uranus is one of the time rulers of a person's life it usually creates a period containing both tension and inspiration. As this unconventional ruler moves around the horoscope and encounters each of the other planets it will open the individual's mind and feelings to new influences. In the process different areas of his life will need to be examined from a fresh angle. Structures he had assumed were permanent may be unexpectedly disrupted. Each planet Uranus comes to represents a problem needing to be resolved, and this provides the individual with an opportunity to inject new energy and ideas into situations that require better understanding and, if necessary, to change them. As a result the individual may alter his activities to ensure more independence.

I tend to relate Uranus to Nataraja, the cosmic lord of the dance and an aspect of the Hindu god Shiva, who controls the motions of the universe and the flow of time. He dances on the demon of ignorance, one foot on the demon's back, the other lifted in the air. When Nataraja brings this foot down, they say time will stop.

Because of the recency of its discovery we cannot call on tradition to learn whether Uranus is strongest as a day or night planet or when rising before or after the Sun. However in Table ♅-1 we see that in the sample those people born during the daytime, specifically those with an occidental Uranus, had values significantly below 50%. Therefore, until contrary evidence becomes available, we will tentatively assume that Uranus is a nocturnal planet, perhaps strongest as an evening star. The low value of 44.2% positive for these 482 directions is strong evidence that Uranus should be treated as a malefic—this does not mean that the planet is itself malevolent but that, very much as Mars and Saturn are experienced, people under its influence more often encounter difficulties than not.

Table ⛢-1:   **⛢ as time ruler: % Positive Years**

Position relative to the ☉	Day birth		Night birth		All	
	N	% Positive	N	% Positive	N	% Positive
Oriental ⛢	125	43.4	125	41.2	250	42.3
Occidental ⛢	119	**39.5****	113	52.8	232	46.0
All	*244*	*41.5****	*238*	*46.7*	*482*	*44.2*

In the sample, as we see in Table ⛢-2, the direction of Uranus to Venus produces a % positive value that is well below the expected 50%. All of the other directions, other than to Neptune, are also below 50%, but not significantly so.

Table ⛢-2:   **% Positive Years when Uranus is directed to the Ascendant & Planets**

⛢ directed to	*Percentage in Sample Experiencing Positive Years when ⛢ is the Time Lord*	
	N	% Positive
⛢ rises	49	40.6
☉	53	39.2
☽	46	43.2
☿	47	40.4
♀	48	**35.8***
♂	42	45.2
♃	53	49.5
♄	48	45.2
♆	48	52.7
♇	48	49.0
All	*482*	*44.2*

Table ⛢-3: **Uranus by sign, natal & to where it is directed**

⛢ natal sign		Sign	Sign to where ⛢ is directed	
N	% Positive Years		N	% Positive Years
37	46.4	♈	27	56.9
61	53.4	♉	53	**37.5***
18	45.2	♊	51	46.1
52	**34.8****	♋	41	46.3
48	49.0	♌	37	39.1
20	33.3	♍	41	55.1
34	37.2	♎	39	37.1
34	42.5	♏	31	55.4
25	39.8	♐	25	47.0
46	49.1	♑	33	41.1
42	49.5	♒	32	42.4
65	40.3	♓	23	35.4
482	44.2	All	433	44.5

As a confirmation of the evidence provided in Table ⛢-2 for the difficulty of the direction of Uranus to Venus, we now see in Table ⛢-3 that when Uranus is directed to a planet occupying any one of the signs in which Venus is strong, Taurus, Libra or Pisces, the % positive is well below 50%.

Uranus natally in Cancer was also associated with a statistically significant low value, but this should perhaps be treated with caution because of the number of years Uranus takes to circle around the zodiac and the many births that will occur during the seven years Uranus takes to pass through each sign.

Table ♅-4: **Uranus by House, Natal & to Where Directed**

♅'s natal house		House	House to where ♅ is directed	
N	% Positive Years		N	% Positive Years
35	49.1	I	49	44.3
44	47.3	II	44	45.2
18	60.3	III	43	50.5
57	41.2	IV	28	54.9
54	46.9	V	26	41.7
24	**71.6***	VI	21	68.9
67	43.2	VII	37	44.0
39	48.7	VIII	29	**24.9****
39	37.2	IX	36	50.2
28	25.8	X	34	39.9
46	39.3	XI	49	40.6
21	32.1	XII	37	36.7
482	44.2	All	433	44.5

Years are likely to be positive when Uranus is located in the 6th house at birth. They are likely to be very difficult when Uranus is directed to a planet in the 8th, a place where this logical and objective time ruler is likely to be greatly at odds with any planet that has become imbued with the house's occult characteristics and ideas.

Table ♅-5: **% Positive when Uranus is the Ruler by its place in the decan sequence**

Place of Uranus in decan	Day		Night	
	N	% Positive	N	% Positive
1	19	**19.0****	14	33.2
2	21	47.4	7	48.7
3	25	54.2	24	54.0
4	47	53.9	14	50.1
5	47	40.4	7	38.1
6	32	36.7	22	50.3
7	18	45.2	16	**18.3****
8	24	**22.6****	6	62.6
9	11	41.1	5	40.6
10	0	0.0	1	0.0
Sum	244	**41.5*****	238	46.7

Uranus as decan ruler is associated with a significant number of difficult years for daytime births when the planet is the first or eighth to rise, the first ten years of life and a person's seventies. Similarly, night births had a significant number of difficult years when in their sixties.

Uranus Rises
(41% positive)

Circumstances are likely to evolve this year to provide the individual with a glimpse of a freedom that he may never before have experienced or, if he has, it was many years ago in his almost-forgotten past. Whether he recognizes what he is being offered or not depends very much on the individual's age and rigidity, on how deeply mired he is in the regularity and security of his everyday life.

The individual is likely to feel different, to begin to suspect that he is unique, and to have an insistent urge for novelty this year. This should be a period of creative awakening, when the person feels completely alive and vibrant, and wants to live a life that is filled with adventure and the unexpected. It is as if he has been given the opportunity to start life afresh. Established structures in his life are liable to be unexpectedly disrupted, and this can cause problems for others. He is restless, liable to rebel against constraint, and will want to do something that is quite different from his everyday life. He may visit a locality that is entirely new to him. Newness and change will come into the life. Nothing will seem impossible. Others may see him as acting in strange ways, becoming eccentric, increasingly odd and unreliable. He will want to break with tradition and experience all the many different facets of this new approach to life and its problems, however trivial others may consider it to be. A change is likely to occur in how he views his relationships with others, and he may seem determined to declare his independence, which can break up his marriage.

Table ⛢-6:   **⛢ Rising: % Positive Years**

⛢ relative to the ☉	Day birth		Night birth		All	
	N	% Positive	N	% Positive	N	% Positive
Oriental ⛢	14	45.2	14	45.2	28	45.2
Occidental ⛢	13	41.7	8	22.6	21	38.1
All	*27*	*43.5*	*22*	*37.0*	*49*	*40.6*

Some examples of events in the sample the year Uranus began ruling the decan:
Oriental Uranus rises in the daytime: *emigrates; unemployed; a warrant is issued for his arrest; he is lionized; partnership ends; his parked car is broken into; travels; overseas visits; protests against authority; converts to Islam; successful coup d'état; learns to swim; involved in a public squabble/a brawl; defends himself in court against ex-wife's accusations.*

Occidental Uranus rises in the daytime: *inherits title; he turns blue & is rushed to hospital; has a deeply profound religious experience; his parents quarrel; wife/mother dies.*
Oriental Uranus rises at night: *he is difficult, unpredictable & strange; unexpected defeat; emigrates; rejects his daughter, never forgives her & never sees her again; he is so feeble & has so high a fever that there are fears for his life; friend scoffs at him in public; graduates.*
Occidental Uranus rises at night: *falls from horse; inflammation of temporal arteries; marriage cancelled; he & his wife are assassinated; problems in everything; leaves home; she feels trapped; end of war, overjoyed he can now return home; wife has an affair; starts astrology.*

Uranus directed to the Sun
(39% positive)

The individual may act in ways now that will surprise others. His individual self is being awakened and his sense of himself is radically changing. As a result this year can be eventful, a time of surprises, pleasant or not according to the relationship the Sun and Uranus have in the natal chart. The individual will be inspired to change his daily routine and fight off restraints he can no longer accept in order to truly liberate himself. His reasons for making these changes will probably be based on rational principles instead of religious sanction and hereditary right.

Table ⛢-7:   **⛢ to ☉: % Positive Years**

⛢ relative to the ☉	Day birth		Night birth		All	
	N	% Positive	N	% Positive	N	% Positive
Oriental ⛢	16	**17.0****	13	41.7	29	**28.1****
Occidental ⛢	12	37.7	12	67.8	24	52.7
All	*28*	*25.8***	*25*	*54.2*	*53*	*39.2*

Those people born with Uranus rising before the Sun, especially in the daylight hours, may find the adjustment to their new situation far more difficult than they imagined. They are likely to become increasingly nervous and restless, more so when they find people in authority checking their desire for unregulated freedom. By contrast, individuals born with an occidental Uranus appear to be given more opportunities to execute their innovations.

Examples of happenings in the sample the year that Uranus came to the Sun:
Oriental Uranus to the Sun in the day: *father dies; humiliated; defeated; financial crisis; rejected; affair; adopts a son; victories in battle; epileptic fit; self-imposed retirement; travels; major crisis; wins a major contract; attacked publicly.*
Occidental Uranus to the Sun in the day: *children are born in the family; quits his job; begins violin lessons; has her first job in government; starts school; coronary embolism; pessimistic; successful analyses; separates from his partner; frequent squabbling.*

Oriental Uranus to the Sun at night: *rejected; first meets the man who will ruin him; goes overseas for studies; burglarized; becomes increasingly dependent on his therapist; deaths in the family.*

Occidental Uranus to the Sun at night: *leaves home, it was too narrow to contain her energy; joins navy; feeling trapped, she leaves her husband & children; becomes a communist; in love; overseas trip; promoted; graduates; meets his spiritual master.*

Uranus directed to the Moon
(43% positive)

The native wants to change the way things have always been. Circumstances may occur this year that will provide him with the opportunity to do things that he has never done before, to break with tradition and restraints from the past. If his Moon is strong any exceptional steps he takes will be to his advantage and the desired change will be accomplished. If the Moon is afflicted results may be less pleasant as his family and influential females may oppose him. Either way, the individual will be willing to fight for his independence.

Table ⛢-8:   ⛢ **to ☽: % Positive Years**

Planets relative to the ☉	Day birth		Night birth		All	
	N	% Positive	N	% Positive	N	% Positive
Oriental ⛢	14	45.2	10	54.2	24	49.0
Occidental ⛢	10	27.1	12	45.2	22	37.0
All	*24*	*37.7*	*22*	*49.3*	*46*	*43.2*
Waxing ☽	11	57.5	10	54.2	21	56.0
Waning ☽	13	20.9	12	45.2	25	32.5

Those people in the sample born with a waxing Moon best survived this direction from Uranus. Day births, especially those with an occidental Uranus or a waning (oriental) Moon had the most difficulties.

Examples of happenings in my sample the year that Uranus came to the Moon:

Oriental Uranus to the Moon in the day: *ordered to leave the USA; separates from his wife; changes his son's school; his ambitions are checked; has a general sense of delay, unable to do all he'd like to do; his mentor dies; escapes assassination attempt; attacked.*

Occidental Uranus to the Moon in the day: *nurse seduces & then thrashes him; pain in his eye; he is bed ridden with a liver complaint; has shingles; he collapses & is no longer sane; scandals; struggles to control his emotions; females born.*

Oriental Uranus to the Moon at night: *betrayed & defeated; intense depression; starts school; in a psychiatric hospital; everyone calls for his resignation; a pleasant time; travels.*

Occidental Uranus to the Moon at night: *marries; divorce; becomes a vegetarian; promoted; resigns from the priesthood; heart attack; hip replacement.*

Uranus directed to Mercury

(40% positive)

Tʜᴇ ʀᴇᴄᴇɪᴩᴛ ᴏʀ ᴅɪꜱᴄᴏᴠᴇʀʏ ᴏꜰ ᴜɴᴇxᴩᴇᴄᴛᴇᴅ ɪɴꜰᴏʀᴍᴀᴛɪᴏɴ ɪꜱ likely to cause a sudden change in how the individual approaches his life. He may have a sudden flash of inspiration that prompts him to drop all else and start gathering evidence to test its validity; he may decide to uproot his family and himself and go to another country; he may quit a long-held safe job and put all of his savings into the manufacture of his or someone else's invention; there are endless possibilities. He may even believe he can discover and understand the fundamental nature of the universe and of his own psyche by means of his own reasoning. He will want to disseminate this newfound knowledge to as many people as possible, wanting others to examine it objectively and provide him with feedback. Whatever the nature of the new information it can cause him to do something out of the ordinary and these actions will probably astonish others. As a result he may end the year living in a different world from the one he was in at the start of these twelve months.

Table ♅-9: ⠀⠀⠀⠀⠀⠀⠀⠀**♅ to ☿: % Positive Years**

Planets relative to the ☉	Day birth		Night birth		All	
	N	% Positive	N	% Positive	N	% Positive
Oriental ♅	11	49.3	13	41.7	24	45.2
Occidental ♅	12	30.1	11	41.1	23	35.4
All	*23*	*39.3*	*24*	*41.4*	*47*	*40.4*
Oriental ☿	13	62.6	9	40.2	22	49.0
Occidental ☿	10	**9.0****	15	42.2	25	**28.9***

Those people in my sample with an occidental Mercury (yes, the numbers are small), especially those born during the day, tended to have more than their share of problems with this direction, their failures seem often to have been the result of becoming a little crazy, and trying to do too much in too great a hurry, impulsively, without any preplanning.

Examples of happenings in my sample the year that Uranus came to Mercury:
Oriental Uranus to Mercury in the day: intensive studies; imprisoned; loss of memory; first introduced to astrology; accepted at military academy; signs a publishing contract; his life-long dream of independence becomes a hideous nightmare; son born; victories in battle; on trial for murder; receives a pension; very sick.
Occidental Uranus to Mercury in the day: moves; his son is wounded; makes his maiden speech in Parliament; his teacher leaves; attends conference; his writings are lost; new job; little income; unsought & unwelcome leisure.
Oriental Uranus to Mercury at night: destroys the old & brings in the new; argues by letter; travels; leaves college; mocks church rituals; psychoanalyzed; passes exams; parents separate; his book receives much attention; practicing writing; imposes a death duty.

Occidental Uranus to Mercury at night: *children born; he is bankrupt; absconds; first house; he is nominated; the ideas in his book are attacked; her brother's ship is sunk but he is safe.*

Uranus directed to Venus
(36% positive)

There will be changes this year in how the individual occupies himself, especially in his leisure hours. He will look for something creative that is different and exciting, and may join up with others seeking the same novelty. Strangers are likely to welcome him into their circle. A whole set of new relationships may result which can bring him into a social situation very different from those he has been a part of in the past. There may be large financial gains. If Venus is afflicted these changes can produce problems with existing relationships.

Table ♅-10: **♅ to ♀: % Positive Years**

Planets relative to the ☉	Day birth		Night birth		All	
	N	% Positive	N	% Positive	N	% Positive
Oriental ♅	11	24.7	13	41.7	24	33.9
Occidental ♅	14	32.3	10	45.2	24	37.7
All	*25*	*28.9*	*23*	*43.2*	*48*	*35.8*
Oriental ♀	11	41.1	11	41.1	22	41.1
Occidental ♀	14	19.4	12	45.2	26	**31.3***

Venus provides problems that Uranus finds difficult to resolve. By her very nature Venus wants life to be harmonious and balanced, in that sense she is ultra conservative, which doesn't fit in too well with the Uranus' desire to replace the past with what is new and intellectually exciting. Most people in the sample experienced problems this year, with diurnal births finding the direction particularly difficult.

Examples of happenings in my sample the year that Uranus came to Venus:

Oriental Uranus to Venus in the day: *excommunicated; father dies; imprisoned; he imprisons the pope; first Caribbean vacation; his enemy is killed; promoted; closes quarterly publication; loss of position; rejects a reunion; others conspire against him; child born; depressed; cerebral hemorrhage.*

Occidental Uranus to Venus in the day: *in love; a year of obsessions; his wife has a heart attack; frustrated; evacuated during wartime; refuses to go to school; swelling from blow completely closes his eyes; emotional confrontations; throat troubles; watching bull fights.*

Oriental Uranus to Venus at night: *humiliated; defeated; tremendous new energy; starts school; he wants a divorce; says that in the beginning was Order & that man created Chaos; damages his left arm; celebrates the end of war; joins RAF.*

Occidental Uranus to Venus at night: *investigating astrology; son has accident; promoted; military training; marries; travels; very involved with communists; he sells his estate.*

Uranus directed to Mars

(45% positive)

This year can contain a major break from the past. The individual wants to kick away all obstacles lying on his path to intellectual freedom. He may even dare the world to stop him breaking down the barriers that he believes imprison him. He wants a revolution, and he wants it now. Often the world simply ignores him and allows him space to make the minor changes he has in mind, but now and then it responds by imposing accidents and perils that can end in catastrophe. Troubles may come from unexpected sources, but they are often the result of the individual being too daring and hasty in his attempt to cut away the ties that he believes restrict him.

Table ⛢-11: **⛢ to ♂: % Positive Years**

Planets relative to the ☉	Day birth		Night birth		All	
	N	% Positive	N	% Positive	N	% Positive
Oriental ⛢	9	50.2	13	34.8	22	41.1
Occidental ⛢	11	41.1	9	60.3	20	49.7
All	*20*	*45.2*	*22*	*45.2*	*42*	*45.2*
Oriental ♂	8	22.6	10	36.2	18	30.1
Occidental ♂	12	60.3	12	52.7	24	56.5

Those born with an oriental Mars had the most difficulties with this direction.

Examples of happenings in my sample the year that Uranus came to Mars:
Oriental Uranus to Mars in the day: erratic sleep; legal losses; accused of sedition; his first writings captivate the public; negotiating independence; he is burnt in effigy; outlawed; hospitalized; bored; meets future wife; flees after assaulting his wife; enjoys an idyllic experience overseas; creates a legal system that will become the basis of most civil law in the modern world.
Occidental Uranus to Mars in the day: researching guilt; addicted to gambling; resulting freedom when his father is absent; breaks with his followers; heavy expenses; in love; death.
Oriental Uranus to Mars at night: wins Nobel Prize; son born; nearly drowns; graduates; mocks pretensions; breaks last powerful link that bound him to traditions of the past; his employer is bankrupt; starts his own business; his mother abandons him; first time away from his mother; severe stroke; his teeth are drilled for the first time.
Occidental Uranus to Mars at night: starts at law school; attends ceremony to bury late king's heart; divorce; cuts links with the West Bank; daughter born (difficult labor).

Uranus directed to Jupiter
(49% positive)

This should be a time of relief from the tension that has accumulated over past years. For some it will even be a time of opportunities and lucky breaks when the individual experiences a sudden change in his destiny, the chance to become all he has ever dreamt of being. He may win a sweepstakes or lottery; this is a year when he could. He will certainly be moved to do something that is completely different from his usual activities. He may try many things that are entertaining and exciting. Perhaps he will be promoted in his job, be recognized for abilities that had previously gone unnoticed, visit a part of the world he has never seen before, emigrate, or have a transforming adventure off the beaten track.

If Jupiter is badly afflicted the relief and opportunities may be missed as he continues to struggle to survive in an unsympathetic world, or he may break rules and attract the attention of an unforgiving authority.

Table ♅-12:

♅ to ♃: % Positive Years

Planets relative to the ☉	Day birth		Night birth		All	
	N	% Positive	N	% Positive	N	% Positive
Oriental ♅	13	48.7	14	45.2	27	46.9
Occidental ♅	11	32.9	15	66.3	26	52.2
All	*24*	*41.4*	*29*	*56.1*	*53*	*49.5*
Oriental ♃	7	64.6	14	38.7	21	47.4
Occidental ♃	17	31.9	15	72.3	32	50.9

Diurnal births in the sample often had problems with those in authority this year.

Examples of happenings in the sample when Uranus came to Jupiter:
Oriental Uranus to Jupiter in the day: protests his rejection due to his skin color; very poor; the church attacks his book; not allowed to take communion; he fears for his sanity; kidney operation; elected; promoted; his library is confiscated; mother dies; buys RV; resurrects quarterly magazine; his leadership is challenged; makes a bad mistake that is morally damaging.
Occidental Uranus to Jupiter in the day: wants to become a priest; writes critique of all things modern; threatened by family cook; mother expels him from the house; writes on pleasure versus reality; depressed; starts school; wife/daughter has surgery.
Oriental Uranus to Jupiter at night: her son is promoted; sexually molested by her stepbrother; writes on education; his brother is bankrupt; fires his long-time assistant; brother dies; travels overseas; goes to college; affair; in poor health; convulsions; mental breakdown.
Occidental Uranus to Jupiter at night: father dies; brother is deaf, home from the war; awarded a medal; in danger of death; successful litigation; learns calligraphy; has a new friend; studies law; promoted; moves; has a new job.

Uranus directed to Saturn
(45% positive)

The individual's old life may come back to haunt him briefly this year. The long-ago past may reappear now, but it does so only to finally to say farewell. He may be shocked by events involving those who are dear to him. There are regrets for those things that were not accomplished in the past, for what was left unspoken; sadness that the opportunity to correct these mistakes has now gone forever. This can cause mental conflicts: it is true that the individual wants to be independent, free from all restraint, but the cost of doing so, the realization that past chapters have now firmly closed and can never be reopened, will trouble him. People die, they go away, and he may feel that it is he who is being rejected. The individual may be forced to be innovative, to rely on his own resources, to drive alone in an otherwise empty car. This is a difficult year during which patient work may come to naught, and he will need to battle to survive a dangerous situation.

Table ♅-13:   ♅ to ♄: % **Positive Years**

Planets relative to the ☉	Day birth		Night birth		All	
	N	% Positive	N	% Positive	N	% Positive
Oriental ♅	10	36.2	14	30.1	24	37.7
Occidental ♅	12	30.1	12	75.3	24	52.7
All	*22*	*32.9*	*26*	*55.6*	*48*	*45.2*
Oriental ♄	13	27.8	13	55.6	26	41.7
Occidental ♄	9	40.2	13	55.6	22	49.3

In the sample night births, especially those with an occidental Uranus, had a greater probability of pleasant years than did those born in the daytime.

Examples of happenings in my sample the year that Uranus came to Saturn:
Oriental Uranus to Saturn in the day: friend dies; wife has a nervous breakdown; his wife kicks him out; accused of murdering his ex-wife & her lover; rejected; humiliated; much criticized; starts an apprenticeship; economic warfare; heavy fines after IRS audit.
Occidental Uranus to Saturn in the day: in a state of shock when his lover dies; unable to walk; headaches & intestinal troubles; in a manic high; arrested & imprisoned for protesting; his work is attacked; moves; has her first garden; father commits suicide; exhausted from political infighting & overwork.
Oriental Uranus to Saturn at night: her sister marries & then dies; becomes very anxious; parents divorce; his wife has an affair; returns home after long absence; paranoia; extensive dental treatment; sees his dead sister; confronted by his lover's father; struggling.
Occidental Uranus to Saturn at night: throws his medals away; moves; nurses her sick husband; receives his doctorate; new job; happy, relaxed; finally has his own house; meets with his idol; travels; orders the cessation of bombardment; re-elected.

Uranus directed to Neptune

(53% positive)

This can be a peculiar year, during it what is strange and unusual may impinge into the individual's life. There can be meetings with foreigners or visits abroad. There may be a change in his thinking, a shift of perspective, a fundamental break with what he had previously believed to be true. He may experience unusual spiritual states or become influenced by religious teachings. He may experiment with mind-altering drugs or become increasingly idealistic and be inspired to forsake his usual humdrum life in order to support a group of refugees, adopt a needy child, or otherwise try to make the world into a better place. He may simply want to investigate different beliefs. For artists, especially painters and musicians, this can be a creative year.

If Neptune is afflicted the above can be dangerous steps for him. He can become confused, perhaps overly dependent on drugs or over influenced by a charismatic religious leader. The changes and journeys that others suggest he makes can be harmful. They can easily weaken him physically. In the sample day births coped with this direction fairly well.

Table ⛢-14: **⛢ to ♆: % Positive Years**

Planets relative to the ☉	Day birth		Night birth		All	
	N	% Positive	N	% Positive	N	% Positive
Oriental ⛢	14	58.1	10	45.2	24	52.7
Occidental ⛢	12	67.8	12	37.7	24	52.7
All	*26*	*62.6*	*22*	*41.1*	*48*	*52.7*
Oriental ♆	14	58.1	12	30.1	26	45.2
Occidental ♆	12	67.8	10	54.2	22	61.6

Examples of happenings in the sample the year that Uranus came to Neptune:

Oriental Uranus to Neptune in the day: *his mother is on trial as a witch; hernia operation; his Declaration of Rights is adopted; resolving contradictions, more freedom & more discipline; his ex-wife remarries; severe headache; arthritis; buys a dairy farm; earns her PhD; crowns himself emperor; spider bite swells ankle; skiing.*

Occidental Uranus to Neptune in the day: *researching symbolism; has a self-pitying sense of victimization; his protector is sent away; writes on incest; tames a wild horse; promoted; in love; arrested for illegal weapons sales; touring by car; financial worries; insomnia; headaches; lectures.*

Oriental Uranus to Neptune at night: *terrified at sea in a full gale; first homosexual experience; meets future wife; believes that allegiance to anything is the beginning of corruption; has a music interest; visits his old home; famine; tranquil; facial tics, some convulsions; she is suicidal.*

Occidental Uranus to Neptune at night: *separated from her sick husband; working like hell on her sculpture; moves; employee steals from her company; sees children she abandoned six years before; loses his assistant; disappointed by his muse.*

Uranus directed to Pluto
(49% positive)

Life will probably never be the same again after this year. Major changes occur but they usually do so quietly, without any great fanfare, and it is only later that the individual will realize that this year contained that moment of demarcation: there was a before and now there is an after, like BC and AD in history, and what was before is gone never to be regained. So many elements of the individual's life will pass away, almost without him realizing this is happening. Children leave home and go away to college, they may return for the holidays but they do so as different people. People retire from the workplace or they start new professions; young men go off to their first jobs; daughters get married. Elements of the individual's life that he believed were permanent are changing. New things are coming into being. This is a year of transformation, when the caterpillar quietly turns into a butterfly. If Pluto is in Leo the individual will probably try to resist these inevitable changes.

Table ♅-15:   **♅ to ♇: % Positive Years**

Planets relative to the ☉	Day birth		Night birth		All	
	N	% Positive	N	% Positive	N	% Positive
Oriental ♅	13	62.6	11	24.7	24	45.2
Occidental ♅	12	52.7	12	52.7	24	52.7
All	*25*	*57.9*	*23*	*39.3*	*48*	*49.0*
Oriental ♇	14	64.6	12	37.7	26	52.2
Occidental ♇	11	49.3	11	41.1	22	45.2

Examples of happenings in the sample the year that Uranus came to Pluto:

Oriental Uranus to Pluto in the day: *stung by a stingray; has a new contract; publishes his best poem; writes the synthesis of his life's work; his eyesight is worsening; his wife becomes manic depressive; his wife divorces him; taking singing lessons; makes an important discovery; peace; plot against him collapses; his son is arrested for assault with a knife; Lyme disease; high blood pressure.*

Occidental Uranus to Pluto in the day: *his parents divorce; moves; studies the source of guilt feelings; divorce; he & his mother flee; promoted; resigns; his first novel is a success.*

Oriental Uranus to Pluto at night: *eye problems; his parents separate; publicly humiliated; ponders the nature of attention; travels; exhibits his work; operation to remedy birth defect.*

Occidental Uranus to Pluto at night: *daughter marries; her first one-woman show is a success; leaves the navy; son is away; large financial gains; war dominates his thoughts.*

Sigmund Freud's Uranus-ruled Decan

Uranus rises in Taurus: The founder of psychoanalysis, Sigmund Freud has an occidental Uranus that is combust the Sun in Taurus in the 7th house. Uranus begins ruling his decan when he becomes fifty years old in 1906. Jupiter his septenary ruler has come to Mars in Libra. For his birthday his friends present him with a medallion with his portrait in profile on one side and Oedipus solving the riddle of the Sphinx on the other. The inscription reads, "He divined the famous riddle and was a mighty man." His daughter Mathilde has an appendectomy. The operation is botched and leaves her in uncertain health. For the first time he plays host to Carl Jung and other important disciples.

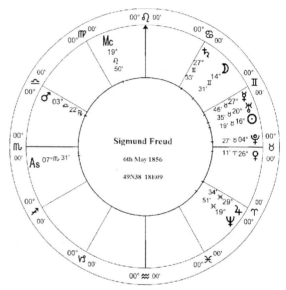

Uranus is directed to the Sun in Taurus: Freud is 51 in 1907 when Uranus comes to his Sun. The two bodies were conjunct at his birth. In his septenary Jupiter has come to his Saturn in Gemini, the sign of Jupiter's detriment. His daughter Mathilde has a worrisome high fever. Freud suspects peritonitis from the previous year's appendectomy. Mathilde is worried that she might be unattractive, and he reassures her. He presides over the first International Congress of Psychoanalysts. He visits England. He separates permanently from Breur, his former partner. He successfully treats the Rat Man, a famous case of obsession. The analysis buttresses his theories postulating the childhood roots of neurosis, the inner logic of the most flamboyant and most inexplicable symptoms, and the powerful, often hidden, pressures of ambivalent feelings. He analyses and cures "Little Hans," a 5-year-old boy who fears a horse would bite him. He also treats a woman with paranoia. He publishes *The Sexual Enlightenment of Children*.

Uranus is directed to Pluto in Taurus: Uranus comes to Freud's Pluto in 1908 when he is fifty-two years old. Jupiter his septenary ruler remains in Gemini, now it is on his Moon. His eldest daughter Mathilde marries. The first psychoanalytical periodical, *Der Zentralblatt*, appears. Freud is planning for the future of his work, and decides that Jung will continue and finish it. He studies paranoia. He is excited by an invitation to visit the United States. He begins writing a general methodology for psychoanalysts. *Creative Writers and Daydreaming* is published. He decides to dig down to the most remote foundation of culture; to determine the moment when the human animal took the leap into civilization by prescribing to itself the taboos indispensible to all ordered societies. He is studying the source of guilt feelings.

Uranus is directed to Venus in Aries: Freud is fifty-three in 1909. Uranus has come to its dispositor. In the septenary Jupiter is at his Mercury in Taurus. His son Martin enters university. Freud amends his basic concept about dreams to read, "A dream is the (disguised) fulfillment of a (suppressed, repressed) wish." He warns against overestimating the significance of symbols in dream interpretation, and introduces the concept of Narcissism. He visits the United States and receives an honorary degree. He is having difficulties with Alfred Adler. At the Nurnberg International Congress he has an emotional confrontation with fellow analysts. He begins a four-year analysis of the "Wolfman," Serge Pankejeff, his most notable patient. He has an insight into the roots of religion and starts working on *Totem and Taboo*. He begins an intense study of Leonardo da Vinci—"the most

beautiful thing I have ever written." He is thinking about the theory of love. He is obsessed with the case of Daniel Schreber, a paranoiac, homosexual judge and physician. This is a year of obsessions.

Uranus is directed to Jupiter in Pisces: In 1910 Uranus comes to Freud's 5th house Jupiter in Pisces. In the septenary Jupiter has arrived at his Sun in Taurus. The emphasis on Jupiter should make this an important year. His eldest daughter Mathilde has a serious operation, and his youngest Anna goes away to a spa to gain weight. Freud holidays in Holland, visits Paris, and then goes to

Sicily with Sandor Ferenczi, who makes the trip disagreeable by trying to turn Freud into a loving father. There are continuing problems with Alfred Adler; his impatience with Adler's tactlessness and unpleasant behavior grows as his qualms about Adler's ideas intensify. The disagreement splits the Association and Adler resigns. Freud speaks at the Nurnberg Congress in a new, chastened mood, which will become permanent, warning his fellow analysts that they all still face demanding, so far unsolved, technical puzzles. He publishes a paper attacking "wild analysis"—merely telling a patient what is wrong does not bring about a cure, resistance must be overcome. His book on Leonardo da Vinci has good reviews. He publishes a paper on Daniel Schreber. He continues his analysis of the Wolfman, but cannot break through the resistance. He writes on the two ways the mind works: the first obeying the pleasure principle, the second reality.

Uranus is directed to Neptune in Pisces: Uranus comes to Freud's Neptune in 1911. He is fifty-five years old. Jupiter is on his Venus in Aries in the septenary. His silver wedding anniversary is celebrated. His final battle of Alfred Adler occurs, and he ejects all Adlerians from the Vienna Association. Freud has persuaded himself that Adler suffers from paranoiac delusions of persecutions. The first strains in his relations with Carl Jung appear. He suffers from a severe and devastating headache. *On the Handling of Dream Interpretation in Psychoanalysis* is published. He writes a speculative paper on the horror of incest.

Uranus directed to Mars in Libra: In 1912 as Uranus comes to Freud's Mars in Libra, Venus assumes rulership of his septenary. His second daughter Sophia marries and he has a sense of loss. He cancels a proposed visit to London when his eldest daughter Mathilde falls ill. He takes his youngest daughter Anna with him to Vienna for a short holiday. He offends Jung and they argue over the meaning of the incest taboo. Jung complains that Freud undervalues him, and then declares his independence in a truculent manifesto. The break is final. Freud becomes preoccupied with ways to ensure the future of his movement. He creates a secret, inner council, and dismisses the editor of *Der Zentralblatt*. He is still unable to break through the Wolfman's resistance. Researching the historical sources of guilt, he finds Matriarchy an obstacle. He completes *Totem and Taboo*, postulating that civilization followed after sons had murdered and eaten their violent primal father, and had made a god out of their victim. He is experiencing violent headaches.

Uranus directed to Saturn in Gemini: Freud is fifty-seven years old in 1913 when Uranus comes to Saturn in Gemini. In his septenary Venus has arrived at Pisces, where it is exalted, on his Jupiter. His daughter Sophie has her first child, a daughter. In a series of lectures, Jung attacks the basic premises of Freud's work, irreparably dividing the leadership of psychoanalysis. Freud is busy rescuing what he can from the wreckage, trying to recapture both his periodical and the organization from Jung. He responds by writing the *History of the Psychoanalytical Movement*, his declaration of war and an outspoken critique of Adler and Jung. He uses pitiless pressure and blackmail on the Wolfman, saying this will be the final year of analysis. As a result his patient gives up his resistance and surrenders "his fixation of being ill." Freud studies and relates the opening scene of King Lear, the judgment of Paris, and the choice of the caskets in the Merchant of Venice—he believes all are really based on the same motif. He goes to Rome and daily visits Michelangelo's statue of Moses, wondering why it should intrigue him so much. *Totem and Taboo* is published and well received. He writes *Narcissism*, a paper that is difficult both to write and for readers to understand. He has headaches and intestinal troubles. He is exhausted from the political infighting and a crowded schedule of patients.

Uranus directed to the Moon in Gemini: In 1914, at the outbreak of the First World War, Freud is fifty-eight years old. Uranus is on his Moon. In the septenary Venus is now in her own sign of Libra, on his Mars. He experiences an unexpected bout of patriotism but worries about his sons and sons-in-law. He protects his youngest daughter Anna from the amorous advances of 35-year-old Ernest Jones, who wants to marry her. His first grandson is born. His critique of Jung in *History of the Psychoanalytical Movement* rids the movement of Jung and his adherents. He is exhilarated by the book's success but still bitterly disappointed by Jung's defection. He struggles to control his emotions. He finally considers that the Wolfman is cured. He writes *Observations on Transference Love*. He is working on his theory of neuroses, and is studying *Macbeth*. He writes that Michelangelo's statue of Moses is a study of self-discipline, control over impulse and rage. The war virtually ruins his practice; potential patients and his followers are away in the army. The war poses an acute danger to the very survival of psychoanalysis; he feels that its immediate future is dark and hopeless. He is depressed.

Uranus directed to Mercury in Taurus: The final year of Freud's Uranus-ruled decan occurs in 1915 when he is fifty-nine years old. In the septenary Venus is on Saturn in Gemini. Europe continues to be at war. Freud is astonished at the hideous spectacle of human nature at war. He is bewildered and has a sense of unease and uncertainty. He anxiously reads the newspapers, waiting for news of his three sons in the army. He dreams of their deaths the day Martin is wounded. He is lonely and misses not having patients. There is little income. The unsought and unwelcome leisure simultaneously lowers his morale and frees time for large-scale enterprises. He feels fatigued, and has a series of erotic dreams. Two papers are published. One on the disillusionment the war has generated, the other on the modern attitude towards death—an elegy for a civilization destroying itself. He continues working on his theory of neuroses but in some obscure way something is going wrong with the book. He discovers the aggressive drive, and gives introductory lectures at the university, summarizing and popularizing psychoanalysis. They are widely read and widely translated.

The following year Freud's Mercury-ruled decan starts.

Napoléon Bonaparte's Uranus-ruled Decan

Uranus rises in Taurus: Napoléon Bonaparte was born with an oriental Uranus in Taurus opposite the ascendant and Jupiter, part of a grand trine with the Mars-Neptune conjunction in Virgo and Pluto in Capricorn. It squares Mercury in Leo, is sextile to its dispositor Venus in Cancer, and its antiscion falls close to the Sun. His was a diurnal birth.

In August 1799 when the oriental Uranus assumes command of the decan General Bonaparte is in Egypt with his invading army, marooned there by the British who have destroyed the French fleet. That same year septenary Mercury is on his Venus in Cancer. Three days after his thirtieth birthday he abandons his army and sails secretly for France. His reception in Paris is cool. Should he be put on trial for desertion? He is angry with his wife Josephine for her affairs while he was in Egypt and threatens divorce, but she soon seduces him and they reconcile. A coup d'état is successful and he becomes one of the three chief executives of the new regime. He installs the Council of State—wreaking havoc with the principle of the separation of powers—brings a long civil war to an end, saves the state from bankruptcy and chaos, changes the code of law, has his few critics silenced, creates national scholarships, and transforms the triumvirate into a dictatorship. He is now First Consul and is living in the royal palace. Wanting a military victory to crown his rule, he crosses the Alps into Italy and defeats the Austrians at Marengo. He opens negotiations with the Pope for the restoration of the Church in France. The British defeat the plague-ridden army he abandoned in Egypt.

Uranus is directed to the Moon in Capricorn: In August 1800 Uranus comes to his waxing Moon in Bonaparte's decan. He is thirty-one years old. Septenary Mercury has also arrived on his Moon. Both rulers coming to the Moon should make this an important year. Austria is forced to accept his terms in the peace treaty signed appropriately at Lunéville, which provides for the territorial reorganization of the Holy Roman Empire. He is negotiating the Concordat between France and Rome to end the schism with the Catholic Church. He escapes an assassination attempt by royalists. He purges the army. His ambitions are checked when Nelson destroys the Danish fleet. He orders the building of a fleet to protect France from England. He is involved in the creation of a new Civil Code (the Code Napoléon).

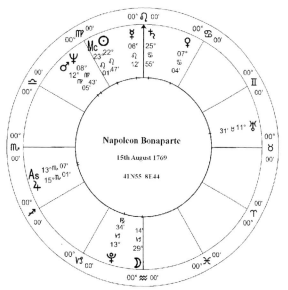

Uranus is directed to Pluto in Capricorn: In 1801 his Uranus is on his occidental Pluto. He is thirty-two years old. Mercury his septenary ruler is now on his Jupiter in Scorpio. He signs the Concordat between France and Rome that ends the schism with the Catholic Church. He creates the Legion of Honor. The Treaty of Amiens is signed with Britain. For the first time in ten years all Europe is at peace. He proclaims a general amnesty for virtually all categories of émigrés, and restructures the French educational system. The Senate extends his term as First Consul by ten years. Republican opposition is virtually ended with the collapse of a generals' plot against him.

Uranus is directed to Jupiter in Scorpio: Bonaparte is thirty-three years old when Uranus comes to his Jupiter in August 1802. Uranus and Jupiter were in opposition at his birth. At the same time his septenary ruler Mercury has arrived at Mars in Mercury's sign of Virgo. The constitution is amended and he is named First Consul for life. He has now won every attribute of royal power save the crown. His phenomenal success in the three years since the Uranus decan began has made France larger than it has ever been and taken him to the point "beyond which no man can go without raising himself to blasphemous heights of power. He has placed himself beside Alexander, Hannibal, Caesar and Augustus." The Louisiana territory is sold to the United States. A French army is expelled from Haiti by the black general Jean Jacques Dessalines. Against his wishes, his brother Lucien marries a divorcée. England violates the Treaty of Amiens and war is resumed. There are rumors of an English-backed conspiracy against him for which he orders the innocent duc d'Enghien to be executed—this is a bad miscalculation, the moral effect on Bonaparte is incalculably damaging, and the murdered duke's ghost will haunt him for the rest of his life.

Uranus is directed to Mars in Virgo: In August 1803 he is thirty-four years old, and Mercury his septenary ruler has come to his Sun in Leo. The Code Napoléon becomes law—it remains the basis of most civil law in the modern world. He orders the Senate to proclaim him Emperor, which it does. He has guns placed on the coast facing England, creates at Boulogne the Grand Army with which he will soon overrun Europe, and plans an invasion.

Uranus is directed to Neptune in Virgo: Napoléon Bonaparte's Uranus comes to his Neptune in August 1804. He is thirty-five years old. This is the year that the diurnal Sun in Leo assumes rulership of his septenary. He crowns himself Emperor in Notre Dame Cathedral, Paris. The extravagant imperial mummery is a theatrical triumph. By the sheer power of his will and his personality he will impose his imperial make-believe on a prosaic world for ten years. Later in the same year he is crowned king of Italy in Milan—the Sun in Leo is beyond any doubt now one of Napoleon's time rulers. England and Russia sign an offensive alliance against France, Austria and Sweden join the alliance later.

Uranus is directed to the Sun in Leo: Uranus comes to Bonaparte's diurnal Sun in August 1805 when he is thirty-six years old. In his septenary the Sun is on Mercury in Leo. The Sun is emphasized in both the decan and the septenary. The alliance of England, Russia, Austria and Sweden are planning to attack him in Italy. There is yet another naval defeat by Nelson and the British navy when his fleet is destroyed at Trafalgar. He abandons his intended invasion of England. There is a financial crisis, which is resolved when he brilliantly defeats Austria and Russia at Austerlitz, and becomes the master of Western Europe. He names his brother Joseph king of Naples and distributes kingdoms to other family members—very much the Leo way of doing things. He has an affair, reorganizes Germany, and has a serious epileptic fit. He adopts Eugene, Josephine's son by her former marriage.

Uranus is directed to Mercury in Leo: Uranus is on Bonaparte's Mercury when he is thirty-seven years old in 1806. The septenary Sun is on his Saturn in Cancer that same year. He defeats the Prussians at Jena and Auerstädt, then the Russians at the bloody Battle of Eylau and again decisively at Friedland. Tsar Alexander makes peace in the Treaty of Tilsit. He creates the Grand Duchy of Warsaw (Poland), to be overseen by France. A son is born to one of his mistresses.

Uranus is directed to Saturn in Cancer: In August 1807 Bonaparte's Uranus comes to his Saturn. Septenary Sun is on his Venus in Cancer. He is thirty-eight years old. He reorganizes the school system in France. His armies invade Spain and Portugal. The British appropriate the Portuguese fleet. Bonaparte retaliates by intensifying economic warfare; he declares that any neutral ship submitting to British orders is subject to seizure by France. He names his brother Joseph king of Spain, makes his general Murat the king of Naples, and creates an aristocracy of merit. A lengthy but unsuccessful Spanish insurrection takes place. A British army lands in Portugal and the French army is forced to evacuate. Peace talks at Erfurt with the Tsar of Russia continue.

Uranus is directed to Venus in Cancer: Bonaparte's Uranus is on its dispositor in 1808 the final year of his decan. He is thirty-nine years old. Septenary Sun is on his Moon in Capricorn. He is discussing peace with the Tsar of Russia at the Congress of Erfurt. French public opinion is sick with anxiety. He recaptures Madrid from insurgents but races back to Paris on hearing news of conspiracies against him organized by Fouché and Talleyrand. After he abolishes the pope's temporal power he is excommunicated. He responds by transporting the pope to France and imprisoning him. Britain starts occupying Portugal. A child is born in Warsaw to Marie Waleswka his Polish lover.

Year	Septenary	Decan
1804	☉Aₛ	♅♆
1805	☉☿	♅☉
1806	☉♄	♅☿
1807	☉♀	♅♄
1808	☉☽	♅♀

For four years starting in 1805 the planet the septenary ruler is directed to in one year becomes the planet that receives the decan ruler in the next. There is a continuing theme at work here.

In 1809 Venus becomes Napoleon's decan ruler.

Chapter 14

Neptune as the Time Ruler

*'Imaginary' universes are so much more beautiful
than this stupidly constructed 'real' one.*
G. H. Hardy, *Mathematician's Apology*

*I know no greater certainty than this:
that all human action is only an extremely imperfect, ridiculously helpless expression
of a hidden internal life of unimagined depths
that presses to the surface without ever being able to reach it even remotely.*
Pascal Mercier, *Night Train to Lisbon*

The intent of Neptune when it is the decan ruler is to introduce the individual to other worlds, to make him aware of another reality, one of unlimited possibilities. In these years there will be increased sensitivity to outside influences, usually far more than has ever been experienced in the past. Individuals can become connected with a world other than the one that is accessible to their senses.

In many ways Neptune is the antithesis of Mars. Mars is the warmongering hawk; Neptune the peace loving dove. Mars is the axe that chops down trees for firewood to heat homes and fuel factories; Neptune is the tree hugger perched high up in the branches in protest. While Mars is always tempted to settle an argument by administering a punch on the opponent's nose, Neptune advocates non-violence and universal peace. Mars has the backing of Charles Darwin and all proponents of survival by the fittest; Neptune has believing creationists ready to plead his case. Mars tends to be selfish and nationalistic, concerned solely with himself, his family and those of his own kind; Neptune sees all mankind as being equal and will go out of his way to help those experiencing poverty and hunger, those who are suffering and in need.

Unfortunately, in Neptune's world things are often not what they seem; Neptune can be inspirational but it can also confuse; what is promised is frequently too good to be true; what is feared is rarely as terrible as one imagines. When Neptune rules the life the individual can be altruistic, charitable, idealistic and artistic but at the same time meet with deceit, subterfuge and duplicity, disguise, stratagem, artifice and displacement. All and everything tends to become exaggerated as Neptune magnifies out of all proportion the effects of the planet to which it is directed.

During the years Neptune rules the decan the individual will discover that things and people are not always as they appear, and that he must learn not to be attached to them.

False reality will be shown up for what it is, and the individual will discover not to accept things at face value.

Neptune has a craving for sensation, for what excites a person, for what it is that allows him to escape the burdens and boredom of the everyday world and live in a world without barriers in which he no longer has any responsibilities. Neptune is involved in all forms of illusion and escapism, of getting away if only for a brief moment from the dullness of mundane reality, of indulging in fantasies, in visions and daydreaming. Depending on the planet to which Neptune is directed this escapism can become an addiction and involve drugs, narcotics or drink; acting a part in the theater or sitting in a darkened cinema mesmerized by those who play their fleeting roles on the silver screen; living in the fantasy of computer games; becoming a fanatic supporter of one's favorite sports team; gambling on cards, the roulette wheel or at the track; and so forth. There are so many ways by which a person will attempt to escape from his everyday world, from the repetitious, uninspiring, hard, degrading, soul-destroying reality of everyday life. Many people simply become lost during these Neptune-ruled years and most never realize it. They are searching for something they have no name for, doing so without a guide.

The craving for power and the desire for omnipotence, wanting to become god-like or to convert non-believers to one's religious beliefs, are also forms of addiction. The one-time prime minister of Great Britain, Winston Churchill liked to quote from Maeterlinck's *Life of the Bee*, on the way one tiny grub, when fed the magical royal jelly in the hive, becomes transformed into a queen. It is the same, he said, with power, which is another sort of royal jelly. Whether a person uses cocaine, crack, royal jelly, or simply one's imagination, the intent is much the same, to become the person one dreams of being, someone other than who he or she actually is.

Table Ψ-1:   **Ψ as time ruler: % Positive Years**

Position relative to the ☉	Day birth		Night birth		All	
	N	% Positive	N	% Positive	N	% Positive
Oriental Ψ	131	**41.4***	105	**40.5***	236	**41.0***
Occidental Ψ	93	52.5	107	43.9	200	47.9
All	224	46.0	212	**42.2***	436	44.2

Neptune is a major influence behind each of the world's religions, and often the Neptune-ruled decan is a time when individuals become increasingly serious about their religious beliefs. At its most beneficial, in those years when it is directed to a planet in Pisces, Neptune can stimulate spiritual changes, which harmonize and reconcile conflicting facets of the person, and allow the true Self to become manifest. Unfortunately, the Neptune-ruled years are also when charlatans who prey on those innocent people who want to believe there is something more to their lives are best able to smell out potential victims.

% **Positive Years**
when Neptune is Time Lord

♆ directed to	N	% Positive
♆ rises	51	53.2
☉	39	41.7
☽	41	48.6
☿	35	54.2
♀	47	46.2
♂	52	**27.8***
♃	45	48.2
♄	42	38.7
♅	38	45.2
♇	46	41.3
All	*436*	*44.2*

When ruling the decan Neptune tends to be associated with difficult years, just 44.2% of 436 were considered as positive in the sample. Neptune must therefore be classified as a malefic. Neptune is most helpful when rising after the Sun, especially for those people born during the daytime. Directions to any one of the planets, with the possible exception of Mercury, indicate a difficult year ahead. The year that Neptune comes to Mars will invariably be one that contains many problems.

Neptune by sign, natal & to where it is directed

♆'s natal sign		Sign	Sign to which ♆ is directed	
N	% Positive Years		N	% Positive Years
66	49.3	♈	25	50.6
32	48.0	♉	58	**35.9**
67	**36.4**	♊	35	41.3
52	38.3	♋	37	36.7
34	42.5	♌	33	43.8
44	45.2	♍	17	37.2
43	56.8	♎	25	39.8
9	20.1	♏	31	49.6
16	56.5	♐	27	50.2
13	41.7	♑	34	53.2
21	43.1	♒	37	41.5
39	41.7	♓	26	41.7
436	44.2	*All*	385	43.0

In the sample, as shown in Table Ψ-3, Neptune has a significant problem when directed to a planet located in Taurus.

The indication in Table Ψ-3 that natal Neptune in Gemini is a significant negative indicator should be treated with caution as Neptune spends far too many years in any one sign for this to be at all meaningful.

Table Ψ-4: **Neptune by House, Natal & to where Directed**

Ψ's natal house		House	House to which Ψ is directed	
N	% Positive Years		N	% Positive Years
2	45.2	I	52	41.7
34	**29.3****	II	33	38.4
78	59.1	III	29	**71.7****
49	36.9	IV	22	**24.7****
65	**36.2****	V	35	43.9
33	54.8	VI	23	59.0
36	57.8	VII	36	45.2
33	52.1	VIII	31	35.0
32	36.7	IX	24	33.9
25	32.5	X	27	40.2
44	37.0	XI	43	**33.6****
5	36.2	XII	30	51.2
436	*44.2*	*All*	*385*	*43.0*

In Table Ψ-4 we see that in the sample natal Neptune was significantly difficult—that is, well below 50%—when in the 2nd and 5th houses. Other statistically significant indicators of difficult years are found when Neptune is directed to a planet occupying the 4th or 11th houses. When Neptune is directed to a planet located in the 3rd house there is a significant indication that the year will be positive.

Table ♆-5: **% Positive when Neptune is the Ruler by its place in the decan sequence**

Place of Neptune in decan	Day		Night	
	N	% Positive	N	% Positive
1	7	13.9	8	21.3
2	51	55.0	39	34.9
3	51	34.3**	20	80.9**
4	49	46.6	23	22.2**
5	20	64.8	24	49.6
6	20	46.3	31	54.9
7	12	56.6	32	37.3
8	14	34.7	26	32.8
9	1	0.0	2	42.9
10	0	0.0	1	0.0
Sum	224	46.0**	206	42.2

When Neptune is the third of the ten to rise after birth it is associated with conflicting results, both statistically significant. These are happenings that occurred when people in the sample were in their twenties. In a daytime chart it is associated with difficult years, while those born at night have it associated with an above-average number of positive years. Even though there are more observations for the day births than for the night ones, there is no reason for saying that one is right and the other wrong, both appear to be correct.

Even though few observations are involved, Neptune as the first to rise after birth does not look at all positive for either day or night births.

Night births with Neptune ruling their thirties (place 4) experienced a significantly high number of difficult years.

Neptune Rises
(53% positive years)

Expect to be somewhat muddled, in something of a fog at times this year and to a varying extent throughout the ten years of this Neptune-ruled decan. The individual's finances may not be as firm as he believed they were, losses are possible and there is a very real danger of being deceived in financial matters. Others may be exerting undue influences on him. He may experience poor health and medical experts could have some difficulty diagnosing what exactly it is that is wrong with him. Mythologizing can become a habit. Everyday life may seem to be missing something that's important and he may be unable to specify exactly what that is; something certainly needs to be changed and he is likely to ask if it is all really worth-while proceeding as he has in the past. Neither the headlines in the papers nor the news on television will be reassuring; the world they describe with such apparent excitement is not where he really wants to be. He may be tempted this year to renounce that outside world and spend his time in his own space, wherever he imagines it might be. Perhaps he'll quit his job in the city and move into the country to raise organic vegetables or find attractive the idea of working with poor, sick or disadvantaged people.

Table ♆-6:   ♆ **to Ascendant: % Positive Years**

♆ relative to the ☉	Day birth		Night birth		All	
	N	% Positive	N	% Positive	N	% Positive
Oriental ♆	18	55.2	12	45.2	30	51.3
Occidental ♆	9	60.3	12	52.7	21	56.0
All	*27*	*57.0*	*24*	*49.0*	*51*	*53.2*

If Neptune is afflicted, or if the ascendant is in Gemini, Virgo or Capricorn, someone he trusts may be deceiving the native. Disillusionment can occur this year. There is the danger also that the individual can lose sight of who he truly is as others increasingly attempt to influence him, especially if he tries to mimic them in thought, word or deed. He is susceptible to disease and can become nervously stressed. This can be a particularly difficult year for those in their teens or twenties; they can become too easily excited and agitated without real cause, and will tend to lack the ability to make plans or to take decisive action.

Examples of happenings in the sample the year that Neptune became the time ruler:
Oriental Neptune rules in the day: *in plane lost in fog; his father kills a man; arrested; proposes universal peace; having difficulty seeing; her husband retires; mental disorder; has a secret ritual; has two mistresses; he is "the votary of licentiousness"; his wife threatens to leave him; leaves her husband & quits her job; kidney transplant; many debts; his dog dies; studies non-violent civil disobedience.*
Occidental Neptune rules in the day: *vows never to drink again; mother blames him for father's death; loss of Christian belief; passes exams; goes overseas for further education; praised; sells his company; visits a brothel; nearly dies from loss of blood.*
Oriental Neptune rules at night: *his father's company is bankrupt; has an undiagnosed illness; goes away to school; his agent is arrested; involved first in Buddhism, then in Sufism; being tutored in religion; loses much money; at a crossroads; she is a love junky; vacations overseas; attempt on his life; elected; first solo flight; aware of his illusionary relationship with women.*
Occidental Neptune rules at night: *mysterious throat infection nearly kills him; stripped of his office; his entire philosophy & beliefs are transformed; gets a new dog; gardening; considers renouncing the world; imprisoned; banished; death.*

Neptune directed to the Sun
(42% positive)

This is likely to be a difficult year during which a person's imagination can become exaggerated. Mythologizing, imaginatively placing oneself into situations where one has greater power than usual, can become a habit. Because he does not see himself clearly an individual's valuation of himself now can be off kilter. He is likely to be extremely sensitive to what others do or say; yet at the same time his self-confidence is weak. Other people can appear threatening, often by their mannerisms or innuendo, and he may feel himself victimized or trapped. All grounds for authority should be questioned, including his religious beliefs, and he is likely to advocate changes that others may consider foolish. He may have a strong desire to resist or disappoint those who want to dictate what he should do. Unexpected honors may be received, for which he may believe himself unworthy. He can acquire an actual distaste for money and money-making this year, yet in typical Neptunian contradiction he'll want enough to get by without having to do or think much about it, his preference being for others to support him so that he can continue to indulge in his mythologizing. An interest in spiritual activities can be awakened this year and mystical experiences may occur. Journeys to distant places are likely, either in the imagination or in reality. He could take to going around in sandals and, just as likely, become involved in scandals.

Table ♆-7:　　　　　　　　**♆ to the ☉: % Positive Years**

♆ relative to the ☉	Day birth		Night birth		All	
	N	% Positive	N	% Positive	N	% Positive
Oriental ♆	12	37.7	6	60.3	18	45.2
Occidental ♆	10	45.2	11	32.9	21	38.8
All	*22*	*41.1*	*17*	*42.6*	*39*	*41.8*

Examples of happenings in my sample the year that Neptune comes to the Sun:
Oriental Neptune to the Sun in the day: *he ceases believing in Free Will, saying the human body is a machine; investigates fundamental Christian beliefs; decides not to be a priest; arrested for assaulting a policeman; sells fifteen paintings; idle; re-elected by a landslide; jailed; his wife leaves him; first time drunk; accused of cheating; his fleet is destroyed; escapes from prison; calls the USA "the greatest cause of violence in the world today".*
Occidental Neptune to the Sun in the day: *typhoid fever; his shop fails; loses his job; emigrates; his parents divorce; separates from his wife; marries; his wife is in hospital; often in trouble; homosexual attraction; all year he is a conscript in the army.*
Oriental Neptune to the Sun at night: *her father safely survives a shipwreck; he commands a minesweeper; he is a naval helicopter pilot; in poor health; her son visits; starts school/college.*

Occidental Neptune to the Sun at night: *not allowed back in the US; refuses to accept the role of the Messiah that others had prepared him for; becomes president; persecuted; buys a large estate; resigns; the film of his book is a flop; reunited with her mother after long separation; becomes Grand Master of Masonic Lodge; living with a woman half his age; bronchitis; her back problems are resolved without the feared surgery.*

Neptune directed to the Moon
(49% positive)

This will not be the easiest of years, and that is mainly due to the individual becoming extremely sensitive now. He may feel humiliated should he discover that those he trusted have been deceiving him, perhaps for a long time. This can bring about some form of hysteria and he may live in a state of terror. He may become extremely touchy; feel neglected and frightened, and can develop a sense of inferiority. He may be tempted to shirk his responsibilities. It can be a year of self-delusion and instability, a time when the inducement to drown one's sorrows in drink or forget them through drugs can become overpowering. Financial problems are likely. His marriage may end, and he can become a victim of theft. The individual is learning not to accept what his feelings says is so.

Table Ψ-8: Ψ **to the ☾: % Positive Years**

Planets relative to the ☉	Day birth		Night birth		All	
	N	% Positive	N	% Positive	N	% Positive
Oriental Ψ	13	41.8	10	54.2	23	47.2
Occidental Ψ	7	25.9	11	65.8	18	50.3
All	*20*	*36.2*	*21*	*60.3*	*41*	*48.6*
Waxing ☾	10	54.2	16	**73.4***	26	66.1
Waning ☾	10	18.1	5	18.1	15	**18.1****

Daytime births can have a particularly difficult time this year, while people born during the night, especially those with a waxing Moon, often avoid these problems. They seem to possess the ability to relax, to sympathize with the troubles of others, and to happily enjoy their own inner thoughts and dreams.

In the sample individuals with a waxing Moon experienced a high proportion of positive years under this direction, while those born with a waning Moon had a completely different experience: for most of them it was a ghastly time.

Examples of happenings in the sample when Neptune came to the Moon:

Oriental Neptune to the Moon in the day: *she spends time in an opium den; major operation to correct spinal nerve damaged lifting a heavy object; humiliated; her husband stops talking to her; rejected for jobs because of his prison record; tells of prison brutality; interest in reincarnation; meets the Pope; audience refuses to listen to him; sees his mother in the nude; she has twins; exhausted; receives Nobel Peace Prize.*

Occidental Neptune to the Moon in the day: *syphilis; mad love affair; financial failure; war starts; loss of control; begins taking an interest in politics; conscripted into army.*

Oriental Neptune to the Moon at night: *serving in the navy; her wedding reception & honeymoon are cancelled; domestic tension; a depressing time; says his memory & concentration seem to be slowly sleeping away; virus infection; giddiness; apart from her parents; sent away to school; travels.*

Occidental Neptune to the Moon at night: *his wife leaves him; hit by a taxi; wins a scholarship; travels overseas to hear Bach's St John Passion; in poor health; refuses to be anyone's guru; loses leadership election; her mother is away; forced to sell his house; gives first account of his experiments.*

Neptune directed to Mercury

(54 % positive)

News may be received that causes nervous excitement. Has he finally won the jackpot? Is the market crashing? Or are these just more fantasies; hopes and fears that should be ignored? The individual's imagination can certainly run away with him this year, and his thinking can get easily confused. He may lose his sense of reality. In all likelihood the information he receives will contradict, undermine or go beyond objective common sense; yet it can cause him some humiliation. He is discovering that most of what he reads or hears has no real meaning for him.

Table Ψ-9:   **Ψ to ☿: % Positive Years**

Planets relative to the ☉	Day birth		Night birth		All	
	N	% Positive	N	% Positive	N	% Positive
Oriental Ψ	14	38.8	4	67.8	18	45.2
Occidental Ψ	7	64.6	10	63.3	17	63.8
All	*21*	*47.4*	*14*	*64.6*	*35*	*54.2*
Oriental ☿	10	54.2	8	56.5	18	55.2
Occidental ☿	11	41.1	6	75.3	17	53.2

This year may change both how a person perceives things and how he expresses his thoughts to others. It is an excellent time for all forms of artistic expression, but the less inspired may experience communication difficulties. Their opinions can be easily ridiculed and ignored.

Night births and those individuals born with an occidental Neptune appear to have the easiest time with this direction.

Examples of happenings in the sample the year that Neptune came to Mercury:
Oriental Neptune to Mercury in the day: *his ideas meet with hostile rejection; meets Sufi leader who totally changes how she perceives things; defeats; his former lover dies; stoned by angry whites; elected to an elite club; much fantasizing; sells paintings; her son is lost in the desert; urges a halt to the bombing in Vietnam.*
Occidental Neptune to Mercury in the day: *visits London docks; much enforced idleness; stateless; talks his way out of being fined; yellow jaundice; doctorate; first political writings; sports success; has a new love.*
Oriental Neptune to Mercury at night: *lists all his sins; travels; founds astrological society; religious crisis; starting to doubt himself.*
Occidental Neptune to Mercury at night: *elopes & marries although legally underage; drafts the Declaration of Independence; rejects the Masters; acquires his first slaves; loses money in stock market panic; writes on life after death; runs away from school; promoted; elected; wants to become a hermit; exhausted; travels.*

Neptune directed to Venus
(46% positive)

This will probably not be an easy year. Any person experiencing it should be careful this year not to renounce his duties for the promise of romance. Because he will want to satisfy the slightest whims of those he loves, others can easily exploit him and financial losses are a strong possibility. Everyday reality may seem asphyxiating and he will want to breathe a different air and be released from what goes on everyday. He will probably indulge in daydreaming. A romantic yearlong voyage around the world would be perfect but few can hope to totally disregard their responsibilities to do that, even if they could afford it. On a positive side, the individual may now gain an insight into different levels of consciousness, and artists should be at the peak of their creativity now.

Daytime births, particularly those with an oriental Venus, had a hard time under this direction.

Table Ψ-10:   **Ψ to ♀: % Positive Years**

Planets relative to the ☉	Day birth		Night birth		All	
	N	% Positive	N	% Positive	N	% Positive
Oriental Ψ	14	38.8	11	57.5	25	47.0
Occidental Ψ	12	45.2	10	45.2	22	45.2
All	*26*	*41.8*	*21*	*51.6*	*47*	*46.2*
Oriental ♀	17	31.9	10	54.2	27	40.1
Occidental ♀	9	60.3	11	49.3	20	54.2

Examples of happenings in the sample the year that Uranus came to Venus:

Oriental Neptune to Venus in the day: *becomes an atheist; goes to college; stabs man in a bar; incorporates his business; appendectomy; audited by IRS; at Sufi retreat; race riots; marries; jailed; he is now able to voice his thoughts; his poetry has unprecedented high sales.*

Occidental Neptune to Venus in the day: *kills his brother in a gun accident; evacuated from home in wartime; has a great sense of release when she leaves school; marries; twice breaks his arm; buys a baseball team; dysentery & diphtheria; mother has still-born twins; catches hepatitis A; barely escapes death.*

Oriental Neptune to Venus at night: *abdicates his throne for love; marries; affairs; divorce; unhappy when ex-lover sells his letters to her; has a vision of God; first communion; his nursemaid straps him to a chair in a dark room; travels; goes to new school/college.*

Occidental Neptune to Venus at night: *cuts his wife out of his will; constant travel; creates a ballet; separated from her mother; insight into different levels of consciousness; crippling financial pressure; first attack of gout; he proves that lightning is a form of electricity; escapes intended execution.*

Neptune directed to Mars
(28% positive)

In the sample this was by far the most difficult year of Neptune's rulership.

Most individuals experienced major problems with this direction. An individual easily gets lost, confused and irritable now. He can become incapable of doing anything useful, unable to help himself or any one else. He should avoid competing with others; they will surely defeat him, perhaps by trickery. It is as if he is in a fog and his hands are tied behind his back. He is powerless to fight. His natural desire for conscious initiative and independence has become eroded. He is too easily induced into a general state of contentment, happy to be lulled by a lullaby. This is definitely not the time to start anything new, an individual will probably lack the energy or inclination to do so anyway, but it can be a good time for future planning. There are also dangers now from flooding and drugs.

Few people in the sample experienced this as a pleasant or positive year. Those born during the daytime experienced a particularly devastating time, one in which they appeared to be under a never-ending attack, missiles being tossed at them from all directions.

Table ♆-11:   **♆ to ♂: % Positive Years**

Planets relative to the ☉	Day birth		Night birth		All	
	N	% Positive	N	% Positive	N	% Positive
Oriental ♆	15	**12.0***	14	25.9	29	**18.7***
Occidental ♆	10	36.2	13	41.8	23	39.3
All	*25*	*21.7**	*27*	*33.5*	*52*	*27.8***
Oriental ♂	13	**20.9***	14	45.2	27	33.5
Occidental ♂	12	22.6	13	20.9	25	**21.7***

People in the sample with an occidental Mars *and* an oriental Neptune invariably had a difficult year.

Table Ψ-12: ## Ψ-♂ Interaction

Neptune-Mars Interaction	Oriental Ψ		Occidental Ψ		All	
	N	% Positive	N	% Positive	N	% Positive
Oriental ♂	14	32.3	13	34.8	27	33.5
Occidental ♂	15	**6.1****	10	45.2	25	**21.7*****
All	*29*	*18.7****	*23*	*39.3*	*52*	*27.8****

Examples of happenings in the sample the year that Neptune came to Mars:

Oriental Neptune to Mars in the day: *six deaths in four months; father is declared insane; hits his head on curb; church becomes a place of torment; shipwrecked; doubts his past beliefs; her hotel is bombed; in prison; an incurable disease is diagnosed; arrested; frequently punished; he is lost & confused; calls for a Day of Penance.*

Occidental Neptune to Mars in the day: *his wife is executed; from being an ideal pupil she starts to loath school; marries; opens a tobacconist shop; first poems; flees rioting; his girl friend leaves him; promoted; collapses.*

Oriental Neptune to Mars at night: *the city is flooded; bullied; explosion on ship; helicopter training in navy; attempt on his life; bullied; meets future husband; nose operation.*

Occidental Neptune to Mars at night: *divorced; she has cancer; hysterectomy; chicken pox; he is ordered to rest; marries; enlarges his house; fails to be nominated; wife/mother dies.*

Neptune directed to Jupiter
(48% positive)

The individual experiencing this direction is likely to be more idealistic and compassionate now than at other times. He will want to explore fresh places and investigate some of the different ways in which other people live and pass their time. He may visit a town or country that is new to him; become involved with a different church or religious group, perhaps with a facet of New Age philosophy; attend classes in order to learn a new language or craft; or take up golf or cycling. Whatever he does, he is expanding his experience because he has become aware that his old world is stale and confining. This should be a happy time of release, an opportunity for people to make a fresh start in their lives. Any interest in spiritual, mystical or religious philosophy may be stimulated now. A danger is that some people in their desire for radical change will take risks when they cannot afford to do so. This year also contains the danger of financial loss and is not really a time for speculating in the markets. The individual is likely to encounter bogus wealth and be presented with hopes and aspirations that bear little correspondence to reality. If Jupiter is in Pisces he is likely to become very confused.

Table Ψ-13:   **Ψ to ♃: % Positive Years**

Planets relative to the ☉	Day birth		Night birth		All	
	N	% Positive	N	% Positive	N	% Positive
Oriental Ψ	14	45.2	10	27.1	24	37.7
Occidental Ψ	7	77.5	14	51.6	21	60.3
All	*21*	*47.0*	*24*	*41.4*	*45*	*48.2*
Oriental ♃	8	33.9	11	57.5	19	47.6
Occidental ♃	13	69.5	13	27.8	26	48.6

Oriental Neptune is associated with a high proportion of difficult years, and occidental Neptune with successful ones, but the numbers are really too few. Like all Neptune phenomena they may be illusionary.

Examples of happenings in my sample the year that Neptune came to Jupiter:
Oriental Neptune to Jupiter in the day: *typhoid fever; released from prison; not allowed to return to USA; her therapist dies; IRA bombs; overnight he is famous; debts; his marriage proposal is rejected; getting fatter; moves; family disgrace; in love; meets US president; overjoyed when segregation is ruled to be illegal.*
Occidental Neptune to Jupiter in the day: *peasant communism is spreading; lobbies for better pay & working conditions; in love; in his first starring role.*
Oriental Neptune to Jupiter at night: *fined for letting his sheep loose; her brother-in-law is caught selling drugs; serving in the navy; sister marries; local council forces her to move house; undergoes surgery; girls bully him; his wife dies.*
Occidental Neptune to Jupiter at night: *fails to get the position he wanted; feeling of emptiness; his plans are rejected; she is an overnight success, a sex goddess; awarded World Peace Prize & distributes the money to the poor; feels the need to transform the direction of her life; re-elected; in great debt; worn out; his mother comes to live with him.*

Neptune directed to Saturn
(39% positive)

This can be something of a 'cold turkey' year, one in which the high flyer is brought sharply down to earth, any excessive behavior being met with a firm slap in the face. It is a time when the individual's idealism and dreams can meet harsh opposition, perhaps even betrayal. It will be a difficult year. The individual is likely to find himself in a place that seems quite alien, a situation for which he is utterly unsuited. Few will take his side and speak up on his behalf. He may have come to that place he tries to avoid during nighttime hours, the source of all his nightmares.

The individual's self-confidence is likely to be undermined. He will have very little sense of well-being. His emotions are inhibited and he can become susceptible to disease. The memory of hurts he experienced in the past will make him fearful now, perhaps even paranoid, and he is aware only of what can again harm him. His perception of the world in which he is now living is likely to become very different from what it was before this year began.

Table Ψ-14:   **Ψ to ♄: % Positive Years**

Planets relative to the ☉	Day birth		Night birth		All	
	N	% Positive	N	% Positive	N	% Positive
Oriental Ψ	15	48.2	10	45.2	25	47.0
Occidental Ψ	4	45.2	13	**20.9***	17	**26.6***
All	*19*	*47.6*	*23*	*31.5*	*42*	*38.8*
Oriental ♄	13	55.6	7	38.8	20	49.7
Occidental ♄	6	30.1	16	28.2	22	**28.8***

In the sample those people born at night, especially those with an occidental Neptune, suffered particularly badly under this direction, for many the year seemed to have consisted of one crisis after another. Those people who were extremely active avoided many of the problems.

Examples of happenings in the sample the year that Neptune came to Saturn:

Oriental Neptune to Saturn in the day: *arrested for stealing a watch; debts; eats & drinks to excess; hunger strike; on protest marches; embarrassed by his parents' poverty; school is pure tedium; his nursemaid is sent to prison; harassed by an ex-lover; gathering a multiracial army of the poor; assassinated.*

Occidental Neptune to Saturn in the day: *fails a screen test; complimented; scandal; grandmother dies; recovers from some form of asphyxiation; in a coma from drug overdose.*

Oriental Neptune to Saturn at night: *broken collarbone when knocked down by a car; resigns; gains a large profit from commodities trading that later prompts a judicial investigation; financial problems; she is in the spotlight; his sister has polio; made partner in her law firm; bullied; his defeatist statements anger the government.*

Occidental Neptune to Saturn at night: *teeth implants take months to heal; financial crisis; flees; her mother is absent all year; major political crisis; expelled from the party; he is elected party leader; his two half-sisters are burnt to death; forced to sell printing office & editorial; organizing defenses; resigns; stripped of his positions.*

Neptune directed to Uranus
(45% positive)

Much depends this year both on the natal aspects of these two planets and on the coincident direction occurring within the septenary. It can be a very exciting year, a boom or bust time, either one of honors or one of defeats. A person's position may be unexpectedly improved or he can find himself in serious trouble. It is as if the individual has just stepped out into a new world. Before he always knew what to do, he had been taught how to fit in, but now he seems to have eluded the control of others and needs to find his own way. There is a fundamental break with the past, and he is likely to be exposed to ideas and situations that are new to him. As a result he can expect to become very confused.

Table Ψ-15:   **Ψ to ♅: % Positive Years**

Planets relative to the ☉	Day birth		Night birth		All	
	N	% Positive	N	% Positive	N	% Positive
Oriental Ψ	13	41.8	7	38.8	20	40.7
Occidental Ψ	8	45.2	10	54.2	18	50.3
All	*21*	*43.0*	*17*	*47.8*	*38*	*45.2*
Oriental ♅	10	36.2	7	64.6	17	47.8
Occidental ♅	11	49.3	10	36.2	21	43.0

Because of the few observations involved, none of the values in Table Ψ-15 stand out as meaningful.

Examples of happenings in the sample the year that Neptune came to Uranus:
Oriental Neptune to Uranus in the day: *a friend drowns; her husband loses his professional license; children born; indecisive; defeated; her marriage turns sour; debts; idle, much reading; fights for the rights of the poor; experiences a moment of initiation & confirmation; the FBI are wiretapping his phone; the motel where he is staying is bombed.*
Occidental Neptune to Uranus in the day: *accused of being a spy; seriously ill; writes against slavery; leaves school; loses his position.*
Oriental Neptune to Uranus at night: *her lover is banished; embarrassed by his lover; serving in the navy; moves; retires; much traveling; marries; finances improve.*
Occidental Neptune to Uranus at night: *honored; IRS claim back taxes; defeated; travels; his theories are disputed; awarded a scholarship; bitterly attacks the USA; assassinated.*

Neptune directed to Pluto
(41% positive)

This is likely to be a difficult year. The individual is being introduced into a strange new environment, one in which he must begin to learn his way all over again. To succeed he will have to change his frame of reference and resolve problems that are entirely new to him. This can prove difficult, at least initially. He will be dazzled by the novelty of his new situation and at the same time acutely aware of the loss of his comfortable past. How he copes with this demand for an extreme inward transformation will determine much of his future life. Those born with an occidental Neptune appear to have slightly less problems than do those with the planet oriental, but all are likely to be confused by the pressure, both internal and external, that is experienced. Finances are likely to be tight.

Table ♆-16:   **♆ to ♇: % Positive Years**

Planets relative to the ☉	Day birth		Night birth		All	
	N	% Positive	N	% Positive	N	% Positive
Oriental ♆	16	33.9	8	33.9	24	33.9
Occidental ♆	12	45.2	10	54.2	22	49.3
All	*28*	*38.8*	*18*	*45.2*	*46*	*41.3*
Oriental ♇	17	42.6	7	38.8	24	41.4
Occidental ♇	11	32.9	11	49.3	22	41.1

Examples of happenings in the sample the year that Neptune came to Pluto:
Oriental Neptune to Pluto in the day: *humiliates himself; saves his daughter from drowning; convinced there is no life after death; forsakes the family tradition of priesthood; lengthy convalescence; meets his future wife; heavily in debt; acquitted of tax fraud; in prison; suicide.*
Occidental Neptune to Pluto in the day: *abdicates; profits from insider trading; gets a job overseas; enlists in the army; acts in several flops; living in careless extravagance; first flight; wounded in a duel; flees revolution; his writings are widely read; appendicitis is wrongly diagnosed.*
Oriental Neptune to Pluto at night: *father/aunt dies; eyesight problems; sister/daughter born; involved in controversy; smallpox.*
Occidental Neptune to Pluto at night: *perceiving life anew; intense pain; writes fifty articles in the year; criticizes weakness of air defenses; poor health; wins scholarship & gold medal; promoted; writing poetry; her mother remarries.*

Mao Zedong's Neptune-ruled Decan

Mao Zedong, the first Chairman of the People's Republic of China, was chairman of the Communist Party of China from 1945 until his death in 1976.

Neptune rises in Gemini: Chairman Mao's Neptune-ruled decan began on his thirtieth birthday in December 1923. Neptune is in the 6th house in Gemini, conjunct Pluto, opposed by Mercury, and sextile to the Moon. His septenary ruler Mars has come to the Moon in Leo. Mao has just been elected one of the five commissars of the Central Committee of the Communist Party of China. He is organizing labor unions and strikes in Hunan.

Neptune directed to Pluto in Gemini: The septenary ruler Mars is at his Jupiter in Taurus. He becomes disillusioned with the revolution and returns to his native village

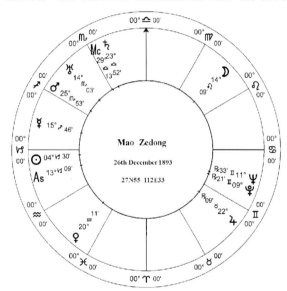

where he encounters a wave of peasant unrest that forces him to appreciate just how much the peasantry were involved in the class struggle. His interest in the revolution is rekindled and, appropriately for the direction to Pluto in Gemini, he becomes acting Propaganda Director of the Kuomintang.

Neptune is directed to Jupiter in Taurus: Mao is thirty-two years old at the end of 1925 when Neptune comes to his retrograde Jupiter. Mars is on his Venus in Aquarius in the septenary. Peasant communism is spreading. General Chiang Kai-shek and his government quarrel with the communists. Mao is becoming increasingly aware of the potential energy of the peasantry. The liberation he finds at work in village after village, with peasants overthrowing their landlords, has a great impact on him. He turns down an opportunity to study in France because he firmly believes that China's problems can be studied and resolved only within China.

Neptune directed to Venus in Aquarius: Neptune is on his Venus throughout most of 1927. Mao is thirty-three years old. Septenary Mars has moved into Capricorn, the sign in which it is it is exalted, to his Sun. The communists split with General Chiang. Chiang massacres communists in Shanghai and then sends soldiers against communists in the country. Mao leads a peasant uprising in Hunan. It fails and pro-Nationalist militiamen capture him. They march him back to their headquarters to be shot. Just in sight of their camp, he breaks loose and flees into a nearby field, where he hides in tall grass until nightfall. He leads his small surviving band of supporters up into the Chingkang-shan Mountains to start the search for power all over again—on his terms. The period is filled with complex wrangling over leadership and policy. He is directed to lead attacks on cities, which end in catastrophic defeat.

Neptune directed to the Sun in Capricorn: Neptune comes to Mao's Sun when he is thirty-four years old. Septenary Mars is now on his Mercury in Sagittarius. The complex wrangling over leadership and policy continues. He is living with 17-year-old He Zichen, the daughter of a landlord. With Zhu De, he organizes an uprising and gains control of Kiangsi, a province on the banks of the Yangtze River.

Neptune directed to Mercury in Sagittarius: Mao is thirty-five in December 1928. Neptune is on its dispositor in the decan, and at the same time Mercury assumes rulership of his septenary. It should be a Mercury inspired year. He is in Kiangsi, reforming farming, educating the peasants, and creating the Red Army. The complex wrangling within the Chinese Communist Party over leadership and policy continues.

Neptune directed to Mars in Scorpio: In December 1929 Mao becomes thirty-six years old. Both rulers, Neptune and Mercury, have arrived at the place of his natal Mars in Scorpio. Mars is part of a five-body grand cross in fixed signs; the Mars-Jupiter opposition being brought together with the Moon-Uranus square by Venus. Both rulers coming to Mars makes this an important year for Mao. The Kuomintang forces execute his sister and his second wife, Yang Kai-hui. Mao marries He Zichen, his third wife. Chiang Kai-shek launches a "bandit extermination" campaign against the communist groups. Mao is directed to lead attacks on cities, and this tactic again ends in catastrophic defeats.

Neptune directed to Uranus in Scorpio: Neptune is on Mao's Uranus when he is thirty-seven years old. In the septenary Mercury has come to Saturn in Libra. Japan occupies Manchuria. Mao's success in Kiangsi proves to be his undoing. The Communist Central Committee moves to Kiangsi from Shanghai and take over control of the province from Mao. The complex wrangling within the Party over leadership and policy continues.

Neptune directed to Saturn in Libra: Mao is thirty-eight in December 1931. Neptune is on his Saturn in the decan, and Mercury is on his Moon in Leo in the septenary. For the sixth consecutive year the complex wrangling within the Party over leadership and policy continues. The Communist Central Committee strip Mao of his posts in the party and army.

Neptune directed to the Moon in Leo: In December 1932 Neptune comes to Mao's waning Moon in Leo. This is the final year of Neptune's rulership of Mao's decan. In the septenary Mercury is on its dispositor, Jupiter in Taurus. Mao's loss of control of the Red Army coincides with another of General Chiang's encirclement campaigns to wipe out the Communists. Previous attempts had failed in the face of Mao's tactics—withdrawing when outnumbered and then launching surprise attacks in overwhelming force on isolated units. Now the other Communist leaders decide to tackle the Nationalists head on, but Chiang has 700,000 men—a seven-to-one advantage—and a German general, Hans von Seeckt, is advising him. Chiang and von Seeckt slowly strangle the Communists within a ring of barbed wire and machine-gun emplacements. 60,000 Red Army soldiers and about one million peasants die.

The following year is the start of the Mao's Moon-ruled decan. Following another disastrous defeat at the hands of Chiang's Nationalists and inspired by the shape-changing Moon, Mao will begin leading the remnants of the Red Army over mountains, rivers and wastelands from Kiangsi in South China on the epochal Long March to Shensi in the North West, a distance of six thousand miles.

Dr. Martin Luther King Jr's Neptune-ruled Decan

Neptune rises in Virgo: One of the leaders in the American civil rights movement, the Baptist minister Dr. Martin Luther King Jr., a day birth, is thirty years old in January 1959 when his oriental Neptune becomes the ruler of his decan. He has just recovered from being stabbed in the chest a few months earlier by a demented woman. Mercury in Aquarius rules his septenary and it has come to Saturn in Sagittarius. By tradition Mercury is weak in Sagittarius. This year he visits India where he studies the non-violent civil disobedience Mahatma Gandhi used successfully against the British and has dinner with Prime Minister Nehru. He then visits Jerusalem and Cairo. This year he writes *The Measure of Man*.

Neptune directed to Pluto in Cancer: In January 1960 Dr King's Neptune comes to Pluto in his decan. He is thirty-one years old. In his septenary Mercury has arrived at his Mars in Gemini Mercury rules Gemini, but Mars is opposed by Saturn and squared by the Moon. He moves with his family from Montgomery to Atlanta, where he is arrested and charged with falsifying his income tax returns. An all-white jury acquits him of tax evasion, but he has spent time in prison. He speaks at the founding conference of the SNCC (pronounced "snick"), the Student Nonviolent Coordinating Committee. King discusses civil rights with presidential candidate Senator John F. Kennedy. The lunch counter sit-in movement begins. He is arrested at the Atlanta sit-in. Charges are dropped for that arrest but he is held for violating probation for an earlier traffic offense and is in prison for two days. John F. Kennedy wins a close presidential election, receiving strong support from black voters.

Neptune directed to Mars in Gemini: In January 1961 Dr King's Neptune comes to Mars in his decan. He is thirty-two years old. Mercury is on his Jupiter in Taurus in his septenary. His third child, Dexter Scott is born. After the initial group of Freedom Riders seeking to integrate bus terminals is assaulted in Alabama, he addresses a mass rally at a mob-besieged Montgomery church. He is arrested in Albany, Georgia and begins serving a 45-day sentence, but leaves jail after an unidentified person pays his fine. After an outbreak of racial violence, he calls for a Day of Penance to atone for the violence. A prayer vigil ends in his

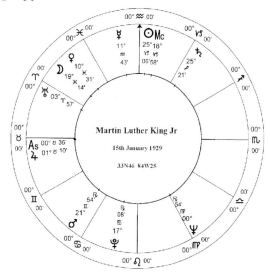

Martin Luther King Jr

15th January 1929

33N46 84W25

arrest. He leaves jail after two weeks and agrees to halt demonstrations.

Neptune directed to Jupiter in Taurus: In January 1962 Dr King's decan ruler Neptune comes to Jupiter. He is thirty-three years old. Mercury is on his Moon in Pisces in his septenary. He is briefly jailed in Albany, Georgia. He meets the president of the United States. The United States Supreme Court rules that segregation is illegal but Southern states and cities continue to practice it by intimidating the blacks.

Neptune directed to Uranus in Aries: In January 1963 Dr King's Neptune comes to Uranus in his decan. He is thirty-four years old. His septenary ruler Mercury is still in Pisces where it is very weak, and has moved to conjunct his exalted Venus. His fourth child, Bernice Albertine, is born. Fearing that Communists are trying to infiltrate the Civil Rights Movement, Attorney General Robert Kennedy authorizes the FBI to start wiretapping King. After violating a state injunction against protests, he is arrested and placed in prison where he writes his "Letter from Birmingham Jail", a passionate statement of his crusade for justice. Birmingham police use fire hoses and dogs against the "Children's Crusade" and over 1,000 youngsters are arrested. Mass demonstrations are suspended. Segregationists bomb the motel where he is staying and the home of his brother. Federal troops come into Birmingham. An assassin kills the NAACP leader Medgar Evans. King again meets with President Kennedy, and addresses the march on Washington for Jobs and Freedom, delivering the most famous of his speeches: "I Have a Dream". He delivers the eulogy for four young black girls killed by a dynamite blast in a Sunday school in Birmingham. President Kennedy is assassinated.

From 1964 until his death in 1968 the planet receiving the septenary ruler's direction will the following year receive the decan ruler's direction—a continuous and unstoppable stream of fate has taken over King's life.

Year	*Septenary*	*Decan*
1964	♀As	♆☽
1965	♀☿	♆♀
1966	♀☉	♆☿
1967	♀♄	♆☉
1968	♀♂	♆♄

Neptune directed to the Moon in Pisces: In January 1964 Dr King's Neptune comes to his waxing Moon in his decan. The Moon is part of a T-cross, squaring the Mars-Saturn opposition. He is thirty-five years old. This year the exalted Venus in Pisces takes over as his septenary ruler. He is arrested in St. Augustine, Florida where he is protesting segregationist violence. *Why We Can't Wait* is published, and the Civil Rights Act becomes law. He briefly meets with Malcolm X. Bodies of three missing civil rights workers are found six weeks after they were arrested and disappeared. He testifies at the Democratic convention on behalf of the Mississippi Freedom Democratic Party. He is exhausted after many months of working for the civil rights movement, and checks into a hospital for a rest and complete physical check-up. He becomes the youngest person to be awarded the Nobel Peace Prize, for his work to end segregation and racial discrimination through civil disobedience and other non-violent means. He travels to Europe where he meets the Pope and receives the Nobel Prize.

Neptune directed to Venus in Pisces: His exalted Venus is emphasized this year. In January 1965 Neptune comes to Venus in his decan, and Venus is on his Mercury in Aquarius in his septenary. He is thirty-six years old. He is honored at an integrated dinner in Atlanta. He leads voter registration campaigns and is jailed. Malcolm X is assassinated. There are race riots. He delivers his famous "How Long, Not Long" speech at the end of the march from Selma to Montgomery. The Voting Rights Act becomes law. Widespread racial violence in Los Angeles results in more than thirty deaths. He goes to LA at the invitation of local groups. He leads a march on Chicago City Hall, and announces the start of the Chicago Campaign. He begins to express doubts about the United States' role in the Vietnam War. The American Jewish Committee awards him the American Liberties Medallion by for his "exceptional advancement of the principles of human liberty".

Neptune directed to Mercury in Aquarius: In January 1966 Dr King's Neptune comes to its dispositor. He is thirty-seven years old. Venus is on his Capricornian Sun in the septenary. Following several successes in the South leading protest marches, he is trying to spread the Civil Rights movement to the North and is in Chicago, where he is attempting to integrate housing. Angry whites stone him: a brick hits him during one march. Racial rioting in Chicago results in two deaths and widespread destruction. He is awarded the *Pacem in Terris* (Latin for 'Peace on Earth') Award, and the Margaret Sanger Award for "his courageous resistance to bigotry and his lifelong dedication to the advancement of social justice and human dignity." He marches in Mississippi to encourage black voting. Stokely

Carmichael ignites controversy by using the "Black Power" slogan, and Dr. King urges a halt to the bombing in Vietnam.

Neptune directed to the Sun in Capricorn: In January 1967 Dr King's Neptune comes to the Sun in his decan. He is thirty-eight years old. Venus is on his Saturn in Sagittarius in the septenary. He is in prison, from where he calls for the rioting to end. In a speech in New York he speaks strongly against the American role in Vietnam, calling the US government "The greatest purveyor of violence in the world today". This speech turns the media against him. He calls for a radical redistribution of economic and political power and launches the Poor People's Campaign.

Neptune directed to Saturn in Sagittarius: In January 1968 Dr King's Neptune comes to his oriental Saturn in this final year of his decan. He is thirty-nine years old. Septenary Venus is on his Mars in Gemini. The two receiving planets, Saturn and Mars, are in opposition, from the 8th to 2nd houses, and the Moon squares them. He speaks to striking sanitation workers in Memphis, and then leads a protest march that is disrupted by violence. He travels throughout the United States in order to assemble "a multiracial army of the poor". In Memphis he delivers his "I've been to the Mountaintop" speech and the next day he is assassinated.

Chapter 15

Pluto as the Time Ruler

A solitary, unused to speaking of what he sees and feels, has mental experiences which are at once more intense and less articulate than those of a gregarious man.

Thomas Mann, *Death in Venice*

He who is unable to live in society, or who has no need because he is sufficient for himself, must be either a beast or a god.

Aristotle, *Politics*

Pluto is the outsider. It is separate from all other forms of planetary life, never truly an involved member of the local system. As such, looking in on the feverishly active life in the human hive, it has the ability to objectively identify what is old and becoming increasingly less useful. Where possible the outdated component is replaced with an improved version. In the process the new is created from the old, and life is extended by way of death. The urge to be separate is a craving for an independent and individualized existence.

Major changes occur during the years that Pluto rules a person's decan, and there will be radical transformations of one's thoughts and objective existence. As it comes to each of the planets on its tour of the individual's horoscope Pluto will encounter different areas of life that are failing to operate as they are intended. Sweeping changes will be called for. It is this ability to identify the need for and the willingness to make fundamental changes in the individual's world that Pluto brings during the years that it governs his decan. All too often the early stages of change mimic deterioration. Cut a chrysalis open, and there is a rotting caterpillar. You will never find that mythical creature that is half caterpillar and half butterfly. The process of transformation often seems to consist almost entirely of decay.

It is a truth of the human condition that each one of us is an outsider. When it comes really down to the nitty-gritty, each one of us is alone. We attempt to run away from this disagreeable fact by taking a mate, by spending time with friends, by becoming involved within our community and with colleagues in the workplace, by attending places where many people are gathered together, but all of these are really distractions, ways we have of pretending to ourselves that we are not alone, that in the final analysis the only person who is totally committed to our well being is oneself. Those others to whom we believe ourselves closely connected each have their own independent lives. They may care for us, they may make sacrifices for us, but they too have independent egos, the I each one of them responds to is not the same as my I or your I. Yes, when we were children, our parents, particularly our mothers, were fully committed to providing for our needs and ensuring we enjoyed good health, received an adequate education and grew into self-responsible adults. One hears of cases in which this doesn't happen but for the most part parents do provide adequately for their children. Yet, even so, the beloved child eventually realizes that he or she is a separate being from his or her loving mother. The son may be the fruit of the mother's womb but he, like his mother, is alone in this world, only able to declare, "Who I am is me!"

Pluto and the Sun are similar in some ways. Both bodies ask the individual to recognize his aloneness and to become self-sufficient. As each one of these two bodies circumnavigates the natal horoscope and encounters the other members of the solar system it will stimulate situations that are aimed at achieving unconditional self-respect, at recognizing one's own limitations, at letting go of unnecessary control, at concentrating one's whole self into whatever one is doing, at being without fear and tolerating uncertainty, at being open and receptive, at recognizing everything as beautiful and precious, and all of the other characteristics that are essential parts of a fully matured and enlightened person.

The years ruled by Pluto, like those ruled by the Sun, are never easy. The individual is likely to experience total upheaval. What happens, and how he relates to these happenings, tells us much about how well he will fulfill the purpose for which he was born.

Table ♇-1:   **♇ as time ruler: % Positive Years**

Position relative to the ☉	Day birth		Night birth		All	
	N	% Positive	N	% Positive	N	% Positive
Oriental ♇	182	52.2	105	46.5	287	50.1
Occidental ♇	51	51.4	124	**35.7***	175	**40.3**
All	233	52.0	229	**40.7***	462	46.4

The changes that occur to an individual at this time should be considered inevitable. Whatever or whoever must depart from a person's life will do so whether he agrees of not. Fewer people are hurt when this fact is accepted. Unfortunately, by accepting this fact, the individual may gain the reputation of bring cruel.

The evidence in Table ♇-1 suggests that Pluto is most positive when it is a diurnal planet, and strongest when it rises before the Sun. The difficulties associated with occidental Pluto in a nocturnal chart are statistically very significant.

**% Positive Years
when Pluto is the Time Lord**

♀ *directed to*	N	% Positive
♀ rises	46	49.1
☉	48	41.4
☽	47	51.9
☿	41	37.5
♀	43	42.1
♂	52	50.4
♃	40	54.2
♄	53	**32.4****
♅	46	59.0
♆	46	47.2
All	*462*	*46.4*

Pluto's directions to Saturn and Mercury indicate difficult years ahead. In these years defenses built over time are likely to collapse and the individual will be left open to all manner of attack. At the same time he is likely to face questions that demand responses never before considered. During Pluto's rule the world in which the individual lives tends to experience drastic change.

Table ♀-3:

Pluto by sign, natal & to which it is directed

♀'s natal sign		Sign	Sign to which ♀ is directed	
N	% Positive Years		N	% Positive Years
33	46.6	♈	27	40.2
103	47.4	♉	47	46.2
126	44.5	♊	30	48.2
91	45.7	♋	34	42.5
40	45.2	♌	35	54.2
4	67.8	♍	31	40.8
7	64.6	♎	39	55.6
10	63.3	♏	47	40.4
4	45.2	♐	33	49.3
10	63.3	♑	34	37.2
3	60.3	♒	27	53.6
31	35.0	♓	32	45.2
462	*46.4*	*All*	*416*	*46.1*

Because of its slow movement around the zodiac, Pluto's natal sign must be meaningless here.

I had hoped the results for the sign to which Pluto is directed would confirm my suspicion that Pluto is strong where Mars is strong, namely in Aries, Scorpio and Capricorn, but there are no indications in the above table that this is so. On the contrary, directions of Pluto to planets in these three signs are associated with the lowest values in the table. However, none of the values in Table ♇-3 are statistically significant.

Table ♇-4:   **Pluto by house, natal & to which it is directed**

♇'s natal house		♇'s natal house	House where ♇ is directed	
N	% Positive Years		N	% Positive Years
33	49.3	I	33	46.6
27	**30.1***	II	46	51.1
40	56.5	III	45	46.2
38	47.6	IV	28	48.4
36	35.2	V	36	47.7
25	61.5	VI	21	43.1
77	48.1	VII	32	53.7
64	59.3	VIII	18	60.3
43	42.1	IX	34	34.6
41	**30.9****	X	34	53.2
35	43.9	XI	52	41.7
3	0.0	XII	37	34.2
462	46.4	All	416	46.1

Pluto in either the natal 2nd or 10th house is a significant indicator of difficult years. The planet is most beneficial when directed to a planet in the eighth house, the house some say it rules, but the numbers involved are too few for significance.

Table ♀-5: **% Positive when Pluto is the Ruler, by its place in the decan sequence**

Place of Pluto in decan	Day		Night	
	N	% Positive	N	% Positive
1	16	44.9	9	30.3
2	10	62.9	20	45.5
3	58	**64.0****	37	39.4
4	41	57.0	54	46.4
5	50	47.6	14	45.5
6	39	**32.3*****	19	33.5
7	15	53.9	48	38.0
8	4	67.4	18	35.5
9	0	0.0	10	45.5
10	0	0.0	0	0.0
Sum	233	52.0	229	**40.7*****

Day births with Pluto as decan ruler experienced significant above-average years in their twenties (place 3) and significant below-average years in their fifties (place 6). With the exception of place 6, day births were associated with much easier years than were night births for each of the different decades or place numbers.

Pluto Rises
(49% positive years)

This year the individual will experience drastic changes in his life and in the lives of those around him. He will probably feel the need to separate himself from others as he struggles to gain some control of what is happening to him. He is no longer simply willing to be just another marionette on a string controlled by fate or other people. He will try to reject restrictions that he accepted in the past. Frustrations that may have been hidden or pent-up can be revealed in the shape of a violent emotional outburst. His finances may suffer. If he is to achieve the success he desires, he will need to get deeper into whatever subject it is that fascinates him and to cease simply flittering around on its surface.

It can be a year in which circumstances contrive matters so that the individual finds peace, calmness and a degree of solitude. The opportunity is there to enjoy a delicious sense of freedom. However, if the person is over dependent on society this will probably be an extremely lonely time.

For some death can occur this year.

Table ♀-6:

♀ Rises: % Positive Years

♀ relative to the ☉	Day birth		Night birth		All	
	N	% Positive	N	% Positive	N	% Positive
Oriental ♀	16	62.2	11	32.9	27	50.3
Occidental ♀	4	45.2	15	48.2	19	47.6
All	*20*	*58.8*	*26*	*41.8*	*46*	*49.1*

Pluto is most favorable when oriental in a diurnal chart.

Examples of happenings in my sample the year that Pluto became the time ruler:
Oriental Pluto rises in the day: *elected to a high position; declared legally insane; joins Masonic Lodge; depressed & terrified; imprisoned; his father's murderers are executed; travels; touring; skin infection; emigrates; assassinations; murdered, with his whole family.*
Occidental Pluto rises in the day: *resigns from his job to become a fulltime astrology researcher; studying; nearly dies from excessive bleeding; mentally he becomes as a child; he becomes paralyzed.*
Oriental Pluto rises at night: *starts at college; first year in London; campaigning for election all year but loses; grueling lecture tour; devastated by death of close friend; family is abandoned by father; father is ill; brother dies; her first novel is published; has an addition built to his house; enjoying his fame; little money; breaks her shoulder; discusses sleep in human evolution; death.*
Occidental Pluto rises at night: *employed again after long time out of work; fails exams; retires; children born; feeling totally rejected; outside events halt his studies; lonely & unhappy; wounded; appendectomy; cancer of uterus.*

Pluto directed to the Sun
(41% positive years)

The individual will need to become fully involved in whatever he does this year; otherwise he can easily become someone's victim. Another may be trying to unduly influence him, to demonstrate his power over him, supposedly for the individual's own good. Obviously, this should not be allowed to happen. As a result he may feel compelled to assert himself, to rebel and demonstrate just how different he is from others. Unfortunately, unless great care is taken, this can bring disastrous consequences to himself, his family, and his friends.

The year can also be a time of regeneration, when new ideas are realized and the individual's position is consolidated. He should have the energy now to work the long hours that may be required for his ambitions to be fulfilled, but he may have to do this alone, without assistance or companionship. An upheaval at his work place may occur during the year.

Table ♇-7:   **♇ to the ☉: % Positive Years**

♇ relative to the ☉	Day birth		Night birth		All	
	N	% Positive	N	% Positive	N	% Positive
Oriental ♇	19	38.1	10	54.2	29	43.7
Occidental ♇	3	30.1	16	39.6	19	38.1
All	*22*	*37.0*	*26*	*45.2*	*48*	*41.4*

The values in Table ♇-7 confirm that this was a difficult year for many people in the sample. Only nocturnal births with an oriental Pluto appear to have enjoyed a fair degree of success. However, the observations are too few for anything to be made of this.

Examples of happenings in my sample the year that Pluto came to the Sun:
Oriental Pluto to the Sun in the day: *she is "the lady nobody loves"; he investigates the collective unconscious; founds cities; lonely; his actions excite widespread horror; disciplines himself & reduces his weight; a bomb is tossed into his house; he studies the electron; his father is dying; living under constant pressure.*
Occidental Pluto to the Sun in the day: *first published writing; expelled from school; hitchhiking.*
Oriental Pluto to the Sun at night: *father is fined for running a monopoly; fame; non-stop work; her parents are away; honored; moves.*
Occidental Pluto to the Sun at night: *loses a finger in shotgun accident; cancer operation; fails exams; on trial; extremely busy, son marries; full of energy; resigns; his own actions set his career back; deaths in the family; war starts.*

Pluto directed to the Moon

(52% positive years)

This can be a disruptive year. The individual may experience intense emotional experiences that can completely overwhelm him. He will want to go off by himself to recover, to analyze what has been happening to him. There will be little time for others, and he is likely to become increasingly private. This can be a period of separations and farewells—teenagers leave home, marriage ties are broken. What he says and does this year may be unpopular. Possessiveness and jealousy are likely to be encountered at some time during the year.

The difference between day and night births in Table ♇-8 for occidental Pluto looks interesting, but unfortunately there are far too few observations for it to be relied upon.

Table ♇-8:   ♇ **to the ☽: % Positive Years**

Planets relative to the ☉	Day birth		Night birth		All	
	N	% Positive	N	% Positive	N	% Positive
Oriental ♇	19	57.1	10	63.3	29	59.2
Occidental ♇	5	72.3	13	27.8	18	40.1
All	*24*	*60.3*	*23*	*43.2*	*47*	*51.9*
Waxing ☽	14	64.6	12	37.7	26	52.2
Waning ☽	10	54.2	11	49.3	21	46.7

Examples of happenings in the sample the year that Pluto came to the Moon:
Oriental Pluto to the Moon in the day: his work is criticized; parents die; loses his job; his theory revolutionizes physics; intense affair; learns to depend on his own intuition; disbands his navy; rejected; retires; very ill from bathing in ice water; convalescing.
Occidental Pluto to the Moon in the day: receives large inheritance on his sister's death; moves.
Oriental Pluto to the Moon at night: prostate surgery; drives across USA; receives a substantial sum for lecturing; father becomes company president; the Altar of Peace is dedicated in Rome; works as a shop clerk; honored.
Occidental Pluto to the Moon at night: loses election; swollen leg; goes into seclusion; honored; fails exams; purchases a village store; enlists in the army; goes into hiding; resigns; upset when she is criticized.

Pluto directed to Mercury

(37% positive years)

This can be a very difficult year. Choices must be made. Finances can suffer and most projects are in danger of failing. It can be a year of persuasion, of trying to get others to act in ways that the individual wants them to. Politicians and writers employed in the advertising industry can benefit now. The individual may become preoccupied with news, possibly confidential, that he receives; it may have shocked him and could tempt him to try to escape his obligations.

Based on what we see in the sample, people born at night with an oriental Pluto are likely to experience particularly difficult times under this direction. Despite the few observations, this result is statistically significant.

Table ♀-8:   ♀ to ☿: % Positive Years

Planets relative to the ☉	Day birth		Night birth		All	
	N	% Positive	N	% Positive	N	% Positive
Oriental ♀	19	42.8	9	**10.0****	28	**32.3***
Occidental ♀	4	45.2	9	50.2	13	48.7
All	*23*	*43.2*	*18*	*30.1*	*41*	*37.5*
Oriental ☿	12	52.7	9	30.1	21	43.1
Occidental ☿	11	32.9	9	30.1	20	31.6

Examples of happenings in the sample the year that Pluto came to Mercury:
Oriental Pluto to Mercury in the day: war starts; qualifies professionally; a time of transition; midlife crisis; completely helpless; in love; physical collapse; she is unpopular; cuts expenditures; fasting; in poverty & gloom; scandal; excess display of remorse; kills a friend in a drunken quarrel; founds cities.
Occidental Pluto to Mercury in the day: acts of bravado; his father is away from home.
Oriental Pluto to Mercury at night: uncle dies; idle, not knowing what to do; joins the Communist Party, "the most neurotic act in my life"; takes mescaline; loses money on stock market; father's business is indicted by government; cruel surprises.
Occidental Pluto to Mercury at night: loses his patronage; his speeches inspire the nation; immensely busy; resigns; moves; studying; becomes prime minister.

Pluto directed to Venus

(42% positive years)

This may not be the easiest of years. The individual may be tempted to try to escape from the dull worries of everyday life through a new romantic interest. A stranger may seek his friendship. A romantic invitation may be received from someone he never suspected of having an interest in him. Existing relationships are disrupted. The native may become utterly fascinated by this new relationship and this can create stresses and strains with those who have stood by him in the past. His affections are changing their direction. A new child, who grabs everyone's attention, may be born into the family.

Table ♀-10:   **♇ to ♀: % Positive Years**

Planets relative to the ☉	Day birth		Night birth		All	
	N	% Positive	N	% Positive	N	% Positive
Oriental ♇	16	50.8	9	20.1	25	39.8
Occidental ♇	5	72.3	13	34.8	18	45.2
All	*21*	*56.0*	*22*	*28.8*	*43*	*42.0*
Oriental ♀	11	49.3	6	30.1	17	42.6
Occidental ♀	10	63.3	16	28.2	26	41.8

None of the values in Table ♀-10 are statistically significant.

Examples of happenings in my sample the year that Pluto came to Venus:
Oriental Pluto to Venus in the day: *father dies; brother wins Olympic medal; he is confronted with the choice of continuing his academic career or following the demands of his inner self; breakdown in his health forces him to give up his job; great financial panic; becomes a full-time pastor; challenges the fraudulent appeal of consensus; first meets her great friend.*
Occidental Pluto to Venus in the day: *first experience of being in hospital; siblings born; studying; graduates; becomes king on the death of his mother.*
Oriental Pluto to Venus at night: *relief following crisis awakens a state of euphoria; her lover leaves her; meets his future wife; emotional crisis; appendicitis; daughter is ill; coalition collapses; wins awards.*
Occidental Pluto to Venus at night: *eating little; sells his estate; distributing her love; stock market losses; tries to obtain patronage; re-elected; row with his son; his wife dies; travels.*

Pluto directed to Mars
(50% positive years)

Power struggles can occur this year. The strong energy the individual possesses now is likely to attract others with similar strong energies, and conflicts can occur. Situations can occur in which he may learn that he doesn't need to be right all of the time, that he can allow himself to be vulnerable without losing the love and respect of others. Even so, wives may leave husbands, and children may run away from home. This could be a good time for planning and organizing new concepts or for increasing the productivity of existing projects.

Table ♀-11:

♀ to ♂: % Positive Years

Planets relative to the ☉	Day birth		Night birth		All	
	N	% Positive	N	% Positive	N	% Positive
Oriental ♀	12	60.3	18	55.2	30	57.3
Occidental ♀	13	48.6	9	30.1	22	41.1
All	*25*	*54.2*	*27*	*46.9*	*52*	*50.5*
Oriental ♂	10	45.2	15	36.2	25	39.8
Occidental ♂	15	60.3	12	60.3	27	60.3

None of the values in Table ♀-11 are significant.

Examples of happenings in my sample the year that Pluto came to Mars:
Oriental Pluto to Mars in the day: *experiments confirm his atomic theory; ill; tension; depressed; a series of catastrophes; at the peak of his fame; honored; travels; to college; borrows money; marries; his sweetheart marries another; retires; works overseas; abandons experiment after it is ridiculed.*
Occidental Pluto to Mars in the day: *father returns after 6-year absence in army; arrested & on trial; decides he needs a philosophy of life; her lover has cancer; brother has TB; wins election; friends die; not allowed to travel abroad; reforming the navy.*
Oriental Pluto to Mars at night: *motionless on his back for six weeks; newspapers report his death; his eye is restored to health; alarmed by his failing writing ability; nearly drowns; in prison in solitary confinement; participates in 9-month-long trial; has a growing sense of desolation; marries; he is ridiculed; arrested for debt; released from insane asylum; moves; concentrates on his work.*
Occidental Pluto to Mars at night: *many defeats; severe depression; leaves college after just three months; punished for lying; mother dies.*

Pluto directed to Jupiter
(54% positive years)

This should be a prosperous year in which the individual is rewarded for past efforts. His progress may be spectacular. He will want to achieve, to improve his life, to better himself, and events now can provide the impetus and opportunity for doing so. The separation or the departure of a key member of the family may occur; it is unlikely to be a trivial leave-taking. The loss may create a major change in the family's future interaction and development, and bring a sense of freedom and relief.

If either planet is badly afflicted there can be a loss of property and social standing. Conflicts with those in authority may occur; these become more likely should the individual wish to achieve his ambitions by taking short cuts.

Table ♀-12:   **♀ to ♃: % Positive Years**

Planets relative to the ☉	Day birth		Night birth		All	
	N	% Positive	N	% Positive	N	% Positive
Oriental ♀	16	62.2	6	75.3	22	65.7
Occidental ♀	6	45.2	12	37.7	18	40.1
All	*22*	*57.5*	*18*	*50.3*	*40*	*54.2*
Oriental ♃	7	64.6	7	38.8	14	51.6
Occidental ♃	15	54.2	11	57.5	26	55.6

In the sample, even with the few observations involved, we see that oriental Pluto was associated with more positive years than was occidental Pluto.

Examples of happenings in the sample the year that Pluto came to Jupiter:
Oriental Pluto to Jupiter in the day: *his paper is the birth of atomic physics; onset of TB; honors; promoted; several near-fatal accidents; first sexual experience, with a prostitute; two affairs; much indecision; major victories; studies astrology; sells his house; teaching; touring.*
Occidental Pluto to Jupiter in the day: *discovers the quantum of action & revolutionizes physics; mother dies; hospitalized; moves; goes to a new school.*
Oriental Pluto to Jupiter at night: *retires; buys his first computer; works in his mother's store; deaths in the family; violent struggle of wills; to be a Protestant or a Catholic?*
Occidental Pluto to Jupiter at night: *defends others; he is completely changed; he perfidiously turns on his mentor; has an a government position after five years in limbo; forced to leave office; periods of extreme pain; away at school; in love; first sees his future home; brother dies; a year of setbacks.*

Pluto directed to Saturn

(32% positive years)

This will be a very difficult year for just about everybody. Anyone achieving success now will do so only after a hard struggle. The individual will have fewer resources available, less help from friends and family. Favors will be hard to come by; others will reject his requests, and there can be showdowns and clashes, misunderstandings that could lead to the opening up of necessary truths. He may recognize his own limitations and be forced to cope with unavoidable failures and unwanted burdens, more responsibilities than he can deal with, and as a result his freedom of movement and action is likely to be severely constrained. Under this direction children can be separated from their parents. They may go away to boarding school, or become refugees in a time of war, sent away into the country to avoid their city's bombing. They will be forced to grow up and become self-responsible much earlier than expected. The individual may become an unwelcome guest in the home of strangers, an unwitting target for the violence of others. Possessions are lost this year, and there is the danger of broken arms and legs.

Table ♀-13: **♀ to ♄: % Positive Years**

Planets relative to the ☉	Day birth		Night birth		All	
	N	% Positive	N	% Positive	N	% Positive
Oriental ♀	26	38.2	11	41.1	37	39.1
Occidental ♀	5	36.2	11	8.1**	16	17.0**
All	*31*	*37.9*	*22*	*24.7***	*53*	*32.4***
Oriental ♄	16	28.2	11	24.7	27	26.8**
Occidental ♄	15	48.2	11	24.7	26	38.2

Those people who were born during the night with an occidental Pluto are likely to experience especially great difficulties this year.

Examples of happenings in my sample the year that Pluto came to Saturn:
Oriental Pluto to Saturn in the day: children born; parents/friends die; retires due to ill health; unexploded bomb on his porch; graduates; awarded honorary degree; persecuted for pacifism; love affair; depressed; excessive work; jealousy; finds his true vocation as a revolutionary; evacuated; his horse dies; he is forced to retreat.
Occidental Pluto to Saturn in the day: his son is arrested for drugs; studies logic; causes death of ex-wife; her husband dies; loses fight with local government; wins comeback fight.
Oriental Pluto to Saturn at night: deaths; grief; proposes the abolition of slavery; ship disaster; sees her son for first time in nine years; works as a store clerk; works overseas; writings published; father has an operation.
Occidental Pluto to Saturn at night: arrested for treason; partner dies; final rupture with friend; heavy debts; much writing; starting to feel his age; humiliated; emergency surgery; bronchitis; cerebral hemorrhage.

Pluto directed to Uranus

(59% positive years)

There are likely to be sudden drastic changes in the world in which the individual is living. And the incidence with which such changes occur may even appear to speed up as the year progresses. New and radically different situations may present themselves, new conditions that the individual will need to assimilate into his life. Things are not at all the same as they were. His health is not as it was. The family is changing. Friends and partners are leaving, separations occur. Unexpected events are likely to happen that emphasize just how much the individual is alone in the world, and how imperative it is that he act and be innovative, taking the necessary steps to becoming completely self-reliant.

Table ♀-14:   **♀ to ♅: % Positive Years**

Planets relative to the ☉	Day birth		Night birth		All	
	N	% Positive	N	% Positive	N	% Positive
Oriental ♀	18	60.3	12	75.3	30	**66.3***
Occidental ♀	4	67.8	12	37.7	16	45.2
All	*22*	*61.7*	*24*	*56.5*	*46*	*59.0*
Oriental ♅	8	67.8	13	55.6	21	60.3
Occidental ♅	14	58.1	11	57.5	25	57.9

Those people in my sample who were born during the night with an occidental Pluto had the most problems this year. Otherwise this was a positive year for most people.

Examples of happenings in my sample the year that Pluto came to Uranus:
Oriental Pluto to Uranus in the day: *wins Pulitzer Prize; breaks with his lover; arrested & exiled; razes a city; factory where he works closes; converts a Rolls Royce into a pick-up truck; defeated; imprisoned; humiliated; moves; earns PhD; wonderful summer; first visits USA.*
Occidental Pluto to Uranus in the day: *insane & paralyzed; first sex; first visit home in six years.*
Oriental Pluto to Uranus at night: *lectures overseas; brother's suicide; working for abolition of slavery; non-stop work; travels; kills cat; father deprives family of all assets; promoted; successful elections; translating; mother dies.*
Occidental Pluto to Uranus at night: *deaths; pneumonia; very tired; elected; avoiding friends; becomes increasingly secretive; qualifies as a Qualified Horary Practitioner; moves.*

Pluto directed to Neptune

(47% positive years)

A person's life may suddenly and inexplicably get out of control this year. He may feel he no longer has any say in what is happening to him. At the same time there is likely to be a degree of disillusionment, which can change how he perceives reality. People the individual trusted in the past he now might find are unreliable. Friends and lovers may reject him. He can become obsessed with an idea or tormented over a decision he must make. There is a certain degree of unreality about much that happens this year and the individual will need to remain calm and flexible if he is to survive it without undue damage to his resources or reputation.

Table ♇-6:   **♇ to ♆: % Positive Years**

Planets relative to the ☉	Day birth		Night birth		All	
	N	% Positive	N	% Positive	N	% Positive
Oriental ♇	21	60.3	9	30.1	30	51.3
Occidental ♇	3	60.3	13	34.8	16	39.6
All	*24*	*60.3*	*22*	*32.9*	*46*	*47.2*
oriental ♆	18	55.2	8	33.9	26	48.6
occidental ♆	6	75.3	14	32.3	20	45.2

There is a large difference in Table ♇-6 between day and night births, but the numbers involved are really too few for this to be relied upon

Examples of happenings in my sample the year that Pluto came to Neptune:
Oriental Pluto to Neptune in the day: *has a terrible feeling of impotence; advocates self-sufficiency; travels; buys a farm/house; founds a city; stabbed in his chest; conceives the idea of the universal brotherhood of men; lonely; lethargic; bitterly cynical.*
Occidental Pluto to Neptune in the day: *frequently in trouble at school; emigrates; lecturing; book published.*
Oriental Pluto to Neptune at night: *falsely accused; forced to move; breaks with her lover; becoming an alcoholic; swaying between Catholicism & Atheism; feels abandoned; death.*
Occidental Pluto to Neptune at night: *father dies; parents separate; daughter marries; badly in debt; goes on a cruise; learns to dance; has a life-threatening ulcer on a kidney; first time on a plane; ignored by her lover; her dog dies; promoted; re-elected; worries.*

Winston Churchill's Pluto-Ruled Decan

Pluto rises in Taurus: Winston Spencer Churchill is not yet Britain's prime minister when Pluto takes over his decan in 1934. Pluto is retrograding in Taurus, opposite Mercury and square to Uranus. Mercury rules his septenary and this year it has come to Saturn in Aquarius[1]. Churchill is sixty years old; he is a member of parliament but a Cassandra out of favor with his party, considered to be 'in the evening of his days' and becoming to be regarded as *passé*, at least by the less perceptive. His speeches of warning this year concentrate upon the threat of German air superiority; he speaks of London being 'the greatest target in the world, a kind of tremendous, fat, valuable cow tied up to attract the beast of prey'. He has recently completed his autobiography, *My Life*. It is published and enjoys good sales. This year, his wife

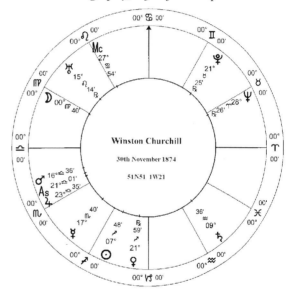

being away on a six-month cruise to South-East Asia, he seems more morose than usual. He is re-elected into parliament and is telling everyone, whether they listen or not, that "Herr Hitler is not to be trusted". Italy invades Abyssinia, and there is a sense of immanent change. This is a junction year for Churchill. He will leave it in a different direction from how he was proceeding when it began. He had hoped to be brought back into the government but is forced to appreciate that this is more difficult than he had first believed. He had earlier seemed more eager to shock the House of Commons than to persuade it, but now he becomes more concerned to broaden his appeal and, without abating his central message that Britain needs to re-arm, does so in a way that embraces those whose hopes are concentrated on the League of Nations and collective security. He opposes the Anglo-German Naval Treaty, which allows Hitler to build up to 35% of British strength.

Pluto directed to Neptune in Aries: Pluto arrives at Neptune in 1935. Churchill is sixty-one years old. The septenary ruler Mercury has come to Venus in Sagittarius, a direction that, because Mercury has come to a sign in which it is in detriment, may involve him in a

---

[1] The chart I use for Churchill has Jupiter as the first planet to rise after his birth. This is the result of my rectification, which was described in Chapter 3.

difficult position involving romance. He is vacationing in Marrakech, but the death of King George V brings him back to London to write a highly paid 4,000-word survey of the reign for a newspaper. He is writing a biography, *Marlborough*. He lectures in Paris, and is upset by the compliant acceptance of Hitler's occupation of the Rhineland. The Spanish Civil War starts. His daughter Diana marries. He is aware of the infatuation of the new king Edward VIII with Mrs. Wallis Simpson and the potential crisis his willfulness and her ambition could bring about, even though the British press has kept this from the public.

Pluto directed to Saturn in Aquarius: Winston Churchill has his occidental Pluto on his Saturn in 1936 when he is sixty-two years old. Septenary Mercury is still in Sagittarius, and has come to his nocturnal Sun, a direction likely to place him in difficult situations

involving matters indicated by the Sun, by tradition the significator of a country's ruler. And so it happens. He is King Edward VIII's advisor at the time the king abdicates the throne. Other members of the House of Commons are overwhelmingly against Churchill's attitude in the matter, and he is humiliated. Otherwise it is a quiet year, the final one of superficial peace, not a satisfactory period for Churchill other than for his writing. During the year he writes sixty-four articles, well over one a week. At the same time he is working on the final volume of *Marlborough* and on *Great Contemporaries*. He is getting bored by his life of semi-retirement and he is coming to feel his age.

Pluto directed to Venus in Sagittarius: Winston Churchill's Pluto comes to its dispositor in 1937 when he is sixty-three years old. This is the year that his nocturnal Sagittarian Sun begins to rule the septenary. He has large financial losses on the New York Stock Exchange and is forced to place his house on the market. A friend assumes these losses. *Arms and the Covenant* is published. He has a row with his son Randolph. He cancels a US speaking tour, paying a substantial penalty, but frequently visits France. He starts writing his *History of the English Speaking Peoples*. *Marlborough* is published. Germany occupies Austria. He is experiencing frequent moods of impotence and gloom. Neville Chamberlain, the British prime minister, meets with Hitler at Berchtesgarten. Churchill assails Chamberlain's 'peace in our time' speech and as a result has a major problem with his constituents. Nevertheless he increases his campaigning against appeasement. The Czechoslovakian crisis prompts him to declare, "This is only the first sip, the very foretaste of a bitter cup that will be proffered to us year by year unless, by a supreme recovery of moral health and martial vigor, we rise again and take our stand for freedom as in the olden times."

Pluto directed to the Sun in Sagittarius: Winston Churchill's Pluto gets to his Sun in November 1938 when he is sixty-four years old. In his septenary the Sun has come to

Mercury in Scorpio. The emphasis this year is clearly on his Sagittarian Sun. He is lonely; his wife is away for three months on a long cruise. Germany contemptuously occupies Czechoslovakia and Italy invades first Abyssinia and then Albania. Newspapers start to demand his inclusion in the Cabinet. He briefly works on his *History of the English-Speaking Peoples* but these are his last months of literary and peaceful life. Germany invades Poland and Great Britain responds by declaring war on Germany. Churchill is immediately offered a place in the War Cabinet and becomes First Lord of the Admiralty where now to his delight he has real executive power. He is extremely busy, filled with excitement and energy, amazing others at the volume of work and the long hours he toils. He is happy when his son Randolph marries. He circumspectly rejects his former king's attempt to involve him in a dispute with his sovereign brother.

Pluto directed to Mercury in Scorpio: Pluto comes to Churchill's Mercury in Scorpio in November 1939. His septenary Sun is on his Jupiter in Libra. Jupiter is the Sun's dispositor, but Libra is a sign in which the Sun is weakened and unwelcome. He is sixty-five years old. The combination of Pluto-Mercury and Sun-Jupiter explains much of what occurs in this memorable year. The first dramatic naval encounter of the war occurs with the destruction of the *Graf Spee* battleship off the coast of Uruguay. He is losing fights within the Cabinet and with the French concerning the conduct of the war. He organizes the ill fated and poorly executed Norwegian campaign—Narvik, the source of Germany's iron ore shipments, is captured but has to be evacuated ten days later. Chamberlain loses the confidence of parliament and Churchill becomes prime minister in the most perilous circumstances in which any PM ever took office. Hitler launches his full offensive against the West, terminating the so-called Phony War by invading Holland, Belgium and France. Churchill visits France several times. France collapses and the defeated British army is evacuated at Dunkirk. He wins an intense battle in the War Cabinet against the defeatist Lord Halifax, his Foreign Secretary. In this fateful summer the climax of his whole life is measured out and given shape by his speeches as he inspires the nation. France surrenders. He has the French fleet crippled to ensure it does not fall into German hands. Victory in the Battle of Britain halts Hitler's dreams of invasion. London is being regularly bombed in the nightly blitz. A welcome breakthrough occurs with the acquisition of an Enigma coding machine, now (as predicted by the direction of Pluto to Mercury) he will soon be able to secretly learn of Germany's plans. Many losses occur at sea. He is immensely busy all year, constantly initiating.

Year starts	Septenary	Decan
11/1938	☉☿	♇☉
11/1939	☉♃	♇☿
11/1940	☉♂	♇♃
11/1941	☉☽	♇♂
11/1942	☉♄	♇☽
11/1943	☉♀	♇♅

Between November 1938 and November 1943, a key period in his country's future, the planet the septenary ruler comes to is the one the decan ruler will meet the following year. It is a fated period, each year building on the previous one.

Pluto directed to Jupiter in Libra: In November 1940 Churchill is sixty-six years old. The septenary Sun is on his Mars in Libra, a direction that suggests the year will be neither peaceful nor successful. There are many visits to different parts of Britain to see the bomb damage. He is delighted when he learns that the Italians have been kicked out of Egypt. It is the first land victory of the war. However this is mostly a year of setbacks: Germany invades Greece and Yugoslavia with the resulting humiliating evacuations of British troops from Greece and Crete; Rommel defeats the British in the North African desert war; HMS Hood and the Bismarck are sunk after an epic sea battle; and Germany attacks the Soviet Union. He flies to Newfoundland for his first meeting with Roosevelt. This is the year when Churchill starts using the V-sign.

Pluto directed to Mars in Libra: Churchill's Pluto comes to his Mars in November 1941. He is sixty-seven years old. The Sun his septenary ruler is on his 12th house Moon in Virgo. He is overjoyed when the Japanese attack Pearl Harbor, which act of aggression forces the USA into the war. Japan commands every ocean except the Atlantic. Hong Kong is lost. The Japanese advance unopposed through British territories in South East Asia. Singapore is lost. Churchill is rapidly losing confidence in the fighting spirit of the British army. Tobruk is surrendered to Rommel. In the House of Commons he manages to beat back a vote of no confidence on how he is handling the war. He twice visits the USA, and also visits Egypt and Russia. His year ends with the Battle of El Alamein, which victory marks the turning of the war. He has a mild heart attack.

Pluto directed to the Moon in Virgo: Churchill's Pluto arrives at his waning Moon in November 1942. The same year his septenary Sun comes to his Saturn in Aquarius, where the Sun is in detriment. He is sixty-eight years old. The heroic phase of his wartime leadership is ending now. He meets Stalin for the first time. The Russians destroy the German army at Stalingrad. There is much traveling this year. He attends a conference in Casablanca, where he falls ill with pneumonia: thirty-one days of illness and convalescence. He then flies to the USA and Canada, and then on to Algiers to celebrate clearing the enemy out of North Africa. Sicily is invaded. He goes to Quebec to confer with Roosevelt. Italy surrenders. He receives an honorary degree at Harvard, and then goes on to Cairo and Tehran to meet with Roosevelt and Stalin. He loses his voice; he is exhausted. It has been a very restless year.

Pluto directed to Uranus in Leo: Winston Churchill is aged sixty-nine in 1943. It is the final year of both his Pluto-ruled decan and his Sun-ruled septenary. Pluto is on his Uranus. The septenary Sun has come to his Venus in Sagittarius. Next year Uranus and Venus will take over the respective rulerships. The year ends an important phase in Churchill's life. He is in Tehran and goes on to Cairo and Tunis. He again catches pneumonia and is very ill, convalescing in Marrakech. There is much less travel this year than in the previous one. The Anzio landing occurs, forty miles south of Rome. He is very tired and is worried about the Soviets' intentions after the war; aware that the USA will not support him against the

USSR; aware also that he is not the man he had been, physically or mentally. The Normandy invasion occurs. V-1 rockets start exploding over London. The even more frightening and destructive V-2 rockets follow them. He disagrees with Roosevelt over invading the South of France. He visits Italy, and then goes on to Russia where he and Stalin split up Eastern Europe.

Uranus begins to rule Churchill's decan the following year.

The Pluto-ruled Decan of Alexander the Great

The Pluto-ruled decan covers Alexander the Great's twenties, his years of conquest. His oriental Pluto is in Aries, the sign in which it appears to be strongest. It is opposed by a waxing Moon in Libra, and squared by the Cancer Sun. The Sun is elevated in the 10th house. The Moon has two key mutual reception, with Saturn by exaltation and with Venus by rulership. Venus herself is conjunct the royal star *Regulus*.

Pluto rises in Aries: Pluto becomes Alexander's decan ruler in July 336 BC, when he is twenty years old. Mars in its final year as the septenary ruler is at its dispositor, the elevated Mercury in Cancer. The direction of Mars to a planet in Cancer invariably indicates a time in which the individual encounters danger. His father is assassinated. Alexander is acclaimed by the army and succeeds his father as king without opposition. He then seeks out and executes the princes of Lyncetis, who are thought to have been behind his father's murder, along with all possible rivals and those who oppose him. All of the lands that his father had conquered rise up in revolt. Alexander is sur-rounded by many dangers. He marches south and defeats Thessaly. The other cities then do him homage. At an assembly of the Greek League in Corinth he is appointed generalissimo for the forthcoming invasion of Asia that his father had been planning. The Pythian priestess proclaims him 'Invincible'. He defeats the Triballi, then the Getae and Illyrians.

Alexander the Great

22nd July 356 BC

40N43 22E35

321

Pluto directed to Uranus in Capricorn: After assuming control of the decan Pluto comes first to Uranus. Mercury becomes the septenary ruler; it is located close to Alexander's Cancer Midheaven. There are rumors of the young king's death. Athens and Thebes with Persian support combine against him. He razes the city of Thebes, killing 6,000 and selling all of the survivors into slavery. Athens immediately submits. Having firmly secured Greece, he crosses the Dardanelles into Asia with his army. He visits Ilium (Troy). He defeats Mennon of Rhodes and the Persian army—this is the first of his four major victories.

Pluto directed to the Moon in Libra: Alexander is twenty-two years old in 334 BC. In the decan Pluto has arrived at his waxing Moon. If Pluto is indeed the ruler of Aries then Libra is its detriment, and this direction to the Moon could endanger his health. With Mercury at his Geminian Mars in the septenary, his military decisions should be effective. Appropriately for Pluto coming to the Moon, he disbands his navy and announces that he will defeat the Persian fleet on land by occupying all of the coastal cities. He conquers Western Asia, and cuts the Gordian Knot. He becomes ill with a fever, very sick from bathing in ice water.

Pluto directed to Jupiter in Virgo: In 333 BC Pluto comes to Alexander's Jupiter in Virgo. He is now twenty-three years old. Septenary Mercury is on his Saturn in Taurus. He routs the Persian army at the Pinarus River, with the Persian ruler Darius fleeing. Alexander then marches south into Syria, captures Damascus, and continues advancing until he reaches Egypt. He again defeats the Persians at the Battle of Issus, which is considered to be his second major victory. He lays siege to Tyre.

 Pluto directed to Neptune in Virgo: In 332 BC twenty-four years old Alexander has Pluto on his Neptune. Septenary Mercury is on his Libran Moon, its dispositor. He storms Tyre, which is considered to be his greatest military achievement. He now holds all Persian ports, giving him absolute command of the eastern Mediterranean and making Macedonia the greatest naval power in the world. He captures Egypt, sacrifices to the sacred Egyptian bull, Apis (or Hapi), and is crowned with the traditional double crown of the pharaohs. He founds the city of Alexandria, which will become the greatest city of the ancient world, and sends an expedition to discover the causes of the annual flooding of the Nile. He visits the oracle of the god Amon where he is saluted as the Son of Zeus, which salutation influences his thoughts and ambitions ever afterward. He is wounded at Gaza. He conceives the idea of the universal brotherhood of men—an idea that will become commonplace in later centuries but at the time is unique, it has been described as possibly the most important intellectual event in the history of the world. He then moves into Mesopotamia.

Pluto directed to Venus in Cancer: Alexander is twenty-five in July of 331 BC. Pluto is on his Venus, and his septenary ruler Mercury is in a powerful place, on his Jupiter in Virgo. He defeats the Persians at the Battle of Arbela, which has been called the most epoch-making of all of the decisive battles of the western world. He occupies Babylon, and then goes to Persepolis and ceremoniously burns down the palace of Xerxes, following a drunken frolic inspired by an Athenian courtesan. He marches into Media and captures its capital.

Pluto directed to the Sun in Cancer: Pluto comes to Alexander's Sun, the same year that septenary Mercury is on his Venus, also in Cancer. He is twenty-six years old. He learns that his opponent, Darius the Persian ruler, has been assassinated and buries him with honors. Alexander is now Lord of Asia, the High King of the Persian Empire. He founds cities. An alleged plot against his life enables him to ruthlessly destroy his second-in-command's family and adherents. Although this strengthens his position, it excites widespread horror. He crosses the mountains into Afghanistan.

Pluto directed to Mercury in Cancer: Pluto comes to Mercury his septenary ruler in 329 BC when Alexander is twenty-seven years old. Septenary Mercury has come to his Sun in Cancer. He defeats a revolt in Bactria. There are food shortages. He defeats the Scythians. In a drunken quarrel, he murders Cleitus, one of his most trusted commanders. When he sobers up afterwards he deeply regrets his deed. His excessive display of remorse leads the army to pass a decree convicting Cleitus posthumously of treason. This event marks a step in his progress towards Eastern absolutism (shown in the septenary by Mercury meeting the Sun, the ruler of the next septenary), and this growing attitude finds its outward expression in his use of Persian royal dress. He founds more cities. Sogdiana is in revolt led by Spitamenes, who is the most determined opponent he ever faces.

Pluto directed to Mars in Gemini: Pluto has come to its dispositor in 328 BC the year the Sun takes over his septenary. He finally defeats Spitamenes. He marries Roxana, the daughter of Oxyartes, whom he also defeats. He is in Bactria. He attempts to impose Persian court ceremonial, involving prostration by anyone entering his presence, but the army decides this implies an act of worship (the Sun now rules his septenary) and that it would be intolerable before a man. Their laughter causes his experiment to founder and he abandons it. He has Arisotle's nephew executed, which causes much resentment.

Pluto directed to Saturn in Taurus: The final year of Pluto's rulership of Alexander's decan is 327 BC as it comes to Saturn. He is now twenty-nine. The septenary Sun is directed to the elevated Mercury in Cancer. He enters India through the Khyber Pass, and wins his last great battle on the bank of Hydaspes (modern Jhelum). His horse dies. He founds two cities. His army mutinies and refuses to go further into India in the tropical rain. He agrees to return to Macedonia and turns back.

The ending of Alexander's Pluto-ruled decan also marks the ending of his years of conquest. He fails to return to Macedonia, dying instead three years later on the homeward journey in 324 BC at the age of thirty-two (the decan ruler Saturn is then directed to Uranus in Capricorn, the Sun is on the Libran Moon in the septenary).

323

Chapter 16

Ruler Pairs

When the principle of the decan is blended with that of the septenary
and ten times seven is reached,
then man is released from all tasks
and dedicated to the enjoyment of happiness.

—Iamblichus, c250-c330

Ages	Number of years	Appropriate Rising Sequence	
		septenary ruler	*decan ruler*
0 - 6	7	1	1
7 - 9	3	2	1
10 - 13	4	2	2
14 - 19	6	3	2
20	1	3	3
21 - 27	7	4	3
28 - 29	2	5	3
30 - 34	5	5	4
35 - 39	5	6	4
40 - 41	2	6	5
42 - 48	7	7	5
49	1	1	5
50 – 55	6	1	6
56 - 59	4	2	6
60 - 62	3	2	7
63 - 69	7	3	7
70 - 76	7	4	8
77 - 79	3	5	8
80 - 83	4	5	9
84 - 89	6	6	9
90	1	6	10
91 – 94	4	7	10
95 - 97	3	7	10
98 - 99	2	1	10

An individual's focus, his direction in life, tends to alter whenever a new planet rises to the ascendant and takes over control of the life. In the decan this change of direction occurs every ten years; in the septenary it does so every seven years. Yet, because ten is not a multiple of seven, the interval between successive changes is quite irregular. As the accompanying table shows, a person who lives to the age of ninety-nine will experience 24 such changes.

There are just two times in a person's life, at birth and at age seventy, as the Neo-Platonist Iamblichus noted nearly two thousand years ago, when both the rulers of the decan and the septenary change in the same year. At all other times, the coming to the ascendant of a new ruling planet by one of the two methods occurs when the other ruling planet is already embedded in the person's life.

One might assume therefore that when such a change occurs the direction in which the in-place ruler wants to lead the individual, having previously been forced to play second fiddle to an earlier ruler, might now start to predominate in the life.

This is not, however, what appears to happen. The two rulers do not act completely in isolation. Yes, the rulers are

Number of years	Frequency	Cumulative Years
1	3	3
2	3	6
3	4	12
4	4	16
5	2	10
6	3	18
7	5	35
All	24	100

complementary. Yes, there are seven alternative worlds a person's septenary ruler will want to create, and there are ten varying directions in which that same person's decan ruler wishes him to go. And yes, there are seventy (seven tens) different paths the combined decan-septenary ruling pair intend the person to follow. However, one person's seventy is not at all the same as another person's three score and ten. Each different planetary ruler has many variations, depending on its birth sign and the natal relationship it has to the ascendant (its house) and to the other planets. The joint rulership of Mars as decan ruler when Saturn is coincidently the septenary ruler, for example, is not the same for everyone. Apart from the aspects and placement of a single planet differing from those of the same planet in another person's chart, the age at which that planet becomes the time ruler is also very meaningful. This is seen from the table on the previous page.

From the previous table we see that the mixture of changing decan and septenary rulers emphasizes the potential importance in a person's life of the three ages 20, 49 and 90, and to a lesser extent the three sets of ages, 28-29, 40-41 and 98-99. At these key ages life will appear to accelerate. What occurs in them can determine so very much about the individual's future life—although one must doubt this with age 90, 98 and 99—and this in turn relates to the planets that rule the decan and septenary in these years, and the planets to which they are directed.

A pair of planets in tight aspect at the moment of birth are usually associated with periods of intense activity, for good or ill depending on the nature of their aspect, when these two planets simultaneously rule a person's decan and septenary.

As a corollary, what might be expected from two planets in tight aspect at the moment of birth will not fully manifest itself in the life if the pair are not coincident rulers.

Each planet is colored by the aspects it has with other planets, and these aspects help or hinder the ability of the planet to manifest itself positively, but it is only the nature of the relationship between a pair of coincident rulers that is meaningful during the years that these two are joint rulers.

Although the septenary rulers repeat after age 49 they do so with different decan rulers than they had earlier. As this repetition of the septenary clearly relates to a loss of strength, both physical and mental, the planetary rulers of the associated decans (planets that are sixth and greater in the sequence of ten) must also relate to this downward trend.

% Positive for the Pairs of Time Rulers

Decan Ruler	Septenary Ruler							
	☉	☽	☿	♀	♂	♃	♄	All
☉	**34.4** *	51.3	40.0	50.7	49.5	56.9	42.9	46.0
☽	58.1	43.9	43.5	**61.8** *	58.2	**65.4** ***	38.5	52.7
☿	43.4	45.2	46.5	58.7	**63.0** *	**66.1** **	49.3	52.2
♀	48.4	52.8	52.3	62.6	47.4	**60.3** *	59.9	53.5
♂	49.5	43.3	55.3	55.5	52.1	54.2	53.8	51.2
♃	**62.3** **	54.5	47.3	54.4	53.7	55.6	45.9	51.9
♄	56.9	46.0	55.2	51.4	43.3	54.0	37.4	49.2
♅	**39.3** *	44.2	53.7	43.4	**60.3** *	55.6	**38.3** *	46.6
♆	49.3	60.3	45.2	41.3	55.2	52.5	49.0	47.3
♇	46.6	44.6	57.1	45.2	45.2	59.0	56.5	49.0
All	49.4	48.2	49.7	52.0	52.6	**58.7** ***	48.0	50.0

In the sample the greatest likelihood of positive years, expressed in percentage terms, occurred when Jupiter was the septenary ruler at the same time that Mercury ruled the decan. The least positive occurred when the Sun ruled both the septenary and decan.

Septenary ruler	Decan ruler	% Positive	Significance indicator	Diurnal or Nocturnal
Jupiter	Moon	74.8	***	Diurnal
Venus	Venus	84.0	**	Diurnal
Sun	Mars	74.7	**	Diurnal
Sun	Jupiter	70.0	**	Diurnal
Jupiter	Mercury	68.4	**	Nocturnal
Mercury	Mars	67.8	**	Diurnal
Moon	Mars	29.0	**	Nocturnal
Venus	Pluto	31.0	**	Nocturnal
Mars	Venus	31.1	**	Diurnal

Nine pairs of rulers qualify for 2 or 3 significance-indicating stars when these pairings of the two rulers are split by whether the birth was diurnal or nocturnal.

The ten pairs of rulers indicated with a * as being of interest although not statistically significant are as follows:

Septenary ruler	Decan ruler	% Positive	Significance indicator	Diurnal or Nocturnal
Venus	Moon	68.5	*	Nocturnal
Sun	Moon	67.8	*	Diurnal
Jupiter	Sun	64.9	*	Nocturnal
Saturn	Uranus	33.5	*	Diurnal
Sun	Uranus	33.9	*	Diurnal
Sun	Sun	33.9	*	Nocturnal
Venus	Neptune	33.9	*	Nocturnal
Sun	Mars	34.8	*	Nocturnal
Sun	Saturn	36.2	*	Nocturnal

Details of each of the different ruler pairings, split by whether the charts are diurnal or nocturnal, together with brief comments and examples of happenings that were observed in the sample in the combination years, follow:

Sun rules both septenary & decan.

For diurnal births this combination can occur only in very old age, when an individual is in his late seventies or older. Nocturnal births usually experience this pairing in early life, before the age of 21. For both, in the sample this was a difficult year.

Sun rules both decan & septenary	N	% Positive
Diurnal	10	36.2
Nocturnal	32	**33.9***
All	42	**34.4***

Examples of happenings to individuals with this pairing in the sample:
Diurnal: *war starts; defeated in elections; his brother dies; completes writing his autobiography; interest in UFOs; death.*
Nocturnal: *starved for first six months as mother couldn't feed her; mother/father/brother dies; brother born; father abandons the family/is found guilty to rape; mother remarries; starts school; formal education ends; sent away to school/from home to avoid the plague; apprenticed; family moves house; she dresses as a man; delivering newspapers; falls from a runaway horse; he nearly dies from malaria; hospitalized with scarlet fever.*

Both the septenary and the decan want the individual to become independent and to stand on his own feet. Several of the above examples have the individual being deprived of expected support and forced to fend for himself.

The Sun was ruling both Isabelle Eberhardt's decan and septenary the year both her brother and her mother died (see page 70); Rene Descartes' mother died; Eva Peron's father deserted the family and was then killed in a car accident; Jeddu Krishnamurti nearly died from malaria; Peter the Great as an eleven-year-old could only stand and watch as those he loved were cut to pieces by the palace guards; and the 84 year-old Emperor Franz Josef mobilized his army and began the mass slaughter known as World War One.

Sun & Moon

Sun & Moon	Sun rules septenary & Moon rules decan		Sun rules decan & Moon rules septenary	
	N	% Positive	N	% Positive
Diurnal	28	**67.8***	26	55.6
Nocturnal	28	48.5	34	47.8
All	56	58.1	60	51.3

Sun rules septenary & Moon rules decan
Diurnal: *mother/wife dies; coronation; marries; leaves his wife; daughter born; lonely; graduates; moves; his book is a best seller; conference held in his honor; promoted; elected president/to Congress; acknowledged as commanding the army; friend dies; death.*
Nocturnal: *father dies; uncle is killed by the police; her son remarries; marries; robbed by highwaymen; wins scholarship; writing; attends theological seminary; purchases a large estate; becomes prime minister/Lord Chancellor; resigns her position; accused of fraud & of being a spy; very unpopular; openly disliked; two knee operations; his health is damaged when he is forced to change his sleeping habits; severe illness; suffers great pain; death.*

Moon rules septenary & Sun rules decan
Diurnal: *marries; son/granddaughter born; honorary doctorate; her first book is published; sells his house; financial worries; overseas visits; elected president; many honors; promoted; increasingly indolent; his heir is assassinated; sister/friend dies; thrown from a horse; suicidal; death.*
Nocturnal: *father/daughter dies; uncle's death makes him rich; marries; son born; divorce; husband is ill; first job; book published; graduates; travels; accused of sedition; has his rival killed; victory in battle; attacked; hospitalized with near-fatal pneumonia; dies when his heart is pierced by the barb of stingray when filming underwater.*

There is a potential conflict between the two rulers in these years. The Sun wants the individual to rise and shine. Moon wants him to care for others. We would expect the Sun to dominate in a diurnal chart; the Moon if the person were born at night. However, that doesn't always happen. Helena Blavatsky, a nocturnal birth, was viciously accused of fraudulent production of psychic phenomena, and of being a Russian spy. Seventeen-year-old Josef Stalin, another nocturnal birth, lost his interest in poetry and priestly studies and began reading Marx. The Australian wild life expert Steve Irwin, a third nocturnal birth, died underwater when the barb of a stingray pierced his heart. Carl Jung, a diurnal birth, was concerned with the question of the psychological nature of evil, at the same time that the religious aspect was becoming magnified in his life and work.

The Sun and Moon were joint rulers when the Moon ruled Ernest Hemingway's decan, which period is described on page 115.

Sun & Mercury

Sun & Mercury	Sun rules septenary & Mercury rules decan		Sun rules decan & Mercury rules septenary	
	N	% Positive	N	% Positive
Diurnal	30	48.2	15	30.1
Nocturnal	45	40.1	37	43.9
All	75	43.4	52	40.0

Sun rules septenary & Mercury rules decan
Diurnal: *becomes a pacifist; he no longer loves his wife; wife/brother/sister/daughter/friend dies; children born; financial problems; receives trust fund; promoted; removed from his command; severely wounded; cancer of the palate; heart trouble; deep depression.*
Nocturnal: *marries; graduates; financial problems; self-employed; becomes famous; he is self-conceited; losing self-confidence; castigated by the press; blackmailed; wife/mother/father dies; concussion; very ill; ruptures his kidneys; depressed; death.*

Mercury rules septenary & Sun rules decan
Diurnal: *separates from his wife; feels helpless; heart attack; seriously ill; defeated; surgery; death.*
Nocturnal: *signs with Motown records; elected to Congress; passes exams; wins prize; at lowest ebb of his life; husband/father/mother/son/sister/daughter dies; daughter born; affairs; accused of being a spy; arrested; in prison; life on the run; sent to Siberia; goes to college; homesick; away from home; argues against free will; father is ill; malaria.*

These two bodies work fairly well together in that the Sun wants the individual to become self reliant while Mercury, in its pose as the agent of death, provides situations in which the individual is forced to stand on his own feet. The deaths of people important to the individual, those on whom he may have relied on in the past, frequently occurred when this combination was present in the sample. A prime example is the deaths of Teddy Roosevelt's wife and mother on the same day, at different locations and from different causes. Bertie Russell was inspired to start writing *Principia Mathematica;* John F. Kennedy received a $1,000,000 trust fund; the writer Colin Wilson got out of the RAF by pretending homosexuality; and Orde Wingate invaded Ethiopia, captured Addis Ababa, restored the king to his throne, and was immediately removed from his command and reduced in rank for disobeying orders.

The Sun and Mercury were joint rulers when the Sun ruled Bertrand Russell's septenary, see pages 79-80. This also occurred when Mercury ruled Carl Jung's septenary, as described on pages 139-140.

Sun & Venus

Sun & Venus	Sun rules septenary & Venus rules decan		Sun rules decan & Venus rules septenary	
	N	% Positive	N	% Positive
Diurnal	18	50.3	23	62.9
Nocturnal	25	47.0	43	44.1
All	43	48.4	66	50.7

Sun rules septenary & Venus rules decan
Diurnal: *promoted; becomes president/emperor; has a house built; works for women's suffrage; authorizes atom bombings; first publishes magazine; marries; divorce; lengthy honeymoon; son born; international business trips; launches magazine; sudden independence & wealth; father/sister/only child dies; friend drowns; mother has a stroke; alone & melancholy; discoveries; buys his first computer; promoted; loses money in mutual funds; sciatica; epileptic fit; death.*
Nocturnal: *financial difficulties; captures treasure fleet; goes into army; father is knighted; sent away to boarding school; marries; husband leaves her; son born; father/mother/wife sick; father/daughter dies; his cares & worries take a toll on him physically; pain from bladder troubles; typhoid; violent sickness; death.*

Venus rules septenary & Sun rules decan
Diurnal: *wins Nobel Prize; marries; son born; witch-hunt instigated by Catholics stops him working; he has no money; meets future wife; election success; becomes famous/Chief Justice; establishes a scholarship in his father's name; losing his hearing; sciatica; death.*
Nocturnal: *graduates; honors; his brother is assassinated; husband/father dies; survives a plane crash; elected senator; a difficult year; given a horse; has house built; tries but fails to get a divorce; his first great love marries another; marries; mother remarries; war ends; frayed nerves; overseas; exhausted; teaching; loses money in financial panic.*

The Sun wants recognition and self-improvement while Venus is concerned with love, art and relating to others. Napoleon Bonaparte remarried and went on a lengthy honeymoon, withdrawing from society and his duties; Oscar Wilde's father was knighted and appointed Surgeon Oculist to Queen Victoria; Albert Einstein, alone and melancholy following the death of his wife, spoke against the USA's aim for world superiority and the indoctrination of its people; and Teddy Roosevelt forced his brother and wife to separate, and had his brother declared insane.

The Sun and Venus were joint rulers when the Sun ruled Bertrand Russell's decan, see pages 86-87. This occurred also in one of the years in which Venus was Jeddu Krishnamurti's decan ruler, see page 171.

Sun & Mars

Sun & Mars	Sun rules septenary & Mars rules decan		Sun rules decan & Mars rules septenary	
	N	% Positive	N	% Positive
Diurnal	23	**74.7****	26	45.2
Nocturnal	39	**34.8***	38	52.4
All	62	49.5	64	49.5

Sun rules septenary & Mars rules decan
Diurnal: *twin daughters born; company merger; becomes serious about his faith; attempt on his life; brother dies/executed; his son drowns; marries; her long-lasting love affair ends; passes exams; earns his PhD; writes four papers that forever change man's view of the universe; conflict with Einstein over uncertainty; stock market crash; brain hemorrhage leaves her semi-paralyzed.*
Nocturnal: *creates large relief sculpture; coronation; becomes Pontifex Maximus; graduates; he is elected president; retires from presidency; Civil War starts; his Emancipation Proclamation frees slaves; arrested; marries; divorce; daughter born; expelled; becomes a Marxist; repairing house; stops meditating; wife/daughter/sister/mother/father dies; a thoroughly depressing time; moves; travels; angry; gallstones removed; heart attack; death.*

Mars rules septenary & Sun rules decan
Diurnal: *financial loss/panic; quarrels with his best friend; fights off attackers; husband is re-elected president; he is elected president; overseas visits; writes on sexuality; book published; teaching; marries; excommunicated; grandmother dies; exhausted; very nervous; his son's horrible death destroys his will to live; bladder infection; violent death.*
Nocturnal: *builds large telescope; fire halts his work; paranoid; son marries; collecting coins; promoted; sister/brother/son/daughter/father/mother/grandmother dies; son/brother/daughter born; overseas visits; he revels in war, victory and gore; witnesses king's execution; writes on murders; defeats invaders; husband resigns from his job; buys a company; becomes a senator; friend is assassinated; hysterectomy; double pneumonia; measles; bronchitis.*

Both rulers are of the same nature, hot and dry, and they combined well in the sample in diurnal charts when the Sun ruled the septenary, but were associated with difficult years in nocturnal charts. Mars brought violence into the lives, especially when it governed the septenary. Maximilian, the brother of Emperor Franz Josef, was executed in Mexico; Konrad Adenauer was arrested, accused of corruption; Abraham Lincoln was president during the Civil War; Sigmund Freud routed ten men, who had shouted anti-Semitic abuse, charging at them with his walking stick; and Johannes Kepler was denied the Lutheran

331

sacraments for refusing to adhere to the Formula of Concord. By contrast Charlie Chaplin first wore his tramp costume in a film and became an instant success.

The Sun and Mars were joint rulers when Mars ruled Abraham Lincoln's decan, see pages 197-198.

Sun & Jupiter

Sun & Jupiter	Sun rules septenary & Jupiter rules decan		Sun rules decan & Jupiter rules septenary	
	N	% Positive	N	% Positive
Diurnal	31	**70.0****	23	43.2
Nocturnal	43	56.8	39	**64.9***
All	74	**62.3****	62	56.9

Sun rules septenary & Jupiter rules decan
Diurnal: *decides he should become "what I myself am"; awarded Nobel Prize; wins Iron Cross; in car accident; very happy; first in his class; marriage ends; marries; honors; in love; refuses to feel inferior; starts new job; his interest in politics starts; finances improve; sells paintings; starts astrology; promoted; writing his autobiography; thigh wound; has difficulty walking; brother-in-law assassinated; wife/friend killed; death.*
Nocturnal: *first goes to USA; she goes overseas to join her lover; elected president; her father becomes king; recognized as his country's premier representative; on cover of* Time *magazine; declares war; victory; in his first film; love affair; beaten by husband; has a record salary; signs contract that will make him rich; marries; his wife leaves him; withdraws from all societies; loses court case; book published; seething paranoia; inflamed kidneys; sister/aunt dies; death.*

Jupiter rules septenary & Sun rules decan
Diurnal: *his wife leaves him; affair; attracted to a new approach to astrology; he is forced to leave the country; elected president; friendship ends; debut as a pianist; rejected by polytechnic; wife/mother/father/brother dies; death.*
Nocturnal: *away to college; falls in love; meets future wife; marries; he is an overnight success; climbing; coronation; buys house; son/daughter/grandson born; attains power; protesting; his brother is assassinated; father dies; responsible for the drowning death of a young woman; burnt by a firework.*

This combination was expected to be associated with successful years, and in general in the sample it was. The individual should be very confident and enthusiastic about all he does, never really believing he can fail. Carl Jung's stated decision following the death of his wife, to become "what I myself am", shows he was alert to the Sun's message. Many of the above examples have the individual attaining worldly success. Bertrand Russell received the Nobel Prize; John Adams was elected president; Condi Rice began working for the US government as an expert on the USSR; Jean Harlow's photo appeared on the cover of *Time* magazine; Colin Wilson became an overnight success with the publication of *The Outsider*; and Aleister Crowley fought his family for independence and won.

The Sun and Jupiter were joint rulers when the Sun ruled Bertrand Russell's septenary, see pages 82-83, and also when Jupiter ruled Arthur Young's decan, see pages 227-228.

Sun & Saturn

Sun & Saturn	Sun rules septenary & Saturn rules decan		Sun rules decan & Saturn rules septenary	
	N	% Positive	N	% Positive
Diurnal	44	53.4	31	52.5
Nocturnal	26	62.6	45	**36.2***
All	70	56.9	76	42.9

Sun rules septenary & Saturn rules decan
Diurnal: re-elected senator; marries; mother dies/has a stroke; very poor; his job is terminated; badly wanting to be independent; wins tennis championship; successful astrological predictions; landlord difficulties; under extreme stress; conscripted into army; studies music; on cover of Time *magazine; his picture is in* Look *magazine; depressed; in waterless desert; foot surgery; severely wounded; accidentally shoots himself; death.*
Nocturnal: elected president; loses election; knighted; grandson born; receives honorary doctorate; daughter marries; marries a wealthy widow; marriage is annulled; joins protest march; learns to fly; opens a tailor shop; vicious attacks on his character; his enemy dies; death.

Saturn rules septenary & Sun rules decan
Diurnal: international fame; father/mother dies; systematic self-analysis; starts a publishing company; melancholy; being slandered; depression; daughter born; divorce; marries; girl friend commits suicide; stops eating meat; abstains from alcohol; becomes president; realizing old ambitions; defeats attempted coup; teeth troubles; death.
Nocturnal: father dies; grieving for her mother; writing biography of his father; in the army; brother commits suicide/marries; her schoolgirl daughter dies in a motorcycle accident; elected prime minister; becomes an ambassador; completely severs bonds with her past; grandson born; secretly converts to the Arian religion; postulates gravity; meets future wife; marries; works as a hospital orderly; escapes an assassination attempt; cerebral spinal meningitis; death.

Both of these rulers are strongest in a diurnal chart. The Sun wants the individual to stand alone, to be recognized for his accomplishments and for who he is; Saturn demands there is a firm foundation from which future accomplishments will evolve. There is fame (*Time* and *Life* magazines, international fame) in the sample, and also some very saturnine happenings among the people in the sample: loss of job, grief, self-analysis, and abstention from meat and alcohol. John Kerry married a wealthy widow; Isaac Newton was elected president of the Royal Society; and Charles Lindbergh made the first solo flight across the Atlantic.

The Sun and Saturn were joint rulers when the Sun ruled Isabelle Eberhardt's decan, see pages 75-78, and also when Saturn ruled Adolf Hitler's septenary, see pages 251-253.

Sun & Uranus

Sun & Uranus	Sun rules septenary & Uranus rules decan	
	N	% Positive
Diurnal	40	**33.9***
Nocturnal	29	46.7
All	69	**39.3***

Sun rules septenary & Uranus rules decan
Diurnal: *promoted; daughter/son born; managing others; wife has surgery/a nervous breakdown; loses election; his mother/father/sister/lover dies; crowns himself emperor; elected governor; emigrates; writing poetry; refuses to return to school; self-imposed retirement; turns blue; stung by a stingray; collapses & is no longer sane; measles; death.*
Nocturnal: *son born; marries; sister marries; father remarries; mental conflict; he is rich; receives D.Sc; he is difficult, unpredictable & strange; mother dies; his wife is assassinated; death.*

Uranus brings a willful streak into the life that can complement the Sun's drive for independence. However, most people in the sample had difficulties with this combination. Some were provided with the opportunity to direct that things be done as they wished. Under this pair of rulers Peter Sellers was described as being "difficult, unpredictable and strange"; Napoleon Bonaparte crowned himself emperor; Ulysses Grant at age thirty-nine was promoted to Brigadier-General, won several battles and then was suspended from his command; Laurence Olivier's wife Vivien Leigh was diagnosed as a manic-depressive and then later the same year won an Oscar for her acting in *Gone with the Wind*; Jimmy Carter was elected Governor of Georgia; the astrologer Arie Mantel emigrated from Holland to South Africa; and Friedrich Nietzsche became insane.

The Sun and Uranus were joint rulers when the Sun ruled Bertrand Russell's septenary as described on pages 83-84, and when Uranus ruled Napoleon Bonaparte's septenary, refer to pages 278-279.

Sun & Neptune

Sun & Neptune	Sun rules septenary & Neptune rules decan	
	N	% Positive
Diurnal	18	55.2
Nocturnal	37	46.5
All	55	49.3

Sun rules septenary & Neptune rules decan

Diurnal: *proposes universal peace; becomes president; brother dies; kills his brother in gun accident; sister/son/daughter born; vows never to drink again; stops drinking milk; has two mistresses; his dog dies; sells his company; idle, much reading; fasts; typhoid fever; pleurisy; diagnosed with incurable cancer; receives a kidney transplant; heart attack; wounded in a duel.*
Nocturnal: *becomes president/vice president/governor; wife dies; financial problems; gets a new dog; sister born/marries/has polio; nursemaid straps him to a chair in a dark room; bullied; away to school; forced to move house; in navy; father is shipwrecked; marries; her lover is banished; meets future husband; divorce.*

The involvement of Neptune as one of the two time rulers stands out in several of the examples listed here, from the proposal of Tsar Nicholas II for universal peace, George W. Bush vowing never to drink again, and King Juan Carlos accidentally killing his brother, to Prince Charles joining the navy, Queen Anne's father being shipwrecked, and Francis Bacon being stripped of his office and imprisoned in the Tower of London. There are also associations with the Sun's rulership of the septenary, several members of the sample achieving high office, and a number of occasions in which circumstances forced the individual to stop relying on others.

Sun & Pluto

Sun & Pluto	Sun rules septenary & Pluto rules decan	
	N	% Positive
Diurnal	31	52.5
Nocturnal	35	41.3
All	66	46.6

Sun rules septenary & Pluto rules decan

Diurnal: *his discovery revolutionizes physics; in an insane asylum; affair; marries; promoted; visits USA; son/daughter born; wife/mother/sister/close friend/stepson dies; in prison; exiled; graduates; loses her job; family firm is sold; defeated; bomb is thrown onto his porch; ill, confined to bed; assassinated; death.*

Nocturnal: *becomes prime minister/senator; election defeat/victory; his speeches inspire the nation; son/daughter/grandchildren born; depression; father has an operation; affair; marries; ridiculed; retires; goes into seclusion; his army mutiny; arrested for treason; uncle/brother dies; uncle dies in fire; he nearly dies from bitter cold/from drowning; death.*

Pluto's presence is apparent in Max Planck's discovery of the quantum, which has transformed physics ever since. The effect of both Pluto and the Sun is evident in the death of Marcus Agrippa, whose brilliant generalship had so often rescued Caesar Augustus in the past. Left to rely on his own abilities, the devastating blow forced Augustus to radically change, and in doing so he became Rome's greatest emperor.

The Sun and Pluto were joint rulers when Pluto ruled Winston Churchill's decan, see pages 317-318; when the Sun ruled Bertrand Russell's septenary, see pages 80-82; and when the Sun ruled Alexander the Great's septenary at the time his army mutinied and forced him to end his conquests, as described on page 321.

Moon rules both septenary & decan

Moon	Moon rules both septenary & decan	
	N	% Positive
Diurnal	21	47.4
Nocturnal	16	39.6
All	37	43.9

Diurnal: *meets future wife & falls in love; mother & sister die in epidemic; mother/father/brother dies; father's suicide; father is convicted of murder; father leaves home; given choice of living with father or mother; brother/sister born; becomes heir to the peerage; writes on female sexuality; his books are publicly burned; her autobiography published; studies the mystery of Jewishness; studying piano; death.*

Nocturnal: *in WWI trenches; in a sordid & impermanent environment; wounded & believed dead; depressed; joins airforce; graduates; brother/sister born; grandmother dies; mother has an affair; father's song success; decides who is to be killed & have their wealth confiscated; his daughter commits suicide; acute asthma attacks; stroke; falls & breaks his thigh; bronchitis; pneumonia; thrombosis; jaundice; suicidal.*

When the Moon rules both septenary and decan there is great emphasis among the examples on home and the family, very much as we would expect.

Tsarina Alexandra, consort of the last tsar of Russia, was six years old when her mother and sister died from a diphtheria epidemic; she changed from being the girl who had been nicknamed Sunny for her warm disposition to one who rarely smiled.

337

Moon & Mercury

Moon & Mercury	Moon rules septenary & Mercury rules decan		Moon rules decan & Mercury rules septenary	
	N	% Positive	N	% Positive
Diurnal	21	51.6	52	45.2
Nocturnal	41	41.9	29	40.5
All	62	45.2	81	43.5

Moon rules septenary & Mercury rules decan
Diurnal: *commands army in war; divorce; fails to win nomination; becomes a senator; espouses pacifism; yachting; learning Spanish; his son has a mental breakdown; fears for his life; death.*
Nocturnal: *given lead billing; has much media attention; attacked by the press; marries; son born/dies; divorce; wife commits suicide; mother is paralyzed; brother/sister divorce; starts new business with her husband; she in one of the 16 out of 488 who survives shipwreck; loses her job; wins election; promoted; becomes a senator; writes autobiography; arrested; moves house; his horse wins the Grand National; becomes a Freemason; donates a kidney to his sick brother; pleurisy; death.*

Mercury rules septenary & Moon rules decan
Diurnal: *leads 6,000-mile Long March across China; graduates; first performs before large audience; knighthood; becomes president; his son is a POW; daughter born; marries; in love; marriage ends; wife has an affair; son/daughter/mother/father dies; loses his job; conscripted into military; promoted; solitary; marooned; stops smoking; sons emigrate; a happy, creative period; writes about discontent, uneasiness & malaise; fails mathematics/French; little money; survives a plane/car crash; fascinated by psychic phenomena; falsifies reports; high blood pressure; concussion; bronchitis; jaundice; pneumonia.*
Nocturnal: *sons divorce; son/daughter born; criticized as being cold & unfeeling; promoted; defeated; mother goes insane; in love; successful prosecutions; arrested; in prison; death.*

The above includes several acts of survival: Mao Zedung leading the remnants of his battered army across China on their exhausting 6,000-mile Long March; Helena Blavatsky's miraculous survival of a shipwreck when going to Egypt; Albert Einstein's escape from Nazi Germany; Benito Mussolini emerging unharmed from a plane crash; and Ernest Hemingway scarred and concussed after several car accidents. Members of the sample with these two rulers were often publicly criticized, one being Queen Elizabeth II on her reaction to the death of Princess Diana.

The Moon and Mercury were joint rulers when the Moon ruled Ernest Hemingway's decan, see pages 115-116. Mercury was ruling the septenary for Bob Dole, as noted on page 43, and for Carl Jung, see page 139.

Moon & Venus

Moon & Venus	Moon rules septenary & Venus rules decan		Moon rules decan & Venus rules septenary	
	N	% Positive	N	% Positive
Diurnal	35	46.5	43	56.8
Nocturnal	54	57.0	33	**68.5***
All	89	52.8	76	**61.8***

Moon rules septenary & Venus rules decan

Diurnal: *writing daily love letters; becomes a senator; builds a place where he can exist for himself alone; studies alchemy; graduates; accused of being anti-Semitic; son/daughter born; mother dies; buys house; loses election/job; captured but rescued; ill, on the verge of madness; death.*

Nocturnal: *little money; financial panic; creates calculus/the science of dynamics; wife/mentor dies; causes his son's death; disinherits his son; son/grandson born; fire destroys his house & possessions; mother's marriage ends; divorce; marries; returns home after long absence; his reputation is irreparably damaged; now he is stone deaf; pleurisy; influenza.*

Venus rules septenary & Moon rules decan

Diurnal: *receives the Nobel Prize; his affair breaks up two marriages; marries; plays Romeo; first real acting break; wife dies; brother is executed; learns to fly; works as journalist; founds a newspaper; first job; decides to specialize in psychiatry; she is increasingly unpopular; loses nomination; criticized as heartless; large gambling losses; robbed & beaten up; travels; gets a dog; orders invasion; becomes a garrulous maniac; jaundice; cystitis; lung cancer; suicide.*

Nocturnal: *publicly confesses to an affair; marries; divorce; becomes editor-in-chief/prime minister; promoted; wins election; loses party leadership; son/daughter born; emigrates; reads his own obituary; father/son/mentor dies; shop keeping; poor & in debt; depression; survives a plane crash; shell-shocked; flying fighter planes in war; to university; his daughter goes mad.*

As both rulers are feminine, nocturnal and moist, they should combine well together. When they rule simultaneously the individual should be able to easily relate to others. The much-publicized whirlwind romance of Larry Olivier and Vivien Leigh that broke up their two marriages is appropriate for the symbolism of the two rulers. Other examples include Ronald Reagan marrying Nancy; Carl Jung getting married; Sigmund Freud becoming engaged; Max Planck receiving the Nobel Prize for physics, and Charlie Chaplin having an affair and reportedly "being very happy". However, under these two rulers, Virginia Woolf, became a garrulous maniac, and was put into a nursing home, violent and screaming.

The Moon and Venus were joint rulers when Venus was the decan ruler for Samuel Pepys, see pages 173-175, and for Jeddu Krishnamurti, as described on pages 170-171.

Moon & Mars

Moon & Mars	Moon rules septenary & Mars rules decan		Moon rules decan & Mars rules septenary	
	N	% Positive	N	% Positive
Diurnal	20	63.3	30	66.3
Nocturnal	28	**29.0****	29	49.9
All	48	43.3	59	58.2

Moon rules septenary & Mars rules decan
Diurnal: *first book published; abstains from alcohol; joins the army; executes top army generals; starts war; exterminating Jews; deep depression; stage fright; resigns his position; facing total defeat; loses election; in love; marries; meets future husband; son/brother born; father/mother dies; death.*
Nocturnal: *on safari in Kenya; blind to his own longing for power; in boat wrecked on rapids; unpopular; sells his estate; has to flee the country; father dies; marries; elected to Congress; bullied; pretends insanity; boxing; shot in the chest but recovers; bad fall from a horse; hit by lightning; stroke; death.*

Mars rules septenary & Moon rules decan
Diurnal: *escapes attempted assassination; affair; father/son/friend/nephew dies; selling newspapers; marries; son/daughter/grandson born; learns how to pick pockets; start of the arms race; she is now famous & wealthy; business success; becomes president; obtains law degree; learns to play violin; appendectomy; eye infection spreads over his whole face; commits suicide.*
Nocturnal: *argues with his partner; carriage wheels run over his legs; sells house at a loss; first car; graduates; changes his job; books published; decides that God does not exist; gives away his belongings; foreign vacation; daughter born; wife/mother/son dies; depressed; hurts his knee; in pain; death.*

Emotional anxiety and impatience can be expected when the Moon and Mars jointly rule a person's life. Those born at night in the sample had very difficult times when the Moon ruled their septenary and Mars was the decan ruler. The beginning of the arms race was a great disappointment to the Danish physicist Niels Bohr who wrote an open letter to the United Nations pleading for peaceful cooperation between the atomic powers; the start of the Korean War confounded this. Teddy Roosevelt was so upset with his protégé President Taft that he decided to run against him, and in doing so he split the party and allowed Woodrow Wilson to become elected. King Hussein of Jordan had to flee from his country following an uprising in which his prime minister was assassinated. Alexander Hamilton, permanently angry that he was viewed as an alien, an outsider, acted as George Washington's ADC during the War of Independence. A sword-swinging Japanese attacked Nicholas II, the tsar escaped with a permanent scar on his forehead.

The Moon and Mars were joint rulers when the Moon was the decan ruler of Ernest Hemingway in 1950, see page 116, and Bob Dole, see page 43. Mars ruling Adolf Hitler's decan when the Moon ruled his septenary is described on pages 201-202.

Moon & Jupiter

Moon & Jupiter	Moon rules septenary & Jupiter rules decan		Moon rules decan & Jupiter rules septenary	
	N	% Positive	N	% Positive
Diurnal	33	52.1	52	**74.8***
Nocturnal	25	57.9	31	49.5
All	58	54.5	83	**65.4***

Moon rules septenary & Jupiter rules decan
Diurnal: *living the pleasant, mindless existence of a wealthy aristocrat; son/twins born; moves; very poor; son/sister dies; joins army; loses election; mother dies; successful prediction of epidemic; attacked by homosexual; researching genetics; wounded in war; multiple injuries from motorcycle accident; smallpox.*
Nocturnal: *avoids friends & distractions in order to study; foils plan to rob & kill him; joins the army; in prison; a pestering fan complicates his life; inheritance makes him rich; has no money; wife/mother/mentor dies; knighted; humiliations; marries; an idealistically happy period; accusations; first public speech; ostracized; hemorrhage; paralyzed; death.*

Jupiter rules septenary & Moon rules decan
Diurnal: *elected president/mayor/party secretary; father/brother dies; has idea of the helicopter; bullied; depressed; fascinated by war; ex-wife dies; touring in RV; rejected by polytechnic; discharged from his post; book published; starts his first job; fails exams; marries; studies overseas; graduates; renounces his citizenship & religion.*
Nocturnal: *autobiography published; elected senator; son/daughter born; defends the freedom of the press; marries; electricity experiments; his home is burgled; mugged; publishes magazine; father dies/is arrested; chronic fatigue; death.*

These two rulers combine particularly well when Jupiter rules the septenary in diurnal charts. It can be a time of important new ideas and a concern for others. Arthur Young conceived the idea of the helicopter, which he later made work, and Edward Bach gave up wealth and fame to go out into the countryside to discover his flower remedies. Ben Franklin began making electrical experiments, and Rene Descartes had a series of vivid dreams that indicated his life mission was to unify the sciences, meaning to work in mathematics. Margaret Thatcher resigned as Britain's prime minister; Josef Stalin became General Secretary of the Communist Party and then, when Lenin died, assumed control of the Soviet Union; and Samuel Pepys became Secretary of the Navy. Alexander Fleming was knighted for his discovery of penicillin, his photo appearing on the cover of *Time* magazine; and Hugh Hefner launched *Playboy* magazine.

The Moon and Jupiter were joint rulers when the Moon ruled Oscar Wilde's septenary, see pages 109-111.

Moon & Saturn

Moon & Saturn	Moon rules septenary & Saturn rules decan		Moon rules decan & Saturn rules septenary	
	N	% Positive	N	% Positive
Diurnal	36	42.7	33	41.1
Nocturnal	19	52.4	21	34.4
All	55	46.0	54	38.5

Moon rules septenary & Saturn rules decan
Diurnal: becomes president/supreme court judge/senator; promoted; marries; marriage ends abruptly; meets future wife; very lonely; nursing the wounded; son/daughter/sister/grandson born; son & daughter arrested; restricts his diet; imprisoned; passive resistance; says "Religion is collective neurosis"; exiled; agitating; burns registration cards in protest; his book outrages Christians & Jews; moves to USA; husband/wife/grandmother dies; obtains professional qualifications; hospitalized in extreme pain; appendicitis; prostate cancer; death.
Nocturnal: at the peak of fame but visibly miserable; depressed; marries; son/daughter born; abuses his son; wife & children leave him; divorce; meets future wife; father dies; father saves his life; affairs; emigrates; very happy; loses weight; naval setbacks; develops a long-lasting terror of the color purple.

Saturn rules septenary & Moon rules decan
Diurnal: fires cannons into mob, killing many; endures a Spartan course of spare diet, thin clothing & hard exercise; starts school; exiled; wins immense wealth; joins army; studying law; wins lengthy legal hearing brought by his ex-wife; his recommendation for an absence of secrecy in nuclear discoveries is ignored; promoted; his son dies; son marries; grandson born; cataracts removed; chicken pox; bladder cancer.
Nocturnal: in icy cold anger he executes his prisoners; elected president/to Congress; sadly resigns his office; divorce; marries; son/daughter born; son/father/grandmother dies; defeated; wins battle; quarrels; both of his arms are badly crushed; his wife has shingles; dropsy; stroke; death.

These are not the easiest of years. Circumstances can prompt the individual to conceal his emotions, for fear of being rejected and hurt. Peter Sellers, at the peak of fame, is said to have been visibly miserable. Astrologer John Addey, a victim of polio, was hospitalized in extreme pain. Tom Paine had run away to sea but his father chased after him and persuaded him not to sail on his intended ship, which sank soon after leaving the harbor.

Warren Harding fathered an illegitimate daughter and was elected president. Queen Victoria's husband, Prince Albert, died and this was the start of a long period of grieving. Mahatma Gandhi made a vow of permanent celibacy, restricted his diet, and created a farm commune. Niels Bohr accepted the opportunity to create an institute for theoretical physics as part of Copenhagen University. Napoleon Bonaparte became a hero overnight when he fired cannons into a Paris mob, killing many.

The Moon and Saturn were joint rulers when Saturn ruled Sir Laurence Olivier's decan, see page 255, and when Saturn ruled the Emperor Augustus Caesar's septenary, described on pages 257-258.

Moon & Uranus

Moon & Uranus	Moon rules septenary & Uranus rules decan	
	N	% Positive
Diurnal	36	40.1
Nocturnal	54	46.9
All	90	44.2

Diurnal: his mother is on trial, accused of being a witch; his mother expels him from the house; starts school; wife/mother/stepdaughter die; brother/sister born; much criticized for his military actions; moves; first meets future husband; marries; watching bull fights; victory in war; graduates; promoted; his library is confiscated; boxing; fears for his sanity; he is insane; his eyesight is worsening; cerebral hemorrhage; death.
Nocturnal: buys own house & separates from future husband; throws knife at father to defend mother; throws away his medals; coronation; arrested; learns calligraphy; employee steals from her company; marries; marriage is cancelled; separated from sick husband; son born; abortion; graduates; becomes Chancellor; goes into Navy; son/father dies; son has pneumonia; heart attack; hip replacement; death.

Life under these two time rulers tends to be volatile. Several examples of dramatic (Uranus) events involving the mother (Moon) are among the above examples. Ernest Hemingway's mother expelled him from the house; the mother of Johannes Kepler was put on trial as a witch, but freed for lack of evidence, and a year later his mother and stepdaughter died; and Josef Stalin intervened in a quarrel between his parents, and threw a knife at his father to stop him punching his mother. Mao Zedung spoke on the correct handling of contradictions among the people. Max Planck obtained a post at the University of Berlin, where he would remain for the rest of his academic life. John Aubrey was arrested and put on trial but won his case despite experiencing great opposition. Augustus Caesar exiled his granddaughter for sexual promiscuity and conspiracy.

The Moon and Uranus were joint rulers when the Moon ruled Ernest Hemingway's septenary, see pages 112-114.

Moon & Neptune

Moon & Neptune	Moon rules septenary & Neptune rules decan	
	N	% Positive
Diurnal	15	48.2
Nocturnal	12	75.3
All	27	60.3

Diurnal: *embarrassed by his parents' poverty; divorce; marries; meets future wife; honors; loses war & abdicates; carves manikin & hides it; works in brass foundry; creates a farm commune; teaching; father dies; in Scientology prison & not allowed to go home.*
Nocturnal: *tours overseas; wins scholarship & gold medal; becomes governor; studies Hatha Yoga; father is honored; her book becomes the Bible for Woman's Movement; death of two half-sisters by burning; death.*

This combination occurred infrequently in the sample. Even so several of the above examples are appropriate for the symbolism of the two ruling planets. Carl Jung, for example, wrote that he was utterly embarrassed when his parents had to seek reduced fees for his education because of their poverty—nowadays, at least in the United States, such an action by parents is normal; Kaiser Wilhelm II abdicated his throne when Germany lost the First World War; and Arthur Young took up Scientology but then found himself imprisoned by the cult and not allowed to return to the USA with his wife.

Moon & Pluto

Moon & Pluto	Moon rules septenary & Pluto rules decan	
	N	% Positive
Diurnal	37	39.1
Nocturnal	30	51.3
All	67	44.6

Diurnal: *first acts in a play; in love; experiments confirm his atomic theory; attacked by a mob; affairs; marries; sister/daughter born; goes to college; imprisoned for pacifism; financial panic; re-elected president; fails to be re-elected; his book is rejected; walking tour in the Alps; in car accident; father dies; insane & paralyzed; onset of tuberculosis; death.*

Nocturnal: loses finger in shotgun accident; fights a duel; fails to get expected promotion; writes a play; emotional crisis; dresses like a dandy; in love; marries; son born; giving people things fills her life; sells his estate; bankrupt; loses money on stock market; his interest in astrology is rekindled; writing poetry; daughter/uncle dies; buys computer; absconds to avoid arrest; stomach infection; cancer of uterus; tonsillectomy; prostatectomy; appendectomy; massive gall bladder attacks; death.

These can be difficult years. John Aubrey absconded when he believed himself in danger of being arrested for debt; Eva Peron, in constant pain and sleeping only two hours nightly, filled her life by giving people things; and Civil War hero, Ulysses S. Grant although re-elected president had to preside over great panic on Wall Street, the Credit Mobilier and Whiskey Ring scandals, and the impeachment of his Secretary of War.

Mercury rules both septenary & decan

Mercury	Mercury rules both septenary & decan	
	N	% Positive
Diurnal	6	60.3
Nocturnal	31	43.8
All	37	46.5

Diurnal: brother/sister born; grandfather becomes a senator; receives an award; death.
Nocturnal: first great recording success; has a leading role in sketches; parents divorce; father remarries; his marriage proposal is rejected; her mother has no maternal feelings; rejects her mother; mother/father/brother/grandparents dies; starts school; found to have a remarkable aura; keeps a journal; fascinated by science; becomes a freemason; goes into army; falls in love; works as a shopkeeper & bookkeeper; stops playing piano after being ridiculed; attacked in newspapers; works as a journalist; measles.

The few observations for diurnal births in the sample are due to Mercury never being far from the Sun and thus rarely the first to rise when the Sun is up in the daytime sky. Among the nocturnal births 13-year-old Krishnamurti was thought to be stupid at school and punished for being unable to learn; 11-year-old Doris Lessing stopped playing the piano when her schoolmates ridiculed her; and 10-year-old Ludwig von Beethoven's mother took him to Holland where he performed on the violin in several private houses.

Mercury & Venus

Mercury & Venus	Mercury rules septenary & Venus rules decan		Mercury rules decan & Venus rules septenary	
	N	% Positive	N	% Positive
Diurnal	34	53.2	21	56.0
Nocturnal	30	51.3	36	60.3
All	64	52.3	57	58.7

Mercury rules septenary & Venus rules decan

Diurnal: learns how when a patient's symptoms are talked out, they are cured; writes on poets; son marries; books published; son/grandson/granddaughter born; father/mother dies; compulsory military service; writes daily love letters; sexual frustration; subservient to his lover, worshipping her; marries; beset with personal worries; takes cocaine; considers himself a failure; wins a prize; his dream of wealth is shattered; loss of home & children; extreme poverty; ostracized when the Church stirs up people against him; his hands are paralyzed; his feet & thighs swell with water-dropsy; scarlet fever; attempts suicide; death.

Nocturnal: Congress override his veto; son/daughter marries; marries; son born; writing poetry; brother/father/grandmother dies; she is left a legacy; becomes queen/president/master magician; conscripted into the army; unhappy, lonely & melancholy; climbing; indulges in fleshpots.

Venus rules septenary & Mercury rules decan

Diurnal: his son is a POW; preoccupied with survival; describing the results of his research; writing; marries; studying geology; traveling alone; victim of fraud; emphysema; miserable; lung operation; brain surgery; has AIDS; death.

Nocturnal: becomes president/senator; first meets future wife; marries; incompatible marriage; divorce; unable to divorce husband; son/grandson/granddaughter born; pays back taxes; great financial losses; court battles for his guardianship; extensive travels; mother/brother dies; switches career plans from writing to sculpture; switches his political party; start of interest in mathematics; graduates; lonely, unhappy & bored; insomnia; paranoia.

Unless one of the two rulers is afflicted or directed to a sign in which it is unwelcome, these are usually pleasant years. Sam Johnson wrote *The Lives of the Poets* under these two rulers; "the most evil man in the world" Aleister Crowley first became interested in magic; Tom Paine returned to the USA after imprisonment in France; Sigmund Freud wrote love letters daily to his fiancée; and Elizabeth II became queen.

Mercury and Venus were joint rulers when Venus ruled Jeddu Krishnamurti's septenary, described on pages 166-168.

Mercury & Mars

Mercury & Mars	Mercury rules septenary & Mars rules decan		Mercury rules decan & Mars rules septenary	
	N	% Positive	N	% Positive
Diurnal	26	59.1	40	**67.8****
Nocturnal	41	52.9	26	55.6
All	67	55.3	66	**63.0****

Mercury rules septenary & Mars rules decan
Diurnal: *inaugurates a new phase in the evolution of human thinking; has the idea of* Peter Pan; *writes on theoretical physics/morals; writing his autobiography; studying by correspondence; starts a diary; introspection & self-analysis; his company builds the world's largest oil rig; inherits title; arrested; brother/daughter/friend/grandfather dies; promoted; earns law degree; running an experimental school; has to avoid war as he is unready; conscripted into army; affair; marries; skiing; buys a sailboat; working long hours; outbreak of boils.*
Nocturnal: *successful bank robbery; beaten up; humiliated; in prison; exiled; granddaughter born; difficulties with his manager; son/mother/sister dies; ex-husband is murdered; interest in the sphinx; in love; marries; legal battle over child support; his wife leaves him; dressing as a woman in private; visits Japan; studying piano tuning & repair; noise nearly drives him insane; works as advertising copywriter; editing crime novels; sells his poems; enlists in the army; at art school; becomes NATO commander/president/prime minister; honored; triumphant success; bronchitis; assassinated; death.*

Mars rules septenary & Mercury rules decan
Diurnal: *wins Nobel Prize; father takes him to court; rejects Hegalian philosophy; marries; son born; first book published; building a house; studying; learning oratory; arrested for inciting a riot; putsch fails; puts down rebellion; in prison/desert; wife/mother/friend dies; becomes president; tonsillectomy; wounded in the arm; throat cancer; death.*
Nocturnal: *accused of mental cruelty; divorce; disruptive love affair; in battle; father/mother dies; son/daughter born; builds a house; moves; graduates; becomes absolute dictator; marries; her first book is published; founds a debating society; conscripted; swaying between Catholicism, Protestantism & atheism; campaigning; fails to become a Fellow; has a new job; financial problems; confused; depressed; paranoid; tonsillitis; syphilis; severe urethra pains; death.*

Mercury and Mars combine well together as time rulers, especially in diurnal charts. These years were times of fighting, and of the deaths of Abraham Lincoln and Reinhold Ebertin, but they were also when Willy Brandt received the Nobel Peace Prize; Josef Stalin successfully robbed banks; poet Ogden Nash was an advertising copywriter; Bertrand Russell and his wife ran an experimental school; 26-year-old Franz Kafka holidayed in Italy and first saw an airplane; J. M. Barrie had the idea for *Peter Pan*; and Doris Lessing's ex-husband was murdered.

Mercury and Mars were joint rulers when Mercury ruled Jung's decan, see pages 141-143; when Mars ruled Abe Lincoln's decan in 1865, see page 198; when Mars ruled Oliver Cromwell's decan, see page 204; and when Mars ruled Hitler's septenary, see pages 199-200.

Mercury & Jupiter

Mercury & Jupiter	Mercury rules septenary & Jupiter rules decan		Mercury rules decan & Jupiter rules septenary	
	N	% Positive	N	% Positive
Diurnal	38	45.2	22	61.7
Nocturnal	50	48.8	45	**68.4****
All	88	47.3	67	**66.1****

Mercury rules septenary & Jupiter rules decan
Diurnal: *discovers wireless radio; his paper on experimental design gets international attention; no home; has no money, humiliated; son born; marries; estranged from his wife; divorce; mother/daughter dies; husband is assassinated; decisively beaten; leaves RAF; emigrates; self-contempt; psychoanalysis; breaks her ankle; rheumatoid arthritis; gall bladder surgery; death.*
Nocturnal: *life is an endless party; she is now a star; honors; becomes president; defeated; emigrates; cursed by her father; mother/daughter dies; mother is insane; catches wife with another man; son/daughter born; career change; bronchitis; paralyzed; mental breakdown; addicted to drugs; death.*

Jupiter rules septenary & Mercury rules decan
Diurnal: *love affair; marries; daughter born; wife/son dies; his theory that the sun rotates is confirmed; arrested; protests apartheid; melancholy; headaches; hurts arm in a machine; surgery for cancer; influenza; death.*
Nocturnal: *conceives of gravity & calculus; among the best years of his life; very popular; studying astrology; in prison; escapes being guillotined; he is a POW; victim of enemy's jealousy; his enemy is assassinated; elected senator; apprenticed to an engraver; graduates; emigrates; has no money; solitary; fights with his mother; marries; son born; father/sister dies; drinking, dancing & flirting.*

Mostly positive periods occurred when Jupiter ruled the septenary. By contrast, the years when Mercury was in this position were not at all easy. There were new discoveries under these rulers, very much as their symbolism would suggest: Gulielmo Marconi discovered wireless radio; Isaac Newton discovered the infinite series and had the ideas of gravity and differentiation; and Johannes Kepler first observed sunspots and confirmed that the sun rotates. There are also examples of the individual being betrayed: Peter Sellers caught his wife in bed with another man; Friedrich Nietzsche, blissfully happy as part of a platonic *ménage a trois*, awoke to find himself abandoned by his love and best friend; and Tom Paine imprisoned in Paris due to Gouvernoeur Morris's intrigues only escaped being guillotined by sheer luck.

This pairing was a devastating one for Jacqueline Kennedy Onassis. She was born with Jupiter in her eighth equal-sign house in Gemini, with Mercury combust in Leo. When Mercury ruled the septenary JFK was assassinated, and when Jupiter had that rulership she herself died.

Mercury and Jupiter were joint rulers when Mercury ruled Carl Jung's decan, see page 141, and when Jupiter ruled Arthur Young's decan, refer to pages 228-230, and Bob Dole's, see page 43.

Mercury & Saturn

Mercury & Saturn	Mercury rules septenary & Saturn rules decan		Mercury rules decan & Saturn rules septenary	
	N	% Positive	N	% Positive
Diurnal	40	58.8	23	35.4
Nocturnal	32	50.8	43	56.8
All	72	55.2	66	49.3

Mercury rules septenary & Saturn rules decan
Diurnal: paper published on his discoveries; emigrates; honors; marries; affair; police confiscate uninsured car; unemployed; editing magazine; very poor; son/daughter/twins born; daughter marries; father dies; defeats; becomes a gunnery officer; severe hemorrhage; death.
Nocturnal: runs over & kills a child; studies occultism in Tibet; defeated; victory; joins navy; founds a shipyard; mother/wife/sons die; son/daughter/brother born; bombing forces him to leave home; goes to college; breaks his nose; prostate & gall bladder surgery.

Saturn rules septenary & Mercury rules decan
Diurnal: his mind is unsettled & his memory confused; studying Greek; defeated; financial losses; affairs; becomes senator; wife/mother/husband/sister dies; stomach trouble; she has a cancerous kidney removed; fever; death.
Nocturnal: studies for the priesthood; explains calculus; sister/daughter/son born; defeated; in her first film; elected senator/Masonic Grand Master; criticized; accused of libel; in battles; the worst time of her life; son/daughter marries; brother/sister/ex-wife/grandmother/friend dies; graduates; marries; divorce; in prison; pleurisy; severely ill; death.

In the sample the joint rulership of Mercury and Saturn often coincided with defeats. There were many deaths, and often a lack of money. In her autobiography Doris Lessing described the period as the "worst time of her life", during which she saw the children she had abandoned six years earlier. These two planets were ruling Prince Charles when his ex-wife Diana was killed in a Paris car crash; when President Millard Fillmore failed to obtain his party's nomination for his re-election; when John Kerry failed to be selected as Bill

Clinton's presidential running mate; and when Hillary Rodham Clinton was defeated by Barack Obama for her party's nomination. Helena Blavatsky received her occult training in Tibet during these years, and Alan Watts was studying for the priesthood. Roy Firebrace had heavy financial losses, Rene Descartes tried to find the secret of life by dissecting animals, and Samuel Johnson's mind is described as being unsettled and his memory confused.

Mercury and Saturn were joint rulers for Carl Jung in 1924, a thought-altering year when Mercury ruled his decan, see page 143.

Mercury & Uranus

Mercury & Uranus	Mercury rules septenary & Uranus rules decan	
	N	% Positive
Diurnal	29	62.4
Nocturnal	35	46.5
All	64	53.7

Diurnal: *his wife says she doesn't love him anymore; overthrows the government; in a brawl; inherits title; denied visa because of his skin color; attempt on his life; abandons & betrays his army; becomes governor; wife dies; awarded PhD; loses his job; tears knee cartilage; kidney operation; death.*
Nocturnal: *revolution starts; marries; wife has an affair; daughter born/marries; studying law; grandmother/brother dies; becomes a vegetarian; nurses her sick husband; humiliated by defeat; rioting; does away with arranged marriages; starts his own business; nearly drowns; death.*

Mercury wants to improve how the individual communicates. Uranus provides new and stimulating situations. The pair should combine well but not all members of the sample found this was so. The joint rulers were not kind to Larry Olivier, who was very shocked when told he had lost his job, and then even more so when his wife, Vivien Leigh, informed him that she didn't love him any more and that she was having an affair with his protégé, Peter Finch. Isaac Newton's security was shattered when his mother abandoned him. Arthur Ashe's visa to visit South Africa was denied because of his skin color; his protest expanded people's awareness of apartheid. Jimmy Carter had "a deeply profound religious experience". John Quincy Adams' father became president, and Chester Arthur became president on the death of James Garfield. Condi Rice was awarded her Ph. D, and Josef Stalin became editor of *Pravda*.

Mercury and Uranus were joint rulers when Uranus ruled Napoleon Bonaparte's decan, see pages 276-278.

Mercury & Neptune

Mercury & Neptune	Mercury rules septenary & Neptune rules decan	
	N	% Positive
Diurnal	46	37.3
Nocturnal	36	55.2
All	82	45.2

Diurnal: *saves daughter from drowning; abandons a sinking ship; arrested; tells press of prison brutality; escapes from prison; much fantasizing; writes against slavery; marries; his shop fails; his writings inspire independence; stabs man in a bar; decides not to be a priest; indecisive; humiliated; hepatitis A.*

Nocturnal: *abdicates his throne; not allowed into the USA; buys large estate; first solo flight; initiates animal shelter; gives prize money to the poor; travels overseas to hear Bach's music; attempt on his life; wife/mother dies; knocked down by a car; broken collarbone; typhoid.*

This was a difficult combination for those born in the daytime. For Tsar Nicholas II it was a disastrous time: first the son he had eagerly awaited was born but found to be a hemophiliac, then he suffered defeats, both in the war against Japan and at home where he reluctantly agreed to create a national assembly. The influence of the two rulers is apparent in many of the above examples. Carl Jung decided he would not follow the family tradition and become a priest, he then had vehement and fruitless discussions with his father who had religious doubts; Martin Luther King went to India to study non-violence; and Charlie Chaplin was accused of being a Communist sympathizer.

Mercury and Neptune were joint rulers when Mercury ruled Carl Jung's septenary, see pages 137-139, when Mercury ruled Thomas Paine's septenary, refer to pages 144-147, and when Neptune ruled the decans of both Mao Zedong and Dr. Martin Luther King Jr., see pages 297-298 and 298-300 respectively.

Mercury & Pluto

Mercury & Pluto	Mercury rules septenary & Pluto rules decan	
	N	% Positive
Diurnal	37	61.1
Nocturnal	31	52.5
All	68	57.1

Diurnal: *cuts the Gordian Knot; military victories; rejected for military service; burnt in effigy; she is very unpopular; wins international award; elected senator; marries; husband dies; rethinks her policies; a bomb is thrown onto his porch; falsely accused of taking bribes; visits site of massacre; fasting; in prison; stabbed; appendicitis.*

Nocturnal: *becomes king; wife/father/enemy dies; loses his patronage; defeated; falls in love; ship he is on sinks; writes many articles; her lover has cancer; heart failure; eye surgery; cerebral hemorrhage; gall bladder removed; death.*

An appropriate example of how these two rulers can combine occurred when Margaret Thatcher, at that time Britain's education minister, 'The Lady Nobody Loves', decided that her policies were not succeeding and that she had to rethink them. Another is the launching by Mahatma Gandhi of India's first nationwide non-cooperation campaign. He said at the time, "non-cooperation with evil is as much a duty as cooperation with good." Nocturnal births in the sample frequently experienced the death of the father.

Mercury and Pluto were joint rulers when Mercury ruled Thomas Paine's septenary in 1778, see page 147, and when Pluto ruled the decans of Winston Churchill and Alexander the Great, described on pages 318-321 and 322-323 respectively.

Venus rules both septenary & decan

Venus	Venus rules both septenary & decan	
	N	% Positive
Diurnal	14	**84.0****
Nocturnal	12	37.7
All	26	62.6

Diurnal: *wins Nobel Prize; writing his autobiography; sister dies; starts school; astrological studies; marries; poetry; working in rice fields.*

Nocturnal: *joins the army; leaves RAF; success in radio; sister born; brother runs away; raped; first car; much vomiting.*

People in the sample born in the daytime found these to be mostly very pleasant years. Night births had it less well: when Peter the Great was three years old his father died, and his world changed. He was no longer the adored son of a father devoted to his mother, but the potentially troublesome offspring of his dead father's second wife. Isabelle Eberhardt was aged ten when her half sister, who had been as a mother to her, ran away from home; with her went the last semblance of order and tidiness.

Venus & Mars

Venus & Mars	Venus rules septenary & Mars rules decan		Venus rules decan & Mars rules septenary	
	N	% Positive	N	% Positive
Diurnal	24	56.5	32	**31.1****
Nocturnal	46	55.1	31	64.2
All	70	55.5	63	47.4

Venus rules septenary & Mars rules decan
Diurnal: *marries; discovers his wife's infidelity; divorce; his wife is hated; daughter born; son dies; teaching; writing is his obsession.*
Nocturnal: *marries; affairs; deserted by her lover; hires his first servant; pay increase; bankrupt; kills his enemies; socializing; much drinking; his face is burnt by fireworks; organizes strikes; exiled; beaten up; edits newspaper; people flock to hear him speak; kidney stone removed; has a cerebral stroke; his legs are paralyzed.*

Mars rules septenary & Venus rules decan
Diurnal: *loses battle; son commits suicide; husband lies to her; arrested for theft; steals gold; IRS audit; nude photos of her are published; exiled; father/mother/husband dies; becomes king/a vegetarian; buys new house; thrown from his horse; laryngitis; death.*
Nocturnal: *wins battles; explains his theory of the tides; grandfather is assassinated; marries; son born; mother remarries; becomes president/governor; promoted; starts a website; wins a lottery; campaigning; leads a failed climb; builds extension to his house; has an emergency hysterectomy.*

Those diurnal births in the sample that had Mars ruling the septenary experienced many difficulties with this combination. The son of Emperor Franz Josef, Rudolf, committed suicide; Hillary Rodham Clinton was devastated by the Monica Lewinsky scandal and the realization that her husband had lied to her; and Napoleon Bonaparte was defeated at Waterloo and exiled to the island of Saint Helena.

Venus and Mars were joint rulers when Mars ruled the author's septenary, as discussed on pages 44-45; when Mars ruled Oliver Cromwell's decan, described on pages 204-206; and when Venus ruled Jeddu Krishnamurti's septenary, see pages 168-169.

Venus & Jupiter

Venus & Jupiter	Venus rules septenary & Jupiter rules decan		Venus rules decan & Jupiter rules septenary	
	N	% Positive	N	% Positive
Diurnal	40	54.2	35	59.4
Nocturnal	48	54.6	58	60.8
All	88	54.4	93	**60.3***

Venus rules septenary & Jupiter rules decan
Diurnal: six-month trip around the world; explains nuclear fission; in a psychiatric clinic; leaves navy; Transcendental Meditation; discovers yoga & a Tibetan teacher; moves to Arabia; becomes a millionaire; taking drugs; father/sister dies; all teeth are removed; amateur dramatics; teaching; daughter born; marries; divorce; starts a life-long study of astrology; experiences dramatic spiritual change; civil disobedience; hip replacement; attempt on her life; attempts suicide; hernia operation; shot in the head.
Nocturnal: wins Nobel Prize; studying nature; his son's murderer is executed; resignation; mother dies; fights a duel over a woman; daughter born; elected president; loss of confidence; death.

Jupiter rules septenary & Venus rules decan
Diurnal: ends civil war; defeated; receives honorary DSc; being slandered; long-term lucrative contract; graduates; marriage ends; father dies; high blood pressure; Lyme disease; suicide.
Nocturnal: awarded Nobel Prize; brother is charged with sodomy; in a love triangle; jealousy; divorce; affair; daughter/brother marries; accusations; quadruples his fortune; comes into his fortune; forced out of group she founded; founds the Theosophical Society; writes lyrics for a successful musical; son born/has TB; becomes president; husband is elected president; ordained as a priest; mother/husband dies; car accident; beaten up by the police; high blood pressure; malaria; nightmares; eye troubles; death.

As one would expect with the two benefics controlling the life, these years are more often positive than not. Andrew Jackson defeated the British in Florida and then again at the Battle of New Orleans; Rene Descartes fought a duel over a woman; the people of Denmark paid for half a gram of radium as a 50th birthday present for Niels Bohr; John Lennon first smoked marijuana; Jimmy Carter's father died, and he left the Navy to run the family's peanut farm; George Appo was involved in a bar fight, shot in the head and almost lost the sight in his left eye; and Mahatma Gandhi became the center of the world's attention when he challenged the British Empire with the Salt March and began his civil disobedience campaign.

Venus and Jupiter were joint rulers when Venus ruled Samuel Pepys' decan, see pages 172-173, and when Jupiter ruled Theodore Roosevelt's septenary, refer to pages 230-231.

Venus & Saturn

Venus & Saturn	Venus rules septenary & Saturn rules decan		Venus rules decan & Saturn rules septenary	
	N	% Positive	N	% Positive
Diurnal	41	52.9	26	59.1
Nocturnal	40	49.7	45	60.3
All	81	51.4	71	59.9

Venus rules septenary & Saturn rules decan
Diurnal: *his wife is assassinated; his book has very large sales; his poem is a success; marries; falls in love & starts a homosexual relationship; discovers principles governing helicopter flight; buys 38-foot power boat; sister/brother/father dies; his girl friend has a heart attack & dies; civil war starts; victory; loss of money to taxes; wins lottery; becomes world champion/an ambassador; graduates; amoebic dysentery; phlebitis; ptomaine poisoning; pneumonia; death.*
Nocturnal: *knighted; discovers penicillin; invents damper for stoves; friend dies; son is an alcoholic; his lectures are published; his mind is dominated by priority dispute; appendicitis; unable to walk; death.*

Saturn rules septenary & Venus rules decan
Diurnal: *studying alchemy; autobiography published; husband has heart surgery; kidney surgery; death.*
Nocturnal: *attains power; opposed by Catholics; exhausting European tour; marries; buys house; affair; girl friend rejects him; sponsors universal pension schemes; loses election; accepts an overseas job; son/daughter born; photography; runs over & kills a colleague; promotions; honors; mother/father/brother dies.*

The people in the sample with this pair as joint rulers enjoyed better years than one might expect. Although in several cases individuals were concerned for the health of their spouses and loved ones, in my sample only Robert Graves' leaving his wife for Laura Riding, and Peter Sellers being rejected by his girl friend, were love relationship problems. Some other events under the rulership of Venus and Saturn: Ernest Hemingway's father committed suicide; the boxer Max Schmeling crashed his motorcycle with his sister riding behind him on the pillion—he survived but she died; Schmeling also won and then lost the world heavyweight boxing championship under the same two planetary rulers; Hillary Rodham Clinton's husband Bill had heart surgery; Woodrow Wilson became president of Princeton; the novelist Thomas Mann was conscripted into the army, and experienced much suffering; Ben Franklin invented the damper for stoves and chimneys; and astrologer Vendel Polich's friend and collaborator, Tony Nelson Page, died.

Venus and Saturn were joint rulers when Venus ruled Jeddu Krishnamurti's decan, as described on page 170. Saturn ruled Bob Dole's decan, see page 43.

Venus & Uranus

Venus & Uranus	Venus rules septenary & Uranus rules decan	
	N	% Positive
Diurnal	21	38.8
Nocturnal	29	46.7
All	50	43.4

Diurnal: breaks with his partner; his work is attacked; son born; son wounded in war; struggling to control his emotions; describes neuroses; works as a corset maker/excise man/journalist; marries; protesting; pessimistic; coronary embolism; liver complaint; father commits suicide.

Nocturnal: exiles his daughter; falls from a horse; becomes president; large book sales; painting; victory; crushing defeat; affair; marries; son/daughter born; son marries; escapes from exile; parents divorce; father/son dies; hernia operation; dysentery; death.

These can be difficult years. During this time Sigmund Freud broke with Jung and then developed his theory of neuroses, defining three great polarities: love and hate, love and indifference, and love and being loved. He considered them to be tensions between activity and passivity, the self and the external world, and pleasure and unpleasure; struggles over impulse and rage. Under the same two rulers the astrologer Cyril Fagan began working in a patent office; Samuel Johnson, bitterly disappointed when he failed to get a headmaster's job, began vehemently protesting against authority, which disturbance prompted a warrant to be issued for his arrest; and 80-year-old Winston Churchill finally accepted the views of his friends and sadly resigned his office as prime minister.

Venus and Uranus were joint rulers when Uranus ruled Sigmund Freud's decan, see pages 275-276.

Venus & Neptune

Venus & Neptune	Venus rules septenary & Neptune rules decan	
	N	% Positive
Diurnal	49	46.1
Nocturnal	32	**33.9***
All	81	41.3

Diurnal: *he is convinced there is no life after death; ceases believing in Free Will; becomes an atheist; harassed by his ex-lover; humiliates himself; husband loses his professional license; conscripted into army; wins a war; his acting is universally criticized; becomes famous; mad love affair; leaves husband & quits her job; has twins; scandal; rioting; friend drowns; mother dies; syphilis; gonorrhea; exhaustion; attempt on her life; painful kidney stone; dysentery; diphtheria; death.*

Nocturnal: *writes on life after death; embarrassed by his lover; she is a love junky; Sufism; sister marries; remodeled house lets in rain; father's company is bankrupt; brother dies; loses party leadership; elected mayor/president/chancellor; eyesight problems; teeth implants; excruciating spinal pain; nose operation; assassinated; death.*

People in the sample, especially those born at night, found these were difficult years. The writer Colin Wilson was in great debt; Ogden Nash's father's company went bankrupt; and Robert Graves lost much money when his agent was arrested for fraud. Other examples include 7-year-old Sigmund Freud humiliating himself by urinating on the carpet in his parent's bedroom; Franz Kafka becoming lost and confused when he found he was not allowed to change colleges; 18-years-old Franz Josef succeeding to the throne after his father abdicated; Isaac Newton's life becoming a nightmare when his mother removed him from school and brought him home to be a sheep farmer; and Lord Byron's poem *Childe Harold* being published: "I awoke one morning to find myself famous".

Venus and Neptune were joint rulers when Neptune ruled Dr. Martin Luther King's decan, see pages 300-301.

Venus & Pluto

Venus & Pluto	Venus rules septenary & Pluto rules decan	
	N	% Positive
Diurnal	29	62.4
Nocturnal	35	**31.0****
All	64	45.2

Diurnal: *becomes senator; declared legally insane; framed; graduates; emigrates; loses his job; borrows money; sexually molested; poverty & gloom; designs an iron bridge; invents smokeless candles; father dies.*
Nocturnal: *sees son she abandoned for first time in nine years; attempt on his life; breaks with her lover; lover/mother/wife dies; severe depression; graduates; avoids friends to work in peace; scrubbing floors in hospital; feels totally rejected; cancer operation; shot in the chest; death.*

These can be difficult years for night births. The separations we expect from any Pluto involvement are apparent among the above examples. Rene Descartes left France for Holland to avoid his friends and work in peace; Doris Lessing, who had just broken with her lover, says that she felt abandoned with her son away at school; and George Appo's lawyer pleaded that he was insane to stop him being sent to prison where his life would have been in danger. Appo ended up being sent to the same insane asylum where his father was an inmate.

Under this pairing 13-year-old Virginia Stephen (better known by her married name, Woolf) was sexually molested by her stepbrother. She was a day birth.

Venus and Pluto were joint rulers when Venus ruled Jeddu Krishnamurti's septenary in 1915, see page 168.

Mars rules both septenary & decan

Mars	Mars rules both septenary & decan	
	N	% Positive
Diurnal	18	65.3
Nocturnal	15	36.2
All	33	52.1

Diurnal: *father remarries; mother tells her to fight back; father/husband dies; son is sentenced to prison; studying law; learning to play piano; whooping cough.*
Nocturnal: *passes exams; translating poetry; learns to swim; brother/sister born; mother dies; brother killed in an air crash.*

This should be a year in which the native has increased energy and begins to discover how to assert himself. Sample members born at night experienced difficulties. The deaths of parents and the births of siblings were frequent occurrences in the lives of people in the sample. Four-year-old Hillary Rodham ran to her mother complaining that another girl was bullying her; her mother sent her back out, telling her to "fight back". Other examples of events occurring when Mars ruled both decan and septenary: six-year-old Virginia Stephen (not yet Woolf) had whooping cough; twelve-years-old Robert Graves, away at boarding school, wrote his first poem; Helena Blavatsky's mother died; Margaret Thatcher's husband died; George Washington's father died; and Mao Zedung made his last public appearance.

Mars & Jupiter

Mars & Jupiter	Mars rules septenary & Jupiter rules decan		Mars rules decan & Jupiter rules septenary	
	N	% Positive	N	% Positive
Diurnal	52	57.4	30	45.2
Nocturnal	44	49.3	40	61.0
All	96	53.7	70	54.2

Mars rules septenary & Jupiter rules decan
Diurnal: *founds oil company; marries; her divorce is a great relief, she feels reborn; wins Iron Cross; famished; black despair; mental depression; mother/sister dies; son born; traveling & teaching; rejected; emigrates; leaves the navy; beaten by sadist; living in country occupied by the enemy; buys a mansion; in seaplane that sinks; publicity stunts; car accident; primal therapy; feuding; blinded by poison gas; broken arm; appendectomy; tonsillitis; death.*
Nocturnal: *son kidnapped & murdered; has a broadened social life; depression; talks to massive crowds; unhappy marriage; daughter marries/dies; parents separate; wins in court; loses his job; becomes wealthy; promotion; declares war; poisoned by his wife.*

Jupiter rules septenary & Mars rules decan
Diurnal: *caught picking a pocket; forms wartime ambulance corps; expands territory; marries; marriage ends; opens new theater; avoiding alcohol; arrested for drunk driving; loses election; moves; passes exams; delivering milk; watch stolen; not allowed to emigrate; wins a sweepstakes; starts her first job; badly beaten up; shot in stomach; has chronic diarrhea; suicide; death.*
Nocturnal: *receives inheritance; increased salary; large commissions; sells his estate; mother dies; theater going; calculus priority argument; floods; promoted; apprenticed to an engraver; food shortage; wins prizes; first homosexual experience; rejects his pregnant wife; death of his rival.*

Gandhi's formation of an ambulance corps during the First World War is a good example of a Jupiter-inspired response in a Martian environment. Another is Abraham Lincoln arguing his first case before the Illinois Supreme Court, although this is surely a Martian action in a Jovian environment. Less happy is young Larry Olivier being frequently beaten by a sadistic schoolmaster. Some other happenings under Mars and Jupiter: John Lennon marrying Yoko Ono and then being found guilty of drug possession; Bertrand Russell in a seaplane that sank, and having to swim in icy water to the rescue boats; Ludwig von Beethoven's hearing becoming so bad that he had the greatest difficulty carrying on a normal conversation; Friedrich Nietzsche experiencing a protracted attack of migraine and sickness and being forced to retire from the university with a pension; Juan Peron's father dying; and James Madison declaring war against England.

Mars and Jupiter were joint rulers when Mars ruled Adolf Hitler's septenary, described on pages 198-199, and his decan, refer to page 202; also when Mars ruled Oliver Cromwell's decan, see page 206, and when Jupiter was Arthur Young's decan ruler, see page 230.

Mars & Saturn

Mars & Saturn	Mars rules septenary & Saturn rules decan		Mars rules decan & Saturn rules septenary	
	N	% Positive	N	% Positive
Diurnal	22	41.1	34	55.9
Nocturnal	49	44.3	40	52.0
All	71	43.3	74	53.8

Mars rules septenary & Saturn rules decan
Diurnal: his letter starts atom bomb research; lacking courage; begins studying astrology; burglary; marries; children born; buys house/new car; father dies; exhausted; becomes a lawyer; mugged; thrombosis; death.
Nocturnal: daughter elopes; receives inheritance; borrows money; honors; declares war; buys house; returns to her roots; discussing loneliness; "life was hell"; mother/sister dies; falls from a horse; infantile paralysis; attempt on his life; murdered; death.

Saturn rules septenary & Mars rules decan
Diurnal: extends military service; first sees poverty, sickness, old age & death; renounces wealth & family; start of Cultural Revolution; turmoil; conscripted into RAF; elected president; mother/father dies; boxing; feels helpless, fearful & unqualified; badly beaten up; leaves school; defeated; imprisoned; ordained; daughter born; in a coma; says religion is due to fear of the unknown; has steel fragments in his eye.
Nocturnal: begins homosexual affair that will end in his total disgrace; founds a bank; advocating military action; civil war; large commissions; burglary; accusations; carpentry; law degree; world tour; marries; battle for survival; lover killed on motorcycle; father/son dies; has VD; sees those he loves cut to pieces; son killed in war/has cancer; accidents; broken bones; falls from horse; erroneously reported dead; badly wounded in battle.

"Life can be hell" in these years. Albert Einstein's letter to Roosevelt explaining the potential of an atomic weapon; Oscar Wilde's involvement with Alfred Douglas; and Mao Zedung's instigation of China's Cultural Revolution are three examples of actions taken that ended in disaster. Other events in these years include: the offices of Charles Carter being destroyed in the London blitz; one of Teddy Roosevelt's sons being killed in the war and his two other sons severely wounded; Helena Blavatsky escaping from an unconsummated marriage; Jack Nicholls' world collapsing when he is told his son had cancer; actress Grace Kelly's marriage to the Prince of Monaco; and Josef Stalin beginning "The Great Terror" in which millions are starved and hundreds of thousands are deported.

Mars and Saturn were joint rulers when Saturn ruled Laurence Olivier's decan, refer to pages 255-257. Mars ruled Bob Dole's decan, see pages 42 and 43.

Mars & Uranus

Mars & Uranus	Mars rules septenary & Uranus rules decan	
	N	% Positive
Diurnal	41	61.8
Nocturnal	31	58.3
All	72	60.3

Diurnal: *burnt in effigy; introduced to astrology; studies black-body radiation; accused of sedition; son/brother born; loses his job; in his first battle; parents divorce; father/mother dies; evacuated; emigrates; large fines following IRS audit; expelled from USA; outlawed; erratic sleep; confused & angry; defeated; uprising suspends his career; touring in RV; elected MP; founds political party; severe headaches.*
Nocturnal: *"The violence all around is crazy"; ends a war; joins RAF; receives fellowship; affair; marries; divorce; first meets father's new wife; moves; elected president; arrested for illegally selling weapons; becomes a communist; son born; successful one-woman show; inflammation of temporal arteries; has a heart operation to remedy a birth defect; death.*

Although a majority of people in the sample had positive years under these two rulers, it can be a difficult time, one in which there can be too much uncontrolled energy around. Sam Johnson had to suspend his literary career during the Jacobite uprising; Tom Paine risked his life when he stood up in the revolutionary Convention and argued that Louis XVI should not be executed—he was immediately shouted down—in England he was burned in effigy; Arie Mantel's work was interrupted and he was evacuated because of the war; Alexander the Great's parents divorced and he and his mother were forced to flee, his position as heir to the throne now in jeopardy; Lyndon Johnson ordered a complete cessation of "all air, naval and artillery bombardment of North Vietnam"; Doris Lessing abandoned her husband and children to became a communist; and Margaret Thatcher first became a member of Parliament.

Mars & Neptune

Mars & Neptune	Mars rules septenary & Neptune rules decan	
	N	% Positive
Diurnal	20	67.8
Nocturnal	21	43.0
All	41	55.2

Diurnal: *researches surface tension of liquids; coronation; selling paintings; marries; returns home; defeats; his house is totally destroyed by bombs; his acting is praised; slipped disk; breaks arm; nearly dies from loss of blood; appendicitis wrongly diagnosed; father away at war.*
Nocturnal: *refuses to accept the role of Messiah; teaches the oneness of all; acquires his first slaves; expelled from seminary; has a vision of God; father/mother/brother dies; becomes a Marxist; proves that lightning is electrical.*

Difficult years were observed when Mars comes to Neptune or Neptune arrives at Mars in the decan, and these were earlier discussed. However, the years when Mars ruled the septenary at the same time that Neptune was the decan ruler were not as difficult as might have been expected. Indeed, although not statistically significant, daytime births in the sample usually experienced these years as positive ones.

The Danish physicist Niels Bohr wrote his doctoral thesis under the influence of these two rulers. The subject he chose, the surface tension of liquids, appropriately combines the two planetary principles. Jiddu Krishnamurti rejected the Masters and said that all grounds for authority should be abandoned. He refused to accept the role of Messiah, and dissolved the Order of Star. William Blake had his first vision of God. Ben Franklin's kite experiment proved that lightning is electrical. Max Planck's house was completely destroyed by bombs that also annihilated his entire scientific records and correspondence.

Mars and Neptune were joint rulers when Neptune ruled Mao Zedong's decan, see pages 296-297.

Mars & Pluto

Mars & Pluto	Mars rules & Pluto rules decan	
	N	% Positive
Diurnal	46	49.1
Nocturnal	30	39.2
All	76	45.2

Diurnal: *receives large inheritance; learning astrology; in love; mother dies; wins Nobel Prize; honors; father is assassinated/defeated; parachute jump; son becomes president; evacuated; expelled; concussion; skin infection.*

Nocturnal: *father abandons the family/becomes company president; son/father/brother dies; affair; marries; daughter born; non-stop work; refuses award; painful opening of his third eye; stroke; broken ankle; death.*

The following examples show just what can occur when Mars and Pluto govern an individual's life. Rene Descartes halted publication of his book when he learnt of Galileo's trial; he became an intellectual in hiding. Colin Wilson's young daughter was briefly missing. His relief at finding her awoke a state of euphoria, and he later theorized that concentrated effort could bring peak experiences out of boredom and misery. Max Planck's highly disciplined work aimed at maximizing the efficiency of light bulbs is another example of the stimuli of these two rulers being combined in a positive way. Ernest Hemingway caused the death of an ex-wife by a brutal phone call that sent up her blood pressure and ruptured a blood vessel. When Alexander Hamilton's mother died, her estranged husband sued for all of her assets, depriving Alexander and his siblings of any benefits. Two other examples show how these two rulers combine in these difficult years are "non-stop work" and "nearly dies from loss of blood".

Mars and Pluto were joint rulers when Pluto ruled Alexander the Great's decan in 336 BC, as described on page 321.

Jupiter rules both septenary & decan

Jupiter	Jupiter rules both septenary & decan	
	N	% Positive
Diurnal	18	55.2
Nocturnal	8	56.5
All	26	55.6

Diurnal: *survives his plane being shot down into the sea; his grandfather is killed by a bomb; father dies; loses respect for his father; parents divorce; marries; travels overseas; defends his dissertation; passes finals; popular; first record released; clog dancing; brother born; writing his autobiography; death.*
Nocturnal: *parents' coronation; father has political problems; brother/sister born.*

Jupiter's role of protector and as the significator of the father is seen in several of the above examples. George Bush Sr. had his plane shot down into the sea; several members of his crew were killed but (protected by Jupiter) he was rescued almost unhurt. The Beatles first record was released, and John Lennon switched from being a potential bum to a success. Ernest Hemingway wrote that he lost all respect for his father when he failed to stand up to his wife's persistent nagging. Margaret Thatcher's father became mayor. Winston Churchill's father resigned as Chancellor of the Exchequer, an act that permanently ruined his career.

Jupiter & Saturn

Jupiter & Saturn	Jupiter rules septenary & Saturn rules decan		Jupiter rules decan & Saturn rules septenary	
	N	% Positive	N	% Positive
Diurnal	41	48.6	41	48.6
Nocturnal	26	62.6	22	41.1
All	67	54.0	63	45.9

Jupiter rules septenary & Saturn rules decan
Diurnal: *son killed in war; forms song-writing partnership; fails to prevent atom bombing; mother killed; performs overseas; arrested; struggling to overcome sexual desires; marries; exiled; heart attack; mistakenly given AIDS-tainted blood; murdered; death.*
Nocturnal: *son killed in war; named Augustus, the Revered One; defeats invaders; enlists in navy; in love; marries; son/daughter born; wife dies; daughter marries; beating his wife; father remarries; new job; graduates; named best British actor; legal problems; loss of self-confidence; liver disease.*

Saturn rules septenary & Jupiter rules decan

Diurnal: *hails the Russian Revolution as start of society based on reason & science; graduates; marries; leaves his job; falsely accused of accepting bribes; receives honorary PhD; wins Pulitzer Prize; elected senator; shocked & humiliated; has a complete mental & nervous breakdown; paternity scandal; sells his farm; sentenced to one year in solitary confinement; emigrates; mother dies; nose operation; spinal operations; death.*

Nocturnal: *prosecutes his friend & mentor, who is executed; loses libel trial; writing crime articles; father/mother/brother/daughter/mentor dies; depressed; attacked as a Catholic sympathizer; bankrupt; humiliated; he is a broken man; in prison; dysentery.*

Jupiter is promoting growth and expansion in these years, while at the same time Saturn is asking the individual to be disciplined and responsible. The two requirements are often in conflict, as several of the above examples demonstrate. Under these two rulers Mao Zedung ordered the start of China's first five-year plan, which emphasized heavy industry, centralized planning, technical expertise and a large defense buildup in the Soviet pattern; Mahatma Gandhi was struggling to overcome his sexual desires; Jiddu Krishnamurti called for a continual revolution, the need for people to awaken from mental lethargy; Peter the Great, by defeating the Swedish army, thunderously announced the birth of a new Russia; by selling his farm, Harry Truman had 'substantial money' for the first time in his life; and John Logie Baird had a complete mental and nervous breakdown, which altered his life's path, prompting him to end trivial pursuits and to concentrate on a greater destiny—the invention of television.

Jupiter & Uranus

Jupiter & Uranus	Jupiter rules septenary & Uranus rules decan	
	N	% Positive
Diurnal	39	55.6
Nocturnal	13	55.6
All	52	55.6

Diurnal: *his life-long dream becomes a hideous nightmare; receives enemy's surrender; writes on pleasure vs. reality; organizes nuclear protest group; his theory is confirmed; first visits USA; wants to be a priest; becomes president; brother runs away from home; she is Debutante of the Year; meets future wife; wife has a heart attack; son/wife dies; sister born/marries; given lucrative contract; arrested; imprisoned; shingles; Lyme disease; high blood pressure; assassinated; death.*

Nocturnal: *becomes president following predecessor's assassination; graduates; son born.*

What a person desires can manifest in these years, sometimes in unexpected ways. Mao Zedung, believing in the power of the human will to overcome material obstacles, proclaimed the policy of "let a hundred flowers bloom". He did not intend full-scale liberalization but hoped that some relaxation of tight controls would encourage Chinese intellectuals to become good Communists. The resulting vast outpouring of criticism that called the Communist Party itself into question prompted him to quickly switch to a tough rectification campaign. Gandhi's life-long dream of independence became a hideous nightmare when India was divided amid appalling carnage. Lyndon Johnson became president following Kennedy's assassination and quickly ordered the bombing of North Vietnamese PT-boat bases; and George Washington received the surrender of the British at Yorktown.

Jupiter and Uranus were joint rulers when Uranus was the decan ruler for Sigmund Freud, see pages 273-275; and for Barack Obama, see page 232-233.

Jupiter & Neptune

Jupiter & Neptune	Jupiter rules septenary & Neptune rules decan	
	N	% Positive
Diurnal	17	47.8
Nocturnal	26	55.6
All	43	52.5

Diurnal: *his father kills a man; arrested for theft; starts to loath school; brother is caught selling drugs; grandmother dies; authorities stop him emigrating; visits a brothel; loss of his Christian beliefs; passes exams; opens a tobacco shop; marries; seriously ill; appendectomy; suicide.*
Nocturnal: *flees from invading army; builds cottage for his daughter; enlarges his house; reelected PM; electricity experiments; attempt on his life; smallpox; death.*

Tom Paine's opening of a tobacco shop, which subsequently failed, is a perfect example of the speculative optimism these two rulers can generate, so much of which can end up in smoke; Winston Churchill lost money in a stock market panic; 13-year-old Glenda Jackson experienced a sudden, marked change—from being an ideal pupil she began to loathe school; George Appo was arrested for stealing a gold watch and sentenced to 30 months hard labor in Sing Sing, where he learned to read and write; and Ernest Hemingway committed suicide;

Jupiter & Pluto

Jupiter & Pluto	Jupiter rules septenary & Pluto rules decan	
	N	% Positive
Diurnal	37	61.1
Nocturnal	12	52.7
All	49	59.0

Diurnal: *a time of transition; his eye is restored to health after several decades of blindness; gets his PhD; revolutionizes physics; marries; daughter born; studying astrology; brother wins Olympic medal; lonely; ends collaboration; fame but little money; arrested for debt; non-stop drinking; breaks with his lover; wins money on horses; midlife crisis; liver disease.*
Nocturnal: *the experience of kundalini completely changes him; arrested; experiences great opposition; son marries; brother commits suicide/has TB/dies; marries; fails exams; death.*

This can be a time of great change. Marriage and death will bring this about. Several members of the sample experienced transforming events: Neils Bohr's atomic theory revolutionized physics; Carl Jung ended his collaboration with Freud; and Krishnamurti experienced kundalini rising through his body. Sam Johnson's recovery of his eyesight was also transforming.

Saturn rules both septenary & decan

Saturn	Saturn rules both septenary & decan	
	N	% Positive
Diurnal	14	38.8
Nocturnal	15	36.2
All	29	37.4

Diurnal: *sees execution by burning of young woman; receives bike for passing exams; parents separate; mother/grandfather dies; a very bad time; learning piano/violin; apprenticed; sister born; choking fits; persistent headaches.*
Nocturnal: *mother/grandfather dies; starved for human warmth; his faculty of total recall is awakened; homesick; joins navy; victimized; sexually assaulted, murdered & left in a concealed grave; learns to defend himself; punished for theft; autobiography published; tonsillectomy; death.*

To survive these chilly years requires a great deal of patience and discipline, which of course is exactly the lesson Saturn teaches. Mary Shelley's mother died at her birth, depriving the child of human warmth; Teddy Roosevelt, humiliated by boys who victimized him, learnt how to box; the parents of astrologer Alexander Marr separated and he lived with his father, which he says was a very bad time, one in which he experienced much suffering; 12-year-old Thomas Paine watched the execution by burning of a 17–year-old woman; and Helena Blavatsky met an initiate who told her something of the work the future had in store for her.

Saturn & Uranus

Saturn & Uranus	Saturn rules septenary & Uranus rules decan	
	N	% Positive
Diurnal	35	**33.5***
Nocturnal	31	43.8
All	66	**38.3***

Diurnal: *tames a wild horse; retires; homesick; legal problems; military defeats; sister born; father dies; fasting; believes his whole life has been a failure; attempt on his life; prison-induced sickness; accused of murdering his ex-wife & her lover; cataracts removed; rheumatoid arthritis.*
Nocturnal: *"in the beginning was Order & man created Chaos"; experiences tremendous new energy; "time only exists if thinking occurs"; starts new job; promoted; meets future husband; loses election; awarded Nobel Prize; marries; divorce; worst time of her life; meets children he/she abandoned; his family & colleagues all call for him to retire; daughter born; unable to cope; mother/sister die; intense depression; kidney failure; in poor health; high blood sugar; death.*

Sample members often revisited the past. Alexander's taming of the wild horse Bucephalus epitomizes the years when these two planets control the life. Saturn wants life to be predictable, orderly and regulated. Uranus wants it to be constantly renewed and always exciting. The result, as Krishnamurti pointed out when he was experiencing this pair of rulers, can too often be chaos. Gustave Mahler's mother and sister died in these years, and the first performance of his 1st Symphony was a failure. Thomas Paine was imprisoned on the word of Gouverneur Morris, the US representative to France, and sentenced to be guillotined. He escaped death by pure luck, but remained in prison for eleven months, lost his memory and was not expected to recover from his prison-induced sickness. Saturn and Uranus were jointly ruling Winston Churchill when his daughter Diana committed suicide.

Saturn & Neptune

Saturn & Neptune	Saturn rules septenary & Neptune rules decan	
	N	% Positive
Diurnal	63	53.1
Nocturnal	33	41.1
All	96	49.0

Diurnal: *in plane lost in fog over mountains; girl friend/wife leaves him; released from prison; honors; emigrates; marries; brother/daughter dies; father becomes president; she becomes her country's first woman PM; reincarnation interest; much enforced idleness; yellow jaundice; his spinal nerve is damaged; death.*

Nocturnal: *abdicates his throne; writing his autobiography; river bursts its banks; elected party leader; exhaustion; bronchitis; mentors die; assassinated; death.*

"Be responsible and fulfill your obligations", Saturn tells the individual. "Follow your bliss", Neptune says. In 1936, under the influence of this pair of rulers, King Edward VIII chose Neptune's path. He rejected the riches and responsibilities of the British Empire and abdicated his throne in order to marry the woman with whom he was besotted.

It is not unusual for a pair of rulers to bring about external situations that demand a reaction from the individual. In 11 AD the river Tiber burst its banks and flooded Rome. The emperor Augustus, then under this planetary pair, was responsible for cleaning up the mess and ensuring that it would not be repeated. Jupiter had come to Neptune in George W. Bush's decan the year New Orleans was flooded. The absence of any involvement by Saturn that year may point to the lack of responsibility observed in how Bush and his government reacted to the hardship the excess water caused then.

Saturn and Neptune were joint rulers when Saturn ruled Laurence Olivier's septenary, on pages 253-255.

Saturn & Pluto

Saturn & Pluto	Saturn rules septenary & Pluto rules decan	
	N	% Positive
Diurnal	22	61.7
Nocturnal	42	53.8
All	64	56.5

Diurnal: *becomes a full-time astrology researcher; elected president; honors; falls out with his mentor; marries; changes party policy; chaotic living conditions; first published writing; father is dying; wife/mother dies; double pneumonia; murdered.*
Nocturnal: *writes his will; arrested for debt; quits his job; turns on his previous mentor; re-elected; mother becomes queen/dies; joins communist party; breaks her shoulder; cancer of uterus; death.*

The rejection of past authority is seen in several of the above examples. Ben Franklin devoted much time and energy to the abolition of slavery, going against what had become a 'right'; Francis Bacon perfidiously turned on his previous generous mentor, the Earl of Essex, and helped have him executed; Sigmund Freud fell out with his mentor; Doris Lessing joined the Communist Party, an act she later called "the most neurotic in my life"; Mao Zedung wrote his first published article, in which he said the vast majority of Chinese constituted a mighty force for change, it was a bridge that led him from a relatively conservative and traditionalist nationalism to a genuinely Marxist viewpoint; and Cyril Fagan resigned from his job in a patent office to become a full-time astrology researcher.

Chapter 17

Summary of Significant Results

The use of planetary sequence described in this book is an approach that will be new to many astrologers. The reader should decide for himself whether or not it fits with the observed happenings in the lives of the examples that have been presented, and then test the concepts explained here within his own life and in the lives of people for whom he has intimate knowledge. If he finds that the combined decan-septenary method does accurately describe past happenings, his next step will be to use it to predict the future.

The author has found that the nature of future events, however these are identified, whether by transits, returns or progressions, by slow-moving planets or by the direction of the angles, are invariably determined within the framework defined by this combined decan-septenary method.

Although the results of statistical significance tests have been presented throughout this book, there is really nothing here that can or should be used as a defense of astrology. The persons whose lives have been analyzed are not at all representative of the general population. It was never the intention of the research that is the basis for this book to substantiate the validity of our ancient art. Instead the author's intent is that these findings and the method described here will improve the astrologer's ability to accurately interpret the combination of planets present at the birth of an individual.

Despite the qualifications concerning the non-randomness of the sample, it is gratifying to see that the traditionally benefic planets, Jupiter and Venus, were associated with the highest probability of positive years, and that directions to Saturn and Pluto relate to an above-average likelihood of difficult times.

These confirmations enable us to have some faith in results that involve the newly discovered planets, Uranus, Neptune and Pluto, for whom no tradition is available. We find that Uranus is strongest at night and when rising after the Sun; that Neptune is also strongest when occidental; and that Pluto differs from these two in that it is strongest in a daytime chart and when it rises before the Sun.

There are some results that differ from those that have been handed down to us from the past. The Sun at night is associated with a significantly high proportion of difficult years, which agrees with Hindu teachings but not with those of the West. Venus is strongest when it is a morning star (visible in the eastern sky before sunrise) or an evening one (visible in the western sky after sunset), which differs from the traditional view that the planet is strongest as an evening star—that is, when west of the Sun. There are also strong indications that Mars is most powerful by day, which contradicts the widely held teaching that it is a nocturnal planet. Whether or not the reader should accept these differences from tradition obviously depends on whether or not he or she accepts the validity of the decan-septenary method.

The following summarizes the most important findings described in this book:

* * * In the sample the following are associated with a very high likelihood (over 99% probability) that the ensuing period would be pleasant and/or successful:

The Moon directed to a planet in the seventh house, Table ☽-4.
The Moon as the fourth of the seven to rise in the septenary, Table ☽-5.
Moon rules decan at the same time that Jupiter rules septenary in a diurnal chart.
Venus oriental in a day birth, Table ♀-1.
Venus occidental in a night birth, Table ♀-1.
Venus directed to a planet in Taurus, Table ♀-3.
Venus natally in the eleventh house, Table ♀-4.
Venus as the third of the ten to rise in the decan by night, Table ♀-6.
Mars oriental in a diurnal chart, Table ♂-1.
Mars fourth of the seven to rise in the septenary by day, Table ♂-6.
Jupiter oriental in a nocturnal chart, Table ♃-1.
Jupiter directed to the Moon or Venus, Table ♃-2.
Jupiter natally in Gemini or Pisces, Table ♃-3.
Jupiter natally in the fifth house, Table ♃-4.
Jupiter directed to a planet in the second house, Table ♃-4.
Jupiter as the fourth of the seven to rise in the septenary, Table ♃-5.
Occidental Jupiter directed to a waxing Moon by day, Table ♃-9.
Jupiter directed to Venus, Table ♃-11.
Saturn as the third of the ten to rise in the decan by night, Table ♄-6.
Uranus as Time Ruler in a diurnal chart, Table ♅-1.

* * *

* * * In the sample the following are associated with extremely difficult periods (over 99% probability):

The Sun natally in the first house at night, see Table ☉-5.

The nocturnal Sun directed to a planet in houses 8-12, Table ☉-5.

The Sun as the first of the ten planets to rise after birth, Table ☉-7.

The nocturnal Sun directed to the ascendant, Table ☉-8.

The waning Moon in a nocturnal chart, Table ☽-1.

The Moon natally in the first house, Table ☽-4.

The Moon as the first of the seven to rise in the septenary, Table ☽-5.

The Moon as the eighth of the ten to rise in the decan by night, Table ☽-6.

The waning Moon directed to an oriental Jupiter, Table ☽-13.

Mars natally in Pisces, Table ♂-3.

Mars as the sixth of the ten to rise in the decan by night, Table ♂-7.

Saturn natally in the fourth house, Table ♄-4.

Saturn as the fifth of the seven to rise in the septenary by day, Table ♄-5.

Saturn as the fifth of the ten to rise in the decan by night, Table ♄-6.

Oriental Saturn directed to the ascendant, Table ♄-7.

Occidental Saturn directed to oriental Mercury at night, Table ♄-10.

Oriental Neptune as Time Ruler, Table ♆-1.

Oriental Neptune directed to occidental Mars, Table ♆-12.

Occidental Pluto as Time Ruler in a nocturnal chart, Table ♇-1.

Pluto as the sixth of the ten to rise in the decan by day, Table ♇-5.

* * *

** **   The following are associated with a significant probability (between 95 & 99%) of being pleasant and/or successful periods:

The nocturnal Sun directed to a planet in the sixth house Table ☉-5.
Diurnal Sun rules the septenary at same time that Mars rules the decan
Diurnal Sun rules the septenary at same time that Jupiter rules the decan
The Moon directed to a planet in the twelfth house, Table ☽-4.
Waning Moon directed to ascendant from Leo in diurnal chart
The Moon natally in the sixth house, Table ☽-4.
The Moon as the third of the ten to rise in the decan by day, Table ☽-6.
The Moon directed to occidental Mercury, Tables ☽-9 & ☽-10.
The waxing Moon directed to an oriental Jupiter, Table ☽-13.
Mercury as the third of the ten to rise in the decan, Table ☿-6.
Mercury rules decan at same time that Mars rules septenary in a diurnal chart
Mercury rules decan at same time that Jupiter rules septenary at night
Venus as the Time Ruler, Table ♀-1.
Venus natally in the fourth house, Table ♀-4.
Venus directed to a planet in the second house, Table ♀-4.
Venus as the fifth of the seven to rise in the septenary by day, Table ♀-5.
Venus rules both decan and septenary in a diurnal chart
Venus as the fifth of the ten to rise in the decan by night, Table ♀-6.
Mars natally in a Fire sign, Table ♂-4.
Mars natally in the seventh or twelfth houses, Table ♂-5.
Mars directed to a planet in the first house, Table ♂-5.
Mars directed to oriental Mercury in a diurnal chart, Table ♂-12.
Oriental Mars directed to occidental Venus in a diurnal chart, Table ♂-14.
Jupiter directed to Mercury, Table ♃-2.
Jupiter directed to a planet in Libra or Scorpio, Table ♃-3.
Jupiter natally in the ninth house, Table ♃-4.
Jupiter as the last of the seven to rise in the septenary, Table ♃-5.
Jupiter as the third of the seven to rise in the septenary by night, Table ♃-5.
Jupiter directed to the ascendant in a nocturnal chart, Table ♃-7.
Occidental Jupiter directed to occidental Mercury by day, Table ♃-10.
Jupiter directed to Venus with either planet in a Mercury-ruled term
Oriental Jupiter directed to oriental Venus, Table ♃-12.
Saturn directed to Uranus, Table ♄-2.
Neptune directed to a planet in the third house, Table ♆-4.
Neptune as the third of the ten to rise in the decan by night, Table ♆-5.
Pluto as the third of the ten to rise in the decan by day, Table ♇-5.

* * *

* * The following are associated with a significant probability (between 95 & 99%) that the period will be difficult:

A nocturnal Sun is the Time Ruler, see Table ☉-1.

The Sun coming to the ascendant in a nocturnal chart, Table ☉-1.

The nocturnal Sun natally in Libra, Table ☉-2.

The nocturnal Sun directed to a planet in Taurus, Table ☉-3.

The nocturnal Sun directed to a planet in an Earth sign, Table ☉-4.

The nocturnal Sun as the first of the seven to rise in the septenary, Table ☉-6.

The nocturnal Sun as the fourth of the ten to rise in the decan, Table ☉-7.

The nocturnal Sun directed to a waning Moon, Table ☉-9.

The nocturnal Sun directed to an oriental Pluto, Table ☉-17.

The Moon natally in the eleventh house, Table ☽-4.

The Moon rules septenary at same time that Mars rules decan at night

Waxing Moon directed to ascendant from Leo at night

Mercury natally in Scorpio, Table ☿-3.

Mercury natally in the twelfth house, Table ☿-4.

Mercury as the sixth of the seven to rise in the septenary by night, Table ☿-5.

Venus as the second of the seven to rise in the septenary by night, Table ♀-5.

Venus rules decan at same time that Mars rules septenary in diurnal chart

Venus rules septenary at same time that Pluto rules decan at night

Mars occidental in a nocturnal chart, Table ♂-1.

Mars natally in a Water sign, Table ♂-4.

Occidental Mars directed to Neptune in a nocturnal chart, Table ♂-17.

Occidental Mars directed to Pluto in a nocturnal chart, Table ♂-18.

Jupiter the second of the seven to rise in the septenary by day, Table ♃-5.

Occidental Saturn directed to Venus in a nocturnal chart, Table ♄-11.

Uranus directed to a planet in the eighth house, Table ♅-4.

Uranus as the first or eighth of the ten to rise in the decan by day, Table ♅-5.

Uranus as the seventh of the ten to rise in the decan by night, Table ♅-5.

Oriental Uranus directed to the Sun in a diurnal chart, Table ♅-7.

Uranus directed to occidental Mercury in a diurnal chart, Table ♅-9.

Neptune directed to a planet in Taurus, Table ♆-3.

Neptune natally in the second or fifth house, Table ♆-4.

Neptune directed to a planet in the fourth or eleventh house, Table ♆-4.

Neptune as the third of the ten to rise in the decan by day, Table ♆-5.

Neptune as the fourth of the ten to rise in the decan by night, Table ♆-5.

Neptune directed to waning Moon, Table ♆-8.

Pluto directed to Saturn, Table ♇-2.

Pluto natally in the tenth house, Table ♇-4.

Oriental Pluto directed to Mercury in a nocturnal chart, Table ♇-8.

Occidental Pluto directed to Saturn in a nocturnal chart, Table ♇-13.

* * * *

Identifying the Sequence of Planets

The planets are usually in the rising sequence indicated by their zodiacal longitudes. However, it is wise to check close conjunctions, especially when either the Moon or Pluto is involved, to confirm which of the two bodies is ahead of the other. If there is any uncertainty, compare the relative arcs of the planets to the next angle the rotation of the earth will bring them to, going in a clockwise direction. The planet that is closest to that angle will be ahead of the other in the rising sequence.

The arcs concerned are those used in primary directions. The formulae are as follows:

(1) For planets in the southeast or northwest quadrants, their next angle being the MC or IC, their sequence is determined by their Right Ascension, RA. The lower the RA the closer the planet is to the angle. Most astrological computer programs provide details of a planet's RA.

$RA = \arctan(\tan L \cos e)$
where L = longitude of planet
$\quad\quad e$ = obliquity = $23.4523 - 0.00013$ (years since $1/1/1900$)

In my own chart the Moon has RA $50°52'$ & Mercury RA $50°53'$. The Moon is therefore closer to the Pisces MC and ahead of Mercury in the rising sequence despite the Moon being further along the zodiac with a celestial longitude of 23♉46 compared to Mercury's 22♉21.

(2) Arc of a planet to the ascendant, applicable for a planet in the northeast quadrant. This is more complex.

$$\text{Arc} = OA_p - OA_{asc}$$

$$OA_{asc} = RAMC + 90$$

$$OA_p = RA_p - AD_p$$

$$\text{where } AD_p = \arcsin(\tan D \tan \varnothing)$$

D = declination = $\arcsin(\cos e \sin B + \sin e \cos B \sin L)$ if B, planet's latitude > 0, and D = $\arcsin(\sin L \sin e)$ when $B = 0$.

$$\varnothing = \text{geographic latitude of the birthplace.}$$

(3) Arc of a planet to the descendant. Required for a planet in the southwest quadrant.

$$\text{Arc} = OD_p - OD_{\text{Desc}}$$

where $OD_p = RA_p + AD_p$ and $OD_{\text{Desc}} = RAMC - 90$

Example: WR was born with three tight planetary groupings: $\mathit{D} \, \sigma \, \mathit{Q}$, $\odot \, \sigma \, \sigma$, and $\hbar \, \sigma \, \Psi$.

$e = 23.4523 - 0.00013(53.5)$
$\qquad = \mathbf{23.4453}$

$RAMC = \arctan(\tan 332.0667 * \cos$
$\qquad 23.4453)$
$\qquad = \mathbf{334.0597}$

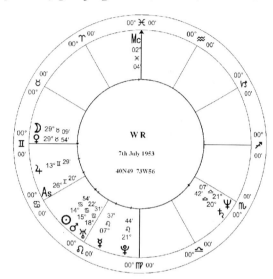

Venus & the Moon

$RA_\mathit{Q} = \arctan(\tan 59.9 * \cos 23.4453) = \mathbf{57.7135}$

$RA_\mathit{D} = \arctan(\tan 59.15 * \cos 23.4453) = \mathbf{56.9337}$

The Moon has the lower RA, indicating that it is closer to the MC. It is therefore ahead of Venus in the rising sequence.

Saturn & Neptune

$RA_\hbar = \arctan(\tan 200.7 * \cos 23.4453) = \mathbf{19.1200}$ [1]
$RA_\Psi = \arctan(\tan 201.1167 * \cos 23.4453) = \mathbf{19.5102}$

Saturn has the lower RA. It is therefore closer to the IC, and ahead of Neptune in the rising sequence.

Sun & Mars

$$OA_{\text{asc}} \quad = RAMC + 90 = 334.0597 + 90 = \mathbf{64.8167}$$

$$\text{Decl}_\odot \ = \arcsin(\sin 104.9 \sin 23.4453) = \mathbf{22.6124}$$

$$AD_\odot \quad = \arcsin(\tan 22.6124 \tan 40.817) = \mathbf{21.0843}$$

$$RA_\odot \quad = \arctan(\tan 104.9 \cos 23.4453) = -73.8266 = \mathbf{106.1734}$$

---

[1] To be strictly correct the RAs of Saturn and Neptune should each be increased by 180° as their longitudes are between 0° Cancer and 0° Capricorn, which of course doesn't alter the relative sizes of their RAs. Such pedantry can be ignored.

$$OA_\odot = RA_\odot - AD_\odot = 106.1734 - 21.1843 = \textbf{85.0891}$$

$$ARC_\odot = OA_\odot - OA_{asc} = 85.0891 - 64.8167 = \underline{\textbf{20.2724}}$$

$$Decl_{\sigma} = \arcsin(\cos 23.4453 \sin 0.95 + \sin 23.4453 \cos 0.95 \sin 105.3667) = \textbf{23.5037}$$

$$AD_{\sigma} = \arcsin(\tan 23.5037 \tan 40.817) = \textbf{22.0621}$$

$$RA_{\sigma} = \arctan(\tan 105.3667 \cos 23.4453) = -73.3243 = \textbf{106.6757}$$

$$OA_{\sigma} = RA_{\sigma} - AD_{\sigma} = 106.6757 - 22.0621 = \textbf{84.6136}$$

$$ARC_{\sigma} = OA_{\sigma} - OA_{asc} = 84.6136 - 64.8167 = \underline{\textbf{19.7969}}$$

As the Mars' arc of 19.7969 is less than the Sun's arc of 20.2724, Mars is closer to the ascendant than is the Sun, and ahead of it in the rising sequence. Mars is in fact the planet that will rise first following the birth.

The birth sequence of the planets not included in the above calculations is determined by their order in the zodiac. The complete sequence is therefore:

$$\sigma \quad \odot \quad ♅ \quad ☿ \quad ♀ \quad ♄ \quad ♆ \quad ☽ \quad ♀ \quad ♃$$

A planet's Longitude, Declination and Right Ascension are usually output by astrological computer programs, together with the Obliquity and the RAMC. In practice therefore, only the AD requires any calculation that goes beyond plus and minus. With the availability of trig functions on inexpensive hand-held calculators, the calculation of AD should not present anyone with a major problem.

Knowing the above formulae does not mean one must use them. I usually don't. Solar Fire provides a Primary Mundane module within its Transits option. Select the following: Directions to Radix and blank the transit and progression options; Primary Mundane under Directions at top right; birth date and 120 years for Period; all ten bodies for Progs; the ascendant and midheaven for Radix; and conjunction and opposition for Aspect Progs. The sequence of planets coming to each angle results.

Appendix B:

Parts of the Decan

Each year within the decan can be split into ten parts the length of each being the time it takes for the Sun to cross thirty-six degrees of the Zodiac. The sequence of the planets ruling these parts is such that the first part is ruled by the planet to which the decan ruler is directed that year, and the final part ruled by the planet to which the decan ruler will be directed the following year. Hence the sequence of parts is in a counter-clockwise direction from the ruling planet.

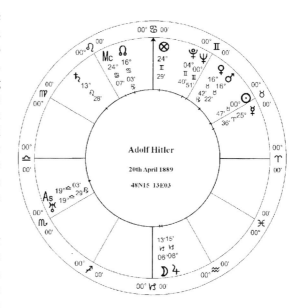

Hitler's mother dies on 21st December 1907, when the transit Sun was in the final degree of Sagittarius. He is then 18 years old and in his decan the Moon has come to Mercury. At his birth the Moon is in the 4th house by equal sign, and Mercury, named after a god of the dead, is in the setting sign.

Parts of Decan for Hitler as his Moon comes to Mercury

Transit ☉	Date Part begins	Part ruler
0° 47' ♉	20th April 1907	☿
6° 47' ♊	28th May	☉
12° 47' ♋	4th July	♂
18° 47' ♌	11th August	♀
24° 47' ♍	17th September	♆
0° 47' ♏	24th October	♇
6° 47' ♐	**29th November**	♄
12° 47' ♑	3rd January 1908	♅
18° 47' ♒	7th February	☽
24° 47' ♓	15th March	♃

As the above table shows, the planet receiving the decan ruler, here Mercury, is allotted the first part of the year. Then, proceeding counterclockwise from Mercury, the parts are ruled in turn at 36° intervals by the Sun, Mars, Venus, Neptune, Pluto, Saturn, Uranus, the Moon and Jupiter. The death of Hitler's mother occurred in the part associated with Saturn.

Transit ☉	Date Piece begins	Piece ruler
6° 47' ♐	29th November 1907	♄
10° 23' ♐	3rd December	♀
13° 59' ♐	6th December	♆
17° 35' ♐	10th December	♀
21° 11' ♐	13th December	♂
24° 47' ♐	17th December	☉
28° 23' ♐	**20th December**	**☿**
1° 59' ♑	24th December	♃
5° 35' ♑	27th December	☽
9° 11' ♑	31st December	♅

Dividing each one of the parts into ten pieces can make a finer split. The length of each of these pieces is then 3°36' measured by the movement of the transit Sun. The sequence of these pieces are now in a clockwise direction from the part ruler to ensure that this same part ruler has the initial piece and the next part ruler will have the final one. For the death of Hitler's mother, the piece is associated with the setting Mercury, the guide of the dead. This period can be described as the Mercury piece within the Saturn part of the Mercury year within the Sun-ruled decan. For young Hitler it symbolized the receipt of sad and depressing news concerning his mother.

Appendix C:

Splitting the Septenary

Each year of the septenary may be split into seven parts in such a way that the planet receiving the time ruler governs the first of these parts and the planet that will receive the time ruler next year governs the last. This means that these sub-rulers are located counter-clockwise from the receiving planet.

The lengths of these planetary parts, in solar degrees, are as follows:

Lengths of Planetary Parts of a Year

Planetary Part	Solar Degrees
☉	53
☽	70
☿	56
♀	22
♂	42
♃	33
♄	84
Total	360

The sequence of rising planets at Hitler's birth is: Moon first, then Jupiter, Mercury, Sun, Mars, Venus and last Saturn.

Hitler's mother dies on 21st December 1907. He is then 18 years old. His septenary ruler is Mercury and on 20th April 1907 it has come to his Venus. At the time of his mother's death the transit Sun has advanced from 1° Taurus to 29° Sagittarius, a distance of 178°. Summing the appropriate solar degrees we have the following dates for when each of that year's parts begins, commencing with that of Venus the planet to which the septenary ruler had come:

The Seven Parts of Hitler's 19th Year

Planetary Part	Solar degrees	Part begins
♀	31	20 April 1907
♄	53	14 May
☽	137	10 August
♃	207	21 October
☿	240	22 November
☉	296	16 January 1908
♂	349	9 March

In September 1907, apparently unaware of the seriousness of his mother's illness, young Adolf leaves home and moves to Vienna where he expects to enter the Academy of Fine Arts. This is in the Moon's part of the year. The Moon is weak in Capricorn and conjunct Jupiter in its fall. He confidently sits the exam at the academy but is shocked by the verdict "test drawing unsatisfactory". The fifth year of a septenary seven can be the time when the individual is forced to recognize that his dreams are not going to be fulfilled. Hitler must now realize that his painting could never be more than a hobby.

Later in that same Moon-governed part of the year he returns home and learns that his mother is dying. He consults doctors and nurses his mother during the Jupiter-ruled part and into the Mercury one. Mercury opposes Hitler's ascendant and as such symbolizes open enemies, at this time the disease about which he can do nothing. As Mercury rules the septenary, this part of the year that begins at the end of November 1907 has to be a very sensitive part of the year.

Each of the seven parts of a year can in turn be split into even finer pieces, as follows:

Seven-way Split of the Parts of a Year, in Days

Type of days	Parts of the year						
	☉	☽	☿	♀	♂	♃	♄
☉	8	10	8	3	6	5	13
☽	10	14	11	4	8	6	16
☿	9	11	9	4	7	5	13
♀	3	4	3	1	3	2	5
♂	6	8	7	3	5	4	10
♃	4	6	5	2	3	3	8
♄	13	17	13	5	10	8	19
Sum	53	70	56	22	42	33	84

To specify when within the Mercury part of 1908 the death of Hitler's mother occurs, the 56 Mercury-governed days are split between the planets, moving now in a clockwise direction to ensure that the final planet in the sequence will be the Sun, the ruler of the next part of the year.

Seven-way Split of Hitler's Mercury Part

Planetary Piece	Solar degrees	Part begins
☿	240	22 November 1907
♃	249	1 December
☽	254	6 December
♄	**265**	**17 December**
♀	278	30 December
♂	281	1 January 1908
☉	288	8 January

The death of Hitler's mother on 21st December 1907 occurs in the Saturn-ruled piece of the Mercury-ruled part of the Venus year within the Mercury-ruled septenary. Saturn is in Leo where it is in its detriment, Mercury closely opposes Hitler's ascendant, and the planet to which the septenary ruler has come, Venus, rules Hitler's ascendant. Aware of this combination of portents an astrologer could only expect Hitler to experience an very unhappy Christmas at that time.

Combining the fine splits of the decan and septenary points to the nature of the event. In the decan, as we've seen in Appendix B, the death of Hitler's mother occurred within the four days indicated by ☽♀♄☿—the Moon as decan ruler has come to his fourth house Mercury, and the Mercury year is split into ten parts of which Saturn rules the part in which the mother died; going even finer in our division we find the death occurring within the four days ruled by Mercury. In the septenary the death is symbolized by ☿♀♀♄—Mercury ruling the septenary has come to Venus and the Venus-year is split into seven parts, the death occurring in the part ruled by Mercury; going even finer and splitting the 56 Mercury-days into seven pieces we come to 13 days ruled by Saturn, within which the death occurred. Both decan and septenary point to the same few days being of a Saturn-within-Mercury or Mercury-within-Saturn type. That could mean concentrated studies or some other Saturn-Mercury manifestation but this pair feature in Moon and Venus periods, which suggests a female within the family is involved. Being aware of the mother's sickness, knowing Mercury's involvement with death, and Saturn's role as the Greater Malefic, an astrologer must expect the period at the end of 1907, around Christmas, to coincide with the death of Hitler's mother, which is what happened.

The 50% Probability Test

This test compares any two numbers of things that are expected to differ from one another only by chance. It is appropriate when comparing positive years against negative ones when the probability of either is expected to be the same, namely 50%.

> X = number of observed cases in the larger class of the sample
> Y = number of observed cases in the smaller class of the sample.
> N = X + Y = sample size

(a) If N = 270 or less: no calculation is required. Simply refer to the tables on the next two pages for the 50% Probability Test. Find the line corresponding to N and then see if the observed Percent (=100*X/N) is greater than either of the three values that are listed. The listed numbers alongside each N in the Table (see next two pages) are the critical values for P = 0.1 (1 in 10), P = 0.05 (1 in 20) and P = 0.01 (1 in 100). P = 0.05 is the probability criterion in standard use in research. If the observed value exceeds the printed number the difference is significant at the stated level and the chance of it having occurred simply due to chance must be questioned. When the observed value is less than the number printed in the Table the difference is not considered to be of statistical significance, and no evidence has been provided that says the two pertinent values differ from each other.

(b) If N is greater than 270 or if use is not made of the Table.
> Calculate the value of $P50 = (|X - Y| - 1)^2 / N$

The higher the value of P50, the less the likelihood of a non-significant assumption being correct.

> If P50 is greater than or equal to 2.706, then P = 0.1 (1 in 10);
> If P50 is greater than or equal to 3.841 then P = 0.05 (1 in 20);
> If P50 is greater than or equal to 6.635 then P = 0.01 (1 in 100);
> If P50 is greater than or equal to 10.828 then P = 0.001 (1 in 1,000).

Example: The waxing Moon at night is associated with 179 positive years and 122 negative ones. Is this meaningful?

$$X = 179, \qquad Y = 122, \qquad N = 301$$

$$P50 = (|179 - 122| - 1)^2/301 = (57 - 1)^2/301 = 56^2/301 = 3136/301 = 10.42$$

The calculated value of 10.42 exceeds the P = 0.01 criteria of 6.635. We can therefore say that the difference is highly significant, the probability that it occurred simply by chance is less than 1 in 100.

Significant Values, 1 in 10 (0.1), 1 in 20 (0.05) & 1 in 100 (0.01) for Binomial Distribution, N = 1 to 135

N	% Significant at			N	% Significant at			N	% Significant at		
	0.10	0.05	0.01		0.10	0.05	0.01		0.10	0.05	0.01
1	*	*	*	46	63.2	65.5	70.1	91	59.1	60.8	64.0
2	*	*	*	47	63.0	65.4	69.8	92	59.1	60.8	64.0
3	*	*	*	48	62.9	65.2	69.6	93	59.0	60.7	63.9
4	*	*	*	49	62.7	65.0	69.4	94	59.0	60.6	63.8
5	96.7	*	*	50	62.6	64.9	69.2	95	58.9	60.6	63.7
6	91.8	98.3	*	51	62.5	64.7	69.0	96	58.9	60.5	63.7
7	88.1	94.2	*	52	62.3	64.6	68.8	97	58.8	60.5	63.6
8	85.2	90.9	*	53	62.2	64.4	68.6	98	58.8	60.4	63.5
9	82.9	88.2	98.5	54	62.1	64.3	68.4	99	58.7	60.4	63.4
10	80.9	86.0	95.7	55	62.0	64.1	68.3	100	58.7	60.3	63.4
11	79.3	84.1	93.4	56	61.9	64.0	68.1	101	58.7	60.2	63.3
12	77.8	82.5	91.3	57	61.7	63.9	67.9	102	58.6	60.2	63.2
13	76.6	81.0	89.6	58	61.6	63.7	67.8	103	58.6	60.1	63.2
14	75.5	79.8	88.0	59	61.5	63.6	67.6	104	58.5	60.1	63.1
15	74.5	78.6	86.6	60	61.4	63.5	67.5	105	58.5	60.0	63.0
16	73.6	77.6	85.3	61	61.3	63.4	67.3	106	58.4	60.0	63.0
17	72.8	76.7	84.2	62	61.2	63.3	67.2	107	58.4	59.9	62.9
18	72.1	75.9	83.1	63	61.1	63.1	67.0	108	58.4	59.9	62.9
19	71.4	75.1	82.2	64	61.0	63.0	66.9	109	58.3	59.8	62.8
20	70.8	74.4	81.3	65	60.9	62.9	66.7	110	58.3	59.8	62.7
21	70.3	73.8	80.5	66	60.9	62.8	66.6	111	58.2	59.8	62.7
22	69.8	73.2	79.7	67	60.8	62.7	66.5	112	58.2	59.7	62.6
23	69.3	72.6	79.0	68	60.7	62.6	66.3	113	58.2	59.7	62.6
24	68.8	72.1	78.4	69	60.6	62.5	66.2	114	58.1	59.6	62.5
25	68.4	71.6	77.8	70	60.5	62.4	66.1	115	58.1	59.6	62.4
26	68.0	71.1	77.2	71	60.4	62.3	66.0	116	58.0	59.5	62.4
27	67.6	70.7	76.6	72	60.4	62.2	65.9	117	58.0	59.5	62.3
28	67.3	70.3	76.1	73	60.3	62.2	65.8	118	58.0	59.4	62.3
29	67.0	69.9	75.6	74	60.2	62.1	65.6	119	57.9	59.4	62.2
30	66.6	69.6	75.2	75	60.1	62.0	65.5	120	57.9	59.4	62.2
31	66.3	69.2	74.7	76	60.1	61.9	65.4	121	57.9	59.3	62.1
32	66.1	68.9	74.3	77	60.0	61.8	65.3	122	57.8	59.3	62.1
33	65.8	68.6	73.9	78	59.9	61.7	65.2	123	57.8	59.2	62.0
34	65.5	68.3	73.6	79	59.9	61.7	65.1	124	57.8	59.2	62.0
35	65.3	68.0	73.2	80	59.8	61.6	65.0	125	57.7	59.2	61.9
36	65.1	67.7	72.8	81	59.7	61.5	64.9	126	57.7	59.1	61.9
37	64.8	67.5	72.5	82	59.7	61.4	64.8	127	57.7	59.1	61.8
38	64.6	67.2	72.2	83	59.6	61.4	64.7	128	57.6	59.1	61.8
39	64.4	67.0	71.9	84	59.5	61.3	64.6	129	57.6	59.0	61.7
40	64.2	66.7	71.6	85	59.5	61.2	64.6	130	57.6	59.0	61.7
41	64.0	66.5	71.3	86	59.4	61.1	64.5	131	57.5	58.9	61.6
42	63.8	66.3	71.1	87	59.4	61.1	64.4	132	57.5	58.9	61.6
43	63.7	66.1	70.8	88	59.3	61.0	64.3	133	57.5	58.9	61.5
44	63.5	65.9	70.5	89	59.3	60.9	64.2	134	57.5	58.8	61.5
45	63.3	65.7	70.3	90	59.2	60.9	64.1	135	57.4	58.8	61.5

Significant Values, 1 in 10 (0.1), 1 in 20 (0.05) & 1 in 100 (0.01) for Binomial Distribution, N = 136 to 270

N	% Significant at			N	% Significant at			N	% Significant at		
	0.10	0.05	0.01		0.10	0.05	0.01		0.10	0.05	0.01
136	57.4	58.8	61.4	181	56.4	57.6	59.8	226	55.7	56.7	58.8
137	57.4	58.7	61.4	182	56.4	57.5	59.8	227	55.7	56.7	58.8
138	57.3	58.7	61.3	183	56.3	57.5	59.8	228	55.6	56.7	58.7
139	57.3	58.7	61.3	184	56.3	57.5	59.8	229	55.6	56.7	58.7
140	57.3	58.6	61.2	185	56.3	57.5	59.7	230	55.6	56.7	58.7
141	57.3	58.6	61.2	186	56.3	57.5	59.7	231	55.6	56.7	58.7
142	57.2	58.6	61.2	187	56.3	57.4	59.7	232	55.6	56.6	58.7
143	57.2	58.5	61.1	188	56.2	57.4	59.7	233	55.6	56.6	58.6
144	57.2	58.5	61.1	189	56.2	57.4	59.6	234	55.6	56.6	58.6
145	57.2	58.5	61.0	190	56.2	57.4	59.6	235	55.6	56.6	58.6
146	57.1	58.5	61.0	191	56.2	57.4	59.6	236	55.5	56.6	58.6
147	57.1	58.4	61.0	192	56.2	57.3	59.5	237	55.5	56.6	58.6
148	57.1	58.4	60.9	193	56.2	57.3	59.5	238	55.5	56.6	58.6
149	57.1	58.4	60.9	194	56.1	57.3	59.5	239	55.5	56.5	58.5
150	57.0	58.3	60.8	195	56.1	57.3	59.5	240	55.5	56.5	58.5
151	57.0	58.3	60.8	196	56.1	57.3	59.5	241	55.5	56.5	58.5
152	57.0	58.3	60.8	197	56.1	57.2	59.4	242	55.5	56.5	58.5
153	57.0	58.2	60.7	198	56.1	57.2	59.4	243	55.5	56.5	58.5
154	56.9	58.2	60.7	199	56.1	57.2	59.4	244	55.5	56.5	58.4
155	56.9	58.2	60.7	200	56.0	57.2	59.4	245	55.4	56.5	58.4
156	56.9	58.2	60.6	201	56.0	57.2	59.3	246	55.4	56.5	58.4
157	56.9	58.1	60.6	202	56.0	57.1	59.3	247	55.4	56.4	58.4
158	56.8	58.1	60.6	203	56.0	57.1	59.3	248	55.4	56.4	58.4
159	56.8	58.1	60.5	204	56.0	57.1	59.3	249	55.4	56.4	58.4
160	56.8	58.1	60.5	205	56.0	57.1	59.2	250	55.4	56.4	58.3
161	56.8	58.0	60.5	206	56.0	57.1	59.2	251	55.4	56.4	58.3
162	56.8	58.0	60.4	207	55.9	57.1	59.2	252	55.4	56.4	58.3
163	56.7	58.0	60.4	208	55.9	57.0	59.2	253	55.4	56.4	58.3
164	56.7	58.0	60.4	209	55.9	57.0	59.1	254	55.3	56.3	58.3
165	56.7	57.9	60.3	210	55.9	57.0	59.1	255	55.3	56.3	58.3
166	56.7	57.9	60.3	211	55.9	57.0	59.1	256	55.3	56.3	58.2
167	56.6	57.9	60.3	212	55.9	57.0	59.1	257	55.3	56.3	58.2
168	56.6	57.9	60.2	213	55.9	56.9	59.1	258	55.3	56.3	58.2
169	56.6	57.8	60.2	214	55.8	56.9	59.0	259	55.3	56.3	58.2
170	56.6	57.8	60.2	215	55.8	56.9	59.0	260	55.3	56.3	58.2
171	56.6	57.8	60.1	216	55.8	56.9	59.0	261	55.3	56.3	58.2
172	56.5	57.8	60.1	217	55.8	56.9	59.0	262	55.3	56.2	58.1
173	56.5	57.7	60.1	218	55.8	56.9	58.9	263	55.2	56.2	58.1
174	56.5	57.7	60.0	219	55.8	56.9	58.9	264	55.2	56.2	58.1
175	56.5	57.7	60.0	220	55.8	56.8	58.9	265	55.2	56.2	58.1
176	56.5	57.7	60.0	221	55.7	56.8	58.9	266	55.2	56.2	58.1
177	56.4	57.6	60.0	222	55.7	56.8	58.9	267	55.2	56.2	58.1
178	56.4	57.6	59.9	223	55.7	56.8	58.8	268	55.2	56.2	58.1
179	56.4	57.6	59.9	224	55.7	56.8	58.8	269	55.2	56.2	58.0
180	56.4	57.6	59.9	225	55.7	56.8	58.8	270	55.2	56.1	58.0

Appendix E:

Comparing Two Observed Percentages

In Table ☉-2 we see that 50.9% of 430 diurnal births experienced positive years when the Sun was the Time Lord. Is this percent really greater than the 44.9% positive years observed in 585 nocturnal births under the same time lord? Can this difference be considered to be a real one or did it occur simply due to random chance, because the number of observations were too few to adequately discriminate between the two percentages?

An important corrolary: is there evidence here to suggest that those born in the daytime experience the Sun as a benefic, while those born at night have it as a malefic?

The necessary steps to take to provide an objective response to this or similar questions follow:

1. Transform the observed percentages into proportions by dividing each of them by 100. Thus 50.9% becomes 0.509, as the larger of the two values being compared we will designate this proportion as p_1. Similarly, 44.9% becomes 0.449, and we will call this proportion p_2.

2. Find the difference between these proportions.
   Here, $p_1 - p_2 = 0.509 - 0.449 = 0.060$.

3. Calculate the Variance of each of the two proportions.
   The formula for the variance is $Var(p_i) = p_i(1-p_i)/N_i$
   Variance of p_1 or $Var(p_1) = (0.509 * 0.491)/430 = 0.24941/430$
   $= 0.000580023$.
   $Var(p_2) = (0.449 * 0.551)/585 = 0.247399/585 = 0.000422904$.

4. Sum these two variances to obtain the Variance of the Difference
   Here $Var(p_1) + Var(p_2) = 0.000580023 + 0.000422904 = 0.001002927$.

5. Calculate the square root of the sum of the two variances, to obtain the Standard Error of the Difference.
   This is $[Var(p_1) + Var(p_2)]^{1/2}$ or the square root of the sum of the two variances.
   Here $SE(p_1 - p_2) = 0.001002927^{1/2} = 0.031669027$.

6. Divide this standard error into the difference $(p_1 - p_2)$ observed between the two proportions at Step 2 above, to obtain the test statistic, usually designated as Z.
   Here, as $p_1 - p_2 = 0.060$, the division of the difference by the standard error, $0.060/0.031669027$, gives $Z = 1.895$.

7. Finally, we examine the following table to see where the calculated test value falls.

Test Value, Z	Significance level	Odds this significance occurs by chance	Meaning of the observed difference
< 1.28	<90%	< 1 in 10	There is no evidence that the two observed values are different. The apparent difference is probably due to chance.
1.28	90%	1 in 10	Interesting but not enough evidence to say that the two values are different.
1.64	95%	1 in 20	The standard level in science. The observed difference indicates the two values are different from each other.
1.96	97.5%	1 in 40	Stronger evidence of a true difference
2.33	99%	1 in 100	Even stronger evidence
2.58	99.5%	1 in 200	A yet stronger indication
3.09	99.9%	1 in 1000	Extremely significant. It is very likely that the observed values really are different. The chances of the observed difference occurring by chance is virtually nil.

The calculated test value of 1.895 falls between 1.64 and 1.96 in the above table. It is therefore higher than the standard value scientists use to evaluate such differences. The actual significance value associated with a Z of 1.895 is 97.094 which indicates the odds to be only 1 in 34.4—obtained by dividing 100 by (100 − 97.094)—that the observed difference between day and night births occurred as the result of chance. We can therefore say that there is statistical evidence in our sample of a true difference in % Positive years between day and night births when the Sun is the time ruler, with day births having a greater number of positive years than did those born during the night. This provides meaningful evidence that the Sun is beneficial for those born during the day, and less so (malefic) for night births.

Appendix F:
An Incomplete List of the Books Consulted

Banville, John. *Kepler.* Boston: David R. Godine, 1984.

Bedford, Sybille. *Aldous Huxley, A Biography.* New York: Carroll & Graf, 1985.

Berry, Reginald. *A Pope Chronology.* Boston: G. K. Hall & Co., 1988.

Bishop, Jim. *The Days of Martin Luther King, Jr.* New York: G. P. Putnam's Sons, 1971.

Blau, Evelyne. *Krishnamurti: 100 Years.* New York: Stewart, Tabori & Chang, 1995.

Boswell, James. *The Life of Samuel Johnson.* London: Penguin Books, 1986.

Campbell, Joseph. *The Hero With a Thousand Faces.* Princeton: Princeton University Press, 1949.

Carso, Clayborne, editor. *The Autobiography of Martin Luther King Jr.* New York: Warner Books, 1998.

Caspar, Max. *Kepler.* Trans. C. Doris Hellman. New York: Dover Publications, 1993.

Clinton, Hillary Rodham. *Living History.* New York: Simon & Schuster, 2003.

Coleman, Ray. *Lennon.* New York: McGraw-Hill, 1986.

Cortázar, Julio. *The Test.* Buenos Aires: Sudamericana, 1969.

Ebertin, Reinhold. *The Combination of Stellar Influences.* Trans. Alfred G. Roosedale. Aalen, Germany: Ebertin-Verlag, 1960.

Ellmann, Richard. Oscar Wilde. New York: Alfred A. Kopf, 1987.

Firmicus Maternus. *Matheseos Libri VIII.* Pub. as *Ancient Astrology Theory and Practice.* Trans. Jean Rhys Bram. Park Ridge, NJ: Noyes Press, 1975.

Franklin, Benjamin. *The Autobiography.* New York: Vintage Books, 1990.

Fraser, Antonia. *Cromwell, the Lord Protector.* New York: Alfred A. Knopf, 1973.

Fraser, Nicholas & Marysa Navarro. *Eva Perón.* London: Deutsch, 1980.

Freud, Sigmund. *The Interpretation of Dreams.* Trans. James Strachey. New York: Avon Books, 1965.

Gay, Peter. Freud, *A Life for Our Time.* New York: Doubleday, 1988.

Gleick, James. *Isaac Newton.* New York: Simon and Schuster, 2003.

Goodwin, Doris Kearns. *Team of Rivals. The Political Genius of Abraham Lincoln.* New York: Simon & Schuster Paperbacks, 2006.

Graves, Richard Perceval. *Robert Graves: The Assault Heroic, 1895-1926.* London: Papermac, 1987.

--------------- . *Robert Graves: The Years with Laura Riding, 1926-1940.* New York: Penguin Books, 1992.

--------------- . *Robert Graves and the White Goddess, 1980-1985.* London: Weidenfeld and Nicolson, 1995.

Graves, Robert. *Goodbye to All That.* Harmondsworth, England; Penguin Books, 1960.

Greennut, R. L. *Revolution before Breakfast.* University of North Carolina Press; ARC edition, 1947.

Hadamard, Jacques. *The Psychology of Invention in the Mathematical Field.* Princeton: Princeton University Press, 1949.

Hand, Robert. *Planets in Transit: Life Cycles for Living.* Rockport, MA: Para Research, 1976.

Hands, Timothy. *A George Eliot Chronology.* Boston: G. K. Hall & Co., 1988.

Hardy, G. H. *A Mathematician's Apology.* Cambridge: Cambridge University Press, 1940.

-------------. *Bertrand Russell & Trinity.* New York: Arno Press, 1977..

Harvey, Ross & Jack Nicholls, "The Search for the Unknown Birthtime." *Considerations* Vol. VII no. 4.

Hephaistio of Thebes. *Apotelesmatics. Book II.* Trans. Robert Schmidt. Cumberland, MD: The Golden Hind Press, 1998

Herndon, William H. & Jesse W. Weik. *Abraham Lincoln: The True Story of a Great Life.* New York: D. Appleton & Co, 1900.

Herold, J. Christopher. *The Age of Napoleon.* Boston: Houghton Mifflin, 2002.

Iamblichus. *Theology of Arithmetic: On the Mystical, Mathematical and Cosmological Symbolism of the First Ten Numbers*, Trans. Robin Waterfield. Grand Rapids, Michigan: Phanes Press, 1968.

Inwood, Stephen. *The Forgotten Genius. The biography of Rober Hooke 1635-1703.* San Francisco: MacAdam/Cage, 2003.

Jayakar, Pupil. *Krishnamurti. A Biography.* San Francisco: Harper & Row,1986.

Jenkins, Roy. *Churchill; A Biography.* New York: Farrar, Straus & Giroux, 2001.

Jung, C. G. *Memories, Dreams, Reflections.* New York: Vintage Books, 1965.

Kanigel, Robert. *The Man Who Knew Inifinity: A Life of the Genius Ramanujan.* New York; Washington Square Press, 1991.

Kobak, Annette. *Isabelle. The Life of Isabelle Eberhardt.* New York: Alfred A. Knopf, 1989.

Langley, Russell. *Practical Statistics simply explained.* New York: Dover, 1971.

Lessing, Doris. *Under My Skin: Volume One of My Autobiography, to 1949.* New York: HarperCollins, 1994.

---------------. *Walking in the Shade: Volume Two of My Autobiography, 1949-.* New York: HarperCollins, 1997.

Lievegoed, Bernard. *Phases: The Spiritual Rhythms in Adult Life.* London: Pharos Books, 1979.

Lutyens, Mary. *Krishnamurti: The Years of Awakening.* New York: Avon Books, 1975.

-----------------. *Krishnamurti: The Years of Fulfillment.* New York: Avon Books, 1983.

-----------------. *Krishnamurti: The Open Door.* New York: Avon Books, 1988.

Lynn, Kenneth S. *Hemingway.* New York: Simon & Schuster, 1987.

Mailer, Norman. *The Castle in the Forest.* New York: Random House Trade Paperbacks, 2007.

Marr, Alexander. *Astrologers, Kings, Politicians and Others.* Buenos Aires: Ediciones Sirio, 1990.

-------------- *Prediction II.* Tempe, Arizona: American Federation of Astrologers, 1985.

-------------- & Isaac Starkman. *Astrologers, Kings, Politicians and Others, Part II.* Miami, Florida: 1995.

Martinez, Tomas Eloy, *Santa Evita.* Trans. Helen Lane. New York: Alfred A. Knopf, 1996.

Massie, Robert K. *Nicholas and Alexandria.* New York: Ballantine Books, 1985.

-------------. *Peter the Great, His Life and World.* New York: Ballantine Books, 1986.

Montgomery, Paul. *Eva Evita.* New York & Chicago: Pocket Books, 1979.

Montefiore, Simon Sebag. *Stalin: The Court of the Red Tsar.* New York: Vintage Books, 2005.

---------------. *Young Stalin.* New York: Alfred A. Knopf, 2007.

Morgan, Ted. *FDR. A Biography.* New York, Simon and Schuster, 1979.

Morris, Edmund. *The Rise of Theodore Roosevelt.* New York: Ballantine Books, 1980.

--------------. *Theodore Rex.* New York: Random House, 2001.

Nelson, Craig. *Thomas Paine. Enlightenment, Revolution and the Birth of Modern Nations.* New York: Penguin Books, 2007.

Neugebauer, Otto & H. B. Van Hoesen. *Greek Horoscopes.* Philadelphia: American Philosophical Society, 1959.

Olivier, Laurence. *Confessions of an Actor.* New York: Simon & Schuster, 1983.

--------------- . *On Acting.* New York: Simon & Schuster,1986.

O'Toole, Patricia. *When Trumpets Call: Theodore Roosevelt After the White House.* New York: Simon & Schuster, 2005.

Page, Norman. *A Byron Chronology.* Boston: G. K. Hall & Co., 1988.

Pearson, John. *The Private Lives of Winston Churchill.* New York, Simon & Shuster, 1991.

Pepys, Samuel. *The Diary of Samuel Pepys in three volumes.* London: Everyman's Library, 1975.

Pinion, F. B. *A Wordsworth Chronology.* Boston: G. K. Hall & Co., 1988.

Plutarch. *The Lives of the Noble Grecians and Romans.* Trans. John Dryden. New York: The Modern Library, 1864.

Renault, Mary. *The Nature of Alexander.* New York: Pantheon Books, 1976.

Ridley, Matt. *Genome: The Autobiography of a Species in 23 Chapters.* New York: HarperCollins, 2006.

Robinson, David. *Chaplin: His Life and Art.* New York: McGraw-Hill Book Co., 1985.

Ruperti, Alexander. *Cycles of Becoming: The Planetary Pattern of Growth.* Davis, CA: CRCS Publications, 1978.

Russell, Bertrand. *Autobiography.* London: Routledge, 1971.

Seymour, Miranda. *Robert Graves, Life on the Edge.* New York: Henry Holt & Company, 1995.

Seymour-Smith, Martin. *Hardy.* London: Bloomsbury, 1995.

Shulman, Irving. *Harlow, an Intimate Biography.* New York: Dell Publishing,1964.

Tranquillus, Gaius Suetonius. *The Twelve Caesars.* Trans. Robert Graves. London: Penguin Books, 1957.

Tolland, John. *Adolf Hitler.* New York: Ballantine Books, 1976.

Tomalin, Claire. *Samuel Pepys, the Unequalled Self.* New York: Vintage Books, 2002.

Weeks, Nora. *The Medical Discoveries of Edward Bach, Physician.* New Canaan, CT., Keats Publishing Inc., 1973.

Wehr, Gerhard. *Jung, A Biography.* Trans. David M. Weeks. Boston: Shambala, 1987.

Westfall, Richard S. *Never at Rest. A Biography of Isaac Newton.* Cambrige University Press, 1980.

Wilson, Colin. *Dreaming to Some Purpose.* London: Arrow Books, 2005.

Wright, Paul. *Astrology in Action.* Sebastopol, California: CRCS Publications, 1989.

Young, Arthur M. *Nested Time: An Astrological Autobiography.* Cambria, CA: Anodos, 2004.

Appendix G: People in the Sample

The following lists the individuals in my sample, separated by day and night births, in order of their planetary sequence, for both decan and septenary. Dates are in New Style, in month-day-year order. The age at which a planet commences its period of rulership is shown by the heading row of each table. To identify the planet to which that ruler comes in each year proceed to the left of the ruler, circling around to the far right when appropriate. Thus Harry Truman, a diurnal birth, became US president on the death of Roosevelt in early 1945 at the age of 61. The decan ruler was Venus in Cancer and that year it came to his Saturn.

DECAN: DIURNAL BIRTHS ANALYZED

Name	Born	0-	10-	20-	30-	40-	50-	60-	70-	80-	90-
Truman, Harry	5. 8.1884	☽♏	☉♉	♆♉	♇♊	☿♊R	♄♊	♀♋	♃♋	♂♌	♅♍R
Obama, Barak	8. 4.1961	☽♊	♀♋	☿♌	☉♌	♅♌	♇♍	♂♍	♆♏	♄♑R	♃♒R
The Buddha	5.11.-564	☽♏	♂♈	☿♈	♃♈	♄♈	☉♉	♇♉	♆♉	♀♊	♅♋
Ashe, Arthur	7.10.1943	☽♎	♂♉	♅♊	♄♊	☿♋	☉♋	♃♌	♇♌	♀♍	♆♍
Appo, George	7. 4.1856	☽♌	♂♎	♆♓R	♃♈	♇♉	♅♉	☿♊	♄♋	♀♋	☉♋
Grant, Ulysses S.	4.27.1822	☽♋	♂♌	♆♑R	♅♑R	♀♓	♇♈	☿♈	♄♉	☉♉	♃♉
Roberts, Martha Ann	6.3.1936	☽♏	♃♐R	♄♓	♅♉	♀♊	☿♊	☉♊	♂♊	♇♋	♆♍
Bush, George Sr	6.12.1924	☽♎	♄♎R	♃♐R	♂♒	♅♓	☿♉	☉♊	♇♋	♀♋R	♆♌
Fagan, Cyril	5.22.1896	☽♎	♄♏R	♅♏R	♂♈	♀♉	☉♊	♇♊	♆♊	☿♊	♃♌
Nietzsche, Frederich	10.15.1844	☽♐	♄♒	♆♒R	♃♓R	♅♈R	♇♈R	♀♍	♂♍	☿♎	☉♎
Huber, Bruno	11.29.1930	☽♓	♅♈R	♃♋R	♇♋R	♂♌	♆♍	♀♏R	☉♐	☿♐	♄♑
Byron, Lord	1.22.1788	☽♋	♅♋R	♆♎	☿♑	☉♒	♇♒	♀♒	♄♒	♃♊R	♂♋R
Alexander the Great	7.22.-357	☽♎	♅♑R	♇♈	♄♉	♂♊	☿♋	☉♋	♀♋	♆♍	♃♍
Johnson, Samuel	9.17.1709	☽♓	♆♈R	♄♋	♅♌	♇♌	☉♍	☿♍	♀♎	♂♎	♃♏
Firebrace, Roy	8.16.1889	☽♉	♆♊	♇♊	♀♋	♂♌	♄♌	☉♌	☿♍	♅♎	♃♐R
Peron, Juan	10. 8.1895	☽♊	♇♊R	♆♊R	♃♌	♀♍R	☉♎	♂♎	♄♏	☿♏	♅♏
DeLorean, John	1. 6.1925	☽♊	♇♋R	♆♌R	♄♏	♀♐	☿♐	♃♑	☉♑	♅♓	♂♈
Franklin, Ben	1.17.1706	☿♒R	☽♓	♆♈	♄♉	♃♋R	♅♌R	♇♌R	♂♐	♀♑	☉♑
Gandhi, Mohandes	10. 2.1869	☿♏	♀♏	♂♏	♄♐	♆♈R	♇♉R	♃♉R	♅♋	☽♌	☉♎
Bush, George W.	7. 6.1946	☿♌	♀♌	♂♍	♆♎	☽♎	♃♎	♅♊	☉♋	♄♋	♇♌
Arthur, Chester	10. 5.1829	☿♏	♀♏	♃♐	☽♑	♆♑	♅♒R	♇♈R	♄♌	♂♍	☉♎
Planck, Max	4.23.1858	☿♉	♀♉	♃♉	♅♉	♇♉	♄♋	☽♍	♂♐R	♆♓	☉♉
Mantel, Arie	8.27.1911	♀♍R	☽♎	♃♏	♅♑R	♄♉	♂♉	♇♊	♆♋	☉♍	☿♍
Barrie, Sir James	5. 9.1860	♀♋	♃♋	♄♌	☽♑	♂♑	♆♓	☿♈	♇♉	☉♉	♅♊
Thatcher, Margaret	10.13.1925	♀♐	♃♑	♅♓R	♇♋	♆♌	☽♌	♂♎	☉♎	☿♎	♄♏
Mao Zedung	12.26.1893	♀♒	♃♉	♇♊	♆♊R	☽♌	♄♎	♅♏	♂♏	☿♐	☉♑
Bohr, Niels	10. 7.1885	♀♏	♆♉R	♇♊R	♄♋	♂♌	♃♍	☽♎	♅♎	☿♎	☉♎
Rice, Condoleezza	11.14.1954	♂♒	☽♋	♅♋R	♃♋	♇♌	♆♎	☿♏	♄♏	☉♏	♀♏R
Cleveland, Grover	3.18.1837	♂♌	♃♌R	☽♌	♄♏R	♆♒	☿♓	♅♓	♀♓	☉♓	♇♈
Taylor, Bill	6.14.1937	♂♏R	♃♑R	♄♈	♀♉	♅♉	☿♊	☉♊	♇♋	☽♍	♆♍
Hemingway, Ernest	7.21.1899	♂♍	♃♏	♅♐R	♄♐R	☽♑	♇♊	♆♊	♀♋	☉♋	☿♌
Paine, Thomas	2. 8.1737	♂♉	♄♊	☽♊	♆♊R	♇♏R	♅♑	☉♒	♃♒	☿♓	♀♈
Wingate, Orde	2.26.1903	♂♎R	♅♐	♄♒	☿♒	☽♒	♃♓	☉♓	♀♓	♇♊R	♆♋R
Schmeling, Max	9.28.1905	♂♐	♅♑	♄♒	♃♊R	♇♊R	♆♋	♀♍	☿♍	☽♍	☉♎
Morin, Jean B.	2.23.1583	♂♋	♆♋R	♅♒	☿♒	♀♓	☉♓	♃♓	♄♓	☽♓	♇♈
Bach, Edward	9.24.1886	♂♏	♆♉R	♇♊R	♄♋	☽♌	♀♍	☿♍	☉♎	♅♎	♃♎
Woolf, Virginia	1.25.1882	♂♊R	♇♉R	♅♍	♀♑	☉♒	☿♒	☽♈	♄♉	♆♉	♃♉
Pope, George	5.21.1688	♃♑R	☽♒	♆♓	♀♉	☿♉	♅♉	☉♊	♂♋	♇♋	♄♎R
Curie, Marie	11.7.1867	♃♒	☽♓	♆♈R	♇♉R	♅♋R	☉♏	♄♏	♀♏	♂♏	☿♐
Gillman, Noah	6.24.1973	♃♒R	♂♈	☽♈	♄♊	☉♋	♀♋	☿♋	♇♎	♅♎	♆♐
Mann, Thomas	6. 6.1875	♃♎R	♂♑R	♄♒R	♆♉	♀♉	♇♉	☉♊	☿♋	☽♋	♅♌
Harlow, Jean	3. 4.1911	♃♏R	♂♑	♅♑	☿♒	☉♓	♀♈	☽♈	♄♉	♇♊R	♆♋R
King, Martin Luther	1.15.1929	♃♉	♂♊R	♇♋R	♆♍R	♄♐	☉♑	☿♒	♀♓	☽♓	♅♈

DECAN: DIURNAL BIRTHS ANALYZED

Name	Born	0-	10-	20-	30-	40-	50-	60-	70-	80-	90-
Hardy, Thomas	6. 2.1840	♃♏R	♄♐R	♆♒R	♅♓	♇♈	♀♉	☿♊	♂♊	☉♊	☽♋
Mondale, Walter	1. 1928	♃♓	♅♓	☽♊	♇♋	♆♌	♀♐	♄♐	♂♐	☿♑	☉♑
Keuhr, Karl	5.13.1899	♃♏R	♅♐R	♄♐R	♀♈	☿♈	☉♉	♇♊	♆♊	☽♋	♂♌
Mountbatten, Louis	6.25.1900	♃♐R	♅♐R	♄♑R	♂♉	☽♊	♇♊	♆♊	☉♋	♀♋R	☿♋
Cromwell, Oliver	5. 5.1599	♃♋	♆♌	☽♍	♄♎R	♂♈	♇♈	♅♈	☉♉	☿♉	♀♊
Franz Joseph, Emp.	8.18.1830	♃♑R	♆♑R	♅♒	♂♈	♇♈R	♀♋	♄♌	☽♌	☉♌	☿♍
Bonaparte, Napoleon	8.15.1769	♃♏	♇♑R	☽♑	♅♉	♀♋	♄♋	☿♌	☉♌	♆♍	♂♍
Polk, James K.	11.2.1795	♃♒	♇♒R	♄♊R	☽♋	♅♍	♂♍	♆♏	☉♏	♀♏	☿♐
Wilhelm II, Kaiser	1.27.1859	♄♌R	☽♏	♀♐	☿♑	☉♒	♆♓	♂♓	♇♉	♅♉R	♃♊R
Carter, Jimmy	10.1.1924	♄♏	☽♏	♃♐	♂♒	♅♓R	♇♋	♆♌	♀♌	☿♍	☉♎
Marr, Alexander	4.12.1919	♄♌R	☽♍	♅♓	☿♈R	☉♈	♂♈	♀♉	♇♋	♃♋	♆♌R
Gillman, Gabi	8. 9.1958	♄♐R	♂♉	☽♊	♀♋	♅♌	☉♌	♇♍	☿♍	♃♎	♆♏
Hefner, Hugh	4. 9.1926	♄♏R	♂♒	♃♒	♀♓	☽♓	♅♓	☿♈R	☉♈	♇♋	♆♌R
Edward VII, King	11.9.1841	♄♑	♂♑	♆♒	♅♓	♇♈R	☽♍	♀♎	☉♏	☿♐R	♃♐
Nicholas II, Tsar	5.19.1868	♄♐R	♃♈	☽♈	♆♈	♂♈	♇♉	☉♉	☿♊	♅♋	♀♋
Rabin, Yitzhak	3. 1.1922	♄♎R	♃♎R	♂♐	☿♒	♅♓	☉♓	♀♓	☽♈	♇♋R	♆♌R
Lennon, John	10.9.1940	♄♉R	♃♉R	♅♉R	♇♌	♀♍	♆♍	♂♎	☉♎	☿♏	☽♒
Ebertin, Baldur	7.21.1933	♄♒R	♅♈	☽♋	♇♋	☉♋	☿♌R	♀♌	♆♍	♃♍	♂♎
Kasmeyer, Joan	9. 7.1933	♄♒R	♅♈R	☽♈	♇♋	♆♍	☿♍	☉♍	♃♍	♀♎	♂♏
Onassis, Jaqueline	7.28.1929	♄♐R	♅♈R	☽♈	♃♊	♀♊	♇♋	☿♌	☉♌	♆♍	♂♍
Vowles, Jacqui	7.28.1931	♄♑R	♅♈	♀♋	♇♋	☉♋	♃♌	☿♌	♆♍	♂♍	☽♎
McCain, John	8.29.1936	♄♓R	♅♉R	♇♋	♂♌	☉♍	♆♍	♀♍	☿♎	♃♐	☽♒
Jung, Carl	7.26.1875	♄♒R	♆♉	☽♉	♇♉	☿♋	♀♋	☉♌	♅♌	♃♎	♂♐
Russell, Bertrand	5.18.1872	♄♑R	♆♈	☿♉	♇♉	♀♉	♂♉	☉♉	♃♋	♅♋	☽♎
Coolidge, Calvin	7. 4.1872	♄♑R	♆♈	♇♉	☽♊	♂♋	♀♋	☉♋	☿♋	♅♌	♃♌
Brandt, Willy	12.18.1913	♄♊R	♇♋R	♂♋R	♆♋R	☽♌	☿♐	♀♐	☉♐	♃♑	♅♒
Marconi, Guglielmo	4.25.1874	♅♌	☽♌	♃♍	♄♒	☿♈	♆♈	☉♉	♀♉	♇♉	♂♉
Baird, John Logie	8.13.1888	♅♎	☽♏	♂♏	♃♏	♆♊	♇♊	☿♌	♄♌	☉♌	♀♌
Hitler, Adolf	4.20.1889	♅♎	☽♑	♃♑	☿♈	☉♉	♂♉	♀♉R	♆♊	♇♊	♄♌
Jackson, Andrew	3.15.1767	♅♈	♂♉	♄♊	♆♍R	♃♍R	☽♍	♇♑	☉♓	☿♈	♀♈
Harrison, W. H.	2. 9.1773	♅♉	♂♋	♄♍R	♆♍R	☽♍	♇♑	♀♑	☿♑	☉♒	♃♓
Huxley, Aldous	7.26.1894	♅♏	♂♈	☽♉	♇♊	♆♊	♃♊	♀♋	☿♋R	☉♌	♄♎
Young, Arthur	11.3.1905	♅♑	♂♑	☽♒	♄♒	♃♊R	♇♊R	♆♋R	♀♎	☉♏	☿♏
Kennedy, John F.	5.29.1917	♅♒R	♂♉	☿♉	♃♉	☉♊	♀♊	♇♋	♄♋	♆♌	☽♍
Buchanan, James	4.23.1791	♅♌	♃♍R	♆♎R	☽♑	♇♒	♄♈	♂♈	☉♉	☿♉	♀♊
Millard, Margaret	9. 6.1916	♅♒R	♃♉R	♇♋	♄♋	♀♋	♆♌	☉♍	☿♎	♂♎	☽♑
Hendrix, Jimi	11.27.1942	♅♊R	♄♊R	♃♋R	☽♋	♇♋R	♆♎	♂♏	☿♐	☉♐	♀♐
Blackwell, Arthur	11.7.1942	♅♊R	♄♊R	♃♋	♇♌	♆♎	☿♏	☽♏	♂♏	♀♏	☉♏
Alexis, Tsarevitch	8.12.1904	♅♐R	♄♒R	♃♉	♇♊	♆♋	♂♋	☉♌	♀♌	☽♍	☿♍
Van Buren, Martin	12.5.1782	♅♋R	♆♎	♂♏	☿♏	♀♐	☉♐	☽♐	♄♑	♃♑	♇♒
Kafka, Franz	7. 3.1883	♅♍	♆♉	♂♉	♇♊	♄♊	♀♊	☿♊	☽♊	☉♊	♃♋
Thornett, David	10.31.1932	♅♈R	♇♋R	♂♌	♆♍	♃♍	♀♍	☉♏	☿♏	☽♐	♄♑
Victoria, Queen	5.24.1819	♅♐R	♆♐R	♃♒	♄♓	♇♓	♂♈	♀♈	☿♉	☽♊	☉♊
Forest, Stephanie	2.14.1958	♅♌R	♇♍R	♃♏	♆♏R	♄♐	♂♑	☽♑	♀♒R	☿♒R	☉♒
Sugarman, Rosalind	6.24.1942	♆♍	☽♎	♀♉	♅♊	♄♊	☿♊R	☉♋	♃♋	♇♌	♂♌
Richardson, Natasha	5.11.1963	♆♍R	☽♐	♄♒	♃♈	♀♈	☉♉	☿♉R	♂♌	♅♍	♇♍R
Harding, Warren	11.2.1865	♆♈	☽♉	♇♉R	♅♋R	♀♎	♄♏	☉♏	♂♏	☿♏	♃♐
Gurion, David Ben	10.16.1886	♆♉R	☽♊	♇♊R	♄♋	♅♎	♀♎	♃♎	☉♎	☿♏	♂♐
Clinton, Bill	8.19.1946	♆♎	♀♎	♃♎	☽♉	♅♊	♄♌	☿♌	♇♌	☉♌	♂♎
Kepler, Johannes	1. 6.1572	♆♊R	♂♎	♄♏	☿♑	♅♑	☉♑	♀♑	♃♓	♇♓	☿♊
Simpson, O. J.	7. 9. 1947	♆♎	♃♏R	☽♓	♂♊	♅♊	♀♋	☉♋	☿♋R	♄♌	♇♌
Freud, Sigmund	5. 6.1856	♆♓	♃♓	♀♈	♇♉	☉♉	♅♉	☿♉	☽♊	♄♊	♂♎R
Twins	1.29.1920	♆♌	♃♌	♄♍	♂♎	♀♑	☿♒	☉♒	♅♓	☽♉	♇♋R
Addey, John	6.15.1920	♆♌	♃♌	♄♍	♂♎	♅♒R	☽♊	♀♊	☉♊	♇♋	☿♋
Washington, George	2.22.1732	♆♊R	♃♎R	♇♎R	♂♏	♅♐	☽♑	☿♒	☉♓	♀♓	♄♈
Hooke, Robert	7.28.1635	♆♏	♄♐R	☽♑	♇♉	♀♋	♂♋	☉♌	♃♌	☿♍	♅♎
Mussolini, Benito	7.29.1883	♆♉	♇♊	♄♊	☽♊	♂♊	♃♋	♀♋	☿♌	☉♌	♅♍
Adams, John Q	7.11.1767	♇♑R	☽♑	♅♉	♄♊	☉♋	♂♌	☿♌	♀♍	♆♍	♃♍

DECAN: DIURNAL BIRTHS ANALYZED

Name	Born	0-	10-	20-	30-	40-	50-	60-	70-	80-	90-
Pierce, Franklin	11.23.1804	♇♓	♂♌	☽♌	♄♎	♀♎	♅♎	♃♏	♆♏	☿♏	☉♐
Louise, Princess	3.18.1848	♇♈	♂♊	♃♋	☽♍	♀♒	♆♓	♄♓	☿♓R	☉♓	♅♈
Taylor, Zachary	11.24.1784	♇♒	♃♒	☽♉	♅♋	♆♎	♂♏	☿♏	☉♐	♀♑	♄♑
Olivier, Laurence	5.22.1907	♇♊	♃♋	♆♋	☽♍	♅♑R	♂♑	♄♓	♀♈	☿♉	☉♉
Blumberg, Leda	7.19.1956	♇♌	♃♍	♆♎	♄♏R	☽♐	♂♓	♀♊	☿♋	☉♋	♅♌
Page, A. Nelson	2.25.1919	♇♋R	♃♋R	♆♌R	♄♌R	☽♑	♅♒	☉♓	☿♓	♂♓	♀♓
Harvey, Axel	2. 6.1940	♇♌	♆♍R	☽♒	☉♒	☿♒	♀♓	♃♈	♂♈	♄♈	♅♉
Jackson, Glenda	5. 9.1936	♇♋	♆♍R	☽♐	♃♐R	♄♓	♀♉	♅♉	☉♉	♂♉	☿♊
Manson, Charles	11.12.1934	♇♋R	♆♍	♂♍	☿♏	♃♏	♀♏	☉♏	☽♒	♄♒	♅♈R

DECAN: NOCTURNAL BIRTHS ANALYZED

Name	Born	0-	10-	20-	30-	40-	50-	60-	70-	80-	90-
Gillman, Natalie	3. 9.1978	☉♓	☽♓	☿♓	♀♓R	♃♊	♂♋	♄♌R	♇♎R	♅♏R	♆♐
Wilson, Woodrow	12.29.1856	☉♑	☿♑	☽♒	♂♒	♀♒	♆♓	♃♈	♇♉R	♅♉R	♄♋R
Andrews, Julie	10. 1.1935	☉♎	☿♏	☽♏	♃♏	♂♐	♄♓R	♅♉R	♇♋	♀♍R	♆♍
Dole, Robert	7. 23. 1923	☉♋	☿♌	♂♌	♆♌	♄♎	♃♏	☽♐	♅♓R	♇♋	♀♋
MacDonald, Ramsey	10.12.1866	☉♎	☿♎	♄♏	♀♐	☽♐	♃♑	♆♈R	♇♉R	♅♋	♂♋
Pubill, Gloria	5. 1.1942	☉♉	☿♉	♄♉	♅♉	♃♊	♂♋	♇♌	♆♍R	☽♏	♀♓
Roland, Lorinda	4.21.1938	☉♉	☿♉R	♅♉	♀♉	♂♉	♇♋	♆♍R	☽♑	♃♒	♄♈
Kerry, John	12.11.1943	☉♐	☿♑	♅♊R	♂♊R	☽♊	♄♊R	♇♌R	♃♌	♆♎	♀♏
Lessing, Doris	10.22.1919	☉♎	☿♏	♅♒R	♇♋	♆♌	♃♌	♂♍	♄♍	♀♍	☽♎
Franz Ferdinand	12.18.1863	☉♐	☿♑	♆♈	☽♈	♇♉R	♅♊R	♄♎	♀♏	♃♏	♂♐
Lincoln, Abraham	2.12.1809	☉♒	☿♓	♇♓	♃♓	♀♈	♂♎	♅♏	♄♐	♆♐	☽♑
Krishnamurti, Jeddu	5.12.1895	☉♉	☿♊	♇♊	♆♊	♀♊	♃♋	♂♋	♄♏R	♅♏R	☽♐
Augustus, Caesar	9.23.63 BC	☉♍	♀♏	☽♑	♄♉R	♂♉R	♇♊R	♅♋	♆♋	♃♋	☿♍
Starkman, Isaac	12.15.1950	☉♐	♀♑	☿♑	♂♒	♃♓	☽♓	♅♋R	♇♌R	♄♎	♆♎
Eliot, George	11.22.1819	☉♏	♀♐	☿♐	♅♐	♆♐	☽♑	♃♒	♄♓R	♇♓R	♂♌
MacArthur, Mary	8.13.1880	☉♌	♀♌	♅♍	♂♍	☽♏	♃♈R	♄♈R	♆♉	♇♉	☿♌R
Graves, Robert	7.24.1895	☉♌	♂♌	☽♌	♀♍	♄♏	♅♏R	♇♊	♆♊	☿♋	♃♋
Sellers, Peter	9. 8.1925	☉♍	♂♍	♀♎	♄♏	♃♑R	♅♓R	☽♉	♇♋	♆♌	☿♌
Peron, Evita	5. 7.1919	☉♉	♂♉	♀♊	♇♋	♃♋	♆♌	☽♌	♄♌	♅♓	☿♈
Blavatsky, Helena	8.12.1831	☉♌	♂♍	♄♍	☿♍	♀♎	☽♎	♆♑R	♅♒R	♃♒R	♇♈R
Descartes, Rene	3.31.1596	☉♈	♅♈	♃♈	♇♈	♀♈	☽♉	♀♉	♂♊	♆♌R	♄♍R
Tyler, John	3.29.1790	☉♈	♅♌R	♂♌	♃♌R	☽♍	♆♎R	♇♒	☿♓	♀♓R	♄♓
Alexandria, Tsarina	6. 6.1872	☽♊	☉♊	♅♋	♃♋	♄♑R	♆♈	♇♉	☿♉	♀♊	♂♊
Beethoven, Ludwig	12.16.1770	☽♐	☿♐	☉♐	♃♑	♇♑	♀♑	♅♉R	♂♊R	♄♌R	♆♍
Schmidt, Helmut	12.23.1918	☽♍	☿♐R	☉♑	♀♑	♂♒	♅♒	♇♋R	♃♋R	♆♌R	♄♌R
Bertiforrt, Solange	3.11.1934	☽♑	♀♒	♄♒	☿♓R	☉♓	♂♓	♅♈	♇♋R	♆♍R	♃♎
Edward VIII	6.23.1894	☽♓	♂♈	♀♉	♇♊	♆♊	♃♊	☉♋	☿♋	♄♎	♅♏R
Monroe, Marilyn	6. 1.1926	☽♒	♃♒	♂♓	♅♓	♀♈	☿♊	☉♊	♇♋	♆♌	♄♏R
Roosevelt, Theo	10.27.1858	☽♋	♄♌	☿♏	☉♏	♀♐	♂♑	♆♓R	♇♉R	♅♊R	♃♊R
Mullette, Julienne	11.19.1940	☽♋	♇♌R	♆♍	♀♎	♂♎	☿♏R	☉♏	♃♉R	♄♉R	♅♉R
Nicholls, Jack	12.12.1920	☿♐	☉♐	☽♑	♀♑	♂♒	♅♓	♇♋R	♆♌R	♃♍	♄♍
Gill, Eric	2.22.1882	☿♓R	☉♓	♀♓	☽♉	♄♉	♆♉	♃♉	♇♉	♂♊	♅♍R
Bacon, Sir Francis	1.22.1561	☿♒R	☉♒	♀♓	♇♓	♃♈	☽♈	♆♉R	♄♊R	♅♏	♂♐
Pepys, Samuel	2.23.1633	☿♒	☉♓	♂♓	♀♈	♃♉	♇♉	☽♌	♅♍R	♆♏R	♄♐
Kelly, Grace	11.12.1929	☿♏	☉♏	♂♏	♄♐	☽♓	♅♈R	♃♊R	♇♋R	♆♍	♀♎
Gladstone, William	12.29.1809	☿♑	☉♑	♂♒	♇♓	♃♈	☽♎	♅♏	♆♐	♄♐	♀♐
Hussein, King	11.14.1935	☿♏	☉♏	♃♐	♂♑	♄♓	♅♉	☽♋	♇♋R	♆♍	♀♎
Nehru, Jawaharial	11.14.1889	☿♏	☉♏	♃♑	♆♊R	♇♊R	☽♌	♄♍	♂♎	♅♎	♀♎
Fillmore, Millard	1. 7.1800	☿♐	☉♑	♇♓	☽♊	♃♊R	♄♌R	♅♍R	♆♏	♀♐	♂♐
Wilson, Colin	6.26.1931	☿♊	☉♋	♇♋	♃♋	♆♍	♂♍	☽♏	♄♑R	♅♈	♀♊
Elliot, Roger	6.25.1937	☿♊	☉♋	♇♋	♆♍	♂♏	☽♑	♃♑R	♄♈	♅♉	♀♉
Eberhardt, Isabelle	2.17.1877	☿♒	♀♒	☉♒	♄♒	☽♈	♆♉	♇♉	♅♌R	♂♐	♃♐
Hoover, Herbert	8.10.1874	☿♌	♂♌	☽♌	♅♌	☉♌	♀♍	♃♎	♄♒R	♆♉R	♇♉
Ross, Diana	3.26.1944	♀♓	☉♈	☿♈	☽♉	♅♊	♄♊	♂♊	♇♌R	♃♌R	♆♎R
Wilde, Oscar	10.16.1854	♀♎	☉♎	☿♏	♂♐	♃♑	♆♓R	♇♉R	♅♉R	♄♊R	☽♌

DECAN: NOCTURNAL BIRTHS ANALYZED

Name	Born	0-	10-	20-	30-	40-	50-	60-	70-	80-	90-
Hayes, Rutherford	10. 4.1822	♀♍	☉♎	☿♏	♂♏	♆♑	♅♑	♇♓R	♄♉R	♃♊R	☽♊
Roosevelt Franklin	1.30.1882	♀♒	☉♒	☿♒	♄♉	♆♉	♃♉	♇♉R	♂♊R	☽♋	♅♍R
Joyce, James	2. 2.1882	♀♒	☉♒	☿♓	♄♉	♆♉	♃♉	♇♉R	♂♊R	☽♌	♅♍R
Peter I, Tsar	6. 9.1672	♀♉	☉♊	☿♊R	♇♋	♃♍	☽♐	♆♒R	♂♓	♅♓	♄♈
Aubrey, John	3.22.1626	♀♓	☉♈	♇♉	♂♊	♅♌	♄♍R	♆♎R	♃♎R	☽♑	☿♓
Hardy, G. H.	2. 7.1877	♀♑	☿♑R	☉♒	♄♓	♆♉	♇♉	♅♌R	☽♐	♂♐	♃♐
Turpin, Ronald	2.27.1936	♀♒	☿♒	♂♓	☉♓	♄♓	♅♉	☽♉	♇♋	♆♍	♃♐
Garfield, James	11.19.1831	♀♎	♂♏	☉♏	☿♏	♆♑	♅♒	♃♒	♇♈R	☽♉	♄♍
Gillman, Michael	10. 1.1985	♀♍	♂♍	☉♎	☿♎	♇♏	♄♏	♅♐	♆♑	♃♒R	☽♉
George VI, King	12.14.1895	♀♏	♄♏	♅♏	☽♏	♂♐	☿♐	☉♐	♇♊R	♆♊R	♃♌R
Gandhi, Indira	11.19.1917	♂♍	☉♏	☿♐	♀♑	☽♑	♅♒	♃♊R	♇♋R	♆♌R	♄♌
Watts, Alan	1. 6.1915	♂♑	☉♑	☿♑	♅♒	♃♒	♇♋R	♄♊R	♆♋R	☽♍	♀♐
Robinson, Wendy	7. 7.1953	♂♋	☉♋	♅♋	☿♌	♇♌	♄♎	♆♎	☽♉	♀♉	♃♊
Nixon, Richard	1. 9.1913	♂♐	☿♑	♃♑	☉♑	♅♒	☽♒	♀♓	♄♉R	♇♊R	♆♋R
Reagan, Ronald	2. 6.1911	♂♑	☿♑	♅♑	☉♒	♀♓	♄♉	☽♉	♇♊R	♆♋R	♃♏
McKinley, William	1.29.1843	♂♏	♀♐	♄♑	♃♒	☽♒	☉♒	♆♒	☿♒	♅♓	♇♈
Ford, Gerald	7.14.1913	♂♉	♀♊	♄♊	♇♋	☉♋	♆♋	☿♌	☽♐	♃♑R	♅♒R
Simone, Nina	2.21.1933	♂♍R	♃♍R	☽♒	♄♒	♀♒	☉♓	☿♓	♅♈	♇♋R	♆♍R
Elizabeth II, Queen	4.21.1926	♂♒	♃♒	♀♓	♅♓	☿♈	☉♉	♇♋	☽♌	♆♌R	♄♏R
Jackson, Michael	8.29.1958	♂♉	♅♌	♀♌	☿♌R	☉♍	♇♍	♃♎	♆♎	♄♐	☽♓
Adams, John	10.30.1735	♂♎	♇♎	☉♏	♀♏R	☿♏	♅♐	♃♑	☽♈	♄♉R	?♊R
Adenauer, Konrad	1. 5.1876	♃♏	☉♑	☿♑	♀♒	♄♒	♂♓	☽♈	♆♉R	♇♉R	♅♌
Pilgrim, Eleanor	1. 6.1937	♃♑	☉♑	☿♒R	♀♒	♄♓	♅♉	♇♋	♆♍R	♂♏	☽♏
Polich, Vendel	4.26.1892	♃♈	☽♈	☿♈R	☉♉	♆♊	♇♊	♀♊	♄♍R	♅♏R	♂♑
Carter, Charles	1.31.1887	♃♏	☿♒	☉♒	♀♒	♂♓	☽♉	♆♉R	♇♉R	♄♋R	♅♎R
Churchill, Winston	11.30.1874	♃♎	☿♏	☉♐	♀♐R	♄♒	♆♈R	♇♉R	♅♌R	☽♍	♂♎
Chaplin, Charlie	4.16.1889	♃♑	☿♈	☉♈	♂♉	♀♉R	♆♊	♇♊	♄♌	♅♎R	☽♏
Tjia, John	8.17.1953	♃♊	♀♋	♅♋	☿♌	♂♌	☉♌	♇♌	♆♎	♄♎	☽♏
Johnson, Lyndon	8.27.1908	♃♌	♂♍	☉♍	☽♍	☿♍	♅♑R	♄♈R	♇♊	♆♋	♀♋
Ebertin, Reinhold	2.16.1901	♃♑	♄♑	☽♑	♀♒	☉♒	☿♓	♇♊R	♆♊R	♂♍R	♅♐
Taft, William H.	9.15.1857	♃♉R	♅♉R	♄♋	♀♌	♂♌	☽♌	☉♍	☿♎	♆♓	♇♉R
Edwards, Michael	5.13.1943	♃♋	♇♌	☽♍	♆♍	♂♓	☉♉	♅♊	☿♊R	♄♊	♀♋
Hamilton, Alex	1.11.1755	♃♍R	♇♐	♂♐	☿♑	☽♑	♄♑	☉♑	♀♑	♅♓	♆♌R
Wordsworth, W.	4. 7.1770	♃♐	♇♑	♂♒	☿♓	☉♈	♀♈	♅♉	♄♋	♆♍R	☽♍
Eisenhower, D. D.	10.14.1890	♄♍	☿♎	☉♎	☽♎	♅♎	♀♐	♂♑	♃♒	♆♊R	♇♊R
Krengel, Elaine	3.23.1935	♄♓	☿♓	☉♈	♅♈	♀♉	♇♋R	♆♍R	♂♎	☽♏	♃♏R
Irwin, Steve	2.22.1962	♄♒	☿♒	♂♒	♃♒	☉♓	♀♓	♅♌	♇♍	☽♍	♆♏R
Gorbachev, Mikhail	3. 2.1931	♄♑	♀♑	☿♒	☉♓	♅♈	♃♋R	♇♋R	♂♋	☽♌	♆♍
Mary Shelley	8.30.1797	♄♋	♂♍	☉♍	♅♍	☿♍	♀♎	♆♏	☽♐	♇♒R	♃♈R
Kennedy, Edward	2.22.1932	♄♑	♂♒	☿♒	☉♓	♀♈	♅♈	♇♋R	♃♌R	☽♍	♆♍R
Madison, James	3.16.1751	♄♐	♂♑	♅♒	☿♒	☉♓	♀♈	♃♉	♆♋R	☽♏	♇♐
Ramanujan Iyengar	12.22.1887	♄♌R	♂♎	♅♎	♀♏	♃♏	☿♐	☉♑	☽♈	♆♉R	♇♊R
Monroe, James	4.28.1758	♄♓	♅♓	♀♈	☉♉	☿♉	♆♌	♂♌	♃♐R	♇♐R	☽♑
Anne, Queen	2.16.1665	♄♑	♆♑	♃♒	♅♒	☉♒	☿♓	♂♓	☽♓	♀♈	♇♊
Marx, Karl	5. 5.1818	♄♓	♇♓	☽♉	☉♉	♀♉	☿♊	♂♋	♅♐R	♆♐R	♃♑R
De Gaulle, Charles	11.22.1890	♅♎	☉♏	☿♐	♀♐	♃♒	♂♒	☽♈	♆♊R	♇♊R	♄♍
Crowley, Aleister	10.12.1875	♅♌	☉♎	♀♎	♃♏	☿♏	♂♑	♄♒R	☽♓	♆♉R	♇♉R
Stalin, Josef	12.16.1878	♅♍R	☽♎	♂♏	☉♐	♀♐	☿♑R	♃♒	♄♓	♆♉	♇♉R
Einstein, Albert	3.14.1879	♅♍R	☽♐	♂♑	♃♒	☉♓	☿♈	♄♈	♀♈	♆♉	♇♉
Lindbergh, Charles	2. 4.1902	♅♐	☽♐	♄♑	♃♑	☉♒	♂♒	♀♓R	☿♓	♇♊R	♆♊R
Dickens, Charles	2. 7.1812	♅♏	☽♐	♆♐	♄♑	☿♑	☉♒	♀♓	♇♓	♂♈	♃♊R
.Gillman, Dhanny	1. 5.1976	♅♏	♀♐	♆♐	☉♑	☿♒	☽♒	♃♈	♂♊R	♄♌R	♇♎
Newton, Isaac	1. 4.1643	♅♏	♆♏	☿♐	☉♑	♀♒	♃♓	♄♓	♂♉	♇♊R	☽♋
Wintle, Prier	8.20.1924	♆♌	☉♌	☿♍	♄♎	♃♐	♂♓R	♅♓R	☽♉	♀♋	♇♋
Kolev, Rumen	11.29.1960	♆♏	☿♏	☉♐	♃♑	♄♑	♀♑	☽♈	♂♋	♅♌	♇♍
Page, Ernest B.	9.15.1913	♆♋	♀♌	☿♍	☉♍	♃♑	♅♒R	☽♓	♄♊	♂♊	♇♋
George V, King	6. 3.1865	♆♈	♀♉	♇♉	☿♉	☉♊	♅♊	♂♌	☽♎	♄♎R	♃♐R
Blake, William	11.28.1757	♆♌R	♂♌	☿♏	♃♐	☉♐	♇♐	♀♑	♄♒	♅♓	☽♋
Barnell, Hal	10.29.1923	♆♌	♂♎	☿♎	♄♎	☉♏	♀♏	♃♏	♅♓R	☽♊	♇♋R

DECAN: NOCTURNAL BIRTHS ANALYZED

Name	Born	0-	10-	20-	30-	40-	50-	60-	70-	80-	90-
Polich, Selma	1.14.1934	♆♍R	♃♎	☽♑	☿♑	☉♑	♂♒	♄♒	♀♒	♅♈	♇♋R
Mahler, Gustav	7. 1.1860	♆♓	♇♉	♅♊	☉♋	♃♌	☿♌	♀♌R	♄♌	☽♐	♂♑
Manning, Trish	10.1.1935	♇♋	♀♍	♆♍	☉♎	☿♏	♃♏	☽♏	♂♐	♄♓R	♅♉R
Clinton, Hillary	10.26.1947	♇♌	♂♌	♄♌	♆♎	☉♏	♀♏	☿♏R	♃♐	☽♓	♅♊R
Charles, P of Wales	11.14.1948	♇♌	♄♍	♆♎	♀♎	☿♏	☉♏	♂♐	♃♐	☽♉	♅♊R
Juan Carlos, King	1. 5.1938	♇♋R	♆♍	☿♑R	♀♑	☉♑	♃♒	☽♒	♂♓	♄♓	♅♉R
Subuh, Muhammed	6. 22. 1901	♇♊	♆♊	☉♊	♀♋	☿♋	☽♍	♂♍	♅♐R	♃♑R	♄♑R
Nash, Ogden	8.19.1902	♇♊	♆♋	♂♋	♀♌	☉♌	☿♍	♅♐R	♄♑R	♃♒R	☽♓

SEPTENARY: DIURNAL BIRTHS ANALYZED

Name	Born	0- 49-	7- 56-	14- 63-	21- 70-	28- 77-	35- 84-	42- 91-
Harvey, Axel	2. 6.1940	☽♒	☉♒	☿♒	♀♓	♃♈	♂♈	♄♈
Truman, Harry	5. 8.1884	☽♏	☉♉	☿♊R	♄♊	♀♋	♃♋	♂♌
Byron, Lord	1.22.1788	☽♋	☿♑	☉♒	♀♒	♄♒	♃♊R	♂♋R
Obama, Barak	8. 4.1961	☽♊	♀♋	☿♌	☉♌	♂♍	♄♑R	♃♒R
Firebrace, Roy	8.16.1889	☽♉	♀♋	♂♌	♄♌	☉♌	☿♍	♃♐R
Harding, Warren	11.2.1865	☽♉	♀♎	♄♏	☉♏	♂♏	☿♏	♃♐
Sugarman, Rosalind	6.24.1942	☽♎	♀♉	♄♊	☿♊R	☉♋	♃♋	♂♌
The Buddha	5.11.-564	☽♏	♂♈	☿♈	♃♈	♄♈	☉♉	♀♊
Grant, Ulysses S.	4.27.1822	☽♋	♂♌	♀♓	☿♈	♄♉	☉♉	♃♉
Baird, John Logie	8.13.1888	☽♏	♂♏	♃♏	☿♌	♄♌	☉♌	♀♌
Appo, George	7. 4.1856	☽♌	♂♎	♃♈	☿♊	♄♋	♀♋	☉♋
Hitler, Adolf	4.20.1889	☽♑	♃♑	☿♈	☉♉	♂♉	♀♉R	♄♌
Peron, Juan	10. 8.1895	☽♊	♃♌	♀♍R	☉♎	♂♎	♄♏	☿♏
Huber, Bruno	11.29.1930	☽♓	♃♋R	♂♌	♀♏R	☉♐	☿♐	♄♑
Marconi, Guglielmo	4.25.1874	☽♌	♃♍	♄♒	☿♈	☉♉	♀♉	♂♉
Roberts Martha Ann	6.3.1936	☽♏	♃♐R	♄♓	♀♊	☿♊	☉♊	♂♊
Jackson, Glenda	5. 9.1936	☽♐	♃♐R	♄♓	♀♉	☉♉	♂♉	☿♊
Johnson, Samuel	9.17.1709	☽♓	♄♋	☉♍	☿♍	♀♎	♂♎	♃♏
Adams, John Quincy	7.11.1767	☽♑	♄♊	☉♋	♂♌	☿♌	♀♍	♃♍
DeLorean, John	1. 6.1925	☽♊	♄♏	♀♐	☿♐	♃♑	☉♑	♂♈
Gurion, David Ben	10.16.1886	☽♊	♄♋	♀♎	♃♎	☉♎	☿♏	♂♐
Alexander the Great	7.22.-357	☽♎	♄♉	♂♊	☿♋	☉♋	♀♋	♃♍
Fagan, Cyril	5.22.1896	☽♎	♄♏R	♂♈	♀♉	☉♊	☿♊	♃♌
Richardson, Natasha	5.11.1963	☽♐	♄♒	♃♈	♀♈	☉♉	☿♉R	♂♌
Nietzsche, Frederich	10.15.1844	☽♐	♄♒	♃♓R	♀♍	♂♍	☿♎	☉♎
Bush, George Sr	6.12.1924	☽♎	♄♎R	♃♐R	♂♒	☿♉	☉♊	♀♋R
Franklin, Ben	1.17.1706	☿♒R	☽♓	♄♉	♃♋R	♂♐	♀♑	☉♑
Bush, George Jr	7. 6.1946	☿♌	♀♌	♂♍	☽♎	♃♎	☉♋	♄♋
Gandhi, Mohandes	10. 2.1869	☿♏	♀♏	♂♏	♄♐	♃♉R	☽♌	☉♎
Arthur, Chester	10. 5.1829	☿♏	♀♏	♃♐	☽♑	♄♌	♂♍	☉♎
Planck, Max	4.23.1858	☿♉	♀♉	♃♉	♄♋	☽♍	♂♐R	☉♉
Mantel, Arie	8.27.1911	♀♍R	☽♎	♃♏	♄♉	♂♉	☉♍	☿♍R
Clinton, Bill	8.19.1946	♀♎	♃♎	☽♉	♄♌	☿♌	☉♌	♂♎
Thatcher, Margaret	10.13.1925	♀♐	♃♑	☽♌	♂♎	☉♎	☿♎	♄♏
Mao Zedung	12.26.1893	♀♒	♃♉	☽♌	♄♎	♂♏	☿♐	☉♑
Barrie, Sir James	5. 9.1860	♀♋	♃♋	♄♌	☽♑	♂♑	☿♈	☉♉
Bohr, Niels	10. 7.1885	♀♏	♄♋	♂♌	♃♍	☽♎	☿♎	☉♎
Rice, Condoleezza	11.14.1954	♂♒	☽♋	♃♋	☿♏	♄♏	☉♏	♀♏R
Huxley, Aldous	7.26.1894	♂♈	☽♉	♃♊	♀♋	☿♋R	☉♌	♄♎
Pierce, Franklin	11.23.1804	♂♌	☽♌	♄♎	♀♎	♃♏	☿♏	☉♐
Young, Arthur	11. 3.1905	♂♑	☽♒	♄♒	♃♊R	♀♎	☉♏	☿♏
Van Buren, Martin	12. 5.1782	♂♏	☿♏	♀♐	☉♐	☽♐	♄♑	♃♑
Morin, Jean B.	2.23.1583	♂♋	☿♒	♀♓	☉♓	♃♓	♄♓	☽♓
Kennedy, John F.	5.29.1917	♂♉	☿♉	♃♉	☉♊	♀♊	♄♋	☽♍
Manson, Charles	11.12.1934	♂♍	☿♏	♃♏	♀♏	☉♏	☽♒	♄♒
Woolf, Virginia	1.25.1882	♂♊R	♀♑	☉♒	☿♒	☽♈	♄♉	♃♉

SEPTENARY: DIURNAL BIRTHS ANALYZED

Name	Born	0- 49-	7- 56-	14- 63-	21- 70-	28- 77-	35- 84-	42- 91-
Louise, Princess	3.18.1848	♂♊	♃♋	☽♍	♀♒	♄♓	☿♓R	☉♓
Cleveland, Grover	3.18.1837	♂♌	♃♌R	☽♌	♄♏R	☿♓	♀♓	☉♓
Thornett, David	10.31.1932	♂♌	♃♍	♀♍	☉♏	☿♏	☽♐	♄♑
Hemingway, Ernest	7.21.1899	♂♍	♃♏	♄♐R	☽♑	♀♋	☉♋	☿♌
Taylor, Bill	6.14.1937	♂♏R	♃♑R	♄♈	♀♉	☿♊	☉♊	☽♍
Gillman, Kennet	6. 7.1937	♂♏R	♃♑R	♄♈	♀♉	☿♉	☽♉	☉♊
Paine, Thomas	2. 8.1737	♂♉	♄♊	☽♊	☉♒	♃♒	☿♓	♀♈
Harrison, W. H.	2. 9.1773	♂♋	♄♍R	☽♍	♀♑	☿♑	☉♒	♃♓
Bach, Edward	9.24.1886	♂♏	♄♋	☽♌	♀♍	☿♍	☉♎	♃♎
Kepler, Johannes	1. 6.1572	♂♎	♄♏	☿♑	☉♑	♀♑	♃♓	☽♊
Wingate, Orde	2.26.1903	♂♎R	♄♒	☿♒	☽♒	♃♓	☉♓	♀♓
Kafka, Franz	7. 3.1883	♂♉	♄♊	♀♊	☿♊	☽♊	☉♊	♃♋
Jackson, Andrew	3.15.1767	♂♉	♄♊	♃♍R	☽♍	☉♓	☿♈	♀♈
Schmeling, Max	9.28.1905	♂♐	♄♒	♃♊R	♀♍	☿♍	☽♍	☉♎
Curie, Marie	11. 7.1867	♃♒	☽♓	☉♏	♄♏	♀♏	♂♏	☿♐
Pope, George	5.21.1688	♃♑R	☽♒	♀♉	☿♉	☉♊	♂♋	♄♎R
Bonaparte, Napoleon	8.15.1769	♃♏	☽♑	♀♋	♄♋	☿♌	☉♌	♂♍
Mondale, Walter	1. 5.1928	♃♓	☽♊	♀♐	♄♐	♂♐	☿♑	☉♑
Taylor, Zachary	11.24.1784	♃♒	☽♉	♂♏	☿♏	☉♐	♀♑	♄♑
Simpson, O. J.	7. 9. 1947	♃♏R	☽♓	♂♊	♀♋	☉♋	☿♋R	♄♌
Olivier, Laurence	5.22.1907	♃♋	☽♍	♂♑	♄♓	♀♈	☿♉	☉♉
Cromwell, Oliver	5. 5.1599	♃♋	☽♍	♄♎	♂♈	☉♉	☿♉	♀♊
Buchanan, James	4.23.1791	♃♍R	☽♑	♄♈	♂♈	☉♉	☿♉	♀♊
Freud, Sigmund	5. 6.1856	♃♓	♀♈	☉♉	☿♉	☽♊	♄♊	♂♎R
Washington, George	2.22.1732	♃♎R	♂♏	☽♑	☿♒	☉♓	♀♓	♄♈
Gillman, Noah	6.24.1973	♃♒R	♂♈	☽♈	♄♊	☉♋	♀♋	☿♋
Harlow, Jean	3. 4.1911	♃♏R	♂♑	☿♒	☉♓	♀♈	☽♈	♄♉
Franz Joseph, Emp.	8.18.1830	♃♑R	♂♈	♀♋	♄♌	☽♌	☉♌	☿♍
King, Martin Luther	1.15.1929	♃♉	♂♊R	♄♐	☉♑	☿♒	♀♓	☽♓
Mann, Thomas	6. 6.1875	♃♎R	♂♑R	♄♒R	♀♉	☉♊	☿♋	☽♋
Page, Tony Nelson	2.25.1919	♃♋R	♄♌R	☽♑	☉♓	☿♓	♂♓	♀♓
Blumberg, Leda	7.19.1956	♃♍	♄♏R	☽♐	♂♓	♀♊	☿♋	☉♋
Polk, James K.	11. 2.1795	♃♒	♄♊R	☽♋	♂♍	☉♏	♀♏	☿♐
Millard, Margaret	9. 6.1916	♃♉R	♄♋	♀♋	☉♍	☿♎	♂♎	☽♑
Keuhr, Karl	5.13.1899	♃♏R	♄♐R	♀♈	☿♈	☉♉	☽♋	♂♌
Hardy, Thomas	6. 2.1840	♃♏R	♄♐R	♀♉	☿♊	♂♊	☉♊	☽♋
Mountbatten, Louis	6.25.1900	♃♐R	♄♑R	♂♉	☽♊	☉♋	♀♋R	☿♋
Addey, John	6.15.1920	♃♌	♄♍	♂♎	☽♊	♀♊	☉♊	☿♋
Forest, Stephanie	2.14.1958	♃♏	♄♐	♂♑	☽♑	♀♒R	☿♒R	☉♒
Martina & Anita	1.29.1920	♃♌	♄♍	♂♎	♀♑	☿♒	☉♒	☽♉
Victoria, Queen	5.24.1819	♃♒	♄♓	♂♈	♀♈	☿♉	☽♊	☉♊
Ebertin, Baldur	7.21.1933	♄♒R	☽♋	☉♋	☿♌R	♀♌	♃♍	♂♎
Marr, Alexander	4.12.1919	♄♌R	☽♍	☿♈R	☉♈	♂♈	♀♉	♃♋
Kasmeyer, Joan	9. 7.1933	♄♒R	☽♈	☿♍	☉♍	♃♍	♀♎	♂♏
Jung, Carl	7.26.1875	♄♒R	☽♉	☿♋	♀♋	☉♌	♃♎	♂♐
Wilhelm II, Kaiser	1.27.1859	♄♌R	☽♏	♀♐	☿♑	☉♒	♂♓	♃♊R
Hooke, Robert	7.28.1635	♄♐R	☽♑	♀♋	♂♋	☉♌	♃♌	☿♍
Coolidge, Calvin	7. 4.1872	♄♑R	☽♊	♂♋	♀♋	☉♋	☿♋	♃♌
Mussolini, Benito	7.29.1883	♄♊	☽♊	♂♊	♃♋	♀♋	☿♌	☉♌
Onassis, Jaqueline	7.28.1929	♄♐R	☽♈	♃♊	♀♊	☿♌	☉♌	♂♍
Carter, Jimmy	10. 1.1924	♄♏	☽♏	♃♐	♂♒	♀♌	☿♍	☉♎
Ne Jame, Joseph	8.25.1933	♄♒R	☿♌	☉♍	♃♍	♀♎	☽♎	♂♎
Russell, Bertrand	5.18.1872	♄♑R	☿♉	♀♉	♂♉	☉♉	♃♋	☽♎
Vowles, Jacqui	7.28.1931	♄♑R	♀♋	☉♋	♃♌	☿♌	♂♍	☽♎
McCain, John	8.29.1936	♄♓R	♂♌	☉♍	♀♍	☿♎	♃♐	☽♒
Brandt, Willy	12.18.1913	♄♊R	♂♋R	☽♌	☿♐	♀♐	☉♐	♃♑
Gillman, Gabi	8. 9.1958	♄♐R	♂♉	☽♊	♀♋	☉♌	☿♍	♃♎

SEPTENARY: DIURNAL BIRTHS ANALYZED

Name	Born	0- 49-	7- 56-	14- 63-	21- 70-	28- 77-	35- 84-	42- 91-
Edward VII, King	11. 9.1841	♄♑	♂♑	☽♍	♀♎	☉♏	☿♐R	♃♐
Hefner, Hugh	4. 9.1926	♄♏R	♂♒	♃♒	♀♓	☽♓	☿♈R	☉♈
Nicholas II, Tsar	5.19.1868	♄♐R	♃♈	☽♈	♂♈	☉♉	☿♊	♀♋
Hendrix, Jimi	11.27.1942	♄♊R	♃♋R	☽♋	♂♏	☿♐	☉♐	♀♐
Blackwell, Arthur	11. 7.1942	♄♊R	♃♋	☿♏	☽♏	♂♏	♀♏	☉♏
Lennon, John	10. 9.1940	♄♉R	♃♉R	♀♍	♂♎	☉♎	☿♏	☽♒
Alexis, Tsarevitch	8.12.1904	♄♒R	♃♉	♂♋	☉♌	♀♌	☽♍	☿♍
Rabin, Yitzhak	3. 1.1922	♄♎R	♃♎R	♂♐	☿♒	☉♓	♀♓	☽♈

SEPTENARY: NOCTURNAL BIRTHS ANALYZED

Name	Born	0- 49-	7- 56-	14- 63-	21- 70-	28- 77-	35- 84-	42- 91-
Gillman, Natalie	3. 9.1978	☉♓	☽♓	☿♓	♀♓R	♃♊	♂♋	♄♌R
Wilson, Woodrow	12.29.1856	☉♑	☿♑	☽♒	♂♒	♀♒	♃♈	♄♋R
Andrews, Julie	10. 1.1935	☉♎	☿♏	☽♏	♃♏	♂♐	♄♓R	♀♍R
Franz Ferdinand	12.18.1863	☉♐	☿♑	☽♈	♄♎	♀♏	♃♏	♂♐
Roland, Lorinda	4.21.1938	☉♉	☿♉R	♀♉	♂♉	☽♑	♃♒	♄♈
De Gaulle, Charles	11.22.1890	☉♏	☿♐	♀♐	♃♒	♂♒	☽♈	♄♍
Krishnamurti, Jeddu	5.12.1895	☉♉	☿♊	♀♊	♃♋	♂♋	♄♏R	☽♐
Kerry, John	12.11.1943	☉♐	☿♑	♂♊R	☽♊	♄♊R	♃♌	♀♏
Dole, Robert	7. 23. 1923	☉♋	☿♌	♂♌	♄♎	♃♏	☽♐	♀♋
Lincoln, Abraham	2.12.1809	☉♒	☿♓	♃♓	♀♈	♂♎	♄♐	☽♑
Lessing, Doris	10.22.1919	☉♎	☿♏	♃♌	♂♍	♄♍	♀♍	☽♎
MacDonald, Ramsey	10.12.1866	☉♎	☿♎	♄♏	♀♐	☽♐	♃♑	♂♋
Pubill, Gloria	5. 1.1942	☉♉	☿♉	♄♉	♃♊	♂♋	☽♏	♀♓
Wintle, Prier	8.20.1924	☉♌	☿♍	♄♎	♃♐	♂♓R	☽♉	♀♋
Augustus, Caesar	9.23.63 BC	☉♍	♀♏	☽♑	♄♉R	♂♉R	♃♋	☿♍
Gill, Eric	2.22.1882	☉♓	♀♓	☽♉	♄♉	♃♉	♂♊	☿♓R
Subuh, Muhammed	6. 22. 1901	☉♊	♀♋	☿♋	☽♍	♂♍	♃♑R	♄♑R
Eliot, George	11.22.1819	☉♏	♀♐	☿♐	☽♑	♃♒	♄♓R	♂♌
Starkman, Isaac	12.15.1950	☉♐	♀♑	☿♑	♂♒	♃♓	☽♓	♄♎
MacArthur, Mary	8.13.1880	☉♌	♀♌	♂♍	☽♏	♃♈R	♄♈R	☿♌R
Crowley, Aleister	10.12.1875	☉♎	♀♎	♃♏	☿♏	♂♑	♄♒R	☽♓
Graves, Robert	7.24.1895	☉♌	♂♌	☽♌	♀♍	♄♏	☿♋	♃♋
Peron, Evita	5. 7.1919	☉♉	♂♉	♀♊	♃♋	☽♌	♄♌	☿♈
Sellers, Peter	9. 8.1925	☉♍	♂♍	♀♎	♄♏	♃♑R	☽♉	☿♌
Tyler, John	3.29.1790	☉♈	♂♌	♃♌R	☽♍	☿♓	♀♓R	♄♓
Blavatsky, Helena	8.12.1831	☉♌	♂♍	♄♍	☿♍	♀♎	☽♎	♃♒R
Mahler, Gustav	7. 1.1860	☉♋	♃♌	☿♌	♀♌R	♄♌	☽♐	♂♑R
Descartes, Rene	3.31.1596	☉♈	♃♈	♀♈	☽♉	♀♉	♂♊	♄♍R
Alexandria, Tsarina	6. 6.1872	☽♊	☉♊	♃♋	♄♑R	☿♉	♀♊	♂♊
Beethoen, Ludwig	12.16.1770	☽♐	☿♐	☉♐	♃♑	♀♑	♂♊R	♄♌R
Schmidt, Helmut	12.23.1918	☽♍	☿♐R	☉♑	♀♑	♂♒	♃♋R	♄♌R
Mullette, Julienne	11.19.1940	☽♋	♀♎	♂♎	☿♏R	☉♏	♃♉R	♄♉R
Bertiforrt, Solange	3.11.1934	☽♑	♀♒	♄♒	☿♓R	☉♓	♂♓	♃♎R
Stalin, Josef	12.16.1878	☽♎	♂♏	☉♐	♀♐	☿♑R	♃♒	♄♓
Edward VIII	6.23.1894	☽♓	♂♈	♀♉	♃♊	☉♋	☿♋	♄♎
Einstein, Albert	3.14.1879	☽♐	♂♑	♃♒	☉♓	☿♈	♄♈	♀♈
Ashe, Arthur	7.10.1943	☽♎	♂♉	♄♊	☿♋	☉♋	♃♌	♀♍
Monroe, Marilyn	6. 1.1926	☽♒	♃♒	♂♓	♀♈	☿♊	☉♊	♄♏R
Roosevelt, Theodore	10.27.1858	☽♋	♄♌	☿♏	☉♏	♀♐	♂♑	♃♊R
Dickens, Charles	2. 7.1812	☽♐	♄♑	☿♑	☉♒	♀♓	♂♈	♃♊R
Lindbergh, Charles	2. 4.1902	☽♐	♄♑	♃♑	☉♒	♂♒	♀♓R	☿♓
Nicholls, Jack	12.12.1920	☿♐	☉♐	☽♑	♀♑	♂♒	♃♍	♄♍
Fillmore, Millard	1. 7.1800	☿♐	☉♑	☽♊	♃♊R	♄♌R	♀♐	♂♐
Bacon, Sir Francis	1.22.1561	☿♒R	☉♒	♀♓	♃♈	☽♈	♄♊R	♂♐
Newton, Isaac	1. 4.1643	☿♐	☉♑	♀♒	♃♓	♄♓	♂♉	☽♋

SEPTENARY: NOCTURNAL BIRTHS ANALYZED

Name	Born	0- 49-	7- 56-	14- 63-	21- 70-	28- 77-	35- 84-	42- 91-
Elliot, Roger	6.25.1937	☿♊	☉♋	♂♏R	☽♑	♃♑R	♄♈	♀♉
Pepys, Samuel	2.23.1633	☿♒	☉♓	♂♓	♀♈	♃♉	☽♌	♄♐
Gladstone, William	12.29.1809	☿♑	☉♑	♂♒	♃♈	☽♎	♄♐	♀♐
Kelly, Grace	11.12.1929	☿♏	☉♏	♂♏	♄♐	☽♓	♃♊R	♀♎
Nehru, Jawaharial	11.14.1889	☿♏	☉♏	♃♑	☽♌	♄♍	♂♎	♀♎
Wilson, Colin	6.26.1931	☿♊	☉♋	♃♋	♂♍	☽♏	♄♑R	♀♊
Hussein, King	11.14.1935	☿♏	☉♏	♃♐	♂♑	♄♓	☽♋	♀♎
Kolev, Rumen	11.29.1960	☿♏	☉♐	♃♑	♄♑	♀♑	☽♈	♂♋R
Juan Carlos, King	1. 5.1938	☿♑R	♀♑	☉♑	♃♒	☽♒	♂♓	♄♓
Eberhardt, Isabelle	2.17.1877	☿♒	♀♒	☉♒	♄♒	☽♈	♂♐	♃♐
Hoover, Herbert	8.10.1874	☿♌	♂♌	☽♌	☉♌	♀♍	♃♎	♂♒R
Gillman, Dhanny	1. 5.1975	♀♐	☉♑	☿♒	☽♒	♃♈	♂♊R	♄♌R
Ross, Diana	3.26.1944	♀♓	☉♈	☿♈	☽♉	♄♊	♂♊	♃♌R
Wilde, Oscar	10.16.1854	♀♎	☉♎	☿♏	♂♐	♃♑	♄♊R	☽♌
Hayes, Rutherford	10. 4.1822	♀♍	☉♎	☿♏	♂♏	♄♉R	♃♊R	☽♊
Peter I, Tsar	6. 9.1672	♀♉	☉♊	☿♊R	♃♍	☽♐	♂♓	♄♈
Manning, Trish	10. 1.1935	♀♍	☉♎	☿♏	♃♏	☽♏	♂♐	♄♓R
Roosevelt Franklin	1.30.1882	♀♒	☉♒	☿♒	♄♉	♃♉	♂♊R	☽♋
Joyce, James	2. 2.1882	♀♒	☉♒	☿♓	♄♉	♃♉	♂♊R	☽♌
Aubrey, John	3.22.1626	♀♓	☉♈	♂♊	♄♍R	♃♎R	☽♑	☿♓
George V, King	6. 3.1865	♀♉	☿♉	☉♊	♂♌	☽♎	♄♎R	♃♐R
Page, Ernest B.	9.15.1913	♀♌	☿♍	☉♍	♃♑	☽♓	♄♊	♂♊
Hardy, G. H.	2. 7.1877	♀♑	☿♑R	☉♒	♄♓	☽♐	♂♐	♃♐
Turpin, Ronald	2.27.1936	♀♒	☿♒	♂♓	☉♓	♄♓	☽♉	♃♐
Garfield, James	11.19.1831	♀♎	♂♏	☉♏	☿♏	♃♒	☽♉	♄♍
Gillman, Michael	10. 1.1985	♀♍	♂♍	☉♎	☿♎	♄♏	♃♒R	☽♉
George VI, King	12.14.1895	♀♏	♄♏	☽♏	♂♐	☿♐	☉♐	♃♌R
Gandhi, Indira	11.19.1917	♂♍	☉♏	☿♐	♀♑	☽♑	♃♊R	♄♌
Watts, Alan	1. 6.1915	♂♑	☉♑	☿♑	♃♒	♄♊R	☽♍	♀♐
Robinson, Wendy	7. 7.1953	♂♋	☉♋	☿♌	♄♎	☽♉	♀♉	♃♊
Adams, John	10.30.1735	♂♎	☉♏	♀♏R	☿♏	♃♑	☽♈	♄♉R
Barnell, Hal	10.29.1923	♂♎	☿♎	♄♎	☉♏	♀♏	♃♏	☽♊
Reagan, Ronald	2. 6.1911	♂♑	☿♑	☉♒	♀♓	♄♉	☽♉	♃♏
Nixon, Richard	1. 9.1913	♂♐	☿♑	♃♑	☉♑	☽♒	♀♓	♄♉R
Blake, William	11.28.1757	♂♌	☿♏	♃♐	☉♐	♀♑	♄♒	☽♋
Nash, Ogden	8.19.1902	♂♋	♀♌	☉♌	☿♍	♄♑R	♃♒R	☽♓
Jackson, Michael	8. 29.1958	♂♈	♀♉	♃♊	☉♋	☿♋	♄♎	☽♓
Ford, Gerald	7.14.1913	♂♉	♀♊	♄♊	☉♋	☿♌	☽♐	♃♑R
McKinley, William	1.29.1843	♂♏	♀♐	♄♑	♃♒	☽♒	☉♒	☿♒
Simone, Nina	2.21.1933	♂♍R	♃♍R	☽♒	♄♒	♀♒	☉♓	☿♓
Elizabeth II, Queen	4.21.1926	♂♒	♃♒	♀♓	☿♈	☉♉	☽♌	♄♏R
Clinton, Hillary	10.26.1947	♂♌	♄♌	☉♏	♀♏	☿♏R	♃♐	☽♓
Adenauer, Konrad	1. 5.1876	♃♏	☉♑	☿♑	♀♒	♄♒	♂♓	☽♈
Pilgrim, Eleanor	1. 6.1937	♃♑	☉♑	☿♒R	♀♒	♄♓	♂♏	☽♏
Polich, Vendel	4.26.1892	♃♈	☽♈	☿♈R	☉♉	♀♊	♄♍R	♂♑
Polich, Selma	1.14.1934	♃♎	☽♑	☿♑	☉♑	♂♒	♄♒	♀♒
Edwards, Michael	5.13.1943	♃♋	☽♍	♂♓	☉♉	☿♊R	♄♊	♀♋
Carter, Charles	1.31.1887	♃♏	☿♒	☉♒	♀♒	♂♓	☽♉	♄♋R
Churchill, Winston	11.30.1874	♃♎	☿♏	☉♐	♀♐R	♄♒	☽♍	♂♎
Chaplin, Charlie	4.16.1889	♃♑	☿♈	☉♈	♂♉	♀♉R	♄♌	☽♏
Tjia, John	8.17.1953	♃♊	♀♋	☿♌	♂♌	☉♌	♄♎	☽♎
Johnson, Lyndon B.	8.27.1908	♃♌	♂♍	☉♍	☽♍	☿♍	♄♈R	♀♋
Wordsworth, William	4. 7.1770	♃♐	♂♒	☿♓	☉♈	♀♈	♄♋	☽♍
Hamilton, Alexander	1.11.1755	♃♍R	♂♐	☿♑	☽♑	♄♑	☉♑	♀♑
Ebertin, Reinhold	2.16.1901	♃♑	♄♑	☽♑	♀♒	☉♒	☿♓	♂♍R
Taft, William H.	9.15.1857	♃♉R	♄♋	♀♌	♂♌	☽♌	☉♍	☿♎
Marx, Karl	5. 5.1818	♄♓	☽♉	☉♉	♀♉	☿♊	♂♋	♃♑R

SEPTENARY: NOCTURNAL BIRTHS ANALYZED

Name	Born	0- 49-	7- 56-	14- 63-	21- 70-	28- 77-	35- 84-	42- 91-
Eisenhower, Dwight	10.14.1890	♄♍	☿♎	☉♎	☽♎	♀♐	♂♑	♃♒
Krengel, Elaine	3.23.1935	♄♓	☿♓	☉♈	♀♉	♂♎R	☽♏	♃♏R
Irwin, Steve	2.22.1962	♄♒	☿♒	♂♒	♃♒	☉♓	♀♓	☽♍
Monroe, James	4.28.1758	♄♓	♀♈	☉♉	☿♉	♂♌	♃♐	☽♑
Charles, P of Wales	11.14.1948	♄♍	♀♎	☿♏	☉♏	♂♐	♃♐	☽♉
Gorbachev, Mikhail	3. 2.1931	♄♑	♀♑	☿♒	☉♓	♃♋R	♂♋R	☽♌
Mary Shelley	8.30.1797	♄♋	♂♍	☉♍	☿♍	♀♎	☽♐	♃♈R
Madison, James	3.16.1751	♄♐	♂♑	☿♒	☉♓	♀♈	♃♉	☽♏
Kennedy, Edward	2.22.1932	♄♑	♂♒	☿♒	☉♓	♀♈	♃♌R	☽♍
Ramanujan Iyengar	12.22.1887	♄♌R	♂♎	♀♏	♃♏	☿♐	☉♑	☉♈
Anne, Queen	2.16.1665	♄♑	♃♒	☉♒	☿♓	♂♓	☽♓	♀♈

Venus directed to:

Ascendant: 20, 152-153, 166, 168, 170, 172, 204, 275, 300
Sun: 21, 43, 45, 154-155, 167, 168, 170-171, 173, 205, 300-301
Moon: 22, 45, 155-156, 167, 169, 171, 174, 206-207, 231
Mercury: 21, 157-158, 166-167, 168, 170, 173, 205, 230, 300
Mars: 21, 45, 158-159, 168, 169, 171, 173, 205-206, 275-276, 301
Jupiter: 23, 45, 160-161, 168, 169, 171, 174-175, 207, 231, 275
Saturn: 21, 44, 45, 161-162, 167-168, 169, 171, 173, 206, 231, 276, 301
Uranus: 21, 163, 171, 174, 231
Neptune: 22, 164, 170, 173-174, 232
Pluto: 23, 165, 170, 174, 231

Mars directed to:

Ascendant: 116, 141, 181-182, 197, 198-199, 201, 204, 230, 255-256
Sun: 42, 45, 142, 169, 183-184, 198, 199, 201, 206-207, 256, 296-297
Moon: 19-20, 44, 142-143, 169, 185-186, 198, 200, 202, 204, 256, 296
Mercury: 42, 45, 142, 168, 187-188, 198, 199, 201, 206, 256-257, 297, 321
Venus: 20, 45, 142, 188-190, 197, 200, 205-206, 257, 296
Jupiter: 20, 43, 45, 142, 190-191, 197, 199+200, 201-202, 205, 256, 296
Saturn: 45, 169, 192-193, 200, 202, 204, 257
Uranus: 169, 194, 202, 207
Neptune: 20, 168, 195, 205
Pluto: 20, 43, 168, 196, 197-198, 207

Jupiter directed to:

Ascendant: 45, 202, 207, 213-214, 227, 230
Sun: 110, 173, 198-199, 214-215, 229, 231, 274
Moon: 111, 173, 216-217, 228, 232, 273-274
Mercury: 109, 173, 199, 217, 218, 229, 231, 274
Venus: 110, 219-220, 229, 231, 232, 274-275
Mars: 141, 172, 220-222, 228, 231, 273
Saturn: 112, 141, 173, 222-223, 228, 231, 273
Uranus: 224, 228-229
Neptune: 225-226, 229-230
Pluto: 43, 226-227, 230

Saturn Directed to:

Ascendant: 42, 143, 238-240, 251, 253, 255, 257
Sun: 43, 45, 170, 240-241, 252, 254, 256-257, 258
Moon: 43, 170, 241-243, 253, 254, 255-256, 257
Mercury: 45, 243-244, 252, 254, 257, 258
Venus: 45, 244-245, 251-252, 255, 257, 258
Mars: 42, 246-247, 252, 253-254, 255, 258
Jupiter: 45, 247-248, 253, 254, 256, 258
Uranus: 45, 248-249, 255
Neptune: 249-250, 256
Pluto: 250-251, 256

Uranus directed to:

Ascendant:	263-264, 273, 276-277
Sun:	113, 264-265, 273, 278
Moon:	265, 275-276, 277
Mercury:	113, 266-267, 276, 279
Venus:	113-114, 267, 274, 279
Mars:	112, 268, 275, 278
Jupiter:	112, 269, 274, 277-278
Saturn:	270, 275, 279
Neptune:	114, 271, 274-275, 278
Pluto:	114, 272, 273-274, 277

Neptune directed to:

Ascendant:	284-285, 296, 298
Sun:	25, 137-138, 146, 254, 286-287, 297, 301
Moon:	138-139, 287-288, 298, 300
Mercury:	138, 144-145, 254, 288-289, 297, 300-301
Venus:	138, 254, 289-290, 296-297, 300
Mars:	45, 255, 290-291, 297, 299
Jupiter:	145-146, 253, 291-292, 296, 299
Saturn:	254, 293-294, 297, 301
Uranus:	137, 146, 294, 297, 299
Pluto:	25, 138, 147, 253-254, 295, 296, 298-299

Pluto directed to:

Ascendant:	23, 147, 168, 307, 317, 321
Sun:	24, 308, 318-319, 323
Moon:	309, 320, 322
Mercury:	310, 319, 323
Venus:	24, 311, 318, 322-323
Mars:	24, 312, 320, 323
Jupiter:	313, 320, 322
Saturn:	25, 314, 318, 323
Uranus:	315, 320-321, 322
Neptune:	147, 316, 317-318, 322